RECORDS OF EARLY ENGLISH DRAMA

David
1990

Records of Early English Drama

HEREFORDSHIRE WORCESTERSHIRE

EDITED BY DAVID N. KLAUSNER

UNIVERSITY OF TORONTO PRESS

TORONTO BUFFALO LONDON

© University of Toronto Press 1990
Toronto Buffalo London
Printed in Canada
ISBN 0–8020–2758–X

Canadian Cataloguing in Publication Data

Main entry under title:

Herefordshire, Worcestershire

(Records of early English drama)
Includes bibliographical references.
ISBN 0–8020–2758–X

1. Performing arts – England – Herefordshire –
History – Sources. 2. Performing arts – England –
Worcestershire – History – Sources. 3. Theater –
England – Herefordshire – History – Sources.
4. Theater – England – Worcestershire – History –
Sources. I. Klausner, David N. II. Series.

PN2595.5.H4H4 1990   790.2'09424'4   C90–094294–0

The research and typesetting costs of
Records of Early English Drama
have been underwritten by the
National Endowment for the Humanities and the
Social Sciences and Humanities Research Council of Canada.

Contents

WORCESTERSHIRE

Records of Early English Drama

The aim of Records of Early English Drama (REED) is to find, transcribe, and publish external evidence of dramatic, ceremonial, and minstrel activity in Great Britain before 1642. The executive editor would be grateful for comments on and corrections to the present volume and for having any relevant additional material drawn to her attention.

ALEXANDRA F. JOHNSTON University of Toronto DIRECTOR
SALLY-BETH MACLEAN University of Toronto EXECUTIVE EDITOR

Acknowledgments

To sum up all; there are archives at every stage to be look'd into, and rolls, records, documents, and endless genealogies, which justice ever and anon calls him back to stay the reading of: – In short, there is no end of it...

Laurence Sterne *The Life and Opinions of Tristram Shandy, Gentleman*, vol 1, chapter 14

The REED editor may be forgiven if, sitting in the record office with a mountain of documents yet to be sifted, he feels with Tristram that there is no end of it. Yet there is an end of it and that this is so is due to the assistance and kindness of a large number of people. Thanking them is very much a 'felix labor.'

First thanks are due to Susan Brock of the Shakespeare Institute, University of Birmingham, who has been my collaborator in a wide variety of ways. She has transcribed and checked documents when I was unable to get to England and has tracked down many of the records in the volume. Her previous work with the Worcester Cathedral rolls gave her an invaluable fund of local knowledge, of which I have taken full advantage.

This volume would have been impossible without the help of my colleagues in the REED office. Anne Quick and Abigail Ann Young checked transcriptions with immense care. Miriam Skey and Theodore de Welles provided constant bibliographical assistance; Miriam Skey also copy-edited the volume and tracked down several records from printed sources. Abigail Ann Young provided both the translations and the Latin glossary and these were checked by Catherine Emerson. The English glossary was prepared by William Cooke and Anne Quick. David Crouch checked the Anglo-Norman text and William Edwards prepared its translation. William Cooke checked the index and the volume was proof-read by Anne Quick, Miriam Skey, and Abigail Ann Young. In the early years of research some of my transcriptions were checked by Edward English and Heather Phillips. I benefited greatly in the preparation of the patrons' biographies from the help of Sally McKee and Elza Tiner. The volume was typeset by William Rowcliffe. The maps were drawn by Michael Waldin.

I owe an especial debt of gratitude to Sally-Beth MacLean, REED's executive editor, for firm but generous guidance through the complex terrain of editing records as diverse as these. In addition she acted as arbitrator in disputes of every possible variety, proving time and again that it is possible to be both consistent and sensible. REED's director, Alexandra Johnston, first convinced me to undertake this project in 1977. Throughout the long research period she was an inspiration, manifesting her faith in the project and in my research just at the times when I was beginning to wonder if Tristram was right.

The research contained in this volume would have been impossible without the kindness of the archivists who not only gave me access to the documents in their care, but put up with an endless succession of questions. My first debt here is to Anthony Wherry, county archivist at the Hereford and Worcester Record Office and his superb staff: in Hereford, D. S. Hubbard, and in Worcester (successively) Margaret Henderson, Elizabeth Howard, and Robin Whittaker. My thanks are no less to Miss Penelope Morgan and Miss E. M. Jancey at Hereford Cathedral Library and to Robin Hill at the Hereford Library; Canon Jeffrey Fenwick gave me free access to the collection of Worcester Cathedral Library, and A. E. A. Phillips, Superintendant Registrar for the Worcester Registration District, helped me with the Worcester civic records while they were still housed in the Guildhall. The following persons assisted me in consulting materials in their collections: Leonard E. Boyle, O.P., Prefect of the Vatican Library; John Creasey, Dr Williams's Library; Edward Higgs of the Public Record Office; Mrs Grace Holmes, the library of St George's Chapel, Windsor Castle; and Geoffrey Pick, Lambeth Palace Library.

I would also like to thank the staff of the following repositories for their help: the Birmingham Reference Library; the Bodleian Library; the British Library; Cambridge University Library; Corpus Christi College Library, Cambridge; the Folger Shakespeare Library; the Lancashire Record Office; the National Library of Wales; the Northamptonshire Record Office; the library of the Society of Antiquaries; the Warwick County Record Office; the muniment room and library of Westminster Abbey; and the York Minster Library. To the staffs of the libraries of the University of Toronto, the Pontifical Institute of Mediaeval Studies, and the Metropolitan Toronto Reference Library I am grateful not only for the use of their collections but for a congenial atmosphere in which to work. The Centre for Medieval Studies at the University of Toronto has been kind to me in unnumerable ways, both large and small.

In the later stages of this research I have been aided by a number of scholars for the checking of transcriptions and in some cases for the transcription of documents. Their accuracy and dedication have saved me from a large number of errors, both of commission and omission. For checking documents in Hereford and Worcester I am grateful to Janet Burton and Christopher Upton; Jodi Ann George, Annette Jacobs, and Julia Merritt gave assistance with checks in London. Michael Heaney of the Bodleian Library kindly helped with documents in Oxford; in addition, his knowledge of early morris dance traditions led me away from some untenable theories about ✓ sixteenth-century Herefordshire's favourite pastime.

Scholars in a wide variety of fields have been generous with information: Pat M.

Hughes gave me the benefit of her unparalleled knowledge of the topography of early Worcester, and Jim Tomkin happily answered questions on early Herefordshire. Each of the following individuals provided information and did me favours of many kinds: B.S. Benedikz, Peter Clark, Frank Collins, Professor Christopher Dyer, Roy Martin Haines, Ian Lancashire, Peter Meredith, Richard Rastall, Nancy Speirs, and Linda Ehrsam Voigts. For help and support in a variety of kinds I am grateful to the following REED editors: John Elliott, Alan Fletcher, Sheila Lindenbaum, John McKinnell, and, in particular, J. A. B. Somerset, whom I often met in the record office and the pub, sharing both the excitement of discovery and the researcher's pleasures.

I am most grateful to the following for formal permission to publish extracts from documents in their possession: the Archbishop of Canterbury, the Bishop of Hereford, the Bishop of Worcester, the Dean and Chapter of Hereford Cathedral, the Dean and Canons of St George's Chapel Royal, Windsor, the Dean and Chapter of Westminster Abbey, the Dean and Chapter of Worcester Cathedral, and the Master and Fellows of Corpus Christi College, Cambridge. I am also happy to acknowledge formal permission from the following libraries and record repositories: the British Library, the Hereford and Worcester Record Office, the Public Record Office, and Dr Williams's Library.

Financial assistance for the volume and the research which has gone into it came from the Social Sciences and Humanities Research Council of Canada, the Connaught Fund of the University of Toronto, and the National Endowment for the Humanities. I am especially grateful to the Department of English and the Centre for Medieval Studies at the University of Toronto for two years of sabbatical leave, and to the SSHRCC (through the REED negotiated grant) for research funding during those periods. A grant from the Jackman Foundation by courtesy of the Reverend Edward Jackman, O.P., historian for the Archdiocese of Toronto, has allowed REED to work closely for the first time with a cartographer in the preparation of the complex county maps.

To Kenn Luby I owe an immense debt of thanks and love for his support and patience, epecially at those times when I felt overwhelmed by the Tristram Shandy syndrome. Finally, it is with great pleasure that I dedicate this collection to my mother and father, Mary Ellis and Neal William Klausner. My father spent most of his career in the department of philosophy at Grinnell College, Grinnell, Iowa, where he served, in later years as Miller Professor of Philosophy, until his retirement in 1975. My mother served as college archivist until her retirement in 1975. The atmosphere of thoughtfulness and love of books which they fostered in my childhood home, along with a reverence for documents of the past, could have provided no better nurture for a REED editor.

Symbols

BL	British Library	LPL	Lambeth Palace Library
Bodl.	Bodleian Library	PRO	Public Record Office
HCL	Hereford Cathedral Library	SHRO	St Helen's Record Office
HRO	Hereford Record Office	WCL	Worcester Cathedral Library
HWRO	Hereford and Worcester Record Office		

A	Antiquarian Compilation
CBA	Council for British Archaeology
DNB	*Dictionary of National Biography*
JEFDSS	*Journal of English Folk Dance and Song Society*
LLB	Bachelor of Laws
LLD	Doctor of Laws
NQ	*Notes and Queries*
OED	*Oxford English Dictionary*
REED	Records of Early Engish Drama
STB	Bachelor of Sacred Theology
STC	A. W. Pollard and G. R. Redgrave (comp), *Short-Title Catalogue ... 1475–1640*
STD	Doctor of Sacred Theology
TRWAS	*Transactions of the Worcestershire Archaeological Society*
TRWNFC	*Transactions of the Woolhope Naturalists' Field Club*
VCH	*Victoria History of the Counties of England*
WHS	Worcestershire Historical Society
Wing	D. G. Wing (comp), *Short Title Catalogue ... 1641–1700*
*	(after folio, page, or membrane number) see endnote
⟨...⟩	lost or illegible letters in the original
[ ]	cancellation in the original
(*blank*)	a blank in the original where writing would be expected
° °	matter in the original added in another hand
⌐ ¬	interlineation above the line

⌊ ⌋   interlineation below the line
^   caret mark in the original
…   ellipsis of original matter
| change of folio or membrane in passages of continuous prose
®   right-hand marginale
†   marginale too long for the left-hand margin

HEREFORDSHIRE

Historical Background

The fertile landscape of Herefordshire is dominated by the River Wye and its tributaries, its borders marked by the harsh facade of the Black Mountains to the west and by the imposing bulk of the Malvern Hills to the east. These natural features, along with great expanses of forested land, especially to the south, not only defined Herefordshire's medieval landscape but governed its transportation and trade.

The slow and meandering Wye rises on the slopes of Plynlimon Fawr in the Cambrian Mountains of central Powys and is already a considerable river by the time it reaches the Herefordshire border at Hay. Passing in a south-easterly direction through Hereford and Ross, it eventually reaches the Severn estuary at Chepstow. The Wye divides the county into two areas with differentiated characters and history. To the north and east the land, though hilly, is highly arable and is protected by the broad expanse of the river. All the major towns of the county lie to the north and east of the Wye. To the south-west of the river the county was largely a frontier territory, open to constant attack from the Welsh and strongly fortified. The eastern, western, and southern borders of the county are well defined; only to the north is the border with Shropshire less clearly marked by any topographical features.[1]

Herefordshire has always been an agricultural county. Only along the eastern slopes of the Hatterrall Ridge, at the south end of the Black Mountains, is the land unfit for cultivation. The harshness of this south-western border contrasts sharply with the soft mass of the Malvern Hills to the east and the relatively flat lands to the north. The county is well watered by an extensive system of small rivers, tributaries of the Wye, among them the Lugg, Teme, Arrow, Frome, and Dore.

Although the Wye was of great importance to the county's transportation system, it presented a variety of navigational difficulties. Most serious was the existence of a series of private and municipal weirs, the last of which was only removed in the nineteenth century.[2] The road system, therefore, was especially important. Principal among the roads leading out from the city of Hereford was the north-south road which ran north from Bristol, crossing the Severn by ferry, thence to Monmouth, Hereford, Leominster, Ludlow, and Shrewsbury. From this road, south of the city, a south-eastern branch led to Ross and Gloucester. A south-western route ran to South Wales, passing through Abergavenny and Pontypool. The most important of the eastern roads ran to Worcester, while a smaller road linked Hereford with Ledbury. To the west ran a road through Hay and Brecon to St David's and another small country road.[3]

Hereford's strategic position on the Welsh border gave it considerable political importance, far out of proportion to its population or wealth. The Welsh had always had a reputation for lawlessness, but Edward I's conquest of Wales in 1282 left the border in relative peace. This border was controlled for the next two centuries by the Marcher lords and although their reputation was also for lawlessness and unruliness, R. R. Davies has shown that they formed a strikingly effective administrative and peacekeeping body.[4] Indeed, much of the county's relationship with Wales was peaceful and the frequent appearance of Welsh personal names in the records attests to the presence of Welsh settlers and migrant workers. On the other hand, complaints to parliament in 1414, 1442, 1445, and 1449 about Welsh looting raids suggest a continuing problem. This border problem seems to have had some racial aspects, as the city was divided by 1450 into 'Welsh' and 'English' factions.[5] The county's reputation can be seen, perhaps in a somewhat exaggerated form, in a letter to Pope Eugenius IV written in 1438 by Thomas Beckington, secretary to Henry VI, over the king's signature. Discussing a possible successor to Bishop Thomas Spofford, Bekynton notes that the cathedral church in Hereford is located 'inter populos non parum natura feroces ac indomitos.'[6] In 1471 a council was appointed to assist the prince of Wales, Edward IV's son, with the administration of the principality; in 1493 a similar council was appointed for Prince Arthur and on his death in 1502 was commissioned to administer the Marches. The Council in the Marches of Wales continued to keep the peace in the border counties throughout the rest of our period.

Through the thirteenth and fourteenth centuries the county's history was dominated by the families of de Bohun and Mortimer and their successive conflicts with the Crown, though both these families died out in the fifteenth century. During the Wars of the Roses, the county was split between the two factions. It was perhaps symbolic of this division that the possessions of the once prominent de Bohun family, the earls of Hereford, were held in part by the Crown and in part by the Lancastrian family of Stafford. Though on the whole the county gentry were probably Lancastrian in their leanings, Richard of York held extensive lands in Herefordshire, retaining local gentry as manorial officials.[7]

Throughout the period Herefordshire remained a moderately prosperous county, though individual land owners may have been quite wealthy. Comparing the 1334 taxation assessments with the subsidy of 1515, R. S. Schofield has shown that although the wealth of the county increased by a factor of almost three, its ranking relative to other counties remained about the same.[8] Wool was Herefordshire's principal commodity. A 1454 petition which ranked the wools of various localities placed the wool of Leominster at the head of the list. Large-scale horticulture reached the county in the early seventeenth century, when, in part through the experiments of John, 1st

Viscount Scudamore, at Holme Lacy, the cultivation of apples became an important industry.[9]

Diocese of Hereford

The diocese of Hereford was established in the late seventh century. Its political influence was overshadowed by that of the great baronial families and it never attained the importance of Worcester. The Cathedral Church of St Ethelbert was not a monastic establishment and was governed by its bishop, dean, and chapter. The diocese was divided into the archdeaconries of Hereford and Shropshire (Ludlow since 1876); most of Herefordshire parishes were contained within the former, which was divided into the seven rural deaneries of Frome, Archenfield, Ross, Weobley, Hereford, Weston, and Leominster. One of the six deaneries of Shropshire archdeaconry (Burford) was largely in Worcestershire.[10]

Perhaps because of its relative remoteness from London and Canterbury, Herefordshire twice became notorious for heterodoxy. The Lollard movement of the late fourteenth century was particularly strong in the county.[11] A century and a half later, the county had continual problems with recusancy. Several major land owners refused to subscribe to the Act of Uniformity in 1569 and the privy council complained with some frequency that Herefordshire's recusants were being treated with too much leniency.[12]

Religious Houses

With few exceptions, Herefordshire's religious houses were small and poor. In contrast to Worcestershire, the county had no large and wealthy Benedictine establishments; most were small Augustinian houses. The sole Benedictine house was Leominster Priory, a cell of Reading Abbey and fully under its jurisdiction. Never a large house, it had ten monks in 1379 and was frequently used by the Reading abbots as a place of discipline for their own monks. Among the Augustinian houses of some importance was Wigmore Abbey, founded, according to tradition, by Hugh Mortimer and connected intimately with the Mortimer family until the fifteenth century. Two small Augustinian convents, Limebrook and Aconbury, were more notable for their poverty than for any other distinctive feature. A set of injunctions to the nuns of Limebrook delivered by Bishop Thomas Spofford in 1437 gives some insight into the life of a small convent, including restrictions on dress and entertainment. The Cistercian house of Abbey Dore, which produced the highest-priced wool in England, declined in importance through the Middle Ages. By the Dissolution it was in decay, housing only eight monks. A few books from its important library survive.[13]

Two friaries were situated within the city of Hereford. The Dominican (Black) friars held land just outside St Owen's Gate until about 1319, when they moved to the

Widemarsh suburb. A large and relatively wealthy establishment, it housed over thirty friars in the fourteenth century. We know far less of the Franciscan (Grey) friars, though their establishment was situated outside Friars' Gate towards the river from about 1250.[14] About twenty books of their considerable library survive.[15]

Boroughs

HEREFORD

The topographical outlines of the medieval city of Hereford can be glimpsed in a number of structures now wholly or partially standing; the castle motte and green, the preaching cross at the site of Widemarsh Gate, fragments of the city wall and, of course, the cathedral itself. A more accurate picture of early Hereford is only now becoming clear in the excavations conducted under the direction of R. Shoesmith.[16] The medieval city was divided into six parishes: St Nicholas', St Peter's, All Saints', St Martin's, St Owen's, and St John's. Although it is now only possible to date the founding of St Peter's parish (1143), the rest of the parochial organization is likely to date from about the same time.[17]

The city's two fords provided access across the river and the name Hereford itself (ford of the army) testifies to the site's strategic importance. The medieval city was surrounded by a wall, mentioned in the Domesday Book, which by the end of the thirteenth century consisted of a stone rampart with seventeen bastions and six gates, all of stone. The names of the city's wards were taken from five of these gates: Friars' Gate, Eign Gate, Widemarsh Gate, Bye Street Gate, and St Owen's Gate. The sixth gate, Wye Bridge Gate, lay at the far side of the stone bridge over the Wye, built about 1100 in the place of an earlier wooden structure and replaced in 1490. The walls and gates stood intact until the Civil War, though after the conquest of Wales in 1282 they were no longer part of an essential defence network. Upkeep for the walls was provided by the imposition of murage grants and tolls, which placed a major burden on both the inhabitants and the traders who brought goods to market. Richard Phelips, six times mayor of Hereford, blamed these tolls for the city's 'contynuall ruyne decay and dishabiting,' because traders 'withdrawith themselfes and resortith to other markettes.'[18]

Within the walls, the northern part of the city was dominated by the market and many of the streets take their names from merchant groups whose wares were sold there. Close at hand were the Tolsey, or customs house, and the Boothall, first referred to in the fourteenth century.[19] North of the market, just inside the city walls ran Jews Street, the home of Hereford's Jewish population. The street is still known as Jewry Lane.[20]

The southern part of the city was dominated by the cathedral and bishop's palace surrounded by the close on the north side and gardens on the south along the river bank. Close to half the acreage of the city was controlled by the bishop and chapter.

The castle stood on the west bank of the Wye, upstream of the cathedral, until it was destroyed by act of parliament in 1654. Leland described its walls as 'highe and stronge and full of great towres.'[21] The city's common land lay predominantly to the north, through Widemarsh Gate and past the houses which Leland called 'the fayrest suburbe of the towne.'[22]

The city received its first charter from Richard I in 1189, a simple grant in fee farm. The privileges of this charter were extended by John, who established a guild merchant, and twice by Henry III. Henry's first charter of 1227 provided for a three day fair on the feast of St Denis (9 October) and the two following days. Thereafter this charter was regularly confirmed and occasionally expanded in minor ways.[23] In 1619, after considerable pressure, James I granted a new charter with provision for a mayor, six aldermen, twenty-four common councillors, and a high steward.[24] In addition to the civic fair in October, the annual bishop's fair was held at the feast of St Ethelbert (20 May).[25]

In 1383, Hereford's chief bailiff was replaced by an elected mayor. In addition to this office, much of the city's administrative business was done by the three members of the Great Inquest. The first member was traditionally chosen by the common council, the second from within the walls, the third from without the walls, though by the sixteenth century the offices had become more hierarchical and the Inquest usually consisted of the mayor and two aldermen. From 1520 on, the council consisted of thirty-one members co-opted for life terms, from which the mayor and aldermen were chosen by seniority.[26] Many of the miscellaneous documents surviving in the Hereford city records are pleas to the Great Inquest, which met on the two annual Law Days at Michaelmas and Easter, and whose authority seems to have covered everything not specifically delegated to another body.

Through most of the Middle Ages, Hereford was a prosperous and thriving provincial city, though the size of its population can only be estimated.[27] The 1377 poll tax returns indicate the number of taxpayers in the city, with Hereford ranked between Great Yarmouth and Cambridge. The number of taxpayers is 1,903 (17,221 in the county).[28]

The cathedral and its various needs provided a significant element of the city's economy. Work on the fabric itself progressed through the thirteenth and fourteenth centuries, employing as many as fifty masons. Although most of these workmen would have been brought in from elsewhere, their provisioning and perhaps their housing would have enhanced the local economy. Miracles at the shrines of St Ethelbert and St Thomas Cantilupe brought pilgrims in great numbers, all requiring food and accommodation. The rest of the town's occupations were dominated by tanning, fulling, and weaving. By the later Middle Ages the cloth industry had become the town's principal business. These two aspects of the city's economy – its cathedral and its cloth trade – explain its rapid growth through the thirteenth century.[29] Even during the Black Death and subsequent outbreaks of plague, the city maintained its prosperity in the cloth trade.[30]

The various occupations associated with the cloth trade were, along with the city's provision industries and other trades, organized by guilds. The best indication of their nature and number is provided by the 1503 list for the Corpus Christi procession, when pageants were mounted by the Glovers, Carpenters, Chandlers, Skinners, Fletchers, Vintners, Tailors, Drapers, Saddlers, Cardmakers, Tanners, Walkers, Butchers, Cappers, Dyers, Smiths, Barbers, Porters, Mercers, and Bakers. A list of 1562 is somewhat different: Carpenters, Corvisers, Goldsmiths, Saddlers, Fullers, Tailors, Butchers, Bowyers and Fletchers, Blacksmiths, Bakers, Drapers, Glovers, Barbers, Dyers, Tanners, Chandlers, and Motley Weavers.[31] There is no evidence that the city had a religious guild like Worcester's Trinity guild. Hereford's prosperity continued even through the political upheavals of the fifteenth century and only came to an end in the mid-sixteenth century. During the first half of the century, most cities suffered a serious economic decline and, if Hereford's contraction was rather later than most, it was no less severe.[32]

LEOMINSTER

Of the county's fifteen other boroughs, only Leominster preserves civic records of importance to this collection.[33] The royal fief of Leominster was transferred by Henry I to the abbey of Reading in 1123 and the Benedictine priory of Sts Peter and Paul remained a daughter house of Reading until the Dissolution. Throughout the Middle Ages, the bailiff and other municipal officers were appointed by the prior as representative of the abbot of Reading.

Leominster received its first municipal charter from Mary in 1554 (confirmed and extended by Elizabeth in 1562).[34] This charter assigned to the borough all privileges previously held by the abbot of Reading and confirmed the borough's fairs. At this time the town had five guilds – Bakers, Butchers, Cordwainers, Tailors and Drapers, and Tanners. The list had grown by 1580 to include Glovers, Mercers, and Walkers and Dyers. The charter was renewed by James I in 1605. Leases from the corporation involved the annual payment of a hen or its equivalent at Christmas, with which the bailiff gave a feast, known as the 'Hen Feast.' References to the celebration are frequent in the Chamberlains' Accounts, occasionally with provision for entertainment.

Households

BISHOP RICHARD SWINFIELD

Relatively few Herefordshire households, whether secular or ecclesiastical, have left extensive records. The principal ecclesiastical household of the county, that of the bishop, rarely attained a position of influence either through land ownership or through political importance comparable to that of the far wealthier bishop of Worcester. Particularly through the earlier Middle Ages, many of the Hereford bishops were firmly under the influence of the powerful Marcher lords, especially the Mortimers and the de Bohuns. With rare exceptions, such as Bishop Adam Orleton (1317–27), their power was local rather than national. The bishops' favoured residence was at Bosbury, some fifteen miles east of Hereford.[35]

Richard Swinfield, a Kentishman, was chaplain to St Thomas Cantilupe from about 1265 until Cantilupe's death in 1282. In 1277, during Cantilupe's episcopate at Hereford, he presented Swinfield to a cathedral prebend. After Cantilupe's death, Swinfield was elected to the bishopric and remained at Hereford until his death at Bosbury in 1317. His private account book survives for the year 1289–90 and gives an extraordinarily detailed picture of the life of a provincial bishop at the close of the thirteenth century.[36]

MORTIMER

The power of the Mortimers in the county dates from the Conquest, when the Norman Ralph de Mortimer was granted the castle of Wigmore by William I in 1074. The family held extensive lands in Herefordshire and Shropshire and rose to national importance after 1247 when Roger Mortimer, 6th Baron Wigmore, acquired through marriage the Marcher lordships of Brecon and Radnor. The family's influence came to a peak in the 1320s, when Roger Mortimer, Lord of Chirk, and his nephew, Roger Mortimer, 8th Baron Wigmore, formed the principal opposition to Edward II. The younger Mortimer was created first earl of March in 1328 after the king's death. The title was forfeit at his attainder and execution in 1330, but was reinstated for his grandson, Roger, in 1354. Edmund Mortimer, 5th earl of March, died 18 January 1424/5, leaving no male heirs.[37]

SCUDAMORE

The Scudamore family, the principal Herefordshire family of the Tudor period, divided into two branches in the late fourteenth century, one at Holme Lacy, the other at Kentchurch. It is the Holme Lacy branch which principally concerns this collection. The manor, a scant five miles south-east of Hereford, was extensively rebuilt during the sixteenth century, possibly by John Scudamore (d. 1571), who served as high sheriff of the county and gentleman usher to Henry VIII. His grandson, Sir John (d. 1623), served in the same capacity under Elizabeth and as member of parliament for the county in six parliaments. Sir John's son, Sir James (d. 1619), served as member for the county in 1604–11 and 1614. He was the model for Sir Scudamour in Book IV of Spenser's *Faerie Queene*. It is his son John (1601–71) who has left us the most records. Serving in parliament for the county in 1621 and 1624, and for the city of Hereford in 1625 and 1628, John was created 1st Viscount Scudamore in 1628. Following his service in parliament, he retired to Holme Lacy, but was called to service in 1635 as Charles I's ambassador in Paris, a post which he held until 1638. In 1639 he again retired to Herefordshire, where he was appointed high steward of Hereford city and cathedral. An extensive correspondence with various London friends who kept him abreast of court events provides a number of references to court plays and masque performances.[38]

Drama, Music, and Popular Customs

Local and Civic Drama

The city of Hereford clearly had a series of pageants in 1503, when a list of them was copied into the Mayor's Book. The list is familiar in its general resemblance to the craft cycles as we know them from York, Towneley, and Chester. Of the twenty-seven pageants, five deal with Old Testament subjects – Adam and Eve, Cain and Abel, Noah, Abraham and Isaac (apparently including Moses), and the tree of Jesse.[39] Twenty of the pageants deal with the life of Christ: the Annunciation, the Nativity, the Adoration of the Magi, the Purification, and Christ and the Doctors. 'ffleme Iordan' must be a baptism pageant, but 'the castell of Israell' is obscure. It could perhaps be a Herod pageant or it might refer to the Israelites in the wilderness, if we assume a confusion of 'castra,' the Vulgate word for the Israelite camps in the desert, and 'castrum,' the Anglo-Latin word for castle. 'Shore Thursday' is likely to be a pageant of Sheer (or Shrive) Thursday, the Thursday before Easter, though if so it is out of order. The following pageants which deal with the crucifixion are not so much given titles as descriptions, the present participles suggesting that these may be descriptions of static tableaux, although the phrasing of the list is not unlike that of the pageant lists from Chester and York.[40] The pageants cover the Entry into Jerusalem, the Arrest, the Buffeting and Scourging, the Crucifixion, Longinus, the Deposition, the Burial, and the laments of the three Marys. 'Milites armati custodes sepulcri' may well be the Resurrection, but the subject matter of the next two pageants ('Pilate cayfas annas & mahounde' and 'Knyghtes in harnes') is unclear and the last, St Catherine and her tormentors, clearly has no place in a Creation to Doomsday cycle. No Hereford church is dedicated to St Catherine.

The loss of the civic records covering the late fifteenth and early sixteenth centuries makes it impossible to establish beyond any doubt the nature of these pageants, but no evidence survives to suggest that they were plays rather than tableaux. The records dealing with the Corpus Christi procession which do survive, while they do mention the pageants, give no suggestion that plays were being performed. Our only record of their production is an entry in the Mayor's Account Roll for 1533–4, in which Thomas Downe is paid for assisting with the Corpus Christi procession 'cum diuersis historijs hoc anno *productis*.' Less than fifteen years later they were no longer a part of the procession, since a 1548 guild ordinance refers to 'dyu*ers* pageaunt*tes*' in the procession of Corpus Christi which 'nowe ys & Are omytted and Surseassed.'[41] The reference to a book of plays ('vni libri de lusionib*us*') in the Mayor's Court Plea Book for 1440? is clearly insufficient evidence for a civic Corpus Christi drama.

The earliest records of drama in Herefordshire are ecclesiastical prohibitions dealing with performances. In September 1286, Bishop Richard Swinfield excommunicated Christians for attending Jewish wedding ceremonies, at which the festivities include 'co*m*edendo. bibendo. ludendo. ioc*u*lando/seu q*u*odcu*m*q*u*e ystrionat*us* officiu*m* ex*er*cendo.' Hereford had a large and wealthy Jewish community until the expulsion in 1290 and Swinfield's description suggests community involvement rather than hired performers.

In 1348 Bishop John Trillek published a letter 'ad prohibend*um* ludo*s* theatrale*s* fieri in eccle*s*iis.' One piece of information is sadly lacking in the letter; the bishop notes as an example the 'ludo*s* s*iu*e inter*l*udia in ecc*l*esia de .l.,' which cannot be specifically identified (though Leominster, Ledbury, and Ludlow are all possible). From the time of Trillek's letter there is a gap of over two centuries in our information. The popular drama again surfaces in the early 1580s, when prohibitions against performances in churches, and later in any place during service time, bring such activities to light in the consistory court records. Herefordshire is unusually rich in these, with 174 volumes of proceedings surviving in varying states of preservation. From the time of the prohibitions they provide a continuous witness to the presence of a popular tradition of parish drama. So in Leominster in 1617, Thomas Waucklen is presented by the churchwardens of Kingsland for acting a play 'vpon the saboath daie at tyme of eveninge praier.' The content of these plays remains obscure, though there is no clear evidence to support the Puritan Philip Stubbs' claim that too many people 'spend the Sabaoth day (for the most part) in frequenting of baudie Stage-playes and enterludes...'[42]

ROYAL VISITS AND CEREMONY

Although royalty passed through Hereford with some frequency, only one official royal entry lies within our period. Henry VII visited Hereford in 1486 towards the end of his first provincial progress. The royal party arrived in Hereford from Worcester on Monday, 15 May, and moved on to Gloucester on Friday, 19 May. Henry's arrival was the occasion for an elaborate pageant with spoken parts for St George, King Ethelbert, and the Virgin Mary.

Travelling Entertainers

MINSTRELS

Bishop Richard Swinfield's household account roll for the year 1289–90 survives and gives us our earliest references to specific performers. On a visitation of the diocese, Swinfield hired a series of performers, largely identified by their instruments and their patrons. A few names complete the meagre picture for this earliest period, including a William Cithariste, whose name appears on a fourteenth-century copy of a cathedral land grant from the middle of the previous century; Peter le harpour, who appears in a Feet of Fines list from 1340; and Richard le Wayte, whose name appears in an Aconbury rental of the early fourteenth century.[43]

What cathedral rolls survive from the fourteenth and fifteenth centuries contain no payments to players and minstrels. The contrast with the wealth of payments in the Worcester Priory rolls for the same period is perhaps indicative of the differences between a secular and a monastic cathedral (and a wealthy one at that).

PLAYERS

It is quite likely that professional players visited Hereford regularly through the latter part of the sixteenth century, but the Mayor's Rolls, the sole surviving documents that might preserve payments to them, record simply an annual blanket payment such as the 1577–8 entry to 'diuersis lusoribus in enterludijs diuersorum generosorum.' The Leominster Chamberlains' Accounts are more fruitful, recording payments to a dozen named companies over the period from 1596 to 1621 and it is very possible that many of these are the same companies that played in Hereford.

We can only guess at possible playing sites in medieval Hereford. One possibility is the Boothall, a large house purchased by the city in 1392 from Henry Cachepole, a wealthy merchant and former mayor. The Boothall was used for a variety of purposes, including a court of pleas, a wool-trading place, and a guildhall for the Mercers, and it could, like the Gloucester 'Bothall,' have been used for play performances.[44] The Guildhall, probably built in 1490, may have been used as well, but we know little of it other than its existence. A new Guildhall was completed in 1602, though its construction was begun at least by 1596.[45]

Waits

Professional musicians sponsored by aristocratic patrons connected with Hereford existed from an early date, as is clear from the entries in PRO: E101/369/6 (1306), in which payments are made to two trumpeters of the earl of Hereford as well as to his wife's organist.[46] However, direct evidence of the Hereford waits does not appear until late in the sixteenth century, when they were hired by county families such as the Scudamores, by other towns like Leominster, and by craft guilds like the Hereford Barbers. From this period there is also a series of letters in the city archives concerning the waits, from which we know the name of at least one member of the ensemble (and one would-be member). There is no indication of their number or their wages, although Roger Squire's letter of 1587 would strongly suggest that although they played 'on diu*ers* instrumentes,' their principal instruments were shawms. — *for outdoor playing*

Popular Customs

THE BOY BISHOP

Hereford Cathedral had a boy bishop for Holy Innocents' Day from the thirteenth century on. A brief indication of his presence is found in a consuetudinal of the late thirteenth century, the text of a passage virtually identical with that of many other cathedral foundations.[47] Payments both in mass-pence and in drink to the 'paruus Episcopus' appear regularly in the cathedral's rolls for the next century and a half.

MORRIS DANCING

'Hereford-shire for a Morris-daunce, puts downe, not onely all Kent, but verie neare ... three quarters of Christendome.' So wrote an ebullient anonymous spectator of a Hereford morris in 1609 and his words are borne out by the records.[48] Although the origins of the morris dance are still a matter of speculation, its ritual character and its connections with the Robin Hood plays (at least in the sixteenth century) have never been disputed.[49] Such a connection is also suggested by a 1618 consistory court prosecution of a Ledbury innkeeper, Edward Hall, the 'actor and morrice dauncer.' Herefordshire documents, especially the ecclesiastical court records, provide a considerable amount of information on morris dancing. The principal information, of course, concerns its geographical distribution, but individual prosecutions both of dancers and of the minstrels who play for them give useful information about other aspects of the tradition as well.

The question of the extent to which women participated in morris dancing remains a matter for discussion, although it is clear that in some localities women or girls did traditionally take part.[50] The Herefordshire records may bear upon this question, for prosecutions of women in connection with dancing are frequent. These prosecutions are, however, ambiguous in character. In many cases they refer merely to dancing on Sundays, often before or during service time, and it is not possible to distinguish between social ('country') dancing and true morris dancing. Similarly, in a few cases in which both men and women are charged, the men are charged with 'dancing the morris' and the women with 'dancing,' perhaps implying a difference in the type of dance involved. The only occasion on which women are charged explicitly in connection with a morris is at Tedstone Delamere in 1602, when several women are charged with 'being at' a morris dance. Following the initial prosecution for dancing the morris, several women are charged 'pro consimili,' but it is not clear whether they are dancing themselves or are merely present at the occasion. Despite these ambiguities, the fact remains that prosecutions of women on the occasion of a morris are frequent, and the possibility of their participation remains open.

Certain parishes clearly had a special interest in and reputation for morris dancing (Avenbury, Tedstone Delamere, Withington, and Yazor, for example), as can be seen from the frequency of prosecutions that occur there. It should also be noted that there are significant differences between them. Withington and Yazor, for example, provide examples of elaborate prosecutions for a large group of dancers on a few occasions, while Tedstone's records are of frequent prosecutions of individuals. Of course, these prosecutions are limited to the period after the early 1580s when dancing on the sabbath became a matter of concern for the consistory court, but there is no indication that the situation as seen in these court cases represents a change from earlier in the century. The frequent prosecutions for fiddling and for piping and taboring are likely connected with morris dancing; in some cases the connection is explicit.[51]

HOODWINKING, COWLSTAVES, AND DISGUISINGS

In addition to the major resource they provide for popular dancing, the Consistory Court Act Books also reveal a variety of local customs, many of which involve some form of disguising. A lord and lady of misrule are recorded in Welsh Newton in 1619. A prosecution is recorded at Bosbury in 1589 for going 'a-hodiwinking,' a term first recorded as a game in 1573.[52] The court clerk specifies the date as Shrove Sunday, so at least in this case it was probably a carnival disguising.

A prosecution at Cradley involves carrying a man on a 'colestaffe,' one of the traditional elements of a charivari. The date is 26 February 1586/7, so this also is likely to be a Shrovetide observance of some kind. The blowing of horns and throwing of grains which accompany the event would be in keeping with the 'rough music' associated with the charivari, a folk custom not at all out of keeping with Shrovetide festivities.[53] Cowlstaff customs are also found in the Worcestershire records.

The Documents

The descriptions of the documents from which records are drawn are sorted principally under four headings: Diocese of Hereford, Boroughs and Parishes, Monasteries,
and Households. Within the Boroughs and Parishes section, civic documents are listed
first, followed by guild, ecclesiastical, and miscellaneous documents. This last
category includes such documents as probate records.

One exception should be noted to the sorting of records by location in the following
list. Descriptions of ecclesiastical court documents have been kept together among
the diocesan documents because the cases they record may refer to a wide range of
locations. Shelfmarks for all documents are given according to the preference of the
individual libraries and record offices.

Diocese of Hereford

EPISCOPAL REGISTER

Until 1984 the bishops' registers were housed in the strong-room of a Hereford lawyer
and were then transferred to the Hereford Record Office. They record episcopal acts,
injunctions, decrees, and decisions and are in excellent condition. The register of
Bishop Richard Swinfield is listed under Hereford in the Boroughs and Parishes section (pp 25–6); the registers of Bishops Adam Orleton and Thomas Spofford are listed
under Monasteries (p 34).

Register of Bishop John Trillek
Hereford, Hereford Record Office, Diocesan archives; 1344–60; Latin; parchment (paper
flyleaves); ii + 267 + ii; 355mm x 220mm; foliated 1–3, 3A, 4–12, 1–61, 65–257 (also a contemporary foliation in roman numerals); parchment covers on pasteboard with modern over-
binding (1935).

VISITATION ARTICLES

Articles of Enquiry of Bishop Herbert Westfaling
ARTICLES | ECCLESIASTI-|CALL TO BE INQVIRED OF | BY THE CHVRCH-

WARDENS | AND THE SWORNE-MEN WITHIN THE | dioces of Hereford in the first visitation of the | reuerend father in God, Harbart Bishop | of the said dioces: this present yeare | M.D.LXXXVI. and in the | XXVIII. yeare of the raigne | of our most gracious soue-|raigne Lady Queene | Elizabeth, &c. | And so hereafter, till the next visitation, | & from time to time to | be presented. | Imprinted at Oxford by Ioseph Barnes | Printer to the vniuersitie. STC: 10215.

Articles of Enquiry of Bishop Herbert Westfaling
ARTICLES: | ECCLESIASTI-|CALL TO BE INQVIRED OF | BY THE CHVRCHWAR-DENS | AND THE SWORNE-MEN WITHIN THE | Dioces of Hereforde in the visitation of the | reuerend father in God, Harbart Bishop | of the saide Dioces: this present yeare | M.D.LXXXXII, and in the | XXXIIII. yeare of the raigne | of our most gratious soue- | raigne Lady Queene | Elizabeth, &c. | And so hereafter till the next visitation, | & from time to time to | bee presented. | Imprinted at Oxford, by Ioseph Barnes | Printer to the Vniversitie. STC: 10215.5.

Articles of Enquiry of Archdeacon Richard Montague
ARTICLES | Ecclesiastical to be enquired | of by the Church-wardens, and | Sworne-men of the Arch-deaconry | of HEREFORD. | In the Visitation of the Worshipfull | Master RICHARD MOVNTAGVE, | Arch-deacon of Hereford this present | yeare 1620. | And in the eighteenth yeare of the raigne of | our most dread Soueraigne Lord King | IAMES. | LON-DON | Printed by IOHN BILL, | 1620. STC: 10218.5.

Articles of Enquiry of Archdeacon Richard Montague
ARTICLES | ECCLESIASTICAL TO | be enquired of by the Church-|wardens and Sworne-men with-|in the °Archdeaconry | of Hereford° | In the Visitation of the °worshipfull Mr Richard | Mountague Archdeacon of | Hereford this present yeare | 1622° | And in the °(20th° yeere of the Reigne of our | most dread Soueraigne Lord | King IAMES.°) | yeare of our Lord 1623°| LONDON | Printed by IOHN BILL. | 1621. | °1623. °[54] STC: 10133.9 (formerly 10219).

Articles of Enquiry of Bishop Augustine Lindsell
ARTICLES | to bee enquired of | within the Diocesse | of | HEREFORD, | In the first Visitation of the Reve-|rend Father in God, | AUGUSTINE, | Lord Bishop of | Hereford. | LONDON, | Printed by THOMAS HARPER. 1634. STC: 10216.

Articles of Enquiry of Bishop Matthew Wren
ARTICLES | TO BE | INQVIRED OF | WITHIN THE DIOCESSE OF | HEREFORD: | In the first Visitation of the Reverend Father in God, | MATTHEW, | LORD BISHOP ⟨OF⟩ | HEREFORD. | Printed at London, by Richard Badg⟨er.⟩ | 1635. STC: 10217.

Articles of Enquiry of Bishop George Coke
ARTICLES | To be enquired of within the Diocese of | HEREFORD, | In the Second and

Ordinary Visitation of the | Reverend Father in God, | GEORGE, Lord Bishop of Hereford. | LONDON, | Printed by THOMAS HARPER. 1640. *STC*: 10218.

ECCLESIASTICAL COURT DOCUMENTS

In 1969 an extensive collection of diocesan material including a vast collection of court records was transferred to the Hereford Record Office. Principal among these is the set of 174 volumes of consistory court acts. These are now listed as Acts of Office, and they document prosecutions of individuals by the consistory court. A further series of eighty-six volumes of Acts of Instance presents cases brought by one individual against another and contains little beyond matrimonial and testamentary disputes. The Acts of Office on the other hand contain frequent prosecutions for the performances of plays and interludes in churches, as well as for morris dancing 'tempore divinorum.' The earlier volumes contain court reports for the whole diocese; later volumes are separated into archdeaconries. Because the borders of the archdeaconries are not contiguous with the county borders the volumes for the Ludlow archdeaconry contain materials relevant to Herefordshire, Worcestershire, and Shropshire. It is clear from the vertical folding of the quires, from the sequence of places visited, and from the dating sequence that individual quires were carried around the diocese by the court registrar and assembled at the end of the year. Some of the volumes are in good condition, but a few of them have practically disintegrated.

Acts of Office
Hereford, Hereford Record Office, Diocesan archives:

Diocese of Hereford

Box 17, vol 66; 1586–7; Latin and English; paper; 268 leaves; 295mm x 195mm; no foliation; remains of vellum cover and leather strap.

Box 17, vol 67; 1587–8; Latin and English; paper; 290 leaves; 305mm x 212mm; foliated to 148 (index on final 24 ff); contemporary vellum binding, back missing, remains of leather strap and buckle.

Box 17, vol 68; 1588–9; Latin and English; paper; 290 leaves; 305mm x 212mm; no foliation; contemporary vellum binding, remains of leather strap and buckle.

Box 24a (formerly 18), vol 70; 1614–17; Latin and English; paper; 210 leaves; 300mm x 195mm; no foliation; cover missing, paper badly decayed.

According to notes scattered throughout, most of the cases bound in this volume have been taken from other volumes without formal headings or other indications of the place of the court or its officials.

Box 24a (formerly 18), vol 71; 1616–18; Latin and English; paper; 375 leaves; 340mm x 198mm; no foliation; vellum cover with cloth ties.

Box 19, vol 72; 1571–9; Latin and English; paper; 229 leaves, last 10 detached; 300mm x 205mm; no foliation; lacks cover (badly faded and stained).

Archdeaconry of Hereford

Box 20, vol 75; 1595–6; Latin and English; paper; 499 leaves; 290mm x 185mm; no foliation; contemporary vellum binding with ties.

Box 21, vol 80; 1602–3; Latin and English; paper; 147 leaves in 4 parts; 310mm x 220mm; part 1: paginated 1–36, 36a–f; part 2: paginated 1–47, 1 unnumbered page between 47 and 48, 48–57, 2 unnumbered pages; part 3: paginated 37–76 (with 1 loose leaf between 68 and 69), 76a, 76b, 2 unnumbered pages, 77–86 (1 loose leaf between 86 and 87), 87–108, 108a–c, 1 unnumbered page, 109–127, 10 unnumbered pages (parts 1–3 inclusive are stitched in a single gathering, followed by a loose single gathering containing 28 unnumbered leaves); part 4: paginated 1–28, 2 unnumbered pages; all leaves are much damaged by damp and dirt; vellum cover labelled 'Liber Correctionis incipit vltimo die Septembris 1602.' No headings are noted beyond the deanery.

Box 22, vol 82; 1605–6; Latin and English; paper; ii + 180; 290mm x 190mm; paginated 1–360; contemporary vellum binding, labelled on spine 'Archidiaconatus Herefo⟨rdie⟩.'

Box 22, unnumbered vol, pt 2; 1609–10?; Latin and English; paper; approximately 200 leaves; 310mm x 200mm; no foliation; in extremely bad condition; remains of vellum binding, in a brown paper wrapper marked 'vol ii.' Generally, the volume notes only the deanery, with no indication of court place and officials. So few dates are legible that the range given is somewhat conjectural.

Box 23, vol 85; 1609–10; Latin and English; paper; 127 leaves; 310mm x 202mm; no foliation; contemporary vellum binding with ties, labelled '1609.'

Box 23, vol 86; 1611–12; Latin and English; paper; 179 leaves; 298mm x 200mm; no foliation; leaves loose owing to deterioration of spine, remains of vellum binding.

Box 23, vol 88; 1612–13; Latin and English; paper; ii + 271 + ii; 308mm x 200mm; modern foliation; bound in modern boards.

Box 24, vol 89; 1613–14; Latin and English; paper; 121 leaves; 308mm x 200mm; no foliation; contemporary vellum binding, labelled 'Herefordie Li⟨b⟩er e⟨x⟩ officio mero 1613.'

Box 24, vol 90; 1618–20; Latin and English; paper; 397 leaves; 308mm x 190mm; no foliation; contemporary vellum covers, labelled 'Detect*a* in sessione gen*er*ali do*mini* e*pisco*pi heref*ordie* Annis do*mini* 1618 et 1619.'

The volume also contains entries for the Worcestershire parish of Ribbesford cum Bewdley.

Box 24, vol 91, pt 2; 1621–2; Latin and English; paper; not possible to count folios accurately; 315mm x 210mm; no evidence of foliation; very badly rotted; remains of contemporary vellum binding.

Box 25, vol 93A; 1627–8; Latin and English; paper; 235 leaves; 310mm x 202mm; no foliation; unbound (loose gatherings).

Box 25, vol 94; 1629–30; Latin and English; paper; 273 leaves; 310mm x 200mm; no foliation; contemporary vellum binding with ties, labelled 'Heref*ordie* Cor*r*ectiones 1629.'

Box 26, vol 96; 1632–3; Latin and English; paper; 430 leaves; 305mm x 205mm; no foliation; parchment cover.

Archdeaconry of Ludlow (Shopshire until 1876)

Box 34, vol 127; 1599–1601; Latin and English; paper; 515 leaves; 290mm x 190mm; no foliation; contemporary vellum binding, labelled 'Liber Correct*ionis* Salop 1599 1600 1601.'

Box 35, vol 129; 1606–7; Latin and English; paper; ii + 239; 305mm x 205mm; paginated 1–453 (10 blank leaves at end); vellum cover, marked 'Salop in cor*r*ection*ibus* penultimo Iulij 1606.'

Box 35, vol 131; 1611–12; Latin and English; paper; 155 leaves; 300mm x 190mm; paginated 1–310; vellum cover, marked 'Salop Liber Cor*r*ectionis 1612°.'

Box 35, vol 132; 1612–13; Latin and English; paper; 200 leaves; 307mm x 205mm; no foliation; vellum cover with cloth ties, marked 'Salop 1613 cor' on back cover.

Box 36, vol 134; 1615–16; Latin and English; paper; 105 leaves; 300mm x 197mm; no foliation; vellum cover with remains of cloth ties, front cover marked 'Salop ⟨....⟩tionis ⟨..⟩ini. ⟨16⟩15,' labelled on spine 'Correct' Salop 1615.'

Box labelled Acts of Office: fragments, Fragment C; early 17th c.; Latin and English; paper; single sheet; original size approximately 270mm x 190mm; torn top and right edge. The document appears to have been mislaid.

Acts of Decanal Court
Hereford, Hereford Cathedral Library; 1619–30; Latin and English; paper; iii + 355 + iii;
294mm x 200mm; modern foliation; modern half leather binding (1953), labelled on spine 'Acts
of the Dean's Court 1619–1630.'

Boroughs and Parishes

Since each volume of the ecclesiastical court documents contains references to a large
number of parishes, they are not listed here repeatedly under the names of individual
parishes, but are grouped together with the diocesan records above.

GOODRICH

Star Chamber Case: Philpot vs Williams et al.

The court of Star Chamber, probably so named from the stars of gold leaf decorating
its azure ceiling, was, in effect, the monarch's privy council meeting as a court, with
the addition of two senior justices.[55] From the time of Henry VII it undertook to hear
a variety of complaints, generally brought by individuals against each other, which
did not fall under the jurisdiction of the local sessions or other courts. These cases
included complaints of assault, unlawful assembly, and libel. Under Elizabeth the
number of cases heard by the court of Star Chamber rose to many times its earlier
case-load with the result that, in the early seventeenth century, stricter limits were
placed on the types of cases the court could hear. Only the Jacobean documents have
been calendared thoroughly; those from the reigns of Henry VII, Henry VIII, and Mary
are briefly calendared in the old catalogues of the Public Record Office, while the very
large number of Elizabethan documents are primarily indexed by the name of the
plaintiff.[56]
    The documents listed here deal with a disturbance on Whit Monday 1607 which
was connected in ways not entirely clear with village revelry – drinking and dancing,
as specified in one of the depositions. The bundle also includes two royal commissions
to take responses from defendants (Items 1 and 6) and two copies of the bill of complaint (Items 2 and 7). For further discussion of the case see the endnotes to the text.

Bill of Complaint
London, Public Record Office, STAC 8/234/10/Item 12; 1609; English and Latin; parchment;
single sheet; 458mm x 607mm; signed by counsel and endorsed.

Answer of Defendant
London, Public Record Office, STAC 8/234/10/Item 9; 1609; English and Latin; parchment;
single sheet; 507mm x 680mm; signed by counsel.

Demurrer of Defendant
London, Public Record Office, STAC 8/234/10/Item 10; 1609; English and Latin; parchment; single sheet; 515mm x 620mm; signed by counsel.

Joint Answers of Defendants
London, Public Record Office, STAC 8/234/10/Item 8; 1609; English and Latin; parchment; single sheet; 435mm x 645mm; signed by counsel.

Answer of Defendant
London, Public Record Office, STAC 8/234/10/Item 11; 1610; English and Latin; parchment; single sheet; 190mm x 288mm; signed by counsel.

Joint Answers of Defendants
London, Public Record Office, STAC 8/234/10/Item 3; 1610; English and Latin; parchment; single sheet; 250mm x 600mm; signed by counsel and three commissioners and endorsed.

Interrogatories for Defendants
London, Public Record Office, STAC 8/234/10/Item 4; 1610; English and Latin; parchment; single sheet; 577mm x 223mm; signed by three commissioners and endorsed.

Examinations on Interrogatories
London, Public Record Office, STAC 8/234/10/Item 5; 1610; English and Latin; parchment; single sheet; 505mm x 275mm; signed by three commissioners and endorsed.

The complaint, found in Item 12, was brought by William Philpot. The various defendants who replied to the bill were John Horsman, Harry Lluellen, John Lynney alias Baker, John Mainston, Thomas Mothewaye, Anthony Philpot, Richard Powell, Thomas Prosser, Edward and William Savacre, John Tovye the younger, George and Philip Vaughan, and Thomas Williams.

HEREFORD

Civic Records

The civic documents of Hereford are now housed in the Hereford Record Office. They have had a chequered history and now comprise a rather spotty collection. From the time of Henry VIII until the early nineteenth century they were kept in the town hall in sheepskin sacks, labelled with the name of the mayor. In 1830 the town hall's cleaner, Esther Garstone, was convicted of selling old documents to local merchants as scrap paper in which to wrap goods. Some documents were recovered from a local butcher, but since no inventory had ever been made of the collection there is no record of what or how much was lost. It is clear from the foliation, for example, that the first 137 folios of the Mayor's Book were lost at this time. The surviving documents were sorted and bound and have been well cared for since. Among the recovered documents were two volumes which form a civic register covering most of the sixteenth century with a gap of about eleven years in the middle.[57] Before they were bound in the middle of the last century they were very likely in loose quires, since they do not appear to be at all complete. The two volumes are now known as the Mayor's Book and the Great Black Book, and civic officials still take their oath of office on the latter. The bulk of the contents is miscellaneous civic decisions, principally those taken at the Law Days, though other information (notably the 1503 pageant list) is also included.

Mayor's Book
Hereford, Hereford Record Office, Hereford City MSS; 1500–30 (a few memoranda for earlier years); English and Latin; paper; iv + 138 + iv; 260mm x 192mm; foliated 138–274 with unnumbered leaf between 166 and 167 and 2 stubs between 181 and 182; 19th c. quarter leather binding in modern slip-case, 'Mayor's Book' on spine. The flyleaf reads 'The proceedings of the Mayor, Steward, the Mayor's Brethren and the Three Inquests at the Law Days from the 16th Henry VII until 21 Henry VIII 1530.'

Great Black Book
Hereford, Hereford Record Office, Hereford City MSS; 1543–92; English and Latin; paper; vi (including table of contents) + 482 + ii; 312mm x 215mm; foliated 2–483; 19th c. calf binding in modern slip-case, 'Great Black Book' on spine. The flyleaf reads 'Minutes of the proceedings of the Mayor & Common Council of the City from 35 Henry VIII 1543 until 31 Eliz. 1589.' It is not, in fact, a minute book.

Civic Miscellanies

The largest surviving collection of records consists of four volumes of miscellaneous papers bound together. Many of these are letters and requests to the mayor and the Inquest; a few include the decision taken on the matter at the bottom of the page. Because of the miscellaneous nature of the collection it is now impossible to tell what may have been lost.

Civic Miscellany 3
Hereford, Hereford Record Office; English and Latin; paper; i + 75 + i; bound papers of various sizes (volume size, 445mm x 355mm); foliated 1–75; 19th c. quarter leather binding in modern slip-case, 'Hereford City MSS. III, Miscellaneous Papers 1513–1593' on spine.

Civic Miscellany 4
Hereford, Hereford Record Office; English and Latin; paper; i + 93 + ii; bound papers of various sizes (volume size, 325mm x 225mm); foliated 1–93; 19th c. quarter leather binding in modern slip-case, 'Hereford City MSS. IV, Miscellaneous Papers 1600–1644' on spine.

Civic Miscellany 6
Hereford, Hereford Record Office; English and Latin; paper and parchment; iii + 92 + ii;
bound papers of various sizes (volume size, 340mm x 246mm); foliated 1–92; 19th c. half
leather binding in modern slip-case, 'Hereford City MSS. VI, Miscellaneous papers 1378–1687'
on spine.

Mayor's Account Rolls

An incomplete series of account rolls covers mayoral expenses for about a century
from roughly 1530 to 1630. The rolls are in good condition and give a useful overview
of the duties and requirements of the office, especially those of a social nature. Until
the accession of Elizabeth they were kept from the Monday following the feast of St
Luke (18 October) until the same date the following year; from 1559 the accounting
year is changed to the more usual Michaelmas – Michaelmas period.

Hereford, Hereford Record Office, Hereford City MSS:

1533–4; Latin; parchment; 2 membranes serial; 625/640mm x 167mm.

1553–4; Latin; parchment; 2 membranes serial; 800/660mm x 156mm.

1577–8; Latin; parchment; 4 membranes serial; 690/680/710/690mm x 180mm.

1580–1; Latin; parchment; 4 membranes serial; 540/570/580/730mm x 185mm.

1582–3; Latin; parchment; 3 membranes serial; 750/760/610mm x 170mm.

1587–8; Latin; parchment; 3 membranes serial; 800/700/670mm x 160mm.

1615–16; Latin; parchment; 3 membranes serial; 650/670/360mm x 160mm.

1627–8; Latin; parchment; 4 membranes serial; 600/640/630/320mm x 140mm.

Mayor's Court Plea Book

Only a few of the records of the mayor's court survive. These are unbound quires
in reasonably good condition and date primarily from the fifteenth century.

Hereford, Hereford Record Office, Hereford Mayor's Court Plea Book; 1440?; Latin; paper;
8 leaves; 320mm x 220mm; no foliation; sewn.

The leaves seem to have been misbound and if reordered 1, 4, 3, 2, 7, 6, 5, 8 give a chronological sequence from 14 April to 20 October. No year is given, but the hand is identical to that of the volume dated 14 October 1439–8 April 1440.

Guild Records

Almost nothing survives of the Hereford guild records. This late account book is the sole representative of extensive guild activity, aside from a few documents addressed to the city preserved in the civic records (especially the Great Black Book and Civic Miscellany 6).

Haberdashers' and Barbers' Company Account and Minute Book
Hereford, Hereford Library, LC 338.6 MSS; 1612–1757; English; paper; 220 leaves; 332mm x 227mm; no foliation; many entries pasted in; contemporary vellum binding and brass clasp.

Ecclesiastical Documents

Cathedral Consuetudines

The Hereford Cathedral Consuetudines include brief directions for the procession of the boy bishop on Holy Innocents' Day. The instructions remain in the Consuetudines as late as the middle of the sixteenth century. There are few substantive differences between the three texts; the Hereford Cathedral Library version has therefore been taken as the base text because of its early date. It has been collated in the notes with the British Library and Corpus Christi College MSS.

Hereford, Hereford Cathedral Library; late 13th c. (after 1264); Latin; parchment; ii + 17 + i (a stub); 275mm x 190mm; foliated 1–17; wooden boards.

London, British Library, Royal 10 A xi; early 14th c. (ff 258v–62); Latin; parchment; iii + 263 + v; 164mm x 235mm; modern foliation; modern binding (1971).

In addition to the Hereford Consuetudines, the volume principally contains a collection of sermons.

Cambridge, Corpus Christi College, 120; c1550; Latin; paper (3 parchment flyleaves); iv + 303 + ii; 310mm x 205mm; paginated 1–606; vellum and leather binding.

In addition to the Hereford Consuetudines on pp 485–519, the volume contains a miscellany of ecclesiastical statutes and inventories.

Register of Bishop Richard Swinfield

Hereford, Hereford Record Office, Diocesan archives; 1283–1317; Latin; parchment; i + 204

+ i; 275mm x 185mm; foliated 1–97, 98A, 98B, 99–109, 110A, 110B, 111–209; 18th c. leather binding on wooden boards, 'Registrum Ricardi de Swinfield' on spine.

Cathedral Mass-pence Rolls

The muniments of Hereford Cathedral Library include an extensive set of rolls detailing payments to clerics for masses. For most of the fourteenth and the early fifteenth centuries these rolls include annual payments, generally of one penny for one mass, to the boy bishop at the feast of the Holy Innocents. The earlier rolls do not specify the obedientiary in charge; the later rolls were kept by the chaplain. Four rolls (R440–R443) are designated by the names of the three manors which supported the chaplain, Diddlebury (Shropshire), Baysham, and Pipe.[58]

Hereford, Hereford Cathedral Library:

R390, roll of Philip de Wytleye; 1302–3; Latin; parchment; 5 membranes; 480mm x 252mm, 405mm x 198mm, 240mm x 170mm, 400mm x 200mm, 580mm x 215mm; attached at top.

R391, roll of Philip de Wytleye; 1306–7; Latin; parchment; single membrane; 332mm x 220mm.

R393, roll of John de la Pounde; 1308–9; Latin; parchment; 3 membranes; 120mm x 112mm, 138mm x 85mm, 320mm x 210mm; attached at top.

R399, roll of John de la Pounde; 1311–12; Latin; parchment; single membrane; 495mm x 225mm.

R401, roll of William de la Felde; 1313–14; Latin; parchment; single membrane; 310mm x 225mm.

R407, roll of William de Blakemare; 1316–17; Latin; parchment; single membrane; 405mm x 270mm.

R408, roll of William de Blakemare; 1319–20; Latin; parchment; single membrane; 470mm x 253mm.

R409, roll of William de Blakemare; 1320–1; Latin; parchment; single membrane; 365mm x 270mm.

R410, roll of William de Blakemare; 1321–2; Latin; parchment; single membrane; 500mm x 230mm.

R411, roll of William de Blakemare; 1322–3; Latin; parchment; single membrane; 357mm x 247mm.

R412, roll of William de Blakemare; 1323–4; Latin; parchment; single membrane; 510mm x 247mm.

R413, roll of William de Blakemare; 1324–5; Latin; parchment; single membrane; 570mm x 258mm.

R414, roll of William de Blakemare; 1327–8; Latin; parchment; single membrane; 597mm x 240mm.

R415, roll of William de Blakemare; 1328–9; Latin; parchment; single membrane; 585mm x 255mm.

R416, roll of William de Blakemare; 1329–30; Latin; parchment; single membrane; 395mm x 250mm.

R417, roll of William de Blakemare; 1330–1; Latin; parchment; single membrane; 630mm x 260mm.

R418, roll of William de Blakemare; 1332–3; Latin; parchment; single membrane; 425mm x 255mm.

R419, roll of William de Blakemare; 1333–4; Latin; parchment; single membrane; 423mm x 225mm.

R420, roll of William de Blakemare; 1334–5; Latin; parchment; single membrane; 520mm x 215mm.

R421, roll of William de Blakemare; 1335–6; Latin; parchment; single membrane; 405mm x 244mm.

R422, roll of William de Blakemare and Thomas Hervi; 1336–7; Latin; parchment; single membrane; 475mm x 262mm.

R423, roll of Thomas Hervi; 1337–8; Latin; parchment; single membrane; 535mm x 280mm.

R424, roll of Thomas Hervi; 1338–9; Latin; parchment; single membrane; 594mm x 260mm.

R425, roll of Thomas Hervi; 1339–40; Latin; parchment; single membrane; 475mm x 260mm.

R426, roll of Thomas Hervi; 1340–1; Latin; parchment; single membrane; 665mm x 270mm.

R427, roll of Thomas Hervi; 1341–2; Latin; parchment; single membrane; 320mm x 255mm.

R428, roll of Thomas Hervi; 1342–3; Latin; parchment; single membrane; 370mm x 280mm.

R429, roll of Thomas Hervi; 1343–4; Latin; parchment; single membrane; 442mm x 295mm.

R430, roll of Thomas Hervi; 1344–5; Latin; parchment; single membrane; 410mm x 242mm.

R431, roll of Thomas Hervi; 1345–6; Latin; parchment; 2 membranes; 405mm x 292mm, 95mm x 292mm; attached at bottom.

R433, roll of Hugh Speed; 1353–4; Latin; parchment; single membrane; 425mm x 220mm.

R434, roll of Hugh Speed; 1354–5; Latin; parchment; single membrane; 425mm x 215mm.

R435, roll of John de Breodon; 1356–7; Latin; parchment; 2 membranes serial; 395/290mm x 230mm.

R436, roll of John de Breodon; 1357–8; Latin; parchment; single membrane; 460mm x 232mm.

R437, roll of John de Breodon; 1358–9; Latin; parchment; single membrane; 710mm x 280mm.

R438, roll of John de Breodon; 1360–1; Latin; parchment; 2 membranes; 425mm x 240mm, 120mm x 130mm; attached at top.

R439, roll of William Knyght; 1361–2; Latin; parchment; single membrane; 425mm x 225mm.

R440, roll for Diddlebury, Baysham, and Pipe; 1372–3; Latin; parchment; single membrane; 315mm x 215mm.

R441, roll for Diddlebury, Baysham, and Pipe; 1373–4; Latin; parchment; single membrane; 470mm x 132mm.

R442, roll for Diddlebury, Baysham, and Pipe; 1374–5; Latin; parchment; single membrane; 485mm x 165mm.

R443, roll for Diddlebury, Baysham, and Pipe; 1375–6; Latin; parchment; single membrane; 425mm x 295mm; 2 cols.

R444, roll of William Knyght, chaplain; 1377–8; Latin; parchment; single membrane; 495mm x 332mm; 2 cols.

R444a, roll of William Knyght; 1378–9; Latin; parchment; single membrane; 505mm x 265mm.

R445, roll of William Knyght; 1379–80; Latin; parchment; single membrane; 50mm x 320mm.

R446, roll of William Knyght, chaplain; 1381–2; Latin; parchment; single membrane; 570mm x 275mm.

R447, roll of William Knyght, chaplain; 1382–3; Latin; parchment; single membrane; 620mm x 282mm; 2 cols.

R448, roll of William Knyght; 1383–4; Latin; parchment; single membrane; 505mm x 290mm; 2 cols.

R449, roll of Thomas Homme, chaplain; 1384–5; Latin; parchment; 2 membranes serial; 450/105mm x 300mm; 2 cols.

R450, roll of Thomas Homme, chaplain; 1385–6; Latin; parchment; single membrane; 600mm x 280mm; 2 cols.

R451, roll of Thomas Homme, chaplain; 1386–7; Latin; parchment; single membrane; 555mm x 285mm; 2 cols.

R452, roll of Thomas Homme, chaplain; 1387–8; Latin; parchment; single membrane; 515mm x 270mm; 2 cols.

R453, roll of Thomas Homme, chaplain; 1389–90; Latin; parchment; 2 membranes serial; 246/434mm x 275mm; 2 cols.

R460, roll of Thomas Homme, chaplain; 1398–9; Latin; parchment; single membrane; 820mm x 290mm.

R467, roll of Roger Jones; 1412–13; Latin; parchment; 2 membranes serial; 565/350mm x 280mm; 2 cols.

R468, roll of Roger Norman; 1413–14; Latin; parchment; single membrane; 640mm x 315mm; 2 cols.

R470, roll of Roger Norman; 1417–18; Latin; parchment; 3 membranes serial; 644/680/270mm x 230mm.

R472, roll of William Jones, chaplain; 1420–1; Latin; parchment; 3 membranes serial; 840/180/670mm x 230mm.

R479, roll of Roger Barboure, chaplain; 1432–3; Latin; parchment; 2 membranes serial; 660/290mm x 248mm.

R480, roll of Roger Barboure, chaplain; 1433–4; Latin; parchment; single membrane; 690mm x 262mm.

R481, roll of John Balle, chaplain; 1435–6; Latin; parchment; single membrane; 720mm x 245mm.

R482, roll of John Balle, chaplain; 1437–8; Latin; parchment; single membrane; 540mm x 246mm.

Cathedral Canons' Bakehouse Rolls

Some further information on the boy bishops is provided by the rolls of the canons' bakehouse, which also controlled the foundation's brewing. These Hereford Cathedral Library rolls include sporadic payments in wine and small beer to the boy bishop. Roll R639, for 1547–8, lacks the payment to the boy bishop, but is otherwise identical with the others.

Hereford, Hereford Cathedral Library:

R630a; c 1470; Latin; parchment; 2 membranes serial; 655/705mm x 268mm; dorse from mb 1.

R632b; 1324–5; Latin; parchment; 2 membranes serial; 690/440mm x 290mm; dorse from mb 1.

R633; 1334–5; Latin; parchment; 2 membranes serial; 820/370mm x 300mm; dorse from mb 1.

R634; 1343–4; Latin; parchment; 2 membranes serial; 710/555mm x 285mm; dorse from mb 1.

R635; 1401–2; Latin; parchment; 2 membranes serial; 550/600mm x 262mm; dorse from mb 1.

R637; 1425–6; Latin; parchment; 5 membranes serial; 680/380/700/620/680mm x 280mm; dorse from mb 1.

R637a; 1463–4; Latin; parchment; 7 membranes serial; 775/630/645/530/630/655/390mm x 230mm; dorse from mb 1.

R637b; 1468–9; Latin; parchment; 5 membranes serial; 730/735/700/715/610mm x 250mm; dorse from mb 1.

R637c; 1470–80?; Latin; parchment; 8 membranes serial; 510/550/725/590/725/655/475/ 295mm x 250mm; dorse from mb 1.

R638; 1543–4; Latin; paper; 7 leaves; 400mm x 310mm; attached at top.

Miscellaneous Documents

Household Accounts of Queen Isabella, Widow of Edward II

London, British Library, Cotton Galba E xiv; 1358–9; Latin; parchment pasted on paper folios; ii + 59 + iii; paper: 240mm x 315mm, parchment: approximately 150mm x 175mm; modern pagination, 1–128; damaged by fire; title on spine: 'Compotus Iohannis de Neubury, Thesaurarii Hospitii Reginae Isabellae. anno 32 E III.'

The First Provincial Progress of Henry VII

Henry VII's royal entry into Hereford in 1486 is described in 'a manuscript from the Cottonian Library' printed by Hearne from Leland's transcript of this MS.[59]

London, British Library, Cotton Julius B xii; 15th–17th c.; English, Latin, and Anglo-Norman; paper (ff 67–82 parchment); iii + 316 + iii; 279mm x 207mm (180mm x 122mm); modern foliation; rebound in brown half morocco with gold lettering.

Account Book of Sir Thomas Walmesley (A)

Thomas Walmesley, justice of the court of common pleas, went on 'all the cercuets of England, except Norfolk and Suffolk,' according to his monument at Blackburn. This account book preserves his expenses riding the Western circuit from July 1596 to March 1601. At the time of Cooper's edition for the Camden Society, it also contained the expenses for the Oxford circuit for 1601, but some of these have since been lost. The Hereford entry formed a part of the Oxford circuit payments and is thus quoted here from Cooper's edition. Both Cooper's edition and the original manuscript are described below.

William Durrant Cooper (ed). *The Expenses of the Judges of Assize Riding the Western and Oxford Circuits, Temp. Elizabeth, 1596–1601.* Camden Society, vol 73 (London, 1858).

Preston, Lancashire Record Office, DDPt 1; 1585–1648; English and Latin; paper; two sections, 24 leaves and 12 leaves; 402mm x 150mm; modern pagination 1–48, 49–72; repaired July 1984, with modern paper covers applied to both sections.

Old Meg of Herefordshire

The preference in Herefordshire for morris dancing is known from many sources, not least the extensive prosecutions in the consistory court act books. None is more striking, however, than this 1609 account of a morris danced entirely by nonagenarians and centenarians.[60]

OLD MEG OF | Hereford-shire, for a | Mayd Marian: | AND HEREFORD | Towne for a Morris-daunce. | OR | TWELVE MORRIS-DANCERS | in Hereford-shire, of twelue | hundred yeares old. | Grata Senectus homini parilis Iuuentæ. | LONDON | Printed for Iohn Budge, and are to be sold at his shop, at | the great South doore of Paules. | 1609. *STC*: 12032.

Star Chamber Bill of Complaint

On the Star Chamber documents, see above under Goodrich (p 21).

London, Public Record Office, STAC 8/50/4; October 1612; English; parchment; single sheet; 430mm x 560mm.

LEDBURY

Letter to William Laud, Archbishop of Canterbury, from Francis Thompson

James I's *The Kings Maiesties Declaration to His Subiects, Concerning Lawfull Sports to be vsed* (popularly known as *The Book of Sports*) and its subsequent reprintings provided much material for the pulpit, both for and against its contents. This private letter from Francis Thompson to the archbishop of Canterbury complains of the Sabbatarian preaching of Henry Page, vicar of Ledbury, against *The Book of Sports*.

London, Public Record Office, SP 16/397; 1638; English; paper; single sheet; 305mm x 198mm.

LEOMINSTER

Chamberlains' Account Books

The civic documents of the borough of Leominster were deposited in the Hereford Record Office in 1974. They form an extensive collection, beginning in the early sixteenth century, though they give only a partial picture of the administration of the borough, since much of the effective civic control lay in the hands of Leominster Priory for which very few records survive.

Hereford, Hereford Record Office:

Book 1; 1571–2; English; paper; 2 leaves; 315mm x 205mm; no foliation; unbound, damaged at bottom.

Book 2; 1572–3; English; paper; 2 leaves; 315mm x 205mm; no foliation; unbound.

Book 3; 1596–7; English; paper; 4 leaves; 305mm x 195mm; no foliation; paper cover, sewn.

Book 4; 1597–8; English; paper; 2 leaves; 315mm x 205mm; no foliation; paper cover, sewn.

Book 5; 1599–1600; English; paper; 4 leaves; 305mm x 200mm; no foliation; paper cover, sewn.

Book 6; 1600–1; English; paper; 4 leaves; 305mm x 200mm; no foliation; sewn.

Book 7; 1602–3; English; paper; 5 leaves; 305mm x 200mm; no foliation; sewn.

Book 8; 1606–7; English; paper; 3 leaves; 305mm x 200mm; no foliation; sewn.

Book 9; 1608–9; English; paper; 8 leaves; 305mm x 200mm; no foliation; sewn.

Book 10; 1613–14; English; paper; 6 leaves; 200mm x 155mm; no foliation; paper cover, sewn.

Book 11; 1616–17; English; paper; 6 leaves; 200mm x 155mm; no foliation; sewn.

Book 12; 1618–19; English; paper; 6 leaves with one insert; 205mm x 160mm; no foliation; remains of paper cover.

Book 13; 1619–20; English; paper; 6 leaves with 3 inserts; 200mm x 155mm; no foliation; paper cover, sewn.

Book 14; 1626–7; English; paper; 4 leaves; 200mm x 155mm; no foliation; sewn.

John Leland's Itinerary

The section on Leominster is missing from the original manuscript of the Itinerary (Bodl.: Gen. Top. e. 8–15), but survives in several later copies, of which this, by John Stow, is the earliest.

Oxford, Bodleian Library, MS Tanner 464e; 1576; English and Latin; paper (inner 4 flyleaves parchment); iii + 147 + iii leaves; 205mm x 145mm; modern foliation, iii + 1–101, 1 blank leaf, 102–146 + iii; leather binding, title on spine at top: 'LELAND/V/' and at foot: 'TANN./464.'

Monasteries

ABBEY DORE

Exchequer Accounts of Edward I
London, Public Record Office, E101/363/18; 1302–3; Latin; parchment; 30 leaves; 210mm x 330mm; modern pagination, 1–60; sewn parchment cover.

LIMEBROOK

Register of Bishop Thomas Spofford
Hereford, Hereford Record Office, Diocesan archives; 1422–48; Latin and English; parchment; 315 leaves; 342mm x 230mm; foliated i–viii (tabula), 1–179, 179A, 180–252, 1–54; soft leather cover, labelled 'Thomas Spofford 1422.'

WIGMORE

Register of Bishop Adam Orleton
Hereford, Hereford Record Office, Diocesan archives; 1317–27; Latin; parchment; i + 108 + i; 285mm x 190mm (ff 80–91A, 95–101: 280mm x 165mm; ff 91B–94: 250mm x 170mm); foliated 1–90, 91A, 91B, 92–107; modern leather binding on wooden boards.

Households

BISHOP RICHARD SWINFIELD OF HEREFORD

Account Roll of Bishop Richard Swinfield

This lengthy account roll covers the household expenses of Bishop Swinfield from Michaelmas to Michaelmas, 1289–90, and includes the travelling expenses associated with a circuit of the diocese.[61]

Oxford, Bodleian Library, MS Lat. hist. d. 1(R); 1289–90; Latin; parchment; 10 membranes serial; 325mm x 252mm of modern parchment at beginning, 720/700/720/725/710/665/705/675/715/675mm x 252mm; dorse from mb 1.

JOYCE JEFFREYS OF HEREFORD

Account Book of Joyce Jeffreys

Joyce Jeffreys, an unmarried woman of considerable wealth, kept this account book for the years 1638–48.[62] It records receipts of annuities and rents from her extensive property in the county and disbursements on her own household expenses, as well as generous gifts to family, friends, dependants, beggars, entertainers, and others. It is a rich source of detail about the life of the county during the early days of the Civil War. The receipts run from ff 1–22 and the disbursements are on ff 25–72. It appears to have been written by Joyce Jeffreys herself. There are a few annotations by a niece or nephew; one of these is dated 1652, a fact which may indicate that she was dead by that year. Although the accounting year is formally Lady Day to Lady Day, she sometimes began her reckoning on 1 April instead of 25 March.

Until 1643, her principal residence was in Hereford, in a rented house on Wide-marsh Street where some of her own property was also located. After that time, when she fled Hereford for fear of the parliamentary forces, her residence was used to quarter troops and she lived in the country with cousins. At the time of the brief royal recapture of Hereford in 1645 she returned to the city where, despite her royalist sympathies, she was ordered either to sell or pull down all her houses on Widemarsh Street, apparently because Waller's troops had used her residence as a firing post against the royalists in 1643. She went back to the country in 1645 and lived on her property at Horncastle.

London, British Library, Egerton 3054; 1638–48; English; paper; 455mm x 190mm; ii + 73; foliated 1–73; 1858 binding of vellum on boards.

MORTIMER OF WIGMORE

Account Roll of Roger, Lord Mortimer

Several Mortimer family account rolls survive in the British Library, of which only one contains material relevant to REED. Roger Mortimer succeeded his father Edmund as Lord Mortimer and earl of March in 1381 at the age of seven. He did homage to Richard II on 18 June 1393, receiving his extensive Irish lands at that time and his Welsh and English lands on 25 February 1393/4, during the period of time covered by this account roll.[63] The roll was printed by W.P. Baildon, who took it to be a royal wardrobe account roll.[64]

London, British Library, Egerton Roll 8738; 1393–4; Anglo-Norman; parchment; 2 membranes serial; 500/370mm x 265mm.

SCUDAMORE OF HOLME LACY

Household Account Books of John, 1st Viscount Scudamore

These volumes contain summary accounts only. Book 1 is arranged under subject headings rather than chronologically. The other books are in two parts, accounts of expenditure covering the period from 1 October to 23 September 'being one whole yeere' (as Book 2 puts it on f 44), with the accounts arranged alphabetically by subject, such as 'Musicke' or 'Mutton.' The second list itemizes expenditure under subject again, but each item is separately dated. In Book 2, all references to performers occur in the first section and are therefore undated within the year. Books 3 and 4 contain entries in both sections.

Book 1
Hereford, Hereford Cathedral Library; 1632–3; English; paper; ii + 48 + ii;
295mm x 183mm; paginated 1–96; modern board binding.

Book 2
Hereford, Hereford Library, LC 647.1 MSS; 1640–2; English; paper; ii + 92 + ii;
307mm x 200mm; no foliation; first 43 leaves have been laminated; late 19th c. half leather
binding, title on spine: 'MSS. Scudamore Accounts 1640–2.'

Book 3
Hereford, Hereford Library, LC 647.1 MSS; 23 September 1641–28 September 1642; English;
paper; ii + 90 + ii; 307mm x 200mm; no foliation; late 19th c. half leather binding.

Book 4
Hereford, Hereford Library, LC 647.1 MSS; 1642–3; English; paper; ii + 81 + ii;
307mm x 200mm; no foliation; late 19th c. half leather binding.

Miscellaneous Papers Relating to John, 1st Viscount Scudamore

This volume of miscellaneous papers is a nineteenth-century assembly of various
documents covering much of the middle part of the seventeenth century. Included
among them, at f 173, are the steward's accounts for Christmas, 1639, spent at the
Scudamore estate of Holme Lacy.

London, British Library, Add. 11044; 1619–71; English; paper; ii + 295 + ii;
292mm x 190mm; foliated 1–295; 19th c. quarter leather binding.

Editorial Procedures

Principles of Selection

It is often difficult to tell from within the confines of the record office what small piece of information may prove to be relevant to the history of drama, minstrelsy, and ceremonial activity. This is especially true in comparatively remote counties like Herefordshire where the available information will suddenly shift from an embarrassment of riches to a barren waste. I have, therefore, tended to err on the side of inclusion, especially in dealing with the acts of the consistory courts. These are often highly repetitive, but they contain an immense amount of information, particularly about morris dancing. Information concerning this activity, for which Herefordshire was especially renowned, is very sparse before the Restoration. It is also sometimes difficult to tell precisely how many of the entries are related to the activity involved; in such cases I have generally included rather than omitted entries.

In transcribing civic accounts I have tended to give extended passages, especially if several references occur near to each other. Frequently, intervening payments provide useful contextual information for the payments concerned with entertainment, often giving some idea of the scale of the occasion and its relative importance. One exception to this practice is in the later accounts which are often summarized in one long sentence with a single sum at the end. In these cases no advantage would be gained by providing surrounding extraneous information. Civic dinners or breakfasts have not been included unless some specific reference to entertainment was made. References to civic regalia (except for waits' liveries) have been omitted also.

Liturgical and semi-liturgical ceremonies within the church, such as processions, bell-ringings, and singing, have been excluded. The sole exception to this is the records dealing with the boy bishop, which have been included because the mimetic nature of the ceremony is clear.

References to disguisings have been included even when it is uncertain whether or not they were meant as entertainment. Ambiguous references to entertainments where the exact kind of entertainment is not clear ('revels,' cowlstaff ridings, hoodwinking, and the like) have been included, though it is not always clear if they were dramatic in nature. The word 'play' in the ecclesiastical court records creates a special problem, since it could carry a variety of meanings. It is entirely possible that many references, especially those lacking further description (eg, Much Marcle, 1618–19) refer to gaming. Sports and games, where they can be clearly distinguished from dramatic activity, have been omitted, including consistory court prosecutions for illegal football playing and frequent civic and churchwardens' account entries for the upkeep of tennis courts.[65]

Household accounts have been dealt with conservatively, omitting references to payments clearly made outside the county. Thus, in the accounts of Sir John Scudamore, payments and records dealing with plays at the court in London or in France during his tenure as ambassador have not been included.[66]

Play texts available in modern editions fall outside REED's scope and therefore I have not included the fragmentary Processus Satanae associated with Limebrook.[67]

Ecclesiastical Court Records

Because the records of the consistory court are highly formulaic and often very abbreviated, it is frequently difficult to understand what actually happened. An outline of the procedures of the consistory court will help clarify some of these difficulties.

A case or 'causa' was commenced against an individual when he or she was presented, detected, or noted for committing a crime. The most official and formal way of bringing an alleged offence to the court was through a presentment in which either the churchwardens or, in some cases, the rector of a parish brought forth a list of any offences known or believed by them to have been committed by members of their parish since the last presentment. The occasion of a presentment was normally the regular visitation of the parish by the diocesan bishop or his deputy and sometimes a list of questions was prepared for the visitation in order to ensure a full presentment. There appear to have been less formal ways in which information could be brought to the court's attention as well. In any event, such proceedings commenced against a person by the court on the basis of information received were called correction cases, or 'ex officio' cases.

After the charge was laid, the accused person was notified to appear in court on or by a certain date. This process had three stages. First a citation was issued by the court for appearance. Next the apparitor, a court officer with the responsibility of serving citations, sought the accused at his or her residence. At this point in the proceedings, personal service of the citation was required. Finally the judge called or summoned the accused in full court and in an audible voice to appear during the session to which he or she was cited. If the accused did not appear, the apparitor was called upon to testify whether or not he had served the citation. If he had done so, and the accused failed to come forward after the judge summoned him or her a total of three times, the accused was declared contumacious, in wilful contempt of the court's authority, and excommunicated.

If the apparitor failed to serve the citation, a new citation was issued and the apparitor was ordered to serve it by whatever ways and means necessary. This citation by ways and means ('vijs et modis') seems normally to have been served by tacking it, and sometimes a copy of the charge, up on the door of the accused's residence. If citation by ways and means failed to produce an appearance on the desired day, the final stage was citation by public decree, 'per publicum edictum,' which seems to have been a citation publicly read in the parish church of the accused on a certain day or series of days. If both these methods failed to produce the accused in court after the judge's threefold call, the accused was considered wilfully to have ignored the summons of the court, was declared contumacious, and excommunicated.

If the accused did incur excommunication at this (or any) point in the proceedings, an extra step was added to the case. Before the original case could be dealt with, the accused had first to appear and be absolved from excommunication. It appears that sometimes the accused was simply late in appearing before the court and arrived after the time appointed but while the court was still sitting. Under such circumstances absolution seems to have been fairly automatic and the case would proceed as though there had been no delay. In other circumstances the accused would have to appear by person or proxy at a later session to seek the benefit of absolution before the case could proceed.

If the accused appeared in person or sent a proxy (who might have been a master, patron, parent, or husband) in response to the citation of the court, the article containing the charge was formally laid against him or her by the judge and then formally either denied or acknowledged.

If he or she acknowleged that the charge contained in the article was true, the court could proceed in one of two ways. The judge could simply warn the offender not to do so hereafter and dismiss the case. Or he could order a public penance, which normally consisted of a confession of the article in the offender's parish church at one or more major services in a set form of words and in a set penitential garb. Sometimes, however, the penance was to be performed only in the presence of the minister and churchwardens and possibly a set number of parishioners. The offender had to return to the court thereafter and certify the performance of his or her penance either by presenting a copy of the schedule of penance, ie, the set form of words used in the confession, which was taken from the court to the church and signed by the minister and wardens after they had witnessed the penance, or by oath. If an offender ordered to do penance did not return to court within the designated period to certify his or her compliance, then excommunication for contumacy was incurred.

If the accused denied all or part of the charge, there were again two courses open to the judge. He might accept the denial on the strength of the accused's oath or he might require formal compurgation. The latter was a variety of proof peculiar to the ecclesiastical courts. The person required to clear him or herself returned to the court on a specified day accompanied by a specified number of compurgators, persons who would take an oath supporting the statements made on oath by the accused. These compurgators were to be of the same sex and of like station with the accused, ie, clerics had to have clerical compurgators and lay persons had to have lay compurgators, preferably fellow parishioners. A public announcement of the date and place set for the compurgation was also required, so that interested third parties might have the opportunity of challenging the compurgators. If the accused could not produce the required number of compurgators, he or she was deemed to have failed in compurgation and was treated as having confessed to the charge. Non-appearance to make compurgation was punished by excommunication.

Presumably, the judge chose whether to issue a warning or order public penance in the case of a confession of fault or whether to accept a simple oath or order compurgation in the case of a denial of the charge on an ad hoc basis. A simple warning to behave better in future might be deemed appropriate on the basis of perceived sincerity of repentance, the likelihood of a recurrence, the perceived gravity of the offence, or the role of the particular accused in that offence. A person of known good character might have his oath accepted whereas a person of known bad morals might have six compurgators required.

After the accused had successfully completed penance or compurgation and delivered any necessary certificates to the judge, the case was normally dismissed. This precluded any further proceedings against the accused for the same charge. There were usually court fees, including the apparitor's fee for delivering the citation, to be paid, although this was not always specified in the court books. The fees could be forgiven a person who could certify poverty.

The court books which record such proceedings tend to be very sparse and laconic. So much of the course of a case was predetermined that repeated formulas were often abbreviated to a word or two followed by 'etc.' A reader very familiar with court procedure would have been able to supply the missing information and in this volume's translations it has been supplied where appropriate in round brackets.

A registrar would prepare pages in advance for recording a court session by writing in the names of the accused who had been cited to appear at that session and some brief description of their alleged crime, usually putting no more than four or five names on a page. Often all the pages for a series of sessions to take place at various places in a diocese or archdeaconry would be prepared at once. The registrar who attended each session (who was not always the same as the one who had made the initial entries) would then use the space left blank to record the progress of each case.

If the accused appeared, the registrar would record the appearance, the plea, and the judge's disposition in as few words as possible. If he or she did not appear, details of the citation process and ultimate appearance or excommunication for non-appearance would be entered briefly. Reappearances to certify penance, perform compurgation, or receive a reserved penalty were recorded in as few words as possible. Each of the new sessions at which an accused person was required to appear may have been recorded by a new registrar. An explicit date, or the phrase 'Quo die' if the new appearance date was specified in the account of the citation, penance, or compurgation, normally signals the start of the record of a new appearance.[68]

Edited Text

The material in this volume has been arranged in the following manner: first, the documents of Herefordshire and Worcestershire have been kept separate. Within each county, the collection follows the same order as the document descriptions, that is, Diocese of Hereford, Boroughs and Parishes, Monasteries, and Households. Localized records in the sections for Boroughs and Parishes and Monasteries are given in alphabetical order of place. Within each locality, documents are ordered chronologically. For a given year, civic records are given first, chamber orders followed by municipal, mayoral, or chamberlains' accounts. Parish accounts and consistory court records are given next and any miscellaneous material is included at the end. There is one minor exception to the alphabetical ordering by place. A small number of extended consistory court prosecutions involve several parishes. If a single parish is indicated as the site of the event, the entire record is given under that location; if the site is not indicated, the record is entered under the parish in which the prosecution took place. Household records are given in chronological order, alphabetically arranged by family name.

As far as possible the layout of the original document has been followed in printing. Marginalia are placed where they occur in the manuscript; places where space has been left for words to be added later are indicated as '(*blank*).' In some documents, notably the Consistory Court Act Books, this strict adherence to manuscript format has not been possible. From their folds it is clear that these books were originally made up of quires carried by the registrar of the court, in his pocket or in a small case, from one sitting to the next. The headings for the cases to be heard were written in before leaving and when, as frequently happened, not enough space had been allowed for the case, the account continues around the margins of the next case, sideways, upside-down, or in any empty space available. The various continuations of the case were often added by a second, third, or even fourth clerk. There seemed little point in preserving this often chaotic arrangement, so these cases have been transcribed as if they were continuous. The paragraphing of the manuscript has been retained, though the lineation has not. Changes in hands have been indicated as simply as possible with raised circles (° °) and, when more than two hands are involved, the details have been given in an endnote.

When more than one copy of a document survive, a collation is given. This collation records only substantive variants, ignoring differences in orthography and abbreviation as well as minor differences in word order. The texts have not been emended, except for errors of extra or too few minims, when the text is corrected and the error indicated in the footnotes. The spelling, punctuation, and capitalization of the originals have been preserved throughout; otiose flourishes and line-fillers have been ignored. Virgules have been printed as / and //. Manuscript braces have generally not been indicated unless they form a significant part of the manuscript's format. 'I' and 'J' have been uniformly transcribed as 'I'; 'ff' has been retained for 'F'. Where it is not possible to tell whether a scribe intended an upper-case or lower-case letter I have given the lower case. With some few exceptions, scribal abbreviations have been expanded, the expansion indicated by italics. In some cases it is not possible to tell if the scribe intended a noun to be singular or plural; in these cases the abbreviation is left unexpanded and is indicated by an apostrophe, eg, 'Item Ministrell' domini Regis.' A few types of abbreviations have not been expanded. These include abbreviations for measures and sums of money (such as 'li.,' 's.,' 'd.,' 'ob.,' 'di.') as well as a few common and current abbreviations ('Mr,' 'viz,' '&c'). Superior letters have been lowered to the line except where they occur with numerals (eg, 'xl^{ti}'). Abbreviated personal and place names have been expanded and the Latin genitive singular of Hereford has been uniformly transcribed as 'Herefordie.' Forms beginning 'Xρ ' or ' χρ ' have been expanded as 'Chr' or 'chr' in 'Christi' or 'christi.'

Dating

Documents have been dated as clearly as possible. Where it is possible to ascertain the time of year in which an event occurred, the single year is given. Most of the account records in this volume used the normal fiscal year from Michaelmas to Michaelmas of the following year. Where this fiscal year is followed a double year (1445–6) is indicated. Where a different fiscal year is followed or accounts are dated irregularly, this information is given in the heading. A split year is given for dates which fall between 1 January and 25 March (Lady Day). Thus, a date given as 20 January 1524/5 indicates 1525 by our present reckoning of a new year on 1 January, but 1524 by the English ecclesiastical calendar, according to which the year changed on 25 March. For simplicity's sake the split year is not used with court cases which begin in one year and end between the following 1 January and 25 March; in those cases a single year is used as the ending date. An example occurs in the Bodenham prosecution dated 1611–12, where the event and subsequent consistory court case cover the period from Whitsun 1611 to February 1611/12.

The dating of the consistory court prosecutions is particularly tortuous. The date of the first hearing of the case is indicated by the 'acta' heading for the relevant archdeaconry at the beginning of each circuit. The dates of further annotations to the case (should it return to the court at a later time) are sometimes included. The most important date, the date of the event or action, is occasionally, though not always, given. Because of the frequent difficulty in dating the action itself, I have consistently entered consistory court cases under the date of the heading, that is, the first hearing of the case. The location of the court and the names of its officials are given where possible, though several of the Act Books appear to be copies entirely lacking such headings. The title 'Sacre Theologie Professor' in the headings to the Act Book entries has been translated by its appropriate equivalent, STD.

Scribes were not always consistent in their use of dates; where there is a question concerning the date given in a document, I have used the manuscript's dating and dealt with the problem in an endnote. Undated records have been kept in their proper sequence since in all cases it has been possible to give an approximate date (most commonly by the name of the official keeping the account).

Gaps in the Records

No matter how exhaustive a survey of the documents of a county may be, we remain at the mercy of time, for our evidence is limited to that which survives, often capriciously. The state of the municipal records for Hereford has already been discussed.[69] Because of the loss of so many records we can have no way of knowing how much information on the Hereford pageants was destroyed in the last century. The almost complete lack of guild accounts further impedes our understanding of the Hereford Corpus Christi celebrations. Among the guild records which may still have existed in the nineteenth century is the Cordwainers' Account Book in which Devlin noted a 1609 payment 'to the Princes players at the request of Mr. Mayor' (*Helps to Hereford History*, p 20). Murray (*English Dramatic Companies*, p 287) quoted the record from Devlin, but no trace of it now exists.

The paucity of surviving churchwardens' accounts is also to be regretted; records from parishes in Worcestershire and other counties suggest that church ales with entertainment were common, but there is no sign of them in Herefordshire, though the Goodrich Star Chamber case of 1607 may well indicate a Whitsun ale. Such accounts as we have often do not indicate receipts at all, summarizing only the inevitable payments for candles, glass, and baldrics for the bells. Quarter sessions records do not survive in any quantity and the number of family and household documents which we do have is relatively small.

Even such documents as we have do not necessarily provide the kind of information we would like. Far too frequently, for example, municipal payments to professional players are merely summarized on an annual basis, a practice which clearly shows how dependent our information is upon bookkeeping practices. Similarly, although they provide a wealth of personal and geographical detail, the ecclesiastical court records rarely tell us much about the details of the performance involved. We are invariably left with a partial picture; moreover, it may well be a distorted one, for the chance survival of a document may give it an apparent weight far out of keeping with its true importance.

In spite of these reservations, the picture is a real one and a judicious reading of these documents will provide a window on the dramatic entertainments, ecclesiastical, parish, and municipal, along the Welsh border.

Notes

1 When not otherwise indicated, much of the descriptive detail is drawn from *VCH*: *Herefordshire*, vol 1, pp 347–405.
2 Keith Kissack, *The River Wye* (Lavenham, Suffolk, 1978), 4–5.
3 Lobel, 'Hereford,' *Historic Towns*, p 1; see also the maps in Brian Paul Hindle, 'Roads and Tracks,' *The English Medieval Landscape*, Leonard Cantor (ed) (London, 1982), 193–217.
4 R. R. Davies, *Lordship and Society in the March of Wales, 1282–1400* (Oxford, 1978), 34–5.
5 Ailsa Herbert, 'Herefordshire, 1413–61: Some Aspects of Society and Public Order,' *Patronage, the Crown and the Provinces in Later Medieval England*, Ralph A. Griffiths (ed) (Gloucester, 1981), 107–12.
6 C. Williams (ed), *The Official Correspondence: Thomas Bekynton*, Rolls Series, vol 56 in 2 vols (London, 1872, rpt 1964), vol 1, p 2.
7 Herbert, 'Herefordshire, 1413–61,' pp 105–6.
8 R. S. Schofield, 'The Geographical Distribution of Wealth in England, 1334–1649,' *Economic History Review*, ser 2, 18 (1965), 483–510, especially p 504.
9 *VCH*: *Herefordshire*, vol 1, p 409.
10 The deaneries and archdeaconries are indicated regularly in the Consistory Court Acts of Office (described on pp 18–21).
11 John A. F. Thomson, *The Later Lollards: 1414–1520* (Oxford, 1965), 24, 48.
12 *VCH*: *Herefordshire*, vol 1, p 380; the privy council's complaints of September 1581 are recorded in *Acts of the Privy Council of England*, ns, vol 13, John Roche Dasent (ed) (London, 1896), 191–3.
13 David Knowles and R. Neville Hadcock, *Medieval Religious Houses: England and Wales* (London, 1971), 69, 115, 179, 278, 281.
14 Knowles and Hadcock, *Medieval Religious Houses*, pp 216, 225.
15 M. R. James, 'The Library of the Grey Friars of Hereford,' *Collectanea Franciscana I*, Publications of the British Society for Franciscan Studies, vol 5 (1914), 114–23.
16 R. Shoesmith, *Hereford City Excavations*: vol 1, *Excavations at Castle Green*, CBA Research Report 36 (London, 1980); vol 2, *Excavations On and Close to the Defences*, CBA Research Report 46 (London, 1982), and vol 3, *The Finds*, CBA

Research Report 56 (London, 1985). See especially vol 2, pp 17–22, 94–5.

17 Lobel, 'Hereford,' p 5.

18 HRO: AE 25/2 LC2180 (deed dated 1535).

19 Lobel, 'Hereford,' p 6.

20 Lobel, 'Hereford,' p 5.

21 Bodl.: MS Tanner 464e, f 68.

22 Bodl.: MS Tanner 464e, f 70.

23 Johnson, *The Ancient Customs of the City of Hereford*, pp 48–58.

24 Martin Weinbaum (ed), *British Borough Charters, 1307–1660* (Cambridge, 1943), 53.

25 Johnson, *The Ancient Customs of the City of Hereford*, p 96.

26 I. M. Slocombe, 'The Government of Hereford in the 16th Century,' *TRWNFC*, 40, pt 2 (1972), 356–72.

27 The calculation of medieval population is notoriously difficult. W. G. Hoskins wrote in 1966: 'In this field the generalizations of the historian working on a national canvas are more than ordinarily useless and misleading' (*English Local History: the Past and the Future* (Leicester, 1966), 11). Although recent research using computer technology and aggregative analysis has improved the situation, it is for the most part on a local level (as Hoskins implies) that some conclusions can be drawn. The most generally accessible figures come from poll tax records and lay subsidy rolls. In some cases these records merely give amounts of money, allowing a rough comparison between boroughs, but in some cases the taxable householders are listed. This is the case with the especially useful 1377 poll tax records. Converting this figure to a population total is more difficult; a conversion factor of about 4.5 to 4.75 has found some general acceptance. See, for example, William George Hoskins, *Provincial England* (London, 1963), 188 and Julian Cornwall, 'English Population in the Early Sixteenth Century,' *Economic History Review*, ser 2, 23 (1970), 32–44. After the introduction of parish registers in the autumn of 1538 information becomes much more readily available, though no less difficult to interpret. Recent work by the Cambridge Group for the History of Population and Social Structure has shown that it is possible to draw some conclusions on a national level. Their researches have tended to confirm a conversion factor of 4.5–4.75 and have provided much clearer guidelines for population estimates on a national, rather than a local, scale. See E. A. Wrigley and R. S. Schofield, *The Population History of England, 1541–1871: A Reconstruction* (London, 1981).

28 The figures for 1377 are given by Josiah Cox Russell, *British Medieval Population* (Albuquerque, 1948), 132, 142. Russell's methodology and conclusions have been superseded by those of Wrigley and Schofield, *The Population History of England, 1541–1871*.

29 Lobel, 'Hereford,' pp 6–8.

30 John Hatcher, *Plague, Population and the English Economy 1348–1530* (London,

1977), 24 concludes that the death rate among the Hereford clergy was about 48%. The later plague outbreaks of the early seventeenth century were serious enough to necessitate restrictions on travel (as at Worcester, see p 303). Such restrictions clearly affected itinerant entertainers of all kinds. See Paul Slack, *The Impact of Plague in Tudor and Stuart England* (London, 1985), 268.

31 Johnson, *The Ancient Customs of the City of Hereford*, p 13; Johnson (p 44) also cites a list of the city's guilds drawn from the will of Bishop John Scory, in which a guild of 'harpers' supposedly appears. The harpers are, however, a ghost and do not appear in the bishop's will. The manuscript of the will (PRO: PROB 10, Box 114, May 1585) appears to be lost, but a microfilm is available at the Public Record Office (PROB 11/68, Brudenell 39).

32 Charles Phythian-Adams, 'Urban Decay in Late Medieval England,' *Towns in Societies*, Philip Abrams and E. A. Wrigley (eds) (Cambridge, 1978), 169.

33 M. W. Beresford and H. P. R. Finberg, *English Medieval Boroughs: A Handlist* (Newton Abbot, Devon, 1973), 122–4.

34 Weinbaum, *British Borough Charters*, p 53; J. Price, *An Historical and Topographical Account of Leominster and It's Vicinity* (Ludlow, 1795), 219–51.

35 J. W. Tonkin, 'The Palaces of the Bishop of Hereford,' *TRWNFC*, 42 (1976–7), 53–64.

36 *DNB*.

37 *The Complete Peerage*, vol 9, pp 251–85.

38 *DNB*; H. Reade, 'Some Account Books of the First Lord Scudamore and of the Hereford Craft Guilds;' J. P. Feil, 'Dramatic References from the Scudamore Papers,' *Shakespeare Survey*, 11 (1958), 107–16; and *The Complete Peerage*, vol 11, pp 572–4.

39 The total number of pageants is not quite clear; twenty-eight sponsors are listed, but the last two are added in another hand. Two sponsors, the Cappers and the Dyers, are listed twice. The list's resemblance to the Corpus Christi cycles was noted by Alan H. Nelson, *The Medieval English Stage* (Chicago, 1974), 182–3.

40 Lawrence M. Clopper (ed), *Chester*, Records of Early English Drama (Toronto, 1979), 31–3 and Alexandra F. Johnston and Margaret Rogerson (eds), *York*, Records of Early English Drama, 2 vols (Toronto, 1979), 16–26, especially pp 25–6.

41 Citations, unless otherwise noted, are from the records text under the appropriate date and place.

42 Philip Stubbs, *The Anatomie of Abuses* (London, 1583), sig L2v (*STC*: 23376).

43 Respectively, HCL: MS 3226/49; BL: Lansdowne 306, f 174v; and PRO: E315/55, f 71v.

44 See Audrey Douglas and Peter Greenfield (eds), *Cumberland/Westmorland/Gloucestershire*, Records of Early English Drama (Toronto, 1986), 253.

45 This Guildhall was pulled down in 1862. A drawing of it appears in Jim and Muriel Tonkin, *The Book of Hereford: The Story of the City's Past* (Chesham, 1975), 85. The construction of the old Guildhall is discussed by H. J. Powell, 'The Booth Hall,' *TRWNFC*, 36 (1958–60), 206; that of the new Guildhall by

N. Drinkwater, 'The Old Market Hall, Hereford,' TRWNFC, 33 (1949), 3.

46 The manuscript contains a list of payments to minstrels who performed at a feast to celebrate the knighting of Edward, prince of Wales, in 1306, including 'Paruo Willelmo organiste Comitisse Herefordie' and 'Les ij Trumpours Le Conte de Hereforde.' See Constance Bullock-Davies, *Menestrellorum Multitudo*, pp 1, 6, 144–5, 171.

47 Chambers, *The Mediaeval Stage*, vol 1, p 358.

48 *Old Meg of Hereford-shire* (London, 1609), sig A4 (STC: 12032).

49 Research into the origins of the morris has until recently been characterized more by enthusiasm than by scholarly rigour and has tended to dwell largely on the question of its ritual origins. Recent work by E. C. Cawte and his associates, 'A Geographical Index of the Ceremonial Dance in Great Britain,' and John Forrest, *Morris and Matachin: A Study in Comparative Choreography* (London, 1984), has assisted in providing a more balanced view. Forrest's work includes a survey of previous scholarship. See also Barbara Lowe, 'Early Records of the Morris in England,' JEFDSS, 8, no 2 (1957), 61–82 and Michael Heaney, 'Early Morris,' *Traditional Dance*, 5/6 (1988), 191–201.

50 Joseph Needham, 'Geographical Distribution of English Ceremonial Dance Traditions,' JEFDSS, 3, no 1 (1936), 15; the question of women's participation in the morris has been discussed at length (though not always from an historical perspective) in the correspondence in *English Dance and Song*, vols 41–3 (1979–81).

51 As John Aubrey noted, 'In Herefordshire &c: parts of the Marches of Wales, the Tabor and pipe were exceeding common: many Beggars begd with it: and the Peasants danced to it in the Churchyard, on Holydayes and Holy-day-eves.' *Remaines of Gentilisme and Judaisme* in *John Aubrey, Three Prose Works*, John Buchanan-Brown (ed) (Carbondale, 1972), 299.

52 The first OED citation, dated 1562, uses the word to indicate simply a covering of the eyes; the later citation (1573) indicates a game, apparently similar to blind man's buff.

53 E. P. Thompson, '"Rough Music": Le Charivari anglais,' *Annales: economies, sociétés, civilisations*, 27 (1972), 285–312; Martin Ingram, 'Ridings, Rough Music and the "Reform of Popular Culture" in Early Modern England,' *Past and Present*, 105 (1984), 79–113, especially pp 85–6; Martin Ingram, 'Ridings, Rough Music and Mocking Rhymes in Early Modern England,' *Popular Culture in Seventeenth-Century England*, Barry Reay (ed) (London, 1985), 166–97. Further information on cowlstaff customs is given in the endnotes: p 275, to HRO: box 17, vol 66, ff [228v, 229]; p 586, to HRO: box 19, vol 72, ff [24v, 25]; p 588, to HWRO: Quarter Sessions Records 110: 21/68, single sheet.

54 Passages marked °...° have been added by hand.

55 J. A. Guy, *The Court of Star Chamber and Its Records to the Reign of Elizabeth I*, PRO Handbooks No 21 (London, 1985), 1, 7.

56 The general history of the court is discussed by Guy, *The Court of Star Chamber*.

See also Thomas Barnes, *List and Index to the Proceedings in Star Chamber for the Reign of James I.*

57   I. M. Slocombe, 'The Mayor's Book and the Great Black Book.'

58   The cathedral records were calendared by B. G. Charles and H.D. Emanuel, 'A Calendar of the Earlier Hereford Cathedral Muniments,' 3 vols (typescript, National Library of Wales, Aberystwyth, 1955); 'A List of Hereford Cathedral Account Rolls, Court Rolls, Rentals & Surveys' (typescript, National Library of Wales, Aberystwyth, 1955). See also Penelope E. Morgan, 'An Index to A Calendar of the Earlier Hereford Cathedral Muniments and List of the Hereford Cathedral Account Rolls, etc' (typescript, Hereford Cathedral Library, 1956); 'An Index of Personal Names to A Calendar of the Earlier Hereford Cathedral Muniments and A List of the Hereford Cathedral Account Rolls, etc' (typescript, Hereford Cathedral Library, 1957).

59   Leland, *Collectanea*, vol 4, pp 197–8.

60   Also printed in *Miscellanea Antiqua Anglicana*, 1 (1814), no 4, 'A Morris Daunce.'

61   Previously edited by John Webb, *A Roll of the Household Expenses of Richard de Swinfield, Bishop of Hereford*, Camden Society, vols 59, 62 (London, 1854–5).

62   John Webb, 'Some Passages in the Life of a Herefordshire Lady during the Civil War,' *Archaeologia*, 37 (1857), 189–223; F. R. James, 'The Diary of Joyce Jefferies, a Resident in Hereford during the Civil War,' *TRWNFC* (1921–3), xlix–lx; R. G. Griffiths, 'Joyce Jeffreys of Ham Castle,' *TRWAS*, ns, 10 (1933), 1–32, 11 (1934), 1–13. James' article relies almost entirely on the earlier one by Webb.

63   *The Complete Peerage*, vol 3, pp 448–9.

64   W. Paley Baildon, 'A Wardrobe Account of 16–17 Richard II, 1393–4,' *Archaeologia*, 65, pt 2 (1911), 497–514.

65   The churchwardens' accounts of Madley are particularly rich in payments for the upkeep of a tennis court.

66   For some of these records, see J. P. Feil, 'Dramatic References from the Scudamore Papers.'

67   Welbeck Abbey MS fragment strips 1a, 2a, 3a–b; 'Processus Satanae,' W. W. Greg (ed), *Collections*, Malone Society, vol 2, pt 3 (Oxford, 1931), 239–50. The fragments, dated by Greg to *c* 1570–80, contain speeches for God and brief cues for other characters.

68   This summary of the procedures of the consistory court was prepared by Dr Abigail A. Young on the basis of the cases edited for these collections and the introduction to *The Archdeacon's Court: Liber Actorum, 1584*, E. R. Brinkworth (ed), vol 1, Oxfordshire Record Society (Oxford, 1942), v–xix, as well as Robert E. Rodes, Jr, *Lay Authority and Reformation in the English Church: Edward I to the Civil War* (Notre Dame and London, 1982), 163–88.

69   See pp 22–5.

Select Bibliography

The Select Bibliography lists works which transcribe documents relevant to REED and works which have proven essential for reference purposes. Works cited in the Introduction and in the Endnotes are, in general, not included here.

Allen, John. *Biblioteca Herefordiensis or a Descriptive Catalogue of Books, Pamphlets, Maps, and Prints, &c. &c. relating to the County of Hereford* (Hereford, 1821).

Bannister, Arthur Thomas. *The Place-Names of Herefordshire* (Cambridge, 1916).

– (ed). *Registrum Ade de Orleton, Episcopi Herefordensis*, A.D. MCCCXVII–MCCCXXVII. Cantilupe Society (Hereford, 1907) and Canterbury and York Society, 5 (London, 1908).

– (ed). *Registrum Thome Spofford, Episcopi Herefordensis*, A.D. MCCCCXXII–MCCCCXLVIII. Cantilupe Society (Hereford, 1917) and Canterbury and York Society, 23 (London, 1919).

Barnes, Thomas G. *List and Index to the Proceedings in Star Chamber for the Reign of James I.* 3 vols (Chicago, 1975).

Blacklock, F. G. *The Suppressed Benedictine Minster and Other Ancient and Modern Institutions of the Borough of Leominster* (Leominster, [1900]).

Bullock-Davies, Constance. *Menestrellorum Multitudo: Minstrels at a Royal Feast* (Cardiff, 1978).

– *Register of Royal and Baronial Domestic Minstrels, 1272–1327* (Woodbridge, Suffolk, 1986).

Capes, W. W. (ed). *Registrum Ricardi de Swinfield, Episcopi Herefordensis*, A.D. MCCLXXXIII–MCCCXVII. Cantilupe Society (Hereford, 1909) and Canterbury and York Society, 6 (London, 1909).

Cawte, E. C. 'The Morris Dance in Herefordshire, Shropshire and Worcestershire,' JEFDSS, 9, no 4 (1963), 197–212.

– A. Helm, and N. Peacock. 'A Geographical Index of the Ceremonial Dance in Great Britain,' JEFDSS, 9, no 1 (1960), 1–41.

Chambers, E. K. *The Elizabethan Stage.* 4 vols (Oxford, 1923).

– *The Mediaeval Stage.* 2 vols (Oxford, 1903).

Cox, John Charles. *Churchwardens' Accounts from the Fourteenth Century to the Close of the Seventeenth Century* (London, 1913).

Devlin, J. D. *Helps to Hereford History, Civil and Legendary* (London and Hereford, 1848).

Dew, Edward N. *Extracts from the Hereford Cathedral Registers*, A.D. *1275–1535* (Hereford, 1932).

– *Index to the Registers of the Diocese of Hereford, 1275–1535*. Cantilupe Society (Hereford, 1925).

Duncumb, J. *Collections towards the History and Antiquities of the County of Hereford*. 5 vols: vol 1 (London, 1804); vol 2 (London, 1812); vols 3 and 4, a continuation by William H. Cooke (London, 1882–92); vol 5, pt 1, a continuation by Morgan G. Watkins (Hereford, 1899); vol 5, pt 2, vols 6 and 7, a continuation by J. H. Matthews (Hereford, 1912–15).

Finucane, R. C. 'Cantilupe as Thaumaturge: Pilgrims and their "Miracles",' *St Thomas Cantilupe, Bishop of Hereford: Essays in his Honour*. Meryl Jancey (ed) (Hereford, 1982).

Frere, Walter Howard and William McClure Kennedy. *Visitation Articles and Injunctions of the Period of the Reformation*. 3 vols (London, 1910).

The Historical Manuscripts Commission. William Dunn Macray (ed). 'The Manuscripts of the Corporation of Hereford,' *The 13th Report of the Manuscripts Commission*. Appendix 4 (London, 1892), 283–353.

James, F. R. 'The Diary [1638–47] of Joyce Jefferies, a Resident in Hereford during the Civil War,' TRWNFC (1921–3), xlix–lx.

Johnson, Richard. *The Ancient Customs of the City of Hereford* (London, 1868; rev ed 1882).

– *A Lecture on the Ancient Customs of the City of Hereford* (Hereford, 1845).

Kennedy, William Paul McClure. *Elizabethan Episcopal Administration: An Essay in Sociology and Politics*. 3 vols. Alcuin Club Collections, 26–8 (London, 1924).

Leather, Ella Mary. *The Folk-Lore of Herefordshire* (Hereford and London, 1912; rpt 1970).

Leland, John. *Joannis Lelandi Antiquarii De Rebus Britannicis Collectanea*. Thomas Hearne (ed). 6 vols. 2nd ed (London, 1774).

Lobel, M. D. 'Hereford,' *Historic Towns*. Vol 1 (London, 1969).

Macray, W. D. *Catalogue of and Index to the Manuscripts of Hereford* (Hereford, 1894).

Morgan, Frederick Charles. *The Regulations of the City of Hereford, including the Assize of Bread and Ale, 1557* (Hereford, 1945).

– 'The Steward's Accounts of John, 1st Viscount Scudamore of Sligo (1601–71) for the Year 1632,' TRWNFC 33, (1950), 155–84.

Murray, John Tucker. *English Dramatic Companies, 1558–1642*. 2 vols (London, 1910).

– 'English Dramatic Companies in the Towns outside of London, 1550–1600,' *Modern Philology*, 2 (1904–5), 539–59.

Parry, Edward. *Royal Visits and Progresses to Wales and the Border Counties of Cheshire, Salop, Hereford, and Monmouth* (Chester, 1850).

Parry, J. H. *Registrum Johannis de Trillek, Episcopi Herefordensis*, A.D. MCCCXLIV–MCCCXLXI. Cantilupe Society (Hereford, 1910–12) and Canterbury and York Society, 8 (London, 1912).

Price, John. *An Historical and Topographical Account of Leominster and It's Vicinity* (Ludlow, 1795).

– *An Historical Account of the City of Hereford* (Hereford, 1796).

Rawlinson, Richard. *History and Antiquities of the City and Cathedral-Church of Hereford* (London, 1717).

Reade, Hubert. 'Some Account Books of the First Lord Scudamore and of the Hereford Craft Guilds,' TRWNFC (1925), 119–33.

Slocombe, I. M. 'The Mayor's Book and the Great Black Book,' TRWNFC, 38, (1965), 149–50.

Smith, [Joshua] Toulmin (ed). *English Gilds*. Early English Text Society (Oxford, 1870).

Smith, Lucy Toulmin (ed). *The Itinerary of John Leland in or about the Years 1535–1543*. 6 vols (London, 1964).

The Statutes of the Realm. A. Luders, Sir T. E. Tomlins, J.F. France, W. E. Taunton, J. Raithby, J. Caley, and W. Elliott (eds). 11 vols. Record Commission (London, 1810–28).

Townsend, George Fyler. *The Town and Borough of Leominster* (Leominster and London, 1862).

The Victoria County History of the Counties of England. *The Victoria History of the County of Hereford*. William Page (ed) (London, 1908).

Walker, D. 'The Bishops' Registers of the Diocese of Hereford, 1275–1539,' TRWNFC, 36 (1958–60), 291–7.

Wickham, Glynne. *Early English Stages, 1300–1660*. 2 vols in 3 pts (London, 1959–72).

– *The Medieval Theatre* (London, 1974).

Williams, W. R. *The Parliamentary History of the County of Hereford* (Brecknock, 1896).

Woodfill, W. L. *Musicians in English Society from Elizabeth to Charles I*. Princeton Studies in History 9 (Princeton, 1953; rpt New York, 1969).

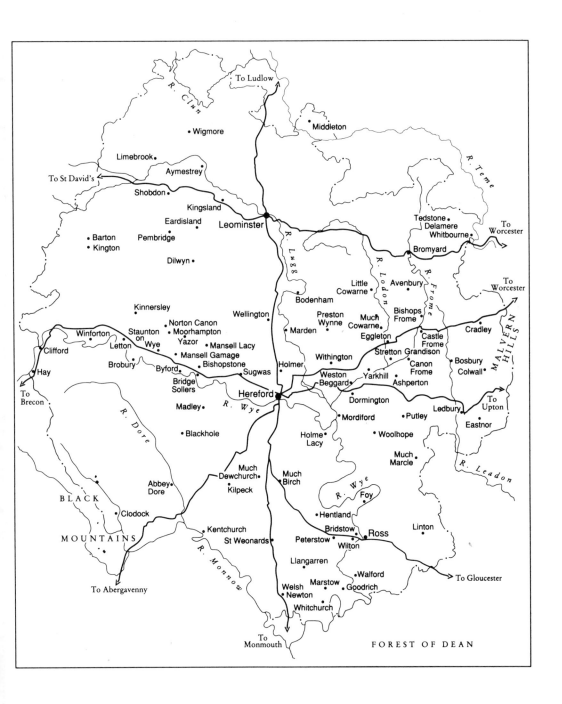

Herefordshire *c* 1600 with principal renaissance roads

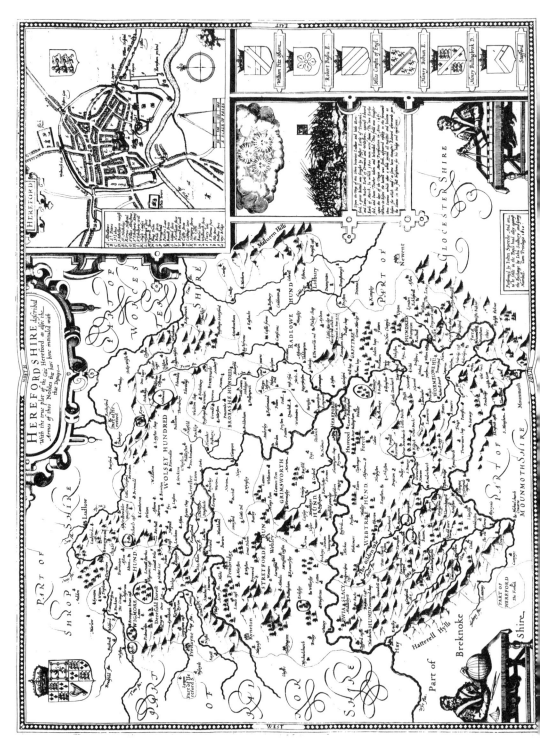

Map of Herefordshire from John Speed, *The Theatre of the Empire of Great Britaine*, by courtesy of the Huntington Library

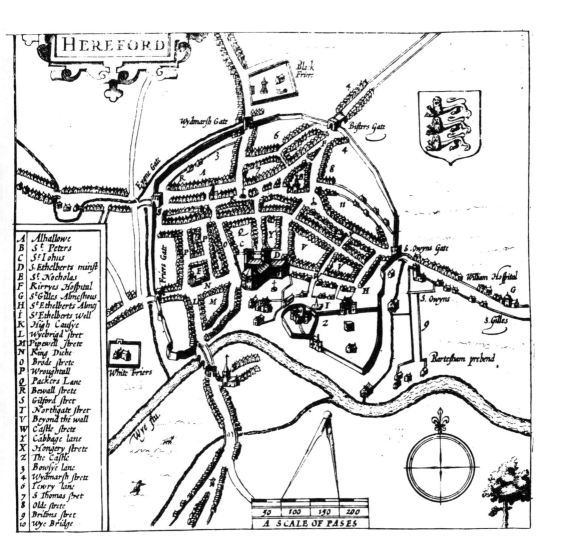

Map of Hereford from John Speed, *The Theatre of the Empire of Great Britaine*, by courtesy of the Huntington Library

Diocese of Hereford

14c. Depositio text in Ordinal

1348
Register of Bishop John Trillek   HRO
ff 91–1v*   *(6 October)*
...

®Ad
prohibend*um*
lud*os* theatral*es*
fieri in
ecclesiis

¶ Quia iux*ta* prophete vocem, domu*m* do*m*ini decet sa*n*ccitudo/ in ea   5
q*ui*cq*uam* excerceri non co*n*uenit quod a cultu religionis fuerit
alienu*m*. Cum *igitur* in ludis theatralib*us* qui *interdum* in ecclesiis fiunt
sc*u*rilitas et t*u*rpiloq*uium* que ab *apos*tolo nedu*m* in templo *dom*ini
q*uo*d dom*us* oracio*n*is teste saluatore fore & vocari debet/ *sed* vbilibet
simplicit*er* prohibent*ur*, aliaq*ue* ad ludibriu*m* pertinencia, ex quib*us*   10
corda fideliu*m* q*ui* in loc*is* eisdem attendere debent sacra solempnia
& de*uo*t*is* or*a*cionib*us* insistere/ ad inania distrahant*ur*, & deuocio
s*u*btrahit*ur* eor*un*dem ut pl*u*rimu*m* interuenire dinoscant*ur*/ in di*u*ini
no*m*inis offensam, & assistenciu*m* seu spectanciu*m* perniciosum
exemplu*m*? nos h*ui*usmodi abusum prout tenem*ur* iuxta sacror*um*   15
canonu*m* sancciones, ne *per* h*ui*usmodi t*u*rpitudi*n*em ecclesie
inq*ui*net*ur* honestas? ab ecclesiis *n*ostre dioc*es*is extirpare cupientes/
tibi *in* virtute *sancte* obed*ienc*ie districte precipim*us* & firmiter
iniungendo mandam*us* quat*inus* h*ui*usmodi ludos siue interludia in
ecclesia de .l. eiusdem *n*ostre dioc*es*is, in qua talia inhonesta frequenc*ius*   20
vt intellexim*us* fieri solebant s*u*b intermi*n*acione anathemat*is* de cetero
studeas prohibere. Quos v*er*o in hac p*ar*te contradictores inueneris
seu rebelles tanq*uam* di*u*ini officij pert*ur*batores denuncies sent*enc*iam
excom*m*unicacion*is* ipso facto dampnabilit*er*/ incurrisse, nich*i*lomin*us*
eos de quor*um* no*m*inibus tibi *per* inquisic*i*onem, quam s*uper* hoc *per*   25
te fieri volum*us*, constiterit/ cites eos seu citari fac*ias* q*uod* comp*ar*eant
cor*am* nob*is* seu Commissario *n*ostro in ecclesia *n*ostra Cathedr*ali*
herefordi*e* .x^{mo}. die post ₍factam₎ citacionem si iuridic*us* fuerit
Alioq*ui*n p*ro*ximo die iuridico sequenti s*uper* h*ui*usmodi rebellione &
contemptu responsuri & iuri parituri ac recepturi quod iusticia   30
suadebit. Certificans nos p*er* .iiij. dies ante t*er*minum h*ui*usmodi eis

per te prefigend*um* quid feceris in premissis per litteras tuas pa*tentes*
h*abentes* hu*n*c ten*orem* aliq*u*o sigillo auctentico consignatas./ Dat*um*
&c.

...

1505: Eleva͂ͅo in   Breviary (Rouen, 1508)   5

1586

Articles of Enquiry of Bishop Herbert Westfaling   STC: 10215
sig B1v

...

41 Whether any Lords of misrule, dauncers, plaiers, or any other   10
disguised persons do daunce, or play any vnseemly parts in the
Church, Church-yard, or Chappell-yard, or whether are there any
playes or common drinking kept in church, or Church-yarde, who
maintaine & accompany such?

...   15

1592

Articles of Enquiry of Bishop Herbert Westfaling   STC: 10215.5
sig B1v

                                                                         20
40. Whether the minister and churchwardens haue suffered any lordes
of misrule, dancers, plaiers, or any other disguised persons to daunce,
or play any vnseemely partes in the church or church-yarde, chappell
or chappel-yarde, if they haue what be the names of such lordes of
misrule, dauncers, plaiers &c. And whether are there any plaies or any 25
drinkings kept in any of the said places, who maintaine and accompany
such?

1620

Articles of Enquiry of Archdeacon Richard Montague   STC: 10218.5   30
sigs A4–A4v
...

30 Whether haue any Lords of misrule, dauncers, players, or any
other disguised person, beene suffered to enter into the Church or
Chappell with games or dances, to the prophaning of Gods house,   35
or into the Church-yards especially in time of diuine Seruice: and if
they haue, what bee the names of such disordered persons?
31 Whether there bee any vnlawfull or prophane excercises I vsed
vpon the Sabboth day, and who gaue them license, whether any doe

---

26/ comon *added by hand in Lincoln College Library copy, N.1.24(1) before* drinkings

vse dancing or such like sports or recreations on the Sabboth day
before the end of all diuine Seruice appointed for that day contrary
to his Maiesties declaration in that behalfe: whether be there any
common drinkings in the Church, and who were present at such
drinkings, or sports, or any that doe sit in Tauernes or Alehouses or   5
Streetes, vpon Sundayes or Holy-dayes, in the time of Morning or
Euening prayer?

...

1622   10

Articles of Enquiry of Archdeacon Richard Montague
STC: 10133.9 (formerly 10219)
sig B1v

33 Whether be there in your Parish any vnlawfull exercises vsed vpon   15
any Sabaoth, or Festivall dayes? whether doe any vse dauncing or
such like sports on the Sabaoth day before the end of all diuine Seruice
appointed for that day? whether be there any common drinking in
your Church? who were present at such drinking, or sports, and
whether any doe sit in the Tauerne, Alehouse, or Streete vpon   20
Sundayes or Holy-dayes in the time of morning or euening prayer?

...

1634

Articles of Enquiry of Bishop Augustine Lindsell   STC: 10216   25
p 6   *(Articles on church property and furnishings)*

7 Whether is your Church or Chappell-yard well fenced, and kept
without abuse: and if not, whose is the default? Hath any person
encroached upon the ground of the Church-yard? hath any used that   30
place, consecrated to an holy use, prophanely or wickedly? Hath any
quarrelled or stricken one another, either in the Church or Churchyard? Hath any person behaved himself rudely, and disorderly in
either, used any filthy or prophane talk, or any other rude or immodest
behaviour in them? Have any Playes, Feasts, Banquets, Suppers,   35
Church-ales, Drinkings, temporall Courts or Leets, Lay-juries,
Musters, or any other prophane usage been suffered to be kept in
your Church, Chappell, or Church-yard? Have any annoyed your
Church-yard, or the fence thereof, by putting in of cattell, by hanging
of clothes, or by laying any dust, dung, or other filthinesse there?   40

...

1635

Articles of Enquiry of Bishop Matthew Wren   STC: 10217
p 4   *(Article on church property and furnishings)*
...

7 Whether is your Church-yard or Chappell yard well-fenced, and   5
kept without abuse? and if not, whose is the default? hath any person
encroached vpon the Church-yard, by setting vp any kinde of building
or fence vpon it, or by opening any doore, gate, or stile into it? hath
any vsed that place (consecrated to an holie vse) prophanely or
wickedly? hath any quarrelled or stricken one another, either in the   10
Church or Church-yard? hath any person behaued himselfe rudely,
and disorderly in either, or vsed any filthy or prophane talke, or any
other rude and immodest behauiour in them? haue any Playes, Feasts,
Banquets, Suppers, Church ales, Drinkings, Temporall Courts, or
L⟨e⟩ets, Lay-iuries, Musters, exercise of dancing, stoole-ball, foot-   15
ball, or the like, or any ⟨o⟩ther prophane vsage, beene suffered to be
kept in your Church, Chappell, or Ch⟨u⟩rch-yard? Haue any annoied
your Church-yard, or the fence thereof, by putting in o⟨f⟩ chattell,
by hanging vp on clothes, or by laying any dust, dung, or other
filthinesse there? When graues are digged, are the bones of the dead   20
piously vsed, and decently interred againe, and laid vp in some fit
place as beseemeth Christians? And is the whole consecrate ground
kept free from swine, and all other nastinesse?
...

                                                                              25

1640

Articles of Enquiry of Bishop George Coke   STC: 10218
sigs [A3–3v]   *(Articles on church property and furnishings)*
...

7 Whether is your Church or Chappell-yard well fenced, and kept   30
without abuse and if not whose is the default? hath any person
incroached upon the ground of the churchyard? hath any used that
place consecrated to an holy use, prophanely or wickedly? Hath any
quarrelled or stricken one another, either in the Church or
Churchyard? Hath any person behaved himselfe rudely, and   35
disorderly in either, used any filthy | filthy or prophane talk, or any
other rude and immodest behaviour in them? Have any playes, Feasts,
Banquets, Suppers, Church-ales, Drinkings, temporall Courts or
Leets, Lay-juries, Musters, or any other prophane usage been suffered

28/ *signature number illegible due to cropping*
36/ filthy | filthy: *dittography; first* filthy *acts as catchword*

to be kept in your Church, Chappell, or Church-yard? Have any annoyed your Church-yard, or the fence thereof, by putting in of cattell, by hanging of clothes, or by laying any dust, dung, or other filthinesse there? And kept free from Swine, and all other nastinesse?

...   5

Boroughs and Parishes

ASHPERTON

1629
Archdeaconry of Hereford Acts of Office   HRO: box 25, vol 94
f [43v]   *(14 October)*   5

Proceedings of the court held in the consistory of Hereford Cathedral
before Master Richard Basset, LLB, deputy to William Skinner, LLD,
official principal and commissary of Francis Godwin, bishop of
Hereford.   10
...

Causae noue   *contra* Philippu*m* Baylies dete*ctum* for playing with his instrument in
nunc de   the tyme of evening prayer the xxx[th] of August last beyng sonday
Mordiford   °quesit*us* 10 Octobris 1629 vijs et modis in p*roximo*°

*Simil*i*ter*   *contra (blank)* Baylies eius fil*ium* presens °Quo die simil*iter*°   15
...

AVENBURY

1588   20
Diocese of Hereford Acts of Office   HRO: box 17, vol 67
f [178v]   *(4 June)*

Proceedings of the court held in the parish church of Bromyard before
Master William Grenewich, deputy, and in the presence of Thomas   25
Crumpe, notary public and registrar.
...

*Citent*u*r.*   Thomas Davy∧⌐ap Bevan⌐ ministrell/. for [b] pipinge in service tyme/
[consocij]   and fetchinge a some*r* poole from Avenbury tempo*re* di*u*inorum/.
consocij.
interessendo.   °cit*atus* p*er* dict*um* ap*paritorem* &c. com*paruit*. dict*us* Thomas Davy   30
18. Iunij./   ap Bevan, & confiten*do* artic*u*lum. &c/. vnde h*a*bet ad confitend*um*

articulum/ &c/ Et ad certificandum in proximo &c./°
...

AYMESTREY

1577/8
Diocese of Hereford Acts of Office   HRO: box 19, vol 72
f [200]*   *(25 February)*

Proceedings of the court held in the parish church of Aymestrey.
...
Thomas bayle parochia de aymesry for dawnsyng at evenyng prayer
the xij of Ianuary. fatetur se abfuisse a vespertinis oracionibus et
Iohannes more taberor Vnde vterque habet vnum f⟨.⟩stig⟨.⟩ etc xxvij°
ffebruarij et solvet xij d. et sic dimittitur
...

BARTON

1606
Archdeaconry of Ludlow Acts of Office   HRO: box 35, vol 129
p 35   *(18 December)*

Proceedings of the court held in the parish church of Ludlow before
Master James Bailie, LLD, *vicar general.*
...
gardiani

citati in
proximo

citati for concealement of Dauncing vppon the saboath Daie &c xviij
die decembris 1606 coram magistro Iacobo Bailie legum doctore &c
comparuerunt et negarunt &c Vnde habent ad melius inquirendum
&c et ad certificandum in proximo &c./ nono die Ianuarij 1606 ad
Idem./ in proximum &c/

BISHOPS FROME

1619/20
Archdeaconry of Hereford Acts of Office   HRO: box 24, vol 90
ff [128v–9]*   *(12 January)*
...

dimissio

Iacobus Poslons & Maria eius vxor for suffering dancing and
minstrelles plaieng in their howse att tyme of eveninge vpon the saboth

41/ eveninge *for* eveninge prayer

daie °quesiti apud ædes suas xvj die decembris predicti &c ad
comparendum xviij eiusdem &c vijs et modis in proximo &c° citati
personaliter per Harris apparitorem die lune vltimo in Bromiard ad
comparendum in loco consistoriali herefordie Quinto die ffebruarij
predicti preconizati trina vice et nullo modo comparuerunt dominus   5
pronunciavit ipsos contumaces reservata pena in proximum xxiiij° die
ffebruarij predicti ad idem in proximum. postea dominus ipsum super
examinacione causarum ipsum dimisit

dimissio   Maria eius pro consimili quinto die ffebruarij predicti comparuit   10
                    personaliter dicta Maria et obiecto ei articulo fassa est articulum esse
                    verum quam confessionem dominus acceptavit et iniunxit ei vnum
Citata in   diem penitencialem more penitenciali et monuit ipsam ad extrahendum
proximo   formam et ad certificandum hoc in loco xxiiij° die ffebruarij instantis
                    xxiiij° die ffebruarij predicti comparuit et dominus ad eius peticionem   15
                    continuavit certificarium in proximum postea iuramentum prestitit
                    that she did not send for any minstrelles nor gave waie vnto them to
                    plaie there vnde dominus ipsam dimisit et admonuit posthac/

dimissio   Iohannes Botchet minstrell   20
                    pro consimili vt supra/ °Citatus in xvij diem decembris predicti &c
                    preconizatus &c excommunicatus/ 12 die Ianuarij 1619 coram
                    magistro Oliuero Lloed legum doctore Vicario generali &c comparuit
                    personaliter et petijt beneficium absolucionis &c et absolutus est &c
                    dein obiecto ei articulo &c fassus est esse verum vnde habet ad   25
                    confitendum articulum in vsuali vestitu coram ministro et gardianis
                    &c et ad certificandum in proximo &c° quinto ffebruarij predicti
                    introducto certificario dimissus |

                    Iohannes Lewis pro consimili   30
dimissio   °Citatus in xv diem decembris predicti &c preconizatus &c
                    excommunicatus° viij° die Martij 1619 iuxta &c apud herefordiam
                    coram magistro Gabriele Wallwin artium magistro deputato &c
                    comparuit personaliter dictus lewis et dominus ad eius peticionem
°citatus°   ipsum absoluit a sentencia excommunicacionis &c deinde obiecto ei   35
                    articulo fassus est articulum esse verum quam confessionem dominus
                    acceptavit vnde habet ad confitendum articulum coram ministro et
certificavit   gardianis die dominico proximo immediate post preces finitas in
pennitenciam   ecclesia ibidem et ad certificandum in proximo secundo
                    ...   40

4/ contumaces: *minim missing* MS   8/ eius *for* eius uxor

f [132v]   *(24 February)*

dimissio   Ricardus Anderos for beinge drinckeing & dauncing at the howse of
Iames Poslance at evening praier tyme/. as marie Poslance vpon her
oath affirmed citatus &c in xxiiij die ffebruarij predicti preconizatus   5
trina vice comparuit personaliter dictus Andrewes et obiecto ei articulo
fassus est articulum esse quam confessionem dominus acceptavit et
iniunxit ei ad confitendum articulum coram ministro et ibidem die
dominico proximo in vsuali vestitutu immediate post lectionem
Evangelij Et monuit ipsum ad extrahendum formam et ad   10
certificandum hoc in loco dimisit die Martij proximo postea dominus
ipsum

dimissio   contra Elizabetham predictam similiter
vxor eius pro consimili xxiiij° die ffebruarij predicti similiter   15
…

Cowarne parva   Ioanna Browne pro consimili xxiiij die mensis ffebruarij 1619 iuxta &c
[L]   apud herefordiam coram magistro Gabriele Wallwin magistro [depu]
dimissio   deputato &c comparuit personaliter dicta Ioanna et examinata causa
dominus ipsam dimisit cum admonicione   20

ffroma Episcopi   Sibilla Browne pro consimili quesita &c in vj^{tum} diem Aprilis predicti
preconizata &c non comparuit vijs et modis in proximo nulla talis.

BODENHAM   25

1611–12
Archdeaconry of Hereford Acts of Office   HRO: box 23, vol 86
f [156v]   *(9 December)*   30

*Proceedings of the court held in the consistory of Hereford Cathedral
before Master James Bailie, LLD, vicar general of Robert Bennett,
bishop of Hereford.*
…

dimissio   Richardus Cronne detectus that he [d] with diuers others vppon   35

7/ esse *for* esse verum
8/ iniunxit: *minim missing* MS
9/ vestitutu *for* vestitu
18/ artium *omitted after second* magistro (?)
23/ nulla talis *for* nullatenus (?)

whitsonday last was a [gu] may gaminge and shotinge of gunes in tyme
of devine service & when the minister was administringe the
sacrement/ °Quo die comparuit et examinata causa dominus iniunxit
ei vnum diem penitentialem in Ecclesia ibidem et ad certificandum in
proximo/ nono die Ianuarij predicti in loco consistoriali &c comparuit   5
et in vim iuramenti &c Et actionem penitencialem &c vnde dominus
eum dimisit/°

...

f [157v]*   10

...

dimissio/   Iacobus Vale de Wellington minstrell
for comminge to Boddenham one the saboth daie, to prophane it, in
playeinge and drinkeing he and his companie in the alehowse diuers
sondaies at tyme of devine service Quesitus [Citatus] in proximo/   15
°nono die mensis Ianuarij predicti comparuit/ obiectoque ei articulo
&c negauit esse verum/ vnde dominus iniunxit ei ad purgandum se
in proximo &c cum bina manu &c facta proclamacione &c Quo 29
die Ianuarij predicti; preconizatus &c non comparuit &c vnde dominus
pronunciauit &c et decrevit citandum fore erga proximum &c dicere   20
causas &c/° vltimo die mensis ffebruarij 1611° iuxta &c in loco
Consistoriali herefordie coram domino vicario generali comparuit
dictus Iacobus Vale et examinata causa dominus ipsum dimisit cum
admonicione &c

...   25

BOSBURY

1589
Diocese of Hereford Acts of Office   HRO: box 17, vol 68   30
f [196v]*   *(29 June)*

*Proceedings of the court held in the consistory of Hereford Cathedral
before Master Francis Bevans.*

                                                                             35
                Richardus Kent habet [vt supra]/ ad certificandum vnum diem
emanavit   penitencialem/ anglice for goyng a hodiwinking on shrove sunday
excommunicacio tempore vespertinarum precum/. Quo die non comparuit/

emanavit   Iohannes Watkis vt supra/   40
excommunicacio Iacobus leeth vt supra/

                ...

f [198]*

...

negat.   Con*tra* eunde*m*/ a Com*m*on dauncer on the saboth day

...

                                                                      5

BROBURY

1616
Diocese of Hereford Acts of Office   HRO: box 24a (formerly 18), vol 70
f [33]*   *(8 September)*   10

Thomas Hulland detect*us* p*er* Rectorem ib*ide*m for vsinge of certen
disorders in his howse one the saboath daies and in the tyme of devine
dimissio   *s*ervice namelie that vpon the viijth daie of September beinge Sondaie
absented himself from devine *s*ervice and sermon at eveninge praier 15
one the saboth daie and retained certen guestes in his howse, dancinge
tiplinge and drinkeinge the whole daie and all tyme of eveninge praier
[⟨.......⟩]   xix° die men*s*is [No] Octobris 1616 in ecclesia Cath*edralis* herefo*rdie*
loco con*s*i*s*toriali ib*ide*m coram vene*rab*ili viro ma*g*istro Iohanne
Richardson sacre theologie p*ro*fessore deputato &c comp*ar*uit 20
p*er*sonali*ter* d*ic*t*us* hulland obiectoq*ue* ei a*rticu*lo fass*us* est a*rticu*lum
esse veru*m* vnde d*omin*us iniu*n*xit ei vnu*m* diem pe*nitencialem* more
pe*nitenciali* Et ad certificand*um* in p*ro*ximo xv° die men*s*is Novembris
p*redicti* comp*ar*uit et d*omin*us sup*er* examina*cione* ipsum dimisit cu*m*
admoni*cione* &c   25

dimissio   Eliza*betha* eius vx*or* pro con*s*i*mi*li xix° die Octobris p*redicti* Simil*iter*
v*t* supra

...
                                                                      30

1616–17
Diocese of Hereford Acts of Office   HRO: box 24a (formerly 18), vol 71
f [313]*   *(7 December)*

Proceedings of the court held in the consistory of Hereford Cathedral 35
before Master Silas Griffithes, STD, *vicar general, and official principal*
of Robert Bennett, bishop of Hereford.

Henricus Iones ffidler de Letton detect*us* p*er* Rectorem de Broburie
for playeinge the whole saboath daie in Broberie and in tyme of 40

3/ eunde*m*: *Richard Caple, gentleman*

dimissio

eveninge praier and sermon h*abe*t ad cer*tificandum* peniten*ciam* xvij°
die Ianuarij [*predicti*] 1616 iux*ta* &c in Ecclesia Cathe*drali* herefor*die*
loco cons*istoriali* ib*idem* coram vener*abi*li viro mag*is*tro Silvano
Griffiths sacre theologie *professore* vicario gener*ali* &c com*paruit*
*p*ersonal*iter* d*ictus* Iones et introduxit formam et in vim iuramenti sui   5
cer*tificavi*t de *p*eractione pen*itencie* iux*ta* &c vnde dimiss*us*
...

CANON FROME

10

1587
Diocese of Hereford Acts of Office   HRO: box 17, vol 66
f [228v]*   *(6 April)*

Proceedings of the court held in the consistory of Hereford Cathedral   15
before Master Francis Bevans, LLD, *and in the presence of Thomas*
Crumpe, notary public and registrar.

18 d.
2 maij./
emanavit
suspencio
[*debet*
feod*um*]

con*tra* Rogeru*m* Hide. notat*us* anglice, for plaieng w*i*th his instrument
in the alehowse (being forbid by the gardians) in the tyme of devyne   20
*s*ervice, sithens lent/ cit*atus* *per* Bullocke &c pu*blice* preconi*z*atus &c
com*paruit,* & confiten*do* arti*cu*lum &c sed nega*vi*t q*uod* non fuit
tempore divi*norum* &c h*abe*t ig*itu*r ad purgand*um* se in prox*imo* &c
cu*m* 4^(ta) manu &c
2. maij com*paruit* et *p*roduxit q*u*osdam Rich*ar*dum Kent, henricu*m*   25
Price, & postea submisit se &c. vnde h*abe*t [v] i diem penit*encialem*
in Ecclesia ib*idem*/ Et ad cer*tificandum* in prox*imo*/
...

CASTLE FROME   30

1615
Diocese of Hereford Acts of Office   HRO: box 24a (formerly 18), vol 70
ff [78v–9]*
...   35
Ric*ard*us Langlius h*abe*t ad cer*tificandum* 2 dies pen*itenciales* for
beinge in an alehowse in the howse of on *(blank)* Ambrose in time
of devine *s*ervice vpon a sondaie before Michaelmas daie Last &c allso
for dancinge °Quo die *p*reconi*z*atus &c nullo modo com*paruit* vnde
ex*comm*unicatus° | 40

dimissio Ric*ard*us Bevie mr Mintridge man *pro* cons*imili*
°Quesit*us* in vlt*imum* diem Maij *predicti* &c vijs et mod*is* in prox*imo*
&c° xxij° di⟨e⟩ Iulij 1616 *predicti* *preconizatus* &c non com*paruit* &c
deinde examinata c*ausa* ⟨d⟩*ominus* ips⟨um⟩ dimisit/
...   5

CLIFFORD

1620
Archdeaconry of Hereford Acts of Office   HRO: box 24, vol 90   10
f [78]*   *(13 July)*
...
Thomas Watkin Owen et Will*imus* Turnor
gard*iani* for not *p*resentinge dancing vpon the saboath daie beinge
admonished by mr Williams and his Curat to forbeare not with   15
standinge they *p*ersistinge and they continewe in *p*rofaning of the
lord*es* saboath at evening praier tyme xiij° die Iulij *predicti*
com*p*aruerunt et ex*aminata* c*ausa* d*ominus* mo*nuit* [ipsum] ips*os* ad
*p*resentand*um* ad *p*roximum eoru*m* presentamenti
                                                                     20

COLWALL

1588
Diocese of Hereford Acts of Office   HRO: box 17, vol 67
f [178]   *(4 June)*   25

Proceedings of the court held in the parish church of Bromyard before
Master William Grenewich, deputy, and in the presence of Thomas
Crumpe, notary public and registrar.
...   30
°paup*er*   Will*imus* Poole de le black hull/ for kepinge pipinge and taberinge
18 Iunij/.°   in domo sua temp*ore* div*inorum*. cit*atus* per dict*um* ap*paritorem* &c.
com*paruit* d*ictus* will*imus* Poole, et confitendo articu*lum* &c. vnde
hab*et* i. diem peniten*cialem* in Ecc*lesia* ib*idem* &c. Et ad cert*ificandum*
in prox*imo* &c.   35
...

f [219]   *(18 June)*

*Proceedings of the court held in the consistory of Hereford Cathedral
before Master William Grenewich.*

...   5

Willimus Poole/ habet ad certificandum vnum diem penitencialem/ for

emanavit
suspensio/
kepinge and dauncinge in domo sua tempore divinorum °Quo die
publice preconizatus non comparuit/°

...

                                                                                                10

1619–20
Archdeaconry of Hereford Acts of Office   HRO: box 24, vol 90
ff [129v–30]*   *(18 December)*

...

Gabriel Pitt iunior   15
for dauncing betweene morninge and eveninge praier die dominico
contrarie to the kinges declaracion/ °18 die mensis Decembris 1619
coram domino Vicario generali &c comparuit personaliter dictus
Gabriel Pit obiectoque ei articulo &c allegatur se fuisse et esse subditum
et subiectum Iurisdiccioni peculiari Prebendarij, de Barton Collwall,   20
tamen fatetur that he did dance prout articulatur within the Iurisdicion
of this cort: vnde dominus ratione delicti et confessionis huiusmodi
iniunxit ei ad peragendum publicam huius sui delicti confessionem
coram ministro et gardianis parochie predicte die dominico proximo
immediate post preces vespertinas finitas°   25

Ricardus Hope iunior pro consimili
°comparuit in ecclesia predicta, et monuit ad certificandum in proximo
°quo die
similiter°
&c 13 viz die Ianuarij proximi hoc in loco coram domino vel &c et
adtunc denuo. compareat ad videndum vlteriorem &c/° xiij° die   30
Ianuarij predicti preconizatus trina vice dictus Hope et nullo modo
comparuit dominus pronunciavit ipsum contumacem et in penam &c
reservata pena in proximum xxiiij° die ffebruarij predicti comparuit
et dominus ad eius peticionem retulit causam ad auditum doctoris Best

                                                                                                35
dimissio
Willimus hould pro consimili/ °quo die similiter° xiij° die Ianuarij
predicti similiter xxiiij° die ffebruarij predicti similiter

dimissio
Willimus Sawford pro consimili/ °quo die similiter° xiij° die Ianuarij

---

7/ *word missing after* kepinge

predicti simil*iter* vt supra xxiiij° die ffebruarij pr*edicti* com*paruit* et examinata *causa* d*omi*n*us* ipsum dimisit./

dimissio

Eliz*abetha* Brooke pro consimili/ °q*u*o die sim*iliter*/ postea dimissi sunt c*um* admonic*ione* &c/° |

5

dimissio

Anna Harbart pro cons*imili*/ °q*u*o die sim*iliter*/ postea dimissi sunt c*um* admonic*ione* &c°

dimissio

Elizabetha Pitt pro cons*imili*/ °q*u*o die sim*iliter*/ postea dimissi sunt c*um* admonic*ione* &c°

10

...

f [131]*

...

15

contra Gabrielem Pitt iu*n*iorem

dimissio

detect*us* for dauncinge on the sonday betwene morninge and eveninge prayer contrarie to the °kinges° ma*i*esties declarac*ion*; Decimo octavo die mens*is* Decembris, Anno d*omi*ni 1619 in loco Cons*is*toriali infra ecclesiam Cath*edral*em herefo*r*die Coram d*omi*no vicario in sp*irit*ualibus g*e*n*er*ali &c pr*esente* me Iacobo Laurence notario publico &c pr*econi*zato d*i*cto Gabriele Pitt ad hos diem &c p*er* publicum edictum in ecclesia p*ar*och*ia*li de Collwall pr*edi*cto die d*omi*nico existen*ti* xij° die mens*is* Decembris pr*edi*cti inter divinorum solemnia &c citat*o* &c com*paruit* p*er*sonaliter dictus Gabriel Pitt et obiecto ei articulo pr*edi*cto allega*vit* se fuisse et *esse* subditu*m* et subiectu*m* iur*i*sdicc*io*ni Prebe⟨n⟩darij peculiaris iur*i*sdicc*io*nis Prebende de Barton Collwall, et tamen fassus est that he did daunce on the sonday betwene morninge and eveninge prayer pro*v*t articulatur within the iur*i*sdic*i*on of this Court quam confessionem ac etiam comp*ar*itionem d*i*cti Gabrielis Pitt iudicial*iter* fact*as* d*omi*n*us* acceptavit quate*n*us &c ac ratione pr*emissoru*m iniunxit eid*em* Gabrieli Pitt ad p*er*agendu*m* publicam h*uiu*smodi sui delicti confessione*m* coram ministro et gard*ianis* p*ar*och*ie* pr*edi*cte die d*omi*nico proxi*mo* immediate post preces vespertinas finitas in ecclesia pr*edi*cta iuxta sched*ulam* concipiend*am* &c et monuit eum ad extrahend*um* dictam sched*ulam* conceptam ac ad certificand*um* de p*er*accione eiusdem ⌐confessionis⌐ hoc in loco decimo tertio die mens*is* Ianuarij proxi*mi* et adtunc et

20

25

30

35

4–5, 7, 10/ dimissi sunt *for* dimissa est

ibi*dem* comp*arendum* personali*ter* ad vidend*um* vlteri*orem* process*um*
fieri in hac causa. °xiij° die Ianuarij p*redicti* preconizatus trina vice et
nullo modo com*paruit* d*ominus* pronu*n*ciavi*t* ipsum contumac*em*
xxiiij° die ffebruarij p*redicti* preconizatus &c com*paruit* et d*ominus*
retulit ca*usa*m ad auditu*m* doctoris Best°   5

CRADLEY

1587
Diocese of Hereford Acts of Office   HRO: box 17, vol 66   10
f [228v]*   (6 April)

*Proceedings of the court held in the consistory of Hereford Cathedral
before Master Francis Bevans, LLD, and in the presence of Thomas
Crumpe, notary public and registrar.*   15

in recept'/   con*tra* Edmund Sheere/. notat*us* anglice./ that vpon the xxvj[th] daie
of ffebruary, 1586. iuxta &c, he & the p*er*sons of the same p*ar*ish
herevnd*er* written, did Cary one willi*am* Pillinger vpon a Colestaffe,
in the tyme of divyne s*er*vice, with blowing of hornes, and throwing   20
of graynes, w*ith* such other like fantasticall toyes, w*hich* ˏ⌜did⌝ hinder
them [for th] from the hearing of divyne pr*a*ier aforsaid.
di*missio*./   ci*tatus* [per ⟨..........⟩] ˏ⌜per⌝ d*ominum* Thoma*m* Higgins [vic*arius*]
clericus/ Curat*us* ibi*dem* &c.
                                                                         25

emanau*it*   con*tra* Willi*mum* Pillinger/ rider/ detect*us* simil*iter*.
emanau*it*   con*tra* Rich*ar*dum Holland/ detect*us* simil*iter*
emanau*it*   con*tra* Thoma*m* Colling*es* iunior/ detect*us* simil*iter* in p*ro*ximo/
emanau*it*   con*tra* Iacobu*m* Colling*es*/ detect*us* simil*iter*.
emanau*it*   con*tra* Robert*um* s*er*vum Ioh*ann*is Warner/ detect*us* simil*iter*.   30

f [229]*

con*tra* Rich*ar*dum Hill ./ detect*us* simil*iter*

...   35

24/ clericus/ Curat*us* *for* clericum Curatum
28/ iunior *for* iuniorem

DILWYN

1589
Diocese of Hereford Acts of Office   HRO: box 17, vol 68
f [149v]   *(7 June)*

*Proceedings of the court held in Hereford Cathedral before Master
Doctor Bevans,* LLD.

...

2 Iulij

Edward*us* hopley [gard*ianus*]./ anglice for suffering Dauncing and
ale selling temp*ore* di*u*inor*um*/ *Citatus* per ap*paritorem* &c. vnd*e*, &
[confest*us* est art*icul*um in]/ confess*us* est art*icul*um &c, vnde h*ab*et
ad agnoscend*um* hu*iu*smodi culpa*m* in proximo/ &c Et ad
cert*ificandum*

...

EASTNOR

1609
Archdeaconry of Hereford Acts of Office   HRO: box 23, vol 85
f [88]*   *(20 December)*

Thomas Wynter
kepeth dauncinge and other disorders in his howse vpon diu*ers*
Saboath daies and sufferinge idel *persons* to play vnsemely part*es*. °20
die mens*is* decembris 1609. comparuit et monitus fuit (ex
confess*ionibus* suis) ad confitend*um* hunc delict*um* su*um* coram
congregatione aliquo die dominico siue festiuo. et ad cert*ificandum*
in proximo/. Postea cum admonic*ione* d*i*mittitur°

dimissio
Citatus in
prox*imo*

Thomas Harnatt
is his minstrell ready at call/ Quo die comparuit & Simil*iter* vt supra.

dimissio
Citatus in
prox*imo*

...

FOY

1621
Archdeaconry of Hereford Acts of Office   HRO: box 24, vol 91, pt 2
f [2v]*   *(14 November)*

Proceedings of the court held before Master Gabriel Wallwin, deputy.

...

contra Thoma*m* Buttongard/ for dauncinge in eveninge prayer tyme/

°xiiij Die Novembris 1621 coram mag*istro* Gabriele Wallweine
Surrog*ato* &c comp*aruit* obiectoq*ue* ei ar*ticulo* &c neg*avit* esse ver*um*:
[vnde h⟨..⟩] Vnde dismiss*us* est donec melius constiterit &c°

...

GOODRICH

1609–10
Star Chamber Bill of Complaint   PRO: STAC 8/234/10/Item 12
single sheet*   *(23 January 1608/9)*

To the kinges most Excellent M*a*iestye
In all humblenes sheweth and informeth vnto yo*ur* most excellent
M*a*iestie yo*ur* most loyall and obedient Sub*iect* William Phelpott of
the parishe of Gooderich in yo*ur* M*a*iesties Countie of Heref*ford* That
whereas yo*ur* M*a*iesties said sub*iect* was appoynted and sworne in the
fifte yeare of yo*ur* M*a*iesties raigne to bee yo*ur* M*a*iesties officer as
Constable of the parishe of Gooderich for the preservac*on* of yo*ur*
M*a*iesties peace and the due execuc*ion* of the said office in all thinges
therevnto belonginge and comanded by yo*ur* M*a*iesties Lawes Soe it
is and it maie please yo*ur* highenes that vpon the mondaye in whitson
week*e* beinge the five and twenteth daie of Maye in the said fifte yeare
of yo*ur* M*a*iesties raigne divers of the Inhabitant*es* and parishioners
of the said Lordshipp and Towne of Gooderich to the number of one
hundred or thereabout*es* then being assembled togeather after dynner
at or neare the Churchyarde of Gooderich aforesaide who did meete
then and there to bee merrye in most neighbourly and friendly sorte
according to the antient custome of the saide towne and Countrey
those holy daies tyme out of mynde vsed w*ith* mirth musique and
dansing w*ith*out entent of hurt to anye personn but to make peace
and love betweene all neighbours if any debate were In w*ith* companye
was then and there one Richard Powell gent*leman* dwellinge in the
next parishe adioyning called Whitchurch in the said Countie of
Heref*ford* and Iohn Guyllim gent*leman* of the parishe of Pitstow neare
adioyning who came then and there to the said Churchyard of
Gooderich to meete and bee merrye w*ith* theire ffriend*es* w*ith*out
entent of hurt to any of yo*ur* M*a*iesties sub*iectes*. And for that one
Richard Powell of Gooderich aforesaid yeoman then kept a victualling

18/ preservacon *for* preservacion: *mark of abbreviation missing*
31/ with *for* which
34/ Pitstow: *Peterstow, Herefordshire*

house at Gooderich aforesaid and made provision of meate and drinke
to enterteyne any persons that should then come thither to bee merrye,
The said Richard Powell gentleman and [one Iohn Lluellen] ⌐Iohn
[H⟨...⟩] Guyllm⌐ went then and there into the house of the said Richard
Powell yeoman at Gooderich aforesaid to banquett and bee merry   5
togeather in your subiectes Companye and in the Company of others
of the chief of the said parishe, And after being togeather there
banqueting for the space of almost one houre or thereaboutes in your
Maiesties peace One Thomas Williams servant to one Edward Savacre
Clerke vicar of Gooderich and other his Accomplices hereafter named   10
or some of them bearinge some displeasure to the said Mr Powell
and Iohn Guyllm vpon former quarrelles betweene them ∧⌐[had]⌐
touchinge certen variances debates & Suytes in the Lawe before had
betweene the said Richard Powell gentleman and one Thomas Guyllm
gentleman a Clerke of the Pettie bagge, in your Maiesties highe Court   15
of Chancery for certen Landes in Whitchurch aforesaid Hee the said
Thomas Williams to the ende to kindle a quarrell therevpon in the
behalfe of the said Thomas Guyllm vpon Confederacie and practize
conspired with [one] ⌐[the said]⌐ one Henry Lluellyn and others and
to make troubles to disturbe the whole Companye then and there   20
assembled togeather the said Thomas Williams did then and there by
the prive Conspiracie and practize of the said Henry lluellen and Iohn
Tovye thelder Iohn Tovye the younger and others the servantes of
the saide Edward Savacre vicar of Gooderich repaired to the said
victualling house at Gooderiche aforesaid aboutes two of the Clocke   25
in the afternoone of the said five and twenteth day of May last past
and intruded into the Company of your saide Subiect and the said
Mr Powell and Iohn Guyllm of sett purpose and to the end to picke
some quarrell with the said Mr Powell and Iohn Guyllm beinge then
and there in your Maiesties peace, and vpon the same meetinge   30
togeather then and there the saide Thomas Williams mynistred wordes
of quarrell to the said Mr Richard Powell and the saide Iohn Guyllim
vpon which wordes some weapon beinge like to bee then and there
drawen in the said house betweene them your said subiect beinge
then your Maiesties said Constable of the said towne of Gooderich   35
aforesaid then and there by vertue of your said subiectes office kept
them asunder and required them then and there on your Maiesties
name to keepe your Maiesties peace And thervpon the said Thomas
Williams having then noe staffe but a dagger at his backe departed
out of the said victualling house in all hast sayinge hee would presently 40
retorne againe and soe departed from thence to the house of the said
vicar his master neare adioyning where it seemed the saide Thomas

Williams had prepared some weapon. Att which tyme and place the
said Henry Lluellen ready in the said Churchyarde had a longe Iavelyn
in his hande prepared to backe and maynteyne anie quarrell of the said
Thomas Williams against the said Mr Powell and Iohn Guyllim And
to that ende the said Henry lluellen then and there in all hast and fury   5
with his Iavelyn came towardes the said house where the said quarrell
was begonne and said to the said Mr Powell and Iohn Guyllm that
hee would haue the blood of some within the said house meaning the
said Mr Powell and Iohn Guyllm as your said Subiect and others there
then conceaved, whervpon your subiect then and there greatlie feared   10
some pretended match to bee contrived to comytt some great [greate]
hurt or murder there and did then and there require and chardge in
your Maiesties name the said Henry lluellen to bee quiett and to keepe
your Maiesties peace and to delyver vp his said weapon which the
said Henry Lluellen then and there refusinge and resisting and   15
threatninge revenge vpon the said Mr Powell and Iohn Guyllim your
subiect and his neighbours present in aide of your Maiesties peace
then and there did arest the said Henry lluellen and then and there
did take away the said Iavelyn from the said Henry lluellen And
therevpon instantly the said Thomas Williams retorned out of the   20
said house of the said Edward Savacre his Master with a longe fforrest
Bill and a dagger towardes the said Mr Powell and Iohn Guyllim then
being in the Churchyarde aforesaide to the ende to assault them And
thervpon your said subiect in the said Churchyarde then also required
the said Thomas Williams to keepe your Maiesties peace which to   25
doe the said Thomas Williams then and there with great Oathes denyed
and assaulted your Subiect with the said Bill to the end to haue
mahumed or hurt your said subiect or the said Mr Powell & Iohn
Guyllm which hee the said Thomas Williams had then doen and
comytted yf your said subiect and other the neighbours in preservacion   30
of your Maiesties peace had not then taken hould of the said Longe
forrest Bill and taken the same away from [him] ⌈the said Thomas
Williams⌉ by vyolence and strong hand whervpon the said Thomas
Williams then and there drewe forth a longe dagger and thrust at your
Subiect to thend to haue killed your said subiect if hee had not broken   35
the saide thrust with his lefte hande whereby the said Thomas Williams
then and there thrust your said subiect verie deepely into his lefte
hand with the said dagger soe that the blood issued aboundantly And
your Maiesties said subiect then and there beinge aided with his
neighbours to keepe your Maiesties peace then and there arrested the   40
said Thomas Williams to thende to haue brought him to some of your
Maiesties Iustices of the peace within the said Countie of Herefford

neare adioyning to put in sureties to aunsweare the said
misdemeanou*r*s com*m*ytted in the said Churchyard and bee
answearable to keepe yo*u*r Ma*ies*ties peace whervpon imediately [one]
ˌʳthe saidˑ Iohn Tovye thelder Iohn Tovy the younger Iohn Horsman
Iohn Lynn⟨e⟩y al*ia*s Baker Iohn Meynsto⟨n⟩ Thomas Mothewaye   5
Thomas Prosser Henry lluellen Phillipp Vaughan and Anthony
Phelpott of Marstow beinge all servant*es* or at the Comand of the
said Edward Savacre they beinge then and there vnlawfully assembled
beinge armed an⟨d⟩ weaponed w*i*th longe staves bill*es* daggers and
other weapons in warlike sort most riotously and routously they then   10
and there knoweng the said Edward Savacre tooke parte and favoured
the said suit*es* of the said Thomas Guyllm against the said Mr Powell
for the said Landes in Whitchurch aforesaid And that there were
former quarell*es* betweene them for the same the said riotous personns
being then and there riotously and routously assembled togeather   15
[and] ʳwithˑ armed weapons as bill*es* staves sword*es* daggers and other
weapons p*re*pared for the said p*re*tenced quarrell to bee had and made
by the said Thomas Williams and Henry Lluellen against the said Mr
Powell and Iohn Guyllim as aforesaid yo*u*r Ma*ies*ties said subi*ec*t then
and there in yo*u*r Ma*ies*ties name chardged and required ayde of your   20
subi*ec*tes neighbours then and there beinge p*re*sent in the saide
Churchyarde of Gooderich to ayde yo*u*r Ma*ies*ties said subi*ec*t in the
keepinge of yo*u*r Ma*ies*ties said peace But the saide Thomas Williams
ˌʳ& his accompliceˑs nothinge respecting yo*u*r Ma*ies*ties Lawes nor
having any regarde to yo*u*r said subi*ec*tes authoritie or office of being 25
yo*u*r Ma*ies*ties Constable hee did then and there assault sore hurt
beate strike and evill intreate yo*u*r Ma*ies*ties subi*ec*t giving him divers
sore hurt*es* and bruses in divers part*es* of his bodie wherby yo*u*r said
subi*ec*t was then and there sore hurte and brused and like to haue
been killed and then not soe satisfied but they then and there haled 30
and pulled forcibly and most violently drewe yo*u*r said subi*ec*t out
of the said Churchyard into an orchard of the said vicar adioyning
to the saide Churchyarde neare to the house of the saide vicar And
the said Phillip Vaughan then and there came w*i*th a long dagger to
the ende to murder yo*u*r said subi*ec*t if some rescous and aide had   35
not beene then and there p*re*sent by the neighbours to defende yo*u*r
saide subi*ec*t from theire vyolence and assault*es* then and there
[performed] ʳmadeˑ and executed vpon yo*u*r said subi*ec*t. And
therevpon the said Phillip Vaughan then and there came behinde the
said Iohn Guyllim and drewe a ffawchin or short sworde of the said   40
Iohn Guylliams to ˌʳthentent toˑ haue doen then and there some hurt*es*
to the said Iohn Guyllim and Mr Powell, And therevpon the said

Thomas Prosser and some other of theire Company by the privitie and
procurement of the said Edward Savacre William Savacre and others
went into the house of the saide vicar and was then and there abetted
by the vicar of Gooderiche to contynue theire misdemeano*u*rs
aforesaide whervpon the said riotous personnes then and there came   5
forthe out of the saide house of the said Vicars armed w*i*th divers
weapons as Iavelyns bill*es* Long pikes staves and other weapons w*hi*ch
were then and there by the saide vicar or his mayde servant*es* in the
saide house delyvered to the saide Iohn Tovye the elder Iohn Tovye
the younger Iohn Maynston Iohn Horsman Iohn Lynney al*ia*s Baker   10
Thomas Mothewaye Phillip Vaughan Richard Powell yeoman and
Henry Lluellen who w*i*th theire weapons to maynteyne the quarrell
ˌ⌐then & there⌐ tooke parte w*i*th the said Thomas ˌ⌐[Guyllm] Williams⌐
against the saide Richard Powell gent*leman* and Iohn Gwyllim wherby
the said Thomas Williams Henry Lluellen and other theire   15
Accomplic*es* had then and there ˌ⌐purposed to haue [murdered]⌐
murdered yo*u*r [Ma*i*esties] said sub*i*ect And the said Mr Powell and
Iohn Guyllim if the neighbours present had not in yo*u*r ma*i*est*ies*
peace defended them from the assault*es* of the saide Thomas Williams
Henry Lluellen and other theire saide Accomplices for as the saide   20
Mr Richarde Powell a very younge gent*leman* havinge only then and
there a verye little dagger and a birdinge peece not chardged w*i*th any
shott And the saide Iohn Guyllim having a short ffawchyn were
inforced to shifte themselves awaye and in great feare to departe for
saveguarde of their lyves or ell*es* they had been then and there ˌ⌐by 25
the said Riotous persons⌐ murdered or otherwise sore beaten
ˌ⌐wounded⌐ hurt or mayhemed ˌ⌐moste grevouslie⌐ All w*hi*ch
Confederacies Conspiracies Mayntenaunces Ryott*es* Rowt*es*
vnlawefull Assemblies Assault*es* Affraies Batteries Hurtt*es* and other
Misdemeano*u*rs aforesaide haue been and are maynteyned procured 30
and abbetted by the saide Edwarde Savacre George Vaughan and
[Edward] William Savacre w*hi*ch being contrarie and against yo*u*r
Ma*i*esties peace Lawes and statut*es* of this yo*u*r Ma*i*esties Realme the
same will growe to the perillous and evill exampl*e* of others in that
Countrey neare Wales to com*m*ytt the like offences and   35
misdemeano*u*rs if some severe ponishment and sharpe Correc*i*on bee
not herein had and provided by yo*u*r Ma*i*estye and yo*u*r most
honorable privie Councell against the saide offendo*u*rs, Maye it
therefore please yo*u*r most excellent Ma*i*estie the premisses considered
to graunt vnto yo*u*r said sub*i*ect yo*u*r highenes most gracious severall 40
writtes of Subpena to bee directed vnto the said Edwarde Savacre
Clerke George Vaughan W*illia*m Savacre Thomas Williams Iohn

Tovye thelder Iohn Tovye the younger Anthonye Phelpott Phillip
Vaughan Henry Lluellen Thomas Prosser Iohn Lynney al*ias* Baker
Iohn Horsman Thomas Motheway Iohn Maynston and Richarde
Powell yeoman comandinge them and every of them therby at a daye
certen and vnder a certen payne therein to bee lymited personally to   5
bee and appeare before yo*ur* Ma*i*esty and yo*ur* highenes most
honorable privie Councell in yo*ur* Ma*i*esties most honorable [privie]
Court of Starchamber to answeare to the premisses And further to
stand to and obey suche [further] order and dire*cci*on therein as to
yo*ur* Ma*i*esties most honorable privie Councell shall seeme most meete   10
And yo*ur* said sub*iect* shall accordinge to his bounden dutye daylye
praie to god for the prosperous and happie reigne of yo*ur* Ma*i*estie
and yo*ur* highenes most noble progenye long to reigne over vs/
                    (signed) °Henshawe°

                                                                            15

dorse

                                                   Phellpott
                                                   *ver*sus
                                                   Williams   20
                                                   & al
                                          A*nn*o 6 Ia*cob*i Regis

            Lune vicesimo Tertio Ianuarij Anno Iacobi Regis
                    (signed) °Edw*ar*d Iones°   25

Star Chamber Answer of Defendant   PRO: STAC 8/234/10/Item 9
single sheet*   *(6 February 1608/9)*

Iur*ata* 6to die ffebr*uarij* Anno sexto Iacobi Regis   30
  °Edw*ar*d Iones°

        The aunswere of Thomas Williams one of the def*endantes*
           to the informa*cion* of William Phellpot Compla*inant*

                                                                            35

The said Defendant the advantage of excep*cion* to the incertayntie
insufficiencie and other imp*erfeccions* of the said informa*cion* to him
nowe and at all times saved and reserved for aunswer saith that the
said William Phellpot the Compla*inant* or informer is and hath bine
of a longe time accompted a trobelsome and Contentious p*er*son   40
delightinge in suy*tes* and vexa*cions* of his poore neighbors and
detestinge and depravinge suche as were of Civill and quiet lief and

behavioure and espechiallie the ministers and professors of the word
of god and that the said William out of his said disposicion hath bred
and mayntayned many Chargeable suytes espechiallie one concerninge
the inheritance of the Powells of Whitchurche in the Com. of Hereford
and to that end hath not onelie Atturned tenant to one Hughe Powell   5
late of Whitchurch father of Richard Powell gentleman in the bill
mencioned and since his death to the said Richard or his vncles with
intention to defeat and defraud Barbara the wief of Thomas Powell
in the bill named and one Bridget Powell her sister Daughters and
Heires of one Walter Powell deceassed of theire lawfull and ancient   10
inheritance contrarie to Iudgementes decree and sentence of Lawe
and equitie as this defendant hath heard but with his daylie invextions
travayle and charges hath greatlie increased the molestacion of the
said Barbara and Bridget and Thomas Gwillim the husband of the
said Barbara and partlie for that Edward Savaker Clarke Preacher of   15
the word of god and Deane of Irchinfield hath affected the said Thomas
Gwillim ˏ⌈beinge his neighbore⌉ for his [godlie] honest and sober
Cariage and partlie for the hatred of the said William Phillpot beareth
to the exercise of the word of god which he desireth not onelie to
interrupte but to prophane with dauncing Drinkinge and other Idle   20
magames the said William Philpot hath extended his hatred towardes
the poore seravantes of the said Edward Savaker namelie towardes
this seelie creature this Defendant beinge lame and almoste blind
whereof he praieth the Consideracion of this honorable Courte which
disposition and inclinacion of the said William Philpot appereth by   25
his defence and comendacion of those meatinge to make meary as he
termeth them in his informacion and for answere to soe muche of
the saide bill as this concerneth this Defendant he saith that true it is
that vpon the munday in the whitson weeke was twelvemonth in the
fifte yere of the kinges maiesties raigne ths England that nowe is one   30
Iohn Mericke and one Iohn Philpot havinge bine ancient acquayntance
of this this Defendant and the one of them havinge bine absent a longe
time out of this defendantes companie and havinge dwelt at Bristoll
the other havinge bine likwise longe absent and havinge dwelt
Worcester and meetinge this defendant at Goodridge in the bill   35
meconed and beinge desirous to drinke with this defendant moved

8/ Powell *for* Gwillim (?)	30/ ths *for* of
18/ of *for* which	32/ this this: *dittography*
21/ magames *for* maygames (?)	34/ dwelt *for* dwelt at
36/ meconed *for* mencioned; *marks of abbreviation missing*	

this defendant to goe with them to the house of Richard Powell in
Goodridge aforesaid beinge an Alehouse where when they and this
defendant ˌ⌈entred⌉ they found the first Rome full of companie
whervppon this defendant went with them into an Inner Roome where
they sawe Iohn and Richard Powell in the bill menconed drinkinge   5
and then ˌ⌈the⌉ said Iohn Mericke Iohn Philpot and this defendant
Callinge for ale whether it were for the hatred that the said Richard
Powell and Iohn Gwillim bare towardes this Defendantes master and
the foresaid Thomas Gwillim his friend or for disdayne that soe simple
a wretch as this defendant should presume to enter the Roome where   10
they were which indeed was ignorantlie donne by this defendant and
without purpose of givinge any kind of offence to anie person livinge
yet the said Iohn Gwillim and Richard Powell some what inraged
and moved beganne to give ill wordes to this defendant without anie
prevocacion asking this defendant whether he came to outface them   15
in their Roome and presentlie without any cause given the said Iohn
Gwillim drewe out a fauchion and the said Richard Powell a poniard
and one William Robertes beganne to drawe his dagger and the said
Iohn Gwillim and Richard Powell presentlie pursued this defendant
and this Defendant for feare and to save his lif fled out of the said 20
Alehouse throughe the Churchard thereto neere adioyninge to the
house of his said Master Edward Savacre and then kepte and hidd
himself a longe time. till aboutes some three of the Clocke in the
afternoone when this Defendant as vsuallie by his said Masters
Commaundement he was wonte to doe this defendant went furth of   25
the said ˌ⌈house⌉ to water horses of his said Master that were tethered
in a pastur⟨e⟩ and to that end this defendant bare with him ane hedge
bill or brier bill with which he vsed to mend hedges and stop[⟨.⟩] and
open Caps and this defendant way lyinge Directlie througe the
Churchyard aforesaid the said William Philpot suddenlie in the said   30
Churchyard assalted this defendant tooke hold of him and soughte
to ta⟨.⟩ from him his said bill and would have dragged this defendant
to the stockes this defendant wonderinge wherefore he soe should
doe and not knowinge the said William Philpot to be ane officer or
Constable or yf he were soe yet this defendant saith he had neither   35
Color nor cause to assalt apprehend and imprison this defendant
wherevpon one Anthonie Philpot of Marsto⟨w⟩ seeinge this defendant

5/ Iohn for Iohn Gwillim (?); see ll. 8, 13, 19 below
5/ menconed for mencioned; mark of abbreviation missing
29/ defendant for defendants
32/ ta⟨.⟩ for tak (?)

dragged and abused the said Anthonie and one Iohn Tovie stayed this
defendant and offred to give bond*es* for this defendant*es* kepinge of
the peace w*h*ich indeed he never attempted to breake or to bringe this
defendant before any Iustice of peace of the said countie and one the
other sid the foresaid Richard Powell and Iohn Gwillim ioyninge w*i*th   5
the said William Phelpot layd hold vpon this defendant and dragged
and pulled him soe that this def*endan*t was almoste trangled betwixte
them and in the said garboyle and strivinge it mighte be this
def*endan*tes dagger beinge pulled out by some of the foresaid p*er*sons
or fallinge out or ther amoungste themselves strivinge for the same   10
or the said William Philpot*es* layinge hold vppon the blade thereof
some scratche mighte fall vpon the said William Phelpot*es* hand or
some drope of blood might vssue but ˏ⌐if the cause was his yt wa⟨s⟩¬
w*i*thout assalte blowe thrust wound or hurt given by this defendant
but this def*endan*t saith that the said Richard Powell then and there   15
offered diu*er*s times to discharge his peece vpon this defendant and
the said Iohn Gwillim then and there strooke at this defendant w*i*th
his fauchion and Charles Gwillim of Pytstow [o] father of the said
Iohn was then there armed w*i*th a longe bill and this defendant fleeinge
frome the said Richard Powell Iohn Gwillim and theire accomplit*es*   20
homeward*es* into the orchard of the said Edward Savacre the foresaid
Richard Powell Iohn Gwillim and William Phillpot w*i*th other theire
accomplit*es* in riotous and vnlawfull mann*er* pursuinge and assaltinge
this defendant the foresaid Iohn Tovie the elder Anthonie Phelpot of
Marstow and Thomas Mothway did indevor to take away this   25
defendant out of the hand*es* of the said William Phelpot Iohn Gwillim
Richard Powell and theire accomplit*es*. And the defendant saith that
the said William Phelpot at the said time and places of the pretended
Mysdemeanors in Goodridge aforesaid in the bill informed of as he
taketh it was noe Constable sworne for or in the said places where   30
the same are sayd to be comitted but vsurped the said office. and he
the said William Phelpot together w*i*th the said Richard Powell Iohn
Gwillim and the rest of their accomplit*es* of theire owne wronge
comitted the ⌐assaltes¬ and ⟨.⟩ riott*es* aforesaid vpon this def*endan*t
and yf anie hurte happened to them or anie of them the same was   35
vpon their owne assalt and begininge but that this def*endan*t knoweth
of noe hurte wound or harme by them receaved. for this defendant
saith that the P*a*riche of Goodridge in the bill menc*i*oned consisteth
of three townshipps the first Glewston and the old mill the second
Hentland the third Hunsum and that all the misdemeanors in the bill   40

7/ trangled *for* strangled   19/ then *for* then and

alleaged and pretended are laid to be Comitted within the townshipp
of Hentland wherefore one Roger Garnons at the time in the bill
menconed and euer since was and is Constable and not the said William
Phelpot And to all the rest of the confederacies practises conspiraces
quarrellinges ministringe woordes of quarrell prepayringe of weapons   5
caryinge or vsinge of weapons assaltes drawinge of anie Dagger
thrustinge of the said William Phelpot in the hand resistance or rescue
made to anie Constable officer or other subiecte of our soveraigne
lord the kinge and to all the riottes Routes vnlawfull assemblies
breaches of the kinges peace and all other offences and misdemeanors   10
wherewith this Defendant by the said bill or informacion is Charged
touched accused or informed or Complayned[ge] of this Defendant
saith he is not gultie of them nor anie of them All which matters this
defendant is readie to averre and prove as this honnorable Courte
shall award and humblie prayeth to be dismissed with his reasonable   15
Costes and Charges in this behalf wrongfullie and without cause
susteyned./

(signed) °I. Hoskyns°

Star Chamber Demurrer of Defendant   PRO: STAC 8/234/10/Item 10   20
single sheet   *(22 June 1609)*

Iurata 22 Iunij Anno septimo Iacobi Regis
    °Edward Iones°

                                                                             25

        The Demurer and answere of Iohn Tovie the
        Yonger to the Informacion of William Phylpote

The said Defendant not confessinge nor acknowledinge anie matter
offence or allegacion in the said Informacion contayned where with   30
this defendant is Charge⟨d⟩ to be true saith that the said Informacion
as for anie thinge touchinge this defendant is vncertaine insufficient
and senselesse therefore demureth therevpp⟨on⟩ and demaundeth the
iudgement of this honorable Courte whether he shalbe Compelled to
make anie further or other answere therevnto and for causes of his   35
Demurer allegeth that he this Defendant is not affirmativelie Charged
with anie offence misdemenor or other matter examinable in this
honorable Courte within the said bill or informacion for this defendant
saith that the said bill or informacion beinge first grounded vpon and
begininge with a forma⟨l⟩ Idle prescripcion pleded for the Inhabitantes   40

3/ menconed *for* mencioned; *mark of abbreviation missing*

of the Lordshipp and towne of Gooderiche tyme out ⟨of⟩ mynde to
assemble themselves at Gooderich together to Daunce drinke and
banquet in the Whitson holiedaies which is not onelie a ridiculus but
an vngodlie Custome alleageth that one Thomas Williams with his
accomplaices therin named, and naminge not this defendant for anie   5
of the accomplaices should intrude into an alehouse at Gooderich the
five and Twentith daie of Maie in the fifthe yere of the kinges maiesties
raigne ouer England and Disturbe or quarrell with one Master Powell
and Master Gwillim as they were drinkinge in the saide alehouse by
the priuitie of this Defendant and others and soe the said Informacion   10
Charginge the said Thomas Williams with some misdemenors for
which the plaintife as Constable alleageth he arrested him this
defendant is ⌐charged¬ to be vnlawfullie and rioutouslie with others
assembled and then is it said that the said Williams and his accomplaices
not naminge this defendant for one, nor naminge them his said   15
accomplaices drewe the Defendant out of the Churchard into the
orchard and it is said the said riotous persons not naming this
defendant had a purpose to murder the Complaynant and the said
master Powell and Iohn Gwillim which beinge all that this defendant
is charged withall This defendant Demurreth in Lawe and abydeth   20
in the iudgment of this honorable Courte whether he shall make ⌐any
further awnswer¬ to the said vncertaine and insufficient Informacion,
Neuerthelesse if by order of this honorable Courte he shall be
ouerruled to make further answere therevnto then the excepcions to
all the insufficiencies of the said bill to this defendant Nowe and at   25
times saved ⌐this defendant¬ saith that the Complaynant bearinge
ancient malice to Edward Savacre one of The defendantes in the bill
and havinge bine an ancient Mayneteyner of suytes and strifes betwixt
Thomas Gwillim in the bill mencioned and others one the one side
And Richard Powell gentleman in the bill mencioned and before him   30
his father one the other side and the Complaynant beynge noe
Constable in the place in the Informacion mencioned where the
Misdemenors in the Informacion mencioned are layde but beinge
Constable in an other Townshipp out of a foreplotted Confederacie
the Complaynant beinge armed with some weapons togeyther with   35
the said Richard Powell gentleman beinge armed with a gunne and
the said Iohn Gwillim gentleman beinge armed with a fouchion or a
short swoord and a longe staffe or a bill or like weapons the
com⌐playnant¬ intendinge and consentinge with the said Powell and
Gwillim and others to doe some Mischief to the said Savacre o[f]r   40
some of his friendes ⌐or servauntes¬ did the daie and Yere in the
Informacion mencioned resort to Gooderiche in the Informacion

named and beinge there sometimes in the Alehouse sometymes in the
Churchard Waytinge theire opportunitie Thomas Williams one of the
Defendant*es* beinge a poore lame and almost blinde creature and
servant to the said Edward Savacre and beinge sent forth through the
Churchyard afforesaid to Water his Masters horses as this Defendant   5
is crediblelie informed the Complay*nan*t William Phelpot vnder collor
of his office of Constableshipp w*hi*ch he had in an other towneshipp
apprehended the said Thomas Williams as this defendant thinketh
w*i*thout cause and of purpose to procure troble and then and there
dragged him towarde*s* the stock and Anthonie Phelpot ˏ⌐the defe*nda*nt¬   10
in the Informac*i*on menc*i*oned beinge a quiet man and verie sufficient
freeholder offeringe to goe alonge w*i*th the said Thomas Williams to
anie Iustice of peace or otherwise to give anie securitie for the peace
in the behalf of the said Thomas Williams and the Complay*nan*t with
ˏ⌐one other¬ Anthonie Philpot his brother and others neu*er*thelesse   15
violentlie hallinge and pullinge the said poore fellowe towarde*s* the
stock*es* this Defendant by the tumult and outcrie beinge called out
of the house of Edward Savacre afforesaid neere adioyninge and
seeinge the said Complay*nan*t and others soe violentlie and
vnresonablelie hawlinge and dragginge [onelie] the said Thomas   20
williams towarde*s* the stock*es* desiringe the Complay*nan*t to stay a
small space till the matter might be resonablelie Debated where at the
first the plaintief Deliu*er*ed the said Thomas Williams to Anthonie
Philpot the defendant and to Iohn Tovie deceased father to this
defendant who quietlie leadinge the said Thomas Williams out of the   25
thronge and multitude of people presentlie as it seemed vpon alterac*i*on
of theire mynde*s* the said Richard Powell gent*leman* offringe diu*er*s
times to discharge his peece vpon this Defendant and the said Thomas
Williams. ⌐he the s*aid* Rich*ard* Powell¬ And they the said Iohn Gwillim
Charles Gwillim William Robart*es* and the Complay*nan*t did assalt   30
the said Thomas Williams and others in most outragious Manner and
were like to have slaine the said Thomas Williams if this Defendant
and others there present had not defended the said Thomas Williams
and kept his ma*i*esties peace w*hi*ch was all that this Defendant did
And to all the rest of the confederace*s* practises conspirace*s* quarrells   35
Caryinge or vsinge of weapons assalt*es* resistance or Rescue made to
anie Constable officer or other subiecte of our Sou*er*aigne lord the
kinge and to all the riott*es* routs vnlawfull assemblies breaches of the
king*es* peace and all other offences and Misdemenors where[fo]⌐with¬
this Defendant by the said bill or Informac*i*on is charged touched,   40
accused or informed or complayned of this Defendant saith he is not
guyltie of them nor anie of them. All w*hi*ch matters this Defendant

is readie to averr and prove as this honorable Courte shall award and
humblie praieth to be dismissed with his costes and Charges in this
behalfe most wrongfully susteined //

(signed) °I. Hoskyns°

Star Chamber Answer of Defendants   PRO: STAC 8/234/10/Item 8
single sheet*   *(16 October 1609)*

°Iur*ata* xvj die octobris 1609 cor*am* Waltero pie et Thoma Iones°

The ioynte and seu*er*all answeares of Anthony Phelpott
Thomas Mothewaye and Harry Lewellin def*endantes* to the bill
or Informac*i*on of William Phellpott Complai*n*ant

The said defendants all advantages of excep*ci*on to the incertaintie
insufficiencye and other imp*er*fec*i*ons of the said bill or Informac*i*on
to them nowe and att all times heereafter saved and reserved for
answeare saye and first the said Anthonye Phellpott for himself doth
saye that the daye and yeare in the bill or Informac*i*on menc*i*on*e*d he
was in the Churche of Goodriche in the Informac*i*on menc*i*on*e*d
ringinge of the bells in the said Churche and one comminge to this
def*endan*t cryinge that a mann was slayne or lyke to be slayne in the
said Churchyard and this defendant therevpon hearinge a great tumult
and outcrye this defendant came foorth in to the said Churchyard
and saw William Phillpott of the ould mill the Complai*n*ant Anthony
Phellpott of the same his brother and Katherin Phillpott of the same
his sister and Thomas Roberts hawlinge and dragginge out Thomas
Williams an impotent man in outragious manner and this defendantt
askinge them what they meant to doe with the poore mann they
answered they mene to have hym to the stockes Wherevpon this
defendant seeinge ˏ⌐the said⌐ Thomas Williams soe abused offred to
be his suertye or [to be] bound for him to bringe hym before any
Iustice of peace of the said Countye or to any other place to answere
to any thinge that should be obiected against hym w*hi*ch he this
defendant did only of purpose to save the life of the said Thomas
Williams by deliu*er*inge him out of the handes of the foresaid William
Phillpott Katherin Philpott his sister and Thomas Roberts but the
foresaid p*er*sones struglinge with the said Thomas Williams and some
others in Compassion layinge hould vpon the said Thomas Williams
to save hym from theyr Cruelty he fell downe over a grave in the

5

10

15

20

25

30

35

40

12/ ew *of* Lewellin *written over other letters*

said Churchyard and soe the said Thomas Williams beinge deliuered
out of their handes and gettinge towardes his masters house through
a Wickgate this defendant shut the gate after hym and this defendant
desiringe the Complainant to staye till the matter might be reasonably
debated betwixt them wherewith the said Complainant and the said   5
other persones at first seemed content but presentlye as it seemed
vpon alteracion of their mindes one Charles Gwillym of Pittestowe
gentleman armed with a longe bill and dagger Iohn Gwillym sonne
of the said Charles havinge a fauchion William Roberts of °Wilton°
armed alsoe and Richard Powell late of Whitechurche gentleman with   10
a gunne ˏ⌈In his hand⌉ offringe divers times to dischardge the said
peece vpon this defendant and the said Thomas Williams and others
and the rest assaultinge the said Thomas Williams and others in most
outragious manner were lyke to have slayne the said Thomas Williams
yf this defendant and others there present had not defended the said   15
Thomas Williams and kept his maiesties peace which was all that this
defendant did and to all the rest of the confederacies practises
conspiracies quarrells caryinge of Weapons vsinge of weapons
resistance or rescue made to any Constable officer or other subiect
of our soveraigne lord the kinge and to all the riotts routs vnlawfull   20
assemblies breaches of the kinges peace and to all other offences and
misdemeanors whereof this defendant by the said bill or Informacion
is charged touched accused or informed or complayned of This
defendant sayth he is not guiltye of them nor any of them: And the
said Thomas Mothewaye for himself doth saye that the daie yeare   25
and place in the bill or Informacion mencioned he seeinge Thomas
Williams in the bill mencioned to have escaped out of the Churchyard
at Goodriche with feare and perill of his lyfe as it seemed to this
defendant seeinge William Philpot Charles Gwillim Iohn Gwillim
Richard Powell William Robertes and other theyr accomplices   30
runninge after hym with violence as it seemed to this defendant
seekinge to kill or hurte hym this defendant shutt a gate that was
betwixt them agaynst the said William Phelpott Charles Gwillim Iohn
Gwillym Richard Powell William Robertes and the rest theyr
accomplices and this defendant keepinge of the said gate to the intent   35
to have them departe without any dainger and to save the lyfe of the
said Thomas Williams one Charles Gwillym of Pittestowe gentleman
came vnto this defendant where he was keepinge the foresaid Wickgate
havinge hys dagger drawen and strickinge at this defendant this
defendant for feare of hurte let goe the said gate and departed awaye   40
which was all that this defendant did And to all the rest of the
Confederacies practises conspiracies quarrellings ministringe wordes

of quarrell *prep*aringe of weapons caryinge or vsinge of weapons
assaults resistance or rescue made to any Constable officer or other
subiects of our sou*er*aigne lord the kinge and to all the riotts routs
vnlawfull assemblies breaches of the king*es* peace and all other offences
and misdemeanors wherew*i*th this defendant by the said bill or   5
Informac*i*on is charged touched accused or Informed or complained
of This defendant saythe he is not guiltye of them or any of them
And this defendant Harry Lewellin sayth he is not guiltye of any
thinge menc*i*oned in the bill or Informac*i*on: And all these defendant*es*
doe saye that the said William Philpott at the said time and place of   10
the *p*retended misdemeanors in Gootheridge aforesaid in the bill
informed of as they take ˌ⌐it⌐ was no Constable sworne for or in the
said places where the same are sayd to be committed but vsurped the
said office vnder ˌ⌐colour⌐ thereof to seeke advantage to imprison and
evill intreat such against whom he bare causles malice and further   15
these defendant*es* doe saie that the *p*arishe of Goodridge in the byll
menc*i*oned consisteth of three Towneshippes the first Glewston and
the ould mill the second Hentland the third Hunsum and that all the
misdeamenors in the bill alleaged and *p*retended are sayd to be
committed w*i*thin the Towne shippe of Hentland whereof one Roger   20
Gar°diner ˌ⌐now decesed⌐° at the time in the bill menc*i*oned [and euer
since] was [and is] Constable and not William Phillpott aforesaid And
all these defendants doe traverse w*i*thout that that any other matter
clause sentence article or allegation in the said bill of Complaint
contained materiall or effectuall in the law °to be° answered vnto by   25
these defendants or any of them and heere not sufficiently answered
vnto confessed and avoyded traversed or denied is true All w*hi*ch
matters these defendant*es* and every of them are redy to averre and
prove as this honourable Courte shall award and humbly praye to be
dismissed from thence w*i*th theyr resonable Costes and Charges in   30
that behalfe most wrongfully sustayned:/

                              (signed) °I. Hoskyns°

dorse
                                                                          35
Iur*ata* Thom*as* M*y*natt
°To the king*es* most excellent ma*i*estie in his highnes court of Stare
Chamber°

Vltimo die Octobris   40
Ded*imus* *p*otestatem inter Willelmum Philpott pl*aintiff* & Anthony
Phillpott et al*ios* def*endantes*
brought in by Thom*as* Gwill*i*m

dorse *(rev)*

Phelpott*es*
versus
Phelpott*es* et al*ios*   5
ded*imus* potesta*t*em

Star Chamber Answer of Defendant   PRO: STAC 8/234/10/Item 11
single sheet   *(27 January 1609/10)*

10

°Iur*ata* 27 Ianuarij Anno 7°Ia*cobi* Reg*is*
   Th*omas* Mynatt°

    The Aunswere of Edward Savaker Clarke one of the Def*endantes*
    to the Bill and informac*ion* of William Phillpott*es* Complai*nan*t   15

The said Defendant savinge to himself now and at all times hereafter
all advauntages of Excepc*ion* to the Incertaynty and insufficiency of
the said bill and informac*ion* by protestac*ion* saieth that the said bill
and informac*ion* is Contrived rather of malice and Iniust displeasure   20
to put the said Defendaunt beinge a Preachinge minister aged and not
fitt for travayle and by his place and Callinge bounde to Continuall
attendance over his flocke and others Comitted to his government
and Charge to vnnecessary travell and Charges in the Lawe then vppon
good grounde or Cause of suict Neverthelesse for a full short and   25
Direct Aunswere to the said Bill and Informac*ion* The said Defendaunt
saieth that hee is not guilty of any the Confederacies Conspiracies
Mayntenaunces Riott*es* Routes Vnlawfull assemblies assault*es* affrayes
batries hurtes abbettinges and other the offences and misdemenors
nor of any of them in the said bill and Informac*ion* Alleaged or   30
wherew*i*th hee is thereby Charged or Chargeable in Manner and forme
as is in the said bill & informac*ion* vntruly surmised All w*hi*ch matters
the said def*endan*t is Ready to averre and prove as this honorable
Courte shall award and therefore humbly prayeth to be dismissed
out of this honorable Courte w*i*th his Reasonable Costes and Charges   35
in this behalf most wroungfully sustayned
                      (signed) °I. Hoskyns°

Star Chamber Answer of Defendants   PRO: STAC 8/234/10/Item 3
single sheet*   *(20 April 1610)*   40

    The ioynte and seu*er*all answeres of George Vaughan

William Savaker Iohn Horsman Iohn Mainston Iohn Lynnye
alias baker Phillip Vaughan Richard Powell and Thomas Prosser
euery of them to the bill and Informacion of William
Phellpott:

5

The said defendants and euery one of them savinge to themselves
now and at all times heereafter all advantages of excepcion to the
incertainty and insufficiencye of the said bill and Informacion by
protestacion saye that the said bill and Informacion is contrived rather
of malice and vniust displesure to put the said defendants to expences   10
and charges in the law then vpon any good ground or iust cause of
suict Neuertheles for full and direct answere to the said bill and
Informacion the said defendantes George Vaughan William Savaker
Iohn Horsman Iohn Mainston and Iohn Lynny alias baker and euery
one of them saithe that they nor any of them are guiltie of any the   15
said Confederacies Conspiracies maintaynances Riotts Routs
vnlawfull assemblies assaultes affrayes bateries hurtes abbetments and
other the offences and misdemeanors ₍or₎ of any of them in the said
bill and Informacion alleaged or wherewith eyther or any of them
are thereby charged or chargeable in manner and forme as is in the   20
said bill and Informacion vntruly surmised. And the said Phillip
Vaughan and other of the said defendants saithe that he beinge in the
Churchyard of Goodriche at the daye in the bill specifyed seinge vpon
the day in the said Informacion mencioned William Phellpott the
Complaynant Anthony Phellpott his brother Katheryne Phellpott   25
theyr sister and Thomas Roberts with great violence haulinge and
pullinge Thomas Williams in this bill mencioned in such furious
manner that they had almost strangled the said Thomas Williams
sayinge that they would carry the said Thomas Williams to the stockes
one that then was in the Company whose name this defendant doth   30
not now remember cast the naked dagger of the said Thomas Williams
vpon the grownd in the said Churchyard of Goodriche and willed
this defendant to take vpp the said dagger and to keepe the same which
this defendant did accordinglye to the intent no mann might be hurte
thereby but his maiesties peace preserued and therewith presently   35
departed out of the said Churchyard into the Orchard of Edward
Savaker Clearke and other of the defendants vnto the said Churchyard
adioyninge holdinge the said dagger in his hands without doyinge or
meaninge to doe any hurte to any bodye wherevpon the said
Complaynant ranne to this defendant with great fury and violence   40
tooke awaye the said dagger from this defendant and then and there
Iohn Gwillym and Richard Powell gentleman in this bill mencioned

and Charles Gwyllim all armed with swordes gunnes bills and other
weapons assalted this defendant and gave him diuers grevous blowes
with theyr weapons and the said Iohn Gwillym gave this defendant
diuers sore blowes with his feete in the bottome of the belly and face
of this defendant and offered to have pulled out his ffauchion which   5
he then had by his side to have slayne this defendant which this
defendant perceauinge and to preuent iminnent dainger of deathe
caught the said ffauchion out of the hand of the said Iohn Gwillym
and kept the same not offeringe any blowe therewith vnto the said
Iohn Gwillym or any others and then the said Richard Powell Iohn   10
Gwillym and Charles Gwillym came violently vpon this defendant
and with their Weapons strake downe this defendant and would have
murthered him yf Rescue had not come all which ⌐done by this
Defendant as aforesaid⌐ as this defendant taketh it was lawfull for
him to doe, And the said Richard Powell and Thomas Prosser and   15
euery of them saye that they are not guiltye of any the said
misdeameanors neyther were they nor any of them in the Churchyard
of Goodriche in the bill mencioned when these ˰⌐supposed⌐
misdemeanors were committed but beinge in the howse of Edward
Savaker Clearke there came in a woman or mayd called Ioan Savakre   20
into the said Edward Savakers howse one of the defendants cryinge
that the said Iohn Gwillym Charles Gwillym Richard Powell and
others had slayne Phillip Vaughan one of the defendants in the said
Informacion Wherevpon the said Richard Powell ˰⌐the defendant⌐ and
Thomas Prosser went out of the said howse takinge with them euery   25
one a staffe which they then found by chaunce in the said howse with
intencion to keepe the kings peace. [as this defendant ⟨...⟩h thinketh]
and as soone as they were out of the doore of the said howse they
fownd the said Iohn Gwillym and Richard Powell and others whose
names they doe not now remember lyinge vpon and oppressinge the   30
said Phillip Vaughan beinge cast downe vpon the grownd and
grovelinge vnder them meaninge as these defendants thinketh and as
the said Iohn Gwillym and Richard Powell gentleman reported to
have murthered the said Phillip Vaughan yf these defendants and one
Iohn Markye the yonger gentleman Iohn Stratford gentleman Thomas   35
Iones and others had not deliuered and rescued the said Phillip
Vaughan and kept them backe from pursuinge the said Phillipp
Vaughan and for all the rest of the Confederacies conspiracies
maintenances riottes routs, vnlawfull assemblies assaltes affrayes

13/ murthered: extra minim MS
32/ these written over this

bateries hurtes abbetements rescues threatning*es* breaches of the peace
and other offences and misdeamenors wherew*i*th the defendant*es* are
charged by the said bill or Informac*i*on and to eu*er*y of them these
defendant*es* Phillipp Vaughan Richard Powell and Thomas Prosser
and eu*er*y of them sayeth they are not guitye of them nor any of them   5
⌐And all these defendant*es* doe traverse and say¬ W*i*thout that that any
other matter thinge clause sentence cause or allegation in the said bill
contayned materiall or effectuall to be answered vnto and heerby not
sufficyently confessed or avoyded trau*er*sed or denyed is true All
wh*ich* matters these defendant*es* and eu*er*ye of them are redye to averr   10
and prove as this Ho*no*rable Courte shall award and humbly prayeth
to be heere hence dismissed w*i*th theyr Costes and Charges in this
wrongfull suict sustayned./

                              (signed) °I. Hoskyns.°

                                                                        15

°Predict*i* defend*e*ntes Iur*a*ti fuer*unt* hinc respons*u*ri xx° die Aprilis
Anno Regni Regis Iacobi nunc &c Octavo Coram nobis/°
(signed) °Gregory Burhill° °Io*h*n Brace° °Iohn Gardner/°

Star Chamber Interrogatories for Defendants   20
PRO: STAC 8/234/10/Item 4
single sheet

          Intergatorryes to be mynistred vnto George Vaughan
          Philip Vaughan and Iohn Horsemen three of the   25
          defend*antes* to⟨.⟩ the Bill of Compl*ai*nt of Willi*a*m Philpotte
          Compl*ainan*t

1   Imprimis whether did the said Phel⟨...⟩⌐lip¬ Vaughan and the other
     defend*antes* Thomas Willi*a*ms Iohn Tovey the yonger Iohn Prychard   30
     and others on the munday in whytson weeke in the ffieft yeere of
     his Ma*iesties* Reigne in thafter noone of the saide day Come forth of
     the house of Edward Savacre Clearke in Gooderych in the Countie
     of Heref*ord* vnto the Churchard then and theare w*i*th bills staffes and
     other wepons to thende to assalt the Compl*ainan*t then beinge   35
     Cunstable of Gooderych and to assalt the said Richard Powell the

─────────────

5/ guitye *for* guiltye
5/ any: *minim missing* MS
10/ u *of* euerye *written over* y
24/ Intergatorryes *for* Interogatorryes

yonger and Iohn Gwillim ye or noe. And what persons Came then
fforth of the said Edward Savacres house and with what wepons and
ffor what Cause and to what ende as you knowe or remember and
whether were you any of these persons which then Came fforth of the
said house with the said wepons into the Churchard declare the truth.   5
Item whether did you George Vaughan with one Thomas Gwyllim
aboutes two yeares past and more at diuers tymes Come to one
messuage or tenemente Called the old Myll in Gooderych aforesaid
to thend to take the possession therof ffrom the Complainantes ffather
ye or noe. And did you affirme that you wold ffyre the house if you   10
Cold not enter the possession ye or noe Declare the truth therof/
Item whether Did you the said Phellippe Vaughan on the munday in
whitson weeke in the after noone Drawe a sword or ffauchion out
of the sheth hanginge at the syde of the said Iohn Gwillim nere the
said Churchard of Gooderich aforesaid ye or noe And whether did   15
you assalt or strike the said Iohn Gwillim or any other with the said
sword or ffauchion ye or noe.
Item whether did you late parte with the said Thomas Williams and
others on the said munday in whitson weeke in the affrey and quarell
then made against the said Complainant and the said Richard Powell   20
the yonger and Iohn Gwillim ye or noe And what wepons had you
then and theare And whether Did you then and theare assalt or strike
at any person or persons And whom did you then assalt or strike at
and with what wepon and ffor what Cause Declare the trueth therof.
Item whether did the Complainant at the daie and place aforesaid   25
arest the defendant Thomas Williams ffor the breach of his Maiesties
peace ye or noe And did you and Diuers others then and theare rescue
and take away the said Thomas Williams ffrom the said arest ye or
noe And who did then and theare rescue and take away by force the
said Thomas Williams ffrom the Complainant as you remember/ And   30
what wepons had you and them then and theare when the said rescue
was made.

        (signed) °Gregory Burhill° °Iohn Brace°
        (signed) °Iohn Gardner°   35

dorse

Phelpottes
versus Vaughan et alios   40
Dedimus potestatem/

Star Chamber Examinations on Interrogatories
PRO: STAC 8/234/10/Item 5
single sheet   *(20 April 1610)*

5

Apud Gotheridge xx° Die Aprilis Anno Regni Domini
nostri Iacobi Dei gracia Anglie ffrancie & hibernie Regis fidei
defensor &c Octavo & Scocie xviij°
The Examynacions and sayeinges of George Vaughan
Phellippe Vaughan and Iohn horsman to the Interrogatories
mynistred by the Complainant William Phelpott and hereunto 10
annexed Taken ˏ⌐vpon theire Corporall othes⌐ the Daye and
yere abovesaid Before Gregory Burghill Clarke Iohn Brace
and Iohn Gardner gentlemen by Vertue of his ˏ⌐highnes⌐
Comission hereunto alsoe annexed And to them and Iohn
Abrahall gentleman   15

George Vaughan of the parishe of Whitchurche in the Countie of
hereford gentleman aged xlv yeres or thereaboutes sworen and
examyned sayeth as followeth

20

1   To the first Interrogatory he sayeth that he cannot depose for that he
was not present at the tyme of suche mysdemeanors surmysed to
have byn Committed but A myle or more Distant from the Churche
yarde of Gotheridge in the interrogatory mencioned

25

2   To the second Interrogatory he sayeth/ That he Did not at the tyme
in the Interrogatory mencioned goe with the sayd Thomas Gwillym
to any suche end mencioned in the said Interrogatory. But sayeth
that beinge Comaunded by the Iustices of the peace of the Countie
of hereford to assiste them was there there twise for the assistinge of 30
the sayd Iustices to geve possession of the sayd messuage And denyeth
that he ever threatened to fire the said house/ *(signed)* °Gregory
Burhill:° °Iohn Brace° °Iohn Gardner°

Phillippe Vaughan of the parishe of Whitchurche in the   35
Countie of hereford yoman Aged xxvj yeres or thereaboutes
sworen and examyned deposeth and sayeth as followeth

29/ e of beinge *written over*
30/ there there: *dittography*

To the first Interrogatory he sayeth/ that he Came not foorth of the
house of the sayd Edwarde Saveaker in any suche manner armed
or with any suche intent at all the sayd tyme or daye mencioned in
the sayd Interrogatory and further sayeth that he knoweth not
what persons came foorth of the sayd house nor thentent of thoose   5
that cam furth nor what weapons any person brought out of the sayd
house

To the second Interrogatory he cannot Depose
                                                                    10
To the thirde Interrogatory he sayeth/ that at the tyme in the
interrogatory mencioned the sayd Iohn Gwillym in the Interrogatory
named strake this examinat with his ffist on the face And further
offered to drawe his falchion from his syd to have wronged or
wounded this examynatt, where vpon he this examinat for his owne   15
savegardge Caught hould of the sayd falchion and gatt the sayd fachion
from the sayd Gwillym, which he onlie kept for a space in his owne
Defence not offeringe any hurte to the sayd Gwillym

To the fourth Interrogatory he sayeth/ That he this examynat tooke   20
noe parte with the sayd Williams in any mysdemeanor agaynst the
sayd Complainant or the sayd Richard Powell or Iohn Gwillym And
that he had noe weapon but onlie as he deposed in the former
interrogatory, neyther Did he this examynat alsaulte or stricke any
person/   25

To the fifte Interrogatory he sayeth/ he knoweth not whether the
Complainant at the Daye and place mencioned in the Interrogatory
Did arest the sayd Williams or not/ for breache of his maiesties peace,
neyther that he this examynat Did rescue the sayd Williams, neyther   30
Doe this examynat remember whether the sayd Williams were rescued
or not/ (signed) °Gregory Burhill° °Iohn Brace° °Iohn Gardner°

     Iohn horsman of the parishe of Gotheridge in the County of
     hereford husbondman aged xxx^tie yeres or thereaboutes   35
     sworen and examyned Deposeth and sayth as followeth

To the first Interrogatory he sayth That he knoweth not what persons
Cam furth of the sayd house weaponed to thentent to asaulte the
Complainant or the sayd Richard Powell or Iohn Gwillym, neyther   40

Did he this examynat see any at all come forthe of the sayd house of
the sayd Edward Saveaker weaponed or vnweaponed at the tyme in
the interrogatory mencioned

To the second and all the Rest of the Interrogatories he this examynat   5
is ignorant/
        (signed) °Gregory Burhill° °Iohn Brace/°
               °Iohn Gardner/°

dorse   10

To the kinges most Excelent maiestie
dedimus potestatem Philpottes inter Vaughan
responsa Georgij Vaughan & aliorum 〈.〉 xv^{na} Pasche in
Camera Stellata ad Partem Phelpott   15
brought in by Iohn Tovye/ xxv^{th} Aprill
                    Iurata Thomas Mynatt

HAY
        20
1617–18
Diocese of Hereford Acts of Office   HRO: box 24a (formerly 18), vol 71
f [288]   *(4 December)*

Proceedings of the court held in the consistory of Hereford Cathedral   25
before Master Gabriel (Wallwin), MA, deputy to Master Oliver Lloid,
LLD, vicar general of Francis Godwin, bishop of Hereford.
   ...
Willimus Meney vsed to plaie one his harpe in the parrishe of the
haie vpon diuers saboath daies in the tyme of eveninge praier °4 die   30
mensis decembris Anno domini 1617 comparuit et negavit Articulo.
postea examinatus [〈..〉] fassus est vnde dominus iniunxit ei 2 dies
penitenciales in Ecclesia predicta more penitenciali &c ad
excommunicatio/ certificandum in proximo./° vj° die ffebruarij predicti preconizatus
&c non comparuit &c neque certificavit &c excommunicatus   35
   ...

13/ dedimus potestatem: *expansion conjectural*
13/ inter *for* versus *(?)*
15/ Partem: *expansion conjectural*
31/ Articulo *for* Articulum

HENTLAND

1586/7
Diocese of Hereford Acts of Office   HRO: box 17, vol 66
f [158v]   *(11 January)*   5

*Proceedings of the court held in the parish church of Leominster before
Master Francis Bevans,* LLD, *vicar general of Herbert Westfaling,
bishop of Hereford.*

...   10

18 d   Edward seymore
8 d   Iohannes morce
          Thomas Blacke
          detecti for dauncing in the churchyard °quo die comparuerunt et
          confessi articulum eundem esse verum/ vnde dominus iniunxit [de p]   15
          eisdem separatim vnum diem penitencialem more penitenciali in
          Ecclesia sua parochiali et ad certificandum in proximo/°

          ...

f [179v]   *(7 February)*   20

*Proceedings of the court held in the parish church of Leominster before
Master Roger Bradshawe, deputy.*

          ...

debet feodum   Edward Seymore/   25
               Iohannes Morce/
               Thomas Blacke/
               detecti pro anglice dauncing infra cimiterium &c habent ad
               certificandum i diem penitencialem more penitenciali in hunc diem/
               °quibus Edwardo Seymor, & Thoma Blacke publice preconizatis &c   30
dimissio   et comparuerunt &c certificaverunt iuxta decretum &c de peractione
               penitencie &c vnde dimissi &c/°

          ...

HEREFORD   35

c 1265
Cathedral Consuetudines   HCL
f 9v*

                                                             40

... Item sciendum quod thesaurarius debet inuenire in festo sancti

Stephani diaconibus. In festo sancti iohannis sacerdotibus cereos
portatiles ad processionem in uesperis & matutinis. & in festo
innocencium pueris candelas & duos cereos coram paruo episcopo....

1286   5

Register of Bishop Richard Swinfield   HRO
ff 39v–40*   *(26 August)*

...

De nupciis
Iudeorum

¶ Ricardus miseracione diuina Herefordensis Episcopus/ dilecto in
christo filio domino .. Cancelario herefordensis vices .. decani eiusdem   10
ecclesie ad presens gerenti, salutem cum benediccione & gracia
saluatoris. Quot & quantis sit plena dispendiis & periculis
christianorum simul & iudeorum adinuicem conuersacio? non solum
iura testantur set & magistra rerum efficax experiencia, manifestat.
quos propria culpa perpetue seruituti dampnatos licet pietas christiana   15
receptet & sustineat pacienter. ipsis tamen christianis pro gracia
contumeliam & pro familiaritate contemptum reddere non verentur.
& quod dictu horrendum est, multipliciter ipsis illudere & in creatoris
sui contumeliam prosilire presumunt. Sane ex frequenti relacione
recepimus quod quidam Iudei hac instanti die Mercurij proxima post   20
festum beati Bartholomei apostoli In Ciuitate Herefordensi quedam
nupcialia conuiuia secundum ritum suum detestabilem prepararunt
ad que/ non nullos christianorum non solum occulte sed palam &
solempniter inuitarunt/ Vt sic fidei christiane cuius hostes gratis
existunt/ detrahere valeant & sinistra simplicibus predicare, ex quorum   25
tam solempni conuersacione ad inuicem/ non est dubium posse
scandalum generari. Cum igitur illius dissimulare opprobrium non
debemus/ qui de summis celorum ad yma mundi descendens, &
tandem mortem subiens temporalem/ probra nostra deleuit? vobis
mandamus in virtute obediencie. firmiter iniungentes quatinus per   30
omnes ecclesias ciuitatis predicte sub pena districcionis canonice hac
instanti die Martis & ipsa die Mercurij faciatis publice inhiberi? ne
quis christianorum huiusmodi conuiuijs cum iudeis interesse presumat.
Et ne aliquos per ignoranciam huius mandati contingat errare quod
absit/ hoc idem per vicos ciuitatis eiusdem faciatis eo modo quo melius   35

Consuetudines collation with BL: *Royal 10 A xi, f 261v (B) and Corpus Christi College,*
Cambridge: 120, p 502 (C):   p 97, l.41 Item] Et C   41 inuenire] inuenire cereos
B   p 98, l.1 diaconibus] dyconibus B   1 *after* sacerdotibus C *adds* [⟨f..is⟩] C

20–1/ instanti die ... apostoli: *Wednesday, 28 August*

conuenit publicari. Contrauenientes uel huic nostro mandato rebelles
siqui fuerint per censuram ecclesiasticam compescendo. valete. Datum
apud Bosebury. vij. kalendas Septembris. Ordinacionis nostre anno
Quarto.

                                                                              5

(6 September)

contra
accedentes
ad ea.

¶ Ricardus dei gracia Herefordensis Episcopus dilecto/ in christo filio
Decano Herefordensis uel eius vices adpresens gerenti, salutem graciam
& benediccionem. Meminimus nos vobis alias scripsisse, & in virtute   10
obediencie firmiter iniungendo mandasse, quatinus per omnes ecclesias
Ciuitatis Herefordensis publice faceretis inhiberi, ne quis
christianorum/ conuiuiis seu conubiis detestabilibus iudeorum
interesse presumeret. sub pena Canonice districcionis. Et ne qui per
ignoranciam nostri mandati/ errare possent mandauimus per vicos   15
Ciuitatis eiusdem eo modo quo melius conueniret inhibicionem
nostram sollempniter publicari. Addentes/ vt contrauenientes/ uel huic
mandato nostro rebelles/ si qui fuerint per censuram Ecclesiasticam
compesceretis in forma iuris. Vnde quia vt postmodum a fidedignis
intelleximus/ quod nonnulli iniquitatis seu rebellionis filii dictorum   20
inimicorum crucis christi nefandis connubiis interesse presumpserunt,
eisdem communicando, ac eos multipliciter honorando & ornando
in christianorum vituperium/ & scandalum/ & contumeliam sui
creatoris/ nostris monicionibus contemptis & etiam vilipensis/ quos
omnes & singulos/ excommunica[ui]mus in hiis scriptis? vobis in   25
virtute obediencie, & sub pena cohercionis canonice firmiter iterato
precipimus & mandamus, quatinus omnes illos qui predictis conuiuiis
seu connubiis intererant comedendo. bibendo. ludendo. ioculando/
seu quodcumque ystrionatus officium exercendo, seu quocumque alio
modo eisdem ad honorem ipsorum communicando in obprobrium   30
fidei christiane? per omnes Ecclesias Ciuitatis & suburbnus diebus
dominicis & festiuis intra missarum sollempnia, pulsatis Campanis/
accensis Candelis/ sic excommunicatos publice denuncietis/ donec ad
gremium sancte Matris Ecclesie redeuntes/ penam pro demeritis
condignam recepturi/ absolucionis ‖ beneficium meruerint obtinere.   35
quorum absolucionem nobis specialiter reseruamus, quicquid circa
eorundem absolucionem actenus fuerit attemptatum, in irritum
reuocantes. Illos vero qui prefatis inimicis christi communicarunt? eos
in equitatura. vectura. ornamentis/ in pannis sericis/ seu deauratis

31/ suburbnus *for* suburbanas

ornarunt/ seu *etiam* honorauerunt? censure sentencie consimil*is*
excom*m*u*n*icacionis proponim*us* innodare. *n*isi infra spaciu*m* octo
dierum a te*m*pore publicac*i*onis presenciu*m*/ deo & Ecclesie p*ro*
commisso tam nefario sat*is*fecerint competente*r*. Q*u*id aute*m* in
premissis feceritis vna *cum* no*m*inib*us* excommu*n*icatorum. nob*is* citra   5
die*m* sa*n*cti Michaelis. distincte & aperte co*n*stari facietis. Proponim*us*
e*n*im i*n* v*es*tri defect*um* seu negligen*ci*am. ne t*an*t*um* scel*us* remaneat
impu*n*itum? per alios d*i*ctam sente*n*ciam execucio*n*i debite dema*n*dare,
si q*uod* absentes negligentes fueritis i*n* premissis. vale*te*. Datu*m*
Bosebir*y*. viij°. Id*us* Septe*m*bris. anno d*omi*ni &c. octoges*imo* sexto.   10
…

1302–3
Cathedral Mass-pence Rolls   HCL: R390
mb 3*   *(Expenses)*   15
…
Ite*m* Die Innocenciu*m* Ep*iscop*o paruor*um*   iiij. d
…

1306–7   20
Cathedral Mass-pence Rolls   HCL: R391
mb 1   *(Expenses)*
…
Ite*m* Ep*iscop*o die Innocenciu*m*   iiij. d.
…   25

1308–9
Cathedral Mass-pence Rolls   HCL: R393
mb 3   *(Expenses)*
…   30
… Et p*ar*uo ep*iscop*o die festi *sanctor*um Innocenciu*m* iiij. d.…
…

1311–12
Cathedral Mass-pence Rolls   HCL: R399   35
mb 1   *(Expenses)*
…
Et p*ar*uo Ep*iscop*o die Innocenciu*m* p*ro* den*arijs*
missal*ibus*   iiij. d.
…   40

1313–14
Cathedral Mass-pence Rolls   HCL: R401
mb 1

...

... Item paruo Ep*iscop*o die Innocenci*um* pro j missa   iiij. d.   5

...

1316–17
Cathedral Mass-pence Rolls   HCL: R407
mb 1   *(First quarter expenses)*   10

...

... Et libe*rasse* p*a*r*u*o ep*iscop*o die innocenci*um* iiij. d....

1319–20
Cathedral Mass-pence Rolls   HCL: R408   15
mb 1   *(First quarter expenses)*

...

... Et p*a*r*u*o Ep*iscop*o pro j miss*a* iiij d.

...

                                                                                   20

1320–1
Cathedral Mass-pence Rolls   HCL: R409
mb 1   *(First quarter expenses)*

...

... Et p*a*r*u*o Ep*iscop*o. iiij d....   25

...

1321–2
Cathedral Mass-pence Rolls   HCL: R410
mb 1   *(First quarter expenses)*   30

...

... p*a*ruus ep*iscop*o die In*n*oce*ncium* iiij. d.

...

1322–3   35
Cathedral Mass-pence Rolls   HCL: R411
mb 1   *(First quarter expenses)*

...

It*em* p*a*ruo ep*iscop*o die innocenci*um* .iiij. d.

...   40

32/ paruus *for* paruo

1323–4
Cathedral Mass-pence Rolls   HCL: R412
mb 1   *(First quarter expenses)*
...
... Item Paruus Episcopus die Innocencium .iiij. d.   5
...

1324–5
Cathedral Mass-pence Rolls   HCL: R413
mb 1   *(First quarter expenses)*   10
...
... Item paruo Episcopo die Innocentium .iiij. d.
...

Cathedral Canons' Bakehouse Rolls   HCL: R632b   15
mb 1   *(External expenses)*
...
Item liberasse in oblaciones parui episcopi die sanctorum Innocencium
viij. d....
...   20

1327–8
Cathedral Mass-pence Rolls   HCL: R414
mb 1   *(First quarter expenses)*
...   25
... Item paruo Episcopo iiij. d.
...

1328–9
Cathedral Mass-pence Rolls   HCL: R415   30
mb 1   *(First quarter expenses)*
...
... paruo Episcopo j. missa iiij. d....
...

5/ Paruus Episcopus *for* Paruo Episcopo

1329-30
Cathedral Mass-pence Rolls   HCL: R416
mb 1   *(First quarter expenses)*

…

… Item paruo Ep*iscop*o j. miss*a*. iiij. d.…   5

…

1330-1
Cathedral Mass-pence Rolls   HCL: R417
mb 1   10

…

… Item paruo Ep*iscop*o j. miss*a* iiij. d.…

…

1332-3   15
Cathedral Mass-pence Rolls   HCL: R418
mb 1

…

… It*em* p*a*ruo Ep*iscop*o j miss*a* iiij. d.

…   20

1333-4
Cathedral Mass-pence Rolls   HCL: R419
mb 1

…   25

… Item p*a*ruo ep*iscop*o die Innocencij iiij. d.

…

1334-5
Cathedral Mass-pence Rolls   HCL: R420   30
mb 1   *(First quarter expenses)*

…

… Item p*a*ruo ep*iscop*o die Innocenc*ium* iiij. d.…

…   35

Cathedral Canons' Bakehouse Rolls   HCL: R633
mb 1   *(External expenses)*

…

It*em* in oblac*ione* p*a*rui ep*iscop*i die s*anctorum* Innocencium .viij. d.…

…   40

26/ Innocencij *for* Innocencium

1335–6
Cathedral Mass-pence Rolls   HCL: R421
mb 1   *(First quarter expenses)*

...

paruo Episcopo .iiij. d....   5

...

1336–7
Cathedral Mass-pence Rolls   HCL: R422
mb 1   *(First quarter expenses)*   10

...

... Item paruo Episcopo Die Innocencium .iiij. d....

...

1337–8   15
Cathedral Mass-pence Rolls   HCL: R423
mb 1   *(First quarter expenses)*

...

... Item paruo Episcopo Die Innocencium .iiij. d....

...   20

1338–9
Cathedral Mass-pence Rolls   HCL: R424
mb 1   *(First quarter expenses)*

...   25

... Item paruo Episcopo Die sanctorum Innocencium .iiij. d....

...

1339–40
Cathedral Mass-pence Rolls   HCL: R425   30
mb 1   *(Expenses)*

...

... Item paruo Episcopo Die Innocencium .iiij. d....

...

35

1340–1
Cathedral Mass-pence Rolls   HCL: R426
mb 1   *(First quarter expenses)*

...

... Item paruo .. Episcopo Die Innocencium pro .j. missa .iiij. d....   40

...

1341–2
Cathedral Mass-pence Rolls   HCL: R427
mb 1   *(First quarter expenses)*

...

Item paruo episcopo die Innocencium .iiij. d.//   5

...

1342–3
Cathedral Mass-pence Rolls   HCL: R428
mb 1   *(First quarter expenses)*   10

...

Item paruo episcopo die Innocencium .iiij. d.//...

...

1343–4   15
Cathedral Mass-pence Rolls   HCL: R429
mb 1   *(First quarter expenses)*

...

... Item paruo episcopo die innocencium. iiij. d.//...

...   20

Cathedral Canons' Bakehouse Rolls   HCL: R634
mb 1

...

...In oblacione parui episcopi pro vino viij. d....   25

...

1344–5
Cathedral Mass-pence Rolls   HCL: R430
mb 1   *(First quarter expenses)*   30

...

... Item paruo episcopo die innocencium .iiij. d./ ...

...

1345–6   35
Cathedral Mass-pence Rolls   HCL: R431
mb 1   *(First quarter expenses)*

...

... Item paruo Episcopo die Innocencium .iiij. d./...

...   40

1353-8
Cathedral Mass-pence Rolls   HCL: R433
mb 1   *(First quarter expenses)*

...

Item .p*aru*o. Ep*iscop*o .iiij. d....   5

...

1354-5
Cathedral Mass-pence Rolls   HCL: R434
mb 1   *(First quarter expenses)*   10

...

... It*em* paruo ep*iscop*o *pro* vna missa .iiij. d....

...

1356-7   15
Cathedral Mass-pence Rolls   HCL: R435
mb 1   *(First quarter expenses)*

...

... Item p*aru*o Ep*iscop*o *pro* .j. m*issa* .iiij. d.

...   20

1357-8
Cathedral Mass-pence Rolls   HCL: R436
mb 1   *(First quarter expenses)*

...   25

Inde lib*erasse* paruo Ep*iscop*o. *pro* .j. m*issa* .iiij. d...

...

1358-9
Cathedral Mass-pence Rolls   HCL: R437   30
mb 1   *(First quarter expenses)*

...

Inde computat lib*erasse* .p*aru*o. Ep*iscop*o *pro* .j. missa .iiij. d....

...

                                                                        35

Household Accounts of Queen Isabella, Widow of Edward II
BL: Cotton Galba E xiv
f 52v   *(9 July)*

...Ioh*ann*i Montsorti Citheredo fac*ienti* menestralc*iam* *suam* coram 40

*dom*ina Regina apud Herefordi*am* de dono eiusdem ix^a die Iulij. vj .s
viij .d....

1360–1
Cathedral Mass-pence Rolls   HCL: R438
mb 1 *(First quarter expenses)*

...

Inde liber*asse* p*ar*uo Ep*iscop*o p*r*o .j. missa .iiij. d....

...

1361–2
Cathedral Mass-pence Rolls   HCL: R439
mb 1 *(First quarter expenses)*

...

Inde liber*asse* p*ar*uo Ep*iscop*o iiij. d....

...

1372–3
Cathedral Mass-pence Rolls   HCL: R440
mb 1 *(First quarter expenses)*

...

¶ P*ar*uus ep*iscop*us p*ro* vna missa   iiij d.

...

1373–4
Cathedral Mass-pence Rolls   HCL: R441
mb 1 *(First quarter expenses)*

...

¶ p*ar*uus ep*iscop*us p*ro* vna miss*a*   iiij d.

...

1374–5
Cathedral Mass-pence Rolls   HCL: R442
mb 1 *(First quarter expenses)*

...

¶ p*ar*uus ep*iscop*us p*ro* vna missa   iiij d.

...

22/ P*ar*uus ep*iscop*us *for* Paruo episcopo
29/ p*ar*uus ep*iscop*us *for* paruo episcopo
36/ p*ar*uus ep*iscop*us *for* paruo episcopo

1375–6
Cathedral Mass-pence Rolls   HCL: R443
mb 1   col 1   *(First quarter expenses)*
...
p*ar*uus ep*iscop*us *pro* vna missa   iiij d.   5
...

1377–8
Cathedral Mass-pence Rolls   HCL: R444
mb 1   col 1   10
...
¶ Inde lib*erasse* p*ar*uo Ep*iscop*o *pro* j. missa   iiij. d.
...

1378–9   15
Cathedral Mass-pence Rolls   HCL: R444a
mb 1
...
¶ Inde computat in lib*eracione* p*ar*uo Ep*iscop*o *pro* vna missa
iiij. d....   20
...

1379–80
Cathedral Mass-pence Rolls   HCL: R445
mb 1   *(Cash payments)*   25
...
₡ Idem comput*at* in soluc*ione* p*ar*uo ep*iscop*o *pro* .j. missa
.iiij. d./...
...

                                                                                    30

1381–2
Cathedral Mass-pence Rolls   HCL: R446
mb 1
...
¶ Inde comp*utat* solut*ionem* p*ar*uo ep*iscop*o *pro* j missa   35
iiij d./...
...

5/ p*ar*uus ep*iscop*us *for* paruo episcopo

1382–3
Cathedral Mass-pence Rolls   HCL: R447
mb 1   col 1   *(First quarter expenses)*

...

¶ Inde comp*ut*at solu*cionem* ˏ⌐paruo ep*iscopo*⌐ pro j missa   iiij d.   5

...

1383–4
Cathedral Mass-pence Rolls   HCL: R448
mb 1   col 1   *(First quarter expenses)*   10

...

¶ Inde comp*ut*at solu*tionem* paruo Ep*iscopo* p*ro* vna miss*a*   .iiij. d.

...

1384–5   15
Cathedral Mass-pence Rolls   HCL: R449
mb 1   col 1   *(First quarter expenses)*

...

Inde comp*ut*at solu*tionem* paruo ep*iscop*o pro j missa   iiij d.

...   20

1385–6
Cathedral Mass-pence Rolls   HCL: R450
mb 1   col 1   *(First quarter expenses)*

...   25

Inde comp*ut*at solu*cionem* paruo Ep*iscop*o pro j missa   iiij d.

...

1386–7
Cathedral Mass-pence Rolls   HCL: R451   30
mb 1   col 1

...

Inde comp*ut*at solu*tionem* paruo Ep*iscopo* pro j missa   iiij d.

...

...   35

1387–8
Cathedral Mass-pence Rolls   HCL: R452
mb 1   col 2

...

Item p*ar*uo Ep*iscopo* pro j miss*a*   iiij d.   40

...

1389–90
Cathedral Mass-pence Rolls   HCL: R453
mb 2   col 2   *(Second quarter expenses)*
…
Item solut' ij° quarterio Parvo Episcopo pro j missa   iiij d.   5
…

1398–9
Cathedral Mass-pence Rolls   HCL: R460
mb 1   *(First quarter expenses)*   10
…
Parvo episcopo pro j missa   iiij d.
…

1401–2   15
Cathedral Canons' Bakehouse Rolls   HCL: R635
mb 1   *(Payments)*
…
In festo sanctorum Innocencium eisdem ix canonicis
& paruo Episcopo   vj s. viij d.   20
…

1412–13
Cathedral Mass-pence Rolls   HCL: R467
mb 1   col 1   *(First quarter expenses)*   25
…
… parvo episcopo   iiij d.
…

1413–14   30
Cathedral Mass-pence Rolls   HCL: R468
mb 1   col 2*   *(First quarter expenses)*

Paruo Episcopo j missa   iiij d.
…   35

1417–18
Cathedral Mass-pence Rolls   HCL: R470
mb 2

…   40
❡ Et computat solutionem paruo Episcopo ibidem

existent*i* in die *sanctorum* Innocenc*ium* hoc anno
accid*ente* *per* d*ictu*m paupiru*m*   iiij d.

...

1420–1   5
Cathedral Mass-pence Rolls   HCL: R472
mb 3

℃ Et soluti*onem* par*u*o Ep*iscop*o ib*i*d*em* existent*i* in die
sanctorum Innocenc*ium* hoc anno accid*ente* *per*   10
d*ictu*m papirum   iiij d.

...

1425–6
Cathedral Canons' Bakehouse Rolls   HCL: R637   15
mb 2 *(Payments)*

...

Et comp*utat* sol*uisse* par*u*o Ep*iscop*o *pro* vino in festo
omn*ium* *sanctorum* Innocenc*ium* accid*ente* infra
temp*us* compo*ti*   viij d.   20

...

1432–3
Cathedral Mass-pence Rolls   HCL: R479
mb 2* *(Allowances)*   25

...

P*ar*vo Ep*iscop*o ib*i*d*em* existent*i* ad j missam infra
tempus compo*ti*   j d. q*u*arter*ium* pars ij^a

...

                                                                          30

1433–4
Cathedral Mass-pence Rolls   HCL: R480
mb 1d *(Allowances)*

...

P*ar*vo Ep*iscop*o ib*i*d*em* existent*i* ad j missam infra   35
tempus compo*ti*   j d. q*u*arter*ium*

...

1435–6
Cathedral Mass-pence Rolls   HCL: R481
mb 1d   *(Allowances)*
…

℃ P*a*ruo ep*iscopo*. ib*idem* exist*enti* ad j missam infra tempus   5
comp*oti*   j d. di. q*uarterium*.
…

1437–8
Cathedral Mass-pence Rolls   HCL: R482   10
mb 1d   *(Allowances)*
…

℃ Paruo Ep*iscopo presenti* exist*enti* ad ⌈j⌉ missam in festo s*anctorum*
Innocenciu*m (blank)*
…   15

1440?
Mayor's Court Plea Book   HRO
f [4v]*   *(30 April)*

20
℃ Eodem die [Thomas lewes Sadeler quor*um*] ⌈Iohan*n*es hanley &
Iohan*n*es Pewte querunt*ur*⌉ vers*us* Thomam ⌈libere condicionis⌉

Memorandum
iiij d.
per pleg*ium*
Iohan*n*is Theo

Sporyo*ur* de p*l*acito detencionis vni libri de lusionib*us* precio ij s. iiij d.
pleg*ij* de p*re*cio Thomas lewes Sadeler & Phil*ipp*us Moseley Et de
re*d*dito att*ach*iandus est p*er* corpus   25
…

1463–4
Cathedral Canons' Bakehouse Rolls   HCL: R637a
mb 3   *(First half of year) (Payments)*   30
…

Et solut*um* ⌈paruo Ep*iscopo*⌉ pro vino exist*enti presenti*
ad missam in festo s*anctorum* Innoc*encium* hoc a*n*no   viij d.
…

35

mb 5d
…

…Et solut*um* p*a*ruo Ep*iscopo* pro j noct*ur*no in festo

23/ vni *for* vnius *(?)*

sanctorum Innocencium ex consuetudine ecclesie
hoc anno   j Commun'
...

1469–70   5
Cathedral Canons' Bakehouse Rolls   HCL: R637b
mb 2   *(Payments)*
...
Et solutum paruo Episcopo existenti presenti ad missam
in festo sanctorum Innocencium   viij d.   10
...

c 1470
Cathedral Canons' Bakehouse Rolls   HCL: R630a
mb 1d   15
...
...Item solutum paruo Episcopo pro nocturna sua in festo sanctorum
Innocencium ex consuetudine ecclesie hoc Anno j Commun'...
...

                                                                    20
1470–80?
Cathedral Canons' Bakehouse Rolls   HCL: R637c
mb 3*   *(First half of year) (Payments)*
...
Et solutum paruo Episcopo pro vino existenti presenti   25
ad missam in dicta prima medietate huius Anni in festo
sanctorum Innocencium   viij d.
...

mb 5d   30
...
Et solutum paruo Episcopo pro eius nocturnis ad
matutina existentia hoc Anno in ffesto inuentionis sancte
crucis ex consuetudine Ecclesie   j Commun'
...   35

1486
First Provincial Progress of Henry VII   BL: Cotton Julius B xii
ff 17–18*   *(15 May)*
...   40
... On the monday the king Remevede And Roode to herforde Wher

A myle And moore oute of the town And ou*er* long brigge the meire
of the towne wi*th* an vj[xx] horse And aboue mette the king And
Receyved hym And further nere the [tow⌐n¹e] towne the frerez of the
saide Citie yaue ther Attendaunce in the procession aft*er* the parish
chirches as accustumed Wi*th* great m*u*ltitude of people of the   5
Countrey [R] Whiche in Reioysing of the king*es* co*m*myng Cried
king henry king henry And holding vp ther handez blessed & prayde
god to prese*r*ue our king And When he entred the gate ther was
ordeyned a pageaunt Of Seint George With a speche as ensueth |

                                                                                        10

Se*int* george   Moost Cristen prince And frende vnto the feith
Supporter of truth confounder of wikkednesse
As people of your Realme holy Reporth And saith
Welcome to this Citie Wi*th*oute eny feintenesse
And thinke verely as ye see her in likenesse   15
That this worme is discomfit by goddes [&] ⌐ayde¹ and myn
So shall I. be your helpe vnto your lives fine
To Wi*th*stonde your Enemyes with the helpe of that blessed virgyn
The Whiche loveth you Right wele I. dar playnly it say
Wherfor ye be right Welcom I. pray god further you in your way   20

Item At the Crosse In the market place Was ordeynede A nother
pageaunt of A king And ij bisshops The whiche sensede the king And
the king of that had this Speche as ensueth

                                                                                        25

Moost vertuouse prince And gracious In gou*er*nance
Not Rigours but m*er*cifull as dauid in his Iuggement
Ethelbert Rex   The people of your Citie Wolde ful fayne your pleasaunce
And prayde me as ther patrone to enforme you of ther entent
My name Is king Ethelbert that sumtyme Was king of kent   30
Whiche in my yong Age loost myn erthly liff
And now am [procto*u*r] protector of this Cathedrall & Citie pre*s*ent
Wherfor I Say Welcome both of man Child & Wiff
And that blessed virgyn that cessith our mortall striff
Abideth your co*m*myng her What I. say you   35
Wherfor I. will not ye tary but I. pray god be wi*th* you

2/ vj[xx]: *ie, sixscore or 120*
13/ Reporth *for* Reporteth
27/ Rigours *for* Rigorous (?)

Item at the entre of the Minster Was the iij^de paiaunt of our lady | With many virgins mervealous & Richely besene And our lady had her Speche as herafter ensueth

®our lady

In the best Wise welcome myn oune true knyght   5
To my Chirche And chapelens of our oune foundacion
Wherfor I. thanke you & pray you both Day & nyght
ffor to kepe And defende from al fraudulent Imaginacion
ffor many thynges I. thanke you The dedes sheweth probacion
Vnto my laude & honour your doth euer atteigne.   10
Wherfor I. thanke you of your good supportacion
Your Rewarde Is behinde It shall come certeyne
That is the blisse of hevyn Wherin my sonne dooth Reigne
That Veraly I promysse you I. haue graunt Afor
Now goo In & see my Chirche I. Will tary you nomore.   15

Item at the entre Within the Chirche doore The Bisshop In
pontificalibus With the Dean & the quere Receyuede the king as in
other cathedrall Chirches Accustumed And on the morne as the king
Went In procession The bisshop of that Same See made A Sermonde   20
declaring The popes bulles touching the kinges & the quenes stile...

1503
Mayor's Book   HRO
f 176*   25

                The paiantes for the procession of corpus christi
                                    b The tanners
                                        the story of Shore Thursday
ffurst Glouers   a Walkers   30
    Adam Eve   the good lord ⌈°ridyng on an
                                   asse°⌉ with xij appostelles
b   [Cayme and abell]   Bochours
Eldest   Cayme abell ⎫
seriant   ⎬ moysey aron the taking of of our lord [to]
                              ⎭ &   35

10/ *word missing after* your
17/ The Bisshop: *Thomas Milling, bishop of Hereford, 1474–92*
28/ b: *this symbol links its line with the line marked* b *(l. 33) in the left hand margin*
30/ a: *this symbol links its line with the line marked* a *(p 116, l. 2) in the left hand margin*
31–2/ ⌈°ridyng on an asse°⌉ *inserted in the same hand as l. 27–31 above*
34/ of of: *dittography*

a

Carpenters
  Noye ship   The Eldest seriant
                                           The Tormentyng of our lord
                                           with iiij tormentoures with
                                           the lementacion of our lady° &   5
Chaundelers   saynt Iohn the euaungelist°
  abram Isack   °Cappers   portacio Crucis
                                           vsque montem Caluarij°
  moysey cum iiij^or pueris   Dyers
                                           ⌜°Ihesus pendens in°⌝ Cruce &   10
Skynners   Smythes
  Iesse   longys with his knyghtes
                                   °The Eldist Sariant // Mari˄⌜a[⟨.⟩⌝ and
fflacchers   Iohannes Euangelista°
  Salutacion of our   Barbours   15
  lady   Ioseth Abarmathia
Vynteners   Dyers
  Natiuite of our lord   Sepultura christi
Taillours   The Eldest seriant
  The iij Kinges of colen   tres marie   20
The belman
  the purificacion of our lady   Porters
  with Symyon   Milites armati custodes sepulcri
drapers
  The – doctours [of q]   Mercers   25
  goyng with the good lord   Pilate cayfas annas
                                       & mahounde
Sadlers   Bakers
  ffleme Iordan   Knyghtes in harnes
Cardeners   °Iorneymen⎫   30
  the castell of Israell   Cappers ⎭
                                       Seinte keterina with [ij]
                                       ⌜Tres⌝ Tormentors°

10/ ⌜°Ihesus pendens in°⌝ Cruce &: *corrected from* portacio Crucis & Iohannes Euangelista
portant' mariam
13–14/ °The Eldist ... Euangelista°: *inserted in a second hand*
30–3/ °Iorneymen ... Tormentors° *inserted in the second hand*

c 1500–20?
Civic Miscellany 6   HRO
ff 12–12v*

    To the Ryght worshypefull Mayer of the Cytay of herefford   5
    And to hys Bretherne./
Shewythe vnto your good mastershyppes your vmble orators the
persons Subscribed beyng Iornemen of thoccupacion of [t] Corvesers
with in this Cytey/ haue obtayned of your mastershyppes predesessors
Mayers And Aldermen of the Sayd Cytey A Composysyon whereby   10
your Sayd Orators were bound to bryng furth Certen torches in the
procession on the Day of Corpus Christi yerelye/ And that your Sayd
orators be Also bound to paye yerlye to the Wardens of the Sayd
occupacon Att xiij hall Dayes with in the Sayd Cytey/ yerelye to be
holden xiij d. ffor the mayntennace of the Sayd torches, And for the   15
Relyeffe of the pore Bretherne of the Sayd occupacion beyng sycke
or in Decaye with in the Sayd Cytey/ And ffor to burye suche pore
bretherne as shuld happen to dye with in the Same./ Whyche good
lavdable orders haue Alwayes ben kepte ffrom the makyng thereof
vntyll nowe of latte that the Wardens of the Sayd occupacion And   20
Certen other frowarde persons in A Cedule hereunto Annexted named
of theyre perverse mynd dyd dystribute And geve Away the torches
of the Sayd Occupacion Att theyre plesure/ And that the Sayd
Wardens haue Alwayes hetherunto Refused and do Refusse./. to make
And yelde to your sayd orators An Accounte of the Receipte of theyre   25
charge Contrary to theyre [chargge] othe thereffore taken And
Contrary to theyre olde Custome thereffore vsed/. And that they
Also wolde breke dyvers ordynnances in the Sayd Composicion
Comprised And by the Lawes off the Realme or Custome of the Sayd
Cytey not ffor bydden which ys to the vtter Impovereshyng of your   30
Sayde orators/ And Contrary to All Ryght And Consyons/. Wherefor
hytt may ples your good mastershyppes to Commaunde the Sayd
Wardens to make Redeliuerye of the Sayd torches And to yelde theyre
Sayd Accounte Accordyng to Iustyce And that your Sayd orators
may Enioye All suche grauntes And libertes in the Same Composicion   35
mencioned And by the kynges magestie | And his moste honorable

12/ procession *corrected from* precession
14/ occupacon *for* occupacion
15/ mayntennace *for* mayntennance
21/ persons *corrected from* presons

Councell nott Abrogatt Accordyng to the porpotte of the Sayd
grauntes to them madde/ And your Sayd orators shall dayle pray to
god for the prosperus Estatte off yowre good mastershyppes long tyme
to Endure.

5

c 1517

Civic Miscellany 6   HRO
f 39*   *(8 May) (Letter from Walter Devereux to the mayor of
Hereford)*

10

Maister Mayer in my mooste hartyst maner I recomend me vnto/ and
to all the Aldremen your brethern of the Cite/ Prayng and desiryng
you all With the hole Commonalte ther to be good and favorable to
thys berer Henry wenston. So it ys. he ys determyned to make within
the Cite a Game or a geve Aill after the custome of the Contre by   15
your lisence/ and in that behalff he hath made labore vnto me to
thentente that I wolde wrytt vnto you for your good wyll and the
favore of your Brethern and Citezens to be hade/ [s] accordyng to
hys suytt made to me as ys before said/ I do desier you and all other
aboue namyd to be favorable and good Maisters vnto hym/ as in   20
gevyng hym leyff to kepe the said game or geve aill/ and that it may
be asmoche to hys provytt as you may cause/ and in thys doyng at
⟨..⟩ instance and for my sake/ I shalbe at all tymes as good lorde and
as frendly to any lover or frende of yours at your request in that shall
ly in me/ No more to you at thys tyme / but Ihesu haue you in hys   25
kepyng/ Wretyn at Rychemonde the viij^th day of May./
                                        By yours assuryd
                        (signed) °Walter Deveroux°

1533–4   30
Mayor's Account Rolls   HRO
mb 1d   *(20 October–19 October) (Allowances)*
...
Item solutis Thome downe servienti ad Clavam domini
Regis ad laborandum processionem ffesti Corporis christi   35
cum diuersis historijs hoc anno productis   vj s. viij d.
...

11/ you *missing after* vnto (?)
18/ [s]: *probably written over another letter*
23/ ⟨..⟩: *probably* my; *edge frayed*

Item solutis Ministrall' domini Regis hoc anno   vj s. viij d.
Item solutis Ministrallorum diuersorum Generosorum   xx s.

...

1543–4
Cathedral Canons' Bakehouse Rolls   HCL: R638
mb 2   *(First half of year) (Payments)*

...

Et solutum paruo Episcopo pro vino existenti ad missam
in prima medietate vnius Anni   j d.   10

...

1548–9
Great Black Book   HRO
ff 27–8*   *(10 December)*   15

Att A Lawday holden Att the Cytey of hereford before Iohn
Warmecombe Esquyer mayor of the Cytey of hereford the xth day
of December in the Second yere of the Raigne of our Soueraigne Lord
Edward the Syxt by the grace of god of England ffraunce and Ireland   20
Kynge Defender of the ffaythe And in erthe Supreme hed of the
Churche of England and Ireland/ fforasmocheas there was before
thys tyme Dyvers Corporacions of Artiffycers craftes and occupacions
in the Sayd Cytey who were bound by the grauntes of ther
Corporacions yerlye to bryng fforthe and Sett foreward dyuers   25
pageaunttes of Ancyentt historyes in the processyon in the sayd Cytey
vpon the Day and ffeast of Corpus christi/ whiche nowe ys & Are
omytted and Surseassed./ Wherfore yt ys Agred Condescended. and
grauntted by the sayd mayour hys bretherne and the thre Enquestes
Sworne at thys presentt Law Day/ And by ther hole Assenttes and   30
Concenttes and by the Auctoryte of the sayd Lawday accordyng to
the Ancyentt Custome of the sayd Cytey. that the sayd [Lawday]
mayour nowe at this presentt Lawday/ And hereafter hys Successors
mayors of the sayd Cytey with the Consentt of hys or ther sayd
Bretherne and the thre Enquestes Shall and may grauntt vnder the   35
Common Sealle of the sayd Cytey vnto all the Artifficers craftes and
occupacions in the sayd Cytey (whiche before this tyme have had
Composycions and grauntes of Corporacions vnder the sayd
Common Seale) Licke Corporacons and Composycyons as they the

2/ Ministrallorum *for* Ministrallis
39/ Corporacons *for* Corporacions; *mark of abbreviation missing*

sayd Artifficers craft*es* and occupac*ions* have had and Enyoyed in
tymes past/ Savyng that all and every of the sayd craft*es* and
Corporacions shall in Stede and place of the Settyng ffurthe of the sayd
pageaunt*tes* on the sayd Day and ffeast of Corpus christi/ yerly
contentt & pay/ Att the ffeast of the Anuncyac*ion* of our lady the   5
vyrgen/ on Anuyte or Certen Som*m*e of money/ [Suche as the same
craft*es*] to the vse and behoffe of the sayd Cytey Suche as the same
craft*es* Artifficers and occupac*ions* & Corporacons shall grauntt to
geve by those graunt*es* of Corporacions as to theym or any of theym
Shall hereafter be grauntted and Delyvered vnder the sayd Com*m*on   10
Seale of the sayd Cytey./ And yt ys ffurther agred and condescendyd
at thes p*re*sentt lawday that ther shalbe yerely | Chosen by the mayor
for the tyme being hys Bretherne And the thre Enquest*es* that shalbe
Sworne yerly at the lawe Day next before the ffeast of Seyntt mychell
tharchangell. Twoo of the Gyldmarchaunt*tes* of the sayd Cytey/   15
whiche shalbe called the Colectours of the Anuytes of the occupac*ions*
in the Cytey of hereford./ on to be Chosen by the ffurst Inquest And
the other by the Second & thyrd Inquest/ who shall by vertue of that
name and offyce Colecte and gather vpp yerly ffor that yere Ensuyng
all the Anuytes & som*m*es of money of the Artifficers and occupac*ions* 20
Incorporat in the sayd Cytey of hereford After the sayd ffeast of
Anuncyacon of our lady by the sayd Corporac*ions* Rese*r*ued./ And
the same shall Dystrybute/ Dyspend & Bestow the same yere
Ensuyng/ in and vpon the Ruynowes and decayed Cawseyes
pamentt*es* Strett*es* & walles and castyng of the Townedyches or suche 25
like Rep*ar*acions in the sayd Cytey/ by the appoyntmentt and order
of the mayor of the sayd Cytey ffor the tyme being/ And that also
the sayd Colectours/ Att the Ende of the sayd yere/ And at the sayd
lawday before the ffeast of Seyntt mychell the sayd Colectours Shall
bryng ffurth A trew and a p*er*ffytt Accompt of all the bestowyng   30
Dyspence and Dystrybucon of the sayde Anuytes & So*m*mes of
money by theym as ys afforsayd to be Receaved in maters And ffactes
before Rehersed. Whiche Accompt So by theym made and Exibeted
shalbe openly Radde and Declared vpon the sayd lawday before the
sayd mayor hys Bretherne and the thre Inquest*es* ffor the tyme being/ 35
And then and thereto Render geve and Delyver vnto the newe
Colectures that shalbe then Elected and chosen/ owtt of hand and

8/ Corporacons *for* Corporacions; *mark of abbreviation missing*
22/ Anuncyacon *for* Anuncyacion; *mark of abbreviation missing*
31/ Dystrybucon *for* Dystrybucion; *mark of abbreviation missing*

withoutt ffurther Delay vpon payne of Imprisonmentt the Rest &
Resydew of [all] suche Sommes of money as by theym was leyved
Receaved and gathered of the sayd Corporacions and by the same
Colectors not bestowed. Dyspended or Dystrybuted in and vpon the
sayd Ruynowes or appeyred Cawseyes pavementtes Strettes walles or   5
pore people in the sayd Cytey of hereford/ provided. alweyes that
the | That the sayd Collectures or any thyng to theym grauntted be
not/ nor shall not be/ Adiugged Reputed or taken to be any thyng
preiudiciall vnto the Chamberleyns of the sayd Cytey in or ffor any
thyng that ys Reserued or grauntted to be payed or gathered to or   10
by the sayd Chamberleyns/ ffor and to the vse or behove of the
Chambour of the sayd Cytey/ by the name of the sayd Chamborleyns
of the sayd Cytey of hereford as yt hathe benne Accustomed in tymes
past/.
...   15

1553–4
Mayor's Account Rolls   HRO
mb 1d   *(23 October–22 October) (Allowances)*
...   20
Item solutis ministralibus domini Regis et Regine
hoc Anno   xx s.

...
Item solutis diuersis ministralibus diuersorum
generosorum hoc Anno   x s.   25
...

1577–8
Mayor's Account Rolls   HRO
mb 3d   *(30 September 1577–6 October 1578) (Allowances)*   30
...
Item solutis diuersis ministralis diuersorum generosorum
hoc anno   xx s.
...
Item solutis diuersis lusoribus in enterludijs diuersorum   35
generosorum hoc anno   xxvj s. viij d.
...

6–7/ that the | That the: *dittography*

1580-1
Mayor's Account Rolls   HRO
mb 4d   *(3 October–2 October) (Allowances)*
…

Item sol*utis* diu*ersis* Ministral*is* diu*ersorum* gen*er*osorum   5
hoc anno   xx s.
…

Item sol*utis* diu*ersis* lusoribus in*ter*lud*iorum* diu*er*sorum
gen*er*os*orum* hoc anno   xx s.
…   10

1582-3
Mayor's Account Rolls   HRO
mb 1d   *(1 October–30 September) (Allowances)*
…   15
Item sol*utis* diu*er*sis ministral*is* diu*ersorum* gen*er*osorum
Hoc anno   xx s.
…

Item sol*utis* diu*er*sis lusoribus in*ter*lud*iorum* diu*er*sorum
gen*er*os*orum* Hoc Anno   xiij s. iiij d.   20
…

1587
Civic Miscellany 3   HRO
f 70*   25

> To the right worshipfull M*aste*r Mayor of
> the Citie of hereford his bretherne,
> and the three Enquest*es* sworne at this
> Lawe Daye,   30
Shewethe vnto your worshippes, that where as by the auncyent
custome of this Citie there hathe byn appoynted waytes to serve in
the same, And that your Orator Willyam Iacson of the seid Citie
hathe served every wynter quarter for the space of these Seaven yeres
paste for a small stipende beynge farre twooe Lyttle to maynetayne 35
hym and his company. And nowe myndynge not to travell into any
place abrode out of the seid Citie. but to serve throwly and contynually
the whole yere, whereunto he will geave his dutifull and diligent
attendaunce, excepte it be by the specyall Lycence of the said mayor
or by his comaundement, by meanes whereof he is to leave all other 40
kynde of travell abrode. and other his busynes, whereby he dyd geate
a great p*ar*te of his Levynge whiche to travell forthe of the seid Citie

he meanethe and will geave over. In tender concyderac*i*on whereof
may hit please your worshippes that hit may be ordered by the same
at this present Lawe daye that your seid orators stypende or wages may
be awgmented and encreaced at your worshippes discression ⸢and to
be quarterly payde⸣ And in so doynge your orator will not onely be   5
the more ready and diligent in his service. as becomethe hym.
Leavynge and puttynge aparte his other pryvate busynes, But also
pray to god for the prosperous estate of this Citie, and for yo*u*r
worshippes well and Longe to governe the same,

10

Civic Miscellany 3   HRO
f 72

To the righte Worshipfull M*aster* Mayor
of the Cytie of here*f*ord his brethren and the   15
thre enquest sworne at this lawe day
In most humble wise besechethe yo*u*r worshippes yo*u*r poore
neighboure & dayly orator Roger Squyre that where by the deathe
of will*i*am Iackson late musyc*i*on and head wayte of this worshipfull
Cytie his Rome is nowe voyde and at yo*u*r worshippes order and   20
disposic*i*on And yo*u*r said orator who from his youthe hathe byn
broughte vp in musycke and dothe *p*resently keepe and meynteyne
s*e*ruant*es* in the arte of musycke to play on diu*er*s instrument*es* is ⸝
Desyrous yf hit may stand w*i*th yo*u*r worshippes pleasures that you
would admyt him to be the wayte of the said Cytie And he trusteth   25
that in shorte tyme he will attayne to suche knowledge in the
Instrument*es* of Shalmes & lowde noyce as shalbe to yo*u*r good
lykinge & contentac*i*on And in graunting to yo*u*r orator this his
humble request he w*i*th his wife Chyldren and famylie will Dayly
pray to god for the *p*rosperous estate of yo*u*r worshippes and of the   30
whole Cytie longe tyme to Contynue
The second Inqueste doth Agre to this byll
The therd in quest dotth agre lickwyse to this byll
The firste inqueste dothe lykewyse agree to this bill/

35

1587–8
Mayor's Account Rolls   HRO
mb 3d   *(2 October–30 September) (Allowances)*
...

Item sol*utis* diu*ersis* lusoribus hoc Anno   XX S.   40
...

1600
Civic Miscellany 4   HRO
f 1

    To the right wor*shi*pfull Iames Smithe esquyre Maior of this Citty   5
    of Hereford, to the Iusti*ce*s of peace of this Citty of Here*fo*rd,
       And the three Inquest*es* sworne at this *p*resent lawe daye.
May yt please your worshipps to consider the humble peti*ci*on of
yowr poore Orator Roger Squyre, a man borne, bred, and continued
in this Citty thees ffourescore yeeres & ode in the loue and favour   10
of you all, and allwayes found you ready to pleasure mee, w*hi*ch
bouldenethe mee once more to *p*resume vppon your worshipps, as
concerninge the waitshippe, w*hi*ch heretofore I was desyred to serve,
w*hi*ch I did not deny, But thought my selfe happy that it lay in mee
to pleasure you, But sithence I was wrongfully defeated vppon no   15
occasion (w*hi*ch is a p*ar*te of my vtter vndoinge), and was allowed
by the Inquest*es* eu*er*y yeere sithence my defeature, and being able
to serve yt as well as now yt is, and w*i*th better creditt. I would
therefore desyre your worshipps (as I haue allwayes done) to graunt
mee the offyce wholly into my hand And in so doinge you do not   20
onely doe a deed of Charity, But also you bynd mee, my wyfe, &
Chylders to pray for the *p*reserva*ci*on of your healthes and the
*p*rosperous estate of this Citty, and this for god*es* love.

                Your poore servaunt to Commaund   25
                    (signed) Roger Squyre

°The second Inqueste Doth alowe hime the Like stipend as he had
beffore°
°The third Inqueste doth the Like as the seconde dothe°   30
°The grete Inquest doth alowe hym a cloke and xx s. to be paid by
the new waites, and that Roger squier shall not by no meanes gather
of any *p*erson any benevolence as one of the citties waites°

1601   35
A *Account Book of Sir Thomas Walmesley*
  Cooper: *Expenses of the Judges of Assize*
  p 49 col 1   *(23 July) (Provisions bought at Hereford)*
  ...
  Item to ye waites of ye cittie   ij s vj d.   40
  ...

1609
Old Meg of Herefordshire   STC: 12032
sigs A3–C3v*

To that renowned oxleach, old Hall, Taborer of Hereford-shire, and   5
to his most inuincible Weather-beaten Nutbrowne Taber, being
alreadie old and sound, threescore yeares and vpward.
   To thee (old Hall,) that for thy Age and Art mightest haue cured
an Oxe that was eaten at Saint Quintins, that for thy warlike Musicke
mightest haue struck vp at Bullen, when great Drummes wore broken   10
heades, thy little continuall Taber, had beene enough to haue put
Spirit into all the Souldiers: Now Tweire-pipe that famous Southre*n*
Taberer with the Cowleyan windpipe, who for whuling hath beene
famous through the Globe of the world, did euer gaine such renowne
and credite by his Pipe and Taber, as thou (old Hall) by striking vp   15
to these twelue hundred yeares Moris-dauncers: Nor art thou alone
(sweet Hall) a most exquisite Taber-man, but an excellent Oxe-leach,
and canst pleasure thy neighbours. The people of Hereford-shire are
beholding to thee, thou giuest the men light hearts by thy Pype, and
the women light heeles by thy Taber: O wonderfull Pyper, O   20
admirable Taber-man, make vse of thy worth, euen after death, that
art so famously worthy in thy life, both for thy age, skill, & thy
vnbruized Taber, who these threescore yeares has kept her |
maydenhead sound and vncrackt, and neither lost her first voyce, or
her fashion: once for the Countryes pleasure imitate that Bohemian   25
Zisea, who at his death gaue his Souldiers a strict command, to flea
his skin off, and couer a Drum with it, that aliue & dead, he might
sound like a terror in the eares of his enemies: So thou sweete Hereford
Hall, bequeath in thy last will, thy Velom-spotted skin, to couer
Tabors: at the sound of which, to set all the shires a dauncing. | 30

     Old Meg of Hereford-shire for a Mayd-marian,
          and Here towne, for a Morris daunce.
   The courts of kings for stately measures: the Citie for light-heeles,
and nimble footing: the Country for shufling dances: Westerne-men   35
for gambouls: Middlesex-men for tricks aboue grou*n*d: Essex-men
for the Hey: Lancashire for Horne-pypes: Worcester-shire for
Bagpypes: but Hereford-shire for a Morris-daunce, puts downe, not

---

12/ Now *for* not   26/ Zisea *for* Zisca
33/ Here *for* Hereford; Here *comes at a line end, but* ford *has been left out at the start of the*
new line

onely all Kent, but verie neare (if one had line enough to measure it)
three quarters of Christendome. Neuer had Saint Sepulchres a truer
ring of Bels: neuer did any Silke-weauer keepe brauer time with the
knocke of the heele: neuer had the dauncing horse a better tread of
the toe: neuer could Beuerley Faire giue money to a more sound   5
Taborer, nor euer had Robin Hood a more deft Mayd-Marian.

If your eares itch after this old (but yet no stale) wonder, let them
itch not more (for why should any mans ears itch longer than is reason)
you shall haue them tickled presently with the neb of my pen.
Understand therefore (if at least you haue so much spare wit left you,   10
as to vnderstand,) that in the merriest Moneth of the yeare, which
last did take his leaue of vs, & in that Moneth, as some report, Lords
went a Maying, the wombe of the | spring being great with child of
pleasure, brought forth (iust about that time) a number of Knights,
Esquiers, and Gallants (of the best sort) from many partes of the land, 15
to meete at a Horse-race neere Hereford, in Hereford-shire. The
horses hauing (for that yeare) run themselues well-nigh out of breath,
wagers of great summes (according to the fashion of such pastimes)
being wonne and lost, and the sports growing to the end, and shutting
vp, some wit (riper than the rest) fed the stomacks of all men (then   20
and there present) with desire and expectation of a more fresh and
liuely meeting in the same place, to be performed this yeare of 1609.
Pleasure and paine had left such deepe print in euery bosome, that
the match was no sooner begotten, but it was borne, time only being
appointed at the due expected houre to bring it forth. The ceremonies   25
which their meeting was to stand vpon, were these, that euery man
should engage himselfe (in his credite) vnder his hand, to bring (this
present yeere) to the place appointed, running horses for the race,
Cockes of the game, to maintaine battails, &. with good store of
money, to flie vp and downe betweene those that were to lay wagers.   30
He that first gaue fire to this sotiable motion, was charged to stand
to his tackling, and to come well prouided, who thervpon (whilest
the mettle of his braines were hot and boyling) vndertooke to bring
a Hobbie-horse to the race, that should out-runne all the Nags which
were to come thither, and to hold out in a longer race, then any would 35
be there.

The circle of time running round, and closing at his fulnesse,
expectation did within fewe dayes make Hereford towne shew like
the best peopled Cittie. Innes were lodgings for Lords: Baucis and

7/ no for not (?)

Philæmons house (had it stood there) would haue beene taken op for
a Knight. The streetes swarmed with people, the people staring and
ioyfully welcomming whole brauies of | Gallants, who came brauely
flocking on horsback, like so many lustie aduenturers. Bath made her
waters to boile vp & swell like a Spring-tide, with the ouerflowing of   5
her owne teares, which fell from her eies through griefe, to see her
dearest guests leaue her for the loue of a horse-race at Hereford. And
so much the greater were her sorrowes, by how much the more
worthie the friendes were whom she lost: for the number of them
being at least two or three hundred. Amongst many of the better   10
rankes, these marched with the foremost.

        Lord Herbert of Ragland.
        Sir Thomas Somerset.
        Charles Somerset.
        Count Arundels &. sonnes.   15
        Sir Edward Swift.
        Sir Thomas Mildemay.
        Sir Robert Yaxley.
        Sir Roger Carey.
        Sir Iohn Philpot.   20
        Sir Edward Lewes.
        Sir Francis Lacon.
        Sir Iames Scudamore.
        Sir Thomas Cornwall.
        Sir Roger Boderham.   25
        Sir Thomas Russell.
        Sir (blank) Bascaruile.
        Sir Thomas Conisby.
        Sir George Chute. |

These were but a small handfull to those rich heapes that there   30
were gathered together. But by these (that had the honour to be the
leaders) you may gesse what numbers were the followers.

The day being come, in which the running horses were to proue
themselues arrant Iades, or to shewe the noblenesse of their breeding:
As much looking there was, asmuch talking, and asmuch preparation,   35
for the Hobbi-horse promised the last yeare, as about dieting the
fairest Gelding this yeare, vpon whose head the heauiest wagers were
layd.

The exercises of this Olympian race, required strength, speede,
lustinesse of courage, and youthfull blood, none but able and actiue   40
bodies could climb ouer such labors. But to performe a race of greater

length, of greater labor, and yet in shorter time, and by feeble
vnexercised, and vnapt creatures, that would be an honour to him that
vndertooke it, that would be to Hereford-shire a glorie, albeit it might
seeme an impossibilitie.

What man would not wonder to see fire strucke out of yce; to see   5
Dead Ashes kindled again, and to yeelde fire; to see Saples trees in
the depth of Winter laden with mellow Apples, and to see those Apples
when they are pluckt and cut, to grow againe. This wonder was as
great, the accomplishment of it as strange.

Age is no bodie (in trials of the bodie) when youth is in place, it   10
giues the other the bucklers: it stands & giues aime, and is content
to see youth Act, whiles Age sits but as a spectator, because the one
does but studie and play ouer the parts which the other hath discharged
in this great and troublesome Theater. It was therefore now plotted,
to lay the Sceane in Age, to haue the old Comedie presented, Fathers   15
to be the Actors, and beardlesse boyes the Spectators. Sophocles
(because he was accused of imbecilitie and dotage, should rehearse
his Oedilpus Coloneus, while the Senate, & his owne wild-brain
sonnes stoode by, and were the audience: And to set out the Sceane
with mirth, as well as with wonder, the state of the whole Act, was   20
put into a Morris-daunce. To furnish which fully & rarely, a Bill of
names able to impannell three or 4. Iuries was giuen & read, but onely
18. were sworne, and had the charge deliuered to them: Those vpon
whose heades the Vous auez was set, being these, that in the next
ranke double their Fyles. viz.   25

The Morris, and all the Officers
attending vpon it.

The running horses being too light of foote for vs to follow, be   30
content I pray to stay with vs, and to march along with our Infanterie
of Hereford, which thus brauely came on.

Two Musitions were appoynted (like the Drum-maior, and Drum-
minor, to strike vp, and to giue the alarum: the one of them was a
Squire borne and all his sons Squires in their cradles. The Instrument   35
he tickled was a trebble Violim, vpon which he played any old lesson
that could be called for: the diuision hee made on the strings, being
more pleasing then the Diapason. In skill he out-shines blind Moone

®Squire of
Hereford,
a Musition.
108.

17/ comma after dotage an error for closing parenthesis (?)
36/ Violim for Violin

of London, and hath out-played more Fidlers, then now sneake vp
& downe into all the Tauerns there. They may all call him their father,
or (if you reckon the yeares rightly which are scored vpon his head)
the Musitions Grandsire, for this tuneable Squire is one hundred and
eight yeares old.   5

Next to Arion (and cheeke by ioule with him in estimation) went
old Orpheus, (as a man might being deceiued, haue taken him) but

®Harrie Rudge
the Taborer.

that hee wanted Orpheus Lute. This was old Hall of Hereford, the
Wayts of three Metropolitane Cities, make not more Musicke | then
he can with his Pipe and Tabor, if at least his head be hard-brac'd   10
with nappie Ale. This noble old Hall, seeing that Apollo was both a
Fidler, and a Quack-saluer, being able to cure diseases, as well as to
harpe vpon one string, would needes be free of two companies as
well he, (that is to say) the sweete companie off Musitions, and that
other which deales in salues and plaisters; for he both beates a Tabor   15
with good iudgement and (with better) can helpe an Oxe if he finde
himselfe ill at ease.

The Wood of this olde Halls Tabor should haue beene made a Paile
to carrie water in, at the beginning of King Edward the sixts raigne:
but Hall (being wise, because hee was euen then reasonably well   20
strucken in yeares) saued it from going to the water, and converted
it in those dayes to a Tabor. So that his Tabor hath made Batchelers

Hall 97.
yeares.

and Lasses daunce round about the May-poll, three-score Sommers
one after another in order, and is yet not worme-eaten. And noble
Hall himselfe, hath stoode (like an Oake) in all stormes, by the space   25
of foure-score and seuenteene Winters, and is not yet falling to the
ground.

4. Whiflers.

The Marshales of the field, were foure: these had no great stomacke
to daunce in the Morris, but tooke vpon them the office of Whiflers.

Thomas Price
of Clodacke
105. yeares.

1   The first of these was Thomas Price of Clodacke, a Subsidie   30
man; and one, vpon whose cheekes age had written, one hundred
and fiue yeares.

Thomas Andros
of Begger
Weston. 108.

2   The second was Thomas Andros of Begger Weston, a Subsidie
man, for he carried vpon his backe, the weightie burden of one
hundred and eight yeares, and went away with them lightly.   35

William Edwards
of Bodenham.
108.

3   The third was William Edwards of Bodenham, (his name is in
the Kings bookes likewise,) & vnto him hath time also giuen the use
of one hundred and eight yeares: And besides the blessings of so many
yeares, the | comfort of a yong wife, and by that wife is his age honored
with a child, of six yeares olde.   40

®Iohn Sanders
102. yeares old.

4   The fourth was Iohn Sanders of Walford, an Iron-worker; the
hardness of which labour could not so wearie and wast his bodie, but
that his courage hath ouercome it, & carried him safely ouer the hie
hill of old age, where she hath bestowed vpon him one hundred and
two yeares.   5

®423. yeares.

These foure Whiflers reckoning with their liues and casting vp what
all their dates which they had spent in the world could make, found
that they amounted to foure hundred and three and twentie yeares;
So that if the rest of their dauncing brother-hood, had come short of
their account, and could not (euery man) make vp one hundred   10
yeares, these offered & weare able to lend them three and twentie
yeares, but the others had enough of their owne, and needed not to
borrow of any man.

Doe you not long to see how ye Morris-dancers bestir their legs
(lift vp your eyes, leape vp behind their heads that stand before you,   15
or else get vpon stalls, for I heare their bells, and behold, here they
come.

®Iames Tomkins,
106. yeeres old.

Of twelue in the whole Teeme, the foreman was Iames Tomkins of
Lengerren, a gentleman by birth; neither loued of fortune, nor hated
of her, for he was neuer so poore as to be pittied, nor euer so rich   20
as to be enuied: when he had bin a dweller in the world fourescore
and eighteene yeares, he maried a wife, of two & fiftie yeares old;
shee brought him a child thats now eight yeares old (liuing,) the Father
himselfe hauing now the glasse of his life running to fill vp, the full
number of one hundred and six yeares.   25

®Iohn Willis
97. yeers old.

After him comes lustily dauncing, Iohn Willis of Dormington, a
bone-setter: he had gotten such skill by placing other mens bones in
order, when they were strucke out of ioynt, that he would neuer
suffer his owne to be | displaced, and by that meanes was so lustie
at legges now, that albeit he carried about him, the full weight of one   30
hundred yeares, yet he was not seene to lye behind his fellewes, but
went foote by foote with the foremost. His dauncing was fit to his
yeares, and his purpose in being one of the Mor is, was both honest
and charitable, for he bestowed his person vpon them, with intent
to be readie at hand if any dislocation should be wrought vpon any   35
ioynt in his old companions) by fetching loftie trickes, which by all
meanes possible they were sworne to auoide. Roome for little Dick

17/ *no closing parenthesis after* come
33/ Mor is *for* Morris
36/ *closing parenthesis after* companions *appears to be otiose*

Phillips, of Middleton; how nimbly he shakes his heeles, wel dancd, old heart of oake, and yet as little as he seemes, his courage is as big,

as the Hobbie-horses, for the fruits of his youth, (gathered long agon,) are not yet withered. His eldest Sonne is at this present foure score yeares of age, and his second Sonne, may now reckon three score: at   5
our Lady day last, he made vp the yeares of his life, iust one hundred and two.

Now falls into his right place William Waiton of Marden, with a

hundred & two yeares at his heeles, and that you may know he neuer swore in his life, he was an old fisher, and of a cleane man an excellent   10 Fowler, the first yeare of King Henrie the eight.

Here slips in William Mosse, who contrarie to his name, had no Mosse at his heeles, little can he say of himselfe, and I as little of him, but that he beares the age of a hundred and sixe.

Now cast your eyes vpon Thomas Winney of Holmer, an honest 15 subsidie man, dwelling close by the towne, he dances with a hundred yeares about him, wheresoeuer he goes, if the Church-yard and

crampe take him not before Midsommer. But how like you Iohn Lace of Madley a Taylor and an excellent name for it. In his youth he was a hosier, & a special good codpiece maker, beling borne before the 20 discension between cloath breeches and veluet breeches, he carries foure score and seuentie Sommers about him, & faine would borrow three yeares of Iames Tomkins to make him a hundred, and Iames may very well spare them, and yet leaue three toward the intrest.

But what say you to Iohn Carelesse you let him passe by you, &   25 seeme as carelesse as he, a man of fourescore and sixteene at Midsommer next, he hath beene a dweller in Homlacie, threescore yeares and two, and knowne to be a tall man, till now he begins to be crooked, but for a bodie and a beard, he becomes any Morris in Christendome.   30

At the heeles of him follows his fellow William Maio of Egelton, an old Souldier, and now a lustie laborer and a tall man, fortie yeares since being grieuously wounded, he carried his liuer and his lights home halfe a mile and you may still put your finger into them, but for a thin skin ouer them; and for all these stormes he arriues at   35 fourescore and seuenteene, and dances merrily.

But looke you who here comes, Iohn Hunt the Hobbie-horse, wanting but three of an hundred, twere time for him to forget himselfe, and sing but O, nothing but O, the Hobbie-horse is forgotten; the

22/ seuentie *for* seuenteen

Maide-marrian following him, offers to lend him seuen yeares more, but if he would take vp ten in the hundred, his company are able to lend them.

®Meg Goodwin of Erdisland. 120.

But now giue way for the Maide-marrian, old Meg Goodwin the 5 famous wench of Erdisland, of who*m* Maister Weauer, of Burton that was fourescore & ten yeares old, was wont to say, she was twentie yeares elder then he, and he dyed ten yeares since. This old Meg was at Prince Arthurs death at Ludlow, and had her part in the dole, she was threescore yeares (she saith) a Maide, and twentie yeares 10 otherwise, thats what you will, and since hath beene thought fit to be a Maide-marrian. |

Iohn Mando 100. yeares old.

Welcome Iohn Mando he was borne at Cradly, a verry good tws hand-sword man, of the age of an hundred at blacke Monday last, and serues in place of Morgan Deede, who climes to that age within 15 foure yeares, here present dwelling in the towne, but he has a great desire to keepe his bed, and be spared.

So here are eighteene persons, that carrie in all places about them eighteen hundred, & thirtie seuen yeares.

1837. yeares

Belike it was a grand-iurie to make vp this Morris-daunce, for more 20 were called, as two men out of Estnor of two hundred nine yeares of age, foure out of Marcle, of foure hundred fiue yeares.

And for a good wager, it were easie to finde in that countie foure hundred persons more, within three years ouer or vnder, an hundred yeares, yet the shire is no way foure and twentie miles ouer. 25

But will you know what fashion was obserued amongst the Musitians, and whats habit the dauncers tooke vpon them, here take a view of both. The Musitians, and the twelue dauncers, had long coates of the old fashion, hie sleeues gathered at the elbowes, and hanging sleeues behind: the stuffe red Buffin, stript with white, 30 Girdles with white, stockings white, and redde Roses to their shooes: the one sixe, a white Iewes cap with a Iewell, and a long red Feather: the other a scarlet Iewes cap, with a Iewell and a white Feather: So the Hobbi-horse, and so the Maide-Marrion was attired in colours: the Wiflers had long staues, white and red. And after the daunce was 35 ended, diuerse Courtiers that won wagers at the race, tooke those colours, and wore them in their hats. |

13/ tws *for* two
27/ whats *for* what

The speech spoken before the Morris.

Ye seruants of our mightie King,
    That came from court one hundred mile
    To see our race, and sport this spring: 5
Ye are welcome, that is our Country stile,
And much good doe you, we are sorie,
That Hereford hath no better for yee.
    A Horse, a Cocke, Trainsents, a Bull,
Primero, Gleeke, Hazard, Mumchance: 10
These sports through time are growne so dull,
As good to see a Morris dance.
Which sport was promised in iest,
But payd as truly as the rest.
    A race (quoth you) behold a race,   15
No race of horses but of men,
Men borne not ten miles from this place,
Whose courses outrun hundreds ten.
    A thousand yeares on ten mens backs,
    And one supplies what other lacks. | 20

The Lenuoy.

This is the Lenuoy (you may gather)
    Gentlemen, Yeomen, Groomes, and Pages   25
    Lets pray, Prince Henrie, and his father,
May outliue all these ten mens ages:
And he that mocks this application,
Is but a knaue past reformation.

                                                      30

    This speech spoken, old Hall strucke vp and the Morris-dauncers
fell to footing, whilest the Whiflers in their office, made roome for
the Hobby-horse.
    And howe doe you like this Morris-daunce of Hereford-shire? Are
they not braue olde youths? Haue they not the right footing? the   35
true tread? comely lifeting vp of one legge, and actiue bestowing of
the other? Kemps Morris to Norwich, was no more to this, then a
Galliard on a common stage, at the end of an old dead Comedie, is
to a Caranto daunced on the Ropes.
    Nestor makes a bragging in Homer, (a kind of blind Poet, that   40
could not see when he did well) of his owne praises, and especially

keepes a prating of his Age. But I would faine read if euer a Homer
of them all, if Nestor at that age (whatsoeuer it was) was able to haue
made one in such a Morris-daunce.

Nay, how many Tailors that skipping from their Shoppe-boords on
Saterday nights, lay waite onelie for weddings on the Sunday   5
following, wasting their Capers many times on filthie rotten Mutton,
and dauncing out their working day-gettings on Holi-day spendings,
how many of these, I say, would be able to set up a Morris at those
yeares, which Hereford here doth reckon? The great Grand-fathers,
Fathers, of three-score such nimble footed Linnen-Armourers will   10
neuer be able to put into the Needle of Life, a Threed so long, so
strong, and so round: no, they eate away their dayes too fast, and
drinke vp their nights in surfeits: hee that can draw out the wire of
his age (in these licentious cockny-endes of the worlde,) to fortie
yeares, is an olde man, and giues vp his cloake for riding on a Hobby- 15
horse, or for playing any youthfull tricks besides.

A Taylor at fortie yeares, is glad to trust to his yard, and walkes
leaning vpon that. A Fencer at thirtie (by reason of his knocking)
takes any foyle, to be a staffe to his age. A waterman at fiftie yeares,
falles from water to drinking of Ale, onely to keepe life and soule   20
togither. A Vintner at threescore, has legges no bigger than a Crane,
they are so wasted with running. But here is a doozen of yonkers,
that haue hearts of Oake at fourescore yeares: backes of steele at
fourescore and ten, ribbes of yron at a hundred, bodies sound as Belles,
and healthfull (according to the Russian prouerbe) as an Oxe when   25
they are trauelling downe the hill, to make that one hundred and
twentie.

These, shewed in their dauncing, and moouing vp and downe, as
if Mawlborne hilles, in the verie depth of Winter, when all their heades
are couered (in steade of white woollie cappes) with snow, had shooke 30
and daunced at some earth-quake.

Shall any man, lay blame on these good old Fathers, because at
such yeares they had not spent all their wild-oates? No, we commend
(as Tully saith) a young man, that smells somewhat of the old signior
and can but counterfeit grauitie in his cheekes; & shall we not heaue 35
vp with praises an old man, that at one hundred & eight yeares end,
can rake his dead embers abroad, and thew some coales of the lustie
Iuuentus glowing in him euen then? Such an olde Mad cappe deserues
better to bee the stuffing of a Cronicle, then Charing Crosse does
for loosing his rotten head, which (through age being wind-shaken)   40
fell off, and was trod vpon in contempt. Were old Stowe aliue, here
were Tabring work enough for his pen: but howsoeuer, so memorable

a monument of man, shall not wither in obliuion, if the sweete Aprill
shewers which drop from the Muses water, can make it grow vp and
flourish.

A dishonour were it to Poets and all pen-men, if acts of this worth
should not Cucomiastically be celebrated and recorded. For heereby   5
the Vertuous are heartned: if you will not belieue me, I will prooue
it by strong reasons. Whoremongers, drunkards, and such like
fellowes, (who are euery hower wrastling with Vices and Villaines,
which are harder to be tripped downe then the Guard) that in their
youthfull dayes spend more at a Tauerne reckoning or in a Vaulting-   10
schoole, in one houre, then their great Grandfathers did (among all
their neighbours) in a whole Christmas. These (I say) drew out a short,
a blacke, a rotten, & gowtie threed of old age. But it is therefore an
argument, that these white-bearded youths of Hereford-shiere, were
neuer giuen to wine or to wenches, both which are sharper then the   15
destinies Sheeres, to cut in sunder the very bottome of the soundest
life.

Old age is to all men for the most part a disease; It is to some the
cough; they do nothing but spit; to some, the Palsey: If these were
rotten, they would shake themselues to peeces: to others, it is the   20
Gowte, they haue not a good legge to throw at a Dogge, and were
ill to be | cowardly souldiers, because they could not runne, vnles
the running Gowte set them forward: But old age in Hereford-shire,⟩
neither spits nor spawles, feeles no aches nor oes in his bones. ⟩

Oh! if all the people in the kingdome, should haue their dayes   25
stretched out to the length of these mens, Clearks and Sextons might
go hang themselues in the belropes: they would haue colde doings:
prodigal heires might beg, they should hardly find an Almanacke that
would tell them when their lands should come to their hands by the
death of their fathers, for they themselues would haue white Beardes,   30
before they could arriue at their full age. It were no hoping after dead
mens shooes, for both vpper leather and soles would bee worne out
to nothing.

As great pittie it were (O old Margaret, or rather new Mayd-
Marion) that all mens wiues (especially those that like Dutch-watches   35
haue larums in their mouths) should last so long as thou hast done:
howe would the world be plagued? Loue would die: the generation
of mankinde, would in a short time be dried vp, & shrunke away to
nothing.

5/ Cucomiastically *for* Encomiastically *(?)*

But a far more lamentable cause of sorow would it be, if Mayden-
heades should stand so long vpon Wenches shoulders as yours (Mother
Marget) hath done vpon your owne, because if they did so, they would
bee seeded (like olde tough Turne-vps) and so not bee worth the
cutting.   5

Alas! what doe I see? Hold Taborer, stand Hobby-horse, Morris-
dancers, lend vs your hands, behold one of the nimble-legd old
gallants, is by chance falne down, and is either so heauy, so weary,
so vnactiue of himselfe, or else fiue of his fellowes are of such little
strength, that all their Armes are put vnder him (as Leauers) | to lift   10
him vp, yet the good olde boyes cannot set him on his feete. Let him
not lie for shame, you that haue (all this while) seene him daunce,
and though hee bee a little out of his part, in the verie last Act of all,
yet hisse at nothing, but rather (because it is begd for Gods sake.)
                  Summi Iouis causa plaudite.   15
                          FINIS.

1612
Star Chamber Bill of Complaint   PRO: STAC 8/50/4
f 2*   *(31 July)*   20

...about*es* the last daie of Iulie now last past one Richard Rodde of
your highnes said Citie of Hereford Corviser, Iohn Perrott of the
said Citie of Here*ford* gent*leman* Thomas Williams of the said Citie
Corviser William Iones of the said Citie yeoman the said William   25
Iones beinge Comonly called Wicked Wyll Alice Grismond of the
said Citie widowe Iohan *(blank)* Mayde servant of the said Alice
Grismond assemblinge to themselves dyvers others Desper*ate* and
vnruly *per*sons to the number of Twelve *per*sons whose names your
Subiecte knoweth not but praieth hee may inserte the same *persons*   30
when theire names shalbee knowne ˏ⌐into this Bill⌐ the said *persons*
or most of them ˏ⌐then⌐ apparrelled in womans apparrell And the said
William Iones al*ias* Wicked Will beinge then apparrelled in the
Apparrell of one ffortune Perrott wief of Robert Perrott gent*leman*
All vnlawfully weap,⌐o⌐ned w*ith* Iavellinges fforrest Bylles and other   35
vnlawfull weapons as well Defensive as invasive ˏ⌐in or about*es* the
said last day of Iuly last past⌐ brake downe the Doores of the said
howse in yo*u*r said Cytie of Hereford ˏ⌐extended as aforesaid⌐ the
same Doores beinge then fast locked And in very furious and
Rebelliouslyke manner entred into the said mesuage [and then and   40
there] And then and there the said william Iones al*ias* Wicked Wyll
apparrelled in Womans apparrell as aforesaid togeather w*ith* the said

Iohn Perrott Richard Rodde Thomas Williams Alice Grismond Iohane
(blank) her Mayde Servant and other vnknowne Ryotours havinge
entred into the said mesuage weaponed as aforesaid Did Assaulte beate
and wounde one Iohn Kington Sibill his wief and Mary Wheeler
Servant*es* and vndertenant*es* of your Subiecte for your Subiect*es* parte   5
of the said Messuage the said One thowsand mark*es* Costes and
Damages beinge not at the tyme or yet satisfied to y*our* Subiecte and
the said William Whitlach or ˏ⌈to⌉ either of them for w*hi*ch debte the
said premisses were extended By w*hi*ch doeinge of the said Ryottors
your good and quiet Subiect*es* of your said Citie were much Terryfied   10
and amazed. In tender Consideraci*on* Whereof and forasmuch as the
said Ryott*es* Routes vnlawfull Assemblyes and other the
misdemeanours aforesaid were Donne and Com*m*ytted since your
Maiesties last and generall and free p*ar*don And for that the same
offences tend to the breache of y*our* highnes peace the Contempte   15
of your gracious Lawes p*ro*vyded against Ryott*es* and Ryotours And
will much incourage other lyke p*er*sons to Com*m*ytt the lyke offences
yf the Ryottours should escape vnpun*n*ished To the end the said
Ryotto*ur*s may receave Condigne pun*n*ishment accordinge to the
qualytie of theire heynous offences by Which Example others wilbee   20
· terrefyed from doeinge or attemptinge the lyke ˏ⌈Ryott*es* and outrages⌉
May yt please yo*ur* most excellent Maiestie to graunte your most
gracious Wrytt of Subpena to bee Dyrected vnto the said Richard
Rodd Iohn Perrott Alice Grismond William Iones al*ia*s Wicked Wyll
Thomas Willyams and Iohane *(blank)* Commaundinge them thereby   25
and everie of them at a Certaine day and vnder a Certaine payne therein
to bee lymited to bee and p*er*sonally appeare before your highnes
and yo*ur* highnes Councell in yo*ur* highnes Courte of Starre Chamber
then and there to answeare And further to [stand to] ˏ⌈receave⌉ and
abyde such ˏ⌈punishment and⌉ order therein as to your highnes and   30
your said Councell shall seeme fytt and convenyent And your highnes
Subiecte shall allwayes pray for your Maiestie in all happines longe
to Raigne and Rule over us

                                        (signed) Walweyne

                                                                                 35

1615
Civic Miscellany 4   HRO
f 21

          To the right wor*shipfu*ll Iames Smith Esq*uie*r Mayor of the   40
          Citty of Hereford with the three in quest and to every of
          them

May it please your good worship to bee advertized That Roger Smith
is thought agood and suffitient man for the supplyance of the place
of one of the waytes of the Citty Yf therfore your worship with the
Three in quest shall give him admittance into the said place hee shall
bee bound to rest   5

°we of the thrid enquest doth [nott] alowe this bill°
°The second in qwest doe allow this bill°
°The great inquest doe allow this bill°
                                                                                         10

                    Your worships humble at Comaund
                                    (signed) Roger Smith

1615–16
Mayor's Account Rolls   HRO   15
mb 3   *(2 October–30 September) (Allowances)*
...
Item solut*is* et dat*is* diu*ercis* lusorib*us* hoc anno   xl s.
...
                                                                                         20

1619–20
Haberdashers' and Barbers' Company Account and Minute Book
Hereford Library: LC 338.6 MSS
f [207]   *(Rendered 6 November 1620) (Disbursements)*
...   25
Item to the waytes at mr Harp*ers*   xiiij d.
...

1627–8
Mayor's Account Rolls   HRO   30
mb 4   *(1 October 1627–6 October 1628) (Allowances)*
...
Item solut*is* & dat*is* diu*ersis* lusorib*us* hoc anno   xx s.
...

18/ diu*ercis for* diuersis

Acts of Decanal Court HCL
f 268   *(26 May)*

*Proceedings of the court held before Master Jones and in the presence
of the registrar.*   5

St Martins   William Powell ffor playing on Saboth dayes vppon his ffiddle

...

1639–41   10
Haberdashers' and Barbers' Company Account and Minute Book
Hereford Library: LC 338.6 MSS
f [187v]   *(6 August 1639–2 August 1641) (Disbursements)*

...

Charges for oure Dinner the 29 of Iuly 1641   xxviij s.   15
Disbursed to the waites and for wine at that time   vj s.

...

1641–2
Haberdashers' and Barbers' Company Account and Minute Book   20
Hereford Library: LC 338.6 MSS
f [186v]   *(Rendered 8 August 1642)*

...

payd to the waytes on the kinges holiday at neight by
consente of the Companie   ij s.   25

...

HOLMER

1619   30
Acts of Decanal Court HCL
f 2v*   *(18 December)*

⟨...⟩ Steevens for not presenting the names of dauncers this last Sommer
&c °18° decembris 1619 coram domino decano &c comparuit et   35
dominus retulit causam ad certificandum articulum determinandam
&c°

...

24/ the kinges holiday: *27 March*

KILPECK

1629
Archdeaconry of Hereford Acts of Office   HRO: box 25, vol 94
f [93]*   *(24 October)*   5

Proceedings of the court held in the consistory of Hereford Cathedral
before Richard Basset, LLB, surrogate, and in the presence of Thomas
Duppa, notary public.

...   10

Kenchurch   *contra* Ricardum watkins detectus for dauncing out of his parishe in
the parishe of Kilpecke on whitsonmunday last °quesitus 16° die
quere de   Octobris 1629 vijs et modis in proximo decimo quarto die mensis
presentibus   Novembris 1629 in ecclesia Cathedrali herefordie loco consistoriali
iure et facto   ibidem coram magistro Iohanne ffreemantle artium magistro deputato   15
dimissio   &c. comparuit personaliter dictus Watkins et obiecto ei articulo fassus
est articulum esse verum quam confessionem dominus acceptauit
quatinus &c et ipsum dimisit cum admonicione°

KINGSLAND   20

1588/9
Diocese of Hereford Acts of Office   HRO: box 17, vol 68
f [65]   *(13 March)*
                                                                            25
Proceedings of the court held in the consistory of Hereford Cathedral
before Master William Grenewich, MA, deputy.
...

Margareta gwillim citata in hunc diem dicere Causas quare penitencie
ei iniungi non debeant ob defectum purgandum [pro] de articulo   30
anglice that she did not daunce die dominico tempore diuinorum.
Quo die publice preconizata comparuit dicta margareta et nullam
Causam allegavit &c vnde dominus iniunxit ei ad confitendum
huiusmodi articulum in Vsuali vestitu et ad certificandum in proximo/
                                                                            35
Iohannes Berry
citatus vt supra, ad ostendum causas vt supra/ quo die comparuit
predictus Iohannes Berry et nullam Causam sufficientem allegauit &c

14–15m/ presentibus, facto: *expansions conjectural*
31/ did not *for* did (?)

vnde dominus [ie] iniunxit ei ad confitendum vt supra/ Et ad
certificandum in proximo/

Iohannes Barrow similiter/
Quo die comparuit &c Et dominus iniunxit ei ad confitendum vt supra/   5
Et ad certificandum in proximo/

Richardus Nelson similiter/
Quo die comparuit &c/ Et dominus iniunxit ei ad confitendum vt
supra et ad certificandum in proximo/   10

f [65v]

emanavit   Anna gwillim suspicione notata anglice for dauncing tempore
excommunicacio   divinorum/ °quo die non comparuit°   15
                    ...

1617
Diocese of Hereford Acts of Office   HRO: box 24a (formerly 18), vol 71
f [356v]*   *(30 June)*   20

Proceedings of the court held in the parish church of Leominster.
...

Thomas Waucklen painter detectus per gardianos de kingsland
acted a plaie with others vpon the saboath daie at tyme of eveninge   25
praier/ °citatus per publicum edictum in vltimum diem Iunij predicti
preconizatus &c non comparuit &c excommunicatus°

KINGTON
                                                                        30
1618
Archdeaconry of Hereford Acts of Office   HRO: box 24, vol 90
f [86v]   *(26 October)*

Proceedings of the court held in the consistory of Hereford Cathedral   35
before Master Gabriel Wallwin, MA, *deputy to Master Oliver Lloid,*
LLD, *official principal and commissary of Francis Godwin, bishop of*
Hereford.
...

                    Catherina Bybyth vidua   40
dimissio   ffor keepinge drinckinge and dauncinge in her howse [in her howse]

in the tyme of Eveninge prayer./ °Quo die com*paruit* personali*ter* d*ict*a
Catherina et obiecto ei ar*ticu*lo fass*a* est ar*ticu*lum esse veru*m* vnde
d*omin*us iniu*n*xit ei vnu*m* diem penitenc*ialem* more penitenc*iali* Et ad
cert*ificandum* in proximo deinde d*omin*us ipsam dimisit cu*m*
admonic*ione*°   5

...

f [93]

...

Walterius Bybith   10
di*missio*   ffor dauncinge die d*omin*ico at eveninge prayer tyme in the house of
Catharine Bybith com*paruit* et neg*av*it d*omin*us *f*acta p*er* eu*m* fide
&c. dimisit eu*m* cu*m* monic*ione* &c

di*missio*   Willimus Driver   15
pro Cons*imili* Simil*iter*

di*missio*   Elizabetha Moore
pro Cons*imili* Simil*iter*

                                                                      20

LEDBURY

1618
Archdeaconry of Hereford Acts of Office   HRO: box 24, vol 90
f [144v]*   *(16 November)*   25

di*missio*   Edwardus hall Inkeeper
hee actor and morrice dauncer, and haue gone out of the parrishe to
other places with gune and drume both in the night to the disturbance
of the king*es* subiectes and the p*ro*fanation of the Saboath daie in the   30
morninge/. °xvj^to die Nove*m*b*ris* &c com*paruit* d*i*ctus Edward Hall,
&c & sup*er* ex*aminacio*ne ar*ticu*li &c/ & confitens &c d*omin*us iniu*n*xit
ei ad confitend*um* ar*ticu*lum in vsuali vestitu &c Cora*m* ministro &
gard*ianis* post preces &c ⌊Et ad cert*ificandum* in proximo/⌋° viij° die
ffebruarij pred*icti* [⟨..⟩] introducta forma cu*m* cert*ificari*o dimiss*us*   35

Edwardus Crocker Corvicer
di*missio*   pro cons*imili* Quo die simil*iter* vt supra vltimo die Ianuarij 1618 iux*ta*
&c apud [her] Ledburie

28/ hee *for* hee being (?)
28/ haue *for* hauing (?)

coram venerabili viro magistro Iohanne Hoskins legum doctore
deputato &c comparuit personaliter dictus Crocker et in vim
iuramenti sui certificavit de peractione penitencie iuxta &c vnde
dimissus

                                                                    5

dimissio   Edwardus hooper pro consimili Quo die comparuit personaliter dictus
             hooper et obiecto ei articulo negavit articulum esse verum vnde prestito
             iuramento de innocencia sua vnde dimissus

             ...
                                                                    10

f [147v]

Iohannes Wilbore ffidler
for drunkenes and [ribl] ribaldry Citetur/
°Citatus in 16. novembris predicti &c non comparuit/°   15

...

1638
Letter to William Laud, Archbishop of Canterbury, from Francis
Thompson PRO: SP 16/397   20
single sheet* *(30 August)*   Puritan – anti – sport.

        To the most Reverend ffather in God William Lord
        Arch Bishopp of Canterbury his grace Primate &c;
The humble petition of francis Thompson gentleman   25
In all duety sheweth That whereas one Henry Page Vicar of Ledbury
in the Countye of Hereford haueing taken vpon him ye Cure of soules
there hath many times vsed diverse and sundrye scandalous and
ignominious speeches in the Pulpitt and elswhere and more especially
vpon the 4th Comandment both by preaching and otherwise hee hath   30
in contempt of ye kings most excelent Maiesties declaracion
concerning the lawfullnes of recreation vpon Sundayes and holye
dayes after time of divine service and in derision and scorne of the
booke sett forth by his Maiestie to that purpose often amongst other
his opprobrious and disgracefull speeches vttered these words   35
followinge concerning the same Videlicet Is it not as lawfull to pluck
at a Cartrope vpon the sabboth day as at a bellrope; Is it not as lawfull
for a Weaver to shoote his shuttle on the Sabboth daye as for a man
to take his bowe to shoote: And is it not as lawfull for a woman to
spinne at her wheele or for a man to goe to plough or Cart as for a 40

26/ Henry Page *underlined*

man on the Sabboth daye to dance that deuilishe round; All which
words and diverse other of the like kinde your petitioner wilbe bound
to proue vnto your grace and the honourable Court of high
Commission;
May it therefore please your grace for the reformacion of the sayde   5
Mr Page and satisfaction of his parishioners Consciences and other
Inhabitants thereabouts who dailye flock vnto him by reason of
Invegling them with such his doctrine to graunt an Attachment or
Letters Missiue to yssue out against him the sayd Page to bringe him
to answere to such articles as shalbe exhibited into the said court   10
against him; And your petitioner as in dutye shall daylye pray for
your graces long life and happie dayes &c

left flap

Book of Sports   15
[⟨....⟩]
August 9 1638

right flap   20

ɪ   I desire Dr Merricke to consider of ye Suggestions of this Petition
and take order for Letters Missiue if he see cause.
                              (signed) °William Cantuarie°
August 30.   25
1638

LEOMINSTER

1534-43   30
John Leland's Itinerary   Bodl.: MS Tanner 464e
f 79*

...

Syns of later dayes it chauncid that the cities of herford and worcester
complainid of the frequency of people that cam to leonminstre in   35
preiudice of bothe their markets in the shire townes and also in
hindringe their drapinge where apon the saturday market was remeuid
from leonminstre and a market on friday was newly assignyd on to
it: syns that tyme the toun of leonminstar hathe decayed/
The commune fame of the people about leonminstar is that Kynge   40
merwalde, and some of his successors had a castle or palace an hill

syde by the towne of leominstre half a mile of by est: The place is now
cawllyd Comfort Castle where now be some tokens of dyches where
buildings hathe bene/
The people of leonminstar there about cum ons a yere to this place
to sport and play/   5
...

1571-2
Chamberlains' Account Book 1   HRO
f [1]*   *(Accounts of John ap Thomas, disbursements)*   10
...
Item paid for iij quartes and a pynt of secke & thre pyntes
of claret wyne   ij s. iij d.
Item paid to mr warmecombes mynstrelles at
mr craswelles   xvj d. 15
...

1572-3
Chamberlains' Account Book 2   HRO
f [3v]*   *(Accounts of Thomas Shoter, disbursements)*   20
...
Item paid for apottell of seck and apottell of clarett wyne
when master Bayly wente to mr warmecombes Before the
henne feast   xx d.
Item paid to the wayes of Herefford for playeng at   25
the Henne feast   xij d.
...

1595
Archdeaconry of Hereford Acts of Office   HRO: box 20, vol 75   30
f [88v]*   *(2 September)*

Proceedings of the court held in the consistory of Hereford Cathedral
before Master Francis Bevans, LLD, *and in the presence of Thomas*
Crumpe, registrar.   35
...

emanavit   Iacobus Waties ministrell notatus anglice (for plaing at Evensonge to
suspensio   the dauncers./ °citatus (ut supra)°

25/ wayes *for* waytes
38/ *no closing parenthesis after* dauncers

Iana Price ⌈alias Spinner⌉

emanavit
suspensio

notata anglice for dauncing tempore precum vespertinarum °citata per
publicum edictum in Ecclesia &c°

Rosa Morries similiter/   5
°[co] quo die comparuit eadem & fatetur articulum vnde dominus
admonuit eum posthac &c°

[pauper]
° dimissio°
dimissio

Anna Mered⟨.⟩ similiter.
°Quo die comparuit. & fatetur articulum vnde dominus admonuit eam   10
posthac &c.°

° dimissio°
monicio
in proximo
dimissio

Iohanna ap pricharde similiter
°Quo die [comparuit & a] super examinacione articuli dominus
admonuit eam posthac &c.°   15

° dimissio°
dimissio

Ioanna Smyth similiter
Quo die similiter/
...
                                                                        20

1596-7
Chamberlains' Account Book 3   HRO
f [3]   *(Accounts of Philip ap Thomas, disbursements)*
...
Item gave the Quens maiesties players the 12 october 1596   xx s.   25
...

1597-8
Chamberlains' Account Book 4   HRO
f [3v]   *(Accounts of Philip ap Thomas, disbursements)*   30
...
Item Gave the Erle of Darby his players   x s.
...

f [4]*   35
...
Item gave my Lorde Schandose players   vj s. viij d.
...

7/ eum *for* eam

1599–1600
Chamberlains' Account Book 5 HRO
f [3]   *(Accounts of Henry Webbe, disbursements)*
...

paid to the lord Staffordes [men] players   vj s. viij d.   5
...

1600–1
Chamberlains' Account Book 6 HRO
f [2v]   *(Accounts of John Frogmor, disbursements)*   10
...

pad to the Queenes Plaiers   xx s.
paid for a gownd for George Eades   xxvj s. viij d.
paid to the Earle of Worcesters plaiers   x s.
paid to Mr Stephens for wyne and sugger bestowed one   15
the Iudges   x s.
paid to my lord Barkley his plaiers   x s.
paid to the lord Dudleis plairs   vj s.
...
                                                              20

1602–3
Chamberlains' Account Book 7 HRO
f [2v]   *(Accounts of William Haynes, disbursements)*
...

Item to the Earle of Huntingtons Plaiers   vj s. viij d.   25
...

1606–7
Chamberlains' Account Book 8 HRO
f [2]   *(Accounts of Edward Wynford, disbursements)*   30
...
Item to the Players   vj s. viij d.
...

12/ pad *for* paid

1608–9
Chamberlains' Account Book 9   HRO
f [3]   *(Accounts of James Hill, disbursements)*
...

Item paied to players by Mr Bailieffes appointment &   5
some of the company   vj s. viij d.

...

Item paied to other plaiers by Master Bailieffes
appointement & some of the company   v s.
...   10

f [4]

...

Item paied to more plaiers by Mr Bailieffes appointment
& others of the company   vj s. viij d.   15

...

1613–14
Chamberlains' Account Book 10   HRO
f [3]   *(Accounts of Otis Nicholles, disbursements)*   20

	li.	s.	d.
...Item to the Ladie Elizabeths players	00	05	00

                                                                           25
f [4]
...

| Item to players at another tyme | 00 | 04 | 00 |

...

                                                                           30

1616–17
Chamberlains' Account Book 11   HRO
f [3]   *(Accounts of John Stead, disbursements)*
...
Item to the Erle of Derbyes players   v s.   35
Item to the Lady Elizabeth her players   x s.
...
Item to the Erle of Sussex players   v s.

...

f [4]

...

| Item to the Princes players | x s. |
| Item to the Queenes H*ighnes*s players | x s. |

...

1618–19
Chamberlains' Account Book 12   HRO
f [3]   *(Accounts of John Lugger, disbursements)*

...

| Item to the Queene players | vij s. |

...

1619–20
Chamberlains' Account Book 13   HRO
f [4]   *(Accounts of John Whitstone, disbursements)*

...

Item to the Earle of Derbies players	vj s. viij d.
Item to the Lady Elizabeths players	x s.
Item to players of the Towne by Mr Baylief his appoyntment	xx s.

...

| Item to the King of Bohemya his players | x s. |

...

1626–7
Chamberlains' Account Book 14   HRO
f [2]   *(Accounts of Rowland Stead, disbursements)*

...

| deliuerd mr Baylief to giue player*es* | 0   05   0 |

...

LINTON

1617
Diocese of Hereford Acts of Office   HRO: box 24a (formerly 18), vol 71
f [207v]*   *(2 September)*

...

dimissio   con*tra* eund*em*/ there is a crime betweene him and his maid *servant*

11/ Queene *for* Queenes   39/ eund*em*: *Henry Nurse*

for keepinge companie and goeinge abroade with his owne maide
servant dancinge vpon the saboath daie and other tymes [⟨..⟩] vnfittinge
secundo die Septembris predicti similiter vt supra./

...

LITTLE COWARNE

1609?
Archdeaconry of Hereford Acts of Office
HRO: box 22, unnumbered vol pt 2
f [78v]*   *(16 December)*

...

dimissio   Iohn Bullock had dauncinge in his ho⟨wse⟩ vpon the Saboath day
dictus Iohannes Bullock & interrogatus sub vi Iur⟨amenti⟩ audivit
citentur ceteri   videlicet that Iohn Rawlins of much Cow⟨arne⟩ [⟨.⟩oms of Stoke lacie]
Citetur   Richard powell of vll⟨ingswick⟩ & others that he remembereth not
Richardus
Powell   [Quam confessionem] ⟨...⟩ &c And on *(blank)* Mason of Bromyard
servius Rogeri   was the ⟨...⟩ Quam confessionem dominus acceptavit & iniunxit ei
Burrox.   vnum d⟨iem⟩ in Ecclesia ibidem etc Et ad certificandum in proximo.
dimissio.   Postea dimissus posthac &c

xvj° die decembris predicti comparuit dictus Powell & negauit
Articulum &c. Vnde habet ad p⟨urgandum⟩ ⟨..⟩ cum 2: manu
honestorum virorum parochie predicte habet

...

LLANGARREN

1616
Diocese of Hereford Acts of Office   HRO: box 24a (formerly 18), vol 70
f [96]*   *(31 May)*

...

dimissio   Gardiani
the youthe of their parrishe hath bynn all waies accustomed to exercise
him selfe in dauncinge vponn ye Saboath daies and holiedaies. And
that divers prophane exercises are used in our parrishe vpon the
ad explanendum Saboath day as in other parrishes/ But we do hope for and pray for
amendement/ °vltimo die Maij 1616 predicti comparuerunt
personaliter Iohannes Gwillim et Iohannes Edwardes et dominus

24/ habet: *redundant*

iniunxit eis ad exhibendum presentamentum in proximo deinde [⟨..⟩]
xxij° die Iulij predicti comparuerunt et dominus super examinacione
cause retulit causam ad [consistorialem ibidem C] proximum
presentamentum gardianorum ibidem vnde dimissi°

5

1628
Archdeaconry of Hereford Acts of Office   HRO: box 25, vol 93A
f [137]*   *(28 May)*

Proceedings of the court held in the consistory of Hereford Cathedral   10
before Master Richard Basset, LLB, *deputy to William Skinner,* LLD,
official and commissary of Francis Godwin, bishop of Hereford.
...
Iohannes drewe detectus for plaieinge on the iewes harpe at praier   ⌐
time xxviij° die mensis Maij 1628 coram magistro Ricardo Basset in   15
legibus bacchalaureo deputato &c in loco consistoriali Herefordie
comparuit personaliter dictus drewe et obiecto ei articulo negauit
articulum esse verum &c tunc dominus iniunxit ei ad purgandum se
in proximo cum 4 manu &c deinde fassus est articulum esse verum et
submisit se &c tunc dominus iniunxit ei vnum diem penitencialem   20
more penitenciali et monuit ipsum ad extrahendum formam et ad
certificandum in proximo xviij° die Iunij proximi
...

f [132]*   25
...
Andreas Milles ⌜minstrell⌝ detectus for dauncing before Evening
prayer on the saboath daie being the 4 of May 1628, and for hiring
a minstrell being a Recusant excommunicated

30

f [140]   *(18 June)*

Proceedings of the court held in the consistory of Hereford Cathedral
before Master John Freemantle, clerk, MA, *surrogate, and in the*
presence of James Lawrence, registrar.   35
...
contra Ianam Simons detectam for dauncing on sonday the 4th of
May before evening prayer the minstrell beyng a recusant
excommunicated habens ad certificandum penitenciam. °Quo die
preconizata &c nullo modo comparuit &c [⟨.....⟩] reservata pena in   40
proximo &c/°

f [143]*

...

dimissio   *contra* Iohann*em* Drew for playing on his Iewes harpe at prayer tyme
h*a*bet ad cert*ifica*ndum pen*ite*nciam. °Quo die s*imilite*r vt supr*a* [⟨....⟩]°
°xxiij° die Augusti 1628 pr*edicti* simil*ite*r°   5

MADLEY

1605
Archdeaconry of Hereford Acts of Office   HRO: box 22, vol 82   10
p 16   *(10 September)*

Proceedings of the court held in the consistory of Hereford Cathedral
before Master James Bailie, LLD, *commissary, and in the presence of*
James Coren, deputy registrar.   15
...
Walter*us* Smyth Edw*ardus* Shep*ard* veteres/ gard*iani*
ad spe*cifi*candum no*min*a vi*delice*t of them that do daunce vppon

dimissio   Sundaies/ and such as haue not rec*eaved* 3 times A yeare/ °habeant ad

excom*municatio* spe*cifi*cand*um* in *proximo* &c 28 Septe*m*bris com*paruerunt* et q*ui*a   20
no*n* specificarunt iux*ta* monic*ion*em ideo excom*municati* 12 Octo*bris*
1605. com*paruerunt* et absolut*i* spe*cifi*carunt no*min*a in script*is*
d*i*missi°
...

   25

p 17*
...
dimissio   veteres gard*iani*
ad spe*cifi*cand*um* no*min*a eor*um* that doe daunce in the Churchyard/
°spe*cifi*carunt vt supra/°   30
...

1622
Acts of Decanal Court   HCL
f 112v*   *(28 September)*   35

Proceedings of the court held before the dean.
...
Rogerus Pigg.

dimissio   for playing on their instrum*entes* before euening prayer on saboath   40
dayes. Quo die com*parui*t cui obiecto ar*ticu*lo pre*dicto* fatetur et vt
supra simil*ite*r d*i*missus./

Iacobus Paine.
pro Consimili./ Quo die similiter dimissus./

Willimus ffoote
for yat as he passed towarde ye church in ye churchyard said he   5
would daunce there in contempt & derogacion of ye
churchwarden./

Idem ffoote
for dauncing before euening prayer time on sonday ye xxith of Iulie./   10
Quo die comparuit cui obiecto articulo predicto negavit &c vnde
dominus iniunxit ei ad purgandum se sua 6ta manu habita
proclamacione &c. et monitus &c./ °Quo die videlicet 12° Octobris
1622 coram magistro Iones &c. preconizatus non comparuit
excommunicatus &c/°   15

Matilda serva Iohannis Seybon.
Pro Consimili./ Quo die introducta citacione executa in ecclesia per
denunciacionem et preconizata non comparuit dominus pronunciavit
ipsam contumacem reservata eius pena in proximum./   20

Iohanna Brampton.
pro Consimili °12° Octobris 1622 coram magistro Iones &c comparuit
et ffassa est &c vnde dominus ex gracia dimisit &c cum admonicione
&c.   25

Andrewe Carwardine William ffoote
pro consimili/° vijs et modis./

Elizabetha Arnoll.   30
pro Consimili./ °Quo die Citata in proximo°
...

f 116v   (26 October)

                                                                      35
Proceedings of the court held before Master Jones, commissary.
...
Willimus ffoote./
for dauncing before euening prayer on a sonday. excommunicatus./
...   40

MANSELL GAMAGE

1609?
Archdeaconry of Hereford Acts of Office
HRO: box 22, unnumbered vol, pt 2   5
f [51] col 1*   *(24 November)*

...

ad pr*econizandum*
Saltatores vi*delicet*
Maria Lurcot/ di*missio*   10
Anna Lurcot/ di*missio*
Alicia Withell/ di*missio*
Elion*ora* serva/ Thome Withell/ [exco*mmunicacio*] di*missio*
Richard Milward/ comp*aruit* di*missio*
Anna Smith/ *preconizata* di*missio* cum admo*nicione*   15
Roger Vaughan pr*econizatus* in pro*ximo*/ di*missio*

col 2

Thomas Churche   20
for dauncinge on Saboath dayes Ci*tatus* p*er* pub*licum* edic*tum*
pr*econizatus* &c 24 die Nove*mbris* pr*edicti* comp*aruit* di*ctus* Thomas
Churche & d*ominus* revoca*vit* excomm*uni*cationem etc./ & [iniu*nxit*
ei] s*uper* ex*aminacione* ar*ticu*li pr*edicti* d*ominus* adiunxit eu*m* that etc
Postea exam*inatus* de cet*eris* saltator*ibus* ib*idem* &c vij⟨.⟩ presunt   25

MUCH BIRCH

1610?
Archdeaconry of Hereford Acts of Office   30
HRO: box 22, unnumbered vol, pt 2
f [110]*

...

Iacobus howell
⟨idem Iac⟩cobus   for dauncinge vt supr⟨a ...⟩ [conp*aruit*] comp*aruit* di*ctus* Iacobus   35
impedivit ⟨...⟩   how⟨ell⟩ &c quia recusa*vit* re*spondere* &c sepius interrog⟨atus⟩ p*er*
et process*us*   Iudice*m* &c d*ominus* pronu*nciavit* eu*ndem* excommunicatum ⟨...⟩
Iudicial'   °xv^{to} die Iulij Anno [⟨...⟩] pr*edicto* comp*aruit* di*ctus* Iacobus howell
⟨..t⟩inge   &c & submisit se &c que*m* d*ominus* absoluit & restituit ⟨...⟩ vnd*e*
the dancers   d*ominus* dimisit eu*m* cum admo*nicione* &c°   40
&c.

24/ adiunxit *for* iniunxit   39m/ &c. *written over other letters (?)*

Phillip Howell.
pro consimili/ Citatus per publicum edictum vt supra ⟨…⟩ comparuit
&c ⟨…⟩ °xv^{to} die Iulij idem Phillipus similiter absolutus cum
admonicione posthac°

… 5

MUCH DEWCHURCH

1609?
Archdeaconry of Hereford Acts of Office   10
HRO: box 22, unnumbered vol, pt 2
f [108v]*   *(16 December)*

…

Thomas Kethewne
⌈xvj^{to} die decembris 160⟨.⟩⌉[1] for dansinge vpo⟨n⟩ Sondaies [and holy   15
daies]/ Quo die comparuit &c confessus est articulum &c. Vnde
dominus iniunxit ei i. diem penitencialem &c. Et ad certificandum in
proximo

MUCH MARCLE   20

1618–19
Archdeaconry of Hereford Acts of Office   HRO: box 24, vol 90
f [237v]*   *(7 December)*

25

Thomas Gorwey for playeinge die dominico citatus &c in vij diem
decembris predicti preconizatus &c non comparuit &c
excommunicatus decimo die mensis decembris 1618 apud herefordiam
coram magistro Gabriele Wallwin artium magistro deputato &c
dimissio   comparuit personaliter dictus Gorwey et dominus ad eius peticionem   30
ipsum absoluit prestito prius iuramento de parendo iure et stando
mandatis ecclesie deinde obiecto ei articulo fassus est articulum esse
verum vnde dominus examinatis causis ipsum dimisit cum
admonicione/

35

Rogerus Parker pro consimili citatus &c per publicum edictum in vij
dimissio   diem decembris predicti preconizatus &c non comparuit &c
excommunicatus vj° die ffebruarij predicti comparuit et dominus ad
eius peticionem ipsum absolvit a sentencia excommunicacionis &c et
super examinacione cause ipsum dimisit cum admonicione   40

dimissio

Willimus Ienkins pro consimili vij° die decembris predicti similiter vt
supra Sexto die ffebruarij predicti comparuit et dominus ipsum absoluit
a sentencia excommunicacionis &c et super examinacione cause ipsum
admonuit posthac

(5 December)

Thomas hamon pro consimili quinto die mensis decembris predicti
[pre] comparuit personaliter dictus hamon et obiecto ei articulo fassus

dimissio

est articulum esse verum vnde dominus iniunxit ei ad confitendum
articulum coram ministro et gardianis ibidem die dominico proximo
in vsuali vestitu immediate post preces finitas in ecclesia ibidem Et
ad certificandum in proximo postea dominus ipsum dimisit cum
admonicione

dimissio

Iohannes Ravenhill pro consimili Quinto die mensis decembris predicti
Similiter vt supra

(18 December)

Willimus Edwardes pro consimili citatus &c in xviij diem decembris

dimissio

1618 in ecclesia Cathedrali Herefordie loco consistoriali ibidem coram
magistro Gabriele Wallwin artium magistro deputato &c comparuit
personaliter dictus Edwardes et obiecto ei articulo fassus est articulum

vide rest/

esse verum vnde dominus admonuit ipsum posthac. °4 Novembris
1620 coram magistro Iohanne Osegoode artium magistro deputato
&c comparuit et dominus ad eius peticionem ipsum absoluit a sentencia
excommunicacionis et audita causa dominus ipsum dimisit cum
admonicione/°
...

NORTON CANON

1622
Acts of Decanal Court   HCL
f 117   *(26 October)*

Proceedings of the court held before Master Jones, commissary.
...
Gardiani ibidem.

they haue not presented ye names of ye tennisplayers & dauncers./
examinati et dimissi

...

1625   5
Acts of Decanal Court   HCL
f 202v*   *(7 October)*

Proceedings of the court held in the dean's consistory of Hereford
Cathedral before Master Jones, subdean, and in the presence of the   10
registrar.

Gardiani ibidem
doe not present the names of the dauncers./ nor doe they present
whether the will of Anne Carpenter be proved, or who is executor   15
therof, they do not answere the 34th article nor do they present where
or when or by whom Anne Olford was married. °Quo die
comparuerunt et dominus ex gracia eosdem dimisit &c°

...

                                                                          20

PEMBRIDGE

1617
Diocese of Hereford Acts of Office   HRO: box 24a (formerly 18), vol 71
f [358v]*   *(2 June)*   25

Proceedings of the court held in the parish church of Leominster.

Ludovicus Thomas daunced in the church porch amongst a companie
of girles of the parrishe not knowne quesitus &c in hos diem et locum   30
preconizatus &c non comparuit &c vijs et modis in proximo citatus
&c per publicum edictum in 3 diem Septembris predicti preconizatus
non comparuit &c excommunicatus

dimissio   Matheus Steade minstrell   35
                  Quo die similiter vt supra postea dominus ipsum dimisit [cum a]
                  ...

PUTLEY

1625

Acts of Decanal Court HCL

f 170v* *(22 October)*

Proceedings of the court held before Master Jones and in the presence of the registrar.

Christopherus Iones.
det*ectus* for dauncing eu*ery* sonday & holieday for the most p*ar*te betweene Easter & lammas °Quo die com*paru*it et fassus est &c vnde d*ominu*s [iniu*n*xit ei] di*misit* eu*m* cu*m* admonic*io*ne &c.°

Alicia Harries for dancing/

Ioh*anne*s Lambert iun*ior*.
pro Cons*imili*. °Quo die si*mi*l*iter*°

Henricus Carpenter.
pro Cons*imili*./ °Quo die si*mi*l*iter*°

Ioh*anne*s Boulcott.
[monitus de solvend*o* sub pen*a* exco*mmunicacionis*]/†
pro Cons*imili*./ °Quo die com*paru*it p*erson*al*ite*r dict*us* Boulcott et ad eius petic*ionem* d*ominu*s eu*m* di*misit* &c./ sol*uit*./°
...

f 174^{a} v* *(19 November)*

...
Alicia Harris.
di*missio* not*atu*r for dauncing vppon Saboath dayes before euening prayer./ 19° Novem*bris* 1625 cor*am* m*agist*ro Osgood surrog*a*to &c. com*paru*it cui obiecto ar*ticu*lo pred*icto* fatetur eu*ndem* esse ver*um* et submisit se &c vnde d*ominu*s ea*ndem* cu*m* admonic*ione* di*misit*./
...

ROSS

1616–17
Diocese of Hereford Acts of Office   HRO: box 24a (formerly 18), vol 71
f [214]   *(9 December)*

*Proceedings of the court held in Hereford Cathedral before Master
Silas Griffith, STD, vicar general of Robert Bennett, bishop of Hereford,
and in the presence of James Lawrence, notary public.*
...

dimissio   Thomas Meiricke iun*ior* glover for dauncing and playinge at vnlawfull
games on the Saboth daie./ °Quo die com*paruit* personali*ter* et su*per*
ex*aminacio*ne ar*ticu*li dimiss*us* est cu*m* admonic*ione* &c.°

dimissio   Iohan*nes* Tayler tapster p*ro* Consimili/ °Cit*atus* in hos diem et locum
&c p*re*conizatus &c excommunicatus° deinde sedente curia com*paruit*
personali*ter* d*ictus* Taillor obiectoq*ue* ei ar*ticu*lo [ne] fass*us* est
ar*ticu*lum esse verum vnde d*ominus* ipsum dimisit cum admonic*ione*

dimissio   Anthonius Harbert p*ro* Consimili./ °quesit*us* &c vijs et mod*is* in
prox*imo* &c° xx° die Ianuarij p*redicti* com*paruit* personali*ter* d*ictus*
Harbett obiectoq*ue* ei ar*ticu*lo fass*us* est ar*ticu*lum esse verum vnde
d*ominus* ipsum dimisit cum admonic*ione*./

dimissio   ffrau*n*ciscus younge Weau*er* p*ro* Consimili/ °quo die com*paruit* et
su*per* ex*aminacio*ne ar*ticu*li dimiss*us* est cu*m* admonic*ione* &c°

dimissio   Alicia Barrett p*ro* Consimili./ °cit*ata* in hos diem et locu*m* &c
p*re*conizata &c nullo modo com*paruit* &c postea d*ominus* eam dimisit
cu*m* admonic*ione* in p*er*sona mariti.°
...

ff [215–15v]   *(10 February)*
...

dimissio   Willimus Meiricke for dancinge die dominico x° die ffebruarij p*redicti*
com*paruit* et obiecto ei ar*ticu*lo fass*us* est ar*ticu*lum esse verum vnde
d*ominus* ipsum dimisit cum admonic*ione*

dimissio   Robertus Meiricke p*ro* cons*imili* decimo die ffebruarij p*redicti*
Simili*ter* vt supra./

alias dimissa   Alicia Meiricke pro consimili |

dimissio   Iohannes Maddox pro consimili decimo die mensis ffebruarij predicti
examinata causa dominus ipsum dimisit cum admonicione

5

dimissio   Walterus Pearce pro consimili decimo die ffebruarij predicti Similiter
vt supra./

dimissio   Thomas Meiricke pro consimili quesitus &c in [quo] decimum diem
ffebruarij predicti preconizatus &c non comparuit &c vijs et modis   10
in proximo deinde xiiij° die ffebruarij 1616 comparuit et fatetur
articulum vnde dominus ipsum dimisit cum admonicione &c

f [249]

15

*Proceedings of the court held in the consistory of Hereford Cathedral
before Master Silas Griffith, STD, vicar general of Robert Bennett,
bishop of Hereford.*

...

Bridstowe   Alicia durley for dancinge at Rosse die dominico decimo die ffebruarij   20
dimissio   predicti comparuit et obiecto ei articulo fassus est articulum esse verum
vnde dominus ipsam dimisit cum admonicione &c

dimissio   Margareta Andros pro consimili decimo die ffebruarij predicti Similiter
vt supra./   25

(3 March)
dimissio./   Aliciam Meiricke pro consimili/ °citata in 3 diem Martij predicti &c
examinata causa dimittitur cum admonicione &c.°

30

1621
Archdeaconry of Hereford Acts of Office   HRO: box 24, vol 91, pt 2
f [41]   *(6 October)*

Proceedings of the court held in Hereford Cathedral before Master   35
*Gabriel Wallwin, MA, deputy to Master Oliver Lloid, LLD, official
principal and commissary of Francis Godwin, bishop of Hereford.*

...

dimissio   Willimus davies the furnishe keeper
for dancing vppon the saboath daie before all service was ended citatus   40
die iovis vltimo in Rosse per Gibbons apparitorem ad comparendum

in hos die*m* et locu*m* et locu*m* preconizatus non com*paruit*
excommunicatus °16 April 1622 in loco officij Registrari*j* Coram
m*a*gistro Evano Iones Surrogato &c pr*esente* me W*illi*mo Rawe
notario pub*l*ico &c com*paruit* m*a*giste*r* Buckly et do*min*u*s* ad eius
peti*cionem* dictu*m* Davies absolvit et di*misit*°   5

...

1629
Archdeaconry of Hereford Acts of Office   HRO: box 25, vol 94
ff [252v–4]*   10

...

Edwardus Keise no*tatur* vt supra [pr*o* cons*imili*] for plaienge vpon
Tewesdaie the xxvjth daie of this instant Maie 1629 at time of eveninge
praier quesit*us* xviij° Iunij 1629 vijs et modis in *pro*ximo °cit*atus* 5
Iulij in p*aro*chi*a* pred*icta* p*er* Ric*ar*d*um* Gibbons app*ar*itorem 14 Iulij   15
*pre*dicti preco*nizatus* et non com*paruit* &c excommunicatus° 23° die
mens*is* Septembris 1629 in ecclesia p*aro*chi*a*li de [⟨...⟩] Rosse coram
m*a*gistro Ric*ar*do Becket in [le] ar*tibus* m*a*gistro deputato &c
com*paruit* p*er*sonali*ter* dictus Keise et do*min*u*s* ad eius peti*cio*n*em*
ipsum absolvit a senten*cia* excommuni*ca*cionis prestito prius   20
iur*amento* de p*ar*endo ⟨i⟩ure &c deinde obiecto ei ar*ti*culo fass*us* est
ar*ti*cu*l*um esse veru*m* et submisit se &c Vnde do*min*u*s* iniu*n*xit ei ad
confitend*um* ar*ti*cu*l*um immediate post [preces] lectione*m* Evangelij
in vsuali vestitu &c et mo*n*uit ad extr*ahendum* et ad cert*ificandum*
in *pro*ximo | 25

Iohannes wilse no*tatur* vt supra pr*o* cons*imili* vl*timo* xviij° die Iunij
instan*tis* in Rosse p*er* Gibbons prout fidem fecit 25° Iunij *pre*dicti
preco*nizatus* et non com*paruit* excom*mun*icatus p*er* m*a*gistr*um* Basset
23° die Septembris *pre*dicti simil*iter*   30

dimissio   Iohannes Machin no*tatur* vt supra for dancinge the morris at time of
eveninge praier cit*atus* xxv° die Iunij instan*tis* vt supra preco*nizatus*
&c et non com*paruit* do*min*u*s* Basset pronu*n*ciavi*t* ipsum contumace*m*
res*er*uatur eius pena in *pro*ximum °14 Iulij 1629 preconizatus et non   35
com*paruit* &c excommunicatus° 23° die Septe*m*bris 1629 *pre*dicti
com*paruit* et absolutus est et di*missus* cum admoni*cione*

1/ et locu*m* et locu*m*: *dittography*

dimissio

Iacobus streete notatur vt supra pro consimili °citatus 5 Iulij 1629 in parochia predicta per Ricardum Gibbons apparitorem 14 Iulij predicti preconizatus comparuit et dominus eum monuit et dimisit./°

dimissio

Thomas Parret notatur vt supra pro consimili 27° die Iunij 1629 in ecclesia Cathedrali herefordie loco consistoriali ibidem [ne] comparuit et obiecto ei articulo negavit articulum esse verum vnde prestito per eum iuramento de innocencia sua | 5

recessit

Leticia Vaughan notatur vt supra pro consimili 10

Iana Currier notatur vt supra pro consimili citata quesita xviij° Iunij 1629 vijs et modis in proximo °citata 2 Iulij 1629 in parochia predicta per Ricardum Gibbons apparitorem. 14 Iulij 1629 preconizata et non comparuit &c excommunicata.° 15

dimissio

Thomas Browne notatur vt supra pro consimili citatus xviij° die Iunij 1629 [vijs et modis in proximo] in Rosse per Gibbons &c ut fidem fecit 25° Iunij predicti preconizatus &c et non comparuit excommunicatus per magistrum Basset 23° die Septembris 1629 predicti comparuit et 20 absolutus est per magistrum Bicket et dimissus est [per] cum admonicione

Robertus Smith notatur vt supra pro consimili quesitus xviij° Iunij 1629 vijs et modis in proximo °citatus 7 Iulij 1629 in parochia predicta 25 per Ricardum Gibbons apparitorem. 14 Iulij 1629 preconizatus et non comparuit &c excommunicatus°|

dimissio

Anna Cater notatur vt supra pro consimili 25° Iunij predicti similiter primo die Septembris 1629 in loco consistoriali herefordie coram 30 magistro Evanno Iones artium magistro deputato &c introducta citacione personaliter executa 26° die Augusti vltimi per Gibbons apparitorem infra parochiam predictam prout fidem fecit preconizata trina vice dicta Cater et nullo modo comparente dominus pronunciavit ipsam contumacem et in penam excommunicacionis 23° die Septembris 35 1629 predicti similiter vt in actu contra Browne

Iohannes Sandie notatur vt supra pro consimili 25° Iunij predicti similiter °citatus j° Iulij 1629 in parochia predicta per Ricardum Gibbons apparitorem. 14 Iulij 1629 preconizatus et non comparuit 40 &c per magistrum Basset excommunicatus°

Wallford   Henricus Baker notatur vt supra for plaieinge at eveninge praier time
                  27° die Iunij 1629 [in] apud herefordiam coram magistro Ricardo
                  Basset in legibus bacchalaureo deputato &c comparuit personaliter
                  dictus Baker et obiecto ei articulo negavit articulum esse verum tunc
                  prestito per eum iuramento de innocencia sua dominus eum dimisit.   5

dimissio   Walterius Garden notatur vt supra for dauncinge at eveninge praier
                  time °27 Iunij 1629 in loco Consistoriali &c coram Ricardo Bassett
                  Surrogato &c comparuit et iuramentum prestitit de innocentia sua et
                  dominus eum dimisit°   10

dimissio   [Ge] Gregorius Harris notatur vt supra pro consimili °27 Iunij 1629
                  in loco Consistoriali &c Coram Ricardo Bassett Surrogato &c
                  comparuit dictus Harris et iuramentum prestitit de innocentia sua and
                  that he was at Evening prayer dominus eum dimisit°   15

                  ff 255–5v*   (28 July)
                  ...
                  Iohannes Bennet iunior
                  de vicinia Rosse notatur for dancinge vpon sondaies and hollidaies   20
per Thomam   at time of eveninge praier & especiallie vpon Tewesdaie 26 maij 1629
Parrot   & especiallie for attinding my lorde vpon the xxviij Iunij 1629 at time
                  of praiers as it is thought °citatus 22 Iulij 1629 in parochia predicta
Willimus Spicer   per Ricardum Gibbons apparitorem 28 Iulij predicti preconizatus et
                  non comparuit &c [excommunicatus] vijs et modis° primo die mensis   25
                  Septembris 1629 predicti comparuit et dominus Iones audita causa
                  ipsum admonuit et dimisit

                  Robertus Younge notatur vt supra pro consimili °abijt°
                                                                                       30
                  Iohannes Mason notatur vt supra pro consimili °citatus 23 Iulij 1629
dimissio   in parochia predicta per Ricardum Gibbons apparitorem 28 Iulij 1629
                  preconizatus et non comparuit excommunicatus. ° deinde sedente curia
                  comparuit personaliter dictus Mason et dominus ad eius peticionem
                  revocavit decretum excommunicacionis deinde obiecto ei articulo   35
                  fassus est articulum esse verum et submisit se &c quam confessionem
                  dominus acceptavit quatinus &c et ipsum dimisit cum admonicione/

dimissio   Walterus Collie notatur vt supra pro consimili °quesitus° |

ne quid fiat contra eundem Probin†
Thomas Probin notatur pro consimili

ne quid fiat contra eum†
Walterus Collie notatur pro consimili   5

Ioanna Bennet notatur pro consimili °citata 20 Iulij 1629 in parochia
dimissio   predicta per Ricardum Gibbons apparitorem 28 Iulij predicti
preconizata.° °28 die mensis Iulij 1629 in loco Consistoriali coram
magistro Iohanne ffreemantle deputato &c comparuit personaliter   10
obiectoque ei articulo &c [negavit] ⌈fassa est⌉ esse verum &c vnde
dominus ipsam admonuit quod deinceps &c Et sicut dimissa est salvis
feodis &c°

ne quid fiat contra eam†   15
°quia infra ætatem legitimam°†
Alicia Bennet notatur pro consimili/
...

f [256]*   20

Willimus Perrocke notatur for dauncinge at eveninge prayer time
vppon Sundaies and hollidaies °quesitus 19 Iulij 1629 28 Iulij predicti
vijs et modis in proximo°

                                                                                25
Carolus Perrocke notatur pro consimili °citatus 19 Iulij 1629 in
parochia predicta per Ricardum Gibbons apparitorem 28 Iulij predicti
preconizatus° °comparuit personaliter dictus Pirrocke et obiecto ei
articulo negavit articulum esse verum et submisit se purgacioni &c
tunc dominus iniunxit ei ad purgandum se hoc in loco primo   30
Septembris predicti cum quarta manu &c facta prius proclamacione
primo die Septembris 1629 predicti in loco consistoriali herefordie
coram magistro Euanno Iones artium magistro deputato &c
preconizatus &c et non comparuit dominus pronunciavit ipsum
contumacem et defecisse in purgacione sua et decrevit ipsum citandum 35
fore ⟨e⟩rga proximum &c.°

Maria Collie notatur pro consimili °quesita similiter°

Alicia Haynes notatur pro consimili °citata in parochia predicta   40

dimissio 23 Iulij 1629 *per* Ricard*um* Gibbons app*arit*orem in *parochia predicta*
28 Iulij *predicti* preconizata° °com*paruit* et simil*iter* vt in actu con*tra*
Ioannam Bennet°

Thomas Webster no*tatur pro* cons*imili* °cit*atus* simil*iter* 28 Iulij 1629   5
dimissio preconizatus° °comparuit *personaliter dictus* Weobster et obiecto ei
ar*ticulo* negavit ar*ticulum* esse ver*um* et submisit se &c tunc d*ominus*
iniu*n*xit ei ad purgand*um* se hoc in loco 4 manu &c f*acta* prius
Septembris proclama*cione* primo die Septembris 1629 *predicti* simil*iter* vt in actu
con*tra* Pirrocke deinde com*paruit* et d*ominus* audita c*au*sa ipsum   10
dimisit cum admonic*ione*°

f [76]*   *(24 October)*

Proceedings of the court held in the consistory of Hereford Cathedral   15
before Richard Basset, LLB, *surrogate, and in the presence of William*
Rawe, notary public.
…

E*dwardus* Keise no*tatur* officio ex pub*lica* fama referen*dus* for
dimissio playinge vpon tuesday the xxvi^th day of this instant May 1629 at time   20
of Eueninge praier h*abe*t ad cer*tificandum* confessionem in hunc diem
°Quo die preconizatus et non com*paruit* &c excommunicatus° °5°
decem*bris* 1629 in ecclesia Cathe*drali* herefor*die* loco cons*istoriali*
ib*idem* coram mag*istro* Ric*ardo* Bicket in ar*tibus* mag*istro* deputato
&c com*paruit personaliter dictus* Keise et introduxit formam et in   25
vim iuramenti sui cer*tificauit* de peractione pen*itencie* iuxta &c vnde
dimiss*us* est postea [⟨..⟩] absolut*us* est°

dimissio Iohan*nes* Wilse no*tatur* vt supra *pro* cons*imili* simil*iter* °Quo die
simil*iter* excom*municatus*° °5° die decem*bris predicti* simil*iter*°   30
…

Willimus perrocke no*tatur* &c for dancinge at Eueninge praier time
vpon sundaies and hollidayes vij*s* et modis in hunc diem °Quo die
renovatur in *proximo* xiiij° die Novem*bris* 1629 introducto [der]   35
decreto vij*s* et modis denu*m* in [viii] viij° die Novem*bris* 1629 *prout*
patet in dorso eiusdem preco*nizatus* trina vice dict*us* Pirrocke et nullo

1/ in *parochia* predicta: *redundant*
36/ denu*m* for demum (?)

modo com*paruit* d*omin*us ffreemantle pronu*nciaui*t ipsum
contumace*m* et in penam exco*mmunicacionis*°

1633
Archdeaconry of Hereford Acts of Office   HRO: box 26, vol 96
ff [426v–7]*   *(29 October)*

Proceedings of the court held in the consistory of Hereford Cathedral
before Master John Dryden, surrogate to William Skinner, and in the
presence of Richard Brasier, registrar.

…

Ioh*anne*s Charles det*ectus* for sufferinge musicke and drinkinge in
his howse in eu*en*inge praier time on sonday 17 ffebr*uarij* si*mi*liter
vt supra. |
Ioh*anne*s Hale det*ectus* for playinge and drinkinge in ye same howse
at ye same time. Si*mi*lit*er.*

…

f [502]   *(30 October)*

Proceedings of the court held in the consistory of Hereford Cathedral
before William Skinner, LLD, and in the presence of Thomas Lawrence,
notary public.

…

al*ias* peregit
peniten*ciam*   con*tra* Nicho*l*aum Gates detect*um* for daunnceing vpon Sundaies &
holy dayes before divine ser*v*ice was ended./

di*mi*ssio   con*tra* Thoma*m* Simondes detectum pro consi*mi*li °11 die mens*is*
decem*bris* p*re*dicti com*paruit* et obiecto ei arti*cu*lo negavit arti*cu*lum
esse veru*m* tunc p*re*stito prius iur*amen*to de innocen*cia* sua dimiss*us*
est/°

nunc de Madeley†
con*tra* Ioha*n*nem Torence detect*um* pro consi*mi*li
…

ST WEONARDS

1609
Archdeaconry of Hereford Acts of Office
HRO: box 22, unnumbered vol, pt 2   5
f [108v]*   *(11 December)*

Proceedings of the court held before Master Gabriel Wallwin, MA,
deputy.

10

excommunicatus: propter ⟨...⟩†
⟨...⟩ xj die Decembris coram magistro Gabriele Walwyn artium
magistro Surrogato

in partibus
p⟨re⟩dic⟨tis⟩
patet ⟨...⟩

W⟨...⟩ M⟨...⟩ners gent ffor dancinge on Saboath dayes &c ⟨xj⟩ die
decembris 1609 comparuit et [p⟨redicto⟩] ⟨...⟩ ipsum absolvit et restituit   15
&c ⟨...⟩
...

SHOBDON

20

1586/7
Diocese of Hereford Acts of Office   HRO: box 17, vol 66
f [218v]   *(9 March)*

Proceedings of the court held in the parish church of Leominster before   25
Master Roger Bradshaw, MA, deputy to Master Francis Bevans, LLD,
vicar general of Herbert Westfaling, bishop of Hereford.
...
contra humfridum Tailer de eadem
[detectus] ⌜notatus⌝ anglice, for keping dauncing and plaieng, for   30
permittinge the same (tempore divinorum) citatus per Iones

8 Aprilis./

apparitorem &c publice preconizatus &c comparuit idem humfridus
Tail⌜u⌝r, & examinatus &c et super examinacione &c/ negavit eundem
&c vnde habet ad introducendum cedulam in proximo ⌜a vicario &⌝
gardianis ibidem &c.   35
...

STRETTON GRANDISON

1616
Diocese of Hereford Acts of Office
HRO: box 24a (formerly 18), vol 71   5
f [277]   *(7 December)*

*Proceedings of the court held in the consistory of Hereford Cathedral
before Master Silas Griffith, STD, vicar general and commissary of
Robert Bennett, bishop of Hereford.*   10

✗   Ricardus Perks a minstrell for playeing on saboth daies in the parish
dimissio   of Stretton gransham and bringing his taber into the Church at divine
service and for vnreuerent behavinge himself vpon admonition given
him./ °Quo die comparuit personaliter et super examinacione articuli   15
dominus ipsum dimisit/°
...

TEDSTONE DELAMERE
                                                                                    20
c 1600
Miscellaneous Visitation Records
HRO: Acts of Office fragments, fragment C
single sheet*
...   25
On Arthure the servaunte of Rodger Conie for dauncinge at tyme of
diu⟨ine⟩ service and did say that moòste parte of the youth of the
parishe did daunce at service tyme and beinge demaundede who they
wer he saide he woulde not name any them/
...   30

1602
Archdeaconry of Hereford Acts of Office   HRO: box 21, vol 80, pt 3
p 60 col 1*   *(1 October)*
                                                                                    35
*Proceedings of the court held in the consistory of Hereford Cathedral
before Master James Bailie, LLD, guardian of spiritualities during
vacancy, and in the presence of James Lawrence, notary public.*
...
Richardus Brooke ⌈et Petrus Corbett⌉ de Avenburye citati   40
per apparitorem &c non comparuerunt &c./ excommunicati

Interogetur de hac turba Luxuriosa presertim de le taborer.

citati Elizabetha Grenewich, Petrus Corbet de Avenbury Richardus
Broke [Thomas Cony Thomas Launcie] ⌐de Avenburie¬, Iacobus
Yong, de tedston predicta interessentes huiusmodi prophanacione ex   5
confessione ipsius Milonis/

col 2

milo Cunny/   10
ffor prophaininge the Saboathe day and dauncinge and revelinge with
morrice daunces tempore divinorum, and namely 8° Augusti vltimo
beinge Sonday, and would not desist albeit he was admonished therof
by mr Grenewiche/ Quo die comparuit, dictus Milo Cunny, qui in
vim Iuramenti examinatus confessus est articulum &c. Vnde dominus   15
inflixit ei [penitenciam] ⌐ad confitendum articulum¬ in Ecclesia ibidem
in vsuali vestitu &c et ad certificandum in proximo/ Et ⌐tenuit¬ ad
denuntiandum nomina ceterorum interessentium &c. °26 die Octobris
predicti preconizato dicto Conney comparuit Thomas Conney pater
ipsius milonis, et in vim Iuramenti sui certificavit penitenciam vnde   20
dimissus dein comparuerunt Thomas Launcie et Thomas Conney et
fatentur etc Vnde habent ad confitendum articulum vt supra et ad
certificandum proximo postea comparuit Corbet et fatetur habet
penitenciam vt supra etc .16. Novembris introducta forma dimisit
eum Thomas Launcie Thomas Conney et Petrus Corbet vnde dimissi   25
⟨....⟩ Certificaverunt in vim Iuramenti./°
...

p 70*   *(16 November)*

30
Avenburie   henricus Boyce for [morning] dauncing the morrice at Tedston and
reveling one the Saboathe daie in time of devine service 16 die
Novembris predicti/ comparuit dictus henricus Boyce [et negavit
habet] et fatetur Vnde habet ad peragendum penitenciam iuxta etc et
ad certificandum in proximo viij. die decembris comparuit et non   35
certificavit et contradat certificarium in proximo

°extra Diocesem°   Willimum Boulter boulter pro simili/

38/ Boulter boulter: *dittography*

Phillippus howles pro simili 16. die Novembris predicti similiter viij
decembris predicti similiter vt supra./

(8 December)
Citatus in proximo† 5

Tedston Richardus Conney pro simili viij decembris predicti comparuit dictus
Dimissio Richardus Conney et negavit vnde monitus est etc.

Citata in proximo†
Dimissio Tacie Richardes pro simili viij die decembris predicti comparuit dicta 10
Tacie et monita est de reformanda se etc.

Citata in proximo†
Dimissio Rebecca Tower pro simili viij decembris comparuit et monita est etc.
15

Citatus in proximo†
Dimissio Willimus Morries pro simili viij decembris comparuit [et monitus] et
negavit articulum Vnde dimissus

Citata in proximo† 20
Dimissio Iane Conney pro simili viij decembris comparuit et monita est etc

Citatus in proximo†
Dimissio Anthonius Conney pro simili viij decembris predicti comparuit et
monitus est etc. 25

Citatus in proximo†
De Cradley Iacobus Henge similiter
...
30

p 75
...
Amburie/ Elizabetha wiet serva willimi Collie notatur for beinge at a morrice
daunce at Tedston one a Sundaie tempore divinorum
35

Iane Somers pro simili
...

33m/ Amburie: Avenbury

1602/3
Archdeaconry of Hereford Acts of Office   HRO: box 21, vol 80, pt 4
p 21*   *(12 January)*

Proceedings of the court held in the consistory of Hereford Cathedral   5
before Master James Bailie, LLD, *commissary during vacancy.*

Avenbury/ | Henricus Boice/

di*missio* Coram m*agistro* w*illimo* Greenewich [di]†
for dauncinge and ⟨...⟩ tyme of devine service ⟨...⟩ Vsq*ue* in hunc diem   10
quoad *certificariu*m p⟨...⟩ °Quo die introduct*o* Certificario per Parat
⟨...⟩ pen*itenci*' *per* quendam ha⟨...⟩ de peractione ⟨...⟩ etc°

Cora*m* m*agistro* w*illimo* Greenewich dep*utato.*
Philippus Howles./   15
pro cons*imili* continuab*atur* certificariu*m* p⟨...⟩e vsque in hunc diem
dimissio | °Quo die introduct*a* forma penitenciali [f] cu*m* certificarijs in dorso
de peract*ione* pen*itencie* etc d*i*missus°

°absolut*us* ad requisicionem M*a*g*is*tri Grenewich gratis°   20

(5 February)
Cradley | °Iacobus Younge / [simi] pro cons*imili* citat*us* per Parrat in 5 ffebr*uarij*
dimissio | *predicti* [de] preconizatus non comp*aruit* etc./° °7° die martij 1602
°Citatus in | coram m*a*g*is*tro St barbe deputato &c comp*aruit* Ricardus Parret et   25
proximo° | pro et in nomine de Younge per dictum Younge in hac parte legitime
excommunicatio | constitut*us* petijt benefici*um* absolu*cionis* dicto Iacobo Younge
cum gracia | impendi &c. vnde dominus ipsum prefat*um* Younge in *per*sona d*icti*
Parret absolvit et c*on*stituit &c et habita caus*e* h*uius*modi debita
consideracione per informacionem m*a*g*is*tri Grenewich ipsu*m* dimisit   30
ab officio suo/°

°Interrogatur vt° | Iocosa Lane pro cons*imili*
excommunicata
   35
cum gracia | °Interrogatur vt supra/°
°Whitborne° | °Richard*us* Brooke / simil*iter* excommunicatus.°
cum gracia | ...

33m/ supra *missing after* vt (?)

p 24   *(2 March)*
...

Avenbury.

dimissio

Citata
in proximo

Elizabetha Wiett *serva* Will*i*mi Collie/
for beinge at a Morrice Dance at Tedston on a Sonday tempore
divinorum °2 martij com*paruit* et fatetur ar*ticu*lum. Unde monit*a* est   5
etc/°

dimissio

Citata in proximo†
Iana Somm*ers* pro cons*imili* °2 martij. m*agiste*r Wallwin dimisit
eandem sub spe amendac*ionis*/°   10
...

1605
Archdeaconry of Hereford Acts of Office   HRO: box 22, vol 82
p 214   *(11 September)*   15

Proceedings of the court held in the consistory of Hereford Cathedral
before Master James Bailie, LLD, *commissary to Richard Bancroft,*
archbishop of Canterbury, and in the presence of James Coren, notary
public and registrar.   20

[Thomas] ⌐Ioh*annes*¬ Wikes detect*us* for receiving Morrice Dauncers
of the parishe of Bromiard And other parishes thereaboute*s* vppon
the Saboath daie at the time of devine ser*ui*ce vi*delice*t at Evening
prayer time./ °Quo die com*paruit* et in vim Iur*amenti* affirmauit q*uod*   25
no*n* [negat] delin*qu*it in ar*ticu*lo *predicto* ideo monit*us* et di*missus*/.°
...

1613/14
Archdeaconry of Hereford Acts of Office   HRO: box 24, vol 89   30
f [69v]   *(23 February)*

Proceedings of the court held in the consistory of Hereford Cathedral
before Master John Richardson, STD, *deputy to Robert Bennett, bishop*
of Hereford.   35
...

Iohannes Wilkes for keepeinge of dancinge, tipling and drinkinge in
his howse diebus dominic*is* °Cit*atus* per app*aritorem* in 23 ffebruarij
1613/ Vt allegavit etc pre*con*izatus non com*paruit*/ excommunicatus°
...   40

WELLINGTON

1613
Archdeaconry of Hereford Acts of Office   HRO: box 23, vol 88
f 156*   5

...

Thomas Iones

excommunicatio for profaning the Saboathe daie in dancing./ °Citatus per publicum
edictum in ecclesia in x diem Maij/ predicti & ex certificario apparitoris
Brooke°   10

...

1620–1
Acts of Decanal Court   HCL
f 55   *(2 December)*   15

*Proceedings of the court held in the dean's consistory of Hereford
Cathedral before the dean.*

...

Marden   [Thomas] ⌐Willimum⌐ Edwardes.   20
for dauncing the morris at Wellington on a saboath day before euening
dimissio   prayer./ °Quo die Citatus et preconizatus non comparuit
excommunicatus° xx° Ianuarij 1620 comparuit ˰⌐coram magistro Iones
&c⌐ ad cuius peticionem dominus eundem absolvit &c tunc obiecto
articulo fassus est vnde dominus ad eius peticionem eundem dimisit 25
cum admonicione &c/

...

WELSH NEWTON

                                                                          30
1619
Archdeaconry of Hereford Acts of Office   HRO: box 24, vol 90
f [176]   *(September)*

Proceedings of the court held in the consistory of Hereford Cathedral   35
before Master Gabriel Wallwin, surrogate, and in the presence of
Thomas Crumpe, registrar.

...

°vide inferius absentem°†
12 Novembris   *contra* Willimum Rice   40

detect*us* for lord of misrule °Quo die com*paruit* et neg*auit* &c vnde
h*ab*et ad purg*andum* se in prox*imo* &c cum 4 manu &c f*acta*
p*r*oclamac*ione* &c 12 die Novemb*ris* p*re*dicti p*re*conizatus &c nullo
modo com*paruit* &c cit*atus* in p*ro*ximo dicere ca*us*as &c quare &c
Cit*atus* in 4 diem decemb*ris* p*re*dicti &c p*re*conizatus &c   5
excom*m*unicatus°

contra Dionisiam Watkins
detecta f*o*r lady of misrule °quesit*a* &c vijs et mod*is* in p*ro*ximo &c
publicat*a* in ecc*le*sia dom*inico* die solis ult*imo* ad septimanam   10
p*re*conizata &c excom*m*unicata°

f [178]*   *(4 December)*
...

contra Thomam fffletcher   15
[ffor] detect*us* for playinge on his instrument in welshe newton in
eveninge prayer tyme & beynge demaunded by the churchwardens
& sworne man whie he did not come to church he answered them
that if they would bring the churche to the place where they played
they would come to church.   20
°quesit*us* &c vijs et mod*is* in p*ro*ximo/ Cit*atus* per publ*icum* edict*um*
&c 28 Novemb*ris* &c p*re*conizatus 4 decemb*ris* 1619. &c nullo modo
com*paruit* &c excom*m*unicatus° °xx° die decembris 1619 in ecclesia
Cath*edra*li herefo*r*die loco cons*is*toriali ib*i*d*em* coram mag*is*tro
Gabriele Wallwin artiu*m* mag*is*tro deputato &c com*paruit* ⟨T⟩homas   25
Phillipps ad cuius petic*ion*em dom*in*us revocavit decretu*m*
excom*m*unicacionis et ex*aminatis* ca*us*is ipsum dimisit cu*m*
admonic*ione*/°

contra eius servuu*m*   30
detect*us* p*ro* cons*im*ili
...

WINFORTON

                                                                             35
1616?
Diocese of Hereford Acts of Office   HRO: box 24a (formerly 18), vol 70
f [26]*
...

Nicholaus Vocle detect*us* per Rectorem ib*idem*/ admonished his   40

parrishion*er* he would he would have noe dancinge die dominico he
answeared he would haue it in despite of S*i*r Priest or S*i*r Parson this
vocle is the chief factor of it vp houlden and mainteygned °refertur ad
vlteriorem *p*resentacio*n*em gard*ianorum* et *p*arochianor*um*°

...   5

WITHINGTON

1619/20
Acts of Decanal Court   HCL   10
f 5v*   *(26 February)*

*Proceedings of court held in the dean's consistory of Hereford
Cathedral.*

...   15

Alicia Berrow
[no] for dauncing on saboath daies before euening prayer./ °cit*ata* in
*p*roxi*m*o vijs et modis 11° Morij 1619 cor*am* do*m*ino decano com*p*aruit
et d*omin*us ex gr*ac*ia eande*m* di*m*isit &c°

                                                                           20

Madley./   Penelope Carwarden.
               pro Cons*imili*./ xi° Martij 1619 com*p*aru*it* cor*am* [cit*ata* *proximo*]
dimissio   d*omi*no decano. &c. Ioh*ann*es Carwarden pater d*i*cte penelopes ad
               cuius peti*c*io*n*em d*omi*nus ex gr*ac*ia eande*m* di*m*isit/
               ...   25

               f 6*
               ...
Preston Win*ne*./ Anna Hodges.
               *p*resent*ata* for dauncing at Withington on saboath daies. °before   30
               *eue*ninge *p*ra*y*er 11° Martij 1619 cor*am* do*m*ino decano com*p*aruit et
               fatetur &c. vnde d*omi*nus ex gr*ac*ia e*a*nde*m* dimisit cu*m* admoni*c*io*ne*
               &c°

Withington   Maria serva Thome ffranke   35
               pro Cons*imili*./ Quesit*a* &c Cit*ata* viis et modis in *p*roximo.
               ...

1/ he would he would: *dittography*
18/ Morij *for* Martij (?)

1620
Acts of Decanal Court   HCL
f 10   *(27 March)*

Proceedings of the court held in the dean's consistory of Hereford   5
Cathedral before the dean.
...
Maria *serva* Thome ffranke
presentata for dauncing on saboath daies./

10

1620/1
Acts of Decanal Court   HCL
f 55v   *(20 January)*

Proceedings of the court held in the dean's consistory of Hereford   15
Cathedral before the dean.
...
Ludovicus Ireland.

Marden   for dauncing the morris at Withington on a saboath day./ xxº Ianuarij
Richardus Crispe 1620 comparuit cui obiecto articulo predicto fassus est &c unde   20
de Moorton   dominus iniunxit ei vnum diem penitencialem et monitus ad
Ieffres./   certificandum in proximo./ 17º ffebruarij 1620 comparuit et revocavit
dimissio   decretum quoad penitenciam et cum admonicione dimisit/
...

25

f 58
...
Richardus Crispe.

Moorton Ieffres for dauncing the morris on saboath dayes/ Quo die comparuit et
                propter eius contemptum dominus eum excommunicavit./   30
...

f 58v   *(17 February)*
...
Willimus Taylor   35
for dauncing the morris on a saboath day at Withington/ 17º ffebruarij.
Citatus et preconizatus non comparuit excommunicatus./

David Iukes pro Consimili.
Quo die comparuit cui obiecto articulo predicto fassus est &c vnde   40

dominus iniunxit ei vnum diem penitencialem iuxta &c et monuit ad
certificandum in proximo./

Willimus Powell.
pro Consimili./ Quo die comparuit &c et fassus est &c. vnde dominus   5
iniunxit vt supra &c

...

Rogerus Miles.
for playing on his fidle.
...   10

    f 60v   (3 March)
    ...

Marden   Willimus Taylor.
for dauncing the morris on a saboath day. excommunicatus./   15

dimissio   David Iukes.
pro Consimili./ monitus ad certificandum penitenciam in hunc diem
Quo die ad Idem in proximo./ Postea comparuit ad cuius peticionem
dominus revocavit penitenciam et ex gracia cum admonicione dimisit./   20

Willimus Powell.
pro Consimili./ similiter./ Quo die comparuit et quia non peregit
dimissio   dominus eum excommunicavit./ 17° Martij absolutus fuit et dimissus./
...   25
dimissio   Rogerus Miles.
for playing on his fidle./ Quo die comparuit cui obiecto articulo
predicto fassus est eundem esse verum vnde dominus iniunxit ei
penitenciam iuxta &c et ad certificandum in proximo./ similiter vt
contra Iukes./   30
...

1622
Acts of Decanal Court   HCL
f 115   *(12 October)*   35

Proceedings of the court held before Master Jones.
...
Robertus *(blank)* le taylor.
for dauncing on ye saboath day before euening prayer./   40

Anna Crumpton.

dimissio

pro Cons*imili*./ °Quo die com*paru*it et ffassa est &c. vnde d*omin*us
iniu*n*xit ei un*um* diem peniten*cialem* &c. iuxta &c et ad *certificandum*
in prox*imo* &c° Postea d*omin*us ea*ndem* cum admonic*one* d*i*misit

5

Maria Tayler.

dimissio

pro Cons*imili*./ °Quo die s*imi*liter vt supra/° Postea simil*iter*./

...

f 118v*   *(9 November)*

10

...

Robertus Beckinsfield le taylor.
for dauncing on ye saboath day before euening prayer./ 9° Novem*bris*
1622 simil*iter* ut *contra* Imme

15

Ioanna Careles.

dimissio

pro Cons*imili*./ Quo die com*paru*it cui obiecto ar*ticu*lo pred*icto*
fatetur eu*ndem* esse ver*um* &c vnde d*omin*us iniunxit ei vn*um* diem
peniten*cialem* more penitenc*iali* iuxta &c et monit*a* fuit ad
certificandum in prox*imo*./

20

Postea d*omin*us revoca*v*it penitenc*iam* al*ias* iniunct*am* et ea*ndem*
d*i*misit./ cum admonic*one* &c.

Ioh*an*nes Ioyner.

dimissio

pro Cons*imili*./ 9° Novem*bris* 1622 simil*iter* vt *contra* Imme. 15to
ffebr*uarij* 1622 com*paru*it cor*am* d*omi*no decano &c ad cuius
petic*ionem* d*omin*us eu*ndem* absolvit &c et allega*v*it se habitasse infra
Prebend*am* de Ewithington vnde d*omi*nus retulit eu*ndem* ad
Prebend*arium* &c.

25

...

30

Edwardus Davis.

dimissio

for dauncing on ye saboath day before euening prayer./ 9° Novem*bris*
1622 com*paru*it et fatetur ar*ticu*lum esse ver*um* &c et submisit se &c

Iane Cerle./

vnde d*omin*us eu*ndem* cum admonic*one* d*i*misit./

35

f 120*   *(7 December)*

Margareta [Tomkins] ⌜Hallinge⌝
for dauncing on the saboath day before euening prayer./ [⟨....⟩]

40

Iana Tomkins.
pro Consimili./

Iana Serle.

pro Consimili./ 7° Decembris 1622 comparuit Iohannes Smith ad cuius   5
peticionem dominus eam dimisit./

...

1622/3
Acts of Decanal Court   HCL   10
f 124   *(15 March)*

...

Margareta Hallinges.
for dauncing vppon saboath dayes./ 15° Martij 1622. [similiter] coram
domino decano &c citata per affixionem presentam⟨enti⟩ super ostium   15
patris sui &c. set preconizata non comparuit dominus eam
excommunicavit &c.

...

1623   20
Acts of Decanal Court   HCL
f 126   *(29 March)*

Proceedings of court held before Master Jones and in the presence of
the registrar.   25

Margareta Hallinges.
for dauncing on saboath dayes./ excommunicata./

...

                                                                                   30

1624
Acts of Decanal Court   HCL
f 158v   *(23 October)*

Proceedings of the court held before Master Jones, commissary.   35
...

Ioanna Ioyner alias Devizer.
detecta for suffering taber playing in her house on Bartholomew day
in time of euening prayer./

...   40

WOOLHOPE

1620
Acts of Decanal Court   HCL
f 35*   *(September)*   5
...
Iohannes Powell fidler.
for playing before euening prayer on saboath dayes vnto the dauncers
videlicet xxvij° Augusti vltimi./
vicarius ibidem   10
Rogerus Butlar ædituus ibidem/
presentati fuere

Putley./   Thomas Iones.
pro Consimili vt supra contra Powell./
...   15

f 35v   *(23 September)*

Proceedings of the court held in the dean's consistory of Hereford
Cathedral before Master Jones.   20
...
Anthonius Wheelar clericus vicarius ibidem
he was a spectator of such as daunced before euening prayer on saboath
dayes. videlicet 27° Augusti vltimi Quo die comparuit cui obiecto
articulo predicto negauit &c vnde dominus iniunxit et monuit eum ad   25
purgandum se 4ta manu clericorum &c./

Rogerus Butlar ædituus ibidem
pro Consimili./ Quo die citatus in ecclesia et preconizatus non
comparuit ideo excommunicatus./ °Postea sedente Curia comparuit   30
et dominus revocavit decretum excommunicacionis &c et dominus
monuit eum ad exhibendum nomina psaltorum et spectatorum in
proximo°

Iohannes Powell.   35
for being the fidler thereat./ Quo die comparuit cui obiecto articulo
predicto fassus est &c [et] ⌐vnde dominus⌐ in vim iuramenti sui
[affirmavit quod] monuit eum ad tradendum nomina saltatorum et

eorum qui presentes fuere tunc et ibidem/ in proximo sub pena./

Putley./   Thomas Iones.
                pro Consimili./
                ...   5

                f 38v   (7 October)

                Proceedings of the court held in the dean's consistory of Hereford
                Cathedral before Master Wallwin, commissary.   10
                ...

                Anthonius Wheelar clericus vicarius ibidem
                he was a spectator of such as daunced on saboath dayes
                [videlicet] before euening prayer videlicet 27° Augusti vltimi./ ad
                purgandum se 4^(ta) manu clericorum in hunc diem/ Quo die facta trina   15
                vice preconizacione et non comparuit dominus pronunciavit
                eum [incidisse] defecisse et pro convicto teneri &c et decrevit
                &c./

dimissio   Rogerus Butlar ædituus ibidem   20
                pro Consimili / monitus est ad tradendum nomina psaltatorum
                et spectatorum ibidem./ Quo die preconizato et non comparente
                nec monicioni parente dominus eum excommunicavit xxi° Octobris
                1620 comparuit coram domino decano &c ad cuius peticionem
                dominus eundem absolvit &c et super examinacione eundem   25
                dimisit./

                Iohannes Powell fidler/ similiter/
                Quo die dominus continuavit causam in proximo et monuit eum
                ad tunc comparendum &c/ Quo die preconizatus non comparuit   30
                excommunicatus./

Putley./   Thomas Iones fidler
                pro Consimili/ Quo die Citatus per Gough et preconizatus
                non comparuit dominus eum excommunicavit ⟨...⟩ per magistrum   35
                Iones &c et super examinacione cause dominus eundem
                dimisit/
                ...

YARKHILL

1588
Diocese of Hereford Acts of Office   HRO: box 17, vol 67
f [215]*   *(17 June)*   5

*Proceedings of the court held in the consistory of Hereford Cathedral
before Master William Grenewich.*
...

Tadington   Iohannes Bidcotte Richardus Bidcot Robertus Bidcot   10
notati anglice/ in piping, and plaing as minstrells (tempore divinorum)

2. Iulij.   in 5ᵗᵒ die Maij. [infra] die dominico existenti, infra parochiam de
yarkill/ in hawlinges Close &c vnde habet [vterque] ⌐quilibet¬ i. diem
penitencialem &c Et ad certificandum in proximo/

    15

YAZOR

1619-20
Archdeaconry of Hereford Acts of Office   HRO: box 24, vol 90
ff [23v-4]   *(13 October)*   20

*Proceedings of the court held in the parish church of Leominster before
Master Gabriel Wallwin, MA, deputy to Master Oliver Lloid, LLD,
official principal and commissary of Francis Godwin, bishop of
Hereford.*   25

Mauncell Lacie/   *contra* Thomam hopkins
°inseretur   detectus per gardianos de yazor for dauncing the morrice betwene
in decanatu   morninge & eveninge prayer on a sonday & goeinge dauncinge out
de Weobley°   of that parishe.   30
    contra Thomam Hodges
    detectus pro consimili
Yazer   *contra* Willimum Lyke
    detectus for dauncinge the morrice betwene morninge & eveninge
    prayer on a sonday & goeinge dauncinge the morrice out of that   35
    parishe.
    contra Iacobum Hodges
    detectus pro consimili|
    contra Annam Lyke
    detecta for dauncinge [of] on the sab⟨oath⟩ day betwene morninge &   40
    eveninge prayer.

contra Elizabetham Hint
detect*a* *pro* cons*imili*.
contra Margaret*am* Wynne
detect*a* *pro* cons*imili*.
contra Ann*am* Watkins   5
detect*a* *pro* cons*imili*
contra Iohann*em* Watkins
detect*us* *pro* cons*imili*.
…

                                                                                    10

f [65]   *(12 November)*
…

gard*iani* ib*idem* v*i*d*e*lic*e*t hugo Stringham Hugo Winney
for havinge a greate morris daunce vpon the saboath daie at eveninge
praier tyme cit*ati* ın xıj diem Novembris 1619 *pre*co*n*izati &c   15
comp*ar*ueru*n*t *pre*fati gard*iani* quibus do*minus* iniunxit su*per*
examin*a*c*io*ne caus*arum* ad comp*ar*endu*m* in loco cons*istoriali* ecclesie
Cathe*dralis* herefordie xix die Novembris instan*tis* ad recipiend*um*
arti*cu*los et mo*n*uit ipso*s* ad tunc interessend*um* ad [⟨..⟩] videndu*m*
vlteriorem *process*u*m*   20

ff [72v–4]*   *(February)*
…

<table>
<tr><td>Maunce llacie</td><td></td></tr>
<tr><td>dimissio</td><td></td></tr>
<tr><td>[kinnerslie]</td><td></td></tr>
</table>

Maunce llacie   Thomas hopkins detect*us* per gard*ianos* de Yazor for dancing the
dimissio   morrice betweene morning and eveninge praier on a sondaie and   25
[kinnerslie]   goeing a dauncing out of that parrishe °2do die ffebruar*ij* 1619 iuxta
                    &c. cora*m* m*a*gistro Osgood surro*gato* &c comp*ar*ui*t* et obiecto
                    arti*cu*lo fassus est etc et do*minus* mo*n*uit eu*m* ad agnoscend*um*
                    eius culp*am* &c eu*mque* mo*n*uit ne posthac &c. eu*mque* dimisit
                    &c.°   30

5 m*a*rtij   Thomas hodg*es* *pro* cons*imili* °quesit*us* in quintu*m* ffebr*ua*r*ij* 1619
                    vijs et modis in proxi*mo* 24 ffebruar*ij* 1619° do*minus* ren⟨ov⟩avit in
                    proxi*mo* cit*atus* person*ali*ter per M*a*rsten app*ari*torem 5 M*a*rtij vltimo
                    ad comp*ar*endum in ecclesia Cathe*drali* herefordie loco consistoriali 35
                    ib*idem* [⟨…⟩] xvj° die M*a*rtij *pre*dicti *pre*conizatus trina vice et nullo
                    modo comp*ar*uit do*minus* pronunc*i*avit ipsum contumace*m* et in pena
                    excommu*n*icac*i*onis

dimissio Yazor   Willim*us* Lyke *pro* cons*imili* °2do ffebruar*ij* 1619 simil*i*ter vt in actu 40
                    contra Thom*am* hopkins.°|

Iacobus hodg*es* viij° die ffebruarij *predicti* simil*iter*. °24 die ffeb*ruarij*
predicti ad idem in prox*imo*°°15 Martij 1619 comp*aruit* et introd*uxit*
formam executi*onis*°

Anna Lyke [*pro* cons*imili*] detect*a* for dauncing on the saboath day   5
betweene morning & evening praier °2do ffeb*ruarij* 1619 Simil*iter* ad
petic*ionem* w*illi*mi Like°

Eliz*abetha* [Hynct p*ro* cons*imili*] Hint p*ro* cons*imili* °2do ffeb*ruarij*
simil*iter* ad petic*ionem* dic*ti* w*illi*mi Like°   10

Margareta Winney p*ro* cons*imili* °5 ffeb*ruarij* 1619 in loco
Cons*istoriali* &c comp*aruit* et fassa est &c d*omin*us accep*tavi*t &c et
iniu*n*xit ei *penitenc*iam vt Bowcott/°°24 die ffeb*ruarij predicti* ad idem
in prox*imo* &c° °postea dimissa est cu*m* admonic*ione*°   15

Anna Watkins p*ro* cons*imili* °2do ffeb*ruarij* 1619 simil*ite*r ad
petic*ionem* Ioha*n*nis Watkins°

Iohannes Watkins p*ro* cons*imili* °2do ffeb*ruarij* 1619. Simil*iter* vt in   20
actu *contra* Thoma*m* hopkins°

Bridg Sollers   Thomas Phillpott*es* for dauncing the morrice on a sondaie betweene
*di*missio   morning and evening praier in th⟨e p⟩arrishe of yazor °5 ffeb*ruarij*
                   1619 in loco Cons*istoriali* d*omin*us con*tinuavi*t in prox*imum*° xj° die 25
                   ffebruarij 1619 iuxta &c in ecclesia Cathedra*l*i herefo*rdie* loco
                   cons*istoriali* herefo*rdie* coram mag*istro* Gabriele Wallwin artiu*m*
                   mag*istro* deputato &c comp*aruit* personal*iter* d*ictus* morris et obiecto
                   ei ar*ticu*lo fass*us* est art*icu*lum esse veru*m* qu*am* confessionem d*omin*us
                   accep*taui*t et ex*aminatis* ca*us*is ipsum dimisit cu*m* admonic*ione*   30

Staunton   Iacobus Blether p*ro* cons*imili* °5° ffeb*ruarij* 1619 in loco Cons*istoriali*
sup*er* Wiam   &c comp*aruit* d*ictus* Blether et obiecto ar*ticu*lo fassus est that he did
                   daunce the morrice on the sabaothday in the p*ar*ishe of yazor on the
*di*missio   sabaoth day before evening prayer ended qua*m* confess*ionem* d*omin*us   35
                   acceptavit &c et iniu*n*xit ei *penitenc*iam iuxta sched*ulam* et mo*n*uit
                   eu*m* ad extrahend*um* forma*m* &c et ad cert*ificandum*° [°2do die
                   ffeb*ruarij predicti* preconizatus &c non comp*aruit* &c°] °[2] 16 Martij
                   1619 di*misit* vt Clarke sequen*tem*. °|

28/ morris *for* Phillpottes *(?)*

dimissio

Iohannes Clerke pro consimili °5° ffebruarij 1619 in loco Consistoriali &c comparuit et similiter vt in actu contra Blether 16 Martij 1619 in loco Consistoriali comparuit et dominus monuit eum &c eumque dimisit°

5

dimissio
Biford

Thomas Powell pro consimili °5° ffebruarij 1619 in loco Consistoriali &c comparuit et fassus est &c similiter vt in actu Bowcott° xj° die ffebruarij 1619 iuxta &c in loco consistoriali herefordie coram magistro Gabriele Wallwin artium magistro deputato &c comparuit et introduxit formam et in vim iuramenti sui certificavit de peractione   10 vnde dimissus

dimissio
Bishopston

Hugo Powell pro consimili °5 ffebruarij 1619 in loco Consistoriali comparuit et fassus &c similiter vt in actu Bowcott° °Quo 24 die ffebruarij predicti comparuit, et (ex gratia) habet diem in proximo   15 &c ad certificandum hoc in loco 16 Martij proximo° °15 Martij 1619 in loco Consistoriali comparuit et dominus [⟨.⟩] audita causa eum dimisit cum admonicione°

dimissio
Mauncell
Gammadg

Thomas Bowcot pro consimili °5° ffebruarij 1619 in loco Consistoriali   20 &c comparuit dictus Bowcot et obiecto articulo fassus est eundem esse verum quam confessionem dominus acceptavit quatinus &c et iniunxit ei penitenciam iuxta schedulam &c quam [confessionem dominus in] schedulam dominus monuit eum ad extrahendum &c et ad certificandum° °24 die ffebruarij predicti coram magistro Wallwine   25 deputato &c in loco consistoriali &c comparuit, quem dominus contumacem pronunciavit in non peragendo penitenciam &c reservata tamen pena in proximum &c° °[2] 15 Martij predicti vt in causa [Bow] Powell°

30

dimissio

Willimus Reygnoldes pro consimili °5 ffebruarij ⌈°1619°⌉ loco Consistoriali &c vt in actu Shepperd 4 ffebruarij 1619 in loco Consistoriali &c comparuit et introduxit formam et de peractione penitencie iuxta certificarium in dorso eiusdem factum fecit fidem°

35

dimissio
Yazor

Iohannes Shepperd for dauncing on a saboath daie betweene morning & evening praier in the parrishe of Yazor °5° ffebruarij 1615 in loco Consistoriali &c comparuit dictus Shepperd et dominus eum

32/ 4 ffebruarij for 24 ffebruarij (?)
37/ 1615 for 1619(?)

iuramento oneravit de fide*liter* *res*pondendo &c tunc interroga*tus*
whether he did daunce on the sabaoth day fassus est that he did soe
daunce on the sabaoth day before eveninge prayer ended & beyng
asked whoe did soe daunce beside nominavit *partes per* gard*ianos* de
yazor al*ias* no*min*atas et affirmavit se nullos alios scire. qua*m*   5
confessionem do*minus* accep*t*avit &c et iniunxit ei pe*ni*ten*ci*am in
vsuali vestitu suo iuxta sched*ulam* &c qua*m* sched*ulam* do*minus*
mo*nuit* eu*m* ad extrahend*um* &c et ad cer*tific*and*um* &c mense Martij
proxi*mo* 15 Martij 1619 in loco Cons*istoriali* com*paruit* et introd*uxit*
formam et fecit fide*m* &c et do*min*us eum dimisit./°| 10

Yazor

Iohannes hodg*es* *pro* cons*imili* quinto die ffebruarij *predicti* com*paruit*
et obiecto ei a*rticulo* fassus est a*rticu*lum esse veru*m* vnde do*min*us
iniu*n*xit ei ad confitend*um* a*rticu*lum in vsuali vestitu cora*m* ministro
et gard*ianis* ibidem die dominico *proximo* immediate post preces   15

dimissio

finit[it]*as* et ad cer*tific*andum in *proximo* secundo deinde do*min*us
ip*s*um dimisit cu*m* admoni*ci*one

dimissio

Ioanna Emmans *pro* cons*imili* °5 ffebruarij 1619 in loco Cons*istoriali*
&c com*paruit* d*i*cta Emmans et obiecto a*rticu*lo negavit a*rticu*lum esse   20
verum in aliquo vnde do*min*us iniunxit ad purgand*um* se in proxi*mo*
hoc in loco 2 manu f*a*cta prius proclama*ci*one &c et mo*nuit* eam adtunc
et ibi*dem* interessend*am* ad vidend*um* vlteriorem processu*m* fieri
postea fassa est that she did daunce before the end of eveninge prayer
on the sabaoth day qua*m* confessionem do*minus* acceptavit quat*inus* 25
&c et iniunxit ei pe*ni*ten*ci*am ˏˈin vestitu suo vsualiˈ iuxta sched*ulam*
ˏˈ&cˈ quam [confess] sched*ulam* do*min*us mo*nuit* eam ad extrahend*um*
&c et ad cer*tific*and*um* in proxi*mo* vi*delice*t 24 huius mens*is*. °°24 die
ffebruarij 1619 cora*m* Wallweine deputa*to* &c dimisit d*i*ctam Ioannam
sub admoni*ci*one &c Vnde dimiss*a* est./°   30

dimissio

Elionora Wheetse
pro cons*imili*/ Simil*iter*. °Quo 24 die ffebr*uarij* *predicti* Simil*iter* vt
supra/°

...   35

Monasteries

ABBEY DORE

1303
Exchequer Accounts of Edward I   PRO: E101/363/18
f 21v*   *(7 April)*

...

❡ Septimo die Aprilis Gerardo vidillatori Menestrallo
domini .. de Suttinges venienti ad Principem vsque Stradle
ex parte eiusdem domini sui & facienti menestralciam
suam coram eodem de dono eiusdem Principis/ in recessu
suo ibidem eodem die   xiij .s. iiij .d.

Menestralli
fflandrie

❡ Amando menestrallo domini Ernaldi de Gardinis/
facienti eodem modo menestralciam suam coram dicto
domino Principe ibidem de dono eiusdem ibidem
eodem die   xx .s.

...

LIMEBROOK

1437
Register of Bishop Thomas Spofford   HRO
f 77*   *(16 June) (Constitution for the convent of Limebrook)* ✔
...

The firste We ordeyne and charge yow that thir thre substancyalle
articles of your professyon that es to say dew obedyence. wylfulle
pouertee. and clene chastytee be obserued and keped contynually:
Obedyence that no sustre professyd go withoute of the precynct and
the closer of your Monastery to any maner of place be nyght or by
day withouten specyall leefe askyd and had of the prioresse or hire
deputee and with on othir honeste sustre on lyke wyse professyd

---

25/ wylfulle *corrected from* wyffulle

forbedyng that the prioresse nor her deputee yife no lycence to noon
of hire sustres her aftir to go to no port townes no to noon othir townes
to comyn wakes and festes. spectales and othir wordly vanytees and
specyally on holydayes nor to be absent lyggyng oute by nyght out
of thair Monastery but with fader and moder excepte causes of   5
necessytee
...

ff 77v–8*

...   10
¶ Also Wee forbede alle maner of mynstrelseys enterludes dawnsyng
or reuelyng with in your sayde holy place and what dysport of
walkyng forward in dewe tyme and place so that yee kepe the dewe
houres and tymes of dyuyne seruyce with inforth and with honeste
compeny and with lycence specyally asked and obteyned | the   15
Pryoresse or suppryoresse in her absence and at yee be two to gyder
at the leest we holde vs content Chargyng yow Prioresse that now
es and al youre successours here after vnder the payne of inobedience
and suspensyon of your Office that yee obserue and kepe this present
ordynaunce in yowr awne persons And that in yow es to make it to   20
be obserued and keeped with al your sustres that now present er and
her after schalbe And at in [c] yche moneth ones in the yeer opynly
in the Chapitr howse all thies ordynaunce distynctly be red called
therto all the sustres that none pretend none ignoraunce vnder the
payn forsaide Wryten in our maner of Whitburn the sextene day of   25
Iune the yeer of our lord Millesimo CCCCxxxvij and the yeer of our
translacion sextend//
...

WIGMORE   30

1318
Register of Bishop Adam Orleton   HRO
f 28* *(30 December)*

                                                                        35
...Item dampnamus consuetudinem seu corruptelam minucionis
sanguinis hactenus observatam, set minuantur quando oportet, & tunc
absque dissolucione aliqua & cantilenis inhonestis, et minutis
deseruiatur secundum ordinacionem Abbatis in victualibus....

2/ no² for ne (?)   3/ spectales for spectacles
3/ wordly for worldly   15/ obteyned for obteyned of

Households

BISHOP RICHARD SWINFIELD OF HEREFORD

1289–90
Account Roll of Bishop Richard Swinfield   Bodl.: MS Lat. hist. d. 1(R)   5
mb 3d*   *(Gifts)*
...

...In solucione facta Willielmo vigili qui recessit tam de dono quam
stipendio/ ij s.... Item Hugoni Cithariste domini Abbatis Radingi/
xij. d.   10
...

...Item iij menestrallis londonii ˄⌜&⌝ ij nunciis/ Regis/ ij. s.... Item
benetto vielatori Londonii/ iij s. Item Cithariste domini Radulphi
Pippard/ ij. s. Item Ricardo Oblatori de Oxonia/ ij. s. Item aliis
wafferariis & menestrallis ibidem/ v s. vj. d. Item Magistro Henrico 15
harparum domini Edmundi de Mortuomari/ xij d....
...Item .ij. menestrallis apud Moneketoun/ ij. d....
...Item harparator' domini Iohannis Tregoz apud Sugwas/ ij. s....
Item Cuidam menestrallo Ioliet apud Colewell/ xij d. Item Pynke
menestrallo apud Colewell/ xij d.   20
...

JOYCE JEFFREYS OF HEREFORD

1637–8   25
Account Book of Joyce Jeffreys   BL: Egerton 3054
f 26   *(7 June) (Disbursements)*
...

gave michaell hearing. ye lord bushops bailiff   15 s.

16/ harparum *for* harparatori

(10 June)
gave the waits there at his feast   1 s.
...

f 28   *(2 October)*   5
...
gave the waites when I dined at ye maiors   1 s.

f 30   *(25 December)*
...   10
gave the waites of the citty   2 s. 6 d.
gave the 2: beedles of the Citty also   8 d.

(27 December)
gave the plaiers at my new howse   5 s.   15
...

1638-9
Account Book of Joyce Jeffreys   BL: Egerton 3054
f 30   *(1 January) (Disbursements)*   20
...
gave S*ir* Iohn Giles ye fidler   j s.
...

(6 January)   25
gave 2: fidlers on twelf day   j s.
...

f 30v   *(February)*
...   30
gave Mrs mary wallwin, mary powell & fidlers   18 d.
...

f 32   *(4 May)*
...   35
mellin at   sent to Mr Henry Mellin: maiore of Herifford   10 s.
ye Law Day   gave the waites: at ye maiors feast   j s.
...

f 33   *(28 May)*

…

at ye play   gave Elyza*beth* Acton to give the musick at M*aster*
Alder*m*ans. at the play   6 d.

…   5

f 33v*   *(1 July)*

…

pamflets   for 2: pamphilletts: one moorning verses vpon Ben*jamin*
Ionsons death & of cantting   j s.   10
for A box to carie them down   8 d.

(30 July)
I paid for cariage downe of these bokes   22 d.

…   15

1639–40
Account Book of Joyce Jeffreys   BL: Egerton 3054
f 36   *(10 January) (Disbursements)*

…   20

gave the waites of heriford   2 s. 6 d.

…

f 37v   *(3 April)*

…   25

gave the waites of heriford at ester   18 d.

…

f 38v   *(22 June)*

…   30

ye faier   gave Elyzabeth Acton: at heriford faier   10 s.
gave Ioyse Walsh ye yonger my god daughter then   2 s. 6 d.
gave a man that had ye dawncing hors   j s.
gave the musisians the same tyme   6 d.

…   35

f 39v   *(7 September)*

…

given megge A dawncer j d. 4: oz: wostid. 15 d.   16 d.

…   40 f 41   *(25 December)*

gave the waites of heriford 3 s. to ye 2: beedles 8 d.   3 s. 8 d.
...

(31 December)
gave Knell. & his fellow fidler Iohn a Tomas   6 d.
...

1640-1
Account Book of Joyce Jeffreys   BL: Egerton 3054
f 41   *(1 January) (Disbursements)*
...
gave a boy that did sing Like a black byrd   3 d.
...

f 43   *(20 April)*
...
gaue the waites of heriford Ester Tewsday   18 d.
...

(28 April)
gave hoddy: for dauncing: j d. & mr danseies maid 6 d.   [13] 7 d.
...

f 46v   *(27 December)*

I gave the waites 3 s. gave Iames prichett j s.   4 s.
...

1641-2
Account Book of Joyce Jeffreys   BL: Egerton 3054
f 46v   *(1 January) (Disbursements)*
...
gave the 2: fidlers 6 d. & Mrs bifords dawghter 6 d.   j s.
...
gave ye [waites] beedles 8 d. to ye waites 3 s.   3 s. 8 d.
...

f 48 *(25 March)*

...

gave megge a dauncer   i d.

...

f 48v *(11 April)*

...

waites   gave the waites, on Ester munday   18 d.

...

f 49 *(18 May)*

...

gave Iohn a Tomas: & Ruell ye fidlers   6 d.

...

f 49v *(30 June)*

...

to the washer woeman 6 d. gave ye worcester waites j s.   18 d.

...

MORTIMER OF WIGMORE

1393–4
Account Roll of Roger, Lord Mortimer   BL: Egerton Roll 8738
mb 2*

Houedene   ...

Item pur j haucelet de blanc satyn embroude   xiiij s.
Item pur j daunsyng doublet de blance satyn embroude   iiij s.

...

mb 2d

W. Venne.   ...

Item en c pommes de oringe d'argent susorrez pur j
daunsynge doublet fait par W. Mallynges et soun
compaignon brouderes poisant ij lb. et di. unc. de pois de
Troie pris la lb. xxviij s.   lvij s. ij d.
Item pur xv welkes et xv muscles pur j haucelyn blank fait

27/ haucelet: *doublet*
37/ haucelyn: *doublet*

par W. Venne pois ix unc. de pois de Troie iiij d. meyns
pris la lb. xxviij s. come desuys   xx s. viij d.
Item pur la facoun et *pur* l'endorreure des pom*m*es
welkes et muscles susditz p*r*is la pece ix d. et hors pris un
de ava*u*ntage   iiij li. xvij s. vj d.   5
Item en xv cokles d'argent blancs *pur* le dit haucelyn
blank pois iiij unc. et di. de pois de
Troie ij d. meins   x s. iiij d.
Et *pur* la facoun de les ditz xv cokles p*r*is la pece iiij d.   v s.

W. Mallynges,   ...   10
tillere.   Item pur l'enbroudure d'une dauncyng doublet de satyn
blank embroudez oue arbres de pom*m*es de oringe p*ur*
l'or et lo*u*r overaigne   c s.

Penston.   ...
Item pur iij aln de lynge toille *pur* haucelyn pris l'aln ix d.   ij s. iij d.   15
Item *pur* iiij aln*n* de Westfall' *pur* stoffure de meisme
le haucelyn p*r*is l'aln vj d.   ij s.
Item pur vj verges de fustien *pur* lynure de meisme le
garnement p*r*is la v*er*ge viij d. ob.   iiij s. iij d.
Item pur ij aln*es* de lynge toile *pur* j doublet *pur* daunsyng   20
p*r*is l'aln*e* viij d. ob.   xvij d.
Item pur ij aln*es* de lynge toill*e* *pur* lynure del dit doublet
p*r*is l'aln*e* xj d.   xxij d.
...

25

SCUDAMORE OF HOLME LACY

1632–3
Household Account Book 1 of John, 1st Viscount Scudamore   HCL
p 37   *(1 January)*   30
...
to the musicke on new yeares day   0   2   6
...
to the dru*m*mer   0   2   6

6, 15, 17/ haucelyn: *doublet*
11m/ tillere: *weaver*
15, 16, 17, 20, 21, 22, 23/ aln, aln*n*, aln*es*, aln*e*: *ell(s): a measure of length; the English ell was*
45 inches
16/ stoffure: *adornment, decoration*
18, 22/ lynure: *lining (from Anglo-Latin 'linura')*

p 38   *(25 March) (Gifts)*

...

to waytes   0   2   6

...

5

p 40

...

to waytes   0   2   6

...

10

p 44   *(25 March)*

...

to the waytes   0   5   0

...

the musick   0   5   0   15

...

p 50   *(Holme Lacy expenses)*

...

Giftes the musicke   0   3   0   20

...

Giftes musicke   0   2   6

...

p 81*   25

Stewardship of Hereford

...

the musick there   0   5   0

...   30

1639
Miscellaneous Papers Relating to John, 1st Viscount Scudamore
BL: Add. 11044
f 173v   *(Christmas) (Gifts)*   35

...

	li.	s.	d.
To those yat brought Presentes	8	3	0
Musicke of Hereforde	4	5	0
Welsh Harpar	0	10	0	40
Blinde Harpar	0	10	0

To the Organist	1	0	0
To ye singing boye	0	5	0
To Mils ye Taborer	0	5	0

...

1640–1
Household Account Book 2 of John, 1st Viscount Scudamore
Hereford Library: LC 647.1 MSS
f 24v   (Holme Lacy and Hereford)

...

Musicke to the wayts of Hereford at Home	0	10	0
to the wayts of Hereford	0	10	0
Total	1	0	0

...

f 25

...

Musick to the fidlers at Christmas	0	10	0
to the same at Candlemas	0	10	0
Total	1	0	0

...

f 42v   (General summary)

Musick	1	0	0

...

1641–2
Household Account Book 3 of John, 1st Viscount Scudamore
Hereford Library: LC 647.1 MSS
f 83   col 1   (Wednesday, 10 September)

...

+Hereford Musicke	0	10	0
+Blinde Harpar	0	2	0

...

f 21v*   (22 September) (Holme Lacy and Hereford)

Gifts To Hereford Musicke	0	10	0			
				0	12	0
Blinde Harpar	0	2	0			

...

1642–3
Household Account Book 4 of John, 1st Viscount Scudamore
Hereford Library: LC 647.1 MSS
f 27   *(Holme Lacy)*

	l.	s.	d.
Musicke			
giuen 2 companies of musick	0	7	0
Total	0	7	0

...

f 37   *(General summary)*

Musick	0	7	0

...

f 37v

Musick	0	2	6

...

f 64v   *(29 December) (Other particulars)*
...

December Blinde Harpar	0	2	0

...

[December] 29 Musicke. a man & a woman	0	1	0

...

f 74v   *(12 January) (Other particulars)*
...

Gifts ye blinde Harpar	0	5	0

...

APPENDIX 1
A Minstrel's Miracle

Records concerning minstrels and their activities are particularly scarce before the fourteenth century. Frequently, those records which do survive involve performers engaged in activities not connected with their performing careers. While the principal interest of this collection is, of course, in the performing minstrel, it seems unwise to ignore entirely documents which record other aspects of individual minstrels' lives. It is for this reason that I have included this account of the miraculous cure of a lame harper on Good Friday 1287. The manuscript in which it is found contains testimony from the canonization hearings of St Thomas Cantilupe, bishop of Hereford from 1268 to 1282.

After Cantilupe's death in Italy on 25 August 1282, his bones and heart were returned to Hereford and buried in the Lady Chapel of the cathedral. Five years later, his chaplain and successor, Bishop Richard Swinfield, arranged for the bones to be moved to a more prominent position in the north transept on 3 April 1287. An extensive series of miracles, beginning on the date of the translation of his remains and numbering seventy-one by the end of the month, formed the principal evidence for Cantilupe's canonization. The canonization proceedings, which lasted from 13 July to 13 November 1307, gathered the testimonies of 205 witnesses and the ceremony of canonization was finally celebrated by Pope John XXII on 16–17 April 1320.

The miracle of Philip the harper took place on 4 April 1287, the day following the translation, and the miracle was described by Juliana Kock, another lame pilgrim. Also present was Gilbert de Chevening, Bishop Swinfield's almoner and one of the custodians of the new tomb. Cantilupe's miracles and canonization are discussed in detail by Ronald C. Finucane, *Miracles and Pilgrims: Popular Beliefs in Medieval England* (London, 1977), 174–8, and 'Cantilupe as Thaumaturge: Pilgrims and their "Miracles",' *St Thomas Cantilupe Bishop of Hereford: Essays in his Honour*, Meryl Jancey (ed) (Hereford, 1982), 137–8. Finucane gives the minstrel's name as Gilbert, but it is clearly Philip in the manuscript.

Vatican City, Biblioteca Apostolica Vaticana, Cod. lat. 4015; 1307; Latin; parchment; 313 leaves; 290mm x 215mm; contemporary foliation, 1–313; tooled leather 19th c. binding.

1287
Canonization Proceedings for St Thomas Cantilupe
Vatican Library: Cod. lat. 4015
ff 169v–70   *(4 April) (Testimony of witness 104)*
...   5

℃ Do*minus* G*ilbertus* de cheueniges presb*yter* perpetu*us* vicar*ius* eccl*esi*a
de mag*n*a markle t*estis* s*up*raiurat*us* respo*n*dit requisit*us* se esse etatis
.xxx. anno*rum* v*el* circa & q*uod* no*n* fuerat de p*ar*entela v*el* fam*i*lia
d*i*cti dom*i*ni th*om*e.

10

℃ It*em* requisit*us* ut narraret siq*ui*d sciebat de miraculo q*uod* in p*er*sonam
pre*di*cte | Iuliane Kock d*i*citu*r* co*n*tigisse dixit q*uod* ipso existente
custode tumuli d*i*cti dom*i*ni Th*om*e & vicar*io* in ecclesia hereford*ie*
anno dom*i*ni .M°. .CC°. Octogesimo septimo. co*n*tigit q*uod* i*n* die
paraseue hora p*ri*me dum pre*di*cta Iuliana staret in d*i*cta ecclesia   15
hereford*ie* in quada*m* sporta de virgulis cu*m* qua sporta aportata fuerat
ad ecclesiam hereford*ie* per ph*i*lip*um* le longe teste*m* s*up*raiuratu*m* &
per qua*n*dam mulierem c*uius* nome*n* dixit se nescire ut miraculose
curaret*ur* ibi me*ri*tis d*i*cti s*an*cti thome pro quo deus in d*i*cta ecc*lesi*a
anteriori tempo*re* iiij°ʳ miracula fuerat operatus. Videns ipsa Iuliana 20
q*uod* q*ui*d ali*us* co*n*tractus pedib*us* qui vocabat*ur* ph*i*lip*us* citharista
& morabat*ur* in ci*ui*tate herefordi*e* et stabat in q*ua*da*m* al*i*a sporta in
d*i*cta ecc*lesi*a herefordi*e*. expecta*n*s in ibi miraculose me*ri*tis d*i*cti s*an*cti
Thome beneficiu*m* recipe*re* sanitatis fuerat in d*i*cta hora prime uidente
ipso teste miraculose curat*us*? & erectus & ambulauerat circa tumulu*m* 25
s*up*radictu*m* absq*ue* aliq*uo* apediame*n*to accensa ipsa Iuliana & ducta
nescit quo feruore per se ipsam absq*ue* ˌaliquo hu*m*ano adiutorio exiuit
de d*i*cta sporta in q*ua* tenebat tibias plicatas & sedebat curua & dimissa
d*i*cta sporta in loco in quo sic stabat in ea. *sed* aliq*ua*nt*u*lu*m* cu*m*
pede a se elongata erecta sine apodiame*n*to & *sine* aliquo adiutorio 30
humano no*n* claudicando pre*di*cta hora venit ad tumulu*m* s*up*radictum
& orauit *i*bidem & optulit ˌ⌐ibi⌐ vnu*m* denari*um* & narrauit ipsi testi
& al*i*js et sp*ecialiter* domi*n*o henrico de S*ancto* Albano custodi tu*n*c
cu*m* ipso teste d*i*cti tumuli et mag*i*stro rogero de Seuenok tu*n*c

6/ ecc*lesi*a *for* ecclesie
14–15/ die paraseue: *Good Friday, 4 April 1287*
16/ cu*m* qua *for* quacum
26/ a *of* apediame*n*to *apparently written over erased letter*
27/ aliquo *written in right margin and keyed to position in text by matching sigla above caret
and in margin*

canonico herefordie iam defuncto quod dictus sanctus Thomas dixerat ipsi Iuliane quod surgeret & ambularet.

...

Saints' Days and Festivals

The following table contains the dates for all the feast days to which reference is made in the documents. The exact dates of moveable feasts are given in textual footnotes. See also the tables in C.R. Cheney, *Handbook of Dates for Students of English History* (London, 1978), 84–161.

Annunciation	25 March
St Bartholomew	24 August
Christmas	25 December
Corpus Christi Day	Thursday after Trinity Sunday, the eighth Sunday after Easter
Easter	Sunday after the first full moon on or following 21 March
Good Friday	Friday before Easter
Holy Innocents' Day	28 December
Holy Cross, invention of	3 May
St John the Baptist, nativity of	24 June
St John the Evangelist	27 December
Lady Day	25 March
Lammas	1 August
St Michael (Michaelmas)	29 September
Midsummer	24 June
New Year's Day	1 January
Pentecost	seventh Sunday after Easter
St Quentin	31 October
Relic Sunday (Hereford)	first Sunday after 7 July
Shore (Sheer) Thursday	Maundy Thursday, the Thursday before Easter
St Stephen	26 December
Whitsunday	*see* Pentecost

Translations

ABIGAIL ANN YOUNG

The Latin documents have been translated as literally as possible. The order of records in the translations parallels that of records in the original. Place-names and given names have been modernized. Surnames have been normalized on a document by document basis. If the same person or family is referred to by different spellings of the same surname in a document, the most common spelling is adopted throughout the translation. If no one spelling predominates, the spelling closest to modern spelling has been chosen. Judges and other court officials, whose names also appear in the modernized 'acta' headings, form a special category. The spelling of their names is based on all the spellings which appear in the manuscript 'acta' headings as well as that of individual documents. Where English names which might be interpreted as either surnames or first names are followed by Latin occupation titles, those occupation titles have been assumed to be descriptions rather than names; thus 'Benettus vielator' has been treated as 'Bennet, a fiddler' rather than 'Bennet Fiddler.' Capitalization and punctuation are in accordance with modern practice.

As in the text, diamond brackets indicate obliterations and square brackets cancellations. Round brackets enclose words not in the Latin text but needed for grammatical sense in English. In the translations of account entries, words also appear in these round brackets to represent the subject and verb known to be governing each entry. These governing phrases were usually written out in full only a few times, at the beginning of each account heading or subheading, for example, 'Gifts and rewards'; they were not repeated for each item. It appears that once a corporate body found a set of formulae which fitted its needs, it tended to repeat those formulae year after year despite changes of accountants or auditors, who doubtless copied them from earlier account books.

In accounts of cases heard before ecclesiastical courts, phrases in round brackets have been used to complete formulae suspended with 'etc,' when the remainder of a formula can be deduced with certainty. See the section on ecclesiastical court procedure in the introduction for a full discussion of such cases. The dates in ecclesiastical court cases, which are normally given according to the English church practice of beginning the year on 25 March, have not been adjusted to agree with the modern historical year.

Not all the Latin in the text has been translated here. Latin tags, formulae, headings, or other short sections in largely English documents are either translated in footnotes or not at all. Individual documents which consist of a single line, or other very short entries, especially those that are part of repetitive annual series, are not translated, unless they present some unusual syntactic or semantic problem. All Latin vocabulary not found in the standard Latin dictionary, the *Oxford Latin Dictionary*, is found in the glossary.

DIOCESE OF HEREFORD

1348
Register of Bishop John Trillek   HRO
ff 91–1v*   *(6 October)*

…

®To keep stage plays from taking place in churches

Because, according to the voice of the prophet, holiness becomes the Lord's house, it is not suitable to do anything in it which would be foreign to the practice of devotion. Since, therefore, in the stage plays which take place from time to time in churches offensive humour and rude language – which are forbidden without qualification by the apostle not only in the Lord's temple, which ought to be and to be called a house of prayer, as the Saviour testified, but everywhere – and other things partaking of mockery – by which the hearts of the faithful who in the same places (*ie*, churches) ought to attend to holy solemnities and concentrate upon devout prayers may be dragged away to vain things and their devotion diminished – are known very frequently to occur as an offence to the divine name and a deadly example to those taking part or looking on; we, wishing to uproot this kind of abuse from the churches of our diocese as we are constrained (to do) by the ordinances of the sacred canons, lest by this sort of coarseness the honour of the church is besmirched, strictly order you by virtue of holy obedience and, firmly enjoining, command that you shall take pains to forbid hereafter, under threat of anathema, such plays or interludes in the church of L. in the same our diocese, in which, as we understand, such dishonourable things used quite customarily to take place. Moreover (we command that) those whom you find (to be) disobedient in this respect or rebellious you shall denounce as having damnably incurred a sentence of 'ipso facto' excommunication, just as disturbers of the divine office (do). I Likewise (we order that) you shall cite, or cause to be cited, those whose names you have learned by the examination which we want you to make on this point to appear before us or our commissary in our

cathedral church of Hereford on the tenth day after the citation has
been made, if it is a court day (and) otherwise on the next court day
following, ready to answer questions about this sort of rebellion and
contempt and to obey the law and to receive what justice demands.
(You shall) inform us by four days before the date fixed for them by
you what you are doing about the foregoing by your letters patent
containing the subject matter of this letter (and) sealed with some
authoritative seal. Given, etc.

...

ASHPERTON

1629
Archdeaconry of Hereford Acts of Office   HRO: box 25, vol 94
f [43v]   *(14 October)*

*Proceedings of the court held in the consistory of Hereford Cathedral
before Master Richard Basset, LLB, deputy to William Skinner, LLD,
official principal and commissary of Francis Godwin, bishop of
Hereford.*

...

New cases Against Philip Baylies, detected for playing with his instrument at time
of evening prayer 30 August last, being Sunday. °(He was) sought on
10 October 1629 by ways and means (to appear) on the next (court
day).°
Now of (the parish of) Mordiford†
Likewise Against *(blank)* Baylies, his son (for being) present. °(He was) likewise
(sought to appear) on that day.°

...

AVENBURY

1588
Diocese of Hereford Acts of Office   HRO: box 17, vol 67
f [178v]   *(4 June)*

*Proceedings of the court held in the parish church of Bromyard before
Master William Grenewich, deputy, and in the presence of Thomas
Crumpe, notary public and registrar.*

...

(His) companions Thomas Davy ap Bevan, minstrel, for piping in service time and

are to be
cited for
being present.
fetching a summer pole from Avenbury in time of divine service.
°Having been cited by the said apparitor, etc, the said Thomas Davy
ap Bevan appeared and, confessing the article, etc. Wherefore he has
18 June
to confess the article, etc, and to certify (his compliance) on the next
(court day), etc.°

...

AYMESTREY

1577/8
Diocese of Hereford Acts of Office   HRO: box 19, vol 72
f [200]*   *(25 February)*

Proceedings of the court held in the parish church of Aymestrey.
...

Thomas Bayle of the parish of Aymestrey for dancing at evening
prayer 12 January. He confesses that he was absent from evening
prayers and John More (the) taborer (was too). Wherefore each of
them has one (day of penance?). On 27 February he will also pay 12d
(of costs) and so is dismissed.

...

BARTON

1606
Archdeaconry of Ludlow Acts of Office   HRO: box 35, vol 129
p 35   *(18 December)*

*Proceedings of the court held in the parish church of Ludlow before
Master James Bailie, LLD, vicar general.*
...

Churchwardens

(They were)
cited (to
appear) on
the next
(court day).
(They were) cited for concealment of dancing upon the sabbath day,
etc. They appeared on 18 December 1606 before Master James Bailie,
LLD, etc, and denied, etc. Therefore, they have to make more thorough
enquiries, etc, and to certify (that they have done so) on the next (court
day), etc. On 9 January 1606 (the case was continued) in the same way
till the next (court day), etc.

BISHOPS FROME

1619/20
Archdeaconry of Hereford Acts of Office   HRO: box 24, vol 90
ff [128v–9]*   *(12 January)*
…

Dismissal

James Poslons and Mary his wife for suffering dancing and minstrels playing in their house at time of evening (prayer) upon the sabbath day. °Having been sought at their home on 16 December aforesaid, etc, to appear on the 18th of the same (month), etc, (they did not appear and were cited) by ways and means (to appear) on the next (court day), etc. °(They were) cited in person by Harris, an apparitor, last Monday in Bromyard to appear at the consistory in Hereford. On 5 February aforesaid (they were) summoned three times and they did not appear in any way (*ie*, neither in person nor by proxy). The lord (judge) declared them contumacious, (but) the penalty was reserved till the next (court day). On 24 February aforesaid (the penalty was held over) in the same way till the next (court day). Afterwards the lord (judge) dismissed him upon an examination of (their) cases.

Dismissal

Mary his (wife) on the like (charge). The said Mary appeared in person on 5 February aforesaid and, when the article had been charged against her, she confessed that the article was true. The lord (judge) accepted this confession and enjoined on her one day of penance in the manner of a penitent and he warned her to copy out the form (for penance) and to certify (her compliance) in this place on 24 February instant.

(She was) cited on the next (court day).

On 24 February aforesaid she appeared, and at her petition the lord (judge) held over (the production of) the certificate till the next (court day). Afterwards she took an oath that she did not send for any minstrels nor give way unto them to play there, whereupon the lord (judge) dismissed her and admonished (her) hereafter (to conduct herself properly).

Dismissal

John Botchet, minstrel
On the like charge as above. °He was cited (to appear) on 17 December aforesaid, etc, (and) having been summoned, etc, (he did not appear, therefore he was) excommunicated. He appeared in person on 12 January 1619 before Master Oliver Lloid, LLD, vicar general, etc, and sought the benefit of absolution, etc (*ie*, from the excommunication for non-appearance), and he was absolved, etc. Thereupon when the (original) article had been charged against him, etc, he confessed that

it was true. Therefore he had to confess the article in the usual garb before the minister and churchwardens, etc, and to certify (his compliance) on the next (court day), etc. ° On 5 February aforesaid (he was) dismissed after the certificate had been introduced.|

Dismissal

John Lewis on the like (charge).
°Having been cited (to appear) on 15 December aforesaid, etc, (and) having been summoned, etc, (he did not appear, therefore he was) excommunicated. ° On 8 March 1619 according, etc (ie, according to English ecclesiastical practice), the said Lewis appeared in person at Hereford before Master Gabriel Wallwin, MA, deputy, etc, and the lord (deputy) absolved him at his petition from the sentence of excommunication, etc. Thereupon, when the article had been charged against him, he confessed that the article was true. The lord (deputy) accepted this confession. Therefore he (Lewis) has to confess the article before the minister and churchwardens next Sunday immediately after prayers are finished in the church there and to certify (his compliance) on the next (court day) following.
...

°(He was)
cited.°

He certified
penance.

f [132v]   *(24 February)*

Richard Andrewes for drinking and dancing at the house of James Poslons at evening prayer time as Mary Poslons upon her oath affirmed. Having been cited, etc, (and) summoned on 24 February aforesaid three times, the said Andrewes appeared in person and, when the article had been charged against him, he confessed that the article was (true). The lord (judge) accepted this confession and ordered him to confess the article before the minister (of his parish) and there (*ie*, in his parish church?) next Sunday in the usual garb immediately after the reading of the Gospel. And he (the judge) warned him (Andrewes) to copy out the form (for penance) and to certify (his compliance) in this place. The lord (judge) afterwards dismissed him on the next (court) day in March.

Dismissal

Against the aforesaid Elizabeth likewise.
(She is) his wife. (Having been cited) in like manner, on 24 February aforesaid, (she appeared and confessed) in like manner.
...

Little Cowarne

Joan Browne on the like (charge). On 24 February 1619 according, etc (*ie*, according to English ecclesiastical practice), the said Joan

Dismissal appeared in person at Hereford before Master Gabriel Wallwin, MA, deputy, etc, and, upon an examination of the case, the lord (deputy) dismissed her with a warning.

Bishops Frome Sibyl Browne (was) sought on the like (charge), etc, (to appear) as of 6 April aforesaid, (she was) summoned, etc, (and) did not appear (Having been cited again) by ways and means (to appear) on the next (court day), (she did not appear) in any way.

BODENHAM

1611–12
Archdeaconry of Hereford Acts of Office HRO: box 23, vol 86
f [156v] *(9 December)*

Proceedings of the court held in the consistory of Hereford Cathedral before Master James Bailie, LLD, vicar general of Robert Bennett, bishop of Hereford.

...

Dismissal Richard Cronne (was) detected that he with various others upon Whitsunday last was may gaming and shooting off guns in time of divine service and when the minister was administering the sacrament. °He appeared on this day and, upon an examination of the case, the lord (vicar general) enjoined on him one day of penance in the church in the same place (*ie*, in his parish) and (he has) to certify (his compliance) on the next (court day). On 9 January aforesaid he appeared in the consistory, etc, and on oath, etc, (he produced the form of penance) and (certified his) performance of penance, etc; the lord (vicar general) therefore dismissed him. °

...

f [157v]*

...

Dismissal James Vale of Wellington, minstrel
For coming to Bodenham on the sabbath day to profane it in playing and drinking, he and his company, in the alehouse various Sundays at time of divine service. (He was) sought (to appear) on the next (court day). °On 9 January aforesaid he appeared and, when the article had been charged against him, etc, he denied that it was true. Therefore the lord (judge) ordered him to clear himself on the next (court day), etc, with two compurgators, etc, after an announcement had been

made, etc. On that day, 29 January aforesaid, having been summoned, etc, he did not appear, etc. Therefore the lord (judge) pronounced, etc (*ie*, pronounced him contumacious), and ordered that he be cited before the next (court day), etc, to show cause, etc. ° On the last day of February 1611 according, etc (*ie*, according to English ecclesiastical practice), in the consistory of Hereford before the lord vicar general, the said James Vale appeared and, upon an examination of the case, the lord (vicar general) dismissed him with a warning, etc.

...

BOSBURY

1589
Diocese of Hereford Acts of Office   HRO: box 17, vol 68
f [196v]*   (*29 June*)

Proceedings of the court held in the consistory of Hereford Cathedral before Master Francis Bevans.

An excommu-
nication was
promulgated.

Richard Kent has to certify one day of penance, in English, for going hoodwinking on Shrove Sunday at time of evening prayers. On that day he did not appear.

An excommu-
nication was
promulgated.

John Watkis, as above.
James Leeth, as above.

...

f [198]*

...

He denies
(the charge).

Against the same, (he is charged with being) a common dancer on the sabbath day.

...

BROBURY

1616
Diocese of Hereford Acts of Office   HRO: box 24a (formerly 18), vol 70
f [33]*   (*8 September*)

Thomas Hulland detected by the rector there for using of certain

Dismissal

disorders in his house on the sabbath days and in the time of divine
service, namely that upon 8 September being Sunday absented himself
from divine service and sermon at evening prayer on the sabbath day
and retained certain guests in his house, dancing, tippling, and
drinking the whole day and all time of evening prayer. On 19 October
1616 in the cathedral church of Hereford in the consistory there before
the honourable man, Master John Richardson, STD, deputy, etc, the
said Hulland appeared in person and, when the article had been
charged against him, he confessed that the article was true. Therefore
the lord
(deputy) enjoined on him one day of penance in the manner of a
penitent and to certify (his compliance) on the next (court day). On
15 November aforesaid, he appeared and, upon examination, the lord
(deputy) dismissed him with a warning, etc.

Dismissal

Elizabeth his wife on the like (charge). On 19 October aforesaid (she
appeared and confessed) in like manner as above.
...

1616–17
Diocese of Hereford Acts of Office   HRO: box 24a (formerly 18), vol 71
f [313]*   *(7 December)*

*Proceedings of the court held in the consistory of Hereford Cathedral
before Master Silas Griffithes, STD, vicar general and official principal
of Robert Bennett, bishop of Hereford.*

Dismissal

Henry Jones, fiddler, of Letton detected by the rector of Brobury.
For playing the whole sabbath day in Brobury and time of evening
prayer and sermon. He has to certify his penance. On 17 January
aforesaid 1616 according, etc (*ie,* according to English ecclesiastical
practice), in the cathedral church of Hereford in the consistory there
before the honourable man, Master Silas Griffithes, STD, vicar general,
etc, the said Jones appeared in person and introduced the form (for
penance) and certified on his oath the completion of penance
according, etc (*ie,* according to the schedule). Therefore (he was)
dismissed.
...

CANON FROME

1587
Diocese of Hereford Acts of Office   HRO: box 17, vol 66
f [228v]*   *(6 April)*

*Proceedings of the court held in the consistory of Hereford Cathedral
before Master Francis Bevans, LLD, and in the presence of Thomas
Crumpe, notary public and registrar.*

18d

2 May

A suspension
was
promulgated.

> Against Roger Hide, noted, in English, for playing with his instrument
in the alehouse, being forbidden by the churchwardens, in time of
divine service since Lent. (He was) cited by Bullocke, etc, (and was)
publicly summoned, etc. He appeared and confessing the article, etc
(*ie*, to be true in part), he nevertheless denied (it in part) because it was
not time of divine services, etc. Therefore he has to clear himself on
the next (court day), etc, with four compurgators, etc.
    On 2 May, he appeared and brought (with him) certain men,
Richard Kent (and) Henry Price, and afterwards he submitted himself
(to the judgment of the court), etc. Therefore he has one day of penance
in the church there and has to certify (his penance) on the next
(court day).
    ...

CASTLE FROME

1615
Diocese of Hereford Acts of Office   HRO: box 24a (formerly 18), vol 70
ff [78v–9]*
    ...

Richard Langlius has to certify two days of penance for being in an
alehouse in the house of one *(blank)* Ambrose in time of divine service
on a Sunday before Michaelmas day last and also for dancing. °On that
day having been summoned, etc, he did not appear in any way (*ie*,
neither in person nor by proxy). Therefore (he was)
excommunicated. °|

Dismissal

Richard Bevie, Mr Mintridge's man, on the like (charge).
°(He was) sought (to appear) as of the last day of May aforesaid, etc,
(and when he did not appear, he was cited) by ways and means (to

appear) on the next (court day). ° On 22 July 1616 aforesaid (he was)
summoned, etc, (and) did not appear, etc. Thereafter the lord (judge),
upon an examination of the case, dismissed him.

...

CLIFFORD

1620
Archdeaconry of Hereford Acts of Office   HRO: box 24, vol 90
f [78]*   *(13 July)*

...

Thomas Watkin Owen and William Turnor
Churchwardens for not presenting dancing on the sabbath day being
admonished by Mr Williams and his curate to forbear notwithstanding
their persisting and they continue in profaning of the Lord's sabbath
at evening prayer time. On 13 July aforesaid they appeared and, upon
an examination of the case, the lord (commissary) warned them to
make presentment at the next (time) for their presentment.

COLWALL

1588
Diocese of Hereford Acts of Office   HRO: box 17, vol 67
f [178]   *(4 June)*

*Proceedings of the court held in the parish church of Bromyard before
Master William Grenewich, deputy, and in the presence of Thomas
Crumpe, notary public and registrar.*

...

° A poor man   William Poole of the *(?)* Blackhull for keeping piping and taboring in
18 June°   his house at time of divine services. Having been cited by the said
                apparitor, etc, the said William Poole appeared and, confessing the
                article (to be true), etc (*ie*, he submitted himself to the judgment of
                the court). Therefore he has (to perform) one day of penance in the
                church there, etc, and to certify (his compliance) on the next (court
                day).

...

f [219]   *(18 June)*

Proceedings of the court held in the consistory of Hereford Cathedral
before Master William Grenewich.

...

A suspension
was
promulgated.

William Poole has to certify one day of penance for keeping and
dancing in his house at time of divine services. °Having been publicly
summoned on that day, he did not appear.°

...

1619–20
Archdeaconry of Hereford Acts of Office   HRO: box 24, vol 90
ff [129v–30]*   *(18 December)*

...

Gabriel Pitt the younger
For dancing between morning and evening prayer on Sunday contrary
to the king's declaration. °On 18 December 1619 the said Gabriel Pitt
appeared in person before the lord vicar general, etc, and, when the
article had been charged against him, etc, he claims that he was and
is under the authority of and subject to the peculiar jurisdiction of the
prebendary of Barton Colwall. Nevertheless he confesses that he did
dance as is said in the article within the jurisdiction of this court.
Therefore the lord (vicar general), by reason of the fault and this
confession, ordered him to carry out a public confession of this his
fault before the minister and churchwardens of the aforesaid parish
next Sunday immediately after evening prayers (are) finished.°

Richard Hope the younger on the like (charge).
°He appeared in the aforesaid church and (the lord vicar general)
warned (him) to certify (his compliance) on the next (court day), etc,

° Likewise on
that day°

that is, on 13 January next in this place before the lord (vicar general)
or, etc (*ie*, or his deputy). And at that time he should appear again to
see the further, etc (*ie*, the further will of the judge in his case).° On
13 January the said Hope (was) summoned three times and did not
appear in any way (*ie*, neither in person nor by proxy). The lord (vicar
general) pronounced him contumacious and under penalty, etc, the
penalty being reserved until the next (court day). On 24 February
aforesaid he appeared and at his petition the lord (vicar general)
referred the case to the judgment of Dr Best.

Dismissal

William Hould on the like (charge). °On that day (*ie*, 18 December)

(he appeared and confessed) in like manner.° On 13 January aforesaid
(he was summoned) in like manner. On 24 February aforesaid (his case
was referred to Dr Best) in like manner.

Dismissal

William Sawford on the like (charge). °On that day (*ie*, 18 December)
(he appeared and confessed) in like manner.° On 13 January aforesaid
(he was summoned) in like manner as above. On 24 February aforesaid
he appeared and, upon an examination of the case, the lord (vicar
general) dismissed him.

Dismissal

Elizabeth Brooke on the like (charge). °On that day (*ie*, 18 December)
(she appeared and confessed) in like manner. Afterwards she was
dismissed with a warning, etc.°

Dismissal

Anne Harbert on the like (charge). °On that day (*ie*, 18 December)
(she appeared and confessed) in like manner. Afterwards she was
dismissed with a warning, etc.°

Dismissal

Elizabeth Pitt on the like (charge). °On that day (*ie*, 18 December)
(she appeared and confessed) in like manner. Afterwards she was
dismissed with a warning, etc.°

...

f [131]*

...

Against Gabriel Pitt the younger

Dismissal

Detected for dancing on the Sunday between morning and evening
prayer contrary to the °king's° majesty's declaration. On 18 December
AD 1619 in the consistory within the cathedral church of Hereford
before the lord vicar general for spiritualities, etc, (and) in the presence
of me, James Lawrence, notary public, etc, after the said Gabriel Pitt
had been cited, etc, by public decree in the aforesaid parish church of
Colwall on Sunday 12 December aforesaid between the solemnities of
the divine services, etc, (and) summoned on this day (and in this place),
etc, the said Gabriel Pitt appeared in person and when the aforesaid
article had been charged against him, he claimed that he was and is
under the authority of and subject to the jurisdiction of the prebendary
of the peculiar jurisdiction of the prebend of Barton Colwall, but he
confessed that he did dance on the Sunday between morning and
evening prayer, as (is stated) in the article, within the jurisdiction of
this court. The lord (vicar general) accepted that this confession and

also the appearance of the said Gabriel Pitt had been lawfully carried out insofar as, etc, and by reason of the foregoing he ordered the same Gabriel Pitt to perform a public confession of this his fault before the minister and churchwardens of the aforesaid parish next Sunday immediately after evening prayers were finished in the aforesaid church according to a form to be drawn up, etc. And he warned him to copy out the said form once drawn up and to certify the completion of the same confession in this place on 13 January next and to appear in person then and there to see the further proceedings to take place in this case. °On 13 January aforesaid (he was) summoned three times and did not appear in any way (*ie*, neither in person nor by proxy), (and) the lord (vicar general) pronounced him contumacious. On 24 February aforesaid, having been summoned, etc, he appeared and the lord (vicar general) referred the case to the judgement of Dr Best.°

DILWYN

1589
Diocese of Hereford Acts of Office   HRO: box 17, vol 68
f [149v]   *(7 June)*

Proceedings of the court held in Hereford Cathedral before Master Doctor Bevans, LLD.

...

Edward Hopley, in English, for suffering dancing and ale selling in time of divine services. Having been cited by an apparitor, etc, he thereupon also confessed that the article, etc (*ie*, that it was true), wherefore he has to acknowledge this fault on the next (Sunday or festival), etc, and to certify (his compliance).

2 July

...

EASTNOR

1609
Archdeaconry of Hereford Acts of Office   HRO: box 23, vol 85
f [88]*   *(20 December)*

Thomas Wynter
Keeps dancing and other disorders in his house upon various sabbath days and suffers idle persons to play unseemly parts. °On 20 December 1609 he appeared and was warned – on the basis of his confession – to

Dismissal.

Cited (to
appear) on
the next
(court day).
Dismissal.
Cited (to
appear) on
the next
(court day).

confess this his fault before the congregation on some Sunday or
festival and to certify (his compliance) on the next (court day).
Afterwards he is dismissed with a warning. °
Thomas Harnatt
Is his minstrel ready at call. On that day (*ie*, 20 December) he appeared
and (was warned) in like manner as above.
...

FOY

1621
Archdeaconry of Hereford Acts of Office   HRO: box 24, vol 91, pt 2
f [2v]*   *(14 November)*

Proceedings of the court before Master Gabriel Wallwin, deputy.
...

Against Thomas Buttongard for dancing in evening prayer time. °He
appeared on 14 November 1621 before Master Gabriel Wallwin,
surrogate, etc, and after the article had been charged against him, etc,
he denied that it was true. Therefore he was dismissed until (the
evidence) was better established, etc. °
...

HAY

1617–18
Diocese of Hereford Acts of Office   HRO: box 24a (formerly 18), vol 71
f [288]   *(4 December)*

*Proceedings of the court held in the consistory of Hereford Cathedral
before Master Gabriel (Wallwin), MA, deputy to Master Oliver Lloid,
LLD, vicar general of Francis Godwin, bishop of Hereford.*
...

Excommu-
nication

William Meney used to play on his harp in the parish of the Hay upon
various sabbath days in the time of evening prayer. °On 4 December
AD 1617 he appeared and denied the article. Afterwards, having been
examined, he confessed. Therefore the lord (deputy) enjoined two
days of penance on him in the aforesaid church in the manner of a
penitent, etc, (and ordered him) to certify (his compliance) on the next
(court day). ° On 6 February aforesaid, having been summoned, etc,

he did not appear, etc, nor did he certify, etc. (He was)
excommunicated.

...

HENTLAND

1586/7
Diocese of Hereford Acts of Office   HRO: box 17, vol 66
f [158v]   *(11 January)*

*Proceedings of the court held in the parish church of Leominster before
Master Francis Bevans, LLD, vicar general of Herbert Westfaling,
bishop of Hereford.*

...

18d   Edward Seymore
8d   John Morce
             Thomas Blacke
             Detected for dancing in the churchyard. °On that day they appeared
             and confessed that the same article was true. Therefore the lord (vicar
             general) enjoined one day of penance in the manner of a penitent on
             the same men individually in their parish church and (ordered them)
             to certify (their compliance) on the next (court day). °

...

f [179v]   *(7 February)*

*Proceedings of the court held in the parish church of Leominster before
Master Roger Bradshawe, deputy.*

...

He owes   Edward Seymore
(his court)   John Morce
fee.   Thomas Blacke
              Detected for, in English, dancing, within the churchyard, etc. They
              have to certify one day of penance in the manner of a penitent as of
              today. °After these men Edward Seymore and Thomas Blacke had
              been publicly summoned, etc, and they appeared, etc, (and) certified
Dismissal   (their compliance) according to the decree, etc, about the completion
              of penance, etc. Therefore (they were) dismissed, etc. °

...

HEREFORD

c **1265**
Cathedral Consuetudines HCL
f 9v*

...Likewise be it known that on the feast of St Stephen the treasurer
should find portable wax torches for the procession at vespers and
matins for the deacons; and on the feast of St John, for the priests;
and on the feast of the Innocents, candles and two wax torches for the
boys (to be carried) before the boy bishop....

1286
Register of Bishop Richard Swinfield HRO
ff 39v–40* *(26 August)*
...

Concerning
Jewish
weddings

Richard, by the divine mercy bishop of Hereford, to his beloved son
in Christ, Sir A.B., the chancellor of Hereford, currently acting as the
deputy of C.D., dean of the same church: greetings together with the
grace and blessing of the Saviour.
Not only do (human) laws testify, but efficacious experience, teacher
in all practical matters, also manifests with how many and what great
wrongs and dangers the daily intercourse of Christian and Jew with
one another is rife. Although Christian piety patiently welcomes in
and supports those who have been condemned to perpetual slavery by
their own sin, nevertheless they do not fear to return to these very
Christians contumely for mercy and contempt for social acceptance
and intimacy. And – what should be more horrible to relate – time
and time again they presume to mock them (*ie*, the Christians) and
rush into contumely of their own creator. In fact, we have learned from
frequent report that some Jews on this very Wednesday next after the
feast of St Bartholomew the apostle have prepared a wedding feast in
the city of Hereford according to their detestable rite. To this (feast)
they have invited not a few Christians not only secretly but openly
and formally so that they can detract from the Christian faith – as
enemies of which they willingly exist – and preach evil things to the
simple. There is no doubt that a stumbling block can arise from such
formal (*or* customary) association together with these people (*ie*,
Jews). Since therefore we ought not to disregard insult to him who
descending from the highest heavens to the depths of the world and
finally by undergoing temporal death wiped away our faults, we order

you by virtue of (your) obedience, firmly enjoining (you) that in all the churches of the aforesaid city upon pain of canonical punishment, on this very Tuesday and the Wednesday itself you shall cause (it) to be publicly forbidden for any Christian to presume to be present at this sort of banquet with Jews. And lest it happen that some err – God forbid – out of ignorance of this order, you shall cause this same (order) to be made public through the streets of the same city in that way which is most suitable, constraining the contraveners or those rebellious to this our order – if there should be any – by ecclesiastical censure. Farewell. Given at Bosbury on 26 August in the fourth year of our consecration (*literally*, ordination).

(6 September)

Richard, by the grace of God bishop of Hereford, to his beloved son in Christ, C.D., the dean of Hereford or his current deputy: greetings, grace, and blessing.

We remember that we have written to you elsewhere and have ordered (you) by virtue of (your) obedience, enjoining firmly that you should cause (it) to be publicly forbidden in all the churches in the city of Hereford for any Christian to presume to be present at the detestable feast or wedding of Jews under pain of canonical punishment. And lest anyone should be able to err out of ignorance of our order, we have ordered that our prohibition be solemnly made public through the streets of the same city in that way which would be most suitable, adding that you should constrain under the form of law the contraveners or those rebellious to this our order – if there should be any – by ecclesiastical censure. Wherefore because, as we have learned afterwards from those worthy of belief, because not a few sons of iniquity and rebellion have presumed to be present at the unspeakable wedding of the said enemies of the cross of Christ, sharing in the same (wedding) and on many occasions honouring and showing respect to them (*ie*, the Jews) to the disparagement and scandal of Christians and the contumely of their own creator, holding our monitions in contempt and even (to be) worthless – each and every one of whom we have excommunicated in these writings – we firmly order and command you again by virtue of (your) obedience and under pain of canonical constraint that, having tolled the bells and burned the candles, you thus denounce publicly as excommunicate during the solemnities of masses through all the churches of the city and suburbs on Sundays and feast days all those who had been present at the

aforesaid feast or wedding, eating, drinking, playing, jesting, or exercising some function or other as an entertainer, or in some other way taking part in the same to the honour of those very (enemies of the cross of Christ) to the insult of the Christian faith until, returning to the bosom of holy mother church, about to receive a fitting punishment for their faults, I they will be worthy to receive the benefit of absolution. We have reserved especially for ourselves their absolution, revoking in anger whatever absolution has been put into effect regarding them up until now. But those who have associated with the aforesaid enemies of Christ, have shown respect to, or even honoured them in riding, in driving, in ornaments, in silk or gilt clothing, we propose to involve in the censure of a like sentence of excommunication unless they make satisfaction in a suitable way to God and the church for committing such a crime within eight days from the time of the publication of the present (letter). You, however, shall cause what you have done in the aforesaid matter, together with the names of the persons excommunicated, to be confirmed to us clearly and openly, before St Michael's Day. For we propose, lest such a great crime remain unpunished through your failure or neglect, to require that the said sentence (be) duly executed by others, if you omit (or) fail (to do) anything concerning the foregoing. Farewell. Given at Bosbury on 6 September in the year of the Lord, etc, (12)86.
...

1316–17
Cathedral Mass-pence Rolls   HCL: R407
mb 1   *(First quarter expenses)*
...
...And (he renders his account, that he) has paid to the little bishop on (Holy) Innocents' Day 4d....

1324–5
Cathedral Canons' Bakehouse Rolls   HCL: R632b
mb 1   *(External expenses)*
...
Likewise (he renders his account, that he) has paid in the little bishop's alms on Holy Innocents' Day 8d....
...

1334–5
Cathedral Canons' Bakehouse Rolls   HCL: R633
mb 1   *(External expenses)*
...
Likewise (spent) on the little bishop's alms on Holy Innocents' Day,
8 d....
...

1357–8
Cathedral Mass-pence Rolls   HCL: R436
mb 1   *(First quarter expenses)*
...
Next (he renders his account, that he) has paid to the little bishop for
one mass 4d....
...

1358–9
Household Accounts of Queen Isabella, Widow of Edward II
BL: Cotton Galba E xiv
f 52v   *(9 July)*

...For John Montsors, a harper, while performing his minstrelsy
before the lady queen at Hereford by gift of the same (lady queen) on
9 July, 6s 8d....

1360–1
Cathedral Mass-pence Rolls   HCL: R438
mb 1   *(First quarter expenses)*
...
Next (he renders his account, that he) has paid to the little bishop for
one mass, 4d....
...

1361–2
Cathedral Mass-pence Rolls   HCL: R439
mb 1   *(First quarter expenses)*
...
Next (he renders his account, that he) has paid to the little bishop,
4d....
...

1377–8
Cathedral Mass-pence Rolls   HCL: R444
mb 1   col 1
…
Next (he renders his account, that he) has paid to the little
bishop for one mass   4d
…

1401–2
Cathedral Canons' Bakehouse Rolls   HCL: R635
mb 1   *(Payments)*
…
(Paid) on the feast of the Holy Innocents to the same nine
canons and to the little bishop   6s 8d
…

1417–18
Cathedral Mass-pence Rolls   HCL: R470
mb 2
…
And he accounts for his payment to the little bishop being
there on Holy Innocents' Day falling in this year
according to the said paper (bill)   4d
…

1420–1
Cathedral Mass-pence Rolls   HCL: R472
mb 3

And (he accounts for his) payment to the little bishop
being there on Holy Innocents' Day falling in this year
according to the said paper (bill)   4d
…

1425–6
Cathedral Canons' Bakehouse Rolls   HCL: R637
mb 2   *(Payments)*
…
And he accounts for having paid to the little bishop for

wine on the feast of all the Holy Innocents falling within
the period of (this) account   8d

...

1440?
Mayor's Court Plea Book   HRO
f [4v]*   *(30 April)*

Memorandum:
4d by the
pledge of
John Theo.

On the same day, John Hanley and John Pewte bring an action against
Thomas Sporyour, (who is) of a free condition, for a plea of detention
for one book of plays, price 2s 4d. Pledges for the price (are) Thomas
Lewes, saddler, and Philip Moseley. And he is subject to bodily
attachment for the return (of the book?).

...

1463–4
Cathedral Canons' Bakehouse Rolls   HCL: R637a
mb 3   *(First half of year) (Payments)*

...

And paid for wine to the little bishop being present at
mass on the feast of the Holy Innocents this year   8d

...

mb 5d

...

...And paid to the little bishop for one nocturn on the
feast of the Holy Innocents according to the custom of
the church this year   one allowance of commons

...

1469–70
Cathedral Canons' Bakehouse Rolls   HCL: 637b
mb 2   *(Payments)*

...

And paid to the little bishop being present at mass on
the feast of the Holy Innocents   8d

...

c 1470
Cathedral Canons' Bakehouse Rolls   HCL: R630a
mb 1d

...

...Likewise paid to the little bishop for his nocturns on the feast of
the Holy Innocents according to the custom of the church this year,
one allowance of commons....

...

1470–80?
Cathedral Canons' Bakehouse Rolls   HCL: R637c
mb 3*   *(First half of year) (Payments)*

...

And paid for wine to the little bishop being present at
mass in the said first half of this year on the feast of the
Holy Innocents   8d

...

mb 5d

...

And paid to the little bishop for his nocturns, at matins,
being on the feast of the Invention of the Holy Cross
this year according to the custom of the
church   one allowance of commons

...

1533–4
Mayor's Account Rolls   HRO
mb 1d   *(20 October–19 October) (Allowances)*

...

Likewise (he seeks allowance of) 6s 8d paid to Thomas Downe, the
lord king's serjeant-at-mace, for working on the procession of the
feast of Corpus Christi together with various stories put on this year
(*or*, together with various visual representations put on this year).

...

Likewise (he seeks allowance of) 6s 8d paid to the lord king's minstrel/s
this year.
Likewise (he seeks allowance of) 20s paid to various gentlemen's
minstrels.

...

1543–4
Cathedral Canons' Bakehouse Rolls   HCL: R638
mb 2   *(First half of year) (Payments)*
...
And paid for wine for the little bishop being (present) at
mass during the first half of one year   1d
...

1553–4
Mayor's Account Rolls   HRO
mb 1d   *(23 October–22 October) (Allowances)*
...
Likewise (he seeks allowance of) 20s paid to the lord king's and
queen's minstrels this year.
...
Likewise (he seeks allowance of) 10s paid to various minstrels of
various gentlemen this year.
...

1577–8
Mayor's Account Rolls   HRO
mb 3d   *(30 September 1577–6 October 1578) (Allowances)*
...
Likewise (he seeks allowance of) 20s paid to various minstrels of
various gentlemen this year.
...
Likewise (he seeks allowance of) 26s 8d paid to various players in
interludes of various gentlemen this year.
...

1580–1
Mayor's Account Rolls   HRO
mb 4d   *(3 October–2 October) (Allowances)*
...
Likewise (he seeks allowance of) 20s paid to various minstrels of
various gentlemen this year.
...
Likewise (he seeks allowance of) 20s paid to various players of
interludes of various gentlemen this year.
...

1582–3
Mayor's Account Rolls HRO
mb 1d *(1 October–30 September) (Allowances)*
...
Likewise (he seeks allowance of) 20s paid to various minstrels of various gentlemen this year.
...
Likewise (he seeks allowance of) 13s 4d paid to various players of interludes of various gentlemen this year.
...

1587–8
Mayor's Account Rolls HRO
mb 3d *(2 October–30 September) (Allowances)*
...
Likewise (he seeks allowance of) 20s paid to various players this year.
...

1615–16
Mayor's Account Rolls HRO
mb 3 *(2 October–30 September) (Allowances)*
...
Likewise (he seeks allowance of) 40s paid and given to various players this year.
...

1627–8
Mayor's Account Rolls HRO
mb 4 *(1 October 1627–6 October 1628) (Allowances)*
...
Likewise (he seeks allowance of) 20s paid and given to various players this year.
...

HOLMER

1619
Acts of Decanal Court HCL
f 2v* *(18 December)*

⟨...⟩ Steevens for not presenting the names of dancers this last summer,

etc. °On 18 December 1619 he appeared before the lord dean, etc, and
the lord (dean) reported that a case should be specified in order to make
the article (*ie*, the charge) more clear, etc. °

...

KILPECK

1629

Archdeaconry of Hereford Acts of Office   HRO: box 25, vol 94
f [93]*   *(24 October)*

*Proceedings of the court held in the consistory of Hereford Cathedral
before Richard Basset, LLB, surrogate, and in the presence of Thomas
Duppa, notary public.*

...

Kenchurch
Ask about
those present
in law and
in fact.

Dismissal

Against Richard Watkins, detected for dancing out of his parish in the
parish of Kilpeck on Whit Monday last. °Having been sought on 16
October 1629 by ways and means (to appear) on the next (court day),
the said Watkins appeared in person in the cathedral church of
Hereford in the consistory there on 14 November 1629 before Master
John Freemantle, MA, deputy, etc, and when the article had been
charged against him, he confessed that the article was true. The lord
(deputy) accepted this confession insofar as, etc, and dismissed him
with a warning. °

KINGSLAND

1588/9

Diocese of Hereford Acts of Office   HRO: box 17, vol 68
f [65]   *(13 March)*

*Proceedings of the court held in the consistory of Hereford Cathedral
before Master William Grenewich, MA, deputy.*

...

Margaret Gwillim (was) cited (to appear) as of this day to show cause
why penances ought not to be enjoined on her on account of a defect
in clearing (herself) from the article, in English, that she did not dance
on Sunday in time of divine service. Having been publicly summoned
on this day, the said Margaret appeared and showed no cause, etc,
wherefore the lord (deputy) enjoined her to confess this article in the
usual garb and to certify (her compliance) on the next (court day).

John Berry
(He was) cited as above to show cause as above. On this day the
aforesaid John Berry appeared and showed no sufficient cause, etc.
Therefore the lord (deputy) enjoined him to confess as above and to
certify (his compliance) on the next (court day).

John Barrow likewise
On this day he appeared, etc, and the lord (deputy) enjoined him to
confess as above and to certify (his compliance) on the next (court day).

Richard Nelson likewise
On this day he appeared, etc, and the lord (deputy) enjoined him to
confess as above and to certify (his compliance) on the next (court day).

f [65v]

An
excommu-
nication was
promulgated.

Anne Gwillim (was) noted on suspicion, in English, for dancing at
time of divine services. °On this day she did not appear.°
...

1617
Diocese of Hereford Acts of Office   HRO: box 24a (formerly 18), vol 71
f [356v]*   *(30 June)*

Proceedings of the court held in the parish church of Leominster.
...
Thomas Waucklen, painter, detected by the churchwardens of
Kingsland.
Acted a play with others upon the sabbath day at time of evening
prayer. °Having been cited by public edict (to appear) as of the last
day of June aforesaid, (he was) summoned, etc. He did not appear,
etc, (and therefore he was) excommunicated.°

KINGTON

1618
Archdeaconry of Hereford Acts of Office   HRO: box 24, vol 90
f [86v]   *(26 October)*

Proceedings of the court held in the consistory of Hereford Cathedral
before Master Gabriel Wallwin, MA, deputy to Master Oliver Lloid,

LLD, official principal and commissary of Francis Godwin, bishop of Hereford.

...

Catherine Bybith, widow

Dismissal

For keeping drinking and dancing in her house in the time of evening prayer. °On this day the said Catherine appeared in person and, when the article had been charged against her, she confessed that the article was true. Therefore the lord (deputy) enjoined on her one day of penance in the manner of a penitent and to certify (her compliance) on the next (court day). Thereafter the lord (deputy) dismissed her with a warning. °

...

f [93]

...

Dismissal

Walter Bybith

For dancing on Sunday at evening prayer time in the house of Catherine Bybith. He appeared and denied (the article). After he had taken an oath, etc, the lord (deputy) dismissed him with a warning, etc.

Dismissal

William Driver

On the like (charge) in a like manner.

Dismissal

Elizabeth Moore

On the like (charge) in a like manner.

LEDBURY

1618

Archdeaconry of Hereford Acts of Office   HRO: box 24, vol 90

f [144v]*   *(16 November)*

Dismissal

Edward Hall, innkeeper

He, being an actor and morris dancer, and having gone out of the parish to other places with gun and drum both in the night to the disturbance of the king's subjects and the profanation of the sabbath day in the morning. °On 16 November, etc, the said Edward Hall appeared, etc, and upon an examination of the article, etc, and confessing, etc, the lord (deputy) enjoined him to confess the article in the usual garb, etc, before the minister and churchwardens after prayers, etc, and to certify (his compliance) on the next (court day). °

On 8 February aforesaid after introducing the form (of penance) with the certificate (he was) dismissed.

Edward Crocker, shoemaker

Dismissal On the like (charge). On that day (*ie*, 16 November) (he appeared and confessed) in like manner as above. On the last day of January 1618 according, etc (*ie*, according to English ecclesiastical practice), at Ledbury the said Crocker appeared in person before the honourable man, Master John Hoskins, LLD, deputy, etc, and certified on his oath the completion of (his) penance according, etc. Therefore (he was) dismissed.

Dismissal Edward Hooper on the like (charge). On that day (*ie*, 16 November) the said Hooper appeared in person and when the article had been charged against him he denied that the article was true. Therefore after he had taken an oath of his innocence (he was) therefore dismissed.
...

f [147v]

John Wilbore, fiddler.
Let him be cited for drunkenness and ribaldry.
°Having been cited (to appear) on 16 November aforesaid, etc, he did not appear.°
...

LEOMINSTER

1595
Archdeaconry of Hereford Acts of Office   HRO: box 20, vol 75
f [88v]*   *(2 September)*

Proceedings of the court held in the consistory of Hereford Cathedral before Master Francis Bevans, LLD, and in the presence of Thomas Crumpe, registrar.
...
An order of suspension was promulgated.†
James Waties, minstrel, (was) noted in English for playing at evensong to the dancers. °(He was) cited as above.°

An order of suspension was promulgated.†
Jane Price, alias Spinner
Noted, in English, for dancing at the time of evening prayers. °(She
was) cited by public decree in church, etc.°

Rose Morries in like manner.
°On that day the same (Morries) appeared and confesses the article.
Therefore the lord (judge) warned her hereafter, etc (*ie*, she should not
dance on Sunday).°

°Dismissal°   Anne Mered⟨.⟩ in like manner.
Dismissal   °On that day she appeared and confesses the article. Therefore the lord
              (judge) warned her hereafter, etc (*ie*, she should not dance on Sunday).°

              °Dismissal° Warning until the next (court day)†
              Joan ap Pricharde in like manner.
Dismissal   °On that day [she appeared and] upon an examination of the article,
              the lord (judge) warned her hereafter, etc (*ie*, she should not dance on
              Sunday).°

°Dismissal°   Joan Smyth in like manner.
Dismissal   On that day (she was warned) in like manner.
               …

LITTLE COWARNE

1609?
Archdeaconry of Hereford Acts of Office
HRO: box 22, unnumbered vol, pt 2
f [78v]*   *(16 December)*
…

Dismissal   John Bullock had dancing in his ⟨house⟩ on the sabbath day.
Let the   The said John Bullock, having been questioned also on ⟨oath⟩, (said
rest be   that he ?) heard, that is, that John Rawlins of Much ⟨Cowarne⟩,
cited.   Richard Powell of ⟨Ullingswick⟩, and others that he does not
                remember, ⟨…⟩ etc (*ie*, were present). And one *(blank)* Mason of
Let Richard   Bromyard was the ⟨…⟩. The lord (judge) accepted this confession and
Powell,   enjoined one ⟨day⟩ (of penance) on him in the church there, etc, and
servant of   to certify (his compliance) on the next (court day). Afterwards (he was)
Roger Burrox,   dismissed (with a warning that) hereafter, etc (*ie*, he should not have
be cited.   dancing in his house on Sunday).
Dismissal

On 16 December aforesaid the said Powell appeared and denied the article, etc. Therefore he has to ⟨clear⟩ ⟨..⟩ (himself ?) with two compurgators, honourable men of the aforesaid parish.
...

LLANGARREN

1616
Diocese of Hereford Acts of Office   HRO: box 24a (formerly 18), vol 70
f [96]*   *(31 May)*
...

Dismissal

The churchwardens
The youth of their parish has been always accustomed to exercise himself in dancing upon the sabbath days and holidays and that various profane exercises are used in our parish upon the sabbath days as in

To explain

other parishes, but we do hope for and pray for amendment. °On the last day of May 1616 the aforesaid (churchwardens), John Gwillim and John Edwardes, appeared in person and the lord (judge) enjoined them to exhibit a presentment on the next (court day). Then on 22 July aforesaid they appeared and the lord (judge), upon an examination of the case, held over the case until the churchwardens' next presentment there. Therefore (they were) dismissed. °

1628
Archdeaconry of Hereford Acts of Office   HRO: box 25, vol 93A
f [137]*   *(28 May)*

Proceedings of the court held in the consistory of Hereford Cathedral before Master Richard Basset, LLB, deputy to William Skinner, LLD, official and commissary of Francis Godwin, bishop of Hereford.
...

John Drewe (was) detected for playing on the jew's harp at prayer time. On 28 May 1628 the said Drewe appeared in person before Master Richard Basset, LLB, deputy, etc, in the consistory of Hereford. When the article had been charged against him, he denied that the article was true, etc. Then the lord (deputy) enjoined him to clear himself on the next (court day) with four compurgators, etc. Later he confessed that the article was true and submitted himself, etc. Then the lord (deputy) enjoined on him one day of penance in the manner of a penitent and warned him to copy out the form and

to certify (his compliance) on the next (court day), 18 June next.
...

f [132]*
...
Andrew Milles, minstrel, detected for dancing before evening prayer
on the sabbath day, being 4 May 1625, and for hiring a minstrel being
a recusant excommunicated.

f [140]   *(18 June)*

*Proceedings of the court held in the consistory of Hereford Cathedral
before Master John Freemantle, clerk, MA, surrogate, and in the
presence of James Lawrence, registrar.*
...
Against Jane Simons, detected for dancing on Sunday 4 May before
evening prayer, the minstrel being a recusant excommunicated. She
has to certify penance. °Having been summoned on that day, etc, she
did not appear in any way (*ie*, neither in person nor by proxy), etc.
Penalty (was) reserved for the next (court day), etc.°

f [143]*
...

Dismissal   Against John Drewe for playing on his jew's harp at prayer time. He
has to certify penance. °On that day (he was dealt with) in like manner
as above.° °On 23 August 1628 aforesaid in like manner.°

MADLEY

1605
Archdeaconry of Hereford Acts of Office   HRO: box 22, vol 82
p 16   *(10 September)*

*Proceedings of the court held in the consistory of Hereford Cathedral
before Master James Bailie, LLD, commissary, and in the presence of
James Coren, deputy registrar.*
...
Walter Smyth, Edward Shepard, the old churchwardens
(They are) to specify names, that is, of them that do dance on Sundays
Dismissal   and such as have not received three times a year. °They have to specify

Excommu-
nication

(these names) on the next (court day), etc. On 28 September they
appeared and because they had not specified (the names) according to
the warning, (they were) therefore excommunicated. On 12 October
1605 they appeared and, having been absolved, they specified the
names in writing and were dismissed. °

...

p 17*
...
The old churchwardens

Dismissal

(They are) to specify the names of those that do dance in the
churchyard. °They specified as above. °

1622
Acts of Decanal Court HCL
f 112v* *(28 September)*

Proceedings of the court held before the dean.
...
Roger Pigg

Dismissal

For playing on their instruments before evening prayer on sabbath
days. On that day he appeared. When the aforesaid article was charged
against him, he confesses and in like manner as above (he was)
dismissed.

James Paine

Dismissal

On the like (charge). On that day (he was) dismissed in like manner.

William Foote
For that as he passed toward the church in the churchyard (he) said
he would dance there in contempt and derogation of the
churchwarden.

The same Foote
For dancing before evening prayer time on Sunday 21 July. On that
day he appeared. When the aforesaid article was charged against him,
he denied, etc, wherefore the lord (dean) enjoined him to clear himself
with his six compurgators after a proclamation had been made, etc,
and he (was) warned, etc. °On that day, that is, on 12 October 1622
before Master Jones, etc, he did not appear when summoned. (He was)
excommunicated, etc. °

Matilda, servant of John Seybon
On the like (charge). On that day, although the citation introduced
(had been) executed in church by an announcement and (although she
had been) summoned, she did not appear. The lord (dean) pronounced
her contumacious (but) her penalty was reserved until the next (court
day).

Tiberton

°Dismissal°

Joan Brampton
On the like (charge). °On 12 October 1622 before Master Jones, etc,
she appeared and confessed, etc, wherefore the lord (judge) graciously
dismissed (her), etc, with a warning, etc.

Andrew Carwardine (and) William Foote
On the like (charge). °(They were cited) by ways and means.

Elizabeth Arnoll
On the like (charge). °On that day (she was) cited (to appear) on the
next (court day).°
...

f 116v   *(26 October)*

Proceedings of the court held before Master Jones, commissary.
...
William Foote
(He was) excommunicated for dancing before evening prayer on a
Sunday.
...

MANSELL GAMAGE

1609?
Archdeaconry of Hereford Acts of Office
HRO: box 22, unnumbered vol, pt 2
f [51] col 1*   *(24 November)*
...

To summon the dancers, that is:
Mary Lurcot – dismissal.
Anne Lurcot – dismissal.
Alice Withell – dismissal.

Elinor, servant of Thomas Withell – [excommunication] dismissal.
Richard Milward – he appeared. Dismissal.
Anne Smith – (she was) summoned. Dismissal with warning.
Roger Vaughan – (he was) summoned on the next (court day and
appeared). Dismissal.

col 2

Thomas Churche
For dancing on sabbath days. (He was) cited by public decree (and)
summoned, etc (*ie*, he did not appear and was excommunicated). On
24 November aforesaid the said Thomas Churche appeared and the
lord (judge) revoked (his) excommunication, etc. And upon an
examination of the aforesaid article, the lord (judge) enjoined him that,
etc. Afterwards (he was) examined about the rest of the dancers there,
etc: seven were present.

7 dancers.

MUCH BIRCH

1610?
Archdeaconry of Hereford Acts of Office
HRO: box 22, unnumbered vol, pt 2
f [110]*
...

The same
James hindered
⟨...⟩ and the
judicial process
⟨...t⟩ing the
dancers, etc.

James Howell for dancing as above ⟨...⟩. The said James ⟨Howell⟩
appeared, etc, (and) because he refused to reply, etc, although often
asked by the judge, etc, the lord (judge) pronounced the same (Howell)
excommunicate ⟨...⟩. °On 15 July in the aforesaid year the said James
Howell appeared, etc, and submitted himself, etc. The lord (judge)
absolved him and restored ⟨...⟩. Therefore the lord (judge) dismissed
him with a warning, etc.°

Philip Howell
On the like (charge).
(He was) cited by public decree as above ⟨...⟩ (and) he appeared, etc.

Excommu-
nication

(He was) dismissed. On 15 July, the same Philip (was) likewise
absolved with a warning.

With remission ...

MUCH DEWCHURCH

1609?
Archdeaconry of Hereford Acts of Office
HRO: box 22, unnumbered vol, pt 2
f [108v]*   *(16 December)*
...

Thomas Kethewne
On 16 December 1605, for dancing on Sundays. On that day he appeared, etc, (and) confessed the article, etc. Thereupon the lord (judge) enjoined one day of penance on him, etc, and to certify (his compliance) on the next (court day).

MUCH MARCLE

1618–19
Archdeaconry of Hereford Acts of Office   HRO: box 24, vol 90
f [237v]*   *(7 December)*

Thomas Gorwey (was) cited for playing on Sunday, etc, (to appear) as of 7 December aforesaid. (He was) summoned (and) did not appear, etc, (and was) excommunicated. On 10 December 1618 the said Gorwey appeared in person at Hereford before Master Gabriel Wallwin, MA, deputy, etc, and at his petition the lord (deputy) absolved him (from the sentence of excommunication) after he had first taken an oath to obey the law and observe the commandments of the church. Then when the article had been charged against him, he confessed that the article was true. Therefore, after examining the case, the lord (deputy) dismissed him with a warning.
[margin: Dismissal]

Roger Parker (was) cited on the like (charge), etc, by public decree (to appear) as of 7 December aforesaid. (He was) summoned, etc, (and) did not appear, etc, (and was) excommunicated. On 6 February aforesaid he appeared and at his petition the lord (judge) absolved him from the sentence of excommunication, etc, and upon an examination of the case dismissed him with a warning.
[margin: Dismissal]

William Jenkins on the like (charge). On 7 December aforesaid (he did not appear) in like manner as above (and was excommunicated). On 6 February aforesaid he appeared and the lord (judge) absolved him from the sentence of excommunication, etc, and upon an examination
[margin: Dismissal]

of the case warned him (that) hereafter (he should not play on Sunday).

(5 December)

Thomas Hamon on the like (charge). On 5 December aforesaid the said Hamon appeared in person and when the article had been charged against him, he confessed that the article was true. Therefore the lord (judge) enjoined upon him to confess the article before the minister and churchwardens there next Sunday in the usual garb immediately after prayers are finished in the church there and to certify (his compliance) on the next (court day). Afterwards the lord (judge) dismissed him with a warning.

Dismissal

John Ravenhill for the like. On 5 December (his case was heard) in like manner as above.

Dismissal

(18 December)

William Edwardes on the like (charge). (He was) cited, etc, (to appear) on 18 December 1618 in the cathedral church of Hereford in the consistory there before Master Gabriel Wallwin, MA, deputy, etc. The said Edwardes appeared in person and when the article had been charged against him he confessed that the article was true. Therefore the lord (deputy) warned him that hereafter (he should not play on Sunday). – On 4 November 1620 he appeared before Master John Osgood, MA, deputy, etc, and the lord (deputy) at his petition absolved him from the sentence of excommunication and, when the case had been heard, the lord (deputy) dismissed him with a warning.

Dismissal

Look for the rest.

…

PEMBRIDGE

1617
Diocese of Hereford Acts of Office   HRO: box 24a (formerly 18), vol 71
f [358v]* *(2 June)*

Lewis Thomas danced in the church porch among a company of girls of the parish not known. (He was) sought, etc, (to appear) as of this day and at this place. Having been summoned, etc, he did not appear, etc. (He was) cited, etc, by ways and means (to appear) on the next (court day). (When he did not appear, he was then cited) by public decree (to appear) as of 3 September aforesaid. (He was) summoned (and) did not appear, etc, (and was) excommunicated.

Matthew Steade, minstrel

Dismissal   On that day (his case was dealt with) in like manner as above.
Afterwards the lord (judge) dismissed him.

...

PUTLEY

1625
Acts of Decanal Court   HCL
f 170v*   *(22 October)*

*Proceedings of the court held before Master Jones and in the presence
of the registrar.*

Christopher Jones
Detected for dancing every Sunday and holiday for the most part
between Easter and Lammas. °On that day he appeared and confessed,
etc. Therefore the lord (judge) dismissed him with a warning, etc.°

Alice Harris for dancing.

John Lambert the younger
On the like (charge). °On that day (his case was dealt with) in like
manner.°

Henry Carpenter
On the like (charge). °On that day (his case was dealt with) in like
manner.°

John Boulcott
[(He was) warned to pay under pain of excommunication.]†
On the like (charge). °On that day the said Boulcott appeared in person
and at his petition the lord (judge) dismissed him, etc. He paid (his
court fee).°

...

f 174ᵃv*   *(19 November)*

...

Alice Harris

Dismissal   She was noted for dancing upon sabbath days before evening prayer.
She appeared on 19 November 1625 before Master Osgood, surrogate,

etc. When the aforesaid article had been charged against her, she confessed that the same (article) was true and submitted herself, etc. Therefore the lord (surrogate) dismissed the same (Harris) with a warning.

...

ROSS

1616–17
Diocese of Hereford Acts of Office   HRO: box 24a (formerly 18), vol 71
f [214]   *(9 December)*

Proceedings of the court held in Hereford Cathedral before Master Silas Griffithes, STD, vicar general of Robert Bennett, bishop of Hereford, and in the presence of James Lawrence, notary public.
...

Dismissal

Thomas Meiricke the younger, glover, for dancing and playing at unlawful games on the sabbath day. °On that day he appeared in person and, upon an examination of the article, he was dismissed with a warning, etc.°

Dismissal

John Tayler, tapster, on the like (charge). °Having been cited (to appear) on this day and in this place, etc, (and) having been summoned, etc, (he did not appear and therefore was) excommunicated.° Later, while the court was sitting, the said Tayler appeared in person and when the article had been charged against him he confessed that the article was true. Therefore the lord (vicar general) dismissed him with a warning.

Dismissal

Anthony Harbert on the like (charge). °(He was) sought, etc, by ways and means (to appear) on the next (court day), etc.° The said Harbert appeared in person on 20 January aforesaid and when the article had been charged against him he confessed that the article was true. Therefore the lord dismissed him with a warning.

Dismissal

Francis Younge, weaver, on the like (charge). °On that day he appeared and upon an examination of the article he was dismissed with a warning, etc.°

Dismissal

Alice Barrett on the like (charge). °Having been cited (to appear) on this day and at this place, etc, (and) having been summoned, etc, she appeared in no way (*ie*, neither in person nor by proxy), etc. Afterwards, the lord (vicar general) dismissed her with a warning in the person of (her) husband. °

...

ff [215–15v]   *(10 February)*

...

Dismissal

William Meiricke for dancing on Sunday. He appeared on 10 February aforesaid and when the article had been charged against him he confessed that the article was true. Therefore the lord (vicar general) dismissed him with a warning.

Dismissal

Robert Meiricke on the like (charge). On 10 February aforesaid (his case was dealt with) in like manner as above.

(She is) dismissed elsewhere.†
Alice Meiricke on the like (charge). |

Dismissal

John Maddox on the like (charge). On 10 February aforesaid, after an examination of the case, the lord (vicar general) dismissed him with a warning.

Dismissal

Walter Pearce on the like (charge). On 10 February aforesaid (his case was dealt with) in like manner as above.

Dismissal

Thomas Meiricke on the like (charge). Having been sought (to appear) as of 10 February aforesaid, etc, (and) having been summoned, etc, he did not appear, etc. (He was cited again) by ways and means (to appear) on the next (court day). Later on 14 February 1616 he appeared and confesses the article. Therefore the lord (vicar general) dismissed him with a warning, etc.

f [249]

Proceedings of the court held in the consistory of Hereford Cathedral before Master Silas Griffithes, STD, vicar general of Robert Bennett, bishop of Hereford.

...

Bridstow
Dismissal

Alice Durley for dancing at Ross on Sunday. She appeared on 10 February aforesaid and when the article had been charged against her she confessed that the article was true. Therefore the lord (vicar general) dismissed her with a warning, etc.

Dismissal   Margaret Andros on the like (charge). On 10 February aforesaid (her case was dealt with) in like manner as above.

(3 March)

Dismissal   Alice Meiricke on the like (change). °Having been cited (to appear) as of 3 March aforesaid, etc, (she appeared and) after an examination of the case she was dismissed with a warning, etc.°

1621
Archdeaconry of Hereford Acts of Office   HRO: box 24, vol 91, pt 2
f [41] *(6 October)*

Proceedings of the court held in Hereford Cathedral before Master Gabriel Wallwin, MA, deputy to Master Oliver Lloid, LLD, official principal and commissary of Francis Godwin, bishop of Hereford.

...

Dismissal   William Davies, the furnish keeper
For dancing upon the sabbath day before all service was ended. Having been cited last Thursday in Ross by Gibbons, an apparitor, to appear as of this day and at this place, (and) having been summoned, he did not appear (and he was) excommunicated. °On 16 April 1622 in the registrar's office before Master Evan Jones, surrogate, etc, and in the presence of me, William Rawe, notary public, etc, Master Buckly appeared and at his petition the lord (surrogate) absolved and dismissed the said Davies.°

...

1629
Archdeaconry of Hereford Acts of Office   HRO: box 25, vol 94
ff [252v–4]*

...

Edward Keise is noted as above for playing upon Tuesday 26 May 1629 at time of evening prayer, (and was) sought by ways and means on 18 June 1629 (to appear) on the next (court day). °Having been cited on 5 July in the aforesaid parish by Richard Gibbons, an apparitor, (to appear) on 14 July aforesaid (he was) summoned and did not appear, etc. (He was) excommunicated.° On 23 September 1629 in the parish church of Ross before Master Richard Bicket, MA, deputy, etc, the said Keise appeared in person and the lord (deputy) at his petition absolved him from the sentence of excommunication, after (his) oath had first been taken to obey the law, etc. Then, when the article had been charged against him, he confessed that the article was true and submitted himself, etc (ie, to the judgement of the court). Therefore the lord (deputy) enjoined him to confess the article immediately after the gospel reading in the usual garb, etc. And he (the lord deputy) warned him (Keise) to copy out (the form) and to certify (his compliance) on the next (court day).|

John Wilse is noted as above on the like (charge) as in the last (case). On 18 June instant (he was cited) in Ross by Gibbons, just as he (Gibbons) swore, (to appear) on 25 June aforesaid. (He was) summoned and did not appear. (He was) likewise excommunicated by Master Basset on 23 September aforesaid.

Dismissal   John Machin is noted as above for dancing the morris in time of evening prayer. (He was) cited (to appear) on 25 June instant as above, summoned, etc, and (he) did not appear. The lord (deputy), Basset, pronounced him contumacious (but) his penalty was reserved until the next (court day). °On 14 July 1629 (he was) summoned and did not appear, etc, (and he was) excommunicated.° On 23 September 1629 aforesaid he appeared and was absolved and dismissed with a warning.

Dismissal   James Streete is noted as above on the like (charge). °Having been cited on 5 July 1629 in the aforesaid parish by Richard Gibbons, an apparitor, (to appear) on 14 July aforesaid (and) having been summoned, he appeared and the lord (deputy) warned him and dismissed him.°

Dismissal   Thomas Parret is noted as above on the like (charge). He appeared on 27 June 1629 in the cathedral church of Hereford at the consistory there and when the article had been charged against him he denied that the article was true. Therefore after he had taken an oath affirming his innocence (he was dismissed).|

(She) went away.   Lettice Vaughan is noted as above on the like (charge).

Jane Currier is noted as above on the like (charge). (She was) cited (and) sought, etc, on 8 June 1629 by ways and means (to appear) on the next (court day). °(She was) cited on 2 July 1629 in the aforesaid parish by Richard Gibbons, an apparitor, (to appear) on 14 July 1629 (and) summoned, and she did not appear, etc. (She was) excommunicated. °

Thomas Browne is noted as above on the like (charge). (He was) cited, etc, on 8 June 1629 in Ross by Gibbons, etc, as he (Gibbons) swore, (to appear) on 25 June aforesaid, (and) summoned, etc, and he did not appear. (He was) excommunicated by Master Basset. On 23 September 1629 aforesaid he appeared and was absolved by Master Bicket and was dismissed with a warning.

Dismissal

Robert Smith is noted as above on the like (charge). (He was) sought, etc, on 8 June 1629 by ways and means (to appear) on the next (court day). °(He was) cited on 7 July 1629 in the aforesaid parish by Richard Gibbons, an apparitor, (to appear) on 14 July 1629 (and) summoned and he did not appear, etc. (He was) excommunicated. °|

Anne Cater is noted as above on the like (charge). On 25 June aforesaid (she was summoned and failed to appear) in like manner. On 1 September 1629 in the consistory of Hereford before Master Evan Jones, MA, deputy, etc, after the citation personally executed on 26 August last by Gibbons, an apparitor, within the aforesaid parish as he swore had been introduced, (and) after the said Cater had been summoned three times and appeared in no way (*ie*, neither in person nor by proxy), the lord (deputy) pronounced her contumacious and under the penalty of excommunication. On 23 September 1629 aforesaid (her case was dealt with) in like manner as in the action against Browne.

Dismissal

John Sandie is noted as above on the like (charge). On 25 June aforesaid (he was summoned) in like manner. °(He was) cited on 1 July 1629 in the aforesaid parish by Richard Gibbons, an apparitor, (to appear) on 14 July 1629 (and) summoned and he did not appear, etc. (He was) excommunicated by Master Basset. °

Wallford

Henry Baker is noted as above for playing at evening prayer time. On 27 June 1629 at Hereford before Master Richard Basset, LLB, deputy, etc, the said Baker appeared in person and when the article had been charged against him he denied that the article was true. Then after he had taken an oath affirming his innocence, the lord (deputy) dismissed him.

Dismissal   Walter Garden is noted as above for dancing at evening prayer time.
°He appeared on 27 June 1629 in the consistory, etc, before Richard
Basset, surrogate, etc, and he took an oath affirming his innocence and
the lord (surrogate) dismissed him.°

Dismissal   Gregory Harris is noted as above on the like (charge). °On 27 June
1629 in the consistory, etc, before Richard Basset, surrogate, etc, the
said Harris appeared and took an oath affirming his innocence and that
he was at evening prayer. The lord (surrogate) dismissed him.°

ff 255–5v*   (28 July)
...
John Bennet the younger
From the neighbourhood of Ross. He is noted for dancing upon
Sundays and holidays at time of evening prayer and especially upon
By Thomas   Tuesday 26 May 1629 and especially for attending my lord upon 28
Parret   June 1629 at time of prayers as is thought. (He was) cited on 22 July
William Spicer 1629 in the aforesaid parish by Richard Gibbons, an apparitor, (to
appear) on 28 July aforesaid (and) summoned and he did not appear,
etc. (He was cited again) by ways and means. On 1 September 1629
aforesaid he appeared and when the case had been heard, the lord
(judge), Jones, warned and dismissed him.

Robert Younge is noted as above on the like (charge). °He went away.°

John Mason is noted as above on the like (charge). °(He was) cited on
Dismissal   23 July 1629 in the aforesaid parish by Richard Gibbons, an apparitor,
(to appear) on 28 July 1629 (and) summoned and he did not appear.
(He was) excommunicated.° Later while the court was sitting the said
Mason appeared in person and at his petition the lord (deputy) revoked
the decree of excommunication. Later when the article had been
charged against him he confessed that the article was true and
submitted himself, etc. The lord (deputy) accepted this confession
that, etc (ie, that the article was true), and dismissed him with a
warning.

Dismissal   Walter Collie is noted as above on the like (charge). °(He was) sought.°|

Let there be no proceedings against the same Probin.†
Thomas Probin is noted on the like (charge).

Let there be no proceedings against him.†
Walter Collie is noted on the like (charge).

Dismissal Joan Bennet is noted on the like (charge). °(She was) cited on 20 July
1629 in the aforesaid parish by Richard Gibbons, an apparitor, (to
appear) on 28 July aforesaid (and), having been summoned,° °she
appeared in person on 28 July 1629 in the consistory before Master
John Freemantle, deputy, etc. And when the article had been charged
against her, etc, she confessed that it was true, etc. Therefore the lord
(deputy) warned her that thereafter, etc. And so she was dismissed, the
costs having been reserved, etc.°

Let there be no proceedings against her†
°because she is under legal age. °†
Alice Bennet is noted on the like (charge).
...

f [256]*

William Perrocke is noted for dancing at evening prayer time upon
Sundays and holidays. °(He was) sought on 19 July 1629 (and then
cited) on 28 July aforesaid by ways and means (to appear) on the next
(court day).°

Charles Perrocke is noted on the like (charge). °(He was) cited on 19
July 1629 in the aforesaid parish by Richard Gibbons, an apparitor,
(to appear) on 28 July aforesaid (and), having been summoned,° °the
said Pirrocke appeared in person. And when the article had been
charged against him he denied that the article was true and submitted
himself to compurgation, etc. Therefore the lord enjoined him to clear
himself in this place on 1 September aforesaid with four witnesses, etc,
after he had made an announcement beforehand. On 1 September 1629
aforesaid in the consistory of Hereford before Master Evan Jones, MA,
deputy, etc, (he was) summoned, etc, and did not appear. The lord
(deputy) pronounced him contumacious and to have failed in his
compurgation, and decreed that he be cited for the next (court day),
etc.°

Mary Collie is noted on the like (charge). °(She was) sought in like
manner.°

Alice Haynes is noted on the like (charge). °(She was) cited in the aforesaid parish on 23 June 1629 by Richard Gibbons, an apparitor, (to appear) on 28 July aforesaid (and), having been summoned, °°she appeared and (her case was dealt with) in like manner as in the action against Joan Bennet.°

Dismissal

Thomas Webster is noted on the like (charge). °(He was) cited in like manner (to appear) on 28 July 1629 (and), having been summoned, ° °the said Webster appeared in person. And when the article had been charged against him he denied that the article was true and submitted himself, etc. Then the lord (surrogate) enjoined him to clear himself in this place with four compurgators, etc, after he had made an announcement beforehand. On 1 September 1629 aforesaid (his case was dealt with) in like manner as in the action against Perrocke. Later he appeared and the lord (deputy) upon hearing the case dismissed him with a warning.°

Dismissal

September

f [76]*   *(24 October)*

Proceedings of the court held in the consistory of Hereford Cathedral before Richard Basset, LLB, surrogate, and in the presence of William Rawe, notary public.
...

Edward Keise is noted 'ex officio' (as) one who should be reported on the basis of public rumour for playing upon Tuesday 26 May 1629 at time of evening prayer (and so) he has to certify (his) confession on this day. °(He was) summoned on that day and did not appear, etc, (and he was) excommunicated. ° °On 5 December 1629 the said Keise appeared in person in the cathedral church of Hereford in the consistory there before Master Richard Bicket, MA, deputy, etc. And he introduced the form and certified the completion of penance according, etc, by his oath. Therefore he was dismissed (and) afterward was absolved.°

Dismissal

John Wilse is noted as above on the like (charge) in like manner. °On that day (he was) excommunicated in like manner. ° °On 5 December aforesaid (his case was dealt with) in like manner.°
...

Dismissal

William Perrocke is noted, etc, for dancing at evening prayer time upon Sundays and holidays, (and cited) by ways and means (to appear) on this day. °On that day (his case) is held over for the next (court day).

On 14 November 1629 after the said Perrocke (was) summoned three times (and) after a decree of ways and means had been introduced, (which had been issued) finally on 8 November 1629 as appears on the back of the same (decree), he did not even appear in any way (*ie*, neither in person nor by proxy). The lord (judge), Freemantle, pronounced him contumacious and under the penalty of excommunication.°

1633
Archdeaconry of Hereford Acts of Office   HRO: box 26, vol 96
f [502]   *(30 October)*

Proceedings of the court held in the consistory of Hereford Cathedral before William Skinner, LLD, and in the presence of Thomas Lawrence, notary public.

...

He performed penance elsewhere.
Against Nicholas Gates detected for dancing upon Sundays and holy days before divine service was ended.

Dismissal
Against Thomas Simondes detected on the like (charge). °On 11 December aforesaid he appeared and when the article had been charged against him he denied that the article was true. Then, after he had taken an oath affirming his innocence, he was dismissed.°

Now of Madley Against John Torence detected on the like (charge).

ST WEONARDS

1609
Archdeaconry of Hereford Acts of Office
HRO: box 22, unnumbered vol, pt 2
f [108v]*   *(11 December)*

Proceedings of the court held before Master Gabriel Wallwin, MA, deputy.

St Weonards
⟨...⟩ on 11 December before Master Gabriel Wallwin, MA, surrogate. Excommunicated for ⟨...⟩.†
It appears in the aforesaid sections ⟨...⟩.†
W⟨...⟩ M⟨...⟩ners gentleman for dancing on sabbath days, etc. On 11

December 1609 he appeared and ⟨...⟩ he (the deputy) absolved him ⟨...⟩
and restored, etc.

...

SHOBDEN

1586/7
Diocese of Hereford Acts of Office   HRO: box 17, vol 66
f [218v]   *(9 March)*

*Proceedings of the court held in the parish church of Leominster before
Master Roger Bradshawe, MA, deputy to Master Francis Bevans, LLD,
vicar general of Herbert Westfaling, bishop of Hereford.*
...
Against Humphrey Tailer of the same (parish).

April

Noted, in English, for keeping dancing and playing, for permitting
the same in time of divine services. (He was) cited by Jones, an
apparitor, etc, (and) publicly summoned, etc. The same Humphrey
Tayler appeared and (was) examined, etc, and upon an examination,
etc, he denied the same (charge was true), etc. Therefore he has to
introduce a schedule (of completion of penance) on the next (court
day) from the vicar and churchwardens there, etc.

...

TEDSTONE DELAMERE

1602
Archdeaconry of Hereford Acts of Office   HRO: box 21, vol 80, pt 3
p 60 col 1*   *(1 October)*

*Proceedings of the court held in the consistory of Hereford Cathedral
before Master James Bailie, LLD, guardian of spiritualities during
vacancy, and in the presence of James Lawrence, notary public.*
...
Richard Brooke and Peter Corbet of Avenbury (were) cited by an
apparitor, etc, (and) did not appear, etc. (They were)
excommunicated.

Let (each one cited) from this wanton crowd be asked especially about
the taborer.

Elizabeth Grenewich, Peter Corbet of Avenbury, Richard Brooke of Avenbury, (and) James Younge of Tedstone aforesaid (were) cited for being present at this kind of profanation on the basis of that Miles' confession.

col 2

Miles Conney
For profaning the sabbath day and dancing and revelling with morris dances at time of divine service and namely on 8 August last, being Sunday, and would not desist albeit he was admonished thereof by Mr Grenewich. On that day the said Miles Conney appeared, who, after (having been) examined on oath, confessed that the article, etc (ie, that it was true). Therefore, the lord (judge) ordered him to confess the article in the church there in the usual garb, etc, and to certify (his compliance) on the next (court day). And he has to declare the names of the rest of those present, etc. °On 26 October aforesaid, after the said Conney had been summoned, Thomas Conney, father of that Miles, appeared and on his oath he certified (Miles') penance: therefore (Miles was) dismissed. Then Thomas Launcie and Thomas Conney appeared and they confessed, etc (ie, that the article was true). Therefore, they had to confess the article as above (ie, in church in penitential clothing) and to certify (their compliance) on the next (court day). Afterward Corbet appeared and confessed; he has a penance as above, etc. On 16 November, after the form (of penance) had been introduced he (the judge) dismissed him (Corbet). Thomas Launcie, Thomas Conney, and Peter Corbet have certified (their penance) on oath, therefore (they have been) dismissed ⟨....⟩°
...

p 70*   (16 November)

Avenbury   Henry Boyce for dancing the morris at Tedstone and revelling on the sabbath day in time of divine service. On 16 November aforesaid the said Henry Boyce appeared and confessed. Therefore he has to do penance according, etc (ie, according to the schedule), and to certify (his compliance) on the next (court day). On 8 December he appeared and did not certify and should deliver (his) certificate on the next (court day).

°Outside the   William Boulter on the like (charge).

diocese.°   Philip Howles on the like (charge). On 16 November aforesaid (he appeared and confessed) in like manner. On 8 December aforesaid (his case was dealt with) in like manner as above.

(8 December)
Cited (to appear) on the next (court day).†

Tedstone   Richard Conney on the like (charge). On 8 December aforesaid the
Dismissal   said Richard Conney appeared and denied (that the article was true). Therefore he was warned, etc.

Cited (to appear) on the next (court day).†

Dismissal   Tace Richardes on the like (charge). On 8 December aforesaid the said Tace appeared and was warned to reform herself, etc.

Cited (to appear) on the next (court day).†

Dismissal   Rebecca Tower on the like (charge). On 8 December she appeared and was warned, etc.

Cited (to appear) on the next (court day).†

Dismissal   William Morries on the like (charge). On 8 December he appeared and denied the article. Therefore (he was) dismissed.

Cited (to appear) on the next (court day).†

Dismissal   Jane Conney on the like (charge). On 8 December she appeared and was warned, etc.

Cited (to appear) on the next (court day).†

Dismissal   Anthony Conney on the like (charge). On 8 December aforesaid he appeared and was warned, etc.

Cited (to appear) on the next (court day).†

Of Cradley   James Henge in like manner.
...

p 75
...
Avenbury   Elizabeth Wiett, servant of William Collie, is noted for being at a morris dance at Tedstone on a Sunday at time of divine service.

Jane Somers on the like (charge).

...

1602/3
Archdeaconry of Hereford Acts of Office   HRO: box 21, vol 80, pt 4
p 21*   *(12 January)*

*Proceedings of the court held in the consistory of Hereford Cathedral
before Master James Bailie, LLD, commissary during vacancy.*

Avenbury

Dismissal

Before Master
William
Grenewich

Henry Boyce
For dancing and ⟨...⟩ time of divine service ⟨...⟩ until today to the extent
that the certificate ⟨...⟩ (allows ?). °On that day after a certificate had
been introduced by Parrat ⟨...⟩ of penance by some ⟨...⟩ of completion
(of penance ?) ⟨...⟩, etc.°
(He appeared) before Master William Grenewich, deputy, (and was
dismissed).

Dismissal

Philip Howles
On the like (charge). The certificate (*ie*, the order for production of
a certificate) ⟨...⟩ was carried over until today. °On that day, after the
penitential form with the certificates on the back about the completion
of penance, etc, had been introduced, (he was) dismissed.°

°Freely absolved at Master Grenewich's request.°

(5 February)
°Cited (to appear) on the next (court day). °†

Cradley

Dismissal

Excommu-
nication

With remission

°James Younge on the like (charge). (He was) cited by Parrat (to appear)
on 5 February aforesaid (and) summoned. He did not appear, etc. °°On
7 March 1602 before Master St Barbe, deputy, etc, Richard Parret
appeared and for and in the name of Younge, having been duly
appointed in this matter by the said Younge, he sought that the benefit
of absolution be bestowed on the said Younge, etc. Therefore the lord
(deputy) absolved him, the aforesaid Younge, in the person of the said
Parret and appointed, etc, and after a due consideration of this case
had taken place through the information of Master Grenewich, he
dismissed him from his office (?).°

°Let her be asked as (above). °†
Joyce Lane on the like (charge).
(She was) excommunicated.

With remission

°Let him be asked as above.°

°Whitborne°   °Richard Brooke. (He was) excommunicated in like manner.°
With remission   ...

p 24   *(2 March)*

...

Dismissal. Cited (to appear) on the next (court day).†

Avenbury   Elizabeth Wiett, servant of William Collie
For being at a morris dance at Tedstone on a Sunday at time of divine
service. °On 2 March she appeared and confessed the article. Therefore
she was warned, etc.°

Cited (to appear) on the next (court day).†

Dismissal   Jane Sommers on the like (charge). °On 2 March Master Wallwin
dismissed her upon hope of amendment.°

...

1605

Archdeaconry of Hereford Acts of Office   HRO: box 22, vol 82
p 214   *(11 September)*

*Proceedings of the court held in the consistory of Hereford Cathedral
before Master James Bailie, LLD, commissary to Richard Bancroft,
archbishop of Canterbury, and in the presence of James Coren, notary
public and registrar.*

John Wikes detected for receiving morris dancers of the parish of
Bromyard and other parishes thereabouts upon the sabbath day at the
time of divine service, that is, at evening prayer time. °On that day
he appeared and on his oath affirmed that he had not offended as in
the aforesaid article. Thus (he was) warned and dismissed.°

...

1613/14
Archdeaconry of Hereford Acts of Office   HRO: box 24, vol 89
f [69v]   *(23 February)*

*Proceedings of the court held in the consistory of Hereford Cathedral
before Master John Richardson, STD, deputy to Robert Bennett, bishop
of Hereford.*

…

John Wilkes for keeping of dancing, tipling, and drinking in his house
on Sundays. °(He was) cited by an apparitor (to appear) on 23 February
1613, as he (the apparitor) claims, etc, (and) summoned. He did not
appear (and) was excommunicated. °

…

WELLINGTON

1613
Archdeaconry of Hereford Acts of Office   HRO: box 23, vol 88
f 156*

…

Excommu-
nication

Thomas Jones
For profaning the sabbath day in dancing. °(He was) cited by public
decree in church (to appear) as of 10 May aforesaid and according to
the certificate of Brooke, an apparitor. °

…

1620–1
Acts of Decanal Court   HCL
f 55   *(2 December)*

*Proceedings of the court held in the dean's consistory of Hereford
Cathedral before the dean.*

…

Marden

William Edwardes
For dancing the morris at Wellington on a sabbath day before evening
prayer. °On that day, having been cited and summoned, he did not

Dismissal

appear. (He was) excommunicated. °On 20 January 1620 he appeared
before Master Jones, etc. At his petition the lord (dean) absolved the
same (Edwardes) (from excommunication), etc. Then, after the article

had been charged (against him), he confessed. Therefore at his petition the lord (dean) dismissed the same (Edwardes) with a warning, etc.

...

WELSH NEWTON

1619
Archdeaconry of Hereford Acts of Office   HRO: box 24, vol 90
f [176]   *(September)*

Proceedings of the court held in the consistory of Hereford Cathedral before Master Gabriel Wallwin, surrogate, and in the presence of Thomas Crumpe, registrar.

...

°See below: he was absent. °†

Against William Rice

12 November

Detected for lord of misrule. °On that day he appeared and denied, etc. Therefore he has to clear himself on the next (court day), etc, with four compurgators, etc, after he had made an announcement, etc. On 12 November aforesaid, having been summoned, etc, he appeared in no way (*ie*, neither in person nor by proxy), etc. (He was) cited (to appear) on the next (court day) to tell the reasons, etc, why, etc (*ie*, to show cause why he should not be deemed to have failed in his compurgation). (He was) cited (to appear) on 4 December aforesaid, etc, (and) summoned, etc. (He did not appear and was) excommunicated. °

Against Denise Watkins

Detected for lady of misrule. °(She was) sought, etc, by ways and means (to appear) on the next (court day), etc; (the citation to appear) was made public in church from last Sunday for a week. (She was) summoned, etc, (and did not appear). (She was) excommunicated. °

f [178]*   *(4 December)*

...

Llangarren

Dismissal

Against Thomas Fletcher

Detected for playing on his instrument in Welsh Newton in evening prayer time and being demanded by the churchwardens and sworn man why he did not come to church, he answered them that if they would bring the church to the place where they played they would come to church.

°(He was) sought, etc, by ways and means (to appear) on the next (court day). (He was) cited by public decree (to appear), etc, on 28 November, etc. (Having been cited to appear, he was) summoned on 4 December 1619, etc, (and) appeared in no way (*ie*, neither in person nor by proxy), etc. (He was) excommunicated.° °On 20 December 1619 Thomas Phillips appeared in the cathedral church of Hereford at the consistory there before Master Gabriel Wallwin, MA, deputy, etc. At his petition the lord (deputy) revoked the decree of excommunication and, upon an examination of the case, dismissed him with a warning.°

Against his servant
Detected on the like (charge).
...

WINFORTON

1616?
Diocese of Hereford Acts of Office   HRO: box 24a (formerly 18), vol 70
f [26]*
...
Nicholas Vocle detected by the rector there (who) admonished his parishioner he would have no dancing on Sunday. He answered he would have it in despite of Sir Priest or Sir Parson. This Vocle is the chief factor of it upholden and maintained. °(The detection) is referred to the next presentment of the churchwardens and parishioners (for more information).°
...

WITHINGTON

1619/20
Acts of Decanal Court   HCL
f 5v*   *(26 February)*

Proceedings of the court held in the dean's consistory of Hereford Cathedral.
...
Alice Berrow
For dancing on sabbath days before evening prayer. °(She was) cited (to appear) on the next (court day) by ways and means. On 11 March

1619 she appeared before the lord dean and the lord (dean) graciously dismissed the same (Berrow), etc. °

Penelope Carwarden

Madley

On the like (charge). On 11 March 1619 John Carwarden, the father of the said Penelope, appeared before the lord dean, etc. At his petition

Dismissal

the lord (dean) graciously dismissed the same (Penelope).

...

f 6*

...

Preston Winne   Anne Hodges

Presented for dancing at Withington on sabbath days °before evening prayer. On 11 March 1619 she appeared before the lord dean and confesses, etc. Therefore the lord (dean) graciously dismissed the same (Hodges) with a warning, etc. °

Withington   Mary, the servant of Thomas Franke

On the like (charge). (She was) sought, etc. (She was) cited by ways and means (to appear) on the next (court day).

...

1620

Acts of Decanal Court   HCL

f 10   *(27 March)*

Proceedings of the court held in the dean's consistory of Hereford Cathedral before the dean.

...

Mary, the servant of Thomas Franke

Presented for dancing on sabbath days.

1620/1

Acts of Decanal Court   HCL

f 55v *(20 January)*

Proceedings of the court held in the dean's consistory of Hereford Cathedral before the dean

...

Lewis Ireland

Richard Crispe of Morton Jeffreys†

Marden

For dancing the morris at Withington on a sabbath day. On 20 January

Dismissal   1620 he appeared. When the aforesaid article had been charged against him he confessed, etc. Therefore the lord (dean) enjoined on him one day of penance and (he was) warned to certify (his compliance) on the next (court day). On 17 February 1620 he appeared and (the lord dean) revoked his decision as far as the penance (was concerned) and dismissed (Ireland) with a warning.

...

f 58
...

Richard Crispe
Morton Jeffreys For dancing the morris on sabbath days. On that day he appeared and because of his contempt the lord (judge) excommunicated him.
...

f 58v   *(17 February)*
...

William Taylor
For dancing the morris on a sabbath day at Withington. On 17 February, having been cited and summoned, he did not appear. (He was) excommunicated.

David Jukes on the like (charge).
On that day he appeared. When the aforesaid article had been charged against him he confessed, etc. Therefore the lord (judge) enjoined on him one day of penance according, etc (*ie,* according to the schedule) and warned (him) to certify (his compliance) on the next (court day).

William Powell
On the like (charge). On that day he appeared, etc, and confessed, etc. Therefore the lord (judge) enjoined as above, etc.
...
Roger Miles
For playing on his fiddle.
...

f 60v   *(3 March)*
...
Marden   William Taylor
For dancing the morris on a sabbath day. (He was) excommunicated.

Dismissal

David Jukes
On the like (charge). (He had been) warned to certify (his) penance
as of this day. On that day (he was warned to do) the same on the next
(court day). Afterwards he appeared. At his petition the lord (judge)
revoked the penance and graciously dismissed (him) with a warning.

William Powell
On the like (charge). (He had been warned) in like manner. On that
day he appeared and because he had not performed (his penance) the
Dismissal   lord (judge) excommunicated him. On 17 March he was absolved and
dismissed.
...

Dismissal   Roger Miles
For playing on his fiddle. On that day he appeared. When the aforesaid
article had been charged against him he confessed that the same was
true. Therefore the lord enjoined on him penance according, etc (*ie*,
according to the schedule), and to certify (his compliance) on the next
(court day). (His case proceeded) in like manner as (that) against Jukes.
...

1622
Acts of Decanal Court   HCL
f 115   *(12 October)*

Proceedings of the court held before Master Jones.
...
Robert *(blank)* the tailor
For dancing on the sabbath day before evening prayer.

Anne Crumpton
On the like (charge). °On that day she appeared and confessed, etc.
Dismissal   Therefore the lord (judge) enjoined on her one day of penance, etc,
according, etc, and to certify (her compliance) on the next (court day),
etc. ° Afterwards the lord (judge) dismissed the same (Crumpton) with
a warning.

Mary Taylor
On the like (charge). °On that day (her case was dealt with) in like
Dismissal   manner as above.° Afterwards (she was dismissed) in like manner.
...

f 118v* *(9 November)*

...

Robert Beckinsfield the tailor
For dancing on the sabbath day before evening prayer. On 9
November 1622 (his case was dealt with) in like manner as (that)
against Imme.

Joan Careles
On the like (charge). On that day she appeared. When the aforesaid
Dismissal article had been charged against her she confessed that the same was
true, etc. Therefore the lord (commissary) enjoined on her one day
of penance in the manner of a penitent according, etc (*ie*, according
to the schedule), and she was warned to certify (her compliance) on
the next (court day).
Afterwards the lord (commissary) revoked the penance enjoined on
another occasion and dismissed the same (Careles) with a warning, etc.

John Joyner
On the like (charge). On 9 November 1622 (his case was dealt with)
in like manner as (that) against Imme. On 15 February 1622 he
Dismissal appeared before the lord dean, etc. At his petition the lord (dean)
absolved the same (Joyner), etc. And he claimed that he resided within
the prebend of Ewithington. Therefore the lord (dean) referred the
same (Joyner) to the prebendary, etc.

...

Edward Davis
Dismissal For dancing on the sabbath day before evening prayer. On 9
November 1622 he appeared and confessed that the article was true,
etc, and submitted himself, etc. Therefore the lord (judge) dismissed
Jane Cerle the same (Davis) with a warning.

f 120* *(7 December)*

Margaret Hallinges
For dancing on the sabbath day before evening prayer.

Jane Tomkins
On the like (charge).

Jane Serle
On the like (charge). On 7 December 1622 John Smith appeared. At

Dismissal   his petition the lord (judge) dismissed her.

...

1622/3
Acts of Decanal Court   HCL
f 124   *(15 March)*

...

Margaret Hallinges
For dancing on the sabbath days. (She was) cited (to appear) on 15
March 1622 before the lord dean, etc, by the affixing of the
presentment to her father's door, but, having been summoned, she did
not appear. The lord (judge) excommunicated (her), etc.

...

WOOLHOPE

1620
Acts of Decanal Court   HCL
f 35v   *(23 September)*

*Proceedings of the court held in the dean's consistory of Hereford
Cathedral before Master Jones.*

...

Anthony Wheelar, cleric, vicar there
He was a spectator of such as danced before evening prayer on sabbath
days, that is, on 27 August last. On that day he appeared. When the
aforesaid article had been charged against him, he denied, etc.
Therefore the lord (judge) enjoined and admonished him to clear
himself with four compurgators (who were also) clerics, etc.

Roger Butlar, churchwarden there
On the like (charge). On that day, having been cited in church and
summoned, he did not appear. Therefore (he was) excommunicated.
°Afterwards, while the court was sitting, he appeared and the lord
(judge) revoked the decree of excommunication, etc, and the lord
(judge) warned him to exhibit the names of the dancers and spectators
on the next (court day).

John Powell
For being the fiddler thereat. On that day he appeared (and) when the
aforesaid article was charged against him he confessed, etc. Therefore

the lord (judge) warned him upon his oath to turn in the names of the dancers and those who had been present then and there on the next (court day) under penalty (of excommunication ?).

Putley

Thomas Jones
On the like (charge).
...

f 38v   (7 October)

Proceedings of the court held in the dean's consistory of Hereford Cathedral before Master Wallwin, commissary.
...

Anthony Wheelar, cleric, vicar there
He was a spectator of such as danced on sabbath days before evening prayers, that is, on 27 August last. (He had) to clear himself with four compurgators (who were also) clerics as of this day. On that day, when he had been summoned three times and had not appeared, the lord (commissary) declared him to have failed (in his compurgation) and that he should be regarded as convicted, etc, and he decreed, etc.

Dismissal

Roger Butlar, churchwarden there
On the like (charge). (He was) warned to turn over the names of the dancers and spectators there. On that day, since he had been summoned and had not appeared nor obeyed the warning, the lord (commissary) excommunicated him. On 21 October 1620 he appeared before the lord dean, etc. At his petition the lord (dean) absolved the same (Butlar), etc, and dismissed him upon an examination (of the case).

John Powell, fiddler, in like manner
On that day the lord (commissary) carried over the case until the next (court day) and warned him to appear at that time. On that day he was summoned (and) did not appear. (He was) excommunicated.

Putley

Thomas Jones, fiddler
On the like (charge). On that day, having been cited by Gough and summoned, he did not appear. The lord (commissary) excommunicated him ⟨...⟩ by Master Jones, etc. And upon an examination of the case, the lord (judge) dismissed him.
...

YARKHILL

1588
Diocese of Hereford Acts of Office   HRO: box 17, vol 67
f [215]*   *(17 June)*

Proceedings of the court held in the consistory of Hereford Cathedral before Master William Grenewich.
...

Tarrington   John Bidcot, Richard Bidcot, (and) Robert Bidcot
Noted, in English, in piping and playing as minstrels at time of divine
2 July   service on 5 May, being a Sunday, within the parish of Yarkhill in
Hawlinges Close, etc. Therefore each one has one day of penance, etc,
and to certify (his compliance) on the next (court day).

YAZOR

1619–20
Archdeaconry of Hereford Acts of Office   HRO: box 24, vol 90
f [65]   *(12 November)*
...

The churchwardens there, that is, Hugh Stringham (and) Hugh
Winney, for having a great morris dance upon the sabbath day at
evening prayer time. Having been cited (to appear) as of 12 November
1619 (and) summoned, etc, the aforesaid churchwardens appeared.
The lord (judge), upon an examination of the case, enjoined them to
appear in the consistory of the cathedral church of Hereford on 19
November instant to receive the articles and he warned them to be
present at that time to see the further process (of the court).

ff [72v–4]*   *(February)*
...

Mansell Lacy   Thomas Hopkins detected by the churchwardens of Yazor for dancing
the morris between morning and evening prayer on a Sunday and going
Dismissal   dancing out of that parish. °He appeared before Master Osgood,
surrogate, etc, on 2 February 1619 according, etc (*ie*, according to
English ecclesiastical practice), and when the article had been charged
(against him) he confessed, etc, and the lord (surrogate) warned him
to acknowledge his fault, etc, and warned him that hereafter, etc (*ie*,
that hereafter he should not dance on Sunday), and he dismissed him,
etc.°

5 March   Thomas Hodges on the like (charge). °(He was) sought (to appear) on 5 February 1619 (and cited) by ways and means (to appear) on the next (court day), 24 February 1619.° The lord (judge) held over (his appearance) on the next (court day). (He was) cited in person by Marsten, an apparitor, on 5 March last to appear in the cathedral church of Hereford in the consistory there. On 16 March aforesaid (he was) summoned three times and did not appear in any way (*ie*, neither in person nor by proxy); the lord (judge) pronounced him contumacious and under penalty of excommunication.

Dismissal Yazor William Lyke on the like (charge). °On 2 February 1619 (he was dealt with) in like manner as in the action against Thomas Hopkins.°|

James Hodges. On 8 February aforesaid (he was dealt with) in like manner. °On 24 February aforesaid (he was cited to appear) at the same place on the next (court day).°°On 15 March he appeared and brought in the form of execution (of penance ?).

Anne Lyke detected for dancing on the sabbath day between morning and evening prayer. °On 2 February 1619 (she was dealt with) in like manner on the petition of William Lyke.°

Elizabeth Hint on the like (charge). °On 2 February (she was dealt with) in like manner at the petition of the said William Lyke.°

Margaret Winney on the like (charge). °She appeared on 5 February 1619 in the consistory, etc, and confessed, etc. The lord (deputy) received (her confession), etc, and enjoined penance (on) her as on Bowcott (see below). °On 24 February aforesaid (she was cited to appear (?)) at the same place on the next (court day).° °Afterwards she was dismissed with a warning.°

Anne Watkins on the like (charge). °On 2 February 1619 (she was dealt with) in like manner at the petition of John Watkins.°

John Watkins on the like (charge). °On 2 February 1619 (he was dealt with) in like manner as in the action against Thomas Hopkins.°

Bridge Sollers Thomas Phillpottes for dancing the morris on a Sunday between
Dismissal   morning and evening prayer in the parish of Yazor. °On 5 February 1619 in the consistory the lord (judge) carried over (the proceedings)

until the next (court day). °On 11 February 1619 according, etc (*ie*, according to English ecclesiastical practice), the said Phillpottes appeared in person in the cathedral church of Hereford in the consistory of Hereford before Master Gabriel Wallwin, MA, deputy, etc, and when the article had been charged against him he confessed that the article was true. The lord (deputy) accepted this confession and, upon an examination of the case, dismissed him with a warning.

Stanton on Wye   James Blether on the like (charge). °On 5 February 1619 in the
Dismissal   consistory, etc, the said Blether appeared and when the article had been charged against him he confessed that he did dance the morris on the sabbath day in the parish of Yazor on the sabbath day before evening prayer ended. The lord (deputy) accepted this confession, etc, and enjoined on him a penance according to the schedule and warned him to copy out the form, etc, and to certify (his compliance). ° °On 16 March 1619 (the lord deputy) dismissed (him) as (he dismissed) Clarke below. °|

Dismissal   John Clarke on the like (charge). °On 5 February 1619 in the consistory, etc, he appeared and (was dealt with) in like manner as in the action against Blether. He appeared on 16 March 1619 in the consistory and the lord (judge) warned him, etc, and dismissed him. °

Dismissal   Thomas Powell on the like (charge). °On 5 February 1619 he appeared
Byford   in the consistory, etc, and confessed, etc, in like manner as in the action against Bowcott. ° On 11 February 1619 according, etc, in the consistory of Hereford he appeared before Master Gabriel Wallwin, MA, deputy, etc, and brought in the form and certified on his oath the completion (of his penance). Therefore (he was) dismissed.

Dismissal   Hugh Powell on the like (charge). °On 5 February 1619 in the
Bishopstone   consistory he appeared and confessed, etc, in like manner as in the action against Bowcott. On that day, 24 February aforesaid, he appeared and he has, by (the lord deputy's) favour, (another) day (appointed) on the next (court day), etc, (and he has) to certify (his compliance) in this place on the next (court day), 16 March. ° °He appeared on 15 March 1619 in the consistory and when the case had been heard the lord (judge) dismissed him with a warning. °

Dismissal   Thomas Bowcott on the like (charge). °On 5 February 1619 in the consistory, etc, the said Bowcott appeared and when the article had

Mansell
Gamadge

been charged (against him) he confessed that the same (article) was true. The lord (judge) received this confession that, etc (*ie*, that it was true), and enjoined on him a penance according to the schedule, etc. The lord (judge) warned him to copy out this schedule, etc, and to certify (his compliance). ° °On 24 February aforesaid he appeared before Master Wallwin, deputy, etc, in the consistory, etc. The lord (deputy) pronounced him contumacious in not having performed his penance, etc; however the penalty (was) reserved until the next (court day), etc. °°On 15 March aforesaid (he was dealt with) as in the case of Powell.°

Dismissal

William Reygnoldes on the like (charge). °On 5 February °1619° in the consistory, etc, (he was dealt with) as in the action (against) Shepperd. On 4 February 1619 he appeared in the consistory, etc, and brought in the form and swore the completion of his penance according to the certificate written on the back of the same (form).°

Dismissal
Yazor

John Shepperd for dancing on a sabbath day between morning and evening prayer in the parish of Yazor. °The said Shepperd appeared on 5 February 1619 in the consistory, etc, and the lord (deputy) imposed upon him an oath to respond truthfully, etc. Then (he was) asked whether he did dance on the sabbath day (and) he confessed that he did so dance on the sabbath day before evening prayer ended and being asked who did so dance besides, he named the parties named elsewhere by the churchwardens of Yazor and affirmed that he himself knew no others. The lord (deputy) received this confession, etc, and enjoined on him a penance in their (*ie*, penitents') usual garb according to the schedule, etc. The lord (deputy) warned him to copy out this schedule, etc, and to certify (his compliance), etc, on the next (court day) in March. On 15 March 1619 in the consistory he appeared and brought in the form and swore, etc, and the lord (deputy) dismissed him. |°

Yazor

John Hodges on the like (charge). On 5 February aforesaid he appeared and, when the article had been charged against him, he confessed that the article was true. Therefore the lord (deputy) enjoined him to confess the article in the usual garb before the minister and churchwardens there next Sunday immediately after prayers

Dismissal

(were) finished and to certify (his compliance) on the next (court day) after. Then the lord (deputy) dismissed him with a warning.

Dismissal

Joan Emmans on the like (charge). °On 5 February 1619 the said Emmans appeared in the consistory, etc, and when the article had been charged (against her), she denied that the article was true in any (part). Therefore the lord (judge) ordered (her) to clear herself on the next (court day) in this place with two compurgators after proclamation had been made beforehand, etc. And he warned her to be present then and there to see the further process (of the law) take place. Afterwards she confessed that she did dance before the end of evening prayer on the sabbath day. The lord (deputy) received this confession that, etc, and enjoined on her a penance in their (*ie*, penitents') usual garb according to the schedule, etc. The lord (deputy) warned her to copy out this schedule, etc, and to certify (her compliance) on the next (court day), that is, the 24th of this month. °°On 24 February 1619 (she appeared) before Wallwin, deputy, etc, (and) he dismissed the said Joan with a warning, etc. Therefore she was dismissed. °

Dismissal

Elinor Wheetse
On the like (charge). (She was dealt with) in like manner. °On this day, 24 February aforesaid (she was dealt with) in like manner as above. °

...

ABBEY DORE

1303
Exchequer Accounts of Edward I   PRO: E101/363/18
f 21v*   *(7 April)*

...

On 7 April, to Gerard, a fiddler, a minstrel of Sir (William) de Sutton, coming to the prince at Straddle on behalf of the same his lord and performing his minstrelsy before the same (prince), of the same prince's gift at his departure from thence on the same day   13s 4d

Minstrels of Flanders

To Amandus, a minstrel of Sir Arnold de Gardin performing his minstrelsy in the same way before the said lord prince there, of the gift of the same (prince) there on the same day   20s

...

WIGMORE

1318
Register of Bishop Adam Orleton   HRO
f 28*   *(30 December)*

...Likewise we condemn the custom, or rather corrupting practice, hitherto observed, of blood letting. Still, (the monks) should be bled when there is need and then without any slackening (of the rule *or* any dissolute behaviour) and dishonourable songs, and food should be served to those who have been bled according to the abbot's order...

BISHOP RICHARD SWINFIELD
OF HEREFORD

1289–90
Account Roll of Bishop Richard Swinfield   Bodl.: MS Lat. hist. d. 1(R)
mb 3d*   *(Gifts)*
...
...In payment made to William, a watchman/wait, who went away, both for a gift and a wage, 2s....Likewise 12d (were spent) for Hugh, harper of the lord abbot of Reading.
...
...Likewise 2s, for three minstrels of London and two grooms of the king....Likewise 3s, for Bennet, a fiddler of London. Likewise 2s, for Sir Ralph Pippard's harper. Likewise for Richard, an almoner (or a maker of eucharistic wafers) of Oxford. Likewise 5s 6d, for other waferers and minstrels there. Likewise 12d, for Master Henry, Sir Edmund de Mortimer's harper....

...Likewise 2d, for two minstrels at Monkton....

...Likewise 2s, for Sir John Tregoz's harper/s at Sugwas.... Likewise 12d, for some minstrel, Joliet, at Colwall. Likewise 12d, for Pynke, a minstrel, at Colwall.
...

MORTIMER OF WIGMORE

1393–4
Account Roll of Roger, Lord Mortimer   BL: Egerton Roll 8738
mb 2*

Houedene
...

Likewise for one doublet of embroidered white satin	14s
Likewise for one dancing doublet of embroidered white satin	4s

...

mb 2d

W. Venne
...

Likewise for one hundred silver gilded oranges for one dancing doublet made by W. Mallynges and his fellow embroiderers weighing 2 lb 1/2 oz Troy weight, (at a) price (of) 28s per lb	57s 2d
Likewise for fifteen whelks and fifteen mussels for one white doublet made by W. Venne, 9 oz Troy weight less four penny-weight, (at a) price (of) 28s per lb as above	20s 8d
Likewise for the making and the gilding of the above mentioned fruit, whelks, and mussels (at a) price (of) 9d each and one extra at no charge	£4 17s 6d
Likewise for fifteen white silver cockles for the said white doublet weight 4 1/2 oz Troy weight less two penny-weight	10s 4d
And for the making of the said fifteen cockles (at a) price (of) 4d each	5s

W. Mallynges, weaver
...

Likewise for the embroidering of one white satin dancing doublet embroidered with orange trees, for the gold and their work	100s

Penston
...

Likewise for three ells of linen canvas for one doublet (at a) price (of) 9d per ell	2s 3d
Likewise for four ells of Westphalian (cloth) for decoration of the same doublet (at a) price (of) 6d per ell	2s
Likewise for six yards of fustian for lining of the same clothing (at a) price (of) 8 1/2d per yard	4s 3d
Likewise for two ells of linen canvas for one doublet for dancing (at a) price (of) 8 1/2d per ell	17d

Likewise for two ells of linen canvas for the lining of the
said doublet (at a) price (of) 6d per ell   22d

...

APPENDIX 1

1287
Canonization Proceedings for St Thomas Cantilupe
Vatican Library: Cod. lat. 4015
ff 169v–70   *(4 April) (Testimony of witness 104)*

...

Sir Gilbert de Chevening, priest, perpetual vicar of the church of
Much Marcle, having been sworn above as a witness, replied when
asked that he was thirty years of age or thereabouts and that he was
not of the kin or household of the said Lord Thomas.

Again when asked to tell whether he knew anything about the miracle
said to have occurred to the person of the aforesaid Juliana Kock he
said that, while he was acting as a guardian of the tomb of the said
Lord Thomas and as a vicar in the church of Hereford in AD 1287,
it happened that on Good Friday at the hour of prime while the
aforesaid Juliana was set in the said church of Hereford on a litter of
twigs – with which litter she had been carried to the church of
Hereford by Philip LeLonge, a witness sworn above, and by a woman
whose name he says he does not know, so that she might be
miraculously healed there by the merits of the said holy Thomas,
because of whom God had worked four miracles in the said church
in the previous period of time – this Juliana – seeing that another
man, crippled in the feet, who was called Philip (the) harper and was
staying in the city of Hereford and was set on another litter in the
said church of Hereford, waiting therein to receive the benefit of
health from the merits of the said holy Thomas, had been miraculously
cured in the said hour of prime in the sight of this witness and made
straight and had walked about the aforesaid tomb without any
hindrance – this Juliana, roused and compelled by some sort of fervent
zeal, got out, without any human aid, of the said litter in which she
used to hold her shins folded and sit bent over, and (was) released
from the said litter in the place in which she used to stay in such a
manner in it, and further in a short time with her foot stretched from
her, made upright without hindrance and without any human

assistance, she came without limping in the aforesaid hour to the abovesaid tomb and prayed there and left a penny there and told this very witness and others, especially Sir Henry of St Alban, then a guardian of the said tomb together with this very witness, and Master Roger de Sevenok, then a canon of Hereford, now deceased, that the said holy Thomas had said to this very Juliana, 'Rise and walk.'

...

ENDNOTES

57–8 HRO ff 91–1v
Trillek was elected in 1344 and served until 1360. He appears to have been a fine administrator; his episcopate covered the period of the Black Death and much of his energy was devoted to the difficulties raised by a devastated clergy. It is unfortunately not possible to identify 'ecclesia de .l.' (l.20), although Ledbury, Leominster, and Ludlow are all possible candidates. Most early histories of Hereford city and diocese noted this document, though it was not included in Chambers' *Mediaeval Stage*.

63 HRO: box 19, vol 72 f [200]
The damaged word in l.14 is at the edge of the page and difficult to read. It appears to be 'fastigat' or 'fustigat;' it is not clear if there is a suspension mark. Although a form of 'fustigatio' (a beating or whipping) might otherwise seem likely, it is most improbable that an ecclesiastical court would impose such a punishment and it seems impossible to recover what Bayle's sentence was.

63–4 HRO: box 24, vol 90 ff [128v–9]
It is difficult to assign a date to these cases. 12 January 1619/20 has been chosen because, although the cases follow an 'acta' paragraph dated 19 October 1619 on f [117], it is clear that 12 January 1619/20 was the first court session at which any of the four accused made an appearance. In fact, the chronology is difficult to unravel. All four persons were cited to make appearances in mid-December 1619: James and Mary Poslons on 18 December, John Botchet on 17 December, John Lewis on 15 December. However, Mary Poslons did not appear until 5 February 1619/20 and James did not appear until (probably) 24 February after the scheduled session, despite the fact that they were apparently both cited to appear on 18 December and 5 February. Botchet appeared on 12 January and 5 February, and Lewis was the last of the four to appear, on 8 March 1619/20. Both Botchet, a minstrel, and Lewis spent the festive seasons of Christmas and Epiphany under excommunication.

66 HRO: box 23, vol 86 f [157v]
It appears that Vale did not appear on 9 December 1611, the session date given in the 'acta' paragraph on f [156] which applies to this entry, although it seems that a report of an attempt to serve a citation on him was made at that session. His first appearance was made on 9 January 1611/12.

66   HRO: box 17, vol 68   f [196v]
'hodiwinking' (l.37) commonly refers to the game of Blind Man's Buff, although the OED also cites 'concealment' and 'deceiving' as meanings in addition to 'blindfolding.' In part because of the date, the 'game' meaning seems less appropriate here and the prosecution may be for a Shrovetide disguising. It is very likely that this is the same Richard Kent as the one who appears as a compurgator on 2 May 1587 in the neighbouring parish of Canon Frome (see p 68, l.25). The eventual absolution from excommunication and dismissal of Kent, Watkis, and Leeth after their performance of penance is recorded on f [226v].

67   HRO: box 17, vol 68   f [198]
This prosecution represents one of a series of seven charges against Caple, ranging from blaspheming the name of God to fornication. The seven charges are repeated on f [227v], where Caple is charged with contumacy for not replying. It appears from a marginal note that the charges were dismissed.

67   HRO: box 24a (formerly 18), vol 70   f [33]
The date, 8 September, is the date of the occurrence as given in the detection, rather than the date of the court session. Volume 70 of the Acts of Office is almost entirely lacking in 'acta' headings and it is therefore impossible to establish the court date.

67–8   HRO: box 24a (formerly 18), vol 71   f [313]
There are two parishes called Letton in Herefordshire; the one referred to here is just over a mile north of Brobury. No details of Jones' court appearance on 7 December are recorded but he must have confessed the article at that time or the penance which he is ordered to certify would not have been given.

68   HRO: box 17, vol 66   f [228v]
Further down the page, an entry in the right margin gives Roger Hide's sworn statement about a brawl in Canon Frome. This note is next to the cancelled entries transcribed under Cradley (p 72, ll.26–30 and endnote). The cases seem unrelated. Richard Kent, who appears here as a compurgator, is probably the same person prosecuted in Bosbury in 1589 (see p 66, l. 36) for going hoodwinking.

68–9   HRO: box 24a (formerly 18), vol 70   ff [78v–9]
This volume contains very few 'acta' headings, so the date of neither the occurrence nor the court session can be established.

69   HRO: box 24, vol 90   f [78]
There is no intervening court session recorded between the 'acta' paragraph dated 19 October 1619 on f [53] and this folio. Nevertheless, the internal evidence that the case was heard at a session in 1620 is clear: by f [74] (see Yazor below, pp 182–6), cases from 1619/20 were being heard and the first case on f [78] is explicitly dated 1 July 1620. Since the session at which this case was heard is dated 13 July, a hearing date of 13 July 1620 has been assumed.

70–2   HRO: box 24, vol 90   ff [129v–30, 131]
See also Bishops Frome, 1619, for another account of the same case. The prebend of Colwall,
here referred to as 'Barton Collwall,' was also called Barton and Colwall. (John Le Neve,
Fasti Ecclesiae Anglicanae 1300–1541: 2 Hereford Diocese, Joyce M. Horn (comp) (London,
1962), 53). See Kathleen Edwards, *The English Secular Cathedrals in the Middle Ages* (Manchester, 1949), 126–8, for a discussion of the acquisition of peculiar jurisdictions by prebendaries. The applicable 'acta' paragraph on f [117] gives a date of 19 October, but it is clear
from internal evidence that the accused parties first appeared in court two months later on
18 December, the date assigned here to the document.

72   HRO: box 17, vol 66   ff [228v, 229]
The phrase 'to ride on a cowl-staff' (compare l. 19) means 'to be set astride a pole and carried
in derision about the streets' (*OED*), one of the traditional elements of a charivari. The puritan
Philip Stubbs notes that it was a common punishment for those who refused to give money
to the lord of misrule: 'And who will not shew himselfe buxome to them, and giue money
for these the Deuils Cognizances, they shall be mocked, and flouted shamefullie. Yea, and
many times carried vpon a Cowlstaffe...' (*The Anatomie of Abuses* (London, 1595), sig P2v;
STC: 23379). The last phrase is not present in the first (1583) edition (*STC*: 23376). For further
discussion of cowlstaves, see Introduction, pp 15 and 47, n 53.
    The entries for Pillinger, Holland, the two Collinges, and Warner's servant (ll. 26–30) have
been cancelled administratively.

73   HRO: box 23, vol 85   f [88]
There are few 'acta' paragraphs in this volume and the last date given to a court session before
this entry is 28 November 1609 on f [58]. Fortunately the date of the court session at which
Wynter and Harnatt made their appearances is recorded explicitly in the case. The citations
recorded in the margins were presumably ordered and served between 28 November and 20
December.

73–4   HRO: box 24, vol 91, pt 2   f [2v]
The 'acta' paragraph for this entry, which is on f [1], is dated 7 October 1621, but internal
evidence makes it clear that Buttongard did not make his first court appearance until 14
November.

74–9   PRO: STAC 8/234/10/Item 12   single sheet
This document is one of three copies of the bill of complaint contained in PRO: STAC 8/234/10,
the other two being Items 2 and 7. Only Item 12 is endorsed on the back by the clerk, Edward
Jones, and signed by the plaintiff's counsel, one Henshawe, according to the Star Chamber's
regulations for bills (see p 79, ll. 14, 25). It is therefore likely to be the original copy of the
bill. (The date in the endorsement is the formal filing date, rather than the date of the drafting
or submission of the bill.) Items 2 and 7 were probably copied to accompany the commissions
of 'dedimus potestatem' sent to prominent persons in the local area authorizing them to receive
the defendants' answers on oath (see below, pp 276–7, endnote to PRO: STAC 8/234/10/Item
8 single sheet). They are signed by the defendants' attorney, George Shelleton. They have
been treated as administrative copies and therefore neither transcribed nor collated.

The precise nature of the events does not emerge with any clarity from the various pleadings, that is, the bill and the various answers. There are unfortunately few proofs; that is, there is only one examination of defendants and no examinations of witnesses. Some things are clear. All are agreed that there were two incidents, one inside the alehouse and one outside, in the churchyard and an adjoining orchard. The principal participants, Philpot, Powell, and Gwillim on one side and Williams, Philpot, Vaughan, and Mothewaye on the other, seem established. The context was clearly a traditional parish festivity of some kind, probably a village Whitsun ale, towards which the two groups demonstrate very different and incompatible attitudes. In fact, the principal defendant, Thomas Williams, in part ascribes a prior animosity between the complainant and his (ie, Williams') master, the vicar, to the complainant's contempt for the word of God as manifested in his approval of dancing and drinking.

Like most cases in the Star Chamber, this one appears to have arisen out of older quarrels which had already taken the principal participants or their friends, families, and superiors into the common law courts and of which we catch glimpses in the defendants' answers and the interrogatory provided by the complainant. It may very well have been filed by Philpot for its purely nuisance value, to put pressure upon his opponents in other cases. An already confusing set of claims and counter-claims is made worse by the fact that the case involves two men named Richard Powell (one a gentleman of Whitchurch and associated with the complainant and the other an innkeeper of Goodrich and associated with the defendants), as well as two men named Anthony Philpot (one the complainant's brother and the other a defendant).

One thing of which we can be quite sure, however, is that behind all the 'uncertainties and insufficiencies' of this case (to borrow the formal wording of the defendants' answers) lies village animosity fed by the increasing influence of puritanism and sabbatarianism. Such local conflicts would, in 1618, lead to the general issuance of James I's *The King's Maiesties Declaration to his Subiects, Concerning lawfull Sports to be vsed* (London: Bonham Norton and John Bill, 1618; STC: 9238.9), 1–9, commonly known as *The Book of Sports*. See also below p 283, endnote to PRO: SP 16/397, single sheet.

It is possible that some of the places described in this case were still standing as late as the 1930s. According to the Royal Commission on Historical Monuments, England, portions of Goodrich vicarage date from the seventeenth century (*An Inventory of the Historical Monuments in Herefordshire*: vol 1, *South-West*, HMSO (London, 1931), 79). An old mill, portions of which were rebuilt in the late seventeenth century from older materials, is also described (p 81): perhaps this was once the site of the Philpot family farm.

79–83   PRO: STAC 8/234/10/Item 9   single sheet
This answer is signed by counsel, I. Hoskyns (p 83, l.18), and also by the clerk, Edward Jones (p 79, l.31), who may have been acting as an examiner and clerk to the local commissioners. Jones also signed Item 10 (p 83, l.24). It is possible that Hoskyns, who signed as counsel the answers in Items 10, 8, 11, and 3 as well, was the distinguished local Hereford jurist, Serjeant John Hoskins (see p 280, endnote to STC: 12032 sigs A3–C3v).

86–9   PRO: STAC 8/234/10/Item 8   single sheet
The commission 'dedimus potestatem' authorizing Walter Pie and Thomas Jones (l.9) to receive the answers of these defendants on oath is PRO: STAC 8/234/10/Item 6. It was in fact

addressed to a group of four men, Pie, Jones, William Ryddall, and Robert Kirle, and required at least two of them to act upon it. It is signed by Cotton, a member of a family whose members seem to have held virtually hereditary clerkships in the Star Chamber; it is also signed by the commissioners. It has not been transcribed due to its purely formal nature: it sheds no light on the suit. This answer is endorsed by Thomas Mynatt (p 88, l.35), who was, like Cotton, a long-time and powerful member of the Star Chamber bureaucracy (see Guy, *The Court of Star Chamber*, pp 13–15). He also endorsed Items 11 and 5.

89–92   PRO: STAC 8/234/10/Item 3   single sheet
This answer, unlike the other answers in Items 9, 10, 8, and 11, is signed by the commissioners authorized by royal writ to receive it on oath from the defendants. That writ, a commission 'dedimus potestatem' (PRO: STAC 8/234/10/Item 1) is addressed to a group of four men, Burfeilde (presumably an error for Burhill), Brace, Gardner, and John Abrahall, the first three of whom acted upon it. Like the other such commission in this case, it is endorsed by the active commissioners and signed by Cotton. These three men also signed the two following Items 4 and 5, an interrogatory and examination also authorized by their commission. The commission has not been transcribed due to its formal nature: it sheds no light on the suit.

97–8   HCL   f 9v
The Consuetudines ordered the treasurer to provide candles for three consecutive feasts: the deacons' feast on St Stephen's Day (26 December), the priests' feast on St John the Evangelist's Day (27 December), and the boy bishop's celebration on the feast of the Holy Innocents (28 December). The Hereford customs regarding the boy bishop were identical to those of many other English cathedrals, such as Lincoln, and were so noted by Chambers, *The Mediaeval Stage*, vol 1, p 358. See also Arthur F. Leach, 'The Schoolboys' Feast,' *The Fortnightly Review*, ns, 59 (1896), 128–41; Edward F. Rimbault, 'The Festival of the Boy Bishop in England,' *Camden Miscellany 7*, Camden Society (London, 1875), v–xxxii. The statute was printed in *Statutes of Lincoln Cathedral*, Henry Bradshaw and Christopher Wordsworth (eds), pt 2 (London, 1867), 67. Three manuscripts of the Consuetudines survive; there are almost no substantive differences between them and the text is therefore printed here from the earliest.
    A: Hereford, Hereford Cathedral Library, c 1265, no earlier than 1264, which date appears in the text. The manuscript contains only the Consuetudines; the REED section appears on f 9v.
    B: London, British Library, Royal 10 A xi, early 14th century. The Consuetudines is on ff 258v–62, the REED section is on f 261v.
    C: Cambridge, Corpus Christi College, 120, c 1550. The Consuetudines is on pp 485–519, the REED section is on p 502.

98–100   HRO   ff 39v–40
Double dots (as in l.10) were used commonly in medieval documents to indicate non-specific names, rather like the use of 'A.B.' in modern legal formulae. The convention could indicate that the addressee's name was not known to the sender (unlikely in this case), or that the letter was addressed to the holder of the office, whoever he might be, to be acted upon in his official capacity.
    Like many English cities, Hereford had a thriving Jewish community until the expulsion of 1290. The Jewish houses, some of which were made of stone, were located primarily along

Jews Street, an extension of Malieres Street, running off Widemarsh Street just inside the city ditch and north of the market place. The street is still known as Jewry Lane. The community appears to have been a comparatively large and important one; at the expulsion, the government officials who took over as creditors listed forty-one Hereford Jews to whom money was owed (two of these are listed as 'of London,' and one as 'of Worcester'). The largest single creditor was Aaron, son of Elias le Blund, who was owed approximately £1300 in a total of 125 separate debts. See B. Lionel Abrahams, 'The Debts and Houses of the Jews of Hereford in 1290,' *Transactions of the Jewish Historical Society of England*, 1 (1893–4), 136–59. The amount of the debt is inexact because some of it is expressed in geese and bushels of corn.

100   HCL: R390   mb 3
E.K. Chambers' discussion of the Hereford boy bishop (*The Mediaeval Stage*, vol 1, pp 336–71) includes the Hereford statute (p 358, n 5) but not the payments in the mass-pence and canons' bakehouse rolls. These were noted by E.M. Leather in *The Folklore of Hereford-shire*, pp 138–9.

110   HCL: R468   mb 1 col 2
In col 1 the scribe began to enter a payment to the boy bishop under the mass-pence payments and crossed it out: 'De quibus solutis pro denarijs missalibus videlicet [Paruo Episcopo] Pensionibus pro xxii missis vij s. iiij d.'

111   HCL: R479   mb 2
The sum given as payment is difficult to interpret (l.28). I have taken 'qart' as the abbreviation for 'quarterium' (farthing), thus putting 'pars' together with 'ijᵃ', but what the 'pars secunda' refers to is unclear.

112   HRO   f [4v]
This document has been linked with the Mayor's Book pageant list of 1503 to provide the foundation for a hypothetical Hereford play cycle. It is a very weak foundation, for there is no reason to connect the two. There are some interesting aspects of the document, however, apart from its record of the existence of a play-book. The fact that the suit is brought by two persons, John Hanley and John Pewte, may suggest that the play-book was not owned privately by one of the plaintiffs, but was owned by a corporation, such as one of the guilds, of which Hanley and Pewte may have been officials.
   The volume has no year date, but contains cases running from 14 April to 20 October and appears to be in the same hand as that of the volume dated 14 October 1439–8 April 1440. If the volumes are consecutive, it is more likely that this undated volume is from 1440 than 1439; if it were the latter the volumes would overlap by a week. If the undated volume is the later of the two, a gap is left from Friday, 8 April to Thursday, 14 April. It seems likely that the scribe has simply begun dating the new volume from the point at which the court began sitting again.

113   HCL: R637c   mb 3
The roll is clearly from the reign of Edward IV, though the exact date is too faded to be legible. The cathedral catalogue assigns the roll to a date after 1470.

113–15   BL: Cotton Julius B xii   ff 17–18

Henry VII's progress began in March of 1485/6, proceeding north to Waltham, Cambridge, Huntingdon, Stamford, and Lincoln, where the king spent Easter week (Easter was on 26 March). He continued north through Nottingham, Doncaster, Pontefract, and Tadcaster to York, where an elaborate pageant was prepared (Johnston and Rogerson, *York*, REED, vol 1, pp 146–52). The herald who kept this account of the progress left the party at York and joined it again several weeks later on Whitsun Eve (13 May) at Worcester, where a pageant had also been prepared (see pp 406–11 and endnote). On Whit Monday the king came to Hereford, where this St George pageant was performed. On the following Friday he went on to Gloucester and then to Bristol for Corpus Christi (25 May), where several elaborate pageants were presented, returning to London on 26 May. See also Douglas and Greenfield: *Cumberland, Westmorland, Gloucestershire*, REED, pp 291–2; Mark Pilkinton (ed), Bristol, REED, forthcoming; and John C. Meagher, 'The First Progress of Henry VII,' *Renaissance Drama*, ns, 1 (1968), 48–73.

The bishop mentioned at p 115, l.17, is Thomas Milling, bishop of Hereford 1474–92.

115–16   HRO   f 176

This document presents many difficulties; several additions and corrections have been made to it and the intent of these is not always clear. I have tried to reproduce the document's layout as accurately as possible in order not to prejudice its interpretation.

There appears to be an erasure on p 116, l.25, in the phrase 'The – docto*u*rs [of q].' The final letter could also be a 'p' with a subscript. It can be seen faintly under normal light and is clearer under ultraviolet. The last line of the document has been cut off in binding; only the faint tops of the ascenders are visible, but there does appear to be a continuation of the previous line.

117–18   HRO   ff 12–12v

There is no clear evidence by which to date this document; the handwriting would place it in the early part of the sixteenth century and it certainly refers to a period before the pageants were dropped in 1548. The date *c* 1500–20 was suggested by William Dunn Macray in his HMC report, 'The Manuscripts of the Corporation of Hereford' (p 304). The corvisers' concern over their obligation to carry torches in the Corpus Christi procession does not include any reference to a dramatic presentation and it seems clear that no play was involved. The 'Cedule' (p 117, l.21) referred to in the text is missing.

118   HRO   f 39

Walter Devereux (*c* 1490–1558) became the first Viscount Hereford on 2 February 1549/50. The year is not given on the document, but it must have been written after 1513–14 when Devereux first became prominent at court. The court was at Richmond in the early part of May in only two years, 1517 and 1522. The former seems the more likely since the court was there for about a month, from the end of April to the end of May, as opposed to a scant two weeks in May of 1522. *Letters and Papers, Foreign and Domestic, of the Reign of Henry VIII*, vol 2, pt 2, J.S. Brewer (arr and cat) (London, 1864), 1034–52.

119–21   HRO   ff 27–8

In this year the celebration of the feast of Corpus Christi, with its attendant procession, was

banned generally in England (ostensibly because of the plague), so the civic administration
had good reason to convert the money which had been spent on the guilds' pageants into a
fee for the maintenance of roads and ditches. It seems clear from the text that the pageants
had been dropped from the procession some time before this civic order.

122–3 HRO f 70
The decision of the Law Day is not preserved on this copy.

It is not possible to assign this document, or the other documents from Civic Miscellanies
3 and 4 on pp 123, 124, and 137–8, to a specific civic accounting year because we do not
know the dates of the Law Days on which they were considered. Therefore only single year
dates are given.

125–36 STC: 12032 sigs A3–C3v
Seventeenth-century accounts describe two occasions on which a Hereford morris was danced
by a group whose combined ages totalled more than 1000 years. The first, which took place
at Hereford in 1609, is described in considerable detail in this pamphlet. The names, parishes,
and ages of the participants are given, with the whifflers and musicians. A list of gentry among
the spectators is given and important Hereford families are represented. The anonymous
author's exuberant style suggests that a certain measure of exaggeration may be involved,
but there is no particular reason to doubt that a morris dance of elderly men (and one woman)
did take place on this occasion.

The second dance is reputed to have taken place in 1613 in the presence of King James I
at Morehampton Park, the home of John Hoskins, MP for the county in 1603, 1614, and
1628, and serjeant-at-law in 1623. The sources for this occasion are less convincing. It is first
described as an indication of the healthful air of the county (and of its inhabitants' vitality)
in Thomas Fuller's *History of the Worthies of England* (London, 1662, 33; Wing: F2440):
'The ingenious Serjeant Hoskin gave an intertainment to King Iames and provided ten aged
people to dance the Morish before him; all of them making up more then a thousand yeares,
So that what was wanting in one was supplied in another. A nest of Nestors not to be found
in another place.' This account is clearly fictional; there is no contemporary record of the
events and no evidence that James was in the vicinity of Morehampton Park at any time during
1613. Hoskins was a well-known local character and it is not at all unlikely that he is the
source of the ghost morris, although there is no evidence that, as W.P. Courtney suggested
('Morris Dancers in Herefordshire,' NQ, 11th ser, 7 (1913), 91), he was the anonymous author
of *Old Meg*.

The two morris dances have been confused since the seventeenth century and modern accounts frequently cite them side-by-side (see, for example, E.C. Cawte's description in 'The
Morris Dance in Herefordshire, Shropshire and Worcestershire,' p 199), although the fictitious
nature of the Morehampton morris had been pointed out as early as 1828 by John Nichols,
who noted that it 'appears to be deficient in authenticity.' Nichols cites *Old Meg* as evidence
for the historical occasion: 'It appears, however, that this assemblage of veteran morris-dancers
really took place at the Hereford races in 1609, when the King was certainly not present, as
the historian of the festival (for an historian it had) has recorded the names of all the visitors
of consequence.' (See *The Progresses, Processions, and Magnificent Festivities of King James
the First*, vol 1 (London, 1828), xix–xx.) Charles Robinson, in his description of

Morehampton, follows Nichols in regarding the incident there as apocryphal. (See *A History of the Mansions and Manors of Herefordshire* (London, 1873), 2–3.)

Old Meg has not gone without notice. James Howell's *The Parly of Beasts* (London, 1660; Wing: H3119), 121, notes that the Welsh border is 'the healthfullest Country on earth,' since 'of late years ther were cull'd out within three miles compasse ten men that were a thousand years between them, one supplying what the other wanted of a hundred years apiece, and they danc'd the Morris divers hours together in the Market-place, with a Taborer before them 103 years old, and a Maid Mariam 105' (p 122). The verbal parallels suggest that Fuller, too, may have known the pamphlet. Sir William Temple used *Old Meg* as an example of the salubriousness of the area in his essay 'Of Health and Long Life' (*The Works of Sir William Temple*, vol 1 (London, 1720), 277), and notes that he took the information from a pamphlet 'written by a very ingenious Gentleman of that County.' Temple concludes that 'Tis not so much, that so many in one small County should live to that Age, as that they should be in Vigour and in Humour to Travel and to Dance.' Hanmer's edition of *The Works of Shakespear*, 6 vols (Oxford, 1770–1) included in the glossary under 'Maid Marian' a note from the Rev Thomas Warton referring to *Old Meg*. This note was expanded into a description of the pamphlet with excerpts by Henry J. Todd in his *Illustrations of the Lives and Writings of Gower and Chaucer* (London, 1810), 272–4, who calls it 'a real account of performers' (p 273).

Following a series of brief notes by others, W.P. Courtney in 'Morris Dancers in Hereford-shire' surveyed the literature surrounding the two morris dances in NQ, 8th ser, 10 (1896), 513; 11th ser, 6 (1912), 106, 356; 11th ser, 7 (1913), 91–2. More recent commentary has been thin on the ground. In addition to Cawte's brief reference, Joan Sharp described the pamphlet in *JEFDSS*, 2nd ser, 4 (1931), 37–40, and Barbara Lowe used its details in 'Early Records of the Morris in England' *JEFDSS*, 8, no 2 (1957), 74–6. Lowe does not mention the Morehampton morris.

Two further references to a morris of the elderly may be unrelated to *Old Meg*. Edward Chamberlayne's *Angliae Notitiae*, 18th ed (London, 1694; Wing: C1835), 49, notes that 'not many years ago, 8 old men danced a Morrice-Dance, all living in one Manour in the West of England, whose ages put together, made 800 years'. This could, of course, be a somewhat garbled version of either *Old Meg* or the Morehampton Park morris, although 'not many years ago' seems an unlikely way of referring to a period of eighty to eighty-five years. The reference was not included in the seventeenth edition of 1692. This dance of eight men could perhaps be a separate occasion and might be the one noted in John Brand's *Observations on Popular Antiquities*, Henry Ellis (ed), 2 vols (London, 1813), 208, danced 'a few years ago' by eight men: J. Corley, 109; Thomas Buckley, 106; John Snow, 101; John Edey, 104; George Bailey, 106; Joseph Medbury, 100; John Medbury, 95; and Joseph Pidgeon, 79. Michael Heaney has kindly examined Brand's annotated copy in the Bodleian, on which Ellis based his edition. The information is included in a MS addition and there is no indication of its source. Zisea (p 125, l.26) is the Bohemian general Jan Žižka (*c* 1376–1424).

The list of gentry among the spectators (p 127, ll.12–29) serves only to confirm that the morris of *Old Meg* may well be historical, for those listed who can be traced were living at the time and many, though not all, had important local connections. Lord Herbert of Raglan, for example, was Henry Somerset, the second son (and heir) of Edward Somerset, earl of Worcester. Sir Thomas Somerset of Badminton, Gloucestershire, was MP for Monmouthshire in 1601, 1604, and 1614; Sir Charles Somerset was his great-uncle. The 'Count Arundels' (l.15) was Thomas Arundell of Wardour Castle, Wiltshire, who was a count of the Holy Roman Empire. His eldest son would have been about twenty-six at the time of *Old Meg*. Sir Thomas Mildmay was the sheriff of Essex in 1608–9. Scudamore, Baskerville, and Coningsby were among the major Herefordshire families; Sir John Scudamore had served regularly as MP until 1597 and Sir Thomas Coningsby had served for Leominster in 1601, 1604, and 1614. Lacon was a Shropshireman and Russell, of Strensham, Worcestershire, served as MP in 1601. Cornwall is likely to be a member of the Cornwall family of Berrington, Herefordshire, several of whose members served in parliament in the sixteenth century.

'Kemps Morris to Norwich' (p 133, l.37) refers here to Will Kemp's morris dance from London to Norwich (*Kemps nine daies wonder. Performed in a daunce from London to Norwich* (London, 1600; STC: 14923). This part of the text (the ninth day) is printed by David Galloway in *Norwich 1540–1642*, Records of Early English Drama (Toronto, 1984), 331–8.

The difficulty of determining whether or not the event actually took place would seem to preclude an attempt to identify the dancers and musicians. However, Squire of Hereford (p 128, ll.33-5m) may refer to Roger Squyre of Hereford (pp 123–4), a city wait who would have been at least 89 years old in 1609. Although none of the whifflers or dancers can be identified as a participant in an actual morris recorded in this collection, several of them bear the same surnames as persons charged with dancing elsewhere. The parishes from which some of them are said to have come are named as sites of dancing or morris dancing elsewhere in the Records or as the home parishes of dancers charged elsewhere such as Madley or Llangaren. In short, even if this dance is completely fictitious or greatly exaggerated, there is sufficient local colour to lend it an air of verisimilitude.

136–7   PRO: STAC 8/50/4   f 2
The first part of this case may be conveniently summarized as follows: John Breinton of Stretton Grandison complains of Walter Grismond of Hereford (deceased) that the said Walter Grismond owed to John Breinton and William Whitlache, draper, of Hereford, the sum of 1000 marks. In default of this sum, the county sheriff delivered to Breinton and Whitlache some of Grismond's property, as specified by an inquisition, to hold until the debt was repaid. Among the properties seized was a messuage situated by the High Cross in Hereford, which John Breinton and William Whitlache held and quietly enjoyed until the last day of July 1612.

The complainant Breinton is the defendant in several other Star Chamber cases of about the same date. The first name of Wallwin, who signed this bill as counsel, is known from his signatures on other bills to have been Walter.

139   HCL   f 2v
There is no 'acta' heading for this entry, but since there is no previous record of either an appearance or a failure to appear, 18 December is probably to be taken as the date of the court session. The change in hand between the charge and the record of the session is therefore probably due to a different registrar accompanying the court than the one who engrossed the charges before the session began.

140   HRO: box 25, vol 94   f [93]
Apparently Watkins did not appear on 24 October, the session date given in the 'acta'

paragraph on f [91], although it seems that a report of an attempt to serve a citation on him was made at that session. His first appearance took place on 14 November, but because it does appear that his case came before the 24 October session, that date is assigned to the entry.

141   HRO: box 24a (formerly 18), vol 71   f [356v]
The date of the court session given in the 'acta' paragraph on f [353] is 2 June, but the internal evidence of the document suggests that Waucklen's case was not considered at all on that date. He was cited to appear on 30 June, when he was excommunicated 'in absentia' for non-appearance.

142–3   HRO: box 24, vol 90   f [144v]
The 'acta' paragraph for these cases on f [142] is dated 26 October 1618. However there is no indication in the entries that the cases were considered before 16 November, when Hall, Crocker, and Hooper all made their first appearances. It is also the session for which Wilbore was cited, although he failed to appear.

143–4   PRO: SP 16/397   single sheet
The Kings Maiesties Declaration to His Subiects, Concerning lawfull Sports to be vsed (STC: 9238.9) was first printed in London on 24 May 1618 and was reissued in 1633 and 1634. The *Declaration*, commonly known as *The Book of Sports*, was a response to the increasing influence of sabbatarianism which held that all forms of pastime on Sundays and holy days were to be prohibited, including sports, dancing, and folk games. Such prohibitions threatened to eliminate all forms of village recreation, since most villagers and agricultural workers were not in a position to engage in any sort of recreation during the work week. The *Declaration*, first promulgated for Lancashire in 1617, was intended to establish a list of permitted forms of sport and recreation. The full text is printed in Greenfield and Douglas, *Cumberland/ Westmorland/Gloucestershire*, REED, pp 365–8. Henry Page, clearly a strict sabbatarian, served as vicar at Ledbury from 1631 to 1663 (J. Duncumb, *Collections towards the History of Hereford*, vol 5 (by Morgan G. Watkins), p 94).

144–5   Bodl.: MS Tanner 464e   f 79
John Leland, the king's antiquary, undertook his survey of the country during the years 1534–43. The original manuscript of his Itinerary (Bodl.: MS Gen. Top. e. 8–15) is missing the section dealing with Leominster. Fortunately, three early transcripts survive with the passage intact; one made in 1576 by John Stow (Bodl.: MS Tanner 464e, f 79), and two made 1628 and 1632 by William Burton (Bodl.: MS Gough Gen. Top. 2, p 106, and MS Bodley 470, f 78). There are no substantive differences between the three copies, though the orthography is markedly different. The Stow text has been selected as the earliest; it was also the text used by Lucy Toulmin Smith for her 1907 edition of the Itinerary to fill the gaps in Leland's original.
    'Kynge merwalde' (p 144, ll.40–1) was Merewald, son of Penda of Mercia and brother of Wulfhere, king of the West Mercians in the region of Herefordshire. Merewald (called St Merewald in Florence of Worcester's pedigrees) was converted by a priest whose vision of a lion allegedly gave Leominster (Leonis monasterium) its name (*Florentii Wigorniensis*

Monachi Chronicon ex Chronicis, Benjamin Thorpe (ed), vol 1 (London, 1848), 33; *Two of the Saxon Chronicles Parallel*, Charles Plummer (ed), vol 2 (Oxford, 1899), 26, 226).

145   HRO   f [1]
James Warnecombe (l.14) was MP for Ludlow in 1554, for Leominster in 1555, for Hereford-shire in 1563, and for the city of Hereford in 1571–2. In addition to a number of other local offices, he acted as Hereford's mayor in 1571–2 and again in 1578–9. He was county sheriff in 1576–7.

The Warnecombe family of Ivington held offices in Hereford and Leominster through much of the sixteenth century. Three Warnecombes in addition to James served as mayors of Hereford: his father Richard in 1525–6 and 1540–1, and his brothers John and Richard in 1548–9 and 1575–6 respectively. The Law Day session concerning the suppression of the Corpus Christi procession (Hereford 1548–9) was presided over by Mayor James Warne-combe. The elder Richard was the city's MP from 1529–36 and 1542–5; John held the same office in 1547. Neither James nor his brothers had male issue and with the death of Richard the line died out. Mr Craswell (l.14) is quite likely the Creswell who served as bailiff of Leominster in 1590 and as MP in 1597 (S.T. Bindoff, *The House of Commons: 1509–1558*, vol 3 (London, 1982), 548–50; P.W. Hasler, *The House of Commons: 1558–1603*, vol 1 (London, 1981), 669 and vol 3, 582–3; W.R. Williams, *The Parliamentary History of the County of Hereford* (Brecknock, 1896), 83).

145   HRO   f [3v]
Leominster's annual hen feast was supported by the payment of two hens or the sum of 1s 6d by all lease holders each Christmas. See George Fyler Townsend, *The Town and Borough of Leominster*, p 84.

145–6   HRO: box 20, vol 75   f [88v]
The phrase 'cit*atus* (ut sup*ra*)' (l.38) probably refers back to the first case on this folio, in which the accused is said to have been cited by the apparitor Crompton.

146   HRO   f [4]
Lord Chandos' players toured the West Midlands during the years 1595–7, and probably included Robert Armin in the company. See p 585, endnote to STC: 772.3 sigs B–C.

149–50   HRO: box 24a (formerly 18), vol 71   f [207v]
This is the second of a series of three prosecutions of Nurse; the others are for unlawful intercourse and for drinking in the company of an excommunicate. According to the 'acta' paragraph on f [199], this case against Nurse should have been considered at the session held on 28 May. But the internal evidence clearly suggests that the case did not come before any session prior to 2 September.

150   HRO: box 22, unnumbered vol, pt 2   f [78v]
This unnumbered volume, pt 2, of the Acts of Office has been severely damaged by damp and is, for the most part, lacking in 'acta' headings. The date given here, 16 December, is

that of the first appearance of Powell, who is named in Bullock's confession, the date of
which cannot be recovered due to the lack of 'acta' headings.

150–1   HRO: box 24a (formerly 18), vol 70   f [96]
Although this volume contains few 'acta' headings, in the absence of any previous mention
of an appearance of a failure to appear, it is probably safe to assume that 31 May is the date
of the first court session at which this case was heard. If so, the change in hand is probably
due to the charge having been engrossed by a different registrar from the one who accompanied
the court. The change in person from third to first in the charge may indicate that it was
taken from a presentment made in the first person.

151   HRO: box 25, vol 93A   f [137]
There is no 'acta' heading for this entry, but it contains quite full information on the session
date and personnel of the court at the time of the accused's first appearance. The date and
court information are drawn from the entry itself and from other information available about
Basset's principal.

151   HRO: box 25, vol 93A   f [132]
Although this case has been entered on a folio containing cases from the session of 2 November
1627 ('acta' paragraph on f [119]) the contents connect it with the case against Jane Simons
first heard in the session of 18 June 1628 (see ll.37–41). The hand of the registrar closely
resembles that of the registrar for that session. It has therefore been placed under 1628 immediately before the first entry for Jane Simons. It seems probable that it was also heard at
the 18 June session before Mr Freemantle (ll.33–5).

152   HRO: box 25, vol 93A   f [143]
The phrases 'similiter vt supra' (l.4) and 'similiter' (l.5) refer to the otherwise unrelated case
written immediately above this one, in which the defendant was excommunicated on 18 June
for failure to certify penance and absolved and dismissed on 23 August. John Drewe must
have been treated likewise.

152   HRO: box 22, vol 82   p 17
'specificarunt vt supra' (l.30) refers to the previous entry dealing with Smyth and Shepard
on p 16 (printed above, ll.17–23).

152–3   HCL   f 112v
The two previous prosecutions are for tennis playing on the sabbath. The phrase 'similiter
dimissus' (p 152, l.42; p 153, l.2) in the prosecutions against Pigg and Paine refers to the
disposition of the first of those cases, in which the defendant is dismissed with a warning.
The entry of an apparent joint prosecution of Carwardine (who is the defendant in one of
the suits for tennis playing) and Foote (p 153, ll.27–8) was written in between the prosecutions
of Brampton and Arnoll in a cramped and hurried hand, which is probably that of the same
registrar as the one who wrote the other material enclosed within raised circles on this folio.
'Tiberton' (p 153, l.22m) could refer to any of the three Tibbertons in Gloucestershire, Shropshire, or Worcestershire, but is most likely the Gloucestershire parish.

154   HRO: box 22, unnumbered vol, pt 2   f [51]   col 1
The early part of this volume has been severely damaged by damp and it is not possible to
search it for court details. It is, in fact, largely lacking 'acta' headings. The date of 24 November
is given in the entry itself as the first court date on which Churche appeared. Clearly it was
not the first date for which he was cited and summoned, because he appears to have been
excommunicated for non-appearance before 24 November.

154–5   HRO: box 22, unnumbered vol, pt 2   f [110]
This volume has suffered considerable damage and it is not always possible to locate and
read 'acta' headings. This entry follows sessions of 11 and 16 December on f [108v], but if
the folios are in chronological order (as they appear to be) the first court appearance must
fall between December 1609 and 15 July 1610, the apparent date of the second court appearance.

155   HRO: box 22, unnumbered vol, pt 2   f [108v]
There is an 'acta' heading at the top of this folio for a session of 11 December, but it is clear
from the text of this entry that 16 December was the first date the accused was cited to appear
on.

155–6   HRO: box 24, vol 90   f [237v]
The most likely explanation of the marginal note 'vide rest/' (p 156, l.25m), is that it was
written after the time of Edwardes' 1620 court appearance by an inquiring registrar who was
reminding himself or someone else to 'look for the rest (of the case),' ie, to look elsewhere
in the court books for the proceedings intervening between Edwardes' court appearance in
1618 and his appearance in 1620 – proceedings in which he had incurred the excommunication
from which he was absolved in 1620. Apparently they could not be found. There is no 'acta'
paragraph intervening between these six cases and the 'acta' dated 27 October 1618 on f [231].
However, internal evidence shows that the accused parties were all cited to appear at sessions
in December: Gorwey, Parker, and Jenkins on 7 December, Hamon and Ravenhill on 5
December, and Edwardes on 18 December. Two of the six were not finally dismissed until
February 1618/19, and Edwardes' case was not disposed of until 1620.

157   HCL   f 202v
General articles for archidiaconal visitations were issued in 1621, published by J. Bill, London,
with blanks left for the archdeaconry and the name of the archdeacon to be filled in (STC:
10133.9). A new set of general articles was not issued until the mid-1630s (STC: 10134). The
34th Article (see l.16) which the churchwardens have not answered deals with working on
the sabbath: 'Whether be there any in your Parish that vse any handie craft, or worke, or
keepe open shop vpon any Sabbaoth or Festiuall day, or that within time of Haruest doe
vpon Holy-dayes labour about their Haruest, or then vse any carriages by Wayne, or otherwise, vnlesse necessity shall require, or the law permit it?' (STC: 10133.9, sig B1v).

157   HRO: box 24a (formerly 18), vol 71   f [358v]
Presumably 'in hos diem et locum' (l.30) and 'Quo die' (l.36) in these two cases refer to the
session of 2 June 1617 described in the 'acta' paragraph on f [353]. However, it was not the

date of the first court appearance for either accused party, although they seem to have been cited to appear then. In fact, it is not possible to say with certainty that either made a court appearance. The antecedent of 'vt supra' (l.36) is not clear; if it refers to the immediately preceding case against Thomas, then Steade must have been dismissed without ever appearing.

158   HCL   f 170v
The case against Alice Harris (l.15) has been added in the left margin.

158   HCL   f 174ᵃv
Although this entry apparently belongs to a session of 3 November (according to the 'acta' paragraph on f 174v), f 174ᵃ is a single sheet added between ff 174 and 175 and so the sequence of 'acta' dates does not necessarily apply. In fact, the date and court officers for this session are given in the body of the entry: 19 November 1625 before Master Osgood, surrogate.

161–3   HRO: box 25, vol 94   ff [252v–4]
It is impossible to be certain of the exact date and location of the session or sessions to which all of these accused were cited, although most seem to have been originally cited to appear on 25 June (Browne, Cater, Machin, Sandie, Wilse) or 27 June (Baker, Garden, Harris, Parret). Currier, Keise, Smith, and Streete did not appear until July, although Currier's and Keise's original citations of 18 June may have been for 25 June as were the other citations issued on that date. As indicated by 'vt supra' (p 161, l.12), Keise was made known to the commissary's office in the same way as the first accused recorded on f[252v], that is, reported on the basis of public rumour concerning the alleged offence, 'officio ex publica fama referendus.'

163–6   HRO: box 25, vol 94   ff [255–5v, 256, 76]
In the case brought against Joan Bennet, the section beginning '28 die mensis Iulij 1629' (p 164, ll.9–13) is added in a third hand. In the case against Charles Perrocke, a third hand begins at 'comparuit personaliter' (p 164, l.28), and in the case against Alice Haynes a third hand begins at 'comparuit' (p 165, l.2). In the case against Thomas Webster, a third hand begins at 'comparuit personaliter' (p 165, l.6), and in the case against Edward Keise, a third hand begins at '5° decembris 1629 (p 165, ll.22–3). Usually such changes in handwriting, and hence in the writer, are signals that a new court session, recorded by a different registrar, has begun. Here that clearly cannot be the case in any instance except in the proceedings against Keise. It is therefore difficult to interpret the changes in handwriting in these cases or their meaning, except to say that they raise the possibility of more than one registrar having been simultaneously employed in recording the proceedings at individual sessions.

166   HRO: box 26, vol 96   ff [426v–7]
'similiter vt supra' (ll.13–14) refers to the first case on f[426v] where the accused is excommunicated for non-appearance. Charles also must have failed to appear and been excommunicated.

167   HRO: box 22, unnumbered vol, pt 2   f [108v]
The top of this page is damaged by dirt and worm holes and is torn, thus rendering parts of the entry illegible. The court details of the session appear just before the entry and

are sufficiently clear to allow a date to be assigned to the accused party's court appearance.

168   HRO: fragment C   single sheet
There is no heading on this single-sheet fragment, but the handwriting is that of a court clerk who wrote many of the volumes during the period 1600–15 and therefore likely dates from the first two decades of the century. Roger Conie (l.26) was one of the churchwardens.

168–9   HRO: box 21, vol 80, pt 3   p 60
The passage in column 2 from the date '.16. Nov*embris*' to the end (p 169, ll.24–6) is inserted in the left margin below the heading of the following case, with the sign '#' used as a mark of continuation. The layout of this case is particularly complicated by later additions. The principal entry, the prosecution of Miles Conney, is written down the right-hand two thirds of the page; the added entries dealing with Brooke, Grenewich, and Corbet are written down the left-hand side of the page below the initial heading.

169–70   HRO: box 21, vol 80, pt 3   p 70
Although Conney, Richardes, Tower, Morries, Conney, Conney, and Henge did not appear until 8 December, the marginal notes recording that they were cited 'in *proximo*' were probably written on or soon after the session of 16 November, at which those citations were probably issued.

171   HRO: box 21, vol 80, pt 4   p 21
The upper right corner of the page is badly damaged, thus causing some parts of the first entry to be illegible. Four hands have been at work on this page. The sections enclosed in raised circles in the cases against Boice (ll.11–12) and Howles (ll.17–18) and the first part of the case against Younge (ll.23–4) are in the second hand. The rest of the case against Younge (ll.24–31), the note immediately above it (l.20), and the entry about Brooke (l.37) and its marginale (l.37m) are in hand three. The marginale next to the case against Lane (l.33m) and the note immediately above the Brooke case (l.36) are in a fourth hand. The marginale '*Citatus in proximo*' (ll.25–6m) was written by the third hand, and was probably recorded between 5 February and 7 March, although the second citation was probably ordered at the 5 February session.

173   HRO: box 23, vol 88   f 156
Although the session described in the 'acta' paragraph for this entry is dated 20 April 1613, internal evidence suggests that this case was only considered at a later session on 10 May, at which Jones failed to appear.

174   HRO: box 24, vol 90   f [178]
It is clear that the first court session to which Fletcher was cited was held on 4 December, even though he failed to appear at that time. Since it was apparently the first session at which his case was considered, the date of 4 December has been assigned to the entry.

174–5   HRO: box 24a (formerly 18), vol 70, f [26]
There is not direct evidence of date for this entry. However, it falls after the record of a

case commencing in June of 1616 and appears to have been written by the same registrar.

175   HCL   f 5v, 6
Although these cases were apparently first considered at the session of 26 February, none of the accused seems to have appeared before the session of 11 March. The 26 February session seems to have been used to record information about citations and the attempt to serve them.

178   HCL   f 118v
The case against Imme to which the registrar refers (l. 14) is on the same folio; on 9 November he was excommunicated for non-appearance. Beckinsfield too must have failed to appear and been excommunicated. Although the expression 'Quo die' (l. 17) in the entry of Joan Careles' case may refer to the date of the session described in the 'acta' paragraph on f 116v, 26 October 1622, the other four accused parties do not seem to have appeared at a session before that of 9 November. Therefore it is perhaps more likely that 'Quo die' has as its antecedent the date of the previous case, that is, 9 November.

178–9   HCL   f 120
The entries on this folio fall between 'acta' paragraphs describing sessions on 26 October and 23 November, but the only internal evidence suggests that John Smith, who appeared on behalf of Jane Serle, did so at a session of 7 December. There is no evidence that Hallinges or Tomkins either appeared or sent a proxy.

180   HCL   f 35
The entries on this folio fall between 'acta' paragraphs describing sessions on 22 July and 23 September. The court session at which Butlar, Jones, and Powell were first considered must have been held after 27 August, the date of the offence, and before 23 September, the date of the entry describing their first court appearance (see f 35v).

182   HRO: box 17, vol 67   f [215]
'Tadington' (l. 10m) is the adjacent parish of Tarrington, rather than Taddington, Gloucestershire, or Teddington, Worcestershire. 'Tarrington' appears in the Domesday Book as 'Tatintune' and forms with medial 'd' or 't' persist through the period.

183–6   HRO: box 24, vol 90   ff 72v–4
In the case against John Shepperd, the passage 'comp*aruit* ... dimisit' (p 185, l. 38–p 186, l. 10) has been added in the left margin because there was no more room left at the foot of the page.
   Most of the accused parties appeared on a series of dates in early February 1619/20: 2 February (Hint, Hopkins, William and Anne Lyke, Anne and John Watkins), 5 February (Blether, Bowcot, Clerke, Emmans, John Hodges, Thomas and Hugh Powell, Reygnoldes, Shepperd, Wheetse, and Winney), and 8 February (James Hodges). Thomas Hodges, although apparently originally cited for 5 February, failed to appear at every court day for which he was cited. Phillpottes was originally cited for 5 February but did not appear until the eleventh.
   The entry on James Blether was written in three different hands and in four stages. The

text enclosed within the first set of raised circles (p 184, ll. 32–7) is that written in a second hand and at the second stage. The cancelled text (ll. 37–8) is written in a third hand and at the third stage; '[2] 16 … sequen*tem*' (ll. 38–9), which represents the fourth stage, is written in the hand of the second.

The entry on Hugh Powell also shows three hands and four stages of annotation. The text enclosed within the first set of raised circles was written in a second hand and at the second stage (p 185, ll. 13–14); the third hand and stage begin at 'Quo 24 die' (l. 14) and end at '16 Martij p*roximo*' (l. 16). The fourth annotation, beginning at '15 Martij 1619' (l. 16) and ending at 'dimisit cu*m* admonicione' (l. 18), is written in the hand of the second.

The entry on Thomas Bowcot follows the same pattern. The text enclosed within the first set of raised circles (ll. 20–5) is written in a second hand and at the second stage; the third hand and stage begin at '24 die ffeb*ruarij*' (l. 25) and end at 'pen*a* in prox*imum* &c' (l. 28). The fourth annotation, '[2] 15 Martij pred*icti* vt in c*ausa* [Bow] Powell' (ll. 28–9), is written in the hand of the second.

The entry on Joan Emmans was written in three hands and at three stages. The text enclosed within the first set of raised circles (p 186, ll. 19–28) was written in a second hand and at a second stage; the third hand and stage begin at '24 die ffebruarij' (ll. 28–9) and end at 'Vnde dimiss*a* est' (l. 30).

187   PRO: E101/363/18   f 21v
There is no longer a place in Herefordshire called Straddle, though the name was common in the Middle Ages. The place name here refers to the Golden Valley of the River Dore and derives from the Welsh for 'the valley of the Dore,' 'ystrat Dore.' There is little doubt that the royal wardrobe payment would have been made for services at the Augustinian Priory of Abbey Dore. The prince (p 187, ll. 8, 10, 14) is the future Edward II.

187–8   HRO   ff 77, 77v–8
Thomas Spofford served as bishop from 1422–48. The Augustinian priory of Limebrook (or Lindbrook) was founded about 1189 and remained a small house for the whole of its existence. At the Dissolution it was allowed to continue until 1539, at which time it housed six nuns (David Knowles and R. Neville Hadcock, *Medieval Religious Houses: England and Wales* (London, 1953), 229).

Spofford's letter is in English since there was no regulation nor any expectation that the nuns be competent in Latin. The dialect of the letter is of some interest, for several features of the language suggest a somewhat more northerly place of origin than Hereford for the scribe, namely 'es' (p 187, l. 25; p 188, ll. 18, 20) for 'is,' 'er' (p 188, l. 21) for 'are,' and more particularly 'at' (p 188, ll. 16, 22) for the conjunction 'that' and 'sextend' (p 188, l. 25) for 'sixteenth.' The MED terms the last form northeast Midland, which is the dialect one would expect a scribe from the extreme north of Hereford diocese to use. It is quite possible that the person who drafted the injunction was more used to writing such orders in Latin and the document's syntax is in a few places complex enough that I include a paraphrase of the second extract: 'Also we forbid all manner of minstrelsy, interludes, dancing, or revelling within your said holy place; and as concerns recreation of walking abroad in due time and place, we are content so long as you keep the due hours and time of divine service within (the convent) and (so long as you walk) with honourable company and with licence specially asked and obtained (of) the prioress or subprioress in her absence, and that there are at least two of you together; charging you, the current prioress, and all your successors hereafter, on the penalty of disobedience (*ie*, of being considered disobedient) and of suspension from your office, that you observe and keep this present ordinance in your own persons and that it is your responsibility to see that it is observed and kept among all your sisters, both current and future, and that once in each month of the year (*possibly* once a year?) all these rules shall be read openly in the chapter house, all the sisters having been called there so that none may pretend ignorance (of them), under the penalty aforesaid. Written in our manor of Whitbourne on 16 June AD 1437 and in the sixteenth year since our translation.'

188 HRO f 28

Adam Orleton's stormy episcopate began in 1317 when he was nominated to the see against the wishes of Edward II. His tenure at Hereford was marked by continual feuding with the king; for a time Orleton was the virtual leader of the queen's party. After Edward's abdication in 1327, Orleton was translated to Worcester and in 1334, to Winchester. He died in 1345. See Roy Martin Haines, *The Church and Politics in Fourteenth-Century England: the Career of Adam Orleton, c. 1275–1345* (Cambridge, 1978).

The Augustinian abbey of Wigmore was founded in 1179 and through its first two centuries had close connections with the Mortimer family. The lack of discipline among its canons was well-known and they were frequently sent to Bristol or Keynsham for disciplinary purposes, as described in the fourteenth-century Wigmore Chronicle (University of Chicago Library: MS 224). The literature on the practice of blood-letting for medical purposes is surveyed by Linda E. Voigts and Michael R. McVaugh, *A Latin Technical Phlebotomy and Its Middle English Translation, Transactions of the American Philosophical Society*, vol 74, pt 2 (1984), 1–7; the practice of regular monastic blood-letting is discussed in Walter Horn and Ernest Born, *The Plan of St Gall*, vol 2 (Berkeley, 1979), 184–8; vol 3, p 52. The connection regularly cited by church authorities (as here by Bishop Orleton) between blood-letting and unseemly recreation and merriment is noted by Horn and Born, vol 2, p 187. See also the payments for 'seyny money' by Prior More of Worcester, pp 307–8.

189 Bodl.: MS Lat. hist. d. 1(R) mb 3d

Swinfield was elected bishop of Hereford in 1282, following the death of St Thomas Cantilupe, and served until his death in 1317. Much of this account roll deals with the bishop's visitation circuit of the diocese, though it is not possible to localize most the entries. The entries are grouped in paragraphs, some of which contain enough information to date them approximately. The first group of entries (ll. 8–10) follows a payment made around the feast of St Thomas the apostle, 21 December; the second group of payments (ll. 12–16) is associated with those explicitly dated within the octave of Epiphany, 6–13 January. Most of the payments in this group are related to the bishop's journey to London and may refer to performances there. The payment at Monkton (l. 17) follows a payment on Easter, 2 April; the fourth group (ll. 18–20) follows a payment made within the octave of Trinity Sunday, 28 May–4 June.

The payment to the abbot of Reading (l. 9) is indicative of the close ties the abbey of St Mary had with Hereford Diocese; Leominster Priory, one of the major houses of the diocese, was a daughter house of Reading Abbey.

Colwall (ll. 19, 20) and Sugwas (l. 18) are both in Herefordshire, the former on the

Worcestershire border at the southwest end of the Malvern Hills, the latter to the west of the city of Hereford. Monkton (l.17) is more of a problem; it is a common enough place name, though it does not occur in the diocese of Hereford. The closest possibilities would seem to be Monkton Combe in Somerset and Monkton Farleigh in Wiltshire. Both lie between Bath and Bradford-on-Avon.

The relationship between minstrels and waferers (l.15) remains uncertain, though they are frequently linked in accounts. The waferer's primary function was the making and presentation of baked delicacies; the presentation of these at a feast seems often to have involved ceremony and minstrelsy. See also Bullock-Davies, *Menestrellorum Multitudo*, pp 44–50; and Richard Rastall, 'Secular Musicians in Late Medieval England,' PHD thesis (University of Manchester, 1968), 187–92.

191   BL: Egerton 3054   f 33v
The pamphlet on Ben Jonson's death (ll.9–10) was probably John Taylor's *A funerall elegie, in memory of the rare, famous, and admired poet, Mr Benjamin Jonson, deceased* (London, 1637; STC: 23759), though it could also have been *Jonsonus virbius: or the memorie of Ben Johnson revived* (London, 1638; STC: 14784).

193–4   BL: Egerton Roll 8738   mb 2
William Mallynges, described here as a 'tillere' (p 194, l.11m), that is, a weaver or, more generally, one who works with cloth and thread, appears to have been a member of Mortimer's household. In Egerton Roll (fragment) 8728 he is paid during May and June of 1378 at Royston and Pontefract while Mortimer is on the commission to treat with the Scots over the custody of the Marches.

195   HCL   p 81
The account book is arranged topically rather than chronologically. It is quite likely that 'there' (l.29) refers to Scudamore's installation as high steward of the city of Hereford.

196   Hereford Library: LC 647.1 MSS   f 21v
The text of f 21v is repeated on f 39v but crossed out.

WORCESTERSHIRE

Historical Background

The history of Worcestershire, even more than that of Herefordshire, has been shaped by its principal river, the Severn, with its tributaries the Avon and the Teme. The Severn was navigable well into Shropshire to the north-west and provided the principal means of transportation for goods to and from the port of Bristol. Accounts dealing with the building of Kyre Park in 1588 show that the transportation of heavy goods cost between three and four times as much by road as by water.[1] Bewdley attained early importance as a major point of transfer of goods from water to road and, in the fifteenth century, as a bridge site, though Worcester's two fords and later its bridge remained the principal crossing places. Heavy goods relying on this waterway included salt from Droitwich and, from the late sixteenth century, coal from southern Shropshire.[2]

The county is divided by the Severn into two contrasting regions. To the east and south lies some of England's richest arable land and consequently the production of crops went hand-in-hand with a relatively large population. To the west and north the land is hillier and more suitable for grazing cattle than growing produce. It is less populous and considerably more heavily wooded. Worcester, at the border between the two regions, was remarkably well-placed as a market for the exchange of goods between these regions.[3]

Like Hereford, Worcester was the apex of an important system of roads. The principal route from London to Wales ran through Oxford and Evesham to Worcester, crossing the Severn there. To the south ran the road to Tewkesbury and Gloucester and from thence to Bristol, though the principal goods route from Bristol to Worcester was by river. Two roads ran north, one to Kidderminster, then north-west to Shrewsbury, the other, originally a Roman road, north-east to Droitwich and Bromsgrove.[4]

Although Worcestershire had frequently been a mustering place for the Welsh wars, after Edward I's conquest of Wales in 1282 the county remained in comparative peace. Life in the late thirteenth-century West Midlands has been reconstructed in considerable detail by R. H. Hilton, who describes a relatively stable economy of secular and ecclesiastical lords and 'knightly families' administering estates of varying complexity, an extensive farming peasantry living in village-based communities, and a network of larger towns whose economy was based both on manufactures and on markets.[5] Among the lords, the ecclesiastical magnates were the most prominent, for Worcestershire was dominated by its wealthy Benedictine foundations. Not until the early fifteenth century was the county's stability seriously disturbed. Then with Glendower's uprising, Worcester again became the mustering place for Henry IV's troops. The king himself came to Worcester twice in 1401 and again in 1403, but with the suppression of Glendower the county again became a quiet provincial region. The last battle of the Wars of the Roses was fought just over the county border, at Tewkesbury, on 4 May 1478. Much of Buckingham's rebellion against Richard III was fought within the county and his defeat was precipitated by an unusual October flooding of the Severn, leaving Buckingham with no route to his targets, Worcester and Bewdley.[6]

With the increasing peacefulness of the Marches the county's political importance became less, although Worcester remained an important provincial city. In the early seventeenth century, Worcestershire men were heavily involved in the Gunpowder Plot. Most of them were captured in the county within the next few years; one, Thomas Habington, was pardoned, restricted to the county, and became in his retirement its first important antiquary. During the Civil War Worcestershire was primarily a royalist stronghold and suffered heavily following the Battle of Worcester in 1651.[7]

The Council in the Marches of Wales

Although a previous advisory council had been set up in 1471 for Edward IV's son, the Council in the Marches was established by 1494 (and probably in 1493), ostensibly as an advisory body to Arthur, prince of Wales, son to Henry VII. After the prince's death in 1502, the Council continued to act as a Commission for the Peace for the Welsh border, though it may have had little real power since the administrative structure of the earldom of March (which fell to the Crown at the deposition of Richard III) still had real control of much of the border country.[8] In 1534 Cromwell appointed Rowland Lee, the formidable bishop of Coventry and Lichfield, to head the council, with a mandate to bring law and order to the Welsh borders. This Lee did with a vengeance, believing hanging to be the best deterrent to the thieving and murder he found under his jurisdiction. The Welsh Act of 1536 (and its refinement of 1543) established most of the Welsh border shires out of the myriad small marcher lordships, ceding some land to the English border counties.[9] The Council and its administrative head, the lord president, became a power almost equal to that of the Council in the North, with wide-ranging administrative and judicial powers in the counties of Cheshire, Herefordshire, Worcestershire, Gloucestershire, Shropshire, and Monmouthshire. The Council was based at Ludlow, in Shropshire, but also met frequently at Shrewsbury, as well as at Bewdley, Worcestershire, and at Worcester. Its precise powers and procedures remain somewhat obscure, although the Council held a commission of oyer and terminer as well as a commission to hear private suits. It acted as an informal court of appeal for the counties' quarter sessions courts and supervised justices of the peace.[10] Under Elizabeth the influence of the Council declined, until it became little more than a law court, though the office of lord president continued to be a politically influential one. The criminal jurisdiction of the Council, its last real vestige of power, was abolished in 1641.[11]

Diocese of Worcester

The diocese was created in 680 by Theodore, archbishop of Canterbury, who broke the see of Mercia into five smaller sees in an effort to form a less unwieldy administrative structure, forming the diocese of Worcester out of the Mercian sub-kingdom of the Hwicce.[12]

As with most bishoprics, the early history of the Worcester diocese is dominated by a series of conflicts, both external and internal, concerned primarily with episcopal rights. Worcester was a relatively wealthy diocese, however, and its bishop came to wield considerable power; the death of a bishop often left the see vacant while the monks, the king, and the pope battled over the new appointment. During these times the prior of Worcester Priory was left in charge of the bishop's spiritualities and the episcopal register was kept 'sede vacante'. Worcester bishops regularly held high diplomatic and civil offices, often leaving the administration of the see to local deputies. A good example is John Alcock (1476-86), who was also president of Edward IV's Court of the Welsh Marches, lord chancellor, and finally (as a reward for his services as chancellor), bishop of Ely. Not all the Worcester bishops were staunch supporters of the Crown, however. The author of one of the earliest documents in this collection, Walter Cantilupe (1237-66), was one of Simon de Montfort's major supporters (and a close friend of Robert Grosseteste), while Adam Orleton (1327-33) was instrumental in the deposition and murder of Edward II. At the end of the fifteenth century, it became clear to Henry VII (and later to Henry VIII) that a strong diplomatic presence at the Vatican was essential. A review of church administration showed that Worcester (along with Hereford and Lichfield) could most easily do without a resident bishop and thus a series of four Italian bishops presided over the see from 1497 to 1535 and the diocese was administered locally by suffragan bishops and deputies.[13]

By 1291 the diocese was divided administratively into two archdeaconries (Worcester and Gloucester) and six deaneries within the county: Worcester, Kidderminster, Evesham, Pershore, Droitwich, and Powick, although from 1268 Evesham was not under the jurisdiction of the bishop.[14] These were subdivided into 115 parishes (in the 1291 survey). A further deanery of Burford in the north-west of the county was under the control of the diocese of Hereford.

Religious Houses

The diocese housed an extraordinary variety of religious houses, ranging from small priories like Dodford, where only the prior was resident, to the great monastic foundations, numbering twenty-one at the time of Valor Ecclesiasticus.[15] These included Benedictine houses such as St Mary's Priory, Worcester, abbeys at Evesham and Pershore, and priories at Great and Little Malvern; the Cistercian abbey of Bordesley; and the Premonstratensian house of Halesowen on the Staffordshire border. Pride of place went of course to the great cathedral priory of St Mary at Worcester; luckily many of its archives survive, giving us an unusually thorough picture of a great ecclesiastical estate through the Middle Ages. The priory was supported in the mid-thirteenth century by twenty-five manors, all within the diocese. It also possessed a good deal of Worcester city property and part of the income of some seventy parish churches. Through most of the period it housed about forty monks. In contrast to such monasteries as Evesham and Pershore, Worcester Priory was transformed rather than destroyed at the Dissolution. Since the priory was attached to the cathedral, the offices of prior and obedientiaries, as well as most of the property belonging to the priory, passed with comparatively little disruption to the new dean and chapter.[16]

Two friaries were established in the city of Worcester, the Franciscans (Grey Friars) coming about 1225 and the Dominicans (Black Friars) some time after 1347.[17] From 1517 Prior William More regularly made at least one annual gift to each of the friaries.[18] At the Dissolution, the Black Friars' property was destroyed entirely, while part of the Grey Friars' buildings were converted to a private dwelling and stand today in Friar Street. The smaller Cistercian convent of Whistones lay in the parish of Claines, just north of the city outside the Foregate. It, too, was mostly demolished at the Dissolution.[19]

Though Worcester never became as notorious a centre for heterodoxy as did Hereford, Wycliffe and his lollards found great sympathy in the region and the registers of Bishops Henry Wakefield (1375–95), Thomas Peverel (1407–19), and Philip Morgan (1419–26) give frequent documentation of action taken against the heresy and its adherents.[20]

In the later sixteenth century, the county was divided about equally between protestant and catholic sympathizers. In 1564 the bishop reported to the privy council that of the city's principal officers, two were protestant and three catholic.[21] The county's catholics were particularly militant and the names of many of the county's most prominent families appear in the recusancy rolls.[22]

Boroughs and Parishes

BEWDLEY

The borough of Bewdley in the parish of Ribbesford lies on the border between Worcestershire and Shropshire. The county boundary was not settled until 1544 and jurisdictional uncertainties made Bewdley a haven for fugitives. The town gained importance as a principal inland terminus of the Severn, navigable as far as Shrewsbury. Goods were brought to Bewdley by land from all over the Midlands to go on to Bristol by boat. It was also a major crossing place. The river was fordable near Bewdley, but the town became far more important after the building of its bridge in 1447 (for contributions towards which the bishop of Worcester granted indulgences of forty days). The royal palace of Tickenhill lay just outside the town and the meetings of the Council in the Marches were frequently held there.[23]

The borough received its first charter from Edward IV in 1472. Henry VII's charter of 1507 provided for a Saturday market and three annual fairs on the feasts of St George (23 April), St Andrew (30 November), and St Anne (26 July).[24] Richard Symonds described its government in 1644: 'The towne of Bewdley is governed with a bayliffe and a justice, he that is bayliffe this yeare is justice the next. Chosen out of twelve aldermen. Two bridgwardens.'[25] The bridgewardens functioned like the chamberlains in other boroughs; they also acted as churchwardens for the chapel. Their accounts survive from 1569 to 1663. The chapel, situated at the foot of the bridge and dedicated to St Andrew, contained three separate chantries (to Sts Anne and Mary, and the Trinity). William Worcestre described the bridge in about 1478 as being 'de Arboribus,' but other records show that it must have been partly of stone construction.[26] The town was reincorporated under a government of bailiff and burgesses in 1605.[27]

DROITWICH

The principal importance of Droitwich lay in its salt deposits. The town received an early, though limited, charter from John in 1215. Though it was regularly confirmed, this charter was not replaced until 1553/4, when Mary granted a new one, including three three-day fairs, beginning on the vigils of the feasts of Sts Philip and James (1 May), Sts Peter and Paul (29 June), and Sts Simon and Jude (28 October).[28] An extensive set of bailiffs' account rolls in the Hereford and Worcester Record Office is concerned primarily with the jurisdiction and ownership of salt deposits.

EVESHAM

The borough of Evesham originated as a monastic foundation and was listed in the Domesday Book as such, under the government of the abbot and convent. Founded in 710, the Benedictine abbey was a wealthy house by the time of the Domesday survey and remained prosperous throughout the Middle Ages. Little information survives on the medieval abbey beyond the well-known Chronicle of the Abbey and the register of Abbot Bromsgrove from the fifteenth century.[29] R. H. Hilton suggests that what evidence survives shows a firm control of the abbey's estates, more so than, for example, at nearby Pershore.[30] The abbey's fine bell tower, all that now remains of its fabric, was built by Abbot Clement Litchfield. Litchfield refused to hand over the abbey and in 1538 was forced to resign in favour of his cellarer, Philip Hawford, who had previously agreed to its surrender. Hawford himself begged that the abbey be allowed to continue as an educational establishment, but his petition was ignored and when the abbey was surrendered in January 1540, it was torn to the ground, leaving only Litchfield's tower standing.[31]

Evesham had been granted a market by Edward the Confessor in 1055 and the Domesday Book also noted that money was collected 'de censu hominum ibi manentium.'[32] The town's urban status is clearly implied by the fact that it sent burgess representatives to the parliaments of 1295 and 1337. The town's medieval government remains obscure, though it is clear that its administration was in the hands of two bailiffs chosen by the town, while the borough court was presided over by a steward appointed by the abbot.[33] In 1546 letters patent were granted to Sir Philip Hoby, who had purchased much of the abbey estates, giving him the right to oversee a view of frankpledge and to hold three annual fairs, among other jurisdictional privileges.[34] Jurisdictional problems became acute under Elizabeth and were not resolved until James' first charter of 1604. This was quickly replaced by a new charter in 1605 providing for a government by mayor, seven aldermen, and twelve burgesses.[35] The town consisted originally of two parishes, All Saints' and St Lawrence, and was surrounded on three sides by the river Avon. The 1605 charter added the parish of Bengeworth, across the river. Like so many towns in the West Midlands, Evesham was principally a market town and a centre of cloth-making.

KIDDERMINSTER

Kidderminster was a royal demesne. The borough received its first charter in 1241, providing for two annual fairs, though a fair had been held as early as 1228. The borough was not incorporated until 1636; prior to that government was by a bailiff elected by twenty-four citizens.[36] In 1640 the inhabitants of Kidderminster complained of their vicar, George Dance, that he was an 'ignorant and weak man, who preached but once a quarter, was a frequenter of alehouses, and sometimes drunk.' Dance agreed that if he were allowed to keep the living, £60 could be paid from it to support a lecturer to preach regularly. The puritan theologian Richard Baxter of Bridgnorth was selected and he spent about a year and a half in Kidderminster.[37] His autobiography, *Reliquiæ Baxterianæ*, printed five years after his death, in London in 1696 (Wing: B1370), contains extensive details of Kidderminster life just before the Civil War.

PERSHORE

The abbey of Pershore was founded as a Benedictine house in the late tenth century, probably reconstituting an earlier foundation. It was never as wealthy a house as Evesham; through much of the Middle Ages the abbey was plagued by serious financial difficulties. Most of the abbey buildings were destroyed at the Dissolution, though the abbey church still stands as the parish church of the Holy Cross.[38]

Pershore manor had been granted to Westminster Abbey by Edward the Confessor and it is there that many of Pershore's records now survive[39]. The borough of Pershore, lying along the Avon, was divided into two parishes, Holy Cross and St Andrew's. Henry II granted it some borough privileges, which were confirmed by John in 1200 and by Henry III in 1227, who added a fair to the grant, to be held on the feast of St Eadburga (15 June). A frequent source of dispute between the abbey and the townspeople was the maintenance of the important bridge over the Avon on the Evesham road at the edge of the town. The dispute was resolved in 1351, dividing the responsibility equally. Though principally a market town, there is also evidence that Pershore had some industry, predominantly the making of woollen and linen cloth and the manufacture of gloves.[40]

WORCESTER

Excavations have shown clearly that Worcester was the site of an important Roman fort, though its remains are few and there is no clear evidence of continuity between the Roman settlement and the medieval town. Always an important fording place, Norman Worcester became a strategic site as the principal river-crossing on the east-west route.[41] In general outline, Worcester's topography was not dissimilar to that of Hereford.[42] The city lay along the east bank of the Severn and was surrounded, like Hereford, by a wall broken by six gates, one leading west over the Severn bridge to the suburb of St John's.[43] Leland described the city's six gates and 'dyvers fayre strets.' Pride of place, he said, went to the bridge, 'a royal peace of worke highe and stronge and hathe 6. greate arches of stone.'[44] Ten parishes made up the city: St Alban's, St Andrew's, St Clement's, St Helen's, St Martin's, St Michael's in Bedwardine, St Nicholas', St Peter's, St Swithin's, and All Saints'. Two of these, St Clement's and St Peter's, were largely suburban. The Severn bridge lay at the south-east corner of the city; north along the river bank lay the quay, the bishop's palace, and the cathedral, with the parish church of St Michael in Bedwardine attached to its south-west corner. Beyond the cathedral stood the castle.

Worcester's first charter was granted by Richard I in 1189. This grant was extended three times by Henry III; in his first charter of 1227 he allowed the formation of a merchant guild and his third charter of 1264 established a civic government with two bailiffs as chief officers.[45] By the late fourteenth century two aldermen and a council of burgesses had joined the bailiffs. Two chamberlains were added some time during the mid-fifteenth century and by 1466 the council was made up of an upper chamber of twenty-four and a lower chamber of forty-eight. It was essentially an oligarchic system, with the low bailiff serving the following year as high bailiff and the new low bailiff chosen by the body of bailiffs and aldermen. After 1496 the bailiffs were selected only from the members of the Twenty-four, all of whom had previously served as members of the Forty-eight.[46]

From the thirteenth century the city was divided into seven wards, generally corresponding to parishes in the city, All Saints', St Andrew's, St Clement's, St Martin's, St Nicholas', St Peter's, and the 'High Ward,' each under the jurisdiction of two constables.[47]

The medieval charter of 1264 remained the basis of Worcester's government until the seventeenth century. The new charter which the city obtained from Mary in 1555 made few significant changes to the city's powers; most important, it failed to give the city the status of a county, a common provision in other major cities. Alan Dyer has shown that such constitutional backwardness was a feature of Worcester's corporation throughout the sixteenth century.[48] Real change came only after some seventy years of pressure in 1621 when a new charter was granted by James I, in which county status was obtained and government by a mayor and aldermen was put in place.[49]

Two sets of very thorough ordinances for the city survive from 1466 and 1496, both drawn up during periods of economic expansion.[50] The earlier set is unlikely to represent new legislation but is rather a copy (perhaps expanded) of a previous set of regulations, since lost. Detailed provisions are made for all facets of city life: the selection and duties of all civic officers, the bailiffs, town clerk, the upper chamber (the Twenty-four) and the lower chamber (the Forty-eight); regulations for keeping the peace, for the assize of bread and ale, for weights and measures of all trades; sanitary regulations for middens and pavements; by-laws governing citizenship, apprenticeship, markets and fairs, and a variety of other civic concerns. Women merchants are held to be independently responsible, games are forbidden in the Guildhall and the orders for the annual Corpus Christi pageants are outlined. The later set of ordinances adds a few details and rearranges some elements of the laws.

The bishop of Worcester had obtained royal consent in 1218 to an annual four-day fair at the feast of St Barnabas (11 June) and in 1223 a regular cloth fair was held on the feast of the Nativity of the Virgin (8 September). Mary's charter in 1555 provided for three market days a week and for four annual fairs: a four-day fair starting on the fifth day before Palm Sunday, a two-day fair on the Friday and Saturday before Low Sunday, a two-day fair at the feast of the Assumption (15 August), and a two-day fair at the Nativity of the Virgin.[51] The Merchant guild established under Henry III's first charter seems to have been the real power in the city, perhaps overlapping considerably with the city's official government, for a 1392 ordinance directs the bailiffs to present their accounts 'in gilda mercatoria eiusdem Ciuitatis.'[52]

Worcester had one religious guild, the guild of the Holy Trinity, responsible by tradition for civic almshouses, the town walls, the Severn Bridge, and the maintenance of a school. The guild was established and confirmed under Henry IV, although a Trinity chantry had been endowed in 1371. The Trinity Hall was in the parish of St Nicholas and the guild has sometimes been called the guild of St Nicholas.[53] When the Trinity guild was dissolved its duties were taken over by the city. In order to ease the financial burden, the city requested that it be granted the lands of the two friaries, Grey Friars and Black Friars, which had been forfeit to the Crown at the Dissolution.[54]

A complete list of the city's medieval craft guilds can no longer be established, but by 1577 there were twelve companies: the Bakers, Brewers, Butchers and Vintners, Chandlers, Fishmongers, Glovers, Innkeepers and Victuallers, Shoemakers, Smiths and Cutlers, Tanners and Saddlers, and, most important, the Drapers and Tailors, and the Mercers.[55] Worcester was through much of its early history a centre for the cloth trade and clothiers made up much of the city's wealthy citizenry, supporting as well such allied trades as Weavers, Walkers (Fullers), Dyers, and Drapers. Leland wrote that 'The welthe of worcestar standithe most by draping, | And noe towne of England at this present tyme makethe so many clothes yerely as worcestar.'[56] This pre-eminence may not have lasted. In 1575 the city orator complained to Queen Elizabeth that within living memory there had been 380 looms in the city, supporting 8000 people, whereas now there were but 160.[57] The orator was undoubtedly exaggerating his figures, but Dyer suggests that there were signs of a recession in the mid-1570s in an otherwise very prosperous business.[58] The Weavers, Walkers, and Clothiers amalgamated into a single guild – the Clothiers' company – in 1590, further consolidating their power as the most prominent company in the city.[59]

The demographic information which survives concerning early Worcester is similar to that for Hereford. In the poll tax of 1377 Worcester ranked between Hull and Ipswich, with a taxable population of 1,557 (16,099 in the county).[60] Working from chantry certificates, W. G. Hoskins calculates a population for the city in 1520 of about 6,000.[61] The next survey of any accuracy was made by the diocesan authorities in 1563, which listed 937 families in the city.[62] Dyer gives clear evidence for a steady increase in actual population from the beginning of the parish registers in 1538–9 until a century later, by which time the figure increased to a total of perhaps 8,000 inhabitants.[63] Charles Phythian-Adams notes a similar level of increase between the taxation returns of 1524–5 and the diocesan survey of 1563 and concludes that Worcester and Derby are likely the only cities in England whose populations were 'either reasonably stable or possibly increasing over this forty-year period.'[64]

Worcester suffered its share of socio-economic disasters, of which the principal was certainly the outbreaks of plague. The Black Death first devastated the country from 1348 to 1357 and recurred briefly in 1361 and 1365. The plague broke out several times in the early sixteenth century, culminating in a serious epidemic in 1558. After a relative lull of several decades, periods of crisis-level mortality began again in 1593–4, leading in the early seventeenth century to a variety of regulations for the control of disease including, from 1631, an annual payment to players to prevent their entering the city. The mortality evidence strongly suggests that the outbreaks of the plague in Worcester were not as severe as in many other cities, though this may have been due to different sanitary regulations or other factors.[65]

Households

THE BISHOP AND THE PRIOR

Worcestershire never had a large landed aristocracy and most of its resources were under the control of the Crown or the church. The county's principal magnates, therefore, were the bishop of Worcester and the prior of the county's wealthiest monastic foundation, Worcester Cathedral Priory.[66] Between them they controlled a considerable proportion of the land and wealth of the county, with extensive holdings within the city of Worcester as well as rural manors. The two estates had originally been administered as a whole, but were separated gradually before the compilation of the Domesday Book.[67] Although the bishop's palace in the city was the official residence, few bishops spent much time there, preferring their manor of Hartlebury to the north.[68] Although the bishop was titular abbot of the priory, the prior was in charge of its administration and since he was resident much of the time in his lodgings in the priory, his importance in the affairs of the city often outweighed that of the bishop. Later priors, like Prior William More in the first half of the sixteenth century, also spent considerable time at their manors outside the city.

PRIOR WILLIAM MORE

Prior More has provided the most lavish source of information on household entertainment in the early sixteenth century. He kept detailed accounts of his expenditures on a weekly basis, beginning in 1518 at the time of his election and continuing until very close to his resignation in 1535. Born William Peers (or Peres) in 1471 or 1472 in the hamlet of 'the More,' in the parish of Lindridge, near Tenbury, More entered the priory of Worcester at the age of sixteen; in 1501 he became kitchener and within three years sub-prior. He was elected prior on 2 October 1518 in which office he remained until 1535. After considerable argument, More resigned at the end of 1535 (returning briefly in 1536). He demanded quite specific terms of Cromwell for his resignation – a quarterly pension, his gear, plate, and chapel stuff, and his favourite manor of Grimley.[69] More is traditionally held to have survived until after 1558 and to have been buried in the church in Crowle, where one of the prior's manors stood; it is more likely, however, that an entry in the Alveston, Warwickshire, parish register indicates his true date of death: 'Anno Domini 1552 ... Willam more was sometyme Prior of Wo'r'cester was buried the xvj[th] of September.'[70]

The Account Book gives a unique (though necessarily partial) picture of the life of a wealthy ecclesiastical estate at the beginning of the sixteenth century.[71] In addition to the priory, More had three principal residences, the manors of Battenhall (about a mile east of the cathedral), Crowle (about four miles north-east), and Grimley (about four miles north). Prior More tended to spend most of his time at his manors rather than in Worcester and their repair, furnishing, and upkeep figure prominently in the accounts.

Many of the documents from his priorate, including the Account Book, give the impression of an able administrator, but this neither was nor is a universal opinion.[72] In 1535–6, More was accused of extravagance by one of his monks, John Musard, but although his accounts suggest considerable expenditure, the circumstances of the accusation cast some doubt on its validity. Musard appears in the Account Book several times in the late 1520s being paid for work in the library, repairing and binding books. In 1531 Musard was imprisoned for theft; 'the takyng of musard' is recorded in an entry for the week of 2–8 July.[73] While in prison, Musard wrote a lengthy letter detailing charges against More, the principal of which is extravagance. No further action appears to have been taken on it, but a number of documents concerning the case are in the Public Record Office.[74]

PAKINGTON

John Pakington, whose father Thomas served as sheriff of Worcester in 1561, came to the notice of Queen Elizabeth during her official visit to the city in 1575. He was invited to court, where his athletic prowess and personal beauty earned him the nickname 'Lusty Pakington.' He was knighted in 1587 and served as deputy lieutenant for the county from 1587 to 1601 and as sheriff in 1595 and 1607. He built an elaborate home on his estate at Westwood Park, Worcestershire, where a portrait of him now hangs.[75] An account book from the estate gives evidence of the hiring of entertainers.

Drama, Music, and Popular Customs

Local Drama

As in Herefordshire, the earliest Worcestershire documents connected with dramatic performance are ecclesiastical proclamations forbidding the performance of, or the attendance at, theatrical presentations. The earliest of these, though its implications are ambiguous, is contained in the constitutions of Bishop Walter Cantilupe. Drawn up in 1240, in the third year of his episcopate, Cantilupe's regulations concerning church-yards prohibit 'ludi inhonesti' in the church grounds. It is not clear precisely what this term means; in the context of private homes and alehouses it is likely to indicate gambling or other games rather than dramatic presentations. The same phrase is used in a 1450 letter from Bishop John Carpenter to John Lawern, formerly a student at Gloucester College, Oxford, and almoner of Worcester Cathedral. There he describes 'ludi inhonesti' as a regular feature of Hockday celebrations, likely referring to the traditional Hockday customs in which the women hold the men for ransom.[76] The priory itself was certainly involved in such festivities, though whether the monks took part in any way in such 'ludi' is not at all clear; the cellarers' rolls are full of Hockday receipts and payments for ale vats and the like, but there is no information concerning who gathered the money or how.

The priory did, however, support dramatic performances of considerable variety. Priory rolls provide ample evidence of parish drama, beginning with the payment in a cellarer's roll of the 1470s to the 'lusores' of six of the city parishes. To this we can add a wealth of payments for parish entertainments of various kinds in Prior More's Account Book, ranging from parish players and shows to singers and dancers, and in one case, a payment to a manorial rather than parochial Robin Hood play.[77] Where the content is indicated, all the parish plays are Robin Hood plays. The purpose of these parish entertainments seems in practically all cases to be fund-raising for the parish; in one case Prior More notes that a play was held 'to the profett of alhaland churche.'[78] A 1563 payment in the city accounts 'Concernyng the settyng furthe of A plaie' suggests that this tradition of parish or civic drama remained active after Prior More's time. As in Herefordshire, the consistory court records provide some further evidence of dramatic performances in churches, as at Tenbury in 1600, though the collection of ecclesiastical court documents in Worcestershire is thin compared to the riches of Herefordshire.

One series of entries in Prior More's Account Book appears to be connected with players in an ecclesiastical household. In order to clarify this tradition, it will be necessary to look more closely at the manuscript itself and at More's accounting methods. Within each weekly entry, household expenses are listed first; they are not itemized and are not included in the final summation (implying, presumably, that they are recurrent expenses which are expected to be similar in nature each week). A typical entry (f 124v) reads:

...

Ebdomada Nona Advent sonday   At Batnall
℃ In primis for expensis on howsolde þis wycke   xxix s. vij d....

...

Normally these entries are not itemized, but occasionally specific expenses are listed, such as the purchase of 'a byff' for feasts. The entries continue almost identically for all eighteen years of the accounts.

The entry of general household expenses is followed usually by entries for gifts, grants, rewards, and gratuities. Often, though not always, the recipients are named or otherwise identified and this section of the accounting includes frequent payments to professional players, minstrels, bearwards, tumblers, jugglers, and other entertainers.

The final section of the weekly accounting lists a wide variety of extraordinary expenses, including repairs to the prior's various estates at Battenhall, Grimley, and Crowle and work on their moats and fish-ponds, as well as major purchases of wine and spices. Here also are placed the payments to what are clearly non-professional entertainers such as parish singers and dancers, and donations to parishes for the performance of plays. These last two groups of entries – the rewards and the extraordinary expenses – frequently overlap and the distinction between them is not always clear.

Through most of the period an addition is regularly made to the first of these three sections. During most of the year it is a payment (normally of 4s) for 'seyny money.' From 1519 to 1530, primarily during the seasons of Lent and Advent, the payment for 'seyny money' is not made and is replaced by a payment of 12d for 'ij pleyeres.'[79] There are some difficulties with interpreting these entries. First, the nature of the payment for 'seyny money' is not entirely clear; E. S. Fegan, the editor of the Account Book, simply called these entries 'allowances for blood-letting,' but this is not sufficient.[80] In 1530 the payments to players cease and the 'seyny money' payments are no longer entered as a separate item. The year's entry begins with the statement 'At this mihelmas the seynys contynowe amongs ye covent for ye yere foloyng.'[81] Entries referring to 'seyny money' in the obedientiaries' rolls make the connection with blood-letting clear and it seems most likely that the money was used to provide a special diet, probably of red meat, for monks who had been bled.[82] This hypothesis is

supported by the reference in the priory accounts of the 1530s to a 'seyny cook.'[83]
The money would not be paid during the fast seasons of Lent and Advent and could
be diverted to another purpose, in this case the hiring of 'ij pleyeres.' What these
players are doing is less certain. There is no suggestion in the Account Book that they
are part of either an entertainment or a play; the only other expenses which are regularly detailed in this section of the entries deal with feasts, such as the purchase of
beef. One possibility is that since the players are hired principally during Lent and
Advent, the two periods of the church year which deal with biblical narrative – the
Nativity and the Passion – the players may have been involved in an annual presentation of these stories. The nature of their performance, however, remains uncertain,
though with only two persons some form of dramatic reading would be more likely
than even a simple staging. There is, of course, the possibility that they are musicians.
Prior More elsewhere refers variously to 'players' and to 'minstrels,' but there is
neither a clear overlap nor a clear boundary between the terms. A table of payments
to 'ij pleyeres' is given in Appendix 3.

Some kind of ecclesiastical interest in, perhaps even participation in, dramatic
performance seems to have survived the Dissolution. In 1576 an inventory of the
cathedral's moveable goods was made and among the linen, vestments, and plate is
a list of eight costumes, headed 'players gere' and including several gowns, jerkins,
a king's costume, and 'the devils apparell.'

Civic Drama

Like Hereford, Worcester had an annual series of civic pageants, though we do not
have a list of them. According to both sets of ordinances (1466 and 1496) they were
five in number and were organized by the craft guilds. According to the 1466
ordinance, the decision as to whether the pageants would go forward each year was
to be taken by the Great Inquest at the Law Day held on Hock Tuesday. The
regulations for these pageants do not indicate that they are part of a cycle of plays
as it is usually understood from the examples at York or Chester, though there is some
evidence, however thin, that may suggest something more than tableaux. In the
ordinances of 1466, the pageants are to 'holden' and are to 'go to do worshipp to god';
the second set of ordinances from 1496 also notes that the pageants go 'in ther pleyng'
and that their 'pleyng' should be divided between Corpus Christi Day, on which three
pageants should be played, and the following Sunday, when the 'other ij pageantes
pley in lyke maner.' This division of playing may indicate that the pageants took an
appreciable period of time. The later council orders of 1566–7 and 1567–8 follow a
similar schedule, moving three pageants to Trinity Sunday and two to the following
Sunday, adding that they are to be played with 'good matter.' The sum of this information is hardly conclusive, but there is at least the possibility that the pageants may
have been more than tableaux or dumb shows. On the other hand, since no guild
accounts survive, there is a complete absence of information dealing with the minutiae

of dramatic performance; most of the municipal regulations concern torches and tapers for lighting the procession.

There is further evidence that the pageants may have been substantial, for the city had two pageant houses. One of these, in the Cornmarket up against the town wall, is far better documented than the other and a series of leases pertaining to it appears in the Chamber Order Books. A further group of leases after 1642 which clarify its position are transcribed as Appendix 1. The other pageant house is much more shadowy and we would not know of its existence except for a civic rent roll of 1606, in which both houses appear.

Some further information on the pageants is provided by one of the civic register volumes. In 1555 the city issued a general ordinance concerning processions, in which the companies were enjoined to process 'in a decent order' and not 'vpon heapes as hereto fore hath ben oft late accustomyd.' The ordinance ends with the direction that all the companies 'shale prepayre there shewes vpon corpus chrysti daye' (not Trinity Sunday). The pageants were ordered to be 'Dryven and played vpon corpus christi day' again in 1559, but in 1566 they were played on Trinity Sunday, indicating that this is probably a change of day. There is no indication either in this register (Civic Miscellany 1) or in the Chamber Order Book of the suppression of these pageants, though the receipt from the Weavers in the city accounts for 1583–4 suggests that they had by that time fallen into desuetude: 'half A yeres Rente for A Tenement where the pageants were.'

A set of 'pleyars garmentes' which appear in the 1556 probate inventory of William Specheley, draper, valued at £30, may very well have been connected with the civic pageants. Specheley was a prominent citizen of a well-known city family and the likelihood that the costumes belonged to him is slim. He was probably storing them for one (or more) of the guilds.

ROYAL VISITS AND CEREMONY

Two royal entries figure within our period. Henry VII visited Worcester in 1486, travelling from Hereford. A civic pageant was prepared for the occasion and although the scribe provided the full text of the pageant (including speeches for Henry VI and a gatekeeper), he noted that he was copying speeches 'Which his grace at that tyme harde not.' It would be interesting to know if the king did in fact read the speeches even though he did not see the pageant. As John Meagher has shown, the pageant represents a subtle and diplomatic apology for the city's involvement (by association, at least) in Humphrey Stafford's plot. Stafford had raised his army in Worcestershire and planned initially to take the city of Worcester as his headquarters. On his way from York to Worcester Henry had stopped in Nottingham in order to commission a court to investigate the whole Stafford affair. Worcester certainly had reason to be anxious about the king's coming and the pageant's frequent references to mercy, as well as its elaborate compliments, are clearly an attempt to assuage the king's wrath.[84]

Far more information survives concerning Elizabeth's visit in 1575; the Chamber Order Book gives a full outline of the city's administrative decisions prior to Elizabeth's arrival, a complete narrative of her visit (including the city orator's welcoming speech), and full accounts of the associated expenditures. A pageant for three boys was presented at the Grass Cross and the town clerk claims to have given the text of their speeches elsewhere in the volume, but there is no sign of it.

Travelling Entertainers

MINSTRELS

The sort of prohibitions promulgated by Bishops Cantilupe and Carpenter do not reflect a general ecclesiastical disapproval of dramatic or mimetic entertainment, as the frequent payments to entertainers of various kinds in the obedientiaries' rolls of Worcester Priory show. These payments begin with the earliest surviving rolls in 1293–4 and continue until the method of accounting changes in the early sixteenth century and payments are summarized in a less helpful manner. They include payments to minstrels, players, and musicians, some associated with a patron, many wholly anonymous. The most frequent term for these performers, 'menestrallus,' does not allow us to be certain of the nature of the performance involved, though their popularity is undeniable.

I have not included miscellaneous documents which refer briefly to minstrels in non-performing capacities. An example would be the commission of 15 June 1468 to Richard Beauchamp and others to compel a lengthy list of persons (including Robert Hanyes of Little Malvern, minstrel) to appear before the court of King's Bench.[85]

PLAYERS

Professional players visited Worcester frequently. Prior More records payments to a wide variety of performers under patronage, including players, minstrels, jugglers, and bearwards. Among these are John Slye and his company, who were Henry VIII's interluders, as well as his minstrels and his juggler, Thomas Brandon. Under Elizabeth, players came to Worcester on a regular basis, though their frequency and identity is often obscured by the town clerk's tendency to summarize his annual entry under 'money geven to players' in a manner similar to that of the Hereford mayoral accounts. As in many cities, payments to travelling companies are replaced in the 1630s with payments to prevent the players from entering the city. The usual excuse of fear of infection may, of course, mask a change in attitude towards the players and their performances.

The normal playing places were the Guildhall and the Trinity Hall, as is clear from several by-laws of the 1620s forbidding their use for plays. A Merchant guild had been permitted by the 1227 charter and as early as 1249 a Richard de la Gyldhall witnessed a document. By 1294 the Guildhall had become the city's law-court.[86] According to a by-law of 1622, it had two playing places, the 'vpper end of the Twone hall,' and the Council Chamber. The relationship between these is made somewhat clearer by the description of the building given by Valentine Green, writing some seventy-five years after its demolition:

The old town-hall was a large structure of timber, of longer extent than the present; it had a piazza in front, adjoining to which, next to Cooken-street, was a range of shops facing the High-street, the back parts of which commanded a view of the Nisi Prius court, in the Guildhall. At the south end of the piazza was another row of shops, adjoining to which was the principal entrance of the hall, down a flight of nearly twenty steps. The body of the hall was open to the roof, and lighted by a large window at the north end. The courts of justice were situated facing each other, at the extreme ends of the hall, and elevated considerably above the level of its general flooring. Internally, on the right of the Nisi Prius court, advancing towards the opposite end, was the prison, the windows of which were under the piazza, and facing the High-street. Nearly opposite to the prison, on the left side of the Nisi Prius court, was the residence of the gaoler, who occupied it as a public-house, over which was a chamber for the petty jury. At the north end of the piazza was the mayor's court, near to the crown bar. Through its entrance the judge was enabled to pass to his seat in the Crown court, without going down the hall steps. Near to this bar a large gallery was provided for auditors at the trials. Over the line of the piazza was the council chamber, a spacious large room, lighted by a series of small windows in front of the building towards the High-street.[87]

The Trinity Hall belonged to the guild of the Holy Trinity. Situated in St Nicholas' parish along Trinity Street, it was used for a variety of purposes; until 1548 it served as the site of the grammar school. The city's principal guild of Weavers, Walkers, and Clothiers began meeting in the hall in 1540; in 1612 it was given to them under provisions made in the will of its owner, Robert Yowle.[88] It was sold by public auction in 1796, reconstructed as a furniture warehouse in 1805, and finally torn down in 1890. A photograph of the hall at the time of its demolition exists in the Worcester Local Studies Library; a part of one of its walls still stands and has been incorporated into the present buildings.[89]

Waits

Worcester's waits are no better documented than Hereford's, for payments to them were not recorded in the city account books. Several pieces of civic legislation pertaining to them make their existence clear, as do occasional payments to them in other places, but most of the details concerning them, including their number, have been lost. A civic order of 1599 hiring a group of musicians as the waits at the bishop's request may imply that they had ceased to exist some time before this. The bishop's involvement may mean that the musicians who are being hired are church musicians, but we cannot be sure of this. Harry Smythe of Worcester, whose 1575/6 probate inventory and will appear in the Records, was probably a musician and may even have been a town wait. He owned 'vyalls,' 'recorders,' and books (presumably of music) valued at a total of £6, which he left to his 'boyes' (probably apprentices). Furthermore, he owned 'players geare' worth 40s – in light of the valuable instruments which he also owned, this may represent liveries or other paraphernalia for waits, rather than the trappings of dramatic entertainers. Worcester's waits did travel; the city of Coventry paid them in 1613, 1623, and 1631, but their life in Worcester remains shadowy.[90] We know the names of a few of them: Thomas Wheeler was hired as one of the waits in 1585 and they were led by John Browne at the time of their eventual suppression by chamber order in 1642.

Popular Customs

Parish dancing and singing appear with great frequency in Prior More's Account Book, though it is not clear what kind of dancing is involved. In many cases it is likely to be country dancing rather than morris dancing, although in one case the number of dancers (seven) would suggest six morris men and a Maid Marian. The information is insufficient to be certain.

The 'colestaff riding' found in Herefordshire appears in Worcestershire also and is again clearly a charivari.[91] The consistory court prosecution for a cowlstaff riding at Lindridge in 1572/3 may very well be a Shrovetide procession as well. We do not know the date of the offence, but the date of the hearing was 6 March. Easter was early that year (22 March) and it is at least possible for sufficient time to have elapsed for the case to come before the court. A quarter sessions memorandum from the parish of Upper Mitton in 1613 also describes a charivari, in this case involving the curate, who is ridden on a cowlstaff. 'Rough music' is indeed involved here, for in addition to the playing of fiddles and the blowing of a horn, one participant rings 'vppon A fryinge panne.' This incident has nothing to do with Shrovetide, for it takes place on 20 October.

The Documents

The descriptions of the documents from which records are drawn are sorted principally under three headings: Diocese of Worcester, Boroughs and Parishes, and Households. In the Boroughs and Parishes section, civic documents are listed first, followed by guild, ecclesiastical, and miscellaneous documents. This last category includes such documents as probate records.

Monastic records from Evesham, Pershore and Worcester have been listed under the appropriate borough headings. One exception should be noted to the sorting of records by location; ecclesiastical court documents have been kept together among the diocesan documents, since the cases each volume records may refer to a wide range of locations.

Access to documents in Worcester in both the Hereford and Worcester Record Office (County Hall) and the St Helen's Record Office is primarily by bulk accession (BA) number, under which the full details of the accession and further reference and shelf numbers can be found. Shelfmarks for all documents are given according to the preference of the individual libraries and record offices.

Diocese of Worcester

EPISCOPAL REGISTERS AND STATUTES

The episcopal registers of the diocese of Worcester are very well preserved, though they contain limited material of REED interest. From 1497 to 1535, Worcester's bishops were Italians; most of them spent very little time indeed in England and their registers are particularly uninformative. The see was frequently left vacant for periods of a year or so, but the register was kept 'sede vacante.'[92]

Register of Bishop Henry Wakefield
Worcester, St Helen's Record Office, BA 2648/4/iv; 1375–95; Latin; parchment (10 of 14 endleaves paper); iii + 170 + xiv; 330mm x 220mm; 3 old foliations, modern pagination 1–367 (including inserts); vellum binding with brass clasps (old calf front cover bound in), 'Registrum Henrici de Wakefield, 1375–95' on cover.

Constitutions of Bishop Walter Cantilupe
London, Lambeth Palace Library, MS 171; 26 July 1240; Latin; parchment; i + 136 + ii; 298mm x 180mm; leather binding. The constitutions are contained on ff 41–7v.

NOTEBOOK OF JOHN LAWERN

The notebook of John Lawern is listed with the episcopal documents since its principal interest lies in a copy of a letter to Lawern from Bishop John Carpenter. Much of the notebook was kept during Lawern's time as a student at Gloucester College, Oxford, though Carpenter writes to him in 1450 as almoner of Worcester Cathedral.

Oxford, Bodleian Library, MS Bodley 692; 1442–50; Latin; paper; ii + 165 + ii; 305mm x 225mm; foliated 1–63a, 63b–84a, 84b–163; leather binding.

REPORT FROM ROGER MAINWARING, DEAN OF WORCESTER, TO ARCHBISHOP LAUD OF CANTERBURY

This decanal report to the archbishop of Canterbury outlines in detail the dean's actions of November 1634 in dealing with the fabric of the cathedral and its possessions, with the present state of its buildings and rents and the conduct of its scholars and almsmen.

London, Public Record Office, SP 16/298; 1634; English; paper; ii + 186 + ii; 320mm x 205mm; foliated 1–189 (the last endleaf is unnumbered); bound in boards, leaves attached with paper strips 45mm in width, 'Domestic Charles I 1635 Sep. 16–30' on spine.

VISITATION ARTICLES

The visitation articles, or interrogatories, which Bishop John Hooper had prepared for Gloucester in 1551 were administered in the following year for the diocese of Worcester during the vacancy of the see. Hooper's articles were especially detailed and provided the basis for many of the visitation articles of the later Reformation.

Visitation of Diocese of Gloucester by Bishop John Hooper
London, Dr Williams's Library, Roger Morrice MSS, L(3); late seventeenth-century copy of lost original dated May, 1551; English; paper; 12 items bound together and separately paginated or foliated, of which Hooper's Articles form Item 3 consisting of 39 + iv leaves; 400mm x 260mm; paginated 1–79; bound in boards with marbled paper, remains of leather cover, volume in extremely poor condition and crumbling, spine gone.[93]

Articles of Enquiry of Bishop John Whitgift
Worcester, Worcester Cathedral Library, A14; 1582–1620; Latin and English; paper; 170 leaves; 300(310)mm x 200mm; several incomplete and erratic foliations/paginations; poor

condition; MS made up of paper booklets (gatherings of 6, 8, 10, etc), some loose leaves; parchment binding.

Articles of Enquiry of Bishop Gervase Babington
ARTICLES | TO BE ENQVIRED | of within the Dioces of Worcester, in the | generall Visitation of the Reuerend Father | in God, GERVASE Lord Bishop | of Worcester: | HOLDEN | In the yeare of our Lord God, | 1607. | AT LONDON, | Printed by Humfrey Lownes: 1607. *STC*: 10367.

Articles of Enquiry of Archdeacon John Johnson
Articles to be inquired | of, by the Churchwardens and Sworne | men, within the Archdeaco*n*arie of Worcester, | in the Visitation of the R*ight* Worshipful, M. Iohn Iohnson | Doctor of Divinitie, Archdeacon of the Archdeacon-|ry of Worcester aforesaid, in this present yeare of our Lorde God. 1609. | At London printed by Ralph Blower, | ANNO DOMINI. 1609. *STC*: 10372.2.

Articles of Enquiry of Archdeacon William Swaddon
ARTICLES | to be enquired of, by | the Church-wardens and | Swornemen, within the Archdea-|conrie of Worcester, | In the visitation of the right | wowshipfull WILLIAM | SWADDON, | Doctor of Diuinitie, Archdeacon of | Worcester. ANNO DOM*INI* | 1615. | Imprinted at London, | 1615. *STC*: 10372.3.

Articles of Enquiry of Archdeacon Hugh Floyd
ARTICLES | TO BE ENQVIRED OF | By the Church-wardens and Sworne- men, within the | Archdeaconry of WORCESTER, in the first visita-|tion of the R*ight* Worshipfull HVGH FLOYD | D*octor* of Divinity, Archdeacon of Worcester. | Anno Dom*ini*. 1625. | AT OXFORD, | Printed by IOHN LICHFIELD, & WILLIAM TVRNER, | Printers to the famons Vniuersity. 1625. *STC*: 10372.6.

Articles of Enquiry of Bishop John Thornborough
ARTICLES | To be enquired of by | the Churchwardens and Swornmen | within the Diocesse of WORCESTER. | In the Visitation of the Right Reuerend | Father in God, IOHN, Lord Bishop | of Worcester, | Holden in the yeare of our Lord God, 1626. | LONDON, | Printed for IOHN GRISMAND, 1626. *STC*: 10368.

Articles of Enquiry of Bishop John Thornborough
ARTICLES | TO BE ENQVIRED | OF IN THE VISITATI- | on of the Right Reuerend Father, | IOHN, by the Prouidence of God, | Bishop of Worcester. | In the yeere of our Lord God, 1632. | °The minister skollemaster and Churchwarde*r*ns⌐ | are to appeare in Kidderminster Church one | Munday the forth of Iune nexte° | LONDON, | Printed for Iohn Grismond, | 1632. *STC*: 10369.

Articles of Enquiry of Archdeacon Edward Thornborough
ARTICLES | TO BE ENQVIRED | OF BY THE CHVRCH-|wardens and Sworne-men

within the Arch-deaconrie of Worcester in the Visita- |tion of the Worshipfull Mr. Edward |
Thornburgh, Arch-Deacon of | Worcester. | Anno Domini. °1634° | LONDON | Printed for
IOHN GRISMOND. *STC*: 10372.7.

Articles of Enquiry of William Laud, Archbishop of Canterbury
ARTICLES | TO BE | INQUIRED OF | IN THE METROPOLITICALL | VISITATION
OF THE MOST | REVEREND FATHER, | WILLIAM, | By GODS Providence, Lord Arch-
Bishop of | Canterbury, Primate of all England; and | METROPOLITAN: | In and for the
Dioces of WORCESTER, In the yeere of | our LORD GOD 1635, And in the second yeere |
of his Graces Translation. | Printed at London, by Richard Badger. | 1635. *STC*: 10370.

Articles of Enquiry of Bishop John Thornborough
ARTICLES | TO BE INQVIRED | OF, IN THE VISITATION | of the Right Reverend
Father, by | Gods providence, IOHN Lord Bishop | of WORCESTER. | IN AND FOR HIS
DIO-|ces of Wercester, in the yeare of our | Lord God, 1636. and in the 20th | yeare of his
Translation. | LONDON, | Printed for Iohn Grismond. 1636. *STC*: 10371.

Articles of Enquiry of Archdeacon Edward Thornborough
ARTICLES | TO BE ENQVIRED | OF AND ANSWERED | unto by the Church-wardens
and | Sworne-men within the Arch-dea-|conrie of Worcester in the Visitation | of the Right
worshipfull Edward | Thornburgh Dr of Divini-|ty Arch-deacon of | Worcester. | Anno
Domini. °1638° | OXFORD, | Printed by LEONARD LICHFIELD. *STC*: 10373.

ECCLESIASTICAL COURT DOCUMENTS

Although the collection of consistory court records from the Worcester diocese is by
no means as extensive as from Hereford, several volumes survive for the early seventeenth century. Several important parishes in the north-west of the county lay in the
deanery of Burford, part of the archdeaconry of Ludlow, diocese of Hereford. Since
these volumes contain a greater proportion of Herefordshire references, they are
discussed in the Herefordshire Introduction (p 20).

Visitation Act Books
Worcester, St Helen's Record Office, BA 2884; 1610–13; Latin, some English; paper; 388
leaves; 286mm x 195mm; modern foliation 1–388; heavily damaged beginning and end.

Worcester, St Helen's Record Office, BA 2760; 1613–17; Latin, some English; paper; x +
444 + x; 310mm x 190mm; foliated 1–444; modern half leather binding (1963), 'Visitation
act book, 1613–17' on cover.

Headings are sparse and rarely give full information about court location and officials.

Visitation Act Book of William Swaddon, Archdeacon of Worcester
Worcester, St Helen's Record Office, BA 2512; 1615–16; Latin, some English; paper; 153
leaves; 290mm x 188mm; paginated 1–306; contemporary vellum binding.

No information is included about court location and officials.

Miscellaneous Consistory Court Papers

Presentments
Worcester, St Helen's Record Office, BA 2302/2(345); 13 June 1624; English; paper; single
sheet; 320mm x 197mm.

Worcester, St Helen's Record Office, BA 2302/2(374); 1624; English and Latin; paper; single
sheet; 320mm x 200mm.

Petition to Bishop John Thornborough
Worcester, St Helen's Record Office, BA 2302/2(414); July 1624; English; paper; single sheet;
305mm x 205mm.

Boroughs and Parishes

BADSEY

St James' Churchwardens' Accounts

From the parish of Badsey in the south-eastern part of the county a fine set of churchwardens' accounts in excellent condition begins very early and covers most of the sixteenth century.

Worcester, St Helen's Record Office, BA 5013/2; 1525–1821; English; paper; 181 leaves;
150mm x 210mm; no foliation; contemporary vellum binding.

BEOLEY

Will of William Sheldon, Dyer
London, Public Record Office, PROB 10 Box 70 1571 – February A–W; 1571/2; English;
paper; 55 leaves; 400mm x 310mm (final 2 ff are 310mm x 205mm); foliated 1–53 (f 2 blank);
parchment cover surrounds roll and bears title 'Will/William Sheldon/February 1571.' Drawn
up January 1569/70.

BEWDLEY

St Andrew's Chapel and Bridge Wardens' Accounts

Bewdley's principal importance lay in its bridge over the Severn and some aspects of its civic administration lay in the hands of the chapel and bridge wardens. Their accounts for almost a century have been preserved. In the early seventeenth century, the wardens changed their accounting year from Annunciation – Annunciation to the more common Michaelmas – Michaelmas.

Worcester, Hereford and Worcester Record Office, BA 8681/236(i); 1569–1663; English; paper; 379 leaves; 320mm x 200mm; paginated 1–758; contemporary vellum binding.

Richard Corbett's Poëtica Stromata

Richard Corbett, bishop of Norwich, composed a satirical poem addressed to John Hammond, vicar of Ribbesford cum Bewdley, who tore down a maypole, probably some time in the 1620s.

POËTICA | STROMATA | OR | A COLLECTION | OF | SUNDRY PEICES | IN | POETRY :| Drawne by The known and approued | Hand of | R. C. | ANNO 1648. Wing: C6272.

DODDENHAM

Quarter Sessions Presentment of Francis Downe
Worcester, Hereford and Worcester Record Office, Quarter Sessions Records 110: 4/36; 1606; English; paper; single sheet; 85mm x 146mm mounted on new paper 87mm x 150mm.

DROITWICH

Bailiffs' Accounts

An extensive collection of municipal accounts (largely bailiffs' accounts) survives from Droitwich, though their principal concern is with the ownership of salt vats and salt-producing springs.

Worcester, Hereford and Worcester Record Office, BA 1006/32/366; 1522–3; English; paper; single sheet; 300mm x 280mm.

Accounts of Edward Davies, Bailiff
Worcester, Hereford and Worcester Record Office, BA 1006/33/596; 1635–6; English;

parchment; single membrane; 642mm x 187mm; endorsed 'Mr Davies his accompts for ye Towne suits.'

John Leland's Itinerary

The section on Droitwich is missing from the original manuscript of the Itinerary (Bodl.: MS Gen. Top. e. 8–15) as well as from the Stow copy of 1576 (Bodl.: MS Tanner 464e), but survives in several later copies, of which this, by William Burton, is the earliest.

Oxford, Bodleian Library, MS Gough Gen. Top. 2; 1628; English; paper; iv + 142; 305mm x 200mm; paginated i–xvi, 1–268 (162 and 163 triple, 67 quintuple); pp 1–226 original pagination, the rest modern; some leaves mutilated and repaired; bound in boards.

EVESHAM

Royal Wardrobe Accounts of Edward I

London, British Library, Add. 7966A; 1300–1; Latin and English; paper and parchment; v + 214 + iv; 210mm x 325mm; foliated in upper right-hand corner (with 10 blank, unfoliated, parchment leaves interspersed throughout MS) 1–17 (index), 1–187; leather binding stamped 'Wardrobe Book 29 Edw. I.'

A Briefe Discourse of Two Most Cruell and Bloudie Murthers

This lurid account of a Worcestershire murder in 1583 includes references to the performance of a play. The anonymous author seems occasionally carried away by theatrical imagery.

A BRIEFE DIS-ICOVRSE OF TWO I most cruell and bloudie I murthers, committed bothe I in Worcestershire, and bothe happe-Ining vnhappily in the yeare. I 1583. I The first declaring, how I one vnnaturally murdered his neigh-Ibour, and afterward buried him I in his Seller. I The other sheweth, how I a woman vnlawfully following the de-Iuillish lusts of the flesh with her seruant, caused him very cruel-Ily to kill her owne Hus-Iband. I Imprinted at London by Roger Warde, I dwelling neere Holburne Conduit I at the signe of the Talbot. I 1583. STC: 25980.

Robert Armin's Foole vpon Foole

Robert Armin's pamphlet was published anonymously in 1600, reprinted in 1605, and again in an enlargement in 1608 entitled A Nest of Ninnies, to which Armin put his own name. Armin was a member of Lord Chandos' players and he includes in this series of tales a story which took place during the players' stop in Evesham, as well as a further tale of his own adventures in Upton on Severn. It is likely that the Grum-ball referred to in the story was Armin himself.

FOOLE | VPON FOOLE, | OR | Six sortes of Sottes. | A flat foole [and] A fatt foole. | A leane foole and A cleane foole. | A merry foole [and] A verry foole. | Shewing their liues, humours and behauiours, with their | want of wit in their shew of wisdome. Not so strange as true | Omnia sunt sex. | Written by one, seeming to haue his mothers witte, | when some say he is fild with his fathers fopperie, and hopes | he liues not without companie. | Clonnico de Curtanio Snuffe. | Not amisse to be read, no matter to regard it: | Yet stands in some stead, though he that made it mar'd it. | LONDON | Printed for William Ferbrand, dwelling neere | Guild-hall gate ouer against the Maiden-head. | 1600. *STC*: 772.3.

KEMPSEY

Royal Wardrobe Accounts of Edward I
See under Evesham, p 319.

KIDDERMINSTER

Autobiography of Richard Baxter

The puritan divine Richard Baxter left some details of Kidderminster life in his autobiography, later published as *Reliquiæ Baxterianæ* (London, 1696; Wing: B1370). The manuscript of the *Reliquiæ* is now split between two libraries; the major portion is in the British Library and one section is in Dr Williams's Library.[94]

London, British Library, Egerton 2570; *c* 1664–91; English; paper; ii + 154 + ii; 358mm x 230mm (many 312mm x 200mm); modern foliation; 19th c. leather binding. The auto-biography covers ff 1–62.

Twelve leaves missing between f 51 and f 52 are now in Dr Williams's Library and a photocopy is at the BL: facsimile 643, foliated 1–12.

LONGDON

Quarter Sessions Petition of William Jeffreys, Constable
Worcester, Hereford and Worcester Record Office, Quarter Sessions Records 110:29/67; 1617; English; paper; single sheet; 410mm x 310mm, only 205mm x 144mm written on.

PERSHORE

View of Frankpledge for Pershore Manor

An extensive collection of documents from the manor of Pershore in the collection of the dean and chapter of Westminster Abbey includes only one of interest, a court record referring to the control of minstrels.

London, Westminster Abbey, Muniment 22088A; 2 October 1572; English and Latin; paper; 2 leaves; 420mm x 305mm.

Abbey of St Mary the Virgin and St Eadburga Monastic Accounts

Account Roll of Abbot John Pypulton
London, Public Record Office, SC 6/Henry vii/1704; 1495–6; Latin; paper; 7 membranes serial; 330/330/330/330/330/330/330mm x 254mm.

REDDITCH

Quarter Sessions Recognizance of John Woodyne
Worcester, Hereford and Worcester Record Office, Quarter Session Records, 110:54/45; 1628; English and Latin; parchment; single sheet; 110mm x 293mm.

SOUTH LITTLETON

St Michael's Churchwardens' Accounts
Worcester, St Helen's Record Office, BA 1284/1; 1548–1707; English; paper; i + 74 + i; 300mm x 195mm; paginated 1–148; 19th c. leather binding, lettered on spine in gold 'South Littleton Churchwardens and Overseers' Accompts 1548 to 1707.'

UPPER MITTON

Quarter Sessions Memorandum
Worcester, Hereford and Worcester Record Office, Quarter Sessions Records, 110:21/68; 1613–14; English; paper; single sheet; 167mm x 275mm.

UPTON ON SEVERN

Quarter Sessions Indictment of John Jones
Worcester, Hereford and Worcester Record Office, Quarter Sessions Records 110:55/31; 1630; Latin and English; parchment; single sheet; 240mm x 315mm; very badly damaged, middle and right portion of lower half almost entirely missing.

Robert Armin's *Foole Vpon Foole*
See the entry under Evesham, p 319–20.

WORCESTER

Civic Records

Worcester's civic records begin in the late fifteenth century and from about 1540 on are fairly extensive. The manuscripts were kept for many years in the Guildhall, but were transferred in 1984 to the St Helen's Record Office. They fall into four groups, of which the most important comprises the two volumes of Chamber Orders, detailing decisions taken by the Twenty-four, the civic administrative body, and other miscellaneous material.

Chamber Order Book 1
Worcester, St Helen's Record Office, BA 9360/A–14; 1539–1601; English and Latin; paper; vi + 214 + viii; 310mm x 210mm; foliated 1–132 (+ 2 unfoliated leaves), 133–210 (+ 2 loose inserts); modern suede binding.

Chamber Order Book 2
Worcester, St Helen's Record Office, BA 9360/A–14; 1602–50; English; paper; ii + 276 + ii; 332mm x 215mm; foliated 4–108 (+ 3 unfoliated leaves), 109–276; modern calf binding (1970).

Civic Account Books

Three account books covering the years 1540–1663 (with a gap from 1600–23), give details about civic income and expenditure. They were kept only on an annual basis and are not very detailed, listing only total sums spent on entertainment, though the later entries do often record payments to professional companies.

City Accounts 1
Worcester, St Helen's Record Office, BA 9360/A–10; 1540–1600; English; paper; i + 254 + i; 305mm x 200mm; no foliation; contemporary vellum binding, 'Audit of City Accounts, 1540–1600 1' on spine.

City Accounts 2
Worcester, St Helen's Record Office, BA 9360/A–10; 1623–39; English; paper; i + 230 + i; 295mm x 190mm; foliated 2–231; contemporary vellum binding, 'Audit of City Accounts, 1623–39 2' on spine.

City Accounts 3
Worcester, St Helen's Record Office, BA 9360/A–10; 1640–9; English; paper; i + 378 + i; 302mm x 190mm; no foliation; contemporary vellum binding, 'Audit of City Accounts, 1640–69 3' on spine.

Civic Ordinances

Two sets of civic ordinances (both dating from the late fifteenth century) are preserved in a single volume. They include similar, though not identical, statutes for the annual pageant procession.

Worcester, St Helen's Record Office, BA 9360/C–2; 1466 and 1496; English; parchment; ii + 53 + ii; 289mm x 190mm; no foliation, 2 fascicles of 24ff and 29ff; 19th c. vellum on boards, 'Ordinances Edward IV' on cover.

Miscellaneous Civic Papers

These two miscellaneous volumes deal principally with legal matters: decisions of the court of frankpledge, lists of jurors and ratepayers, changes in by-laws, etc.

Civic Miscellany 1
Worcester, St Helen's Record Office, BA 9360/A–6; 1552–68; English and Latin; paper; iii + 352 + xi; 280mm x 190mm; foliated 1–352; 18th c. calf binding, 'Frankpledge Orders of the Council of the Marches/Army Musters/Miscells. 1552–1568 I' on cover.

Tolls, subsidies, views of frankpledge, council orders, wages, lists of ratepayers, assessments, musters, etc are included.

Civic Miscellany 2
Worcester, St Helen's Record Office, BA 9360/A–6; 1623-1710; English and Latin; paper; ii + 106 + ii; 375mm x 235mm; paginated 1–33 only, 2 fascicles of 50 ff and 56 ff; 19th c. vellum on boards, 'Liber Legum' on cover.

By-laws, views of frankpledge, lists of jurors, etc are included.

Rent Roll

This single rent roll is the only one to survive dated before 1812.

Worcester, St Helen's Record Office, BA 9360 A–17; 1605–6; English; paper; single sheet; 325mm x 265mm

Pageant House Documents

The Chamber Order Books contain frequent references to the pageant houses; this lease involves the adjacent property, in part defined by its relationship to the pageant houses.

Lease
Worcester, St Helen's Record Office, BA 5234/23(ii); 20 February 1492/3; Latin; parchment;
single sheet; 267mm x 280mm.

Worcester Priory and Cathedral Documents

Obedientiaries' Account Rolls

At the time of the Dissolution, Worcester was both a monastic and a cathedral
foundation and so the transition from prior and obedientiaries to dean and chapter
was relatively easy. Although a large book-burning was held in the courtyard of the
cloisters, an extraordinary amount of pre-Dissolution material has survived. The collection includes over a thousand account rolls, which have recently been catalogued
under the direction of Dr B. S. Benedikz of the Birmingham University Library.[95]
A few Worcester rolls have also surfaced in other collections.

Cellarers' Account Rolls

The cellarer was responsible for a good deal more than the mere provisioning of the
monastery. He was, in effect, the bursar of the foundation; he paid the wages of manorial officers and priory servants, and was in charge of repairs to the fabric of the
monastery, pensions, and provisions for journeys; he also fulfilled other duties not
specified to other officers and was in charge of entertaining guests in the prior's
absence. The accounts were kept from Michaelmas to Michaelmas.

Worcester, Cathedral Library, C51a; 1293–4; Latin; parchment; 1 membrane, written in two
columns; 707mm x 303mm; Hugo de Inteberge, cellarer and bursar.

Worcester, Cathedral Library, C482; 1313–14; Latin; parchment; 2 membranes serial;
699/490mm x 306mm; 2 cols; damaged at top; John de ⟨...⟩, cellarer.

Worcester, Cathedral Library, C606; 1337–8; Latin; parchment; 1 membrane (first membrane
missing); 800mm x 261mm; Robert de Westone, cellarer.

Worcester, Cathedral Library, C58; 1338–9; Latin; parchment; 2 membranes serial;
776/640mm x 271mm; dorse written from membrane 1; Robert de Westone, cellarer.

Worcester, Cathedral Library, C59; 1344–5; Latin; parchment; 2 membranes serial;
905/299mm x 290mm; dorse written from membrane 1; Robert de Westone, cellarer.

Worcester, Cathedral Library, C60; 1345–6; Latin; parchment; 2 membranes serial;
810/714mm x 275mm; dorse written from membrane 1; Robert de Westone, cellarer.

Worcester, Cathedral Library, C61; 1346–7; Latin; parchment; 2 membranes serial; 642/675mm x 263mm; dorse written from membrane 1; Robert de Westone, cellarer.

Windsor, St George's Chapel Library, xi E 37; 1347–8; Latin; parchment; 2 membranes serial; 780/445mm x 254mm; dorse written from membrane 1; Robert de Westone, cellarer.

Worcester, Cathedral Library, C53a; 1351–2; Latin; parchment; 2 membranes serial; 734/589mm x 205mm; dorse written from membrane 1; Thomas de Barndeslegh, cellarer.

Worcester, Cathedral Library, C74; 1391–2; Latin; parchment; 2 membranes serial; 703/737mm x 242mm; dorse written from membrane 1; Thomas Dene, cellarer.

Worcester, Cathedral Library, C77; 1395–6; Latin; parchment; 4 membranes serial; 944/888/843/472mm x 301mm; William Power, cellarer.

Worcester, Cathedral Library, C92; 1449–50; Latin; parchment; 4 membranes serial; 728/766/635/724mm x 285mm; Isaac Ledbury, cellarer.

Worcester, Cathedral Library, C97; 1466–7; Latin; parchment; 4 membranes serial; 846/790/883/554mm x 260mm; Robert Multon, cellarer.

Hereford, Cathedral Library, R707; c 1470–80 (date torn off); Latin; parchment; 6 membranes serial; 740/725/725/730/850/850mm x 285mm; Nicholas Hanbury, cellarer.

Hereford, Cathedral Library, R707a; 1470–1; Latin; parchment; 4 membranes serial; 880/790/750/580mm x 283mm; Walter Frauncis, cellarer.

Almoners' Account Rolls

The almoner was in charge of the distribution of alms and of special gifts, such as the allowance given to the monks on Maundy Thursday. He was also in charge of the almonry school, which was distinct from the cathedral school.

Worcester, Cathedral Library, C201; 1463–4; Latin; paper; 2 membranes serial; 411/417mm x 291mm; William Hodynton, almoner.

Worcester, Cathedral Library, C208; 1489–90; Latin; parchment; 3 membranes serial; 603/635/657mm x 272mm; John Newtowne, almoner.

Priors' Account Rolls

The prior paid the expenses of his own household, his own journeys, food, and entertainment, and his own guests. He also provided food and entertainment for important guests of the monastery.

Worcester, Cathedral Library, C396; 1444–5; Latin; parchment; 3 membranes serial; 719/607/17mm x 233mm; John Hertylbury, prior.

Worcester, Cathedral Library, C397; 1446–7; Latin; parchment; 2 membranes serial; 830/425mm x 255mm; damaged; John Hertylbury, prior.

Worcester, Cathedral Library, C398; 1447–8; Latin; parchment; 3 membranes serial; 520/644/207mm x 223mm; John Hertylbury, prior.

Worcester, Cathedral Library, C399; 1451–2; Latin; parchment; 2 membranes serial; 619/430mm x 216mm; John Hertylbury, prior.

Worcester, Cathedral Library, C401; 1463–4; Latin; parchment; 2 membranes serial; 777/129mm x 289mm; badly damaged; Thomas Musard, prior.

Worcester, Cathedral Library, C402; 1464–5; Latin; parchment; single membrane; 769mm x 327mm; Thomas Musard, prior.

Worcester, Cathedral Library, C403; 1469–70; Latin; parchment; 2 membranes serial; 720/477mm x 270mm; Robert Multon, prior.

Worcester, Cathedral Library, C404; 1470–1; Latin; parchment; 2 membranes serial; 749/378mm x 238mm; Robert Multon, prior.

Hereford, Cathedral Library, R708; 1471–2; Latin; parchment; 2 membranes serial; 620/560mm x 290mm; Robert Multon, prior.

Worcester, Cathedral Library, C405; 1472–3; Latin; parchment; 2 membranes serial; 609/489mm x 241mm; Robert Multon, prior.

Worcester, Cathedral Library, C406; 1478–9; Latin; parchment; 2 membranes serial; 913/467mm x 304mm; dorse written from membrane 1; Robert Multon, prior.

Worcester, Cathedral Library, C407; 1481–2; Latin; parchment; 2 membranes serial; 742/400mm x 286mm; Robert Multon, prior.

Worcester, Cathedral Library, C409; 1486–7; Latin; parchment; 3 membranes serial; 552/628/596mm x 239mm; Robert Multon, prior.

Worcester, Cathedral Library, C411; 1490–1; Latin; parchment; 3 membranes serial; 610/670/484mm x 261mm; Robert Multon, prior.

Sacrist's Account Roll

The sacrist's duties included the upkeep of the cathedral treasure and furnishings and the provision of hosts, wax, gloves, incense, and vestments. He was also in charge of some processions, notably that of Corpus Christi.

Worcester, Cathedral Library, C425; 1423–4; Latin; parchment; 2 membranes serial; 520/427mm x 290mm; John Clyve, sacrist.

Cathedral Account Books and Inventories

Through the sixteenth and early seventeenth centuries, accounts were much less carefully kept and appear in large paper volumes, generally bound with inventories, chapter acts, and miscellaneous documents.

Inventory
Worcester, Cathedral Library, B1872; 3 December 1576–4 December 1578; English; paper; single sheet; 300mm x 205mm, 2 cols.

Accounts
Worcester, Cathedral Library, A12; early 16th c.; Latin and English; paper; i + 175 + i; 320mm x 220mm; foliated 1–23, 23, 24–144, 144, 145–173; 19th c. suede binding (spine much damaged). Inventories, accounts, and register.

Accounts
Worcester, Cathedral Library, A26; early 17th c.; English and Latin; paper; 10 fascicles bound together: iii + 45, 56, 38, 32, 44, 44, 44, 20(defective), 17(defective), 41 + ii; 320mm x 200mm; foliated by fascicle; 19th c. suede binding.

City Parish Documents

St Michael's in Bedwardine Churchwardens' Accounts
Worcester, St Helen's Record Office, BA 2335/16b (iii); 1543–1603; English; paper; iii + 122 + iii; 305mm x 210mm; foliated 1–122; parchment wrapper (resewn), 'St Michael 1543 to 1603 inclusive' and '1543 to 1603' on cover.

Miscellaneous Documents

Gerald of Wales' *Gemma Ecclesiastica*

The *Gemma Ecclesiastica* of Gerald of Wales (Giraldus Cambrensis), written about 1198, is a set of exemplary tales in two 'distinctiones,' the first treating the sacraments, the second the clerical life. Among the stories of the first book is this tale of a Worcester priest lapsing inadvertently into a popular song while celebrating mass. The Lambeth

Palace manuscript preserves the unique copy of the text, as well as a number of other works of Gerald.

London, Lambeth Palace Library, MS 236; early 13th c.; Latin; parchment; ii + 167; 260mm x 180mm, 2 cols; foliated 1–111 (book 1), 112–168 (book 2); decorative capital at beginning of each chapter; calf binding.

First Provincial Progress of Henry VII

See under Hereford, *The First Provincial Progress of Henry VII*, p 31.

John Davis' Memoir of his Imprisonment

This narrative of a boy who reads his Bible in English and composes a ballad about tonsured priests was utilized by Foxe, though in a considerably abridged form.[96]

London, British Library, Harley 425; 1546; English; paper; i + 145 + viii; 320mm x 200mm; foliated 1–145; leather on board binding, 'John Fox Collections vol. x.' on spine.

Probate Records

The vast collection of probate records for Worcester were not systematically searched, though wills for all likely names were inspected. In addition to these a random search of fifty wills produced nothing.

Probate Inventory of William Specheley, Draper
Worcester, Hereford and Worcester Record Office, Probate records BA 3585 1556:152A; 1556; English; parchment; single sheet; 603mm x 163mm.

Probate Inventory of Edward Crosby, Draper
Worcester, Hereford and Worcester Record Office, Probate records BA 3585 1559:269; 1559; English; paper; 10 leaves; 390mm x 153mm; no foliation; sewn.

Will and Probate Inventory of Harry Smythe
Worcester, Hereford and Worcester Record Office, Probate records BA 3585 1575:97; 1575.
   Will: English; paper; single sheet; 304mm x 200mm; no endorsement or seals.
   Probate Inventory: English; paper; 4 membranes serial; 409/409/400/21mm x 155mm.

Will of Richard Evans of Bredon
Worcester, Hereford and Worcester Record Office, Probate records BA 3585 1594:28m; 1594; English; paper; single sheet; 390mm x 150mm.

Will and Probate Inventory of Edward Archbold
Worcester, Hereford and Worcester Record Office, Probate records BA 3585 1618:154; 1618.
   Will: English; parchment; single sheet; 542mm x 670mm; no endorsement or seals.
   Probate Inventory: English; paper; 8 leaves; 390mm x 155mm; no foliation; sewn.

Quarter Sessions Records

Quarter Sessions Indictment of John Hart
Worcester, Hereford and Worcester Record Office, Quarter Sessions Records 110:42/53;
1607; Latin, some English; parchment; single sheet; 53mm x 260mm.

Proceedings of the Council in the Marches of Wales

Although originally constituted as an advisory body, through most of its history the
Council operated primarily as a court, hearing a wide range of cases. The cases
recorded in this volume were heard during Trinity term, 1617, from 16 June to 21 July.

London, British Library, Royal 18 B vii; 1617; English and Latin; paper; 34 leaves;
290mm x 180mm; modern pencil foliation 1–34; signed on f 34 by 'Tho: Chamberlyn' and
'H. Tounesend' under the date '21° Iunij. 1617', which is an error for 'xxj° Iulij. 1617', which
appears at the top of the leaf. Now bound in with MS Royal 18 B viii, which is unrelated.

Household Documents

ACCOUNT BOOK OF PRIOR WILLIAM MORE

Perhaps the most important single document in the Worcestershire collection is the
Household Account Book kept by William More during his priorate from 1518 to
1535. Kept on a weekly basis with considerable care, the accounts record in great detail
payments for every aspect of the prior's household life. More made hundreds of payments to players, minstrels, tumblers, bearwards, and other entertainers of all kinds.
Folios 1–28 deal primarily with receipts, though some expenses on visitations are
included and a list of the prior's servants in 1527 appears on folio 6v. Expenditures
are detailed on folios 29–157. The last twenty-four folios of the manuscript have been
torn out, but the final entries for the summer of 1535 cannot be far from the end of
More's tenure of office. Because of the importance of this volume and because it raises
some difficulties of interpretation, a fuller account of Prior More and his journal is
given on pp 304–5 and 307–8. E.S. Fegan, who edited the Account Book for the
Worcestershire Historical Society, thought that three different scribes were responsible for writing the volume. This is unlikely; the whole volume appears to be in the
same hand, excluding some scribbled and irrelevant additions from later in the
century. The scribe occasionally uses a display hand, especially for quarterly

summations and, as is likely in a weekly account book, there are frequent additions and annotations at a later time.

Worcester, Cathedral Library, A11; 1518–35; English and Latin; paper; i + 158 + i; 207mm x 312mm; foliated 1–121a, 121b–157; modern quarter leather binding (1913), contemporary vellum wrappers bound in.

ACCOUNT BOOK OF SIR JOHN PAKINGTON OF WESTWOOD PARK

Worcester, St Helen's Record Office, BA 3835/16(ii)3; 1584; English; paper; 10 leaves; 205mm x 150mm; foliated 1–10.

Editorial Procedures

The editorial procedures which have been observed throughout the volume are discussed in the Introduction to the Herefordshire records on pp 37–43 above and should be consulted with reference to the Worcestershire records as well. There are, however, procedures which apply primarily to the Worcestershire records and these are considered below.

Principles of Selection

All documents dealing with the two Worcester pageant houses have been included, as they provide our only information on the precise location of the houses; those documents (primarily leases) which post-date 1642 are transcribed in Appendix 1.

I have tried to err on the side of generosity in giving material from Prior More's Account Book. I have discussed above More's accounting procedures and the difficulty of interpreting some of his entries (especially the regular household payments to two players); because of these ambiguities I have generally included other ambiguous entries, such as payments to an individual which appear adjacent to a payment for entertainment.

Following the procedure of the REED *Devon* volume, I have included references to church ales. Though the records often do not specify this, it is often clear that some form of entertainment was involved in these festivities. In addition to a relatively small number of church ales in churchwardens' accounts, the largest number of references to these festivities occur in Prior More's Account Book.

I have omitted the regular payments in the Worcester Priory sacrist's rolls for the carrying of banners around the feretory at Rogation and for torch-carrying on Corpus Christi, since these were purely liturgical ceremonies.[97] For similar reasons I have not included the anonymous description of Prince Arthur's funeral procession from Bewdley to Worcester in 1502.[98] I have also omitted a relatively well-known record quoted by Murray among the Worcester city records for 1573–4: 'that money shall be allowed to the players the last somer by the audition at the next audyte, by their discretion.' Murray is quoting here from Noake, who presumably was quoting from either the Civic Accounts or the Chamber Order Book. There is no such entry in either volume for 1573–4 or for any other year.[99]

Edited Text

The genitive singular of the Latin word for 'Worcester' has been uniformly transcribed as 'Wygorn*ie*.' When – rarely – the word is written out in Worcester documents, the scribes show a preference for this form over 'Wygorniensis.' I have tried to be as consistent as possible in the expansion of abbreviations, utilizing where possible the scribe's normal form when writing the word out in full. Especially in Prior More's Account Book this has meant that some sigla have been transcribed in more than one way; for example, the usual '-er' abbreviation is in some words consistently spelled '-ur' when written out, as in 'pepur.'

Dating

The weekly accounting period of Prior More's Account Book is not always consistent and it is clear that the scribe did not consider it to be vitally important. The accounting week began on either Saturday or Sunday. The Account Book begins with a relatively consistent Saturday-to-Friday accounting period, perhaps because More was installed on a Saturday, but this soon breaks down and in later years there is a distinct preference for a Sunday-to-Saturday period. In a very large number of cases it is not possible to tell clearly which period the scribe has in mind and for this reason I have consistently given the dates corresponding to a Sunday-to-Saturday week. This should not be taken to indicate precision on the part of the scribe; occasional further discrepancies in the dating are discussed in the endnotes. More's scribe often gives corroborative information ('fryday cristmas day') which allows these dates to be checked internally.

   If a document can be dated within a decade, I have generally kept it in the body of the text. Hereford Cathedral Roll R707 (a Worcester Priory cellarer's roll) is an example; the date has been torn away, but the cellarer's name, Nicholas Hanbury, is there. He appears with some frequency in Worcester rolls of the late 1470s and early 1480s, and the document is therefore transcribed in its approximate place in the sequence of cellarers' rolls. When such a record can be dated within a decade, I have placed it at the beginning of the decade.

Gaps in the Records

Although the records for Worcestershire are in general more abundant than those for Herefordshire, there remain some important gaps. We have no civic accounts for Worcester before 1540 and the book for 1600–23 is missing. Despite the importance of the Worcester guilds, no guild accounts survive from our period. Rather more churchwardens' accounts survive than in Herefordshire, but it is still not a rich collection. Ecclesiastical court books are preserved only for the years 1610–17; the records of Worcestershire parishes in the deanery of Burford, diocese of Hereford, show that much information would have been preserved in the court books of the period 1580–1610.

An important gap in the Worcestershire documents is the records of major county families. The considerable surviving records of the Talbot family of Grafton (largely in the British Library) include very few household account books and contain nothing of REED interest. Two household account books for the Beauchamp family survive, one at Warwick and one at Longleat, but they contain no REED material. The remaining bulk of the Beauchamp papers which are available to the public are receivers' accounts which contain no relevant material at all. The well-known account book of the duke of York's estate at Hanley Castle for 1409–10 similarly contains no REED material within the county.[100]

The caveats outlined in the Introduction to the Herefordshire records obtain, of course, for the Worcestershire records as well. First, the picture should not be taken as complete, though it may well be as complete as possible. Second, the chance survival of an individual record may distort its importance, implying uniqueness in an event which may in fact have been quite common, or, conversely, giving an impression of normality to an event which was unusual. With these two points borne in mind, the records give a good picture of the history of dramatic entertainment in the provincial West Midlands.

Notes

1 Mrs Baldwyn-Childe, 'The Building of the Manor-House of Kyre Park, Worcestershire (1588-1618),' *The Antiquary*, 21 (1890), 204–5. Carriage of stone by river from Shropshire to Bewdley cost '18d the tonne'; from Bewdley to Kyre Park over land, the cost rose to '5s for every tonne.'

2 *VCH: Worcestershire*, vol 2, pp 250–1; vol 4, p 305; *VCH: Shropshire*, William Page (ed), vol 1 (London, 1908), 454.

3 See Dyer, *The City of Worcester*, pp 70–1. T.R. Slater and P.J. Jarvis (eds), *Field and Forest: An Historical Geography of Warwickshire and Worcestershire* (Norwich, 1982) includes recent work on the medieval geography of the county. When not otherwise indicated, much of the detail in the Introduction is drawn from the essays of the *VCH: Worcestershire*, especially J.W. Willis Bund, 'Ecclesiastical History,' vol 2, pp 1–92 and 'Political History,' vol 2, pp 197–233; F.M. Stenton, 'Topography: City of Worcester,' vol 4, pp 376–420; and A.F. Leach, 'Schools,' vol 4, pp 473–540.

4 *VCH: Worcestershire*, vol 4, p 383. Richard Grafton, *An Abridgement of the Chronicles of Englande* (London, 1570; *STC*: 12151) includes a list titled 'The high wayes from any notable towne in England to the Citie of London. And lykewise from one notable towne to an other...'; see also the maps in Brian Paul Hindle, 'Roads and Tracks,' *The English Medieval Landscape*, Leonard Cantor (ed) (London, 1982), 193–217.

5 R.H. Hilton, *A Medieval Society: The West Midlands at the End of the Thirteenth Century* (London, 1966), 1–2, 26, 50.

6 *VCH: Worcestershire*, vol 2, pp 209–10.

7 *VCH: Worcestershire*, vol 2, pp 209–17, 224; Philip Styles, 'The City of Worcester during the Civil Wars, 1640-60,' *Studies in Seventeenth Century West Midlands History* (Kineton, 1978), 213, 250–1.

8 Penry Williams, *The Council in the Marches of Wales under Elizabeth I* (Cardiff, 1958), 6–15.

9 Williams, *Council of the Marches in Wales*, pp 15–27.

10 Williams, *Council of the Marches in Wales*, pp 47–59, 186–91, 316–20.

11 Penry Williams, 'The Activity of the Council in the Marches under the Early

Stuarts,' *The Welsh History Review*, 1 (1960–3), 140–2; C.A.J. Skeel, 'The Council of the Marches in the Seventeenth Century,' *English Historical Review*, 30 (1915), 22.

12   Margaret Wilson, 'The Hwicce,' *The Origins of Worcester*, Philip Barker (ed), *TRWAS*, 3rd ser, 2 (1968–9), 21–5; A.H. Smith, 'The Hwicce,' *Franciplegius: Medieval and Linguistic Studies in Honour of Francis Peabody Magoun Jr*, Jesse B. Bessinger and Robert P. Creed (eds) (New York, 1965), 56–65. Christopher Dyer, *Lords and Peasants in a Changing Society: The Estates of the Bishopric of Worcester, 680–1540* (Cambridge, 1980), 7–38 outlines the early history of the diocese.

13   *VCH: Worcestershire*, vol 2, pp 19–20, 30–1, 39–42.

14   Hilton, *A Medieval Society*, p 9; *VCH: Worcestershire*, vol 2, pp 89–90. The abbey was under the jurisdiction of the apostolic see in spiritual matters and of the Crown in temporal matters. See the Register of Bishop Simon Montacute, *SHRO*: BA 2648/2 (iii), ff 25–5v.

15   *VCH: Worcestershire*, vol 2, map facing p 90.

16   *Registrum sive Liber Irrotularius et Consuetudinarius Prioratus Beatæ Mariæ Wigorniensis*, William Hale Hale (ed), Camden Society, 91 (London, 1865), i–iii; Knowles, *The Religious Orders in England*, vol 3, p 389.

17   David Knowles and R. Neville Hadcock, *Medieval Religious Houses: England and Wales*, 2nd ed (London, 1971), 229, 219.

18   Prior More's Account Book indicates that the gifts were paid in December.

19   Pat M. Hughes, 'Houses and Property in Post-Reformation Worcester: A Topographical Survey,' *Medieval Worcester: An Archaeological Framework*, M.O.H. Carver (ed), *TRWAS*, 3rd ser, 7 (1980), 271–3, 276–7.

20   Marett, *A Calendar of the Register of Henry Wakefeld*, pp 144–5, 150–2. The Peverel and Morgan registers have not been printed.

21   Dyer, *The City of Worcester*, pp 237–8.

22   *VCH: Worcestershire*, vol 2, pp 51–5; Vincent Burke, 'The Economic Consequences of Recusancy in Elizabethan Worcestershire,' *Recusant History*, 14, pt 1 (1977), 71–7; John Humphreys, 'Recusancy in Worcestershire, 1558–1603,' *Studies in Worcestershire History* (Birmingham, 1938), 174–87.

23   *VCH: Worcestershire*, vol 4, p 310.

24   R.C. Gaut, *A History of Worcestershire Agriculture and Rural Evolution* (Worcester, 1939), 61.

25   *BL*: Add. 17062, f 25.

26   Cambridge, Corpus Christi College Library, 210, p 189; see also John R. Burton, *A History of Bewdley* (London, 1883), 27.

27   Philip Styles, 'The Corporation of Bewdley under the Later Stuarts,' *Studies in Seventeenth Century West Midlands History*, (Kineton, 1978), 43–5.

28   *VCH: Worcestershire*, vol 3, p 74; Martin Weinbaum, *British Borough Charters*

1307–1660 (Cambridge, 1943), 123; Gaut, *History of Worcestershire Agriculture*, p 62.

29 *Chronicon Abbatiae de Evesham ad Annum 1418*, William Dunn Macray (ed), Rolls Series, 29 (London, 1863); the surviving material has been assembled by George May, *A Descriptive History of the Town of Evesham* (Evesham, 1845), 91–133; see also R.H. Hilton, 'The Small Town and Urbanisation – Evesham in the Middle Ages,' *Midland History*, 7 (1982), 1–8.

30 Rodney Hilton, 'A Rare Evesham Abbey Estate Document,' *Class Conflict and the Crisis of Feudalism: Essays in Medieval Social History* (London, 1985), 101.

31 The abbot and convent argued that the abbey's situation, buildings, lack of debt, and (not least) exemption from the bishop's control, made it an ideal educational establishment. See *Letters and Papers, Foreign and Domestic, in the Reign of Henry VIII*, vol 13, pt 2 (1538, Aug – Dec), James Gairdner (arr and cat) (London, 1893), entry no 866; *VCH: Worcestershire*, vol 2, pp 125–6.

32 *Domesday Book: Worcestershire*, Frank and Caroline Thorn (eds) (London, 1982), chapter 10, section 1.

33 *VCH: Worcestershire*, vol 2, p 372; R.H. Hilton, 'The Small Town and Urbanisation – Evesham in the Middle Ages,' pp 2, 6.

34 *VCH: Worcestershire*, vol 2, p 374.

35 Weinbaum, *British Borough Charters*, p 123; May, *A Descriptive History of the Town of Evesham*, pp 257–61.

36 Gaut, *History of Worcestershire Agriculture*, p 40; Weinbaum, *British Borough Charters*, p 124.

37 *DNB*, 'Richard Baxter.'

38 *VCH: Worcestershire*, vol 2, pp 127–30; vol 4, pp 156, 159.

39 Hilton, *A Medieval Society*, pp 28, 34; Barbara Harvey, *Westminster Abbey and its Estates in the Middle Ages* (Oxford, 1977), 125.

40 Pershore's economy is discussed by R.H. Hilton, *The English Peasantry in the Later Middle Ages* (Oxford, 1975), 81–2, 90–1; see also *VCH: Worcestershire*, vol 4, pp 151–2 and Gaut, *History of Worcestershire Agriculture*, pp 40–1.

41 M.O.H. Carver, 'The Site and Settlements at Worcester,' *Medieval Worcester: An Archaeological Framework*, TRWAS, 3rd ser, 7 (1980), 19–20.

42 Recent archaeological work has given a much clearer view of the details of Worcester's topography. See M.O.H. Carver (ed), *Medieval Worcester: an Archaeological Framework* and Philip Barker, *The Origins of Worcester*, TRWAS, 3rd ser, 2 (1968–9), especially pp 35–7.

43 There is some uncertainty over the number of gates. Leland specifies six, but there is evidence of seven, two of which (Trinity Gate and Friars' Gate) were only posterns. Leland omits Friars' Gate from his list in Bodl.: MS Tanner 464e, f 85. See also Barker, *The Origins of Worcester*, p 35.

44 Bodl.: MS Tanner 464e, f 84v.

45 *VCH: Worcestershire*, vol 4, pp 380–2.

46 Dyer, *The City of Worcester*, pp 190–1.
47 *VCH: Worcestershire*, vol 4, p 389; Dyer, *The City of Worcester*, p 202.
48 Dyer, *The City of Worcester*, p 195; *VCH: Worcestershire*, vol 4, p 381.
49 Dyer, *The City of Worcester*, p 194.
50 SHRO: BA 9360 C-2.
51 Gaut, *History of Worcestershire Agriculture*, pp 41, 62.
52 SHRO: BA 9360/A23 Box 4, 1392, Ordinance for the Better Regulation of the Bailiffs and the Rendering of their Accounts.
53 *A Survey of Worcestershire by Thomas Habington*, John Amphlett (ed), vol 2 (Oxford, 1899), 424–6. An early seal reproduced by Toulmin Smith suggests that the guild may at one time have been called the St Nicholas guild, though the Commissioners' Reports of 1545–6 and 1548–9 refer to it only as 'the Guyld of the holy Trynyte within the said parishe [of saynt Nicholas]....' Smith, *English Gilds*, p 202; H.F. Westlake's *The Parish Gilds of Mediaeval England* (London, 1919) does not mention either the St Nicholas or the Holy Trinity guild. See also *VCH: Worcestershire*, vol 4, pp 478–9.
54 Dyer, *The City of Worcester*, p 218.
55 SHRO: BA 9360, View of Frankpledge, vol 2, f 107, cited in Dyer, *The City of Worcester*, p 149.
56 Bodl.: MS Tanner 464e, ff 85v–6.
57 References to this and other records can be found in the Records under the appropriate date and place.
58 Dyer, *The City of Worcester*, p 109.
59 Dyer, *The City of Worcester*, pp 115–16.
60 The discussion of the difficulties of estimating local populations in the Introduction to the Herefordshire records, p 45, note 27, applies equally to Worcestershire. The ranking lists are given by Josiah Cox Russell, *British Medieval Population* (Albuquerque, 1948), pp 132–3, 142, though his interpretation of the data can no longer be accepted; see also J.A. Johnston, 'Developments in Worcester and Worcestershire 1563–1851,' *TRWAS*, 3rd ser, 5 (1976), 51–5.
61 W.G. Hoskins, *Provincial England: Essays in Social and Economic History* (London, 1963), 72.
62 T.R. Nash, *Collections for the History of Worcestershire*, vol 2, Appendix, p cxvii.
63 Dyer, *The City of Worcester*, pp 20–9.
64 Charles Phythian-Adams, 'Urban Decay in Late Medieval England,' *Towns in Societies: Essays in Economic History and Historical Sociology*, Philip Abrams and E.A. Wrigley (eds) (Cambridge, 1978), 173.
65 Dyer, *The City of Worcester*, pp 44–6; Paul Slack, *The Impact of Plague in Tudor and Stuart England* (London, 1985), 60–3; E.A. Wrigley and R.S. Schofield, *The Population History of England, 1541–1871: A Reconstruction* (London, 1981), 653; Ian Roy and Stephen Porter, 'The Population of Worcester in 1646,' *Local Population Studies*, 28 (1982), 32–43.

66   Hilton, *A Medieval Society*, pp 26–30; the household of the bishop is described
      by Roy Martin Haines, *The Administration of the Diocese of Worcester in the First
      Half of the Fourteenth Century* (London, 1965).

67   C. Dyer, *Lords and Peasants in a Changing Society*, pp 18–19.

68   Dyer, *The City of Worcester*, p 15; *VCH: Worcestershire*, vol 3, p 381.

69   There is some question about what More actually received. The Worcestershire
      antiquary John Noake claimed that Grimley was denied to More and that he was
      given Crowle manor instead, though he gives no source for this information.
      Green says he 'had the manors of Crowle and Grimley settled on him for life.'
      John Noake, *The Monastery and Cathedral of Worcester*, pp 203–4 as cited by
      Knowles, *The Religious Orders in England*, vol 3, pp 344–5; Valentine Green,
      The History and Antiquities of the City and Suburbs of Worcester, vol 1, p 221.

70   *DNB*, 'William More'; Knowles, *The Religious Orders in England*, vol 3,
      pp 108–26, 344–5. The Alveston parish register is now at Warwick, Warwickshire
      County Record Office: DR65/1, p 9.

71   Knowles, *The Religious Orders in England*, vol 3, pp 109–11. See Ethel S. Fegan
      (ed), *The Journal of Prior William More* for a modern edition of this account book
      or journal.

72   Knowles' portrait of More is, on the whole, that of a competent administrator,
      though his career was hardly spotless. In 1525 the tenants of Henbury brought
      action for nepotism against the prior as surveyor of the estates, charging that he
      had made a preferential grant of land to his brother, Robert Peers. A riot broke
      out when Peers attempted to visit his holdings and the case eventually went to
      Star Chamber (PRO : STAC 2/21/136, STAC 2/26/138). See also C. Dyer, *Lords
      and Peasants in a Changing Society*, pp 161, 296–7; R. A. Houlbrooke, 'Women's
      Social Life and Common Action in England from the Fifteenth Century to the
      Eve of the Civil War,' *Continuity and Change*, 1, pt 2 (1986), 171–89, especially
      p 178.

73   More Account Book, f 129.

74   *Letters and Papers, Foreign and Domestic, in the Reign of Henry VIII*, vol 9 (1535),
      James Gairdner (arr and cat) (London, 1886), entries 51, 52, 90, 108, 204, 497;
      vol 10 (1536), James Gairdner (arr and cat) (London, 1887), entry 216. This last
      is Musard's letter to Cromwell from prison.

75   *DNB*, 'Pakington.'

76   Hockdays were celebrated on the second Monday and Tuesday after Easter.

77   Week of 23–9 July 1531, f 129; the tenants of the manor of Cleeve Prior present
      a Robin Hood Play.

78   Week of 6–12 July 1533, f 143v.

79   A 1318 entry concerning the monastery of Wigmore in the register of Adam
      Orleton, bishop of Hereford, draws a connection between the practice of blood-
      letting and the singing of 'cantileni inhonesti.' See above, p 188.

80   Fegan, *The Journal of Prior William More*, p v.

81 More Account Book, f 131, as transcribed in Fegan, *The Journal of Prior William More*, p 336.

82 A considerable amount of money was involved in the 'seyny' payments. The following entry occurs under the heading of 'monks' wages' in the accounts of Thomas Asteley, pittancer, for the year 1521–2 (Worcester Cathedral Library: Roll C412):

> ...Et solut*um* domino priori et Convent*u* pro eor*um* Minucio*ni*b*us*
> cum duplicib*us* dicti domini prioris voc*atur* Seny money p*er*
> ann*um*   lviij s. viij d....

83 The 'seyny' cook appears in the 'lyvereys of bred,' in which the food allowances are specified for various priory officials and employees, as in Worcester Cathedral Library: A12, f 114 (not dated):

> lyvereys of bred as heraf*ter* foloweth'
> ...
> Item to the seyny cooke iiij yoman past loffe
> ...

84 John C. Meagher, 'The First Progress of Henry VII,' *Renaissance Drama*, ns, 1 (1968), 60–7.

85 PRO: C66/521, mb 15d; see also *Calendar of Patent Rolls: Edward IV – Henry VI, 1467–1477* (London, 1900), 101–2.

86 VCH: *Worcestershire*, vol 4, pp 381–2.

87 Green, *History and Antiquities of Worcester*, vol 2, pp 6–7 (note).

88 Nicholas Orme, 'The Medieval Schools of Worcestershire,' TRWAS, 3rd ser, 3 (1978), 48; VCH: *Worcestershire*, vol 2, p 287 and vol 4, p 491; *A Survey of Worcestershire by Thomas Habington*, John Amphlett (ed), vol 2 (Oxford, 1899), 426; J.M. Gutch, 'The Clothiers' Company of Worcester,' pp 253–4.

89 Pat M. Hughes, 'Houses and Property in Post-Reformation Worcester,' *Medieval Worcester: An Archaeological Framework*, M.O.H. Carver (ed), TRWAS, 3rd ser, 7 (1980), 277.

90 R.W. Ingram (ed), *Coventry*, Records of Early English Drama (Toronto, 1981), 386, 417, 431.

91 See Herefordshire Introduction, p 47, note 53. Further information on the charivari is given in the endnotes: p 275, to HRO: box 17, vol 66, ff [228v, 229]; p 586, to HRO: box 19, vol 72, ff [24v, 25]; p 588, to HWRO: Quarter Sessions Records 110: 21/68, single sheet.

92 The registers are listed by David M. Smith, *Guide to Bishops' Registers of England and Wales* (London, 1981), 215–31.

93 The librarian of Dr Williams's Library, Mr John Creasey, has generously supplied

the new dating for this manuscript. He assigns it to the late seventeenth century and probably pre-1694 rather than post-1694.

94   Geoffrey F. Nuttall, *The Manuscript of the Reliquiae Baxterianae*, Dr Williams's Library, Occasional Paper No 1 (London, 1954).

95   B.S. Benedikz and Susan Brock, 'Worcester Cathedral Library, Catalogue of Muniments, Class A' (Birmingham University Library, typescript, 1977); Susan Brock, 'Worcester Cathedral Library, Catalogue of Muniments, Class B' (Birmingham University Library, typescript, 1981); G.M.B. Pick, 'Worcester Cathedral Library, Catalogue of Muniments, Class C' (Birmingham University Library, typescript, 1981).

96   John Foxe, *Actes and monuments of these latter and perillous dayes, touching matters of the church. Now againe, recognised, perused, the fift time imprinted.*, 2 vols (London, 1596), 1879–80 (STC: 11226). The tale does not appear in earlier editions.

97   The form of these entries is generally as follows: '...Et sol*utum* portantib*us* vexillas cu*m* dracone dieb*us* Rogation*is* iiij s. iiij d. Et solut*um* portant*ibus* luminaria circa feretru*m* in festo Corporis Chr*isti*...' (Sacrist's Accounts 1501–2, WCL: Roll C426, mb 2.)

98   Transcribed by John Leland: see Hearne (ed), *Joannis Lelandi Antiquarii De Rebus Britannicis Collectanea*, vol 5, pp 373–81.

99   Murray, *English Dramatic Companies*, p 408; Noake, *Worcester in Olden Times*, p 131.

100 Northampton, Northamptonshire Record Office: Westmorland (Apethorpe), 4.xx.4.

Select Bibliography

The Select Bibliography lists works which transcribe documents relevant to REED and works which have proven essential for reference purposes. Works cited in the Introduction and in the Endnotes are, in general, not included here.

Amphlett, John. *An Index to Dr. Nash's Collections for a History of Worcestershire* (Oxford, 1894–5).

Barnard, E. A. B. 'Churchwardens' Accounts of the Parish of South Littleton, Worcestershire, 1548–71,' TRWAS, ns, 3 (1925–6), 60–106.

– *The Prattinton Collections of Worcestershire History* (Evesham, 1931).

– and W.H. Price. *Churchwardens' Accounts of the Parish of Badsey, with Aldington, in Worcestershire from 1525 to 1571* (Hampstead, 1913).

Blair, Lawrence. *English Church Ales as Seen in English Churchwardens' Accounts and Other Archival Sources of the Fifteenth and Sixteenth Centuries* (Ann Arbor, 1940).

Bond, Shelagh (ed). *The Chamber Order Book of Worcester, 1602–50*. WHS, ns, 8 (Leeds, 1974).

Bullock-Davies, Constance. *Register of Royal and Baronial Domestic Minstrels: 1272–1327* (Woodbridge, Suffolk, 1986).

Burton, John Richard and F. S. Pearson. *Bibliography of Worcestershire*. WHS (Oxford, 1898–1907).

Chambers, E.K. *The Elizabethan Stage*. 4 vols (Oxford, 1923).

– *The Mediaeval Stage*. 2 vols (Oxford, 1903).

Cox, John Charles. *Churchwardens' Accounts from the Fourteenth Century to the Close of the Seventeenth Century* (London, 1913).

Duignan, W. H. *Worcestershire Place Names* (London, 1905).

Dyer, Alan D. *The City of Worcester in the Sixteenth Century* (Leicester, 1973).

– 'Probate Inventories of Worcester Tradesmen, 1545–1614,' *Miscellany 2*. WHS, ns, 5 (Worcester, 1967), 1–67.

Fegan, Ethel S. (ed). *Journal of Prior William More*. WHS (London, 1913–14).

Frere, Walter Howard and William McClure Kennedy. *Visitation Articles and Injunctions of the Period of the Reformation*. 3 vols. Alcuin Club Collections, 14–16 (London, 1910).

Fry, Edmund Alexander (ed). *A Calendar of Wills and Administrations Preserved in the Consistory Court of the Bishop of Worcester*. Vol 1, 1451–1600. WHS (Hertford, 1904) and British Record Society, 31 (London, 1904–10).

Green, Valentine. *The History and Antiquities of the City and Suburbs of Worcester*. 2 vols (London, 1796).

Gutch, J. M. 'The Clothiers' Company of Worcester,' *British Archaeological Association*. Proceedings at Worcester, August 1848 (London, 1851), 243–60.

Habington, Thomas. *A Survey of Worcestershire by Thomas Habington*. John Amphlett (ed). 2 vols. WHS (Oxford, 1894–9).

Halliwell-Phillipps, James Orchard. *Outlines of the Life of Shakespeare*. 2 vols (London, 1884).

Hamilton, Sidney Graves (ed). *Compotus Rolls of the Priory of Worcester of the XIV & XV Centuries*. WHS (Oxford, 1910).

The Historical Manuscripts Commission. W. J. Hardy (ed). 'The Records of the County of Worcester,' *Report on Manuscripts in Various Collections*. Vol 1 (London, 1901), 282–326.

– Reginald L. Poole (ed). 'Muniments in the Possession of the Dean and Chapter of Worcester,' *The 14th Report of the Manuscripts Commission*. Appendix 8 (London, 1895), 165–203.

Hollings, Marjory (ed). *The Red Book of Worcester*. WHS (London, 1934–50).

Hooper, John H. 'The Clothiers' Company, Worcester,' *Associated Architectural Societies' Reports and Papers*, 15 (1880), 331–9.

Kennedy, William Paul McClure. *Elizabethan Episcopal Administration: An Essay in Sociology and Politics*. 3 vols. Alcuin Club Collections, 25–7 (London, 1924).

Knowles, David. *The Religious Orders in England*. 3 vols (Cambridge, 1948–59; rpt 1971).

Leach, Arthur F. *Documents Illustrating Early Education in Worcester, 685 to 1700*. WHS (London, 1913).

Leland, John. *Joannis Lelandi Antiquarii De Rebus Britannicis Collectanea*. T. Hearne (ed). 6 vols. 2nd ed (London, 1774).

Marett, W. P. *A Calendar of the Register of Henry Wakefeld, Bishop of Worcester 1375–95*. WHS, ns, 7 (1972).

Mawer, Alan and F. M. Stenton. *The Place-names of Worcestershire*. English Place-Name Society, vol 4 (Cambridge, 1927).

Murray, John Tucker. *English Dramatic Companies, 1558–1642*. 2 vols (London, 1910).

– 'English Dramatic Companies in the Towns Outside of London, 1550–1600,' *Modern Philology*, 2 (1905), 539–59.

Nash, Treadway R. *Collections for the History of Worcestershire*. 2 vols (London, 1781–2).

Nichols, John. *The Progresses and Public Processions of Queen Elizabeth*. 3 vols (London, 1823).

Noake, John. 'Ancient Worcester Cordwainers' Company,' *The Gentleman's Magazine*, 3rd ser, 3 (1857), 317–19.
– 'The Deanery and the Trinity Hall, Worcester,' *Associated Architectural Societies' Reports and Papers*, 21, pt 1 (1891–2), 75–97.
– *The Monastery and Cathedral of Worcester* (London and Birmingham, 1866).
– *Notes and Queries for Worcestershire* (London and Birmingham, 1856).
– *The Rambler in Worcestershire; or Stray Notes on Churches and Congregations.* 2 vols (London and Birmingham, 1851–4).
– *Worcester in Olden Times* (London, 1849).
– *Worcestershire Nuggets* (Worcester, 1889).
– *Worcestershire Relics* (London and Worcester, 1877).
Orme, Nicholas. 'The Medieval Schools of Worcestershire,' TRWAS, 3rd ser, 6 (1978), 43–51.
Smith, [Joshua] Toulmin (ed). *English Gilds*. Early English Text Society (Oxford, 1870).
Smith, Lucy Toulmin (ed). *The Itinerary of John Leland in or about the Years 1535–1543*. 6 vols (London, 1964).
The Victoria History of the Counties of England. *The Victoria History of the County of Worcester*. J. W. Willis-Bund (ed). 4 vols (London, 1901–24).
Whitehead, David. *The Book of Worcester* (Chesham, 1976).
Wickham, Glynne. *Early English Stages: 1300–1660*. 2 vols in 3 pts (London, 1959–72).
– *The Medieval Theatre* (London, 1974).
Williams, W. R. *The Parliamentary History of the County of Worcester* (Hereford, 1897).
Willis Bund, J. W. *Worcestershire County Records. Division I. Documents Relating to Quarter Sessions. Calendar of the Quarter Sessions Papers*. Vol 1, 1591–1643. WHS (Worcester, 1900).
– with John Amphlett (eds). *Lay Subsidy Roll for the County of Worcester, Circ. 1280*. WHS (Oxford, 1893).
Wilson, James Maurice (ed). *Accounts of the Priory of Worcester, 1521-2*. WHS (Oxford, 1907).
– *The Liber Albus of the Priory of Worcester*. WHS (Worcester, 1919).
– and Cosmo Gordon (eds). *Early Compotus Rolls of the Priory of Worcester*. WHS (Oxford, 1908).
Woodfill, Walter L. *Musicians in English Society from Elizabeth to Charles I*. Princeton Studies in History, 9 (Princeton, 1953; rpt New York, 1969).
Woof, Richard. *Catalogue of Manuscript Records & Printed Books in the Library of the Corporation of Worcester* (Worcester, 1874).

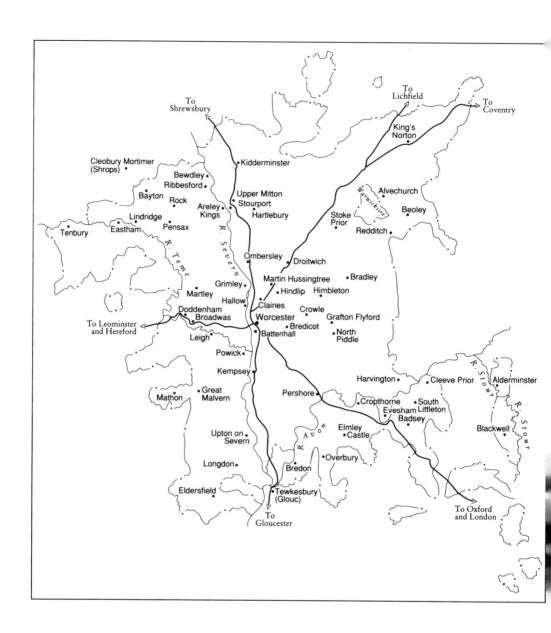

Worcestershire *c* 1600 with principal renaissance roads

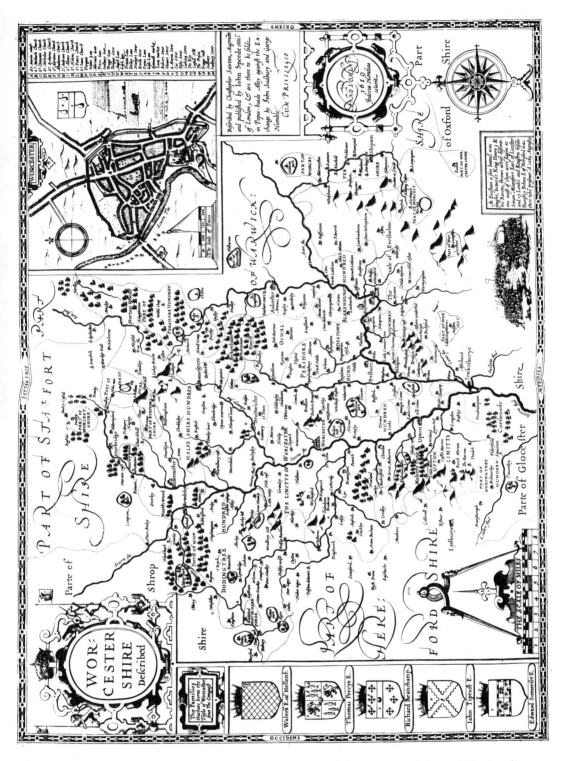

Map of Worcestershire from John Speed, *The Theatre of the Empire of Great Britaine*, by courtesy of the Huntington Library

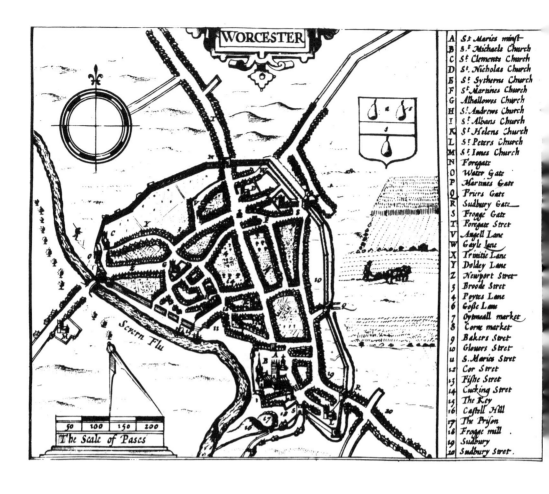

The legend on the map reads:

A St. Maries minst
B St. Michaels Church
C St. Clements Church
D St. Nicholas Church
E St. Sytherns Church
F St. Martines Church
G Alhallowes Church
H St. Andrews Church
I St. Albans Church
K St. Helens Church
L St. Peters Church
M St. Iones Church
N Foregate
O Water Gate
P Martines Gate
Q Friers Gate
R Sudbury Gate
S Frogge Gate
T Foregate Strcet
V Angell Lane
W Gayle Lane
X Trinitie Lane
Y Doldey Lane
Z Newport Strcet
3 Broode Strcet
4 Poytes Lane
6 Goße Lane
7 Oytmeall market
8 Corne market
9 Bakers Strcet
10 Glouers Strcet
u S. Maries Strcet
12 Cor Strcet
13 Fiße Strcet
14 Cucking Strcet
15 The Key
16 Caftell Hill
17 The Prifon
18 Frogge mill
19 Sudbury
20 Sudbury Strcet.

Severn Flu

50 100 150 200
The Scale of Paces

WORCESTER

Map of Worcester from John Speed, *The Theatre of the Empire of Great Britaine*, by courtesy of the Huntington Library

Diocese of Worcester

1240

Constitutions of Bishop Walter Cantilupe   LPL: MS 171
f 41v*   *(26 July) (Part 1, On the state of the church: Chapter 4,*
Concerning churchyards)

...   5

Cimiteria quoque que corpora continent saluandorum quorum multa
iam purgata stolam sue glorificacionis exspectant. inhoneste credimus
brutorum animalium sordibus deturpari. Preterea etiam precipimus
quod honeste claudantur sepe uel muro: canonice compellendis ad
hoc faciendum hijs ad quos eorum clausio noscitur pertinere.   10
¶ Rectoribus etiam ecclesiarum & sacerdotibus inhibemus, ne ipsi in
dictis ecclesiarum atriis animalia sua pascant uel etiam intrare
permittant. Quod si presumpserint grauiter se nouerint puniendos.
¶ Ad seruandam quoque tam cimiterij quam ecclesie reuerenciam
prohibemus ne in cimiterijs uel alijs locis sacratis uel etiam alibi diebus   15
dominicis mercata teneantur uel sanguinis cause tractentur/. nec ludi
fiant inhonesti. maxime in sanctorum vigilijs & festis ecclesiarum quod
sanctis pocius in dedecus cedere nouimus: quam honorem
presumptoribus etiam & sacerdotibus qui hec fieri sustinuerint
canonice cohercendis. Nec in cymiterijs edificia nisi forsan hoc tempus   20
hostilitatis exegerit nulla fiant. & si facta fuerint dirruantur

...

Collation with BL: Cotton Claudius A viii (C) f 210:   6 que] *C omits*
7 inhoneste] inhonestum *C*   8 Preterea] Preter *C*   11–12 Rectoribus *etiam ...*
ecclesiarum] *C omits*   12 sua] *C omits*   18 vigilijs ... dedecus] *C omits*   19
&] *C omits*   19 fieri sustinuerint] sustinuerint fieri *C*

21/ exegerit *corrected in left margin from* exegere

f 45v*   *(Chapter 29, Concerning wanton behaviour)*

... ¶ Queratur *etiam* an *in* omnib*us* ecc*l*esij*s* canon misse sit rite
correct*us*. Prohibem*us etiam* clericis ne i*n*tersint ludis inhonestis u*el*
correis u*el* ludant ad aleas u*el* taxillos nec sustineant ludos f*ier*i de rege   5
& regina nec arietes leuari? nec palestras publicas f*ier*i. nec gildas
inhonestas & precipue mercator*um* & peregrinor*um* quas om*n*ino
fieri prohibem*us* p*er* q*ue* m*u*lta peric*u*la nouim*us* peruenisse....

f 47v   *(Part 2, On the correction of priests: Chapter 33)*   10

Ad hoc statuim*us* ne dieb*us* festiuis & solempnib*us* carragia fiant seu
mercata & si qui *in* hoc deliq*u*isse rep*er*iant*ur* & moniti no*n* desistant
ad cap*itulu*m euocentur & *ibi*dem grauiter pu*n*iantur hoc idem de
mercatis ludis placitis in locis sacris ne fiant statuim*us* obseruandu*m*....   15
...

1391
Register of Bishop Henry Wakefield   SHRO: BA 2648/4/iv
ff 86–6v*   *(20–1 November) (Orders for the appointment and*   20
conduct of stipendiary chaplains)
...

...nec eis in naui ecc*l*esie in qua admissi fuerint I vt *prefertur* seu in
Cimeterio aut alias in campo liceat tunc vagari Et si sup*er* hijs per
eos quos ecc*l*esij*s* tunc p*re*esse contigerit commoniti fu*er*int & correpti   25
ceruices suas contra ipsos propterea non erigant nec tumidos se
ostendant q*uo*dq*ue* correpcio*n*is hui*usmod*i occasione contra Rectores
vicarios seu eor*um* vices gerentes hui*usmod*i alios qui in insolencijs
suis eis assistant ipsosq*ue* foueant nullatin*us* commouebunt *sed* hijs
omnib*us* supradictis se exhibebunt humiles. reuerenciam debitam q*ue*   30
impendant. Dicti vero p*res*b*y*teri dictis do*m*inicis diebus & festiuis
vel si corpus alicui*us* defuncti affu*er*it. demu*m* post lectum maioris
misse Evangelium missas suas incipiant & non prius nisi de licencia
Rectoris vel vicarij aut alterius vices g*er*entis spiritu*a*liter preobtenta
P*res*b*y*teri quoq*ue* prefati Rectorib*us* vel vicarij*s* ecclesiar*um* vel   35
Capellar*um* vbi celebrauerint non detrahant *sed* discant cum psalmista
pone*re* custodiam ori suo Item q*uo*d tabernas spectac*u*la aut alia loca

Collation with BL: Cotton Claudius A viii (C), f 213v: 6 gildas] gildales C
8 peric*u*la nouim*us* peruenisse] nouim*us* peric*u*la p*er*uenisse C

14/ no*n* *corrected in left margin from* in

inhonesta seu ludos noxios & illicitos non frequentent *sed* more
sacerdotali in habitu se *h*a*b*eant & in gestu ne ipso*rum* ministerium
quod absit vitup*er*io scandalo seu defectui *h*a*b*eat*ur*....

...

5

1450
Notebook of John Lawern   Bodl.: MS Bodley 692
f 163v*   *(6 April) (Letter from John Carpenter, bishop of Worcester,
to John Lawern)*

10

⟨.....⟩missione di*u*ina Wygorn*ie* ep*isco*p*us*. dilect*is* nobis in Christo
filijs Magistro Ioha*n*ni Lawarn' ⟨sac⟩re Theologie *professo*ri.
Elemosinario ecclesie no*st*re Cath*edralis* Wygorn*ie*. Necno*n* vniuersis
et ⟨singulis⟩ rectorib*us* vicarijs ac cap⟨ell⟩anis curat*is* q*u*ibuscu*m*q*ue*
per no*st*ram dioc*e*sem constitut*is* Salutem ⟨.......⟩dicc*i*onem. Repleuit   15
amaritudi*n*e interiora m*en*tis no*st*re exertus mestitie rumor ⟨de⟩
pestifera coruptela ho*m*ines vtriusq*ue* Sexus ad residiuac*i*onem
reductiua qua*m* nullu*m* v*est*rum quod dolent*er* referim*us* latere
putamus. q*u*alit*er* vno certo die heu vsitato. hoc Solempni festo
paschat*is* transacto? mulieres ho*m*in*es*. Alioq*ue* die ho*m*ines mulieres   20
ligare ac cet*er*a media vtinam non inhonesta *vel* deteriora[re] facere
m⟨enti⟩unt*ur*. et excretere lucru*m* ecclesie fingentes. *Sed* dampnum
a*n*ime Sub fucato colore lucrantes. q*u*oru*m* occasione pl*u*ra oriu*n*t*ur*
Scandala. Adult*er*iaq*ue*. & A*l*ia crimina committu*n*t*ur* enormia in dei
ma*n*ifestam offensam. committenciu*m*q*ue* A*n*imar*um* periculu*m* valde   25
graue. et alior*um* perniciosum exe*m*plu*m*: Nos igit*ur* volentes.
quatenus. nob*is* co*n*cesserit Altissim*us* huic morbo canceroso & ficte
p*er*feccioni de oportuno prouideri remedio. ne Sub hui*u*smodi
si*m*ulatio*n*e deuoc*i*onis effigie turpia grauiora de cetero committant*ur*
Vobis coniu*n*ctem et diuisim committim*us* & mandam*us* firmit*er* Sub   30
pena inob*e*diencie & co*n*temptus iniungentes quatin*us* omnes &
Sing*u*los nostros vtriusq*ue* Sexus subditos in gen*er*e peremptorie
moneat*is* q*u*os nos etia*m* tenore presenciu*m* Sic monem*us*. vt ab
hui*u*smodi ligac*i*onibus & ludis inhonestis dieb*us* hacten*us* vsitatis
vocatis co*mmun*it*er* hok dayes vt predicit*ur* cessent & desistant S*u*b   35

11/ ⟨.....⟩missione: *left margin badly stained, affecting the beginning of first 4 lines, several*
words illegible in each line
21/ media *for* media via *(?)*
30/ coniu*n*ctem *for* coniu*n*ctim
31/ contemptus: *mark of abbreviation omitted*
35/ hok dayes *underlined*

pena excommunicacionis maioris in contrauenientes vel non parentes huiusmodi monicionibus nostris absque fauore. verumeciam cum iuris rigore acriter fulminande. Vobis insuper mandamus Sub pena iuris quatinus premissa statim post recepcionem presencium in sermonibus et ecclesis vestris predictis tempore diuinorum cum maior ffuerit populi multitudo ibidem publice intimetis. Ac de nominibus & cognominibus delinquencium post monicionem vestram. ymmo verius nostram eis legitime factam in premissis. Nos vel presidentem Consistorij nostri Wygornie aliquo die consistoriali citra festum pentecostes proximum futurum per vestras litteras patentes autentice Sigillatas. Seu alias personaliter viua voce distincte ⟨...⟩ certificetis. Datum Sub Sigillo nostro ad causas in Castro nostro de hertylbury Sexto ⟨die⟩ Aprilis Anno domini millesimo CCCC^mo quinquagesimo. & nostre consecracionis anno Septimo

...

1551–2
Copy of Visitation of Diocese of Gloucester by Bishop John Hooper,
May 1551   Dr Williams's Library: Roger Morrice MSS, L(3)
p 12*

...

4 Item. Whether they talke, walke, molest, unquiete or grieve the Minister whiles he is at the Divine Service, within the Church, or Church Yard, with any noise, brute Cryes clamours, Playes, Games, Sports, Dancing or Suchlike.

...

1577
Articles of Enquiry of Bishop John Whitgift   WCL: A14
f 47*

...

29. Item, whether any lords of misrule or players do daunce ⟨...⟩ any unseemly partes in the church or churchyarde; or whether there any plays or common drinkinge kept in church or churchyard: who maintaine and accompany such

...

5/ ecclesis *for* ecclesijs
33/ are *or* be *missing after* there

1607

Articles of Enquiry of Bishop Gervase Babington   STC: 10367
p 11*   *(Articles concerning the parishioners)*

17 Whether haue you or your Predecessors, Churchwardens there   5
suffered since the 25. day of September 1605. any playes, feastes,
banquets, Church-ales, Drinkings, or any other profane vsages, to
be kept in your Church, Chappels, or Churchyard, or bels to be
rung superstitiously vpon holidaies or Eues abrogated by the book
of common-praier, contrary to the 88. Canon?   10
...

1609

Articles of Enquiry of Archdeacon John Johnson   STC: 10372.2
sig A4   15
...
14 Whether any Dauncers players of Enterludes or such like, or any
other doe Daunce play or vse any vnseemly parts or games, or sell
any victualls or other Marchandise in the church or churchyard or
doe vse to sit in the street, tauernes, Alehowses or at home during 20
seruice time and exercises of gods Worship. and is there any that suffer
any such in their Houses at seruice time, and who be they: or be
there any feastes, drinckings, Churchales, temporall Courtes, laye
Iuries, musters, or other prophane vsage in the Church or churchyard
or any superstitious ringing of belles. vppon holidaies or Eues   25
abrogated by authoritye.
...

1615

Articles of Enquiry of Archdeacon William Swaddon   STC: 10372.3 30
sig A3v   *(Articles concerning the church and churchyard)*
...
5 Are your Bels, Belropes, and Clocke, in good repayre, and well
ordered? Is your Churchyard well fenced and decently kept? Is it not
prophaned with fighting, brawling, chiding, gaming, dancing,   35
playing, or with vnlawfull Cattell, or otherwise; and how, and by
whome, and in whose default?
...

1625

Articles of Enquiry of Archdeacon Hugh Floyd   STC: 10372.6
sig A4v   *(Articles concerning the church and churchyard)*
...

7 Are your Bells, Bell-ropes, and clock in good repair, and well   5
ordered? Is your Churchyard well fenced and decently kept? Is it not
prophaned with fighting, brawling, chiding, gaming, dancing, playing
or with unlawfull cattle, or otherwise; and how, and by whom, and
by whose default?
...   10

sigs B3v–4   *(Miscellaneous articles)*
...

74 You shal further present whether any in your parish vpon Sundaies
or Holydaies, do vse any dancing, plaies or other sports or pastimes   15
whatso ever, before all Seruice on those daies be fully ended: and are
the same | vsed by any of another parish or by any which haue not
the same day been at diuine prayers in there own parish Church, who
be they which haue offended in any of the premisses?
...   20

1626

Articles of Enquiry of Bishop John Thornborough   STC: 10368
pp 3–4   *(Articles concerning the church and churchyard)*
...   25

6 Are your Bells, Bell-ropes, and Clocke in good repayre, and well
ordered? Is your Churchyard well fenced and decently kept? Is it not |
prophaned with fighting, brawling, chiding, gaming, dancing,
playing, or with vnlawfull cattell, or otherwise: and how, and by
whom, and by whose default?   30
...

1632

Articles of Enquiry of Bishop John Thornborough   STC: 10369
p 4   *(Articles concerning the church and churchyard)*   35
...

7 Are your Bels, Bell-ropes, and Clocke in good repaire, and well
ordered? Is your Churchyard well fenced and decently kept? Is it not
prophaned with fighting, brawling, chiding, gaming, dancing,
playing, or with vnlawfull cattell, or otherwise, and how, and by   40
whom, and by whose default?
...

1634

Articles of Enquiry of Archdeacon Edward Thornborough
STC: 10372.7
sig A4v

7 Are your Bells, Bel-ropes, and Clocke in good repayre, and well
ordered? Is your Churchyard well fenced, and decently kept? Is it
not prophaned with fighting, brawling, chiding, gaming, danceing,
playing, or with vnlawfull Cattell, or otherwise; and how, and by
whom, and by whose default?

...

1635

Articles of Enquiry of William Laud, Archbishop of Canterbury
STC: 10370
p 11   (*Articles concerning the churchwardens and sidesmen*)

1 Whether you and the Church-wardens, Quest-men, or Side-men
from time ⟨to⟩ time, doe, and haue done their diligence, in not suffering
any idle person to bide either in the Church-yard, or Church-porch,
in Seruice or Sermon time, but ca⟨u⟩sing them either to come into
the Church to heare Diuine Seruice, or to depart, and n⟨ot⟩ disturb
such as be hearers there? And whether they haue, and you doe
diligently see the parishioners duely resort to the Church euery Sunday
and Holiday and there to remaine during diuine Seruice and Sermon?
And whether you or your predecessors, Church-wardens there, suffer
any playes, Feasts, drinkings, or any other prophane vsages, to be
kept in your Church, Chappell, or Church-yards, or haue suffered
to your and thei⟨r⟩ vttermost power and endeauour, any person or
persons to be tipling or drinking in any Inne or Victualling house in
your Parish, during the time of Diuine Seruice or Sermon, on Sundayes
and Holidayes?

...

1636

Articles of Enquiry of Bishop John Thornborough   STC: 10371
sigs B3–3v   (*Articles concerning the churchwardens and sidesmen*)

1 Whether you and the Church-wardens, Quest-men, or Side-men
from time to time, do and haue done their diligence, in not suffering
any idle person to abide either in the Church-yard, or Church-Porch,
in Seruice | or Sermon time, but causing them either to come into

the Church to heare diuine Seruice, or to depart, and not disturbe such
as be hearers there? And whether they haue, and you do diligently see
the Parishioners duely resort to the Church euery Sunday and
Holiday, and there to remain during Diuine Seruice, & Sermon: and
whether you or your predecessors, Church-wardens there, suffer any   5
Playes, Feasts, Drinkings, or any other prophane vsages, to be kept
in your Church, Chappell, or Church-yards, or haue suffered to your
& their vttermost power and endeauour, any person or persons to
be tipling or drinking in any Inne or Victualling house in your parish,
during the time of Diuine Seruice, or Sermon, on Sundaies and   10
Holidaies?

...

1638
Articles of Enquiry of Archdeacon Edward Thornborough   15
STC: 10373
sig [A4v]   *(Articles concerning the church and churchyard)*

7 Are your Bels, Bell-ropes, and Clocke in good repayre, and well
ordered? Is your Church-yard well fenced, and decently kept? Is it   20
not prophaned with fighting, brawling, chiding, gaming, dancing,
playing, or with unlawfull Cattell, or other wise? if yea, how? and
by whom, and by whose default?

...

Boroughs and Parishes

ALDERMINSTER

1612
Visitation Act Book   SHRO: BA 2884
f 26v*   *(23 October)*

...

Officium domini contra Christoferum Hawten
detectus ffor beinge at a bearebaytinge one the Sabaoth daye. °23

excommunicacio octobris comparuit et fassus est. vnde dominus injunxit ei canonicam
emanauit penitentiam in linteis semell et semell in consuetis vestibus. et ad
vocent gardiani certificandum in proximo 13 Novembris excommunicatus°
ad
presentandum ...

f 27*   *(4 November)*

...

Officium domini contra Thomam Greene
ffor beinge at the bearebaytinge °at Laughton non comparuit

excommunicatio excommunicatus°

Officium domini contra Richardum Bowlton
ibidem similiter/ similiter °excommunicatus°

ALVECHURCH

1611
Visitation Act Book   SHRO: BA 2884
f 161*   *(July)*

...

Officium domini contra Edward Bartlemewe alias heath

10/ linteis: *extra minim* MS   29/ mewe *of* Bartlemewe *written over* -us *sign*

excommunicacio for playing an interlude with divers others at the tyme of divine service
emanavit
° absolutus°   citatus per coombie non comparuit excommunicatus
                 ...

f 161v   *(31 July)*   5

...

Officium domini contra Radulphum Lyddiat
detectus for playeinge in a stagge playe vppon the Sabaoth dayes and
vppon St Peters daye in time of divine seruice vltimo Iulij 1611
Dimissio   Comparuit [per] dictus Radulphus Lyddiat et fatendo culpam dominus 10
             Cum monicione eum dimissit

ibidem

excommunicacio Officium domini contra Iohannem Liddiatt
emanavit   similiter excommunicatus
certificarium   15

ibidem   Officium domini contra Iohannem Lilley
               similiter dimissus cum monicione

dimissio

ibidem   Officium domini contra Richardum davis
               similiter dimissus cum monicione   20

dimissio

               Officium domini contra Willimum More
ibidem   s⟨im⟩iliter Quo die Citatus per Combey post⟨ea⟩ Comparuit reseruata
excommunicacio pena in proximum. °22 Novembris excommunicatus°

                                                                                      25

ARELEY KINGS

1613
Archdeaconry of Ludlow Acts of Office   HRO: box 35, vol 132
f [41]*   *(8 June)*   30

*Proceedings of the court held in the parish church of Ludlow before
Master James Bailie, LLD, vicar general.*
...

[Contra]   Contra eundem ffranciscum   35
               he rod uppon a bull at Areley wake contra decus, et dignitatem
               clericalem./

9/ St Peters daye: *probably feast of Sts Peter and Paul, 29 June*

BADSEY

1533-4
St James' Churchwardens' Accounts   SHRO: BA 5013/2
f [30]   *(Rendered 19 April 1534) (Accounts of Robert Smith* 5
and Thomas Mores)

...

Item reseuyd of ye [yong m⟨.⟩ys] maydys gederyng   iiij s. x d. ob.

...

Item reseuyd for ye churche ale   xxiij d. 10
Item reseuyd of ye yonge maydys gederyng   xij d.

...

Item reseuyd of ye gederyng of ye yonge maydys
thys yere   ix d.
...   15

1534-5
St James' Churchwardens' Accounts   SHRO: BA 5013/2
f [31]   *(Rendered 11 April 1535) (Accounts of Thomas Placum*
and Robert Smith, churchwardens)   20
...

Item reseuyd of ye maydes gederyng   iiij s. j d.

...

Item reseuyd for ale   iij s. iij d.
Item reseuyd of ye lytyll maydys   viij d. ob. 25
...

f [31]*

Item payyd for barley a stryke & halfe   ix d. 30
...

1535-6
St James' Churchwardens' Accounts   SHRO: BA 5013/2
f [31v]*   *(Rendered 30 April 1536) (Accounts of Thomas Placum* 35
and Robert Smith)
...

Item reseuyd of ye yongemenys gederyng   ij s.
...

Item reseuy⟨d⟩ of ye maydes gederyng   iiij s. j d.
…

1536–7
St James' Churchwardens' Accounts SHRO: BA 5013/2   5
f [32v]   *(Rendered 15 April 1537) (Accounts of William Harentun and*
Thomas Welles)
…
Item reseuyd[e] of ye lytyl maydes   viij d.
…   10

f [33]
…
Item payyd for a stryke of barley & a halfe   ix d.
…   15
Item payyd for wax & makyng of ye lytyll maydes
tapur   xij d.

1537–8
St James' Churchwardens' Accounts SHRO: BA 5013/2   20
f [33]   *(Rendered 5 May 1538) (Accounts of Thomas Placum*
and Robert Smith)
…
Item reseuyd of Ihon ponter for church ale   vii⟨..⟩
Item reseuyd of ye grete maydes   iij s. iij d.   25

1538–9
St James' Churchwardens' Accounts SHRO: BA 5013/2
f [33v]   *(Rendered 20 April 1539) (Accounts of Robert George*
and Thomas Welles)   30
…
⟨Item⟩ reseuyd of gederyng money   xxiij d. ob.
…

f [34]   35
…
Item payyd for barley   ij s. ix d.
…

1540–1
St James' Churchwardens' Accounts   SHRO: BA 5013/2
f [34v]*   *(Rendered 1 May 1541) (Accounts of John Pegyn, Senior
and John Pegyn, Junior)*

...   5

Item reseuyd for ale   ij s. vj d.

...

1552–3
St James' Churchwardens' Accounts   SHRO: BA 5013/2   10
f [40v]   *(Rendered 16 April 1553) (Accounts of William George
and Thomas Robardes)*

...

Item payyd for barley iiij stryke   v s.

...   15

1554–5
St James' Churchwardens' Accounts   SHRO: BA 5013/2
f [41]   *(Rendered 28 April 1555) (Accounts of Thomas Smith
and John Smith)*   20

...

Item payyd for ij stryke of barley   iij s. & iiij d.

...

Item reseuyd for ye churche ale   xxv s. iij d. qu.

...   25

1556–7
St James' Churchwardens' Accounts   SHRO: BA 5013/2
f [42]   *(Rendered 2 May 1557) (Accounts of Nicholas Grove
and William Crumpe)*   30

...

Item payyd for a stryke of barley   iij s. & iiij d.

...

Item reseuyd of the churche ale   viij s. j d.

...   35

1571-2
St James' Churchwardens' Accounts   SHRO: BA 5013/2
f [4v]*   *(Rendered 20 April 1572) (Accounts of William White
and Thomas Wells)*

...& at the church aell at whitsontyd   X S.

...

BAYTON

1611/12
Archdeaconry of Ludlow Acts of Office   HRO: box 35, vol 131
p 88   *(26 February)*

Proceedings of the court held in the parish church of Ludlow before
Master Silas Griffithes, STD, deputy of James Bailie, LLD, official
principal.

dimissio   Willimus Phillipes
was present At a bull baiting at Baiton die dominico/ monitus fuit ad
comparendum hodie ad respondendum &c
Quo die comparuit dictus Willimus Phillipes et super examinacione
cause dominus ipsum dimisit cum admonicione

...

BEOLEY

and tapestry weaver.

1571/2
Will of William Sheldon, Dyer   PRO: PROB 10 Box 70 1571—Feb. A—W
f 53*

...

Item I doe give unto everye one of my five musycians foure [fouer]
pounds to be paid with in two yeres after my dethe/ or yerre if my
Dethe be satisfied.

...

1611
Visitation Act Book   SHRO: BA 2884
f 160   *(5 July)*

Officium domini contra Iohannem Butcher

for proclayminge a playe in the Church one the Sabaoth daye.
°comp*aruit* et fassus est vnde d*ominus* injunxit ad agnoscend*am* culp*am*
[cor*am* mi*n*istro et] juxta form*am* scedule. et ad cert*ificandum* in
proximo° °27 Septemb*ris* precon*i*zatus non cert*ifi*cando

excommunicacio excommunicatus°   5

…

BEWDLEY

1570–1   10
St Andrew's Chapel and Bridge Wardens' Accounts
HWRO: BA 8681/236(i)
p 29   *(4 June 1570–10 June 1571) (Accounts of Richard Gye
and Gilbert Aston)*

…   15

Item paid in the churche to the plaiers   xvj d.

…

1571–2
St Andrew's Chapel and Bridge Wardens' Accounts   20
HWRO: BA 8681/236(i)

p 45   *(10 June 1571–14 June 1572) (Accounts of Gilbert Aston and
Matthew Parckes)*

…   25

Item p*ai*d vnto the quenes plaiers in the church   vj s. viij d.

…

1573–4
St Andrew's Chapel and Bridge Wardens' Accounts   30
HWRO: BA 8681/236(i)
p 62   *(3 May 1573–23 May 1574) (Accounts of William Monoxe,
William Hollmar, and Matthew Parckes)*

…

Item payd to my lorde of lesters pleyars   viij s.   35

…

1575–7
St Andrew's Chapel and Bridge Wardens' Accounts
HWRO: BA 8681/236(i)
p 97   *(12 June 1575–2 June 1577) (Accounts of Henry Iamber
and John Mylward)*   5
...

Item payd for pavenge at the bolrynge and for nayles
to nayle bordes in the stypell   iij d.
...

                                                                                      10

p 98

...

Item paid to symon mit for mendinge the bollrynge   viij d.
...

                                                                                      15

1593–4
St Andrew's Chapel and Bridge Wardens' Accounts
HWRO: BA 8681/236(i)
p 238*   *(25 March–24 March) (Accounts of Robert Iudge
and Thomas Bulson)*   20
...

Item paid to my Lord President his players   xx s.
...

1598–9   25
St Andrew's Chapel and Bridge Wardens' Accounts
HWRO: BA 8681/236(i)
p 264   *(25 March – 24 March)*
...

Paid the 22 of desember 1598 to the erle of Pembrockes   30
Players geuen them   x s.
...

1603–4
St Andrew's Chapel and Bridge Wardens' Accounts   35
HWRO: BA 8681/236(i)
p 312*   *(19 June 1603–20 August 1604) (Accounts of John Bennett)*

Item payd to them that playd on the waytes at the
Cominge in of the Lorde Zowche   ij s.   40

Item payd to the Ringers at the same time   xij d.

...

1606–8
St Andrew's Chapel and Bridge Wardens' Accounts   5
HWRO: BA 8681/236(i)
p 331*   *(10 December 1606–April 1608)*

...

payd for the beare at my lordes cum*m*ing   xiiij s. vj d.
...   10

1615–16
St Andrew's Chapel and Bridge Wardens' Accounts
HWRO: BA 8681/236(i)
p 399*   *(29 September–29 November?) (Accounts of Richard Clare*   15
and Richard Whitcott)

...

It*em* giuen to mie lordes players   xx s.
...

                                                                                        20

Diocese of Hereford Acts of Office
HRO: box 24a (formerly 18), vol 70
f [136v]*   *(5 September)*

...

dimissio/   Ioha*nn*es Brigges for dancing die do*m*inico/ Quinto die Septembr*is*   25
Bewdley   predicti com*paruit* et super exa*m*inacione arti*cu*li dimiss*us* est c*um*
              admonic*ione* &c/

1616–17
St Andrew's Chapel and Bridge Wardens' Accounts   30
HWRO: BA 8681/236(i)
p 403   *(30 November–21 November) (Accounts of Edward Tombes*
and William Hopkins)

...

It*em* payd [to] att Mr Baylifes Comand to ye King*es*   35
Trumpeters   xj s.
...

c 1620
Richard Corbett's Poëtica Stromata   Wing: C6272
pp 97–102*

AN
EXHORTATION
To Mr. John Hammon minister in the parish of
Bewdly, for the battering downe of the Vanityes of
the Gentiles, which are comprehended in a Maypole; written by a Zealous Brother
from the Black-fryers. *~ see note*

near Kidderminster

against Puritan preaching

The mighty Zeale which thou hast new put on,
Neither by Prophet nor by Prophetts sonne
As yet prevented, doth transport mee so
Beyond my selfe, that, though I ne're could go
Farr in a verse, and all Rithmes haue defy'd
Since Hopkins, and old Thomas Sternhold dy'de,   *psalter*
(Except it were that little paines I tooke
To please good people in a prayer-booke
That I sett forth, or so) yet must I raise
My Spirit for thee, who shall in thy praise
Gird up her Loynes, and furiously run |
All kinde of feet, saue Satans cloven one.
Such is thy zeale, so well dost thou express it,
That, (wer't not like a Charme,) I'de say, Christ blesse it.
I needs must say 'tis a Spirituall, thing
To raile against a Bishopp, or the King;
Nor are they meane adventures wee haue bin in,
About the wearing of the Churches linnen;
But these were private quarrells: this doth fall
Within the Compass of the generall.
Whether it be a Pole painted, and wrought
Farr otherwise, then from the wood 'twas brought,
Whose head the Idoll-makers hand doth croppe,
Where a lew'd Bird, towring upon the topp,
Lookes like the Calfe at Horeb; at whose root
The unyoak't youth doth exercise his foote;
Or whether it reserve his boughes, befreinded

5

10

15

20

25

30

35

26/ Spirituall,: *misplaced comma*
36/ Calfe at Horeb: *Exodus 32*

By neighb'ring bushes, and by them attended:
How canst thou chuse but seeing it complaine,
That Baalls worship't in the Groves againe?
Tell mee how curst an egging, what a sting |
Of Lust do their unwildy daunces bring?   5
The simple wretches say they meane no harme,
They doe not, surely; but their actions warme
Our purer blouds the more: for Sathan thus
Tempts us the more, that are more Righteous.
Oft hath a Brother most sincerely gon,   10
Stifled in Prayer and contemplation,
When lighting on the place where such repaire,
He viewes the Nimphes, and is quite out in's prayer.
Oft hath a Sister, grownded in the truth,
Seeing the iolly carriage of the youth,   15
Bin tempted to the way that's broad and bad;
And (wert not for our private pleasures) had
Renounc't her little ruffe, and goggle Eye,
And quitt her selfe of the? Fraternity.
What is the mirth, what is the melody   )   20
That setts them in this Gentiles vanity?   /
When in our Sinagogue wee rayle at sinne,
And tell men of the faults which they are in,
With hand and voice so following our theames, |
That wee put out the side-men from their dreames.   25
Sounds not the Pulpett, which wee then belabour
Better, and holyer, than doth the Tabour?
Yet, such is unregenerate mans folly,
Hee loves the wicked noyse, and hates the Holy.
Routes and wilde pleasures doe invite temptation,   30
And this is dangerous for our damnation;
Wee must not moue our selves, but, if w'are mov'd,
Man is but man; and therefore those that lov'd
Still to seeme good, would evermore dispence
With their owne faults, so they gaue no offence.   35
If the times sweete entising, and the blood
That now begins to boyle, haue thought it good
To challenge Liberty and Recreation,
Let it be done in Holy contemplation:
Brothers and Sisters in the feilds may walke,   40

19/ the?: *misplaced query*

Beginning of the holy worde to talke,
Of David and Vriahs Lovely wife,
Of Thamar, and her lustful Brothers strife;
Then, underneath the hedge that woes them next,
They may sitt downe, and there Act out the Text. | 5
Nor do wee want, how ere wee liue austeere,
In Winter Sabbath-nights our lusty cheere;
And though the Pastors Grace, which oft doth hold
Halfe and howre long, make the provision cold,
Wee can be merry; thinking't nere the worse   10
To mend the matter at the second course.
Chapters are Read, and hymnes are sweetly sung,
Ioyntly commanded by the nose, and tongue;
Then on the worde wee diversly dilate,
Wrangling indeed for heat of zeale, not hate: 15
When at the length an unappeased doubt
Feircely comes in, and then the light goes out,
Darkness thus workes our peace, and wee containe
Our fyery spiritts till wee see againe.
Till then, no voice is heard, no tongne doth goe,   20
Except a tender Sister shreike, or so.
Such should be our Delights, grave and demure,
Not so abominable, not so impure
As those thou seek'st to hinder, but I feare
Satan will bee too strong; his kingdomes, here.   25
Few are the righteous now, nor do I know |
How wee shall ere this Idoll overthrow,
Since our sincerest Patron is deceast
The number of the Righteous is decreast.
But wee do hope these times will on, and breed   30
A Faction mighty for us; for indeede
Wee labour all, and every Sister ioynes
To haue Regenerate Babes spring from our Loynes:
Besides, what many carefully haue done,
Getting the unrighteous man, a righteous sonne.   35
Then stoutly on, let not thy Flock range lewdly

2–3/ Of David ... strife: *2 Samuel 11, 13*
9/ and *for* an
20/ tongne *for* tongue
25/ kingdomes,: *misplaced comma*

In their old Vanity, thou Lampe of Bewdly.
One thing I pray thee, do not too much thirst
After Idolatryes last Fall; but first
Follow this suite more close, let it not goe
Till it be thine as thou would'st haue't: for soe   5
Thy Successors, upon the same entayle,
Hereafter, may take up the Whittson-Ale.

1625–6
St Andrew's Chapel and Bridge Wardens' Accounts   10
HWRO: BA 8681/236(i)
p [482]   *(29 September–28 September) (Accounts of James Nash
and Francis Gilding)*

...

Item paid the 2ᵈ of aprill at the proclayming of the King   15
by master Bayliffes Appointment for 2 drommes &
a ffiffe   00 02s. 6d.

...

1642–3   20
St Andrew's Chapel and Bridge Wardens' Accounts
HWRO: BA 8681/236(i)
p [590]   *(Account rendered 14 November 1643)*
(Accounts of Mr Milton)
...   25
paid for a drum by master Bayliffes appointment   0 11 6

...

BRADLEY

                                                                     30

1617/18
Visitation Act Book   SHRO: BA 2760
ff 321v–2*   *(27 February)*
...
contra Thomam Paddye   35
detectus for dauncinge vppon whitsontewsdaye in time of devine
service °citatus per wall non comparuit &c 13 martij dimissus cum
dimissio   monicione°|

(13 March)
contra Iohannem Sale
Simiłiter °13 martij citatus per wall non comparuit &c° 15 martij 1617
dimissus cum monicione

contra Wiłłimum Sale   Comparuerunt et submiserunt
Simiłiter °citatus [vij] non   se et dominus injunxit ad
certificavit reservatur in   agnoscendum culpam coram
proximum°   ministro gardianis et [sex] 4ᵒʳ
                                         parochianorum et ad
contra humfridum ffaukes   certificandum in proximo
Simiłiter °Simiłiter°

contra wiłłimum Lewe
Simiłiter °citatus et dimissus°
...

BROADWAS

1624
Consistory Court Presentment   SHRO: BA 2302/2(345)
single sheet*   *(13 June)*

To the worshipfull Doctor Helmes Chancellor
for the diocesse of Worcester:
Wheareas Robert Price of Brodwas victualer, (notwithstanding
admonition duely given hath not ceacesed to prophane the sabbath
daye by selling ale on the same daye & that [day] in tyme of divine
service – and by suffering disorderes in his house as daunceing all the
tyme of [pra] prayers on Sondaye last bₐʳeˡinge the xiijᵗʰ of this instant
Iune as allso at divers other tymes hee hath suffered the like abuses,
wee therefore according to our office & dutyes in that behalfe doe
present the crime before your worship.
Wee doe allso present ffloris Serman musician for breaking the sabbath
the xiijᵗʰ day of Iune aforesaid by playing vpon his musick & in tyme
of divine service one that daye
Wee doe allso present William Bodenham [a singleman] ʳCooperˡ late
of Brodwas but now of dodenham for abusing our minster of Brodwas

26/ (notwithstanding: *no closing parenthesis*

with many vncivill wordes & abusive speeches, the which crime was
committed & doon beefore Easter laste at which tyme hee the said
Bodenham then was commorant in Brodwas

       (signed) Iohn: Goldwell   Churchwardens of Brodwas
         curate ibidem   *(signed)* Thomas Stockin 5
                   the marke of Thomas Coomely
                          TC

CROWLE

10

1611
Visitation Act Book   SHRO: BA 2884
f 251   *(10 May)*

...

Dimissio   Officium domini contra Richardum Chaundler   15
excommunicatio ffor playeinge on his fiddle one Low sundaye last tempore divinorum
absolutio   iniunctus ad peragendum penitentiam secundum formam schedule
dimissio   °excommunicatus°

...

20

f 252v*

°[non sollucionem Officium domini contra Richardum Auster Iohn Horniblow °[Iordan
non certificando Dison] Iohn Davies [Humfridum Bowling Ed]°
excommunicati
⟨........⟩]°   ffor dauncinge tempore divinorum °vijs et modis &c comparuerunt 25
° dimissio°   et fassi sunt. vnde dominus injunxit eis canonicam penitenciam [Iuxta]
in consuetis vestibus Iuxta formam et ad certificandum in proximo°
°certificaverunt xviij° Iulij 1611 idem et dimissi/°

...

30

DODDENHAM

1606
Presentment of Francis Downe
HWRO: Quarter Sessions Records 110:4/36   35
single sheet

ffrancis Downe of Dodnam kepeth A Common Alehowse without

7/ *Coomely signed with his personal mark*   26/ injunxit: *abbreviation mark omitted*

licence, Resetteth lewde persons; Where by it ys suspected the church
ys Robbed by some of them, And two very good Sirplices stolen fforth
of the same Church:/ He hireth one Bruton A lewde and Bad persone
to play there Holiedayes and the sabboth dayes in prayer tymes. yt
cawseth mens sonnes & servauntes ffrom theyer good Busines:/   5
                                                    °Billa vere°

DROITWICH

1522–3   10
Bailiffs' Accounts   HWRO: BA 1006/32/366
single sheet

...

to a bearward   Item payd to a b[r]erward   xlij d.

...   15

waytes of   Item to the waytyes of warwheyc   xij d.
warwic

...

1538   20
John Leland's Itinerary   Bodl.: MS Gough Gen. Top. 2
p 114

There be at this present tyme three sault springs in the towne of
Wiche, whereoff the principall is within a butt shoote of the right   25
ripe of the river, that there cometh downe, & this springe is double
as profitable in yelding of sault liquour as both the other. Some say
that this spring did fayle in the tyme of Rich de le Wich Bishop of
Chichester and that after by his intercession it was restored to the
profitt of the ould course; such is the superstition of the people, in   30
token whereoff, or for the honour that the Wichemen and saulters
bare vnto this Richard their cuntriman, they vsed of late tymes on
his daye to hang about this sault spring or well once a yeere with
tapestry, & to have drinking games & revels at it. There be a great
number of sault cotes or furnaces about this well, wherein the sault   35
water is decoct & brought to the perfection of pure white sault.

®Richard
de la Wiche
dyed 2 April
1253 37.H3

5/ sonnes: *minim missing* MS
6/ Billa vere *for* Billa vera
28/ Rich *for* Richard

1635–6
Accounts of Edward Davies, Bailiff   HWRO: BA 1006/33/596
mb 1d*

...

More to ffrauncis Allexanders and his Company expended   5
in Castinge open the Commons att Midsommer   10 1 6

...

ELDERSFIELD

                                                                          10

1624
Consistory Court Presentment   SHRO: BA 2302/2(374)
single sheet*

...

⟨....⟩dum prior   for that he hath in a prayer before his sermon vsed certaine &   15
Eldersfild   scandalous speeches towardes the Kinge. [Videlicet that he] comparuit
dictus Mr Prior et saith that he doth not remember that he hath at
any time vsed any such speeches or preched at all againste him but
that he ever hath & will accordinge to his dutie prayc for the Kinges
prosperous estate & if that hath vnwittingely lett/ any [such] wordes   20
which might geve occasion of any such conceite or construction
amongste the auth⟨orit⟩ie he is very sorry for it ⟨...⟩ that he will
publikely [⟨...⟩] certifie to the parishners that Kinge had licensed
sportinge & dancinge after eveninge prayer ˏˊaccordinge ⟨...⟩ the
Iustices had interpreted it at the ⟨....⟩¹ & that at that time they might   25
vse it
Comparuit Walter. Vnderhill de Eldersfild et previo Iuramento allegat
that upon a Sabaoth day aboute St Peeters tide was twelve month Mr
Prior in his prayer before the sermon prayed to god to turne the Kinges
harte from profanes. & that often times in his sermons he inveyeth   30
against dancinge vppon the Saboth day as a prophane [p] sporte.
(signed) Walter Vnderhill

...

Thomas ˊBrutonˋ comparuit et previo Iuramento testificavit similiter
per omnia.   35
                    signum Thome Bruton

15m/ ⟨....⟩dum: *name lost due to tear in sheet*
20/ he *omitted before* hath
23/ the *omitted before* Kinge
36/ *Bruton signed with his personal mark*

EVESHAM

1300-1
Royal Wardrobe Accounts of Edward I   BL: Add.7966A
f 66*   *(20 November–19 November)*

...

vidulatores **C**   Gilberto de Eboraco & Willelmo Hathewy
vidulatoribus facientibus menestralciam suam coram
Rege de dono ipsius Regis videlicet predicto Gilberto
xiij s iiij .d. & predicto Willelmo vj s. viij ⌈d⌉. per manus
proprias ibidem secundo die Aprilis   Summa xx .s.

...

1582/3
A Briefe Discourse of Two Most Cruell and Bloudie Murthers
STC: 25980
sigs A4v–B2 *(1 January)*

A most cruel and bloody Murder, committed on New-yeares euen
last past, beeing the last day of December, 1582 in the town of Esam
in Worcester shire, by one Thomas Smith a town dweller, vpon his
neighbor Robert Greenoll, who when he had cruelly murdered him,
made a graue in his Seller, & there buried him.

In Esam, a hansome market Town in Worcester shire well known
dwelled two youngmen, who by their vsual trade were mercers, as
in ye country they call them so yat sell all kind of wares: the one of
them they called Robert Greenoll, a bacheler, & of such an honest
conuersation, as he was not onely wel belooued in the Towne where
he dwelt, but also of those who had euerie market day accesse thither,
for their needfull necessaries, so yat he was as wel customed as any
occupier in ye towne. The other was called Thomas Smith, of
indifferent welth likewise, & son to one of the most substantial men
in ye towne, & ioyned in mariage | with a gentlewoman of very good
parentage: so yat he likewise was well thought on of most & least.
This Thomas Smith, seeing Greenoll haue so good vtteraunce for his
wares, and so well esteemed in ech companie: if not vppon this cause
alone, though chiefly it bee accounted so, he began to enuy the
prosperous estate of him beeing his neighbour and frend, and the
Deuill so farre ruled the course of his enuious intent, as nothing wold
suffise the desire thereof, but onely making away of Greenoll by
death which though hee had no reason for, yet suche was the

perswasion of the euill spirite with him. Manie platformes were laid,
a thousand deuises canuazed ouer by this lewde man, which way he
might woork the death of his frendly neighbor: at last as the Deuill
wanteth no occasions to helpe man forward to his own destruction,
so he presented Smith with a fit oportunity, whereby he might execute   5
ye sum of his bloody will. And as the repining at our neighbors
prosperity, is not onely monstrous, but a deuilish nature | So had
this man compassed a monstruous and most deuilish deuise, the verie
conceite whereof is able to astonish the heart of a Iewe, or Mahomitans
recreant, and this it was as followeth.   10
   On New-yeares euen laste past, this Thomas Smith longinge and
desiringe the end of his vnnaturall will, bearing the image of a frendlie
countenaunce in the face, but the verie perfecte shape of Iudas trecherie
in his hart, inuited his neighbour Greenoll to his house, where he
promised to bestowe a quart of wine and an apple vpon him: saying   15
further, they woulde passe awaye the Euening pleasauntly in frendlie
talke and drinking together. Greenoll beeing one desirous of eche
mans frendship, and much the rather of his beeing his neighbour,
and one of the same trade himself was: nothing mistrusting the
villanous treason, hyd vnder so smooth a show of neighberhood,   20
gaue him thanks, promising to come to him at night, & not to faile
him. This pleased well the bloud-thirsting man, so that home he went
to determine | the Instrument to doo the deede withal, & then downe
into his Seller hee goes, to dispose a place wherein he might conuay
the body when hee had slayne him: there he digged a graue about   25
fiue or seuen ynches deepe, thinking there to burie him that he should
neuer be founde. It drew toward night, when as a play was cryed
about the Towne, whereto both old and young did hastely repaire:
& this Smith hauing a boye that serued him in his Shop, fearing leaste
the boye shoulde perceive anie thinge, gaue hym money, and bad   30
him goe see the Play: & bring him the whole report of the matter.
This he did in the presence of Greenol who was come according to
his promisse to keepe him companie: & the boye hauing fetcht a quarte
of wine and Apples as his maister willed him, ran merrily to see the
Play, leauing Greenol & his maister by the fire pleasauntly talking.   35
They twoo thus sitting alone, did drink to ech other verie familiarly,
tyll at last, Greenol stouping to turne an apple in the fire, a fit time
that Smith es|pied to accomplish his will: who taking an yron pestell
wherewith hee vsed to beate his spice in the morter, and which he
had laid by him ready for the nonce, with this pestel (as Greenoll   40
stouped to turne the Apple) he gaue him twoo suche mightie blowes
on the heade, as hee fell down backward to the ground, yeelding foorth

a verie pittifull and lamentable groane. Smith hearing him to giue such
a wofull groane (as himselfe said to me, when I came to him into the
prison) began to enter into some sorrowfulnes for the deede, wishinge
that hee mighte recouer againe: but when he perceiued he had smote
him so sore, that ther was no hope of his recouerie, he tooke the pestel   5
againe, and gaue him three or four more cruell strokes about the heade,
whiche made him lie trembling and shaking in such pittifull manner,
as would haue made a hearte of Adamant to melte in griefe: for to
beholde how life and death made strife together, life for the sweetenes,
to resist death his bitternes, wyth many a gaspe for breath, with   10
strugling | and often folding his armes together: then laye this Innocent
and martyred coarse. Not suffised with this, the bloody murderer
taketh a knife, and therewith cut the throate of Greenol, but as Smith
himselfe saith, he did not cut the wez*a*nd, but pierced the skin
somwhat: and then would haue stabbed him to the heart w*ith* the   15
knife, but missed and smote him on the shoulder blade, whervpon
he strooke againe, and then indeede pierced him to the heart: what
a cruell and monstrous harde heart had hee, that coulde endure this
rufull Stratageme? when he had suffised his bloody mind, vpon his
freend and loouing neighbour, hee drewe him down into his Seller,   20
where his graue was readie prepared for him, and there buried him:
which beeing doone, he smoothed it ouer so finelye with a Trowell
that Playsterers vse, so that it could be hardly discerned, and because
he would woorke the surer, hee tooke Bayles of Flax which laye in
his Seller, and so shaked the shellinges thereof on ye floore in all places,   25
as no one coulde saye, | (but he that knewe it) where the graue was,
setting likewise Drifats & Chests ouer it, so that he iudged it should
neuer be found. Afterward he went and tooke water, wherewith he
washed and dryed his house so clean in euerie place, ye one drop of
blood could not be espied: behold how subtilly hee wente to woorke,   30
but God, who in no case will haue bloudie murder hidde, preuented
all his craftie pollicies.
    Smith hauing thus plaide his tyrannous pageant, & hauing taken
Greenols keyes of his shop from him, wente thither and likewise
robbed it, bringing a great deale of the goods from the*n*ce into his   35
owne house. But this by the way is to bee considered, that in the
Towne of Euesam, all the time of Christmas, and at no other time,
there is watche & ward kept, that no misorder or il rule be committed
in the Towne, which doubtlesse is a verie good and commendable
order. To one of the watchmen had Smith giuen this watch-woord,   40
See and see not: which was onelie to this ende, that hee | might goe
by them vnseene, when he caryed the goods out of Greenols shop

to his owne house. On the morrowe when it was knowen that Greenols
shop was robde, question was made thorowe the Towne, who was
abroade that nighte that might bee suspected, because of the Playe that
was in the Towne: vppon which demaund, the watchman to whom this
message was sente, declared howe Thomas Smith was abroad somewhat 5
late, and sent him this watch-word, See and see not, but was meant
thereby hee could not gather. Upon this, Smith was sent for before
the chiefe of the Towne, and demaunded if he knew where Greenol
was, for that it was reported he had beene in his house ouer-night,
and since that time no man could tell anie tidinges of him: moreuer 10
his shop was robbed as that night, and that Smith beeing abroad, and
sending such a by-word See and see not, to one of the watchmen, yt
was a shrewd presumption against him to bee somewhat faultie in
the matter. So after his aunswere that hee knewe I not where Greenol
was become, and by his late walkinge and woordes sente to the   15
watchman, no harme was meante: they said that they would goe to
searche his house, whervpon Smith aunswered, that his house they
could not as then see, because his wife was at Kinges Norton, a Towne
not farre Thence, and she had the keyes of his howse: but (quoth
hee) if you will search my Seller you maye, and so tooke the keyes 20
from his girdle and threw them vnto them. Then went certayne that
were appointed, to search Smiths Seller, whence they were comming
again without finding such matter as they looked for: till by chaunce
one of them happened to espye a little piece of earth, as it were new
broken out of the grounde, lying vnder the nethermoste staire, which 25
he taking vp, said it were good to see where any earth was latelye
broken there aboute, for if they chaunced to finde the place, some
thing might come to light woorth ye beholding. Upon this councel
they began all to looke earnestlye about the Seller, I if they could
find the place where that Earth had been broken vp. At last they   30
remooued the Chests & Dryfats, where they felt the ground more
soft then all the rest: which caused them (suspecting somewhat) to
fall to digging, where presently they found Greenoll buryed, not past
six or seuen inches deepe, and looking vppon him, beheld how cruelly
and vnnaturally he had beene murdered. These newes brought to the 35
Baylifs of ye towne, where Smith was kept till they returned: not
without great lamentation for this bloody deed, of all that knew or
heard thereof, he was sent to Worcester Gaole wher he remained till
such time as the crueltie of his vnneighbourlike deede might be
determined by Iustice. When ye Assises came, ye apparaunt truth of 40

6/ but was *for* but what was   11/ as *for* at (?)

his offence layd before the Iudges, he was condemned to the death,
which he suffered very lately since: but yet by the earnest intreatie of
his Freendes, who were of great wealth and credit, the seueritie of the
lawe was not altogether ministred, for | wheras he should haue beene
hanged in chains, he had more fauour shewd him, he was hanged to   5
death, and afterward buryed.

Thus my Freendes, haue you heard the true discourse of this most
bloody & monstrous act, accordinge as in great greefe, with like
sorowe for the deed, him selfe dyd vtter it, both vnto me and diuers
other being present, Preachers, and Gentlemen. And truly thus much   10
I must say, for the man truely he was both a hansome and well featured
a Youngman as one shall lightly see, his Father of good wealth, and
one of the chiefs in the Towne of Esam, and hee had beene marryed
not past eight weeks by crebible reporte, before he did the deed, to
a Gentlewoman of very good Parentage, who no doubt remaineth in   15
great greef for this vnlooked for mischaunce, she being merry abroade
with her Freends, when her Husband at home committed this cruell
deed: I commit it to the Iudgement of all vertuous Women, what a
greefe it was to her, when first | she heard of these vnhappy newes…
…   20

1600
Robert Armin's Foole vpon Foole   STC: 772.3
sigs B–C*

                                                                        25

A Cleane Foole.
How Iacke Miller the cleane foole, ventred ouer the Seuerne a foote
in much daunger.

In the towne of Esom in Worcestershire Iacke Miller being there
borne, was much made of in euery place: it hapned that the Lord   30
Shandoyes Players came to towne, and vsed their pastimes there,
which Iacke not a little loued, especially the clowne whome he would
imbrace with a ioyfull spirit, and call him grumball (for so he called
himselfe in Gentlemens houses, where he would imitate playes dooing
all himselfe, King, Clowne, Gentleman and all hauing spoke for one,   35
he would sodainly goe in, and againe returne for the other, and
stambring, so beastly as he did, made mighty mirth: to conclude he
was aright innocent without any villany at all.)

When these Players as I speake of, had done in the towne they
went to Partiar, and Iacke swore he would goe all the world with   40

14/ crebible for credible   40/ Partiar: Pershore

Grumball, that he would: it was then a great frost new begun and the
euen was frozen ouer thinly: but heere is the wonder the gentleman
that kept the Hart (an Inne in the towne) whose back-side looked to
the way that led to the riuer side to Partiar, and lockt vp Iacke in a
chamber next the Hauen where he might see the players passe by, and   5
they of the towne loath to loose his company, desired to haue it so.
But he I say seeing them goe by, creepes through the window, and
sayde I come to thee Grumball: the Players stood all still to see further,
he got downe very daungerously, and makes no more a doe but boldly
ventures ouer the Hauen, which is by the long bridge as I gesse some   10
forty yardes ouer: tut hee made nothing of it, but my heart aked to
see it, and my eares heard the Ize crackt all the way: when he was
come vnto them, I was amazed, and tooke vp a brickbat (which there
lay by) and threwe it, which no sooner fell vpon the Ize but it burst:
was not this strange that a foole of thirty yeeres was borne of that   15
Ize which would not indure the fall of a brickbat: yes it was wonderfull
me though: but euery one rating him for the deed, telling him it was
daungerous: he considered his fault, and knowing faults should be
punished, he entreated Grumball the clowne whom he so deerely
loued to whip him but with rosemary, for that he thought wold not   20
smart: but the Players in iest breecht him till the bloud came, I which
he tooke laughing: for it was his manner euer to weepe in kindnes,
and laugh in extreames, that this is true, my eyes were witnesses being
then by.
...   25

GRAFTON FLYFORD

1615/16
Visitation Act Book of William Swaddon, Archdeacon of Worcester 30
SHRO: BA 2512
pp 195–6*   *(24 February)*
...

deinde d*omin*us decrevit pen*itenc*iam peragend*am* cora*m* ministro et
gard*ianis*/†   35
+ Georgius Heming
detect*us* for ˄⌐setting & suffering⌐ daunsenge in his newe barne floore
the 18 daye of Iune 1615 at time of devine s*er*vice °xxiiijto die ffebr*uarij*
1615 coram d*omi*no Archi*di*acono comp*aru*it et obiecto ei ar*ticu*lo et

2/ euen: *Avon*   17/ me though *for* me thought
5/ Hauen: *Avon*

dimissio

fass*us* est arti*cu*lum et submisit se &c vnde d*ominus* inflixit ei ad
agnoscend*um* delictu*m* coram ministro et tota congregac*ione* tempo*re*
div*in*orum die dominico proximo immediate post lectionem sec*un*di
Capitis et ad cert*ificandum* in proximo° °dein*de* cert*ificaui*t de
per*accione* pen*itencie* et d*imissus*° 5

Con*tra* Robertum Heminge

dimissio

for dauncing there at that time xxiiij^(to) die ffebr*uarij* 1615 comp*aruit*
et fassus est q*uod* pr*esens* fuit cum saltor*ibus* ˏ⌐sed non¬ tempo*re*
div*in*orum vnde d*ominus* dimisit eund*em* cum monic*ione* quia fecit 10
fidem de veritate premiss*orum*

\+ Con*tra* Rad*ul*phum king*es*

citatus ap*ud*
North Piddle

°pro simili xxiiij^(to) die ffebr*uarij* 1615 cit*atus* in ecclesia p*er* m*agist*rum
Stonehall pro*v*t ipse prius in Iudit*io* affirmavit vnde pub*lice* 15
prec*onizatus*/ non comp*aruit* et quia pauperinus d*imissus* ad
informa*cionem* m*agistr*i Stonehall tam quoad pena*m* si sit nocens &c°

\+ Con*tra* w*illimu*m Elletes

dimissio

°pro simili xxiiij^(to) ffebr*uarij* 1615 cit*atus* in ecclesia p*er* m*agist*rum 20
Stonehall pro*v*t ipse prius affirmavit pub*lice* prec*onizatus* non
comp*aruit* reservata pena in prox*imum* deinde d*imissus* fuit cu*m* forma
pauperis/°

Lawford
citatus in
proximo

\+ Con*tra* Thomam Haye 25
pro si*m*ili °haye abijt ex relac*ione* Smith app*aritoris*.°

\+ Con*tra* Thomam Woolner

dimissio

pro simili °xxiiij^(to) die ffebr*uarij* 1615 Comp*aruit* et fassus est arti*cu*lum
vnde d*ominus* eum dimisit cum monic*ione*/.° 30

[*citata* in
proximo]

\+ Con*tra* Alicam Heming mu*lierem*/
pro simili °18° Ian*uarij* 1616° °Mortua ex relac*ione* ⟨...⟩ app*aritoris*/° |

\+ Con*tra* Thomam Dugard musician 35
for playing to the dauncers at that time °xxiij^(to) ffebr*uarij* 1615 iux*ta*
&c. comp*aruit* et obiecto ei arti*cu*lo fassus est q*uod* absens fuit a

dimissio

precibus vespertinis et quoad aliam p*artem* hu*ius*modi arti*cu*li negavit
eund*em* in vim iuram*enti* sui vnde d*ominus* inflixit ei ad agnoscend*um*

15/ Iuditio *for* Iudicio
32/ mu*lierem*: *expansion conjectural*

16/ pauperinus: *extra minim* MS
36/ xxiij^(to) *for* xxiiij^(to) (?)

delict*um* coram ministro et gard*ianis* iuxta formam sibi tradend*am*
&c/.° °dein*de* cert*ificavi*t de perac*cione* penitencie et d*imissus*°

+ Con*tra* Walter*um* Arnoll

<table>
<tr><td>dimissio</td><td>pro simili/ xxiiij^{to} die ffebruarij 1615 similiter</td><td>5</td></tr>
</table>

pro simili/ xxiiij^to die ffebr*uarij* 1615 sim*iliter*   5
°Quere pro no*m*inibus alior*um*/ qui tunc temp*oris* saliebant &c°

GREAT MALVERN

1613   10
Visitation Act Book   SHRO: BA 2760
f 330*   *(7 October)*

Officiu*m* d*o*mini *contra* Georgiu*m* ffarse al*ias* Barber
ffor playenge on his drum in s*er*vice time to drawe the youth from   15
excommunicacio Church to the offense of minster and the better disposed of the p*ar*ishe
emanavit   °vijs et mod*is* 7 octob*ris* no*n* comp*aruit* excom*m*unicatus°
...

KEMPSEY   20

1300–1
Royal Wardrobe Accounts of Edward I   BL: Add. 7966A
f 66v*   *(20 November–19 November)*
...   25
Gigatores Regis Hen*rico* & Girardo Gigatorib*us* Allemann*is* menestrall*is*
R*egis* de dono R*egis* per m*anus* proprias apud Kemeseye.
xxix° die aprilis cuilib*et* eor*um* .xiij .s. iiij .d.   xxvj .s. viij .d.
...
          30

KIDDERMINSTER

1641
Autobiography of Richard Baxter   BL: Egerton 2570
ff 3v–4*   35
...

¶ 38 Whilst I was thus employed between outward labors & inward
tryalls, Satan stird up a little inconsiderable rage of wickedness ag*ainst*
me. The Towne having bee*n* formerly Eminent[ly] for vanity, had
yearly a Shew, in w*h*ich they brought forth ye painted formes of   40
Gyants & Such like foolery, to walk about ye streetes with: And

though I said nothing ag*ainst* yem, as being not simply evill, yet on
everyone of those daies of ryot, ye rabble of ye more vicious sort had
still some spleen to vent ag*ainst* me, as one p*art* of their game. And
once all ye ignorant rowt were rageing mad ag*ainst* me, for preaching
ye doctrine of Original Sin to yem, & telling yem y*at* Infants before   5
regeneration I had so much guilt & corruption as made yem loathsome
in ye eyes of God. Whereuppon they vented it abroad ye Country
y*at* I preached y*at* God hated or loathed Infants; so y*at* they railed
at me as I passed through ye streets: The next Lords day I cleared &
confirmed it & shewed yem y*at* if this were not true, their Infants   10
had no need of Christ of Baptisme or of renewing by ye Holy Ghost:
And I asked yem whether they durst say y*at* their Children were
saved without a Saviour, & were no Christians, & why they baptized
yem, with much more to y*at* purpose; & afterward they were ashamed
& as mute as fishes.//   15
...

1642
Autobiography of Richard Baxter   BL: Egerton 2570
f 12   20
...

¶ 61 When I had ben at Gloucester a month my neighbors of
Kederminster came for me home, & told me y*at* if I staid any longer
ye people would interpret it either y*at* I was afraid uppon some guilt,
or y*at* I was ag*ainst* ye King: So I bid my Host (Mr Dorney ye Towne   25
Clark) & my friends farewell, & never came to Gloucester more.
When I came home I found ye beggarly drunken rowt in a very
tumultuating disposition; & ye Sup*er*iors y*at* were for ye King did
animate yem, & the people of ye place who were accounted Religious,
were called Roundheads & openly reviled & threatened as ye Kings   30
enemies (who had never medled in any cause ag*ainst* ye King): Every
drunken sot y*at* met any of yem in ye streets would tell yem [we
shall take an order with ye Puritans ere long.]

✓   And just as at their Shews & wakes & Stageplayes, when ye drink &
ye spirit of ryot did worke together in their heads, & ye Crowd   35
encouraged one another, So was it with yem now; they were like a
company of stags at rutting time, or like tyed mastiffes newly Cosed.
& fled in ye face of all y*at* was Religious yea or Civil, w*hi*ch came
in their way...

32–3/ [we ... long.]: *no deletion; square brackets are original punctuation*

LEIGH

1611
Visitation Act Book   SHRO: BA 2884
f 304v   *(27 September)*   5

...

con*tra* eund*em* Io*hannem* Browning
for being p*resente* at a playe made in a howse at service tyme one a
Saboath day./
...   10

LINDRIDGE

1572/3
Diocese of Hereford Acts of Office   HRO: box 19, vol 72   15
f [24v]*   *(30 January)*

*Proceedings of the court held in the parish church of Whitbourne before
John Scory, bishop of Hereford, and in the presence of Edward
Langford, notary public and principal registrar.*   20

...

thomas p*ar*kar al*ias* tynckar p*ar*ochia de stockton cit*atus* &c
pers*on*al*iter* no*n* com*paruit* ideo excommunicatus postea s*ecundo*
m*artij* com*paruit* et fatet*ur* that he did play vpon the taber. vnde
d*omin*us inflixit sibi pen*itenc*ias [q*uod*] die d*omin*ico proximo in   25
ecclesia de estham et die d*omin*ico sequenti in ecclesia de lyndryge.
xxvij° m*artij* pu*b*lice preconizatus no*n* com*paruit* ideo sus*pensus*
postea com*paruit* et certificavit et sic d*im*issus

f [25]*   *(2 March)*   30

...

offic*ium* d*o*mini con*tra* Willi*mum* Morton de eadem com*paruit*
s*ecu*ndo m*artij* et fatet*ur* that he was one of them that caryed the
coole staffe, vnde d*omin*us monuit et inflixit pen*itenc*ias vi*delicet* die
d*omin*ico proximo in ecclesia de lyndryge. et die d*omin*ico sequenti   35
in ecclesia de Estham et c*ertificando* xxvij° m*artij*, quibus die et loco
pu*b*lice preconizatus no*n* com*paruit* ideo sus*pensus*

22/ stockton: *Stockton on Teme, Worcestershire*
26, 36/ estham, Estham: *Eastham, Worcestershire*
26,35/ lyndryge: *Lindridge, Worcestershire*
32/ de eadem: *parish of Lindridge, named in previous, otherwise unrelated case on f [25]*

LONGDON

1617
Petition of William Jeffreys, Constable
HWRO: Quarter Sessions Records 110:29/67   5
single sheet*

        To the righte worshipp*fu*ll the kinges ma*iesties*
        Iustices of the peace, for the Countie of Worcester.
        The humble peticion of William Iefferis.   10
Sheweth to your worships, That whereas the Inhabitant*es* and youth
of Longdon, Have every yeare, vpon the Saboth daie, in the som*m*er
time vsed to sport themselves w*i*th maygames, Morrices, and
dawncinges, by reason whereof many rude Ruffions, and drunken
Companions, have comen thither, from other townes adioyneinge,   15
to the said sport*es* and have made much quarrellinge, redye to murther
one an other. As vpon a Saboth day 1614 some of ffortingtons men
comeinge to the said sport*es*, made an affray there, and gave one a
broken heade, And vpon a Saboth daie 1615 some of Elsfild*es* men
comeinge to the said sport*es*, made an affray vpon the Smithes man   20
of longdon, whereby the townesmen there, have beene much tro*u*bled,
to parte the said affrayes, to keepe the peace and to bringe ˏ⸢them⸣
before some of his ma*iesties* Iustices for this Countie, the principall
actor, in w*hi*ch last menc*i*onyd fray was one Sandye of Elsfield, who
sythence hath cut of his neighbours arme, for doeinge the office of   25
Constable vpon him a litle before. And whereas on a Saboth daie
1615 there was much sport made in longdon, by morrices, and
dawncing*es*, and because at eveninge pray*er*s the same day, they were
forced to cease their sport*es*, some of the youth of longdon, p*ro*cured
a poore woman then beinge excomunicated, to goe into the Church   30
in s*er*vice time, and made an other poore boy to followe after her
into the Church, and there to tell the minister (beinge then sayinge
the s*er*vice of allmightie god) That this excomunicate p*er*son was in
the Church, hopeinge thereby to put an end of god*es* s*er*vice, That
soe they might againe retorne to their sport*es*, all w*hi*ch beinge done   35
by this excomunicate p*er*son and poore boy, as they were directed,
The minister was Thereby interrupted in god*es* s*er*vice, and the whole
congregac*i*on much disturbed. And whereas vpon Trenitie sunday
1616 the dawncinge againe takeinge place in longdon aforesaid, your

19, 24/ Elsfild*es*, Elsfield: *Eldersfield*
39/ 1616: *underlined in* MS

poore peticioner being ˄⌈then⌉ constable there, for the preventinge and
suppressinge of these abuses, endevored peaceably to take the
Minstrell there playinge, and to punish him vpon the Statute against
Rogues Therevpon one of the dawncinge Companie, strake vp your
peticioners heeles and said he would breake your peticioners necke   5
down the stayers there if I departed not from them, and lett them
alone, Whereby your peticioner beinge thus terrified by them
departed. And afterwardes many other abuses were comitted that
yeare, by the said companie, to longe here to relate vnto you. And
wereas nowe againe this present yeare 1617 they vse againe their   10
dawncinge sportes vpon euerie Saboth daie, whereby it is to be feared
the like quarrelles may ensue as afore, to the greate dishonor of
almightie, and contempt of his maiesties lawes and proclamacion
against the same. May it therefore please your worshipes the premisses
consydered to make some order in this your open Cessions, for the   15
suppressinge of the prophanacion of the lordes daie and withall to
give Comaundment to the highe constable of the limit to see the same
executed and your peticioner shall ever pray to god, for you, in
worshipe longe to endure.

        °bene gerendo [pro] versus Sandy and the Constable to bringe   20
        all morrice dauncers which dawnce in tyme of divine service
        before Mr Iefferey.

                           vnlawfull games &c.°

MARTIN HUSSINGTREE   25

1617
Visitation Act Book   SHRO: BA 2760
f 113   *(17 December)*
...   30

contra magistrum Griffinum Glinn
detectus for [sufferinge] ⌈causinge⌉ a puppett playe ˄⌈to be⌉ in the
Chauncell °17 Decembris citatus per Coombie non comparuit

[°excom-
municacio°]   [excommunicatus] vnde dominus decrevit eum suspendendum fore ab
      officio et beneficis° 20 decembris 1617 super submissione dicti Glynn   35
° suspencio°   in Pallatio domini Episcopi Idem dominus Episcopus revocavit
° revocatur°   Suspencionem contra eum alias latam &c et monuit eum ad
      Comparendum proximo die Iuridico videlicet 16 Ianuarij proximo in
      Consistorio. °comparuit et fassus est vnde dominus injunxit ad
      comparendum coram domino episcopo in post meridiem citatus per   40

13/ God *omitted after* almightie   35/ beneficis *for* beneficio

Coomby no*n* comp*aruit* excommunicatus refertur ad d*ominum*
episco*pum* in post meridiem° °deinde d*ominus* eum absoluit et iniu*n*xit
ad Comparend*um* in proximo/°

MATHON

1624
Petition to Bishop John Thornborough   SHRO: BA 2302/2(414)
single sheet*   *(July)*

To the Right Reverend ffather in God the Lord Bishopp of
Worcester.
Right Reverend ffather in God, my humble duty remembred &c.
Whereas divers yong people of our p*ar*ish of Mathon are summoned
vnto yo*ur* Lordshipps Consistory Court at Wor*cester*, there to
appeare the Nineth day of this instant moneth of Iuly, for daunceinge
vppon the Sabbath day before Eveninge prayer. May it please your
Lordshipp to be aduertised, that I sawe not anie such thinge putt in
practise by them At anie time this summer but onely vppon Whitson
munday. our yong people in this respect are verie orderly and carefull,
takeinge noe further libertie then is by the Kings Ma*i*estie allowed
for their recreations vppon the Sabbath day, beinge conforme in
comeinge to devine service vpon those daies wherein they daunce.
May it please yo*ur* Lordshipp to be alsoe advertised, that some of
those whoe are cited into the Court are noe dauncers, some are
dwellinge in Herefordshire, some in other p*ar*ishes and not in Mathon;
wherevpon I doe coniecture that this complaint was grounded vppon
noe iust foundation. The Apparitor sent me his Warrant and his Letter,
chardeginge me to summon them to the Court at my p*er*ill, certifyinge
me that he was com*m*aunded by yo*ur* Lordshipp, M*a*ster
Chauncellour and Mr Warmstrey to doe soe. But I thinke it was his
informac*i*on onely, and that he did vsurpe your Lordshipps authority.
In regard whereof (beinge willinge to asist my p*ar*ishioners in anie
thinge that is iust, honest and Lawfull and not otherwise) I doe most
humbly beseech yo*ur* Lordshipp to dischardge these p*er*sons
summoned to the Court, and to free them from the wrong that is
offered them, and that yo*ur* Lordshipp would be pleased to allowe
them such Lawfull libertie as the moste p*ar*te of the p*ar*ishes haue
w*i*thin yo*ur* Lordshipps diocesse, for their recreations, behaue⸝ ⌐inge⌐
themselues moderately and duely observeinge the times of prayer and
I shall euer rest bound vnto yo*ur* Lordshipp for the same, faithfully

1/ Co *of* Coomby *written over other letters now illegible*

promiseinge yo*u*r Lordshipp, that if anie shall offend, to informe
against them my selfe, and to doe my best endauour to cause them to
be punished for an example to others. Thus hopeinge that yo*u*r
Lordshipp wilbe pleased to graunt me this fauo*u*r in giveinge me a
dischardge for our yonge people at this time, I committ your   5
Lordshipp to the protection of the Almightie.
          Your Lordshipps in all humble
          dutie to be commanded
    (signed)   Edward Reese Curat*us*.

                                                                          10

PERSHORE

1495–6
Account Roll of Abbot John Pypulton   PRO: SC 6/Henry VII/1704
mb 7   *(External expenses)*   15

... Et in donis & regard*is* dat*is* Ministrall*is* do*m*ini R*egis* et al*iorum*
do*m*inor*um* vj li....

1572   20
View of Frankpledge for Pershore Manor
Westminster Abbey: Muniment 22088A
sheet 2, col 2   *(2 October)*

Sartayne peynes that we being the twelue men are agreid vpon this   25
Corte being holden the second day of octobre in the xiiij yere of the
quenes ma*i*estie that now ys
...
Item we Are Agreid that eu*er*y ˏ⌐man that kepes⌐ vytteling
howse or alehowse wythin this Lete shall suffer nor   30
meynteyne or keape Any mans sonnes or se*r*vaunts ˏ⌐or
mynstrells⌐ wythin theire howsis at the due tyme of se*r*vis
[nor allso] nor also af*ter* [nyght] viij of the clocke in
the nyght to keape them from theire masters howsis in
paine of   X S.   35
...

1612/13
Visitation Act Book   SHRO: BA 2884
f 279   *(12 February)*   40
...

Parshore   Offici*um* do*m*ini con*tra*   for playing of a stage play on the
St Cruc*is*   Ioh*anne*m George   Saboath day at tyme of divine service

egrotat/

Iohannem Cosnet   12 ffebruarij 1612 ⌜Cosnett⌝
Thomam Morris vt Cosnet   Comparuit et dominus iniunxit ei ad
Rogerum Edge vt Cosnet   agnoscendam culpam coram
Richardum Nashe vt Cosnet   ministro gardianis et [sex] ⌜decem⌝
                                 parochianis iuxta &c post preces   5
                                 matutinas et ad Certificandum in
                                 proximo/

Richardum Bell
12 ffebruarij 1612 citatus in ecclesia provt patet per Certificarium   10
preconizatus non comparendo reservata pena in proximum

Matheum Davies vt Cosnet

Iohannem Greneway vt Cosnett/ plene/   15

egrotat/

Samuelem Costell
Citatus in ecclesia &c reservata pena in proximum/

f 280   20
...
Officium domini contra Willimum Phelpes
✓ detectus for beinge a ministrell did play at the said stage play.
dimissio   Comparuit personaliter dictus Phelps et previo iuramento negat yat
✓ he played tempore divinorum, and was at part of evening prayers   25
vnde dominus eum ex gracia dimisit cum monicione &c

Officium domini contra Thomam Sharman
Similiter 12° ffebruarij 1612. Comparuit et dominus eum iniunxit ad
agnoscendum culpam coram ministro gardianis ˌ⌜iuxta formam⌝ et ad   30
Certificandum in proximo./ °reservata pena in proximum./ 12 martij
1612 proximum./°
...

REDDITCH   35

·

1628
Recognizance of John Woodyne
HWRO: Quarter Sessions Records 110:54/45
single sheet   *(20 October)*   40

Wigornie   Memorandum quod vicesimo die Octobris Anno Quarto Regni
sessiones   Domini nostri Caroli dei gratia Anglie Scotie ffrauncie et Hibernie

regis fidei defensor*is* &c Iohan*ne*s Woodyne de Redditch in Com*itatu*
predicto victualer in *propria persona* sua venit Cor*am* nob*is* Iohan*ni*
Culpep*er* et E*dwardo* Cookes Ar*migeris* duob*us* Iusticiar*ijs* dic*ti*
dom*ini* regis ad pace*m* in dic*to* Com*itatu* Conservandu*m* assignat*is* et
Recognovit se debere dic*ti* dom*ini* regis decem libras et Thomas Sore   5
husbandman et E*dwardus* Vaughan yeoman ambo de Redditch
predicta tunc et ibidem in *proprijs personi*s suis, similiter venerunt
vt manucaptor*es pro predicto* Iohan*ne* Woodyne et recognoverunt
vterque separatim similit*er* sub pæna quinque librar*um*: Quas
Concesserunt de bonis et catallis terris et Tenement*is* suis ad vsu*m*   10
ipsius dom*ini* regis nunc heredu*m* et Successor*um* suor*um* levari si
idem Iohan*ne*s Woodyne defecerit in Condic*i*one sequent*i*./

The Condic*i*on of this recognisaunce is such that Whereas thaboue
bounden Iohn Woodyne is admitted and Allowed by thabouesayd   15
Iustices to keepe a Com*m*on alehouse or victualinge house for the
space of one whole yeare next ensuinge the Day of the Date hereof
& noe longer in Redditch aboues*aid*, yf therefore the *said* Iohn
Woodyne shall not suffer any vnlawfull Playes or Games to bee vsed
within his house nor any evill Rule or Order to bee kept *with*in the   20
same duringe the tyme of his s*aid* licence but to behaue himselfe therein
(in eu*er*y Respect) accordinge to his Ma*ie*sties Lawes in that behalfe
prouided That then this Recognisaunce to bee voyde and of none
effect Or els to stand in full fource and strength:/
       (signed)   John Culpep*er*   25
                 Edwarde Cookes

RIBBESFORD

1616   30
Archdeaconry of Ludlow Acts of Office   HRO: box 36, vol 134
ff [35–5v]* *(30 July)*

*Proceedings of the court held in the parish church of Ludlow before
Master Silas Griffithes, STD, vicar general of Robert Bennett, bishop* 35
of Hereford.

dimissio   Thomas Weav*er* detect*us* for dauncinge the morris vppon the Lord*es*
               day and providinge himself for it at the tyme of devine s*er*vice and
               sermon and for many misdeameanors then com*m*itted   40

2/ Conservandu*m for* Conservanda*m*   3/ dic*ti* dom*ini* regis *for* dicto domino regi
6/ predic*to*: *extra superscript* d

°[29] 30 die Iulij 1616 in ecclesia de Ludlowe coram domino Vicario
generali &c comparuit personaliter dictus Thomas Weaver obiectoque
ei articulo fassus est esse verum et submisit se &c/ vnde dominus eum
admonuit quod posthac &c et sic dimissus est.°

dimissio   Iohannes Budd pro consimili
              Quo die similiter

dimissio   Willimus Lake alias lloid pro consimili
              Quo die similiter

dimissio   Willimus Sparrie pro consimili
              Quo die similiter

dimissio   Thomas Nashe pro consimili
              Quo die similiter

dimissio/   Edwardus Parker pro consimili
              Quo die similiter |

              (23 September)
dimissio   Thomas Lucas Iunior pro consimili citatus &c in xxiij diem [Ses]
              Septembris 1616 preconizatus &c non comparuit &c deinde examinata
              causa dominus ipsum dimisit./

              Thomas Hayward Iunior pro consimili citatus &c personaliter in xxiij
              diem Septembris predicti preconizatus &c non comparuit &c
              excommunicatus

              (5 September)
dimissio   °Iohannes Brigges pro consimili Quinto die Septembris predicti
              comparuit et in vim iuramenti purgavit se &c vnde dimissus est causa°
              ...

Diocese of Hereford Acts of Office   HRO: box 24a (formerly 18), vol 70
f [129v]*   (5 September)
...
Thomas Aston senior
affirmed that stage plaies were made by the holie ghost and the [wod]
woord of god was but mans Invencion.

Citatus in
proximo
°vide inferius°

°5 die Septembris predicti in ecclesia parochiali de Ludlow coram domino Vicario generali &c comparuit personaliter dictus Thomas Aston obiectoque ei articulo &c negavit esse verum Vnde habet ad purgandum se in proximo &c cum sexta manu &c facta proclamacione &c hoc in loco xxiij videlicet die instantis Septembris sub pena iuris/ et decrevit Iohannem hailes citandum fore in speciali &c 23 die Septembris 1616 in ecclesia de Ludlowe coram domino Vicario generali &c comparuit dictus Aston cui dominus ex gracia assignauit vt supra in proximo 15 videlicet die Octobris predicti hoc in loco, prefato Iohanne Hailes monito &c°

23 Septembris   5

                                                                                   10

...

f [138]*   *(15 October)*

Thomas Aston senior/ habet ad purgandum se cum vj^{ta} manu &c   15
super articulo that he affirmed not that stage plaies were made by the holie ghost and that the woord of god was but mans inven⟨ti⟩on decimo quinto die Octobris 1616 in ecclesia de Ludlowe coram venerabili viro magistro Silvano Griffiths sacre theologie professore vicario generali &c comparuit personaliter dictus Aston et produxit in   20 compurgatores suos quosdam Iohannem Gillam et Iohannem Stephens facta intimacione et nulla contradictione habita dictus Aston iuramentum prestitit de innocentia dictique compurgatores de eorum respective credulitate vnde dominus pronunciavit &c et ab officio suo dimisit/   25

dimissio

1618
Archdeaconry of Hereford Acts of Office   HRO: box 24, vol 90
f [279v]*   *(11 November)*

                                                                                   30

Proceedings of the court held in the parish church of Ludlow before Master Gabriel Wallwin, MA, deputy of Master Oliver Lloid, LLD, vicar general of Francis Godwin, bishop of Hereford.

...

Thomas Gunghe for beinge disgised contrary to the 30 article °citatus   35
&c per publicum edictum in xj die Novembris predicti preconizatus &c non comparuit &c excommunicatus°

3m/ inferius: *see below, f [138]*

ROCK

1613–14
Archdeaconry of Ludlow Acts of Office   HRO: box 35, vol 132
ff [73v–4]*   *(14 December)*   5
…

Cleburie
mortimer

[ffranciscus] ⌐Willimus⌐ Mundaie de eadem detectus per gardianos de
Roke for acting a stage plaie vpon a Sundaie after Evening praier./.
Quesitus in xiiij diem decembris predicti &c vijs et modis in proximo
&c Citatus in [⟨..⟩] viij diem ffebruarij predicti &c ex certificario   10
apparatoris &c preconizatus &c excommunicatus/ |

(18 January)
[Georgius] ⌐Iohannes⌐ Bathe de eadem pro consimili
xviij die Ianuarij 1613 in ecclesia de Ludlowe coram docorem   15
Griffithes deputato &c comparuit obiectoque ei articulo &c fassus est
esse verum.
…

f [105v]   *(8 February)*   20
…

dimissio/
Neensavag./

Thomas Watmor/ ⎫	contra Walter Pother./ per
Willimus Norden. ⎬ interessent	profanandum Sabbatum
Thomas Turnor. ⎪	videlicet for [not] acting
Johannes Turnor. ⎭	vpon a stage at the Rock viijº 25
Richardus Piper. ⎫	die ffebruarij 1613:
Richardus Piper. ⎬	comparuit Coram Doctore
Thomas Warrold ⎭	Griffi⟨ths⟩ Surrogato &c &

confessus est articulum &c
vnde dominus infl⟨ixit⟩ ei   30
penitenciam iuxta formam
scedule &c .i. diem
penitencialem in ⟨parochiam⟩
[ibidem]ᴧ⌐de Rock⌐. Et ad
certificandum in proximo/   35
°deinde dominus ipsum
dimisit cum admonicione/°

7/ ⌐Willimus⌐: *3 minims* MS   24/ d *of* Norden *written over* g
16/ docorem *for* doctore   26, 27/ Richardus Piper, Richardus Piper: *probably dittography*

SOUTH LITTLETON

1553
St Michael's Churchwardens' Accounts   SHRO: BA 1284/1
p 10   *(24 May–15 May) (Accounts of Thomas Pyrry and John   5
Leygge – Receipts)*

...

Item recevyed for owr chwrche Ale   iij s. vij d.

1554   10
St Michael's Churchwardens' Accounts   SHRO: BA 1284/1
p 11   *(16 May–4 June) (Accounts of John Busshell and Richard
Panter – Receipts)*

...

Item Recevyd for owr chwrche ale thys yere   ij s. iij ⟨d.⟩   15
Item Recevyd that the maydons dyd gethur thys yere   ij s. iij d.
Item Recevyd for ij strycke of malt that was lefte on
browed for the profett of owr churche   iij ⟨...⟩

...
                                                                        20

1555
St Michael's Churchwardens' Accounts   SHRO: BA 1284/1
p 13   *(5 June–26 May) (Accounts of Richard Kirtley and John
Busshell – Receipts)*
                                                                        25
...

Item recevyd that the ˏ⌜youmen⌝ and maydens dyd gethur
thys yere for the profett of owr churche   xiiij d.
Item recevyd for owr chwrche ale thys yere   *(blank)*

...
                                                                        30

TENBURY

1600
Archdeaconry of Ludlow Acts of Office   HRO: box 34, vol 127
f [133]   *(8 July)*   35

*Proceedings of the court held in the parish church of Ludlow before
Master Francis Bevans, LLD, vicar general, and in the presence of James
Lawrence, notary public and deputy of Master Thomas Crumpe,
registrar.*
                                                                        40
...

°dimissio°   ffranciscus walker for making a plaie in the churche. °dimittitur &c.°

Iohannes Mason similiter

° dimissio°   °Quo die comparuit et super examinacione articuli dimittitur cum
admonicione &c.°

UPPER MITTON

1613/14
Quarter Sessions Memorandum
HWRO: Quarter Sessions Records 110:21/68
single sheet   (10 January)*

Bounde to Appeare at these Sessions, 10° Ianuarij 1613
Iohn Hucke of Overmitton in the Countye of Worcester walker
Thomas ffrancklin of the same walker
William Hardman of Hartlebury in the Countie of Worcester weaver/
These three with divers other vppon Wensdaye 20. October 1613
betwixt ix. and .x. of the Clocke in the night, beinge gathered together
at the house of Thomas Hucke in Mitton tooke Mr Thomas Smithe
Curat of Mitton and by violence putt him vppon a Cowlestaffe and
Caried him vp and downe ⌜the towne⌝ and caused fidlers beinge then
in company to playe by them, and ⌜one⌝ range vppon A fryinge panne
another blewe A horne, and the rest followed makinge A great
disorderly noise to the great disturbance of all the neighborhood
there about

chiaverie

UPTON ON SEVERN

1600
Robert Armin's Foole vpon Foole   STC: 772.3
sigs C–Cv*
...
How Iacke the cleane foole sung his song of Derries fayre in diuers
places, where he made great sport.
Iacke Miller welcomed to all places, and bar'd of none, came to a
Gentlemans, who being at dinner, requested him for mirth, to make
him a play, which hee did, and to sing Derries faire, which was in
this manner: First it is to be noted, he stutted hugely, and could neither
prenounce b nor p, thus he began.

As I went to Derries faire, there was I ware of a Iolly begger,

Mistresse Annis Master Thomas vnder a tree mending of shoone,
Mistresse Annis Master Thomas hight braue beggers euery one.

And so forward: but the iest was to heare him pronounce braue
beggers, and his quallity was after he began his song, no laughing could   5
put him out of it: standing by noting his humour that b and p plagued
him, bad him say this after him, which Iacke said he would doe.

Buy any flawne, pasties, pudding pyes, plumbe pottage, or pescods:
O it was death to Iack to do it, but like a willing foole he felte it:
buy any, buy any, fla flawne, p p p pasties, and p p p pudding p p   10
p p pyes, p p p, &c.

And euer as he hit on the word he would pat with his finger on
his other hand, that more and more it would make a man burst with
laughing, almost to see his action: sometime he would be pronouncing
one word while one might go to the doore and come againe. But euer   15
after Gentiles would request him to speake that, where before Derries
fayre was all his song.

He came not long after (to this I am witnes, because my eares heard
it) to a Gentlemans not farre from Vpton vpon Seuerne: where at the
Table (amongst many gallants and Gentlewomen, almost the state of   20
the country) hee was to iest and sing, especially they intreated him
for his new speech of the pees: which hee began in such manner to
speake, with driueling and stuttering, that they began mightily to
laugh: insomuch that one proper Gentlewoman among the rest,
because shee would not seeme too immodest | with laughing, for such   25
is the humour of many, that thinke to make all, when God knowes
they marre all: so she straining her selfe, though inwardly shee laughed
hartily, gaue out such an earnest of her modesty, that all the Table
rung on it: Who is that sayes one? not I sayes another, but by her
cheekes you might finde guilty Gilberto, where he had hid the brush: 30
this iest made them laugh more, and the rather that shee stood vpon
her marriage, and disdained all the gallants there, who so hartily
laught, that an olde Gentlewoman at the Table tooke such a conseit
at it with laughing, that had not the foole been, which stood (by
fortune) at her back and was her supporter, being in a great swound,   35
shee had fallen to the ground back-ward: but downe they burst the
windowes for ayre, there was no little boote to bid runne, shee was
nine or tenne daies ere she recouered that fit on my knowledge: thus
simple Iack made mirth to all, made the wisest laugh, but to this day
gathered little wit to himselfe.   40

...

1629
Indictment of John Jones   HWRO: Quarter Sessions Records 110:55/31
single sheet*   *(24 June)*

Wigorni*a*   ¶ Iur*ati* pro d*omi*no Rege sup*er* sacr*amentu*m suu*m* present*ant* quod   5
Ioh*anne*s Iones nup*er* de p*ar*ochia *san*cti Michael*is* in Bedwardine in
Com*itatu* Wigorn*ie* laborer machinau*it* quomodo popul*us* d*omi*ni
Regis nunc Subtilissime potuit legem huius Regni Anglie subvertere
& adnullare vicesimo quarto die Iunii Anno regni d*omi*ni Caroli nunc
Regis Angl*ie* &c quinto apud vpton sup*er* Sabrinam in Com*itatu*   10
Wigorn*ie* deceptive & f*a*lse *litter*⟨is⟩ contraf*acti*s sub nomine Henrici
Harbert milit*is* magistr*i* revellor*um* anglice master of the Revells hunc
tenorem continen*tibus* videl*icet* To all Mayors Sheriffes Iustices of
the peace Bayliffes Co⟨nstables⟩ and all other his ma*ie*sties officers
true Leighmen and subiec*tes* and to eu*ery* of them greeting know yee   15
that whereas the king*es* most excellent ma*ie*stie hath graunted vnto
the mast⟨er⟩ Commission vnder the greate Seale of England Giveing
thereby charge with full power and authoritie to the Master of the
Revells and his deputy for the ordering ⟨...⟩ and putteing downe of
all & eu*ery* Playes Players & Playmakers As of all other shewes   20
whatsoever in all places within his ma*ie*sties Realme of England as
well w⟨ithin⟩ as without I have by these *presentes* lycenced and
authorised Iohn Iones Anne his wief Richard Payne Richard Iones
and their assistance To sett forth and shew a ⟨...⟩ Motion with dyvers
storyes in ytt As alsoe tumbleing vaulteing sleight of hand and other   25
such like feates of Activety Requyreing you and eu*ery* of you in ⟨...⟩
suffer and p*er*mytt the said Iohn Iones Anne his wief Richard Payne
Richard Iones and their assistanc*es* quietly to passe and to try their
said shewes with ⟨...⟩ Trumpett*es* as they or any of them shall thinke
fitteing for the same from tyme to tyme and att all tyme & tymes   30
without any of yo*u*r lett*es* or molestac*ion* with ⟨...⟩ places of
Iurisdicc*ion*. Townes Corporate Citties or Boroughes whatsoever
within the Realme of England They behaveing them selves
ho⟨nestly...⟩ lawes of this Realme and fo⟨...⟩ shew on the Sabboth
Day or in the tyme of divine service you affordeing them yo*u*r Ten⟨...⟩   35
Schoolehowses or some other Com⟨...⟩soever either Stage Players or

19/ ⟨...⟩: 6 mm   34/ ho⟨nestly...⟩: 25 mm
24/ ⟨...⟩: 6 mm   34/ fo⟨...⟩: 25 mm
26/ ⟨...⟩: 6 mm   35/ Ten⟨...⟩: 30 mm
29/ ⟨...⟩: 8 mm   36/ Com⟨...⟩: 80 mm
31/ ⟨...⟩: 10 mm

such as make shew of moc*i*ons ⟨...⟩ any of yo*u*r Citties T⟨...⟩ Cor⟨...
im⟩medyatly frome mee or confir⟨m⟩ed ⟨...⟩ That forthwith you s⟨...⟩
Mayors Sheriff*es* Iustic*es* ⟨...⟩ Chamberleyne of the king*es* ma⟨iestie...⟩
Such Condigne punishm*ent* as in yo*u*r discr⟨etion...⟩ ensueing the date
hereof Given att h⟨...⟩ fiefte yeare of the Raigne of o*u*r most gracious   5
s⟨oueraign...⟩ Ac c*um* idem Ioh*annes* Iones dict*um* F*alsum* script*um*
sic ⟨...⟩ qualit*er* dict*um* f*alsum* script*um* potuisset sigillare v⟨...⟩
apposuit & annexit & C*um* f*alsum* script*um* sic ut prefert⟨...⟩ sup*er*
Sabrinam pred*ictam* in Com*itatu* pred*icto* ac in diuersis ˏ┌alijs┐ locis
eiusd⟨em...⟩ Regis ligeis & subditis recepit in d*icti* d*omi*ni Regis nunc   10
con⟨...⟩ contra formam statut*i* in hu*ius*modi casu edit*i* & provisi
...

WORCESTER

15

1186–90
Gerald of Wales' Gemma Ecclesiastica   LPL: MS 236
f 51v*   *(Distinction 1, chapter 43)*
...

Q*u*od saltationib*us* & cantilenis in ecclesiis & cimiterijs pop*u*li vacare   20
non debent.
Quod aut*em* saltacionib*us* & cantilenis in s*an*ctor*um* solempnitatib*us*
pop*u*li uacare non debeant circa ecclesias & cimiteria. sed tant*um*
diuinis officijs? h*abemus* ex concilio Toletano de consecratione
distinctione iijª. Religiosa consuetudo est quam uulgus per s*an*ctorum   25
solempnitates ag*ere* consueuit. Pop*u*li qui deb*ent* diuina officia
attendere saltacionib*us* turpib*us* inuigilant. cantica non sol*um* mala
canentes. s*ed* & religiosor*um* officijs obstrepu*erunt*. Hoc *etenim* ut
ab omnib*us* prouincijs depellat sacerdot*um* ac iudic*um* a concilio

---

1/ ⟨...⟩: 35 mm	5/ h⟨...⟩: 200 mm
1/ T⟨...⟩: 10 mm	6/ s⟨oueraign ...⟩: 185 mm
1–2/ Cor⟨... im⟩: 105 mm	7/ ⟨...⟩: 170 mm
2/ ⟨...⟩: 50 mm	7/ v⟨...⟩: 160 mm
2/ s⟨...⟩: 240 mm	8/ prefert⟨...⟩: 150 mm
3/ ⟨...⟩: 230 mm	10/ eiusd⟨em...⟩: 140 mm
4/ ma⟨iestie...⟩: 215 mm	11/ con⟨...⟩: 130 mm
4/ discr⟨etion...⟩: 200 mm	25/ Religiosa *for* Irreligiosa

27/ non sol*um* mala: *written* non mala sol*um* *but two last words marked for inversion of order by scribe*
29/ depellat *for* depellatur

sancto cure committatur. Vnde August*inus*. Nemo in oratorio aliquid
agat nisi ad q*u*od f*a*ct*u*m est unde & nomen habet. Exemplum de
sacerdote qui in anglia Wigornie finib*us* his n*o*stris dieb*us* interiectam
quandam cantilene particulam ad quam sepius redire *con*sueuerant
quam refectoria*m* seu refractoriam uocant ex reliquijs cogitacionu*m* 5
& quonia*m* ex habundantia cordis os loqui solet q*ui*a tota id nocte
in choreis circiter ecclesiam ductis audierat? mane ad missam
sacerdotalib*us* indutus & ad aram stans insignitus p*ro* salutatione ad
pop*u*l*u*m sc*i*l*i*cet domin*us* uobiscum. eandem anglica lingua coram
*om*nibus alta uoce modulando p*ro*nunciauit in hunc modum. Swete 10
lamman dhin are. Cui*us* hec dicti me*n*s *e*ss*e* potest. Dulcis amica tua*m*
poscit amator opem. Hui*us* aut*em* euentus occasione ep*isco*pus loci
illius Will*e*l*mus* sc*i*l*i*cet de Norhal sub anathematis *inter*minatione
pupliceper sinodos & capitula prohiberi fecit. ne cantilena illa p*ro*pter
memorie refricationem que ad mente*m* facinus reuocare poss*et*? de 15
cet*er*o p*er* ep*isco*patum suu*m* canetu*r*...
...

1293–4

Cellarer's Account Roll WCL: C51a   20
mb 1   col 2*   *(Prior's expenses)*
...
...It*em* menestrall' die Nat*iui*tatis b*e*at*e* mar*ie*. xviij. d....

1313–14   25

Cellarer's Account Roll WCL: C482
mb 1   col 2*   *(Gifts and grants)*
...
...It*em* cuidam Menestrallo .vj. d....

                                                                    30
1337–8

Cellarer's Account Roll WCL: C606
mb 1*   *(Gifts and grants)*
...
...Item in donis datis tribus Menestrall*is* Comit*is* Lancastrie xviij. 35

p 395, l.26–p 396, l.1/ Religiosa ... committatur: *Gratian*, Decretum, *Tertia Pars De
Consecratione, D III c 2, Corpus Iuris Canonici, Emil Friedberg (ed), 2nd ed, vol 1 (Leipzig,
1879), col 135*
1–2/ Nemo ... habet: *Augustine of Hippo, Epistula 211.7*, Epistulae, *Corpus Scriptorum
Ecclesiasticorum Latinorum, Al. Goldbacher (ed), vol 57, Sec 2, pt 4 (Leipzig, 1911), 361*
5/ ex reliquijs cogitacionu*m* for inter reliquias cogitacionum (?)
6/ ex habundantia ... solet: *Matthew 12.34*

den.... In donis datis Menestrall' Comitis Warr*ui*ci iij s. iiij den.... In
don*is* Citharedo Comit*is* Warr*ui*ci ⟨....⟩... In donis d*o*m*i*ni Prioris
Menestrall' apud la More iiij den....

...
5

1338-9
Cellarer's Account Roll   WCL: C58
mb 2*   *(Gifts and grants)*

...

...In ij. Menestrall*is* Comit*is* Warr*ui*ci iiij s.... Dat*is* Menestrall' die   10
installac*i*onis d*o*m*i*ni p*ri*or*is* ij s....

...

1344-5
Cellarer's Account Roll   WCL: C59   15
mb 2*   *(Gifts and grants)*

...

...Item menestrall' eiusdem iiij s. Item Citharedi Regine ij s.... In
don*is* d*o*m*i*ni p*ri*or*is* . iiij menestrall*is* Comit*is* Warr*ui*ci in eb*domada*
paschali vj s. ⌜viij d⌝ Item iij aliis menestrall*is* in festo corpor⟨is christi⟩   20
v. s.... Item menestrall' Ioh*a*nnis atte Lee vj d.... Item da⟨tis⟩
menestrall' in torn*o* d*o*m*i*ni p*ri*oris iij s. vj d.... It*em* menestrall' die
palm*arum* vj d.

...
25

1345-6
Cellarer's Account Roll   WCL: C60
mb 2*   *(Gifts and grants)*

...

...Item Menestrall' d*o*m*i*ni Hugonis Despens*er* iiij. s.... Item   30
Menestrallis d*o*m*i*ni Edmundi de Hereforde ij. s.... Item Menestrallis
ad pascha xij. d. Item Menestrallis in festo corp*o*ris ch*ri*sti ij. s.... In
don*is* dat*is* Menestrall' Ioh*a*nnis Talbot p*er* vices xviij. d.... Item
Citharedi abb*a*tis de Gloucest*ri*a p*er* ij vices iiij. s.... In donis

2/ Prioris: *Wulstan de Bransford, prior of Worcester 1317–39*
19–20/ eb*domada* paschali: *28 March–4 April*
20/ festo corpor⟨is christi⟩: *3 June*
22/ p*ri*oris: *John de Evesham, prior of Worcester 1340–70*
22–3/ die palm*arum*: *28 March*
32/ pascha: *27 March*
32/ festo corporis christi: *26 May*
34/ abb*a*tis de Gloucest*ri*a: *Adam of Staunton, abbot of Gloucester 1337–51*

menestrallis apud Clyue & Blacwelle in torno prioris vj. s. vj. d....

...

1346-7
Cellarer's Account Roll   WCL: C61
mb 1d   *(Gifts and grants)*

...

Item donis datis menestrallis domini W〈.......〉 & aliorum magnatum
xj s. ij d.

...

1347-8
Cellarer's Account Roll
St George's Chapel Library, Windsor: xi E 37
mb 1d   *(Expenses)*

...

Item Menestrall' abbatis Gloucestre ij s. Item Menestrall' Iohannis
Talbot ij s. Item Menestrall' in 〈aliis〉 diuersis festis ij s.... Item
〈Menestrall'〉 Comitis Arundel ij s.... Item Menestrall' in torno 〈domini
prioris ij s.〉...

...

1351-2
Cellarer's Account Roll   WCL: C53a
mb 1d   *(30 September–7 September) (Expenses)*

...

...In donis datis Ministrell' Comitis Warwich' xij d. Item ministr'
Abbatis Eueshame ij. s ...

1391-2
Cellarer's Account Roll   WCL: C74
mb 2   *(29 September–26 March) (Gifts and grants)*

...

...Item. in. dono. minstrall'. ad. comunam. domini Prioris. ij. s.

...

1/ prioris: *John de Evesham, prior of Worcester 1340–70*
17/ abbatis Gloucestre: *Adam of Staunton, abbot of Gloucester 1337–51*
20/ prioris: *John de Evesham, prior of Worcester 1340–70*
28/ Abbatis Eueshame: *William de Boys, abbot of Evesham 1345–67*

1395-6
Cellarer's Account Roll WCL: C77
mb 3 *(26 September 1395-30 September 1396) (Gifts and grants)*

...

...Item in dono ministrall*is*. eiusdem. precepto. d*o*m*i*ni pri*o*r*is* iij s.   5
iiij d....

...

1423-4
Sacrist's Account Roll WCL: C425   10
mb 2 *(External expenses)*

...

...In dono ludentib*us* die Corpor*is*. chr*is*t*i* .iij. s. iiij. d....

...

                                                                              15

1445-6
Prior's Account Roll WCL: C396
mb 3* *(Gifts and grants)*

...

...Item M*y*nstrell' d*o*m*i*ni Reg*is* ap*u*d Beuerey xiij s. iiij d. Item d*o*m*i*ni   20
duc*is* Gloucestr*ie* x s. Item d*o*m*i*ni duc*is* Warr*ui*ci vj s. viij d. Item
vn*i* M*y*nstrell*o* d*o*m*i*ni duc*is* de Bockyngham xx d. Item M*y*nstrell'
d*o*m*i*ni Ep*i*scop*i* de durham xx d. Item M*y*nstrell' d*o*m*i*ni de W. iij s.
iiij d. Item alijs diu*ersis* ad diu*ersas* vices xx d. Item M*y*nstrell' d*o*m*i*ni
Duc*is* de Excet*er* vj s. viij d. Item M*y*nstrell' d*o*m*i*ni de Salysbury vj s.   25
viij d. Item M*y*nstrell' d*o*m*i*ni de Suffolch x s.... Item diu*ersis*
ludent*ibus* ville in nocte Epipha*n*ie vj s. viij d....

...

1446-7   30
Prior's Account Roll WCL: C397
mb 1 *(Gifts and grants)*

...

...Item Ministrell' d*o*m*i*ni duc*is* Eboraci xx d. Item Ioh*anni* Lynley
mynstr⟨...⟩ ij⟨.⟩... Item Ministrell' d*o*m*i*ni duc*is* Eboraci vj s. viij d.   35
Item Ministrell' d*o*m*i*ni duc*is* de Bockyngham vj s. viij d. Item

---

5/ eiusdem: *the previous payment is to William Beauchamp*
13/ die Corporis. christi: *22 June*
35/ mynstr⟨...⟩ ij⟨.⟩: *partially obscured by an ink blot, c 30 mm in diameter*

ministrell' domini Marchionis de Sowtheffolke x s. Item j Citherazatori
domini Roulondi Leynthale xx d.... Item j Citherazatori viij d. Item
j alii Citherazatori xij d.... Item Ministrell' domini Regis xiij s. iiij d....

mb 2

...Item ludent' in festo corporis christi xiij s. iiij d....
...

1447–8
Prior's Account Roll   WCL: C398
mb 2*   *(Gifts and grants)*
...
...Item Ministrell' ville Wygornie in prima dominica aduentus domini
xij d.... Item Ministrell' domini Comitis de Arundell iij s. iiij d. Item
Ministrell' domini Edmundi Hungerford iij s. iiij d. Item j Ministrello
domini Walteri Deverose xx d. Item j Ministrello domine ducisse
Warrewych xx d.... Item Ministrell' domini Walteri Deverose xx d....
...

1449–50
Cellarer's Account Roll   WCL: C92
mb 4   *(Gifts and grants)*
...
...Item in donis datis mimis & histrionibus ville wygornie ad festum
Natale domini xij d....
...

1451–2
Prior's Account Roll   WCL: C399
mb 1*   *(30 September – 30 September) (Gifts and grants)*
...
...Item ministrell' Willelmi Lucy militis ij s. Item Ministrell' ducis
⟨de⟩ Bockyngham vj s. viij d. Item Ministrell' domini Comitis Warruici
vj s. viij d....

7/ festo corporis christi: *16 June*
14/ prima...domini: *3 December*

mb 3

...

Item Ministrell' domini ducis Excetrie vj s. ⟨....⟩...

...

5

1463–4
Prior's Account Roll   WCL: C401
mb 1   *(Gifts and grants)*

...

In donis datis diuersis ffamulis domini Regis et Ministrallis eiusdem   10
ad diuersas vices hoc Anno vna cum donis datis diuersis famulis ducum
Comitum et aliorum magnatum hoc Anno vij li. xix s. ij d....

...

Almoner's Account Roll   WCL: C201   15
mb 2   *(Petty expenses)*

...

...In donis datis diuersis ludentibus in estate iij s....

1464–5   20
Prior's Account Roll   WCL: C402
mb 1   *(Gifts and grants)*

...

In donis datis diuersis famulis domini Regis et Regine et Ministrallis
eorundem vna cum donis datis diuersis famulis ducum et Comitum   25
Baronum et aliorum magnatum vj li. xix s. ij d....

...

1466
Civic Ordinances   SHRO: BA 9360/C–2   30
f [1]*   *(14 September)*

Ordinaunces Constitucions And articles made by the kynges
comaundement and by hole assent of the Citesens inhabitantes in the
Cyte of Worcestre at their yeld marchaunt holden the Sonday in the   35
feste of the Exaltacion of the holy Crosse the yere of the reigne of
kynge Edward the fourth after the conquest the vj^te.

...

f [6v]

xxij

Also it myght be ordeined a Substanciall rule that .v pagentes amonge
the craftes to be holden yerly and ⌈shuld⌉ not be to seche [when] when
ˏ⌈thei⌉ shuld go to do worshipp to god And to the Cite and to better　5
and more certenly kept then they haue be bifore this tyme vppon
peyn of euery Crafte founde in defaute of xl s. the oon half to be
payd to the Bailly And the other half to the Comyn tresour. and that
the Stewardes of euery Crafte that ben contributory shull be called
to the accompte to knowe the Charge so that the Stuardes of euery　10
crafte may haue levey as for ther parte in peyne of hym that ys founde
in defaute iij s. iiij d. half to the Bailly And half to the Comyn tresour.
Also that yerly at the lawday holdyn at hokday that the grete enquest
shall provide and ordeyn wheþer the pageant shuld go that yere or
no And so yerly for more surete　15
...

ff [19–19v]
...

lxxviij

Also it ys ordeynd by this present yeld/ that all maner of Craftys　20
withyn the seid Cite that haue pageantes goynge to the worshippe of
god and profite and encrese of the seid Cite. And also all the Craftes
that ben contributory to the same And to the lightz of torches and
Tapers amonge the seid Craftes vsyd in the seid Cite haue and enyoie
there good feithfull and trew approved customs and vsages in　25
Susteynynge ther Pageantes lightes and other neccessaries to ther
craftys of Reason and custom belongynge or apperteyninge. the
Comyn weele welfare and prosperite of the seid Cite Accordynge to
the kynges lawes alwey | kept and forseyn also that yf eny persone
Straunger comynge to the seid Cite beynge A Craftisman of eny Craft　30
afore named dwellynge withyn the seid Cite beynge a freman or
kepynge a Shoppe Happen desirynge to hold Crafte as a Maister
withyn the seid Cite or Subarbez of the same At his furst entree ther
he to Comyn with the wordeyns of the same Crafte that he desireth
ther to occupie and by them as reson And conscience will after the　35
custom of ther Crafte to be demened as well for his entre as for yerly
payment to ther pageantes and lightz and in lyke wise all Iorneymen
Strangers comynge to the seid Cite after xiiij. nyghtes of his abidynge

in the same to be Spoken *with* by the wardens or kep*er*s of the Craft
that he canne or ex*er*cisith and for the same to be contributorye to ther
pageant*es* and light*es* and other Iornemen of the seid Craft*es* yerly doth ✓
paye and satisfie and what p*er*sone that denyeth this therof notice to
be made to the Baill*y* And to the kep*er*s of the articles of the yeld they   5
to reforme w*ith*out accion or redresse suche maters as the matier of
Reson shall require and that eu*er*y Crafte havynge the name of pageant
shull fynde oon Cresset yerly brennynge to be born biforn the Baill*y*
of the seid Cite in the vigill of the natiuite of Seynt Iohn Bapt*iste* at
the Comyn Wacche of the seid Cite and the wardeyns of the seid   10
Crafte and all the hole Crafte shall wayte vppon the seid Baill*y* in the
seid Vigill at the seid wacche in ther best arraye harnesid vppon peyn
of eu*er*y man so failynge vn lasse then he haue a Sufficient depute of
xl d. and often tymes as he be founden in defaut the oon half to the
Baill*y* and the other half to the Comyn treso*ur*. and that eu*er*y   15
Craftesman aforeseid that *p*roposeth to Set vp*p*e Crafte w*ith*yn the
seid Cite that he paye to the wardeyns Steward or Maist*er*s of the
same not excedynge xiij s. iiij d. In peyn of theym or hym of eu*er*y
Stuard warden or Maist*er* that doth the contrarie xl s. half to the Baill*y*
And half to the Comyns   20

f [21v]   *(Calendar)*

...

xxij   Item that v. pageaunt*es* be hadd amonge the Craftes. and that the
              Steward*es* And the contributories ther to belongynge make accomptes   25
              as trouth require*th*

...

f [23v]

...   `   30

lxxviij   Item how all man*er* Craft*es* artifecers and ther contributories w*ith*
               ther lightes And pagent*es* shall be ruled and demeaned

...

1466–7   35
Cellarer's Account Roll   WCL: C97
mb 3*   *(Gifts and grants)*
...
...Item Di*u*ersi*s* Ludentib*us* in villa Wigorn*ie* ij s. hoc a*n*no Item

diuersis Ludentibus apud Claynes Aston' & Poywyke hoc anno iij s....

...

1469–70
Prior's Account Roll WCL: C403   5
mb 2 *(Gifts and rewards)*
...

Et computat in donis datis ffamulis domini Regis et seruientibus ac
ministrallis diuersorum generosorum dominorum pro tempore huius
compoti ut patet per quaternum eiusdem domini prioris xxv li. iij s. 10
xj d. ob....

...

c 1470–80
Cellarer's Account Roll HCL: R707   15
mb 5* *(Gifts from the king)*
...

...Et datis lusoribus Ecclesiarum omnium sanctorum sancte Elene
sancti Swithuni [&] sancti Albani sancti Petri & sancti Michaelis in
Wigornia videlicet cuilibet Ecclesie xij d. vj s.... Et datis [lusoribus] 20
Iohannis Yonge vicecomiti pro labore suo circa inquisitionem factam
de vasto... Et datis tempore hokday Couet' mendicantium pro torticijs
fiendis in diuersis Ecclesiis xij d....

...

25

1470–1
Prior's Account Roll WCL: C404
mb 2 *(Gifts and rewards)*
...

...Et in Rewardis Ministrallis domini Regis & aliorum dominorum 30
per tempus huius Compoti xxj li. ⌈x li. xiij s. iiij d.⌉ ...

...

Cellarer's Account Roll HCL: R707a
mb 3 *(Gifts and rewards)*   35
...

...Et in dono diversis ludentibus in villa Wygornie hoc Anno xx. d....

...

8/ ffamulis domini Regis: *corrected from* domini Regis ffamulis
21/ Iohannis *for* Iohanni (?)
22/ Couet' *for* Conuentu *or* Conuentibus (?)

1471–2
Prior's Account Roll   HCL: R708
mb 2   *(Gifts and rewards)*

...

...Et in rewardis dat*is* m*i*nstrall' dict*i* d*omi*ni Reg*is* Duc*is* Clarencie &   5
alior*um* d*omi*nor*um* p*ro* temp*or*e hui*us* comp*oti* xij li. xix s.
ix d....

1472–3
Prior's Account Roll   WCL: C405   10
mb 2   *(Gifts and rewards)*

...

...Et in don*is* dat*is* diu*er*sis Ministrall*is* d*omi*ni Reg*is* Regine Principis
Duc*um* Clarencie glowcestr*ie* & alior*um* d*omi*nor*um* et magnat*um*
xj li. viij s. vj d....   15

...

1478–9
Prior's Account Roll   WCL: C406
mb 1d   *(Gifts and rewards)*   20

...

Et comp*utat* sol*utum* in donis dat*is* s*er*uient*ibus* d*omi*ni Reg*is* Regine
Principis duc*is* Gloucestr*ie* diu*er*sis famul*is* diu*er*sor*um* d*omi*nor*um*
& diu*er*sis Mimis predictor*um* vna cum donis dat*is* diu*er*sis
deferent*ibus* exennia & al*ias* soluc*iones* vt p*atet* p*er* quatern*um* d*omi*ni   25
Prior*is* & Ioha*n*nis Broke hoc anno xxiiij li. xviij s. viij d....

...

1481–2
Prior's Account Roll   WCL: C407   30
mb 2   *(Gifts and rewards)*

...

...Et in donis siue Reward*is* dat*is* ffamulis d*omi*ni Reg*is* Regine d*omi*ni
principis duc*is* Glowcestr*ie* duc*is* Eboraci Comitis Northhu*m*brie
Comit*is* de Aru*n*dell diu*er*sis leg*is* perit*is* ac Ministrall*is* predictor*um*   35
d*omi*nor*um* vna cum don*is* dat*is* diu*er*sis deferent*ibus* Redd*itus* & alias
soluc*iones* cum donis et Exemijs. vt in Quaterno p*re*dicti Prioris
xxix li. vij s....

1486

First Provincial Progress of Henry VII
BL: Cotton Julius B xii
ff 13v–17* *(14 May)*

...   5

...This doon I had leve for to departe/ At Wytsone even at Whiche
tyme I. came to the king*es* grace At Worcest*er* Wher as I. vnderstande
Wer ordeynede certeyn paiant*es* And speches like as ensuen Whiche
his grace at that tyme harde not &c.

10

Welcome ˌ⸢nevew⸣ Welcome my Cousyn dere
Rex   Next of my blood descended by alyau*n*nce
Henricus vjᵘˢ   Chosen by grace of god both fer & ner
To be myn heir in Englande and in fraunce |
Ireland Wales with al the Ap*er*tenau*n*ce   15
of the hole tytle Which I Su*m*tyme had
Al is thyn owne Wherfor I. am Right glad

I am Henry the vj^th Sobre And sad
Thy great vncle Su*m*tyme of England king   20
ffull xxxix yeres This Realme my silf I. had
And of the people had the gou*er*nyng
Slayne was I. martir by great t*or*menting
In Chartesey buriede. translate vnto Windesore
Ther logge I now & Arst ther Was I. bore.   25

Mek And m*er*cifull was I. eu*er*more
ffrom Crueltie refreynyng And from vengeaunce.
God hath me Rewardede largely therfor
And gentil Cosyn Sith thou hast this chaunce   30
To be myn heire vse Wele my gou*er*nau*n*ce [pitie]
Pytie W*ith* m*er*cy haue alwey in thy cure
ffor by meknesse thou shalt longest endure

Aduertise Wele What founde Is in scripture   35
The gospell seith Whoso right Well it markes
Mercifull men of m*er*cy may bee sure
ffor god him self this Writeth And seith al clerk*es*
pr*e*served m*er*cy aboue all his Werk*es*
Now for his sake shewe It to free & bonde   40
And He shall guyde thee both by see & Lande. |

And Here thou may dere Cousyn vn⌐dre⌐stande
This poore Citie With humble Reuerence
A poore bill haue put into myn hande
Becheching me of my benevolence.
It to declare to thy magnyficence   5
Wherto I. muste my pitefull herte enbrace
And this procede Whos luste to here in place

Humbly besechith your high And noble grace
Your poore subiectes liegmen & Oratours   10
Wher late befell A lamentable case.
A gentilmann detectede With Riottours
Making suggestyon ayenst you & youres
Contryved falsely by his Informacion
Shewing so largely by his Communicacion   15

That of your grace he had grauntede his pardon
By great Charter of lif goodes & landes
Desiring heder to come for his devocion
To offer at our lady Wher that she standeth   20
By Ignorance thus bee they brought in bandes
Beseching you moost mekely or ye passe
Graciously pardon theym this trespasse.

ffor greatly greven theym [this trespasse] both mor & lasse   25
So many men by oon to be deceyuede
Your oune Citie that neuer pollutede Was
Is now defiled for she hath hym Receyuede
Your saide Subgettes that al this hath perceyuede |
Enclyne theymsilf And to your Mercy calle .   30
Seing they haue a Warnyng perpetuall

And from this tyme after what euer befalle
They Will entende to put theym silf in devoure
You for to please both olde yonge greate & smale   35
With al ther seruice your high grace to Recouere
And your saide Oratours promysse to pray for euer
ffor Your noble estate and prosperitie
long to contynue In Ioye And felicitie
                                                                      40

And now swete Henry doo some What for me
I stod for vj And now ye stande for vij

ffau*or* thoos folk that fele adu*er*sitie
God Wille Rewarde the therfor high In heven
Now as myghty lyon bere the Even.
Whos noble Angre In his Cruell Rage
To prostrate people neu*er* Wolde doo damage   5

That he may this W*ith* al his counseill sage
Here I. beseche the Holy trynytie
And the Swete moder Whiche in her tendre Age
Bare god & man in pure V*ir*ginitie   10
And ye both seint*es* of myn affynytie
Oswolde & Wolstan Right holy confesso*ur*s
pray for my good sone king henry at al houres

Heuenly fader that art of power moost   15
And thou/ his sonne Appro*r*ede vnto witte |
O thou swete spirite named The Holy goost
Thre p*er*sones in on godhede Suerly knytt
ffor king henry the vij I. me submytt
beseching you to graunte hym in this place   20
Power Wisdome And al foyson of grace.

O hevenly lorde Celestiall god durable
Aboue al king*es* hauyng p*re*emynence
Both iij & on and vndeseuerable   25
I the beseche for thy magnyficence
King Henry the vij to kepe from al offence
Graunt him longe liff in vertue the to please
And al his Dayes for to Reigne in peas.

                                                              30
O Et*er*nal god that made al thing of nought.
ffader And sonne and holy goost ful preste
Beholde the hande maide Whiche they iij haue Wrought
And namely thou my so*n*ne Whiche soke my breste
Henry the vij pres*er*ue at my Requeste   35
Englande my Dowre so forte rule & guyde.
Therby to Wynne the blisse that eu*er* shal abide

O Henry moche art thou beholde to vs
That thee haue Reysede by our oune elec*c*ion   40

16/ Appro*r*ede *for* Approuede

Bee thou therfor mercifull And graciouse
ffor mercye pleasith moost our affeccion
ffolow king henry Whiche Is thy proteccion
As Welle in Worke as in sanguinitie

5

And In this Worlde it Wille rewarded bee/. right Welle
If thou serue god in loue & drede./ |
Hauyng compassion of theym that hath nede
Euerlasting Ioye shalbe thy mede
In heven Aboue Wher al seintes Dwelle

10

Loquitur Ianitor Ad Ianuam
Ecce Aduenit dominator dominus
Et Regnum in manu eius potestas & Imperium
Venit desideratus cunctis gentibus

15

To Whom this Citie both al & some
Sspeking by me biddeth hertely Welcome
And as I. cane Welcome I. shall expresse
Beseching your grace [f] pardon my simplenesse.

20

Quis est ille qui venit so great of price
I thought Noe Whiche came late from the flodde
Or it is Iason With the golden flece
The noble mount of Riches & of goode
Manly of dede manerly meke of mode

25

Or it is Iulius With the trivmphe of victorie
To whom I. say Welcome most hertely

Welcome Abraham Whiche Went from his kynnerede
Of al this lande to take possession

30

Welcome ysaac that sumtyme shulde haue be dedde
And Now is heire to his fader by succession
Welcome Iacob opteynyng the benesoun
Whiche many yeres dwelled with his vngle true
ffleyng his Countrey from drede of Esau

35

Welcome Ioseph that was to egipte sold |
ffrely Welcome oute of the depe Cesterne
Welcome Dauid the myghty lion bolde
Chosen of gode this Realme to Rule & gouerne

40

17/ Sspeking for Speking

Whiche in the felde great goly did prosterne
And al his Enemyes ouercome in fight
god being guyde that yave him strength & myght

Welcome Scipio the Whiche toked hanyball   5
Welcome Arture the very britan kyng
Welcome defence to England as A walle
Cadwaladers bloddde lynyally descending
Longe hath bee towlde of suche A prince comyng
Wherfor frendez If that I shalnot lye.   10
This same is the fulfiller of the profecye.

Whiche he is this mor pleynely to expresse
Henry the vij chosen by grace & chaunce
ffor singular beautie & for high prowesse   15
Now to be king of Englande & of fraunce
And prince of Wales with al thappertenaunces
lord of Irelande moost famous of Renoune
With al the titill perteynyng to the Coroune
                                                                 20
And now Welcome our noble souueraigne lorde
Better Welcome was neuer prince to vs
We haue desirede long god to Recorde
To see your moost noble persone graciouse
Welcome myghty pereles And moost famous   25
Welcome comyng byding gooing And alweys/ knowen
In token Wherof I. yelde to you the keyes. |
Now al this Citie seith Welcome to your ovne.

And on Wittsonday Went In procession And hard his dyuyne seruice   30
In the Cathedrall Chirche of the said Citie having no Roobez of estate
vpon hym but A gowne of cloth of golde of Tissue lynede with blake
Satene. The Bisshop of that see did the dyuyne seruice In pontificalibus
And In the procession comyng towarde the quere Ayene The bisshop
Went Into the pulpitt And made a bref & a fructifull Sermonde in   35
Conclusion of the Whiche declarede the popez bulles touching the
kinges & the quenes Right And the confirmacion of the same present
ther The bisshop of Ely & of excester The duc of Bedeforde The
Marques of dorset Therle of lyncolln Therle of Oxinforde The Vicount

18/ Renoune: *3 minims* MS
31/ In: *three minims* MS

Welles The lorde ffitz Water Sir William Stanley Called lorde
Chaumberlayn The lorde husey chieff Iugge of the kinges benche And
great nomber of knyghtes And esquiers And of other people And byfor
dyner In his Chaumber Sir Thomas Towneshende Iustice knyght And
at the Tyme accustumed on that Day he had his largez cried by his   5
officers of Armes &c...

...

1486–7
Prior's Account Roll WCL: C409   10
mb 3 *(Gifts and rewards)*

...

Et computat in regardis datis seruientibus Domini Regis & seruientibus
aliorum Dominorum Hoc anno superueniencibus per plures Videlicet
infra tempus compoti vnacum Regardis datis diuersis deferentibus   15
exhennias & minstrallis prout particulariter plenius patet in quaterno
dicti domini nunc Computantis hoc Anno L li. x s. iiij d.

...

1489–90   20
Almoner's Account Roll WCL: C208
mb 1 *(External payments)*

...
...Et in regardis datis Lusoribus in festo Natali domini viij d....
...   25

1490–1
Prior's Account Roll WCL: C411
mb 2 *(Gifts, rewards, and alms)*

...   30
Et in regardis datis servientibus domini Regis ducis Bedefordie
Ministrallis Lusoribus diuersorum dominorum generosorum ad
Sessionem Iusticiariorum domini Regis necnon amatoribus &
benefactoribus & pluribus alijs deferentibus exhennia cum elimozinis
datis Scolaribus & magis indigentibus ut patet per quaternum dicti   35
domini prioris xxxvij li. v s.

...

4/ Sir Thomas Towneshende: *error for Sir Roger Townshend, justice of Common Pleas (?)*

1492/3
Lease of Property Adjacent to the Pageant House
SHRO: BA 5234/23(ii)
single sheet*   *(20 February) (Lease)*

Omnibus christi fidelibus ad quos hoc presens scriptum indentatum
peruenerit Willelmus Lane & Thomas Cirkeyn balliui domini Regis
Ciuitatis Wygornie Iohannes ffrethorn & Iohannes Ionys aldermanni
eiusdem ciuitatis Ricardus Cetull & Thomas Wighan camerarij
eiusdem Willelmus Ioly Iohannes Mores Iohannes Payne Ricardus   10
Mors Iohannes Malpas & Thomas Swynerten Ciues eiusdem ciuitatis
salutem in domino/ Noueritis nos ex assensu & concensu tocius
communitatis Ciuitatis predicte tradidisse concessisse & ad firmam
dimisisse Ricardo Griffith Carpinter vnam vacuam placeam terre
situatam in mercato granorum ciuitatis predicte proximam portam   15
sancti martini ibidem continentem in longitudine a muro ciuitatis
predicte ex parte orientali in partem occidentalem viginti octo pedes
regales & in latitudine a muro porte predicte ex parte boreali in partem
australem quindecim pedes regales/ Tradidimus eciam & concessimus
predicto Ricardo Griffith altram vacuam placeam terre situatam in   20
parte australi mercati predicti continentem in longitudine a muro
ciuitatis predicte ex parte orientali in partem occidentalem Triginta
octo pedes regales & in latitudine a domibus vocatis le pageantehouses
ex parte australi in partem borealem duodecim pedes regales/
Tradidimus etiam & concessimus predicto Ricardo Griffith aliam   25
vacuam placeam terre situatam in longitudine inter predictas vacuas
placeas terre & in latitudine inter murum predictum & domum mercati
ibidem/ habendas & tenendas predictas vacuas placeas terre prefato
Ricardo Griffith & assignatis suis a festo annunciacionis beate marie
virginis proximo post datum presencium usque ad finem termini   30
Octoginta vnius annorum extunc proximorum sequencium & plenarie
complendorum/ Reddent inde annuatim Camerarijs Wygornie qui pro
tempore fuerint duos solidos sterlingorum ad duos anni terminos
videlicet ad festa sancti Michaelis archangeli & annunciacionis beate
marie virginis equis porcionibus/ Et predictus Ricardus Griffith &   35
assignati sui denouo facient et construent infra septem annos proximos
sequentes datum presencium super duas placeas terre predictas duo
tenementa quorum altrum continebit duo spacia sumptis suis propriis
& expensis/ & eadem tenementa sic constructa bene & sufficienter
reparabunt sustentabunt & manutenebunt sumptis suis propriis et   40
expensis ac usque in finem termini sui predicti bene & sufficienter
reparata dimittent/ Necnon portabunt & soluent omnia alia onera

predictas placeas terre spectancia seu soluenda per totum terminum
supradictum/ Et predictus Ricardus Griffith & assignati sui non
concedent nec dimittent statum siue terminum suum predictarum
placearum terre nec alicuius inde parcelle nisi solomodo Ciuibus vel
Ciui predicte Ciuitatis & infra dictam ciuitatem manentibus vel 5
manenti & illi vel illis cui vel quibus Camerarij nostri qui pro tempore
fuerint assensum suum prebebunt/ Et si contingat predictum redditum
aretro fore & insolutum in parte uel in toto post aliquid festum
prenominatum quo solui debeat per spacium unius mensis/ Extunc
bene licebit camerariis nostris qui pro tempore fuerint in predictis 10
placeis terre intrare & distringere & districciones si que fuerint capte
licite asportare effugare & penes se retinere quousque de predicto
redditum unacum arreagia eiusdem si que fuerint plenarie fuerint
satisfacta & persoluta/ Et si predictus redditus in parte uel in toto
aretro fuerit & insolutus post aliquid festum prenominatum per 15
spacium quarterij unius anni/ vel si predicta duo Tenementa non
fuerint de nouo constructa per terminum prius limitatum/ vel si eadem
Tenementa non fuerint bene & sufficienter reparata sustentata &
maintenta/ aut si idem Ricardus Griffith seu assignati sui concesserint
seu dimiserint statum siue terminum suum predictarum placearum 20
terre aut alicuius inde parcelle contra formam predictam/ Tunc bene
licebit Camerariis nostris Ciuitatis predicte qui pro tempore fuerint
pro se & communitate ciuitatis predicte in predictis placeis terre & in
quamlibet inde parcellam reintrare dictumque Ricardum Griffith &
assignatos suos abinde totaliter expellere & amouere & in presentem 25
statum nostrum reassumere/ hijs indenturis in aliquo non obstantibus/
Et nos uero dicti balliui aldermanni Camerarij Ciues & tota
communitas Ciuitatis predicte predictas placeas terre prefato Ricardo
Griffith & assignatis suis modo & forma premissis contra omnes gentes
warantizabimus & per terminum predictum defendemus per presentes/ 30
In cuius rei testimonium vni parti harum indenturarum penes
predictum Ricardum Griffith remanenti/ Nos predicti balliui
aldermanni camerarij & Ciues assensu communitatis ciuitatis predicte
sigillum nostrum commune apposuimus/ altri uero parti earundem
indenturarum penes nos predictos balliuos aldermannos Camerarios 35
Ciues & communitatem ciuitatis predicte remanenti predictus
Ricardus Griffith Sigillum suum apposuit/ hijs testibus Iohanne Porter
Iohanne Croke Thoma Grene Thoma Radnor Willelmo Codon &
aliis/ Datum wygornie vicesimo die mensis ffebruarij anno regni regis
henrici septimi post conquestum anglie Octauo 40

subscripsi Codon

1496
Civic Ordinances   SHRO: BA 9360/C-2
f [25]   *(18 September)*

Ordynaunces. Constitucions And articles made and Enacted by the   5
hoole assent and Consent off the Citesens Inhabitauntes within the
Citie off worcestre liberte & ffraunchis off the same at their yelde
merchaunt holden yn the yeld hall of the forseid Citie the Sonday
next Aftur the ffest off the Exaltacion of the holy Crosse the yere of
the reigne of owre most drad & soueryan Lord Kyng Henry, the   10
vij^th after the Conquest the xij^th

...

f [28v]

...   15

ix.
pageantes.

Also hit is ordenid a substanciall reule that v pageantes among the
Craftis yerely be not to seche When they shuld goo to do worship
to god & to the Citie & to be better and more certenly kepte then
they haue byn by for this tyme vpon peyn of euery crafte founde in
defaute off xl.s. the oon halfe to be paied to the bailly & the other   20
half to the comen tresur and that the Stewardes of euery crafte that
byn contributory shull be callid to the accompte to knowe the charge
of the seid pageant so that the stewardes of euery crafte may make
levye as for ther parte in peyn of hym that is found in defawte xl. d.
half to the bailly & halfe to the comen tresour and that the masters   25
in oon pageant/ pay egallye and the Iorneymen pay as hit hathe ben
of old tyme among them vsed nor oon more than another And that
euery pageant goo in ther due ordre in procession & in ther pleyng
and that the iij furst pageantes pleye in ther due ordre vpon Corpus
christi day & the other ij pageantes pley in lyke maner vpon the Sonday   30
next followyng vpon peyn of that pageant that brekyth his due corse
for euery tyme to be leyveydid of ther Stewardes xl. s. in manere &
forme forseid And also that euery of the xxiiij^ti goo in ordre the seid
Corpus christi daye & on Trinite Sonday in procession in ther best
Arraye in peyn of euery man beyng absent & seen in the Citie the   35
same day by fore the procession & is not Syke in boody forfett
xx s. to the comen Tresur//

...

ff [35–6]   40

...

xxviij

Also it is ordeynd that all manere Craftes within the Citie of Worcestre
that haue pageantes goyng to the lawde & worship of god & for profite

®Craftys

& encresse of the seid Citie And also all the Craftes that ben
contributory to the same & to the lightes of Torchis & Tapurs Among
the seid Craftes vsid haue & enyoye their good feithefull & true
Approved Custumes & vsages in susteyning ther seid pageantes lightes
& other neccessaries to þer Craftes of Reson belongyng or   5
Apperteyning And euer that hit is affermyd at this present yeld that
no maner person from hensfurth shall occupy ne set vp eny occupacion
or Crafte Within this Citie nor liberte of the same as a master vnlesse
he be furst sworen & Admytted fre man of the seyd Citie & be
inhabitant within the same or liberte ther of And that fully performed   10
& don hit shall be lefull to euery suche person to occupie or set vp
eny crafte or occupacion without eny interrupcion or withseyng of
eny man So that he paye furthe with vn to the Stewardes or Wardens
of the seid Crafte that he desireth to occupie for his admyssion to
the same – xiij. s. iiij. d. & xij. lb. wex be sides all other paymentes   15
whiche I shall yerely growe to his Charge by Reson of pageantes lightes
and other neccessaryes by fore rehersid Provided allewey that euery
Apprentice within this Cite or liberte of the same which hath truly
servid his Apprentiswod by the hoole terme of vij yeres & is sworen
& admytted ffreman as ys by fore shewyd shall ymmediatly pay vn   20
to the Stewardes or Wardens of the Crafte whiche he was Apprentice
vn to but vj. s. viij. d. & vj. lb. wex besides all other paymentes afore
Rehersid And yf eny suche Apprentice wull be ffree to eny other
Crafte then he was Apprentice vn to Then he shall Content & pay
in hand to the Stewardes or Wardens of the same xiij s. iiij. d. xij.   25
lb. wex & all other yerely charges & paymentes by for specified
Provided also that the Masters of the Crafte of euery pageant & all
the masters which ben Contributory to the ⌈same⌉ shall fromhensfurth
egally pay to ther pageantes lightes & other neccessaries by fore
rehersid no master more than Another And all Iorneymen shall in   30
lyke maner pay to the same as hit hath byn by for this tyme vsid &
Accustumed And what person that denyeth this Ther of Notyce to
be made vn to the Ballies Aldremen & Chamburleyns of the seid Citie
for the tyme beyng They to ordre & Reforme hit as the mater of reson
shall require And ouer that hit is ordenid that euery crafte within this   35
Citie Desiryng to be privelagid Which byfor this yeld hath not be
admytted ne Affermyd as a Crafte within the same shall pay at this
yeld for his liberte & admyssion vj. s. viij. d. to the commen Tresur
And as mony as commyth after this yeld be fore eny other yeld be
grauntid desiryng ⌈þe same⌉ shall pay xiij. s. iiij. d. in forme byfor   40
rehersid Also hit is ordenid that no inhabitant within this Citie nor
liberte of the same ffromhensfurth Sill eny ware or merchandise at
eny feyre tyme withyn the Cemytory or Churcheyard of the

Wach.

milsumner
nonfrez.

Cathedrall churche of owre lady of wurcestre yn peyn of
disfraunchesing Hit is ouer that Affermyd at this present yeld that
✓ euery Crafte havyng the name of a pageant shall ffynd on Cresset
[yerely brennyng to be born be fore the Ballies of the seid Citie in the
vigill of the Natiuite of seynt Iohn Baptist At the comen wathe of the   5
seid Citie And the Wardens or Stewardes of the seid crafte & all the
hoole Crafte in their due ordre & corse after ther going in their
pageantes oon Corpus christi day shall wayte vpon | the seid Baillies
yn the seyd vigill At the seid wache in ther best arraye herneysid vpon
peyn of euery man so ffaillyng vnlesse then he haue A Sufficient depute   10
xl. d. half to the baillies & half to the Comen Tresur And of the hed
Stewardes of euery pageant yf they se not the due corse & ordre kepte
as is by fore rehersid C s. wher of xx. s. shall be paied to the Baillies
& iiij. li. to the comen tresur
...   15

f [37v]* *(Ordinance 30)*

...

Revelles

Gedering
to alys.

...And there be ffromhensfurth no Revelles of pleyes of eny persons
strangers for gederyng of eny money within the Citie In peyn of the   20
baillie yf they or eny of them suffur hit to be Don for euery tyme vj
s. viij d. to the comen tresure And that no inhabitaunt within the
Citie geder money to no playes church alis ne to no person Dwellyng
out of the Citie or liberte of the same vpon payn of vj. s. viij. d. for
euery tyme taken in Defaute half to the baillie & half to the comens   25
provided that euery man may Revell play & Disgysse for the avauntage
of eny churche or of eny other inhabitaunt within the Citie or liberte
of the same as often as nede shall require And þat no man shote gonnys
within the Citie to the Disturbance of his neyburs without he be
required by the baillie in tyme of nede In peyn of xl d. for euery   30
tyme founden with the Defaute half to the baillie & half to the comens
...

f [43v] *(Calendar)*

...   35

ix.

Also that the .v. pageantes be vsid provided that iij. of them go on
Corpus christi day And the other ij. the sonday next followyng And
the Stewardes of euery crafte þat byn contributory shall be callid to
the Accompte And þat euery master pay egally And þat euery of the
xxiiij^ti goo in procession on Corpus christi day & on Trinite Sonday   40
in ther best arraye

f [45]

...

Also that euery person desiring to occupie or set vp eny crafte as a
Master within the Cite or liberte of the same shall be demeanid with

.xxviij.   all for his entre And all Masters of on pageant pay egally to the pageant   5
And that no Citezen sill no manere ware at feyre tymes in seint Mary
Churcheyerd & how Craftes shall waite vpon the bailly at ther comen
Wache at Midsomer & how euery Crafte shall demene them self

...

Also that the price of ale be. as hit is assessid at euery law day or at   10
eny other tyme by the counsell chamber And that ther be contynued
a Cowle to mete ale withall And that ther be but ij. bruers vpon þe
law day in the grete Enquest And that the Ale Tasters be chosin vpon
the eleccion day & they wekely present the defautes of þe bruers And

.xxx.   that no foreyn by no barley ne malt by for his houre And þat the   15
bruers occupie but on Oste And that ther be no Revelles nor pleys
of eny persons stangers Within the Cite And þat no Inhabitant Geder
to no Ales oute of the Cite And þat no person shote gunnys And
that. no inhabitant by to sill eny manere Wood Within vij myles of
the Cite Except grete tymbur & asshe   20

1517–18
Cathedral Accounts   WCL: A12
f 56v   *(Prior's accounts)*

...   25

Item in donis datis Nuncijs. Mynstrellis domini regis. Regine & Alijs.
(blank)/

...

1546   30
John Davis' Memoir of his Imprisonment   BL: Harley 425
ff 69–70*

The yere of our Lorde 1546, and in the last yere of kinge Henry the
eight in the citie of Worcetour was there a childe caled Iohn Davis   35
of the age of [12] twelve yeres and under, [l] who. dwelled with one
mr. Iohnson a poticary his ownckle with whome allso dwelled one
Peter. Goffe prentice whiche in the tyme of the vi. articles woulde
Reade the testament in Inglishe and suche godlye bookes as he then
coulde gett. His mistris manye tymes hering hym so reade would   40

17/ stangers *for* strangers

moste sharplie. revile him ffor she was then and is still to this daye
an obstinate papist. at length. she disclosed the same. to one of her
Secte. & affinite a zolye stowte champion, indewed with more Riches
then wisdome. or godlie zeale. and thus consoulting together. theye
Invented with their adherents the [⟨...⟩] canons of the cathedrall   5
churche with the chauncelour. that. Tyme being whose name was
Iohnson chauncelor. to docter Heath then bishopp of Woorcetour
to intrap and snare the sayde Peter yf theye might by anye meanes
heare hym or see hym [l] with having anye. testament or other godly
booke but he perceyving their purpose kept him sellf owt of their   10
danger notwithstanding. to urge hym this worthie wise man Thomas
Parton. would reade openlie in the streat sytting at his dore or ells
lening at his shopp window, that all men passing by might hear. a
booke named The hunting of the hare with curres and bandoges. a
Trym. tragedie. dowbtles and more estemed with the popes   15
champions. then the bible or booke of the lorde. But when he
perceived he coulde not apprehend the saide Peter. to hurte hym he
would sometyme thretin hym. that yf he cawght him reding suche
bookes as he harde saye he did reade by the conffession of his mistres
[he] that he would make him twine or untwine but his threatninges   20
prevailed him not ffor he was sircomspecte and kept him owt of their
bloody ffingers. notwithstanding, their thirst coulde not be quenched
withowt blood by meane whereof. they shortly invented a newe
interprise and bycawes. the spite that Alice Iohnson bare to Iohn.
Davis her husbands next kinsman to whome shee supposed the saide   25
Thomas Iohnson her housband woulde leave some porcion of his
goods, having no child as it was like ffor god had made her barren
and he had no other kinsman as he would often saye in all the wourld
whiche increassed The more the deadly hate of his wyf ffor she never
loved him bicawes her housband so tendered him and that appered   30
at the death of the sayd Thomas Iohnson ffor she cawsed her
housband. to revoke that hee did give him by will either being past
memorye. or ells specheles, a good note of her love. But shortlie after
these papestes. attempted. to bringe. their longe-loked purpose to
passe by one Alice wif to Nicholas Organmaker. alias brooke. and   35
Oliver their sonne. that the said Oliver should ffawne ffreendshipp
of the said Iohn Davis as thowghe hee weare verye. desirous and ioyfull
of his company manye tymes saieng I woulde wee had some good
Inglish bookes to reade ffor my mother cannot abide this pilde pristes
nor their popish service but had I good bookes. I coulde please her   40
well to reade everye night. Then said Iohn Davis I will bringe a Booke
with me and so he ded bringe a Testament and reade unto them Then

they requested him to leve the booke behinde hym but he said the
booke was not his. − neyther could he so doe. then thei requested him.
to tell them what abuses weare in the churche and howe hee did like
the vj. Articles and he breefflie toulde them what he thowght but I
cannot now tarye said hee least I be shent. Then thei sayd Bicawes ye   5
should avoyd blame ffor comyng hether wright your mynde but hee
sayd I have no such leisour nor place yet would I gladly. do yt to
doe you good but to-morow I shall to peryewood ffeeldes. to gather
eyebright. to still & yf Oliver & you will gather ffor me I will wright
all my mynde And they agreed so to doe and on the morow. every   10
one of them according to their promyse made mett in the ffieldes and
the sayd Iohn Davis. did wright his hoole mynde uppon the sixe
articles. and made them allso a ballet caled come Downe ffor all your
shaven crown But at lengthe. this longhiddin conspiracie burst owte
ffor incontinent this woman within one halfe howre she browght.   15
this wrightinge to the sayd parton and the sayd thomas parton
disclozed the same to the chauncelour & register & other pristes which
laide their heads together and towlde them howe they might bringe
their. pourpose to pass and cawsed the sayd Thomas Iohnson his
ownckle to be their instrument. to trye whether yt were his hand or   20
no and he under the coulor of ffriendshipp came to the sayd childe
saieng I have kept the at the gramer skoole a great while and am minded
to have you to keepe the shopp for your aunte is not in quiet with
peter bicawes of his bookes wherefore I must putt hym awaye but
before I so doe let me see how you can wright So he [to] tooke penn   25
and paper and wrote these verses ffolowing | Of all treasur cunning
is the fflower loke uppon Diogenes whiche was both wyse and [said]
sad to obtayne this treasur cunninge what labour that he had. So hee
toke this wrighting & went to these papists but whether he he knewe
but the ffirst newes that he harde was earlye in the morning his ownkle   30
bid him make cleane the stable in the leche streat, and hee asked leve
to gather herbes but hee sayd naye there are Inowghe. to still this
two daies of yesterdaies gathering wherefore get you to the stable.
And he obeyed hym knowing his ffacte was browght to light, and
that no good was ment to him, but trouble but he no sooner entered   35
the stable. but ye boye oliver cam after hym saieng, Iohn Davis I
praye you reade this same [once] wrighting once or twice over that
I maye learne to reade it to my mother perfectlie but he perceiving
his Iudas-like trick sayde. get the hence I must doe my busynes but
he was so importune in requesting that he could not bee ridd of him.   40

29/ he he: *dittography*

then stept he into a litle howse and there he spied Thomas parton and
his ownckle Iohnson stonding under. a wall harkening, thinking
to have taken them reding the fforesayd wrighting but when he
perceyved their trechery have thie mother and thou dealt thus Iudasly
with me Take this ffor thie paynes and lent him two or thre blowes   5
with a brome and he cryed. then came theye in running sayeng What
is the matter then sayd Oliver Mr. Iohnson, I woulde have had your
boye to have reade this wrighting whiche he made yesterday and hee
woulde not. Then sayd parton what wrighting is that let me see but
parton knew yt right well but sayd so ffor a cullor. Then did they   10
fforce Iohn Davis to reade the same beffore them. Then sayde parton
neighbour Iohnson yee have. well bestowed your money to bring
upp suche. an herytique so yonge as hee is Then sayd Iohnson I loked
ffor ioye of him having no childe of my nowne nor kinsman that I
knowe but nowe he shall have as he hathe deserved And so parton   15
laide handes. on him. and his ownckle bownde his armes behinde
hym and browght hym to the towleshopp, in the citie of Worcetour
mr. Dooding and mr. Richard. Dedicote being bayliffes till the next
Mighellmas. after. Then was he commaunded to the ffreemans prison
at whiche. tyme one Richard howborough brother in law to Richard   20
bullingham which bullingham is brother to the reverend ffather in god.
nicholas bishop of linkcolne being keper of the prison cam abowght
nyne of the clock as the custum was to see their prisoners saffe and
sayd merely Thow hoorson how wilt thow doe they will burne the.
and he sayd [y] They can do no more then God will suffer them.   25
Tushe [h] sayde he prove by the candle how thou canst abide the
ffire And he did soo sayeng I am not affraide of the ffire And so he
helde his ffinger a good space the other holding the candle not willing
to hurt him till at length with admyracion he sayde ffelest thow not
the heate and he sayde no but he woulde skarse beleve him till he   30
had lokid and sawe he was not so muche as skorched. So he locked
the. dores sayeing god night. Shortly after there came a nother prisoner
into the same prisoner ffor what cawes he knewe not but it ffortuned
the prisone being half timbred. or rather better some of the clay of
the wall was ffalen so that this prisoner sayd to the keeper [he] this   35
heritique boye hathe broken the wall to steall owte by meanes wherof
he was put in an Inner prison caled the peephole but yet without
Irons untill Mighelmas Till one Robart yowle was chosen lowebaylef
a ioly catholik whiche quicklie bestowed his charite uppon him laieng
on a payer of bolts that he coulde not lifte up his small legs but lening   40

31/ muche: *minim missing* MS   33/ prisoner *for* prison

on a staff slipp them fforward uppon the grownde the beneffete
whereof is an extreame colde in his anckles to this day whiche he
shall cary to his grave Moreover he was ffayne to lye on the colde
grownd in those boltes having not so muche as a lock of strawe nor
clothe to cover him withall but two shippeskins fforthermore one   5
ffeerefilde a waker coming nightlie. thorowgh the guildehall to go to
the prive as he sayd woulde come and call this child at the hold whether
of his owne mynde or sett on by some other papest he knewe not
but these weare his woordes whie doste thow not recant thow wilt
be ffeared one tyme or other. as I have by robing The Devill, which   10
is like a raged colte whiche hath ledd me abowght this hall all night
or now and at length lawgh me to skorne and sayd howgh hoo Others
would come, and say thow shalt be burned thow heretique this weke,
and that weke this daye and tomorow ffurthermore nether mother
nor none of his kinn that durst come at him. at length to ease his   15
payne theye put into the same prison to him to beare him company
bicawes he was alone one attaynted of treason caled William Taylour
being a madman and owt of his wittes who in his ffrontique fittes
would many tymes profer to thrust him in with a knyf whiche the sayd
madman had to cutt his meate withall. moreover there came to pristes   20
canons of the cathedrall churche [⟨…⟩] the one calle Iolyf the other mr.
Yewer. To them was browtht his wrighting against the six articles
and his ballet called come downe which after they harde yt reade and
had resoned with him they burst owte in a pelting chaf sayeing God
hathe disclosed the in tyme being such a ranck heritique at this age   25
but god hath cut the of. else hadest thow bene the notablest herytique
in all christindome. thus in a great ffury threatning ffier and ffagot
& yat shortly they departed whether theie ware sent to the bishopp
or no he knewe not but shortly after mr. Iohnson the chauncelor sate
in the guildhall uppon the said Iohn and there were browght in his   30
accusers and were sworne and [18] ⌈24⌉ men were sworne and went
on his quest and ffownd him gilty but he never cam [a] before the
chauncelor this did he. to make all things in a redines against the
comyng of the Iudges that there might be no delay but spedye
execucion ffor the whiche cawes sake he was sent to the common   35
jayle and there did lye amonge theves and murtherers but god
prevented theire poorpos and toke awaye kinge Henrye the eight owt
of this troblesom woorlde yet notwithstanding he was araigned being
holden upp in a mans armes at the barr. The Iudges being portman.
and marven which when they perceived that they coulde not burne   40
him woulde have had him presently whipped. Then stept upp Iohn
bourne then esquire and sayd And please you my lordes he hathe

bene sore inowghe whipped allredy. Thus had he no ffarther troble
saving he laye in pryson a weke after many woulde have had him awaye
ffrom the barr and especially a priste but the sayd Iohn bourne toke
him whome and the gentlewoman his wyf. did anoynte his legges her
owne selfe with oyntment [and] wh*i*ch leges were styf and numbde 5
by reson of the Irons. ffor he laye in prison ffrom the 14. of August
[to the] till within [14] 7 daies of Ester. And the said mr. Bourne
travailed to bringe him to beleve in the sacrament sayeing it was
Christes verye fflesh and blood in fourme of bread ffor yf Christ sayd
he should have given us his bodye rawe in ffleshe and blood we shoulde 10
have abhorde yt but at lengthe sayd his wyf Let [his] us put awaye
this herytique, [like] least he mare my sonne Anthony. Moreover in
the dayes of queene marye he was accused by six protestantes and so
constrayned to depart the contry traveling paynfully unknown to any
and solde his patrimony wh*i*ch god had sent him by his parentes to 15
releve him in that tyme of necessite to the wh*i*ch provident god be
all hono*u*r and glory for ever muche more myght be spoken of his
last troble but for breveties sake.

→ 1548- *Caihclnd* – E l e u *a* t i o *rechembed*

1555–6   20
Probate Inventory of William Specheley, Draper
HWRO: BA 3585 1556:152A
mb 1*   *(26 February)*

The true Invetoryes of all the moveable good*es* of William Specheley 25
of the Cettie of worcest*er* draper deceased the xij^th daye of ffebruary
An*n*o d*o*m*i*ni 1555/ praysed by Iames hybbens Richard badlam
George Massye & Iohn Smythe the xxvj daye of ffebruary in the yere
Above wrytten

...   30

The pleyars rayment   Item the pleyars garment*es* And all the other Tyreme*n*t
belongy*n*g tothe same pr*e*ysed at   xxx^ti li.
             Som*m*a xxx^ti li.

...   35

Civic Miscellany 1 SHRO: BA 9360/A-6
f 272v   *(29 April)* *(Council order)*
...

At alle gen*er*all processions all the Councell in decent order doo goo
in procession & All Companis & ffellowshipp*es* & Reward*es* & other † 40
Item Hit is forther ordeynyd for good order hereaft*er* to be had &
continuyd w*i*thin the sayed cytey that whe*n* & as oft as it shale fortune

any generall processione hereafter to be hade within the sayd cyttey
that then the hole company of the commune counsell of the sayed
cytey shalbe present at [th] the same & shale kepe such decent order
in the same procession as heretofore hathe byne accustomyd & that
the stewards of all other [⟨.⟩] companeys & feloships with in the sayed   5
cytey shale lykwyse be at the sayed processione & shale orderly go
in a decent order one aftur a nother as hereaftur shalbe a poyntid by
the ballifes & not vpon heapes as hereto fore hath ben oft late
accustomyd vpon payne of forfaycture of euery feloshype or
companye offendinge contrary to this acte to losse xx s. and that all   10
companeis shale prepayre there shewes vpon corpus chrysti daye as
hathe bine of ould time accustomyd etc.

1559
Civic Miscellany 1   SHRO: BA 9360/A-6   15
f 292v   *(10 April) (Council order)*

Item hit ys ordeyned that the pageantes shalbe Dryven and played   *how?*
vpon corpus christi day this yere acordinge to the auncyent Custom
of this Cyte And that euery one of the commune councell of this   20
citte shall goe in procession vppon corpus Christi daye in theyr lyueres
accordinge to ther Cawlinge and auncient custom off this citte vppon
payn of forfettin of iij s. iiij d. bye ordre of them making defalte
...
25

1559–60
Probate Inventory of Edward Crosby, Draper
HWRO: BA 3585 1559:269
f 1   *(15 November)*

30

The trewe inventory of all the goo⟨...⟩ Cattell late Edwarde Crosbys
of the parishe of Saint Swythins within the cytty of worcester draper
take preysed and valued by Phillipe nicoles thomas harley Iohn
butcher & Raphe bagnall the xv^{th} day of novembre anno/ 1559
...
35

f 5

Inprimis a englyshe byble a testament and a boke of the
pistles & gospels and a lute praysed at   ix s. iiij ⟨d.⟩   40
          Summa ix s. iiij d.
...

1562-9
City Accounts 1   SHRO: BA 9360/A-10
f [82v]   *(Allowances to chamberlains)*
…

…to Henry Hybbyns toward*es* his grete charg*es* Conc*er*nyng the   5
settyng furthe of A plaie in septembre xx s.…

1566-7
Civic Miscellany 1   SHRO: BA 9360/A-6
f 334v   *(6 May) (Council order)*   10
…

vacat   Item that the pageant*es* shalbe played thys yere vpon trynyty sonday
three of them & other ij pageants vpon the sonday followinge with
as good matter & order as before tyme they haue byn played or better
at the charg*es* of the occupacions accustomed vpon [py] payne as in 15
the acte of the yeld ys menc*i*onyd

1567-8
Civic Miscellany 1   SHRO: BA 9360/A-6
f 338   *(30 October) (Council order)*   20
…

Item that the Pageauntes shalbe played this yere vppon Trynyti
sundaye thre pageauntes and vppon sunday next after too pageauntes
with as good matter and order as before tyme they have ben played
or better at the charges of the occupacions accustomed thereunto   25
vppon payne in the Acte of the yelde ys expressed
…

1568-9
Chamber Order Book 1   SHRO: BA 9360/A-14   30
f 104v*   *(17 December)*
…

lyuereys of   In primis it is agreed That the Awditors Mr Baylyff*es* & their breethern
musicions   in the Ende of the Awdite shall by their discressions take order
touchyng the lyue*r*eys of the music*i*ons   35
…

33/ Mr Baylyffes: *John Moore and Edmund Burrey, high and low bailiffs for 1568-9*

1572–3
City Accounts 1   SHRO: BA 9360/A-10
f [114v]   *(Allowances to chamberlains)*
…

…Item Allowed to M*aste*r Low Baylie for the last players iij s. iiij d….   5

1575
Chamber Order Book 1   SHRO: BA 9360/A-14
ff 122–3*   *(16 July)*

10

Ciuitas
Wigorn*ie*

Att A Convocac*i*on & co*m*en councell holden Att the yelde
hall of the said citie in the councell chamber ther the sixtenthe
day of Iulij in the Seventeenthe yeer of the raigne of our
soue*r*aigne Ladye Elizabeth by the grace of God England
ffraunce & yrland Queene defendor of the faith &c.   15

the iiij gates
to be colored

In p*r*imis ffor asmoche as it is reported That the Queenes ma*i*estie will
come to this Citie, hit is agreed That before her ma*i*esties com*m*yng
The fower gates shalbe sett in some decent Colo*u*r vz. in an ashe colo*u*r
w*i*th her ma*i*esties Armes. bothe w*i*thin & w*i*thout.

for removyng
dunghills
& tymber/,
to pave their
soiles &
pr*o*vide gravell

Item That eue*r*y p*er*son havyng any donghills or myskyns & tymber   20
w*i*thin the lib*er*ties shall cause the same to be carried awey w*i*thin ten
daies next And so shall kepe cleane their soyles & pave the same w*i*th
all convenyent Spede And That eue*r*y inh*a*bitaunt of the foregate
streete, the highe streete/ the brodestreete, Newport streete & so ou*er*
the bridge vnto the ende of the lib*er*ties, the Heethe lane. Sudbury   25
streete to the ende of the lib*er*ties there, shall pr*o*vide gravell for their
soyles

howses to
be colored

Item That eue*r*y Inh*a*bitaunt w*i*thin the lib*er*ties of this citie shall
furthew*i*th whitlyme & colo*u*r their howses with comelye colours

The yeld hall
to be colored

Item that the Chamberlaynes shall sett out verry comely w*i*th colours   30
the froonte of the yeld hall w*i*th gildyng the Queenes Armes

the maces to
be gilte

Item the [fyv] fouer maces & the Aldermans staff shalbe gylte on the
hedes, the fethers & knott*es*

too pageaunt*es*
to be dressed

Item too pageaunt*es* or stages to be sett forward vz. the one at the
grasse crosse & the other in Saint Albons streete ende at saynt Ellyns   35
churche
Mr Bell to be spoken w*i*th for the orac*i*on †
Item Mr Bell as depute to S*i*r Iohn Throkmo*r*ton knyght our Recorder
to be spoken w*i*th touchyng the orac*i*on And to be rewarded for his
paynes   40

5/ M*aste*r Low Baylie: *John Combey (1572–3)*

the grasse crosse with other to be putt in colors †

Item the grasse crosse & the crosse without sudbury to be sett in colors to gether with the Kynges pycture at Sudbury gate

The baylyffes aldermen & high chamberlayne to be in scarlett with their horses & the Residue in lyuereys on fote/

Item that our Bayliffes Master Aldermen & the high Chamberlayne In scarlett & to haue their horses in a redynes at Saltelane ende in the foregate streete to meete her maiestie And to beare their maces on horseback before her maiestie. And that the rest of the nomeber of the xxiiijᵗⁱ That hath ben baylyffes. in scarlett gownes faced with blak satten with doublettes of satten on foote & the other the residue of them | In Murrey in grayne And the xlviij in their lyuerey gownes of Violett in grayne faier & comelye with the rest of the freemen & euery occupacion by hym self in their gownes & other decent apparell on a rowe on the easte syde of the said street And before euery occupacion their streamers to be holden

the lyuerey gownes viewed

Item that the lyuerey gownes of euery company of the Chamber to viewed by Master Baylyffes & their breethern to be comelye & decent

Mr Dighten high Baylyff to be alowed towardes his charges

Item That Mr Dighton beyng highe baylyff Att the next Chamber after the Queenes maiesties departure from this Citie shalbe by this howse considered either with money or some other recompence In consideracion as well for takyng apon hym the charge of his office for this yere as also towardes his extraordynary charges duryng her maiesties beyng heere.

A cupp to be bought & the gyfte to her maiestie

Item a faier cupp to be bought at London for the presentyng the gyfte to the Queenes maiestie And xl li. in soueraignes & Angells of her owne coyne or stampe

fees rewardes to be paied

Item That Master highe baylyff shall see all officers & seruantes of the Queenes maiestie to be paied their Accustomed fees & rewardes

A cupp for Master Controller

Item A cupp worthe x li. to be provided & bought to present Sir Iames Crofte Knyght countroller of the queenes maiesties howse for his councell & fryndshipp shewed to this Citie

The charges to be leveyed

Item it is agreed That CCxij li. shalbe leveyd towardes the charges in receavyng the Queenes maiestie as folowyth

In primis to be borowed out of the Threasury of the cytie xx li.

Item to be leveyed by the Way of taxe of the chamberes of the cytie lxxxxvj li.

vz. of euery of xxiiij xl s. & of euery of the xlviijᵗⁱ xx s.

wherof were paied butt xxxij li. in consideracion of ther povertie †

Item of the Inhabitauntes commoners & Cytesyns of the Cytie lxxxxvj li.

4m/ The baylyffes: *Christopher Dighton and Richard Sparkes, high and low bailiffs for 1574–5*
15–16/ Chamber to viewed: be *omitted after* to

Collectors of the xxiiij^ties charge   Richard Nicolls
                                                         Richard Dawkes

Collectors of the xlviij^ties charge   Robert Crosbye
                                                         Thomas Loyte

Item Master Baylyffes shall nominat the Assessors of the Commonaltie   5
towardes their charg⟨e⟩ as folowyth |
The Asseses of euery Warde

col 1

                                                                        10
The Highe   Iohn Parton
Warde   Stephyn whitfoot   With the constables
xx li.   Thomas Warner
                 Thomas Hareley
                                                                        15
Allhallow   Iohn Harte
Warde   Thomas Sponer   With the constables
xx li.   Thomas Antony
                 Thomas Portit
                                                                        20
Saynt   Thomas Handeley
andrews   ffrauncys Nott   With the Constables
warde   Iohn Taf⟨t⟩e
xiij li. vj s.   Thomas Mate
   viij d.   25

col 2

St martens   Thomas Adams
Warde   Iohn Archald   With the constables   30
xiij li. vj s.   William Blagden
   viij d.   Iohn Bradshawe

St Peters   Peter Humfrey
Warde   William Cullanbyne   With the constables   35
xij li. vj s.   Robert Sheperde
   viij d.   Willimus Wythe

St Nicholas   Robert Howsman
Ward   Hugh Hollynhedd   With the constables   40
xiij li. vj s.   Antony Wythye
   viij d.   William Iakson

St Clementes	Hugh Chadock	With the constables
iij li.	Harry Kynyett	

Item it is agreed that ther be [euer] in a reddynes xvij post horses
throughe the cytye & reddy to serue.   5

The highe Warde iiij post horses	St Nicholas Ward ij
Allhallow Ward iiij	St Clementes Ward j
S^taynt Androws Ward ij	
St Martens Ward ij	
St Peters Ward ij	10

ff 123–8* *(13 August)*

The order of receavyng
The Queenes maiestie with a   15
brief discource of her contynewaunce
heere

Memorandum on Saterday the thirtenthe day of August in the yere
of our Lord god one thowsand fyve hundred seventie fyve And in   20
the yere of the raigne of our most victorious & soueraygne Lady
Elizabeth by the grace of god of England ffraunce & yirland Quene
defendour of the faithe &c. The same her Highenes came towardes
this Citie from the Castle of Hartlebury wher she did rest the nyght
before, in her progresse betwene vij [of] & viij of the clock in the   25
afternoone of the same saterday And did alight at a howse neere to
the same Citie called | Whistons farme Ther to Attier her [sef] self
in that respecte of of her wyllyng good mynde to shewe her self
coumfortable to the Cytesyns & to a grett nomber of people of all
countreys abowt ther assembled, And after a litle space her maiestie   30
came rydyng apon her Palfrey towardes the said Citie And in the
confynes of the liberties of the same citie beyng at Salt Lane ende Mr
Christofer Dighton & Mr Richard Sparke Baylyffes of the said Citie
Mr Thomas Heywood & Mr Iohn Coombey Aldermen of the same
And Mr George Warberton Highe Chamberlayne of the Citie   35
aforesaid to gether with one Mr William Bellue master of arte,
supplyeng the place & roome of Sir Iohn Throkmorton Knyght

11/ S^taynt: *dittography; the scribe has written both the abbreviation and the full form of the word*

31/ of of: *dittography*

recorder of the said Citie to gether with others to the nomeber of xij
persons who had ben baylyffes all in skarlett gownes faced with black
satten And the residue of the nomeber of the xxiiij in Murrey in grayne
gownes And all the xlviij^ti in violett in grayne gownes, And all other
occupacions all occupacions standyng on a rowe on the easte syde of   5
the foregate streete, in their best apparell havyng seuerally their
streamers holden before euery occupacion And stretchyng vp verry
neere to the foregate [of] And at the presence of her maiestie
approchyng neere to the said confynes of the said Liberties, The said
Baylyffes And all the residue aforesaid on their Knees, The said Mr   10
Bellue ⌜our oratour⌝ kneelyng betweene the said Baylyffes began in
gratfull woordes & fewe speeches on the Cities behalf to yelde vp
our liberties vnto her maiesties handes by their maces, And the said
Mr Dighton kyssyng his mace delyuered the same to her maiestie,
The which, she bowyng her body towardes hym receaved, with a   15
cheerfull countenance And sayed. hit was verry well, And so the
residue videlicet Master lowe Baylyff Master Aldermen in like maner
yeldyng vp their maces & the said Highe Chamberlayne the Aldermans
staff The which all/ she receaved [&] as before & redelyuered the
The ⟨O⟩racion   same ageyne seuerally vnto them After which doone They all resorted   20
ageyne to their places, And all kneelyng The said Mr Bellue, began
his Oracion, which oracion dothe appere verbatim in the begynnyng
of this book for lack of paper | In the ende of whiche Oracion the
people cried with Lowde voyces, God save your grace, god save your
maiestie. Vnto whom she with a cherfull countenance sayde often   25
tymes. I thanke you, I thank you all. This oracion beyng ended And
as well of her highnes as of all the rest of the nobles & honourable
& others attentyvely harde And by her highnes with a pryncelie
countenance specially noted & well liked of as her gaue wytnes And
also for that dyuers honourable ⌃⌜afterward⌝ willed to haue copies   30
therof, which was doone accordynglie. The said Baylyffes aldermen
& highe Chamberlayne makyng most lowly obeysance & countenance
towardes her highnes, The said Mr Bellue (receavyng from the said
Mr Dighton the syluer cupp with his cover dooble gylte worthe ten
The gyfte   poundes xviij s. ij d. the fairest that mought be fownde in London   35

4–5/ all other occupacions all occupacions: *dittography*
16/ countenance: *mark of abbreviation missing*
29/ as her: *word such as* face *or* voice *omitted after* her
35/ fairest: *underlined in* MS

and in the same cupp xlᵗⁱ pound*es* in half sou*er*aigne of her owne
quoyne & *s*tampe the w*hich* the said Mr Dighton all the tyme of the
said orac*i*on helde openly in his hande) did p*r*esent hir ma*i*estie
therwith vsyng or vtteryng certen fewe speeche & word*es* to her
highnes good likyng   5

And she receavyng the same gaue them thank*es* most hartelie And
the said Baylyff*es* Aldermen/ orato*u*r, & the highe Chamberlayne
havyng their horses reddy by the fyve *ser*iaunt*es* apparaled all in one

The placyng of
the officers lyu*er*ey of turkye colo*u*r, mounted on horse back & were placed by
one of the gentlemen vsshers next before the Lord Chamberlayne   10
beryng her ma*i*esties sworde before her v*idelicet* next next before the
Lord Chamb*er*layne bothe the said baylyff*es*, then the too aldermen
And next before them the orato*u*r, & the highe Chamberlayne, The
sayde officers carrieng their maces, And then her ma*i*estie did ryde
foreward toward*es* the grasse crosse with lightes plentefully p*r*ovided   15
by the Citesyns at their doores besides the garde & others apoynted
by order of the howse carrieng staff torches, Att whiche crosse ther
was a pageaunt or stage verry comely deckydd by Mr Raphe Wyatt
& Mr Thom*a*s Heywood apoynted for that purpose, with three boyes

The stage at
the Grasse
crosse vtteryng verry verry good & dilectable matter in their speeches, The   20
effecte whereof do appeere in the begynnyng of this booke, wherv*n*to
The st⟨..⟩e &
saynt Ellyns
churche her highnes & the rest did geue verry attentyve [y]eare And so ended
Tho with grett cryeng of the people (as before,) god save ⟨you⟩r gr⟨ace⟩
| She still thanked the people with a cherefull countenance. her ma*i*estie

° the three
children w*hich*
prono*u*nced the
speeches wer
William Colles
the highe
shrifes sone
& heir &
William Wyatt
after Tounclarke
Iohn Wyatt° to say⟨nt⟩ Ellyns churche ende wher ther was one other stage or   25
pageaunt likewy⟨se⟩ deckyd by the said p*er*sons, Att whiche place
her ma*i*estie & the rest of the hono*u*rable with as good likyng as before
And many meery speeches & counten*a*nce proceeded from her
ma*i*estie in heeryng of three boyes ther apoynted, The effecte of whos
speeches do also appere in the begyn*n*yng of this booke amongst the   30
others before, with the like cryeng of the people and her ma*i*esties
cherefull woord*es* toward*es* the people as before And so good likyng

11/ next next: *dittography*
24/ countenance: *mark of abbreviation missing*
24/ her maiestie: came *missing after these words* (?)
27m/ pronounced: *mark of abbreviation missing*
28/ countenance: *mark of abbreviation missing*
31m/ after Tounclarke: *actually written interlinearly in text next to which marginale lies and connected by a line to its place within the marginal text*

of the matter (as beyng fowle & rayny wether she called for her cloke
& hatt & tarried the ende/

And from thence she passed towardes the Cathedrall churche. And
in enteryng in to the porche Nicholas [Bussh] Bullyngham the lord
Buysshopp of Worcettur with Doctour Wilson the deane &
prebendaries & the rest of the quyer, The buysshopp in his rochett,
The deane & the rest in their surpleses in the same porche saluted
her maiestie And one of the scholers of her schole ther pronounced *Oration*
an oracion in Lattyn, whervnto she was Attentyve & therof took
verry good lykyng, which oracion ended: she on her knees harde   10
ther certen seruice for that tyme apoynted & made her praiers And
after a gyfte geven to her maiestie in a purse of crymson velvett
wrought with gold beyng xx li. in gold in it she entered in to the
churche with grett & solempne singyng & musick with cornettes &
hakebuttes with a canapy boren ouer her And so vp in to the chauncell   15
wher she diligently viewed the Tombe of Kyng Iohn to gether with
the chappell & tombe of her deere vncle ⌐late¬ Prynce Arthur all
rychelye & Bewtyfully Adourned And from the Churche her maiestie
passed towardes the buysshops palaice And after she came in to the
grett chamber Master Baylyffes Master aldermen the said oratour &   20
highe Chamberlayne kneelyng as she came by them did putt downe
their maces And she bowyng her hedd towardes them thanked them
for her myrthe And offered her hande vnto them to kysse, which
doone they departed, And on soneday the fouerteenthe day of
Auguste her maiestie her maiestie was disposed to ryde in her Cotcher   25
or wagen to the Cathedral churche to here seruice & sermon with
the noble men & others on horseback before Master Baylyffes
Aldermen our oratour & highe Chamberlayne carrieng their maces
on horseback & placed nixt before the seriauntes | Att Armes And
then the Lord Chamberlayne carieng her sword before her ma⟨iestie⟩   30
And after her The Lord Robert Dudley yerle of leycettur Master of
her highnes horses folowyng her with her Leere palfrey in hande And
then the noble women, ladies, maydens of honour & the waytyng
maydens all on horsebak And the people beyng Inumerable in the
streetes & Churchyarde crieng to her maiestie God save your maiestie   35
god save your grace Vnto whom she rysyng shewed her self at bothe

2/ ende/: *virgule apparently serves as a closing parenthesis*
24/ fouerteenthe: *mark of abbreviation missing*
25/ her maiestie her maiestie: *dittography*

sides of her [catche] Cotche vnto them And often tymes saide I thanke
you, I thanke you all And so the Masters of the Citie standyng in their
scarlett gownes at the ende of the highe streete turnyng in to the
churchyarde her maiestie proceeded in to the Churche yarde & churche
with a cherefull countenance And at three seuerall places in the   5
Churche beyng apon the grestes or stepps she turned her self back
shewyng her self vnto the people who crieng God save your maiestie

In the Quyer
she also with a lowde voyce gaue them hartie thankes as before And
in to the chauncell And beyng setteled in her traves or seate rychely
decked & adourned in the vpper ˏ⌐ende⌐ of the chauncell next to Prince   10
Arthurs chappell And heryng a grett & solem noyse of syngyng of
seruice in the quyre bothe by note & also plaieng with Cornettes &
hakebuttes which beyng fynyshed Mr Doctour Langworthe a
prebendary ther did reade the pystle And Mr Doctour Wylson deane
did rede the gospell And whiche ended Doctor Bullyngham   15
buysshopp of Worcettur did preache before her maiestie And the
nobles & others beyng present & a grett Audience, Whiche fynyshed
her maiestie retorned ageyne to the pallace in like order as before &c.

On the
Moneday
Memorandum on the moneday morenyng The said Baylyffes
Aldermen oratour [& Chamberlaynes] with their breethern, for that   20
they had founde grett favour And were moch bounde for many
Sir Iames
Crofte Master
Countroller
desertes to Sir Iames Crofte knyght Countroller of her maiesties
howshold & one of her maiesties pryvye councell lieng at Mr Stayners
& wher he kepte his howse did go vnto hym who honourably
enterteyned them And toke them all by thandes And our oratour   25
presented hym with a faier peece of gilte enchaced plate in maner of
Tankerd ⌐with a cover⌐ worthe vj li. viij s. j d. And besought his honour
to accepte the same as a sklender token of their grett good will &
[thak] thankefulnes for his honourable favour whiche he verry
modestlie at the first refused but with some Intreatie he accepted the 30
same And promesed to love them as | his good neighbors And foynd
them in any thynge that he could do them good in that they hereafter
shalbe bold with hym

Apon Tuysday
Apon Twysday the xvj.th day of August her highnes did ryde
towardes Hynlypp to Mr Abyngtons howse to dynner with a grett   35
nomeber Amongst whom bothe the baylyffes Aldermen oratour &
highe Chamberlayne did ryde in their scarlett gownes carrieng their
said maces before her maiestie in Sampsons fylde without the forgate
(beyng a made wey) vnto the ende of our liberties And turnyng back
ageyne And lyghtyng from their horses to haue doon their duties on   40
their knees, And for that the wayes were fowle/ her maiestie said vnto

them, I pray you kepe your horses & do not alight/ And at her
maiesties commyng homewardes towardes the Citie The said Baylyffes
aldermen oratour & highe chamberlayne mett her maiestie as before
without the citie abowt viij of the clock in yevenyng And so did beare
their maces before her maiestie vnto the Palace gate, she rydyng on   5
horseback [out] her cotche beyng present & fowle weather, with a
cherefull pryncely countenance towardes her subiectes prayeng for
her maiestie, ye with turnyng her horse on euery syde & coumfortable
speeches to her subiectes did geue verry hartie thankes dyuers &
oftentymes (Every howse in the streetes havyng both candles in   10
lanternes/ torches & candles burnyng on euery syde, besides a grett
nomeber of staff torches carried on euery side of her by her garde,
which all gaue a mervelous light./

And on wendisday the xvijth day of August Master Baylyffes Master
Aldermen, our oratour with certen of their breethern did go to the   15
Lord Robert Dudley yerle of Leycettur & Master of the Queenes
maiesties horses lieng in Master Doctour Bullyngham⟨.⟩ howse a
prebendary of the said Churche And the said our oratour declared
vnto the sayde yerle, My lord, Master Baylyffes and their breethern
are come to see your honour And to bydd your honour verry humbly   20
wellcome to this Citie And in token of their poore good wills they
haue brought to your honour too gallons of Ipocras beseechyng you
to beare your honourable favour towardes this Citie And therapon
the yerle tooke them all by the handes | And thanked them hartelie
And said as folowyth. I assuer you, tis a citie That I Love with all   25
my harte And if I may any wey do it good you shall fynde me willyng
and reddy And so bade them all fare well./

And on Thursday the xviijth day of August Master Baylyffes Master
Aldermen & oratour with other their breethern came to the yerle of
Warwyke to wellcome his honour with the like present to whom the   30
oratour spake in effecte as before to the yerle of Leycettur And he
likewise gaue them grett thankes And tooke them all by the handes,
And saied This is a proper citie, hit is pytty it shuld decay & become
poore And for my parte I will devise some way to do it good And
so very hartelie bade them farewell And the same day They did the   35
like to the yerle of [Suffolk] Sussex Lord Chamberlayne, for that he
came but ouer nyght. And beyng in his bedd & somewhat disseased,

7/ countenance: *mark of abbreviation missing*
8/ with *for* which
13/ light./: *virgule apparently serves as closing parenthesis*

Mr William
Ceysill Lord
Thresarour

her maiestie
rydyng to
hallowe viewed
the horses
in pytchcrofte

At hallowe
parke

ffryday the
xixth day

Seturday the
xxth day
her maiesties
departure

sent them verry hartie thankes by his secretary but they spake not with
hym And likewyse the same day They saluted Sir William Ceysill
knyght Lord Threasurer, for that he came likewise but the night before
lieng in the deanes howse who came vnto them and did take them all
by the handes And thanked them all for their gentle curtesie.   5

And the same day after dynner her maiestie rode to Hallowparke
beyng Mr Abyngtons on her palfrey, And beyng on Hynwykes hill
she viewyng Prytchecrofte & all the fyldes adioynyng [The] the Citie
And the commoners ther did agree to kepe seuerall [for] ⌈of⌉ her horses
& the horses of her whole trayne & retynewe/ And turnyng her palfrey   10
merveled to see such a nomber of horses to gether, whervnto it was
answered by her footemen & others cytysyns beyng present, That it
was a common grounde & kepte seuerall for her maiesties horses &
of her retynewe & trayne, for the which she gaue the citie grett thankes,
Duryng which tyme [ther] of her maiesties abode here ther were   15
pastured/ by credible reporte above xv hundred horses & geldynges,
[besides] without paieng any thyng therfore savyng finall rewardes
to watchemen who kepte them day & nyght/ which was but j d. for
a horse for iiij hundred horses/ the noble mens horses were pastured
in seuerall pastures by them selfes neere vnto the citie/ And thankes   20
be to god; Amongst the said grett nomeber of horses & geldynges
not one horse or geldyng was either stolen strayed awey, or peryshed/
And after her maiestie came to hallowe parke, she hunted And with
her bowe she kylled one buck & strak [the] ⌈an⌉ other buck, which
beyng recouered she called for Mr Abyngton askyng hym, how buckes 25
be kylled, And said/ too buckes And then said she Lett one of the
buckes be brought to the one baylyffes howse And the other buk to
the other baylyffes howse, with a better good turn ⏐ which buckes
were brought the baylyffes howses Accordynglye.

And on fryday the xixth day of August in the After noone her   30
maiestie rode to Battenhall parke, Intendyng to hunt ther, but for
that she fownd the game verry scarce, she retorned ageyne without
huntyng at all and That where her maiestie was apoynted by her gestes
to haue departed from this on Wendisday the xvijth day of this August.
ffor the good likyng that her maiestie had of this Citie/ of the people   35
& of her place she tarried heer vntill this seturday the twentith day
And abowt three in the clock in the after noone her maiestie disposyng
to ryde awey The Baylyffes aldermen oratour & highe chamberlayne

25/ how *for* how many   26/ And said *for* And he said

rode before her maiestie in scarlett & in their places ⌐carieng their
maces⌐ as before at her receavyng throughe the streetes beyng
replenyshed with people cryeng to her maiestie & prayeng for her And
also she chierfully & comfortably spekyng to the people & thankes
gevyng with a lowde voyce. And havyng a wey made vp the stublefylde ₅
beynde the barne beyonde the crosse at Twexbury lane ende towardes
Battenhall Parke The freemen of the Citie stoode a rowe in their
gownes or best apparell And above them the xlviij in their gownes
of violett in grayne And then some of the [xl] xxiiij not havyng ben
baylyffes in murrey in grayne And all the rest that had ben baylyffes ₁₀
in Scarlett stretchyng to the Topp of the hill ther ⌐att which place⌐

woordes vttered [And] The baylyffes aldermen oratour & highe Chamberlayne alighted
at her
departure & knelyng the oratour spake thees Wordes, Most gracious soueraigne
beyng some what more then the vttermost confynes of our strayt
liberties to our no litle greef, with out your highnes further ₁₅
commaundement, we ar to leave your Ioyfull presence, most humblie
beseechyng your hignes to pardon all our defectes of dutie happened
either for want of Abilitie or through Ignoraunce And we humbly
thank your maiestie for your pryncely favour towardes vs, beseechyng
you to contynew our good & gracious soueraigne/ And no subiectes ₂₀
shall more hartelie pray for your maiestie Longe to lyve and happelie

all or the to rayne ouer vs, then we, Then said her maiestie Masters I thanke
more parte of
her officers you all verry hartelye for your paynes And I thanke you for the grett
seruantes cheere you made to my menn/ for they talk gretlie of it And I pray
were fested you commend me to the whole citie And thanke them for their verry ₂₅
good will & paynes And I assuer you, you all pray so hartelie for
me as I feare you will by your prayers make me lyve to longe but I
thank you all & so god be with you, And so departed with teres in
her yes And the people with a lowde crye/ saied God save your maiestie
And so proceeded towardes Battenhall And throwe battenhall parke ₃₀
through made wayes/ with a grett trayne bothe before & | behynde
And so to Elmeley Bredon wher she lay that nyght An⟨d⟩ all day/
And so Master Baylyffes & aldermen ⌐on foote⌐ with their brethern
& the whole cha⟨rge⟩ returned to gether to the tollshopp And from
thence departed home to their howses with grett Ioye, that her maiestie ₃₅
with the rest of the nobles, the trayne with the officers of the howse
⌐& her men⌐ had geven the citie so good reporte of good likyng of
this citie And of their Interteynement by the citesyns.

commendacions   And on moneday at the vttermost parte of the countie betwene the
put by her
Elmeley and the castle of Suydley in the presence of the shreeve ⌐beyng ₄₀

maiestie on
moneday the
xxij day

by her Lord
buysshops
report

Mr Edmond Colles esquyer & other[1] gentlemen of the shere ther
takyng their leave & recognisyng their duties, & of the gentlemen of
Gloucestershere ther receavyng her maiestie, She said to the Lord
Buysshopp of Worcettur, my Lord I wold talk with you/ who alighted
from his horse, To whom after some private talk had by her maiestie   5
vnto hym. She sayed, my Lord I pray you commend me hartelie
to the baylyffes of worcettur & to their breethern and to the whole
citie, And I thanke them hartely for my good interteynement And
for the good chere they made my men, And then said the Lord
buysshopp hit may please your maiestie. So it is their trade is not so   10
good as it hathe ben for the meyntenaunce of their lyvyng/ but their
poore good wills & hartes your maiestie hathe, And then sayd she,
I perceave that verry well And I like as well of them/ as I haue liked
of any people in all my progresse/ ye in all my lyff/ The which
coumfortable commendacions & sayenges of her maiestie towardes   15
this citie, when the Lord buysshopp retorned back to this citie/ callyng
for the baylyffes & certen of their breethern vnto hym, his Lordship
vttered vnto them the said pryncely & Lovyng speeches of her
maiestie, prayng them to vtter the same to the residue And so will I
as I meete with them./   20

The noble
mens names
attendyng
her maiestie
at Worcestur

Sir William Cecill Knyght Lord of Burghley & Lord Thresurour of
England
The Lord Thomas Ratclyff yerle of Sussex Lord chamberlayne to the
quenes maiestie
Th Lord Ambrose Dudley, yerle of Warrwyke   25
The Lord Robert Dudley, yerle of Leycettur & Master of the Queenes
maiesties horses
Sir ffrauncys Knolles Knyght Thresurer of the quenes maiesties
howshold
Sir Iames Crofte. Knight. controller of the same   30
Sir Thomas Smythe. Knight. chief secretary to the queenes maiestie
Mr ffrauncys Wallsyngham esquyer the other secretary to her maiestie
Sir Edward Sutton Lord Dudley
Sir Charles howard Lord of Effyngham, And Lord Chamberlayne,
in the absence of ⌜the yerle of Sussex⌝   35
The Lord Harry Seymer sone to the Duke of Somersett decessed
The Lord Straynge sone & heyer apparaunt to the yerle of Darby
Sir Thomas Sakvile Knyght, Lord Buckhurst |

⟨Buy⟩s⟨sho⟩pps

Doctour Bullyngham buysshopp of Worcettur
Doctour Scorye buysshopp of hereford   40

Doctour Cheyny buysshopp of Gloucester
Doctour Bentan buysshopp of lychefild & coventree
Doctour ffreake bysshopp of Rochester, Amner to the quenes maiestie
& electe. Buysshopp. of Norwy⟨ch⟩
Doctour Wylson one of the Masters of the courte of requestes   5

Ladyes
of Honour

The Lady. marques of Northampton Widowe Late wyff to William
Par late marques of Northampton
The Lady countes of Sussex
The Lady countes of Warrwyke
The Lady Vere sister to the yerle of Oxford   10
The Lady Bourser sister to the yerle of Bathe
The Lady Howard wief to Lord Dudley
The Lady Hunsdon wief to S (blank). cary Lord Hunsdon
The Lady Cobham ⌈wief to the⌉ warden of the fyve portes
The Lady Stafford widow late wyff to Sir William Stafford decessed   15
The Lady Patchett

            The Accoumpte of Mr Christofer Dighton high baylyff

Receytes

In primis his receytes As appereth by his billes as by his
billes Annexed more at Large appereth   clxxxxviij li. xvj s. iiij d.

he prayeth
allowaunce
as folowyth

In primis for a gylte cupp ⌈with a cover⌉ geven vnto the   20
Queenes maiestie wayeng xxix vnces xiij quarters at vij s.
iiij d. the vnce   x li. xviij s. ij d.
More in gold with the same cupp geven to her maiestie   xl li.
Item a can cupp gylt geven to Master Countroller sir
Iames Crofte waieng xix vnces & half a quarter at vj s.   25
viij d. the vnce   vj li. viij s. j d.
        Money geven in rewardes to the Queenes maiesties officers

gyftes &
rewardes

In primis to the harbengers   xx s.
Item to too seriauntes at armes   xl s.
Item to the eight ffootemen, as they say, in respecte of the   30
fyve maces offered to the quenes maiestie/ ys their fee   v li.
>Item to the Trompeters   l s.
Item to the Cotchemen & litter men   xxx s.
Item to the way men, videlicet the makers of wayes   x s.
Item to the ordynary messyngers of the Queenes   35
chamber   xl s.
>Item to the yerle of Leycesters mucisians   vj s. viij d.

13/ S (blank). cary: Sir Henry Carey

Item to the yomen of the male   x s.

Item to Osland brynger of the sworde in to the liberties   x s.

Item to Mr Gascoyne poste Master   xx s.

Item to the Knyght marshall for his fee xiij s. iiij d.

And [⟨.... s.⟩] | 5

Item to the Clerk of the markett of the Queenes howshold   xl s.

Item to his men   vj s. viij d.

Item to the gentlemen of the Bottels   xx s.

Item to the black garde   xx s.

Item to the Quenes maiesties bakers   vij s.   10

Item to the officers of the boylyng howse   vj s. viij d.

> Item to the Queenes musicions   xl s.

Item to the post maisters man   ij s.

Item to [t]hym that caried the sworde furthe of the liberties   x s.

Item to the Queenes maiesties porters   .   x s.   15

Item to Mr Morall for vj cote clothes for fyve seriauntes

& the bellman   iiij li. v s. vj d.

Item geven to them the brought the too buckes killed at

Hallowe parke by the quenes maiestie, to bothe the

baylyffes howses   x s.   20

Item to Mr Lupton for his paynes for & devisyng &

instructyng the childern in their speeches on the too stages   iiij li.

Item to his man for wrytyng   x s.

Item to George Warberton for luptons chargies his wief

& man & their horses   xxxiij s. iiij d.   25

Item to Mr Haywood for trymmyng of the sixe childern

⌈5⌉ in the too stages with xij s. [s] to the childern ⌈5⌉ for

their labour & for hurte doone apon silke borowed/ as

appereth by his bill   xxxj s. vij d.

Item to Iohn Davies for all his payntyng at the tollshopp   30

& other wise for the citie as appereth by his bill   xvj li.

Item to Mr Bell the oratour in considracion of his Iorneys

to Master Countroller to the courte at Kyllyngworth,

& his paynes   xx li.

Item to Mr dighton, for mr Bells diett & his too men for   35

xij days & his horsemeate   xliiij s.

Item to Mr dighton for Ipocras geven to the Lordes &

others of the privie councell & other charges as appereth

by his bill   viij li. iiij s. v d.

charges layd   Item paied to George Warberton & Iohn Edwardes   40
out by the
chamberlaynes   chamberlaynes for theyr bill of charges leyd out for the

citie agenst the Queenes ma*i*esties com*m*yng
to Worcett*u*r   xiiij li. xviij s.

The sum*m*
of the
charges –
Clxxiij
viij s. 4 d.

Which said seu*er*all sum*m*es to gether w*i*th dyu*er*s other
small sumes ⌐amounteth to Clxxiij li. viij s. iiij d.⌐¹ / as
appereth by his billes/ And his receytes, deliberatly   5
examyned & all thyng*es* allowed/ ther remaynyth in Mr
Dightons h*an*ds xxv li. w*hi*ch xxv li. to gether w*i*th v li. ys
alowed to the same Mr Dighton as appereth in the next
chamber.

                                                                       10

ff 9–10*   *(13 August) (Oration to the queen)*

firste began, I will brieflie dyvert to y*ou*r ma*i*esties noble progenito*ur*s
to whom this poore citie hath byn especially bounde, wherin albeit
I myght say moche, as touchyng the first foundac*i*on & peoplyng of   15
the same And howe it grewe vp to a florishing estate and of the
scituac*i*on therof, beyng alweys a frontier and Bulwarke of balde &
obedient s*er*uiceable subiect*es* agenst the sundry invasions & vndue
attempt*es* of the Welshemen, who at this day to their grett
com*m*endac*i*on & p*er*petuall prayse lyve in most dutifull obedience 20
and cyvell societie w*i*th vs vnder y*ou*r ma*i*esties most m*er*cifull
gou*er*nement, I will for hono*ur* sake begyn with worthy
worf[e] ⌐a⌐rius, first christen Kynge of Martia or medle England, who
of his Kinglie affecc*i*on towardes this towne abowte nyne hundred
yeres paste by his charter gunted & made Worcester a Citie. Abowt   25
which tyme the inh*a*bitau*n*tes here first began their marte of wooles
& trade of clothynge w*hi*ch eu*er* synce and to this day is ⌐the⌐ onelie
relief & meyntenau*n*ce of this Citie, After whom Offa. Edgar. Henry
the second. Richard the firste, Richard the seconde. Edward the
seconde and Edwarde the fourthe of like pryncelie favo*ur*, endewed   30
this citie w*i*th sundry charterz liberties & pryvileg*es* to the great
aduau*n*cement of this poore com*m*on Weale, of all whom, as we ar
bounde to make reu*er*ent remembraunce for thankfull deserte So most
especially of y*ou*r ma*i*esties nearest & dearest progenyto*ur*s namelie
that pollytike prynce, y*ou*r ma*i*esties grauntfather Kynge Henry the 35
seventhe y*ou*r highnes father of famous memory Kinge Henry the

5m/ li. *missing after* Clxxiij (?)
25/ gunted *for* graunted
26/ inh*a*bitau*n*tes: *extra minim* MS; *mark of abbreviation missing*

eight. That prince of grettest hope, Kinge Edwarde the sixte your
maiesties brother and Quene Mary your highnes dearest sister of whos
grett & Kyngly favour has this citie happelie fealte so pleased it that
second Salamon your highnes grauntfather in his kynglie person. to
gether with the Queene his wyff. the countes of Rychemonde his   5
mother And prynce Arthur your maiesties derest vncle, to visite this
citie. Wheer duryng the tyme of his abode. hit pleased his highnes
so thankfully to Accepte of the poore good will and Loyall affeccion
of the Citesyns as at this day ther remayne in Regyster of Recorde
Amongst sondry comfortable speeches witnessyng the same, And as   10
we haue iuste cause with the whole body of this realme generally to
reioyce of your maiestie and the vnspeakable benefyttes that god in
his mercy hathe blessed vs therby. So haue we specially occasion to
be thankfull to the same, not onelie for the confirmacion &
corroboracion of all our former charteres liberties & privileges. but   15
also for that your maiestie in your carefull breaste moche tenderyng
the vertuous educac⟨ion⟩ of youthe in the feare of god And with
pryncelie pittie pro⟨vided⟩ | for the needy estate of christes poore
membres haue not onelie graunted vs the havyng of a freeschoole
within this Citie, but also graciously increased the stipend therof and 20
meyntenaunce of certen poore people for euer to be relieved amongst
vs, A worke first entended by the charitable devocion of certen good
Citesyns here And now lastely enlarged augmented and confirmed
by your highnes, By thes most bountyfull benefytes by your maiesties
noble progenitours of worthiest memory and by your highnes   25
conferred vnto vs, which for avoydyng prolixitie we may not
particulerly remember to gether with the paynfull labour Industrye
and diligence of good Citesyns. This Citie of Longe tyme so increased
in wealthe substaunce & bewtifull buyldynges And became so
fortunate in the trade of clothyng, as by the onelie meanes therof in   30
good & freshe memory of man ther were here vsed and meynteygned
for the said trade of clothyng three hundred and fowerscore grett
loomes/ wherby eight thowsand persons were well meyntyned in
wealth & abilitie besides Masters & their childern? Then florisshed
this Citie and became populus, then were the inhabitauntes here no   35
lesse able then reddy for seruice of their prynce and countrey, then
frended with many, But why remember we the tyme past with such
commendacion of the florisshyng estate therof, or why do we shewe
your maiestie of thinges that Late were & now ar not with that grief
of mynde may we remember that Worcettur one of the most   40
aunncientest Cities of your Kyngdome was some tyme wealthy

bewtifull and well inhabited, synce at this day your maiestie shall see
and fynde the wealthe wasted and decayed, the bewty faded, the
buyldynges ruyned The three hundred & fowerscore Loomes of   how 160
clothyng comen to the nomeber of one hundred & threescore, and
therby above fyve thowsand persones that were lately well wrought   5
& relieved now wantyng the same So that of all that was ther. is allmost
no thyng lefte but a ruynous Citie or decaied, Antiquities such as we
see the chaunges of [f⟨.....⟩e] fortune and chaunce of tyme, All which
we wayle not with intent to crave any of your maiesties liberalitie
wherwith to be releaved especialy at such tyme as it hathe pleased   10
the same by paynfull travell to vysytt our Citie, but therby to showe
our wante of habilitie so worthelie to receave your maiestie as to your
Highnes person apperteygnyth nether bewayle we our losses to come
by any other meanes then by casually of vnlooked for trobles, as the   & Coventry's
breache of faytheles merchauntes and restraynt of trafyque, with   15   decline
trafyque beyng now restored by your maiesties pryncely providence
breedyth in vs an assured hope shortelie to see the restitucion of our
former florisshyng estate. to the hyndraunce wherof ther remaynyth
one especiall apparaunt Impedyment by the nomeber of pyrates apon
the seas And they not to be accoumpted of for seyng your maiestie 20
hathe prepared to your self so myghty a navye as neuer any of your
noble progenytours earste had the like. So may your highnes when
so euer it shall seeme good to the same very easly daunte & represse
thos Robbers that your subiectes may with safetye sayle & ⟨..⟩se their
trafyque | To the perfeccion of this hope your maiesties commyng to   25
this Citie with whos ioyfull presence, it hath pleased god to bewtifie
the same doothe bothe boo⟨..⟩ and as it were pronosticate vnto vs the
conuersion of all our aduerse fortune in to a more happy & prosperous
estate. In the ioyfull daies of whos coronacion. this worthy Citesyn
then & now vnder your maiestie Chief officer therof the whole citie   30
did so reioyce & so effectually sygnyfie the same by theffuse expence
of their wealthe as the like is neuer remembred to be doon. And
therfore no merveile thoughe their heavy hartes be now in happy
hope, and revived from the clowdy cares of their Aduertisitie, ffor
due proffe wherof may it like your Highnes to beholde the populus   35
concourse of the multitude, the greedy yes cast apon your maiestie
on euery syde the wayes & streetes filled with companyes of all ages
desierous to haue the fruycion of your ioyfull presence, the howses

christofer
dyton a
grate wise
man and
⟨.⟩arefull for
the Citie

14/ casually for casualty   34m/ ⟨.⟩arefull: probably carefull
15/ with for which   34/ Aduertisitie for Aduersitie

& habitacions Lately ryson from their rufull ruyn to a more lyvely and
freshe furnyture, briefly the vniuersall assent of all estates yelde an
assured hope, evident token & perfytt proffe of eeche good thinge
worthie suche a prynce/ So as we may soothely say o Soueraigne for
our selves & the whole body of this realme that if all iuste lawes had   5
not cast apon your maiestie the Inheritaunce & rightfull succession
in this Kingdom we myght my Lordes in merite most iustlie haue

Regum liber
1 capitulo
x° & then
she said none
suche none
suche

elected her maiestie thervnto And haue said with the prophett Samuell,
Beholde see ye not whom the Lord hath chosen and howe ther is not
a like vnto her among all the people One whom & whos most prudent   10
& pollitique gouernement with humble obedience we ioyfully caste
our cares vowyng for our partes with vnfayned hartes the willyng
expence of our goodes and lyves at your maiesties commaundement.
In token of which bounden dutie & Loiall good will to your highnes
syth habilitie is farr inferior and seruyth not to make a sufficient   15
signyficacion therof. The Baylyffes & Cytesyns heere present your
maiestie with this poore peece & small porcion therin conteyned most
humblie beseechyng your highnes to accepte the same not as the grett
alexandr Accepted the sowdiers gyfte nor as the valiaunt Artaxerxes
the litle water gyven by the symple sotte But as Quene Elizabeth in   20
whome is the fulnes of pryncely benygnytie is wonte to accepte the
simple presentes of her subiectes Whos highnes God preserue in
blessyd lyffe in Roiall raigne in Nestors yeres among vs.

at her
maiesties
departure

Memorandum That a fewe wordes vttered by oratour with answer
thervnto by her maiestie do appere in the ende of this booke, Amonge   25
other matters written of the whol⟨e⟩ Discource of her maiesties beyng
heere. Expressa per me Edward Danniell

loose insert 2
                                                                                30
⟨......⟩ at the quenes maiesties commynge to worssetter

loose insert 2v

money Ressevid and borrowed ffor the vse of the cittie as followethe   35
hearafter

8/ ed of elected corrected from ⟨..⟩3
8m–10m/ Regum...x°: 1 Samuel 10.24
24/ w written for v of vttered and first stroke crossed out

Ressevid of [xxj] xxiij*tie* of the xxiiij*tie* at xl s. the pese
amo*unti*ng to   [xlij li.] xlvj li.
M*e*morand*um* that there is vnpaid [m*a*ster hie baylie m*a*ster lowe
bailie &] mr Dedicott
Resseved of the companie of the xlviij*tie* af*te*r the rate of   5
xx s. the pese   xlviij li.
Resseved & borrowed owt of Mr yowl*es* monye in the
tresorie   xvij li.
Resseved & borrowed owt of the corporacio*nes* monye
owt of ye tresorie   xj li.   10

payd/   Ressevid of Richard Hem*my*nge for the companye of
        the m*e*rsers   ij li.
payd/   Resseved of the occupazione of the drapers   iij li.
payd/   Resseved of the wevers   xiij li. vj s. viij d.
payd/   Resseved of the brewers   ij li.   15
payd   Resseved of the chawnlers   ij li.
payd   Resseved of the showmakers   iij li.
payd/   Resseved of the walkers   vj li. xiij s. iiij d.
            Som*me* amo*unti*ng to j C viij li. the Rest vnp*ai*d Cxxij li.
Rec*eve*d of Mr Gibbes of Mr yowl*es* money byng leyed   20
out for wood ⌐wh*i*ch was at the begynnyng delyured to
Mr ffleet & Mr Iames.⌐   vij li.
R*essev*ed of m*aste*r chamberlens for one whole
yeares Rent of mr Rules landes dew att mekellmass
1575/yeare   viij li. xiiij s. 4 d.   25
           the some of all this bill
                Cxxxvj li. xiiij s. iiij d.

insert 3
                                                                                         30

⟨.......⟩ monye Resseved of the constabl*es* as ffollowethe

insert 3v

mony R*essev*ed of the constabell*es* as followythe   35
R*essev*ed of Roger strete and Rechard Whellor
constabell*es* of sent androw*es* warde in mony   ix li. viij s. vj d.
R*essev*ed of Iho*n* ashey and Iho*n* Well*es* constabell*es* of
sent petter*es* in mony   vij li. x[iij] s. viij d.
R*essev*ed of edward barbar and his fellow Rechard   40

hemyng constabel*les* of alhallow ward in a cownt of
thayr charge   [xij li.] ⌈xiij li. vij ⟨s.⟩ iiij d.⌉
R*esseved* of edward hyck*es* and wyll*iam* hylken*es*
constabell*es* of sent martan*es* in a cownt of
thayr charge   vij li. [vj s. x d.][°vj s. x d.°]   5
R*esseved* of semond bathe and Robert withe
constabell*es* of sent necollys ward in acownt of
thayr charge   [iiij li. iiij s.] ⌈v li. viij s.⌉
R*esseved* of howmfray h⟨..⟩l and Ih*on* fesher
constabell*es* of the hye warde in a cownt of   10
thayr charge   [xijj li. xiij s. iiij d.] ⌈xiij li. v s. iiij d.⌉
R*esseved* of fransses hott constable of sent clemens in a
cownt of his carge   [xviij s. vj d.] ⌈xix s.⌉
                  °Som*me* am*ounting* to liiij li. xvij s. ij d.°
                                                57 li. 5 s. 8 d.   15

R*esseved* of hewthe chanlor and his fellow
Howmfray Tom*es* stewyerd*es* of the walker*es* for thowes
walker*es* y*at* ar nott of the chamber as a perythe by a
nother bill here vnto anyxste/   iij li. xvj s. iiij d.
                                                61 li. 2 s.   20

°Som*me* of all the Resseyt*es* in bothe these bylles as
apperythe more at Large is/ | C lxxxxviij li. xvj s. iiij d.
Some of the wholl chardges   173 li. 8 s. 4 d.
So Restethe clere the some of xxv li. viij s.°

                                                                         25

1575/6
Will and Probate Inventory of Harry Smythe   HWRO: BA 3585 1575:97
mb 1 *(Inventory)*

                        The trewe Inuetorye of harrye smythe   30
                            late desessed w*ith*in
                            the cittie of worst*er*
                                1575

...
                                                                         35

mb 2*
...
Item for the players geare valewd at   xl s.
Item for the vyalls & the books vallewd at   iiij li.

13/ carge *for* charge   30/ Inuetorye: *extra minim* MS

Item for the recorders valewed at   ij li.

…

single sheet* *(Will)*

5

…Item I will and bequethe vnto my wyff Katheryne whom I do make
my Sole exsekutrix all my goods withe in my howse movable and
vnmovable that is my owne/ also I geve vnto her all my tymber where
soever yt dothe lye & my wares that are readie made & all my tolles/
also I geve vnto my boyes all my Instruments bothe vyalls & Recorders 10
& theyr boks vpon the consyderazion that they will vse theyr selfes
well towards theyr dame/…

Probatum wigornie coram Iohanne langford legum doctore et dicti
domini Nicholai wigornie Episcopi comissario executrice xxj° die   15
mensis Ianuarij secundum computacionem ecclesie Anglicane 1575/
habet exhibere Inventarium citra xxx^{um} Ianuarij proximum. deinde
[p] Septimo die mensis februarij 1575 exhibuit Inventarium ad
summam lxxxxvj li. xv s. j d

20

1576–7
Chamber Order Book 1   SHRO: BA 9360/A-14
f 133v*   *(22 March)*

…

Richard
Dyrham
to haue for
euer a parcell
of ground in
the corne
market/

Item it is agreed That a lease be made to [William blagden &] Richard 25
Dyrham ˎ⌈& his heires for euer⌉ of a parcell of grounde adioynyng
William blagdens howse in the corne markett conteynyng in lengthe
from the new streete vnto the Pageon howse lxx foot in bredeth from   ⟨K4.⟩
the said streete in bredyth three foote & di. & so nokwise vnto the
said Pageon howse & ther no bredyth for that it meetyth with the   30
sill of the Pageon howse paieng [xx s. for a fyne] for that & his porche
xx s. for a fyne & xxij d. a year

…

Cathedral Inventory   WCL: B1872   35
f 1v*

An Inventorie of the plate and other thinges belonginge to the
Cathedrall church of Worcester taken by Thomas Wilson Doctor of

19/ summam: missing minim MS

Dyvynyty and Deane there and Thomas Bastard thresorer of the said
churche and others of the chapiter the 3 day of December Anno 1576,
Anno Elizabeth xix°

col 1   5

Inprimis 3 goblettes with a couer all gylte
Intem 2 saltes gylte
Item A flatt boule gylte
Item two cuppes with couers parcell gylte   10
Item two white syluer cuppes with couers.
Item fyve spones with knuppes.
        and one other to be Answered by Doctor Lewis.
Item ix playne spones.
Item A syluer present potte for the communinion   15
Item two syluer Cuppes & a plate for the communion.
Item three garnysshe of pewter vessell.
Item 2. present pottes
Item 3. chargers.
Item 4. dosen table napkyns   20
        and 5. odde lost at thaudyte 1578.
Item 3. new course tableclothes
Item 6. olde table clothes
Item 2. table towels

                                                                                        25
col 2
                                for the quyer
Inprimis tenne veluet Cuyssons
Item 2. cussyons of tyssue
Item 4. Cussyons of freres   30
Item an olde cussyon to kneele vpon.
Item 2. pulpitt clothes of tysshew
Item 2. coueringes for the communion table
        the one of tyssew thother of flowres
Item 4. white cussyons. and 3. of   35
        white and grene damaske
Item a paule of blacke veluett
Item a canapie bought when the quene was here

8/ Intem for Item
15/ communinion: *dittography: the scribe wrote the abbreviation for the syllables* communi
but then repeated ni

Item 3. Longe carpettes to sytt vpon at Sermons

Item a white cope.

Item one new clothe for ye communion table and an other old one for
ye same

Item 4. new cupbord clothes bought by mr Carington thresorer.   5
    4° december anno 1578

players gere

A gowne of freres	gyrdles	A womans gowne
A Kings cloke of Tyshew		A Ierkyn and a payer of breches 10
A lytill cloke of tysshew		A gowne of silk
A Ierkyn of greene		2 Cappes and the devils apparell ✳

1583–4

Chamber Order Book 1   SHRO: BA 9360/A-14   15
f 156   *(19 March)*

…

Civitas   Item it is agreed that master Bailiffes & master Aldermen master
Wigornie   Chamberlaines mr Dighton mr fflete & others have the Surveyinge
              of the Pageant howse & therevppon to set downe howe far forth the   20
              buildinges shall extend & what yearely Rent shalbe reserued.

…

City Accounts 1   SHRO: BA 9360/A-10
f [157]   *(Allowances to chamberlains)*   25

…

Item of the wevers for half A yeres Rente for A Tenement
where the pageants were   xviij d.

…

                                                              30

Chamber Order Book 1   SHRO: BA 9360/A-14
f 157v   *(25 September)*

…

A lease   Item it is further agreed that Richard Dyrram haue a lease of the grant
granted to   of this Chamber of the vacant place where the pagantes do stand for   35
Richard Dyrram
of the place   the terme of threescore & one yeares in Consyderacion that he shall
wher the   buyld the same/ paing therefore yearly the rent of xiij s. iiij d./ &
pagantes   that Master [Chamberlens haue the] Baylyffs Master Aldermen &
do stand

18/ master Bailiffes: *Richard Hall and Robert Steyner, high and low bailiffs for 1583–4*

Master Chamberlens shall haue the apoynting how far foorth he
shalbuyld there/

(signed) Walter Iones

1585-6

Chamber Order Book 1   SHRO: BA 9360/A-14

f 161v   *(17 December)*

...

<table>
<tr>
<td valign="top">Thomas Wheler
the musitian to
be reteyned for
playinge the
waytes of
this Cytie</td>
<td>Item it is agreed & ordred that master Baylyffs master Aldermen &
[master Cha] others theyre brethren whome they shall rule vnto them
shall call before them Thomas Wheler the musysian and make
agrement with him for playinge the waytes of this Cyttye yearly ffrom
the ffeast of Saint Michaell vntill the ffeast day of the puryficacion
of the blessed virgin Marye, & that therefore he have such yearly ffee
of the Citie as the sayd officers & theyre brethen shall thinke
conuenient & shall sett doune vppon such conference as aforsayd.</td>
</tr>
</table>

(signed) Walter Iones

...

1586-7

City Accounts 1   SHRO: BA 9360/A-10

f [168]

...

Item geven to the Quenes players   x s.

...

1587-8

City Accounts 1   SHRO: BA 9360/A-10

f [173v]*   *(Allowances to chamberlains)*

...

...Rewardes to the Quenes players & to others, expences at the
Trynytie Hall...

...

1589-90

City Accounts 1   SHRO: BA 9360/A-10

f [182v]*   *(Allowances to chamberlains)*

...

...money geven to players...

...

9/ master Baylyffs: *Robert Steyner and Ralph Boughton, high and low bailiffs for 1585-6*

1590–1
City Accounts 1 SHRO: BA 9360/A-10
f [186]* *(Allowances to chamberlains)*
...
...money geven to players... 5
...

1591–2
City Accounts 1 SHRO: BA 9360/A-10
f [188v] *(Allowances to chamberlains)* 10
...
Item bestowed vppon the Quenes Trompeters & players   iiij li.
...

1594 15
Will of Richard Evans of Bredon HWRO: BA 3585 1594:28m
single mb dorse* *(Presented 18 May) (Inventory)*
...
A rapier & an ould [⟨.......⟩] ruffe band more bookes vz.
passio*nes* planetar*um*, mathematicall Iuell, use of the 20
globe Surveigh of land the comedie of midas 2 pap*er*
bookes, other bookes & pap*ers*   ij s

by John Lyly (1592 *prbl.*)

...

1595–6 25
City Accounts 1 SHRO: BA 9360/A-10
f [209v]* *(Allowances to chamberlains)*

...for money paied by them to the Quenes plaiers & to other noble
mens plaiers... 30

1596–7
City Accounts 1 SHRO: BA 9360/A-10
f [215]* *(Allowances to chamberlains)*
... 35
...money gyven to the Quenes players, and to Certen noble mens
players...

1597–8
City Accounts 1 SHRO: BA 9360/A-10
f [221]* *(Allowances to chamberlains)*
...

...To the Quenes plaiers, & other noble mens plaiers...   5

...

1598–9
Chamber Order Book 1 SHRO: BA 9360/A-14
f 203v* *(26 January)*   10
...

waight*es*
of ye Citty
elected

It ys fynallie ordered that the Cornitors or Musicions (in regard of
the Lord Buishops request) be allowed the waightes or Musicions for
this Citty, and att the Audit to have such benevolence or guift as
shall seeme fitt to M*aster* Baylief*es* their brethren and the Auditors 15
of this Citty accordinge to their discrecions and as they shall deserue/
And further to take the benevolence of eu*ery* Citticen of this Cittie
as hath ben accoustumed.

...

                                                                           20

City Accounts 1 SHRO: BA 9360/A-10
f [228]* *(Allowances to chamberlains)*
...

Item they praie further Allowance for wyne & suger
gyven to the Earle of Darbie the lord Busshop Sir Iohn   25
parkinton Sir henry Bromley m*aster* Recorder, for
Cheses bestowed at the Courte and ⌐money⌐ gyven to
noble mens plaiers   xxj li. ij s. ix d.

...

                                                                           30

1599–1600
City Accounts 1 SHRO: BA 9360/A-10
f [234]* *(Allowances to chamberlains)*
...

...for money gyven vnto [plaiers], the waite plaiers & other plaiers...   35

...

15/ M*aster* Bayliefes: *George Stinton and William Kings, high and low bailiffs for 1598–9*

1605–6
Rent Roll   SHRO: BA 9360/A-17
p 6*

Saint Martins warde   5
[& in all   In p*ri*mis of Mr Durant for a Tenement sometyme a
Sts warde]   pagent howse adioyninge to his owne howse   xiij s. iiij d.
of Him for a Tenement sometime Hills adioyninge to the
towne wall nere to St Martins gate   iiij s.
of Him for grounde w*i*thowt ˏ⌈St⌉ Martins gate vnder   10
the towne wall   O xx d.
of Him for the porche of his howse   O xij d.

...

of the wardens of the weavers for a howse late a
pagent howse   ij s.   15

...

1607
Indictment of John Hart   HWRO: Quarter Sessions Records 110:42/53
single sheet*   20

⟨Wi⟩gorn*ia*   ¶ Iur*ati* pro d*o*m*i*no Rege sup*er* sacr*a*ment*um* suu*m* presentant q*u*od
quida*m* Iohann*es* Hart de Anserwick in Com*itatu* p*re*dicto laborer
quinto die Iunij Anno regni d*omi*ni n*ost*ri Iacobi dei gra*ci*a Angl*ie*
Scotie ffranc*ie* & hib*er*nie Regis fidei defensor*is* &c vide*licet* Anglie   25
ffranc*ie* & hib*er*nie quinto & Scotie xl° infra messuag*ium* suu*m*
scituat*um* in anserwick predict' in com*itatu* p*re*dicto diu*er*sis alijs
dieb*us* & vicib*us* t*a*m antea q*ua*m postea in d*i*cto messuagio suo
custodiuit & h*a*buit diu*er*sa ioca illicita vide*licet* dauncinge ˏʟtempore
divine servitie celebrate⌡ necnon d*i*ctis die & anno & diu*er*sis alijs   30
dieb*us* & vicib*us* in d*i*cto messuagio suo hospita int*er* diu*er*sas p*er*sonas
male fame & conversac*i*onis honeste in magn*um* nocument*um* totius
populi d*o*m*i*ni Regis nunc ac contra pacem d*i*cti d*o*m*i*ni Regis nunc
coron*am* & dignitat*em* suas &c./
William payton proc'   35

1617
Proceedings of the Council in the Marches of Wales   BL: Royal 18 B vii
f 1v*

...   40

ffiftlie your Ma*ies*ti*es* Attournie attending this Court exhibited an

30/ honeste *for* inhoneste

informac*i*on, against one Mr Atwood & diuers others, who by Mr Atwoods encoragement, became enterlude players in the Saboth daie, in Contempt of your highnes authoritie, being prohibited by speciall warrant in writing From one Mr ffleete the next Iustice of Peace adioyning. Wee did vpon hearing of this Cause (For example to others   5 and to sanctifie the Saboth) com*m*itt them to Prison and fined them.

...

f 29v   *(15 July)*

...   10

Wigorn*ia*   Marmaduke llyod ar*miger* Enform*ant*
®Misdemeanors   Anthony Atwood &c D*efendante*s
on the
Sabboth day.

1617/18
Chamber Order Book 2   SHRO: BA 9360/A-14   15
f [60]   *(20 February)*

...

°Robert   A Lease graunted to Robert Durant of a sling or peece of ground
Durants   from S*aint* Martins gate under the Towne Wall to begin after the
leasse°   expirac*i*on of an old lease heretofore made unto mr Richard Durant 20
                his father for & during the Tearme of one & Twenty yeres w*i*th the
                reser*u*ac*i*on of ffive shilling*es* rent p*er* Ann*um* & with such
                Couenaunt*es* as are Conteyned in the former lease.

1618   25
Will and Probate Inventory of Edward Archbold
HWRO: BA 3585 1618:154
single sheet*   *(Will)*

...Item I geave vnto Mary my dawghter ... Item I geave vnto her ye   30
virginalls vsuallie placed in ye Parlo*ur*. And my will & meaning is,
y*a*t ye bedding and other p*ar*ticuler things mency*o*ned in ye former
bequeste, shall be delivered vnto her at her age of xxj^tie yeres complete,
or sooner if she shall be sooner bestowed in maryage.... xviij° Aprilis
1616   35
        °per Edwardum Archbold al*ia*s Archpole seniorem.°
            °Probatu*m* Wigorni*e* 4to Iulij 1618./ p*er*. Executorem
            nom*i*natu*m* cora*m* M*a*gistro Christoph*er*o H⟨...⟩
            legu*m* doctore &c Reuerendi p*atr*is d*omi*ni Iohann*i*s
            Wigorni*e* E*pisco*pi Vicario &c°   40

11/ llyod *for* lloyd

f [1]   *(2 September) (Inventory)*

An Inventary of all ye plate, readie coyne, chattells & goodes
whatsoever of Edward Archbold gent*leman* late whilest he lived,
dwelling w*i*thin ye precinct of ye Cathrall Church of Worcest*er* which   5
sythence his decease, are co*m*me to ye handes or knowledge of Edward
Archbold his Son*n*e & Executor: valued & prysed as heereafter
followethe.

...
                                                                                 10

f [2v]   *(Goods in the hall)*
...
It*em* one paire of virginalls   40 s.
...
                                                                                 15

1618–19
Cathedral Accounts   WCL: A26
f 77*   *(Extraordinary payments)*
...
Payd to goodma*n* Stanton the Musitian for playinge on   20
the Cornetts in the Quyre   xx s.
...

1622
Civic Miscellany 2   SHRO: BA 9360/A-6   25
p 24   *(Council order)*
...
Ballett*es* 63

Item that noe p*er*son whatsoeu*er* shall from henceforth be tollerated
or suffered to bringe to this Cyttie vppon the market days or aney
other days aney ballett*es* & w*i*thin this Cyttie & libe*r*ties of the same   30
to singe the same wherevppon much damage & p*re*iudice may ensue
to maney of the king*es* ma*i*esti*es* lege people./
...

p 28   35
...
° apres 94   71°
° No playes to
  be suffered

Item yt is ordered that noe playes bee had or made in the vpper end
of the Twonehall of this Cyttie nor Councell Chamber vsed by anie
players whatsoever, And that noe players bee had or made in Yeald

5/ Cathrall *for* Cathedrall   38/ Twonehall *for* Townhall
39/ players *for* playes

in the night
tyme nether
att the vpper
Inne of
the Hall°

by nyght tyme, And yf anie players bee admytted to play in the Yeald
hall to bee admytted to play in the lower end onelie vppon paine of
xl s. to bee payd by Master Maior to the vse of the Cyttie yf anie shalbee
admytted or suffered to the Contrarie

...   5

1623–4
City Accounts 2   SHRO: BA 9360/A-10
f 17v   *(Allowances to chamberlains)*

...   10

Item for money given to the kinges Players   xx s.
Item for money given to the kinges Players at
another time   x s.

...

                                                                                      15

1624–5
City Accounts 2   SHRO: BA 9360/A-10
f 26   *(Allowances to chamberlains)*

...

Item they are allowed the money which the last yeare by Master Maiors   20
appointment the did give to Players videlicet
To the kinges Revelers   xv s.
To kinge Charles his servantes when he was Prince –   xiij s. iiij d.
To the Ladie Elizabeths servantes   x s.

...   25

f 27v   *(Gifts)*
...

Item they are allowed for two gallandes of sacke three
gallandes of Clarret wyne six pound of ffigges three   30
pound of sugar, and for Cakes diet bread Simnells and
money given to a Trumpetor a drummer and to Poore
men for carrige of foormes and table boordes for to [er]
make a scaffold which was spent and given at the time that
kinge Charles was proclaimed in the presence of the   35
Iudges of Assizes   xlj s. iiij d.

...

20/ Master Maiors: *Elias Rawlinson, mayor in 1624–5*

1625–6
City Accounts 2   SHRO: BA 9360/A-10
f 40   *(Allowances to chamberlains)*

...

✓ Payed and Given to the Lord Dudleys Players   x s.   5

...

1626
Civic Miscellany 2   SHRO: BA 9360/A-6
p [39]   *(9 October)* *(Council order)*   10

...

°noe plaies   Item wee doe order, that noe plaies shall bee acted by night in the
by night°   Trinitie hall of the Cittie aforesaid vppon paine of fourtie shillings
                to bee paied by the master & wardens of the Companie of weavers &
°94°
                walkers to the vse of the Corporacion: [nor in the Townehall or any   15
°deuant 72°   other hall, by night vppon the like paine to bee paied for everie default
                by master maior & master Aldermen to the vse of the Corporacion
                of the Cittie]

1627–8   20
City Accounts 2   SHRO: BA 9360/A-10
f 119   *(Chamberlains' receipts)*

...

Item they yeald accounte of money by them receaued of
the mountebanke to the vse of the poore   lviij s. ix d.   25

...

1630–1
City Accounts 2   SHRO: BA 9360/A-10
f 113v   *(Gifts and presents)*   30

...

Item given to the Kinges maiesties players by Master
Mayors Direccion to prevente theire playenge in this   ✗
Citie for feare of infeccion   xiij s. iiij d.

                                                                            35

17/ master maior: *John Smith, mayor in 1625–6*
32–3/ Master Mayors: *Thomas Chetle, mayor in 1630–1*

1631–2
City Accounts 2   SHRO: BA 9360/A-10
f 124   *(Gifts and presents)*
...

Item given to the kin*ges* Ma*iesties* players beinge twoe   5
✓ Companies to prevent theire playenge in the Citie by the
appointment of the late m*aster* Maior and Aldermen   XX s.
...

f 125   10
...

Item payed to the kinges Ma*iesties* players by the
✓ appointement of the late m*aster* Maior to prevent theire
playenge within this Citie   XX s.
...   15

1633–4
City Accounts 2   SHRO: BA 9360/A-10
f 151   *(Gifts and presents)*
...   20

Item they are allowed x s. that was given to a Companie of
Players to prevent theire playenge within the Cittie as by
a note vnder the late m*aster* Maiors hand appeareth   x s.
...

                                                                                           25

1634
Report from Roger Mainwaring, Dean of Worcester, to Archbishop
Laud of Canterbury   PRO: SP 16/298
p 84*   *(November)*

                                                                                           30
To ye moste Reuerend father in God ye Lorde Archbishop of
Canterburie His Grace; Primate of All Englande and Metropolitane?
        An accounte giuen of what seruice ye now Deane of worcester
        did att His Maiesties Cathedrall there: what tyme hee first cam
        thither in Nouember Last: 1634.   35
...

7/ late m*aster* Maior: *Thomas Chetle, who had been mayor in 1630–1*
23/ late m*aster* Maiors: *John Nash, who had been mayor in 1632–3*
35/ 1634: *underlined*

5 A perfect Inuentorie taken of all ornaments vestements and
Implements of ye church as well sacra; as focalia:
6 Diuerse vestements and other ornaments of ye church as Copes
Carpetts and fronts being Turned into Players Capps and Coates and   K
Imployed to yat vse by ye direction of Mr Nathaniel Tomkins; I   5
caused to be burned; and ye Siluer extracted putt into ye Treasurie
of ye church:
...

1635–6
Civic Miscellany 2   SHRO: BA 9360/A-6
p [55]   *(9 May) (Council order)*   10
...
Glasse windowes in the Councell Chamber be mended & the same
to bee kept from drinking & plaiers †   15
Item wee doe further order for asmuch as wee finde the glasse
windowes in the Councell Chamber to bee much broken and the
Cyttie thereby suffereth much damage, And that noe plaies nor plaiers
bee suffered to haue any vse thereof nor any Tiplinge or Drinkinge
bee suffered there by which meanes those inconveniencies happen   20
but that the Chamberlaines forthwith putt the same in repaire And
the keyes thereof to bee kept for the Citties vse vppon paine of Tenne
shillings for euery time offendinge.

City Accounts 3   SHRO: BA 9360/A-10   25
f 178v   *(Gifts and presents)*
...
Item given by Master Maiors Appointement to a
Company of Players that they should forbeare to play
within this Cittie   XX S.   30
...

1639–40
City Accounts 2   SHRO: BA 9360/A-10
f [13v]   *(Gifts and presents)*   35
...
Item given to a Companie of players the 14th of August to

4–5/ being Turned ... Tomkins: *underlined*
28/ Master Maiors: *William Beauchamp, mayor in 1635–6*

prevent theire playenge in the Citie   vj s. viij d.

...

1640-1
Civic Miscellany 2 SHRO: BA 9360/A-6
p [71]* *(Council order)*

49

° x stet°

Item that noe person whatsoever shall from hencforth bee tollerrated
or sufferred to bringe to this Cittie vppon the Markett daies or any
other dayes any Balletts and within this Cittie and liberties of the
same to singe the same wherevppon much damadge and preiudice
may ensue to many of [the kings maiesties Liege] ⌐hi⟨s⟩ ⟨...⟩¬ people/

...

p [76]

...

° 74 stet°

Item wee doe order that noe plaies shalbe Acted by night in the
Trinity Halle of the Cittie aforesaid vppon paine of xl s to be paid
by the Master and wardens of the Company of weavers and walkers
to the vse of the Corporacion

...

1642
Chamber Order Book 2 SHRO: BA 9360/A-14
f 211 *(17 November)*

Civitas
Wigornie

Att a Chamber there holden the xvij^th day of November in the xviij^th
yeare of the kinges maiestes Reigne

...

Suppressia
of waits

It is ordered that Iohn Browne & his Companie of musicians called
the waites be suppressed from playing of their instrumentes about
the Citty in the morning, And that they may not expect any
recompence for their paynes And that the Chamberlaynes are desired
to giue notice vnto them of this order./

12/ s of hi⟨s⟩ *obscured by ink blot*

Households

PRIOR WILLIAM MORE OF WORCESTER

1518–19
Account Book of Prior William More WCL: A11
f 29v   *(14–20 November)*   5
...

                    Ebdomada vj.^{ta}

℃ In primis for expens*is* on howsowle [⟨......⟩]   xx s. ij d. ob.
...

Item in Rewardes to þe kynges harper   ij s.   10
...

f 30   *(12–18 December) (Worcester)*
...
                    Ebdomada x^a   15
℃ In primis expens*is* on howsolde þis wycke   xv s.
...

Item rewarded to A harper of þe dewkes of bokyngham   xij d.
...
                                                                      20

f 30v*   *(26 December–1 January) (Worcester)*

            Ebdomada j^a In Natale do*m*ini °1518°
In primis for howsolde at þe cristmas wycke xxxj s. xj d. j ox pr*ice*
xix s. iiij d.   25
Item in expe*ns*is of Mawmesey & Rumney [þe] ⌐on⌐
cristmas day at ny3th   xiiij d. iiij d.
Item rewarded to syngares of carralles at cristmas day
at ny3th   xvj d.

8/ howsowle *for* howsowld

þe sargeantes & þe Alderman sargeant †
Item rewarde to þe Sargeantes vjs viij d. to þe Alderman
sargeant   xx d.
Item payd to Richard skryuener for wrytyng   v s. viij d.
Item rewarded for carralles   iiij d. iiij d. ij d.   5
                                                         j d. iiij d. ij d. ij d./

...

Item rewarded to syngares of carralles A pon   xij d. v d. iiij d. xij d.

...

                                                                              10

(2–8 January) (Worcester)
                              Ebdomada ij^{da}
xj s. x d. .   ⦗ In primis for expensis on howsolde þis wycke þe bayles dyned with
me/ xxxviij s. ix d. ob. ⌐Item spyce al maner x s. v d.¬ j ox price xix
s. iiij d.   15

...

Item in rewardes to pleyeres ⌐childern¬ when þe balys with ther
company dyned with me xij d. Item to syngers of carralles xx d. Item
rewarded to iiij pleyeres A pon þe Epiphani day [of] belongyng to
sir Edward beltenop iij s. iiij d....   20
Item for malmesey A pon twelphday   xvj d.

...

(9–15 January) (Worcester)
                              Ebdomada iij^a   25
iiij s.   ⦗ In primis for expensis on howsolde þis wike   xij s. v d.
iij d.
...

Item payd for certen geere belongyng to Roger
kny3th   vj d. xij d. ⌐a shete¬

                                                                              30

f 31v*   (6–12 March) (Worcester)
...

                    Ebdomada xj^a in quinquagesima
⦗ In primis for expensis on howsolde   xxx s. [j d.] vij d. ob.
In rewardes to Mynstrelles Apon quyttides sonday   ij s. x d.   35
...

8/ date or festival missing after A pon
13/ þe bayles: John Smith and John Hall, high and low bailiffs for 1518–19

f 33*   *(17–23 April) (Worcester)*

...

Ebdomada iiij^{ta}

❧ In primis for expensis on howsolde   xx s.

...   5

Item payd to Iohn taylour for certen warke & stuff   vij d.

Roger Kny3thes Item payd for Roger Kny3thes coote of moteley with   *Fool's coot*
coote   þe makyng xj s. vj d.

Item payd to mawte catur for wasshing of þe seyd
Rogeres geere for iij quarteres   xij d.   10

...

f 33v*   *(1–7 May) (Worcester)*

Ebdomada vj^{ta}   15

❧ In primis for expensis on howsolde þis wycke   xv s.

...

Item rewarded to Wyett & his son Mynstrelles   xiiij d.

...   20

(8–14 May) (Worcester)

Ebdomada vij^a

❧ In primis for expensis on howsolde þis wycke   xvij s. x d. ob.

þe kynges   Item to þe kynges Mynstrelles   x s.
mynstrelles
...   25

Item for rewardes at Stoke vj s. v d. with þe
churche ale

...

f 34*   *(5–11 June) (Worcester)*   30

...

Ebdomada xj^a

❧ In primis for expensis on howsolde   xxviij s. iij d.

Item in rewardes to A Mynstrell & to danyell of
parshor xvj d. apon our dedicacion day   35

...

(12–18 June) (Worcester)

Ebdomada [x] xij^a

❧ In primis for expensis of howsolde   xxx s. iij d. ob.   40

Item in rewardes to þe pleyeres of seynt Myhelles ij s. Item to þe seyd
churche of seynt myhel v s. iiij d.

   ...

f 34v   *(19–25 June) (Worcester)*   5

Ebdomada xiij^a

In primis for expensis on howsold	xxij s. x d. ob.
Item in rewardes to Robyn whod & hys men for	
getheryng to tewkesbury bruge	iij s. iiij d. 10
Item in rewardes to T Walker xx d. Item iiij d.	

   ...

(26 June–2 July) (Worcester)
Ebdomada prima post Natiuitatem sancti Iohannis Baptiste °1519°   15
℃ In primis for expensis on howsolde   xx s. ij d.

   ...

Item to þe kynges Iogyller   xvj d.

   ...

Item to Iohn morys iij s. to Rafe of þe castell fryur mensinger   20

   ...

Item payd for ij shurtes for Roger Kny3th	xvj d.
Item to hys laundar iiij d. Item for makyng of hys coote	xij d.

   ...

                                        25

f 35*   *(Worcester)*

Ebdomada ij^a

℃ In primis for expensis on howsolde	xxij s. iiij d. ob.
...	30
Item rewarded to A Iogellar of þe kynges	xvj d.

   ...

(Worcester)
Ebdomada iij^a   35
℃ In primis for expensis on howsolde   xv s. x d. ob.

   ...

Item in rewardes to grymley churche Ale	iij s.
Item for rewardes & expensis at Stoke	iiij s. iiij d.
Item for A peyer of sheowes to Roger Kny3th vj d. to his lawnder	40
iiij d.	

   ...

(*Worcester*)
Ebdomada v^{ta}
℃ In primis for expensis on howsold þis wycke   xxij s. x d. ob.
Item rewarded to ij Mynstrelles of my lord
of Shrewesbury   xx d.   5
...

f 35v*   (*Worcester*)
...
Ebdomada ix^a   10
℃ In primis for expensis on howsolde xxj s. vj d....
...
Item to A Mynstrell belongyng to þe master of þe
kynges horsses   viij d.
...   15

f 36*   (*Worcester*)
...
Ebdomada x^a
In primis for expensis on howsolde   xiiij s. iiij d.   20
Item rewarded to A seruant of my lord cardinalles
A syngar   xx d.
...

Ebdomada xj^a   25
℃ In primis for expensis on howsold   xvj s. vj d. ob.
Item in expensis to þe parkares ale at seynt gylez with
þe offrynges   ij s. iiij d.
...
                                                                        30

(4–10 September) (*Worcester*)
Ebdomada xij^a
℃ In primis for expensis on howsolde xlj s. þe Natiuite of
our Lady.
...   35
Item to mynstrelles on our lady day þe Natiuite   xx d.
Item to Master fryur iij s. iiij d. to Martley pleyeres iiij d.
...

13–14/ master of þe kynges horsses: *Sir Henry Guildford served as master of the King's Horse
from 6 November 1515 to 18 July 1522*
21/ my lord cardinalles: *Thomas, Cardinal Wolsey*

1519–20
Account Book of Prior William More   WCL: A11
f 38*   *(4–10 December) (Worcester)*
…

Ebdomada x^a   5

℃ In primis for expens*is* on howsolde þ*is* wycke xviij s. ix d. ob. vnde
of pleyer*es* xij d.
…

(11–17 December) (Worcester)   10
Ebdomada xj^a
℃ In primis for expens*is* on howsolde xvj s. ix d. vnde xij d. for ij pleyers
…

f 38v   *(18–24 December) (Worcester)*   15

Ebdomada xij^a
℃ In primis for expens*is* on howsolde xxj s. xj d. vnde of ij pleyer*es* xij d.
…
                                                                     20
(Quarterly summary)
Expens*a* hospicij hoc q*uater*no   xiiij li. ix d. ob.
vnde rec*eved* of Seyny money & pleyer*es*   xxxj s. viij d.
…
                                                                     25
(25–31 December) (Worcester)
°1519°   Ebdomada prima in Natale d*omi*ni q*uod* exta‸⌈t⌉ in
die d*omi*nica hoc Anno
℃ In primis for expens*is* on howsolde xxvj s. x d. Item An ox pr*ic*e
xx s. vj d.   30
Item in Reward*es* for caral*les* on cristmas day x d./ carral*les* on Monday
xiiij d.
…

…Item for mawmesey þe balyes & citie beyng in þe ⌞grete hall on
crist day viij   35
Ite*m* waffur*es* þe same tyme   iij d.⌟
…

34/ þe balyes: *Edward Luddington and Richard Carn, high and low bailiffs for 1519–20*
35/ d *missing after* viij(?)

f 39*   *(1–7 January) (Worcester)*

Ebdomada ij^{da} in Circumcisione domini

…

Item for expensis on howswold ˏ⌈þis wyck⌉ A pon Neweyeres day þe   5
bali ˏ⌈e⌉s And þe brethrene dyned with me lxxvij s. ⌊vnde seyny money
iij s. iiij d.⌋

…

Item to syngers of carralles Apon Neweyeres day   ij s. iiij d.
…   10
Item to Richard chylde for Mawmesey when þe balyes &
citeyzens dyned with me   xiij d.

…

(8–14 January) (Worcester)   15
Ebdomada iij^a
℃ In primis for expensis on howsolde þis wycke xij s. x d. vnde se⟨yny
money…⟩
Item rewardes   iiij d. ij d. x d. iiij d.
Item rewarded to Wyett þe Mynstrell at grymley   xij d.   20
…

f 39v   *(15–21 January) (Worcester)*

Ebdomada iiij^{ta}   25
℃ In primis for expensis on howsold þis wycke xxvij s. vj d. vnde seyny
money iiij s.
Item rewardes to iiij pleyeres of Master beltnops   iij s. iiij d.
…

                                                                                 30
f 40*   *(12–18 February) (Worcester)*

Ebdomada octaua
℃ In primis for expensis on howsold þis wicke ix s. v d. ob. vnde iij s.
iiij d. seyny Money   35
Item rewarded to iiij pleyeres of Evesham   iij s. iiij d. / xij d.
…Item ij Mynstrelles kynges & his felow   xij d.
Item for Rumney & Mawmesey   viij d. xij d. x d. vj d.
…

(19–25 February) (London, Worcester)

Ebdomada ix^a

℃ In *primis* for expen*sis* on howsolde þis wycke *(blank)*

...

Item to Iohn harper Mynstrell A pon quyttid   5
sonday   viij d./ iiij d. vj d.

...

f 40v*   *(11–17 March) (Worcester)*

10

Ebdomada xij^a

℃ In *primis* for expen*sis* on howsold *(blank)*

Item rewarded to þe kyng*es* Iugeler & his blynd

harper will*iam* more   vj s. viij d.

...   15

f 41v*   *(29 April–5 May) (Worcester)*

...

Ebdomada vj.^{ta}

℃ In *primis* for expen*sis* on howsolde xxxj s. iiij d. vnde seyny Money   20
iij s. iiij d.

...

þe kyng*es*   Item to þe kyng*es* Mynstrell*es*   x s.
Mynstrell*es*

...

25

f 42*   *(3–9 June) (Worcester, Battenhall)*

...

Ebdomada x^a in die *sancte* trinita*tis*

In *primis* for expen*sis* on howsolde xxv s. iij d. vnde seyny money

iij s. vj d.   30

...

Item rewarded to Will*iam* benett And to his

company at þe *pro*session tyme beyng/ at batnall

with me at dyner & supper for þ*er* recreation

eu*ery* on iiij d. S*um*m*a*   ij s. iiij d.   35

f 42v*

...

Item rewardyd to synger*es* of þe towne iiij d....

...   40

(17–23 June) (Worcester)
Ebdomada xij^a

In *primis* for expens*is* on howsold this wycke xijj s. vj d. ob. vnde
seyny money iiij s.

...   5

Item to pleyer*es* of seynt peturs iiij d. / ij d. viij d. vj d. iiij d. iiij d.
x d. xij d. ⌈William taylo*ur*⌉

...

f 43   *(1–7 July) (Worcester)*   10

...
Ebdomada ij^{da}

❡ In *primis* for expens*is* on howsolde xij s. iiij d. vnde seyny money
iiij s. viij d.

...   15

❡ Item payd for a shurte to Roger Kny3th viij d. Item a peyer of showes
vj d. & to his lawnder ₐₗfor mydsum*mer* q*u*arter₎ iiij d.

...

f 44   *(12–18 August) (Worcester)*   20

Ebdomada octaua

❡ In *primis* for expens*is* on howsolde xviij s. ⌈vij d.⌉ vnde seyny money
iiij s. viij d.

...   25

Item to Iohn taylo*ur* for makyng & lynyng of a pey*er*
of sleves   vj d.
Item for a shurte to Roger kny3th   viij d.

v days

...

                                                                      30

1520–1
Account Book of Prior William More   WCL: A11
f 45v   *(21–7 October) (Worcester)*

...
Ebdomada iiij^{ta}   35

❡ In *primis* for expens*is* on howsolde ix s. vj d. vnde seyny money iiij s.

...

iij days

Item for a pety coote & a pey*er* of sock*es* to Roger kny3th
w*ith* þe makyng   ij s. ij d.

...   40

f 46   *(11–17 November) (Worcester)*

...

Ebdomada vij[a]

℃ In primis for expensis on howsolde xiiij s. iij d. vnde seyny money iiij s.

...   5

Item rewardes xxj d.. xx d. iiij d. iiij d. ij d./ a peyer of shos to Roger
kny3th vj d./ iiij d.

...

f 46v*   *(18–24 November) (Worcester)*   10

Ebdomada octaua

℃ In primis for expensis on howsolde viiij s. vij d. ob vnde Seyny Money
iiij s.

...to þe kynges Ioguler iij s. iiij d.   15

...

(2–8 December) (Worcester)

Ebdomada x[a]. aduentus Domini

℃ In primis for expensis on howsolde xxxvj s. iij d. ob. Apon aduent 20
sonday ⌈&⌉ our lady day &c.

...

Roger Kny3thes ⎰Item payd for vj styckes & A halff of Motley xx d. þe stycke for Roger
coote   ⎱Kny3thes coote x s. x d. the makyng to Iohn taylour xij d.

...   25

(9–15 December) (Worcester)

Ebdomada xj.[a]

℃ In primis for expensis [of] on howsolde xij s. vj d. vnde of ij pleyeres
xij d.   30

...

ff 47–7v*   *(16–22 December) (Worcester)*

Ebdomada xij.[a]   35

℃ In primis for expensis on howsolde xviij s. iij d. vnde pleyeres xij d.

...

(Quarterly summary)

Summa in Expensis hospicij in hoc quaterno ix li. v s. ij d. vnde seny   40
Money & pleyeres in þe aduent xxxviij s. viij d.

...

(23–9 December) (Worcester)
Ebdomada prima in Natale domini °1520°

℃ In primis for expensis on howsold xxvj s. ⸢xvj d.⸣ viij d. vnde pleyeres
xij d./ vltra A byff xviij s. iiij d.
Item rewardes for caralles on cristmas day ⸢dyner⸣ xiiij d. at supper   5
viij d.
...
Item for wyne to dyner on cristmas day j quarte of mawmesey ⸢iiij
d. to brawne⸣ for þe balyffes at ny3th in þe grete hall ij dosen of
wafurnes. A pottell of osey. & A potell of rumney/ xij d.   10
Item to carroldes A pon seynt [N] Iohns day   viij d. ij d./ viij d.
Item rewarded to William þe lewter for his syngyng & pleyng in þe
cristmas wycke nil hic
Item Swete wyne iij d. ij d. iij d./ rewardes xij d.
...   15

(30 December–5 January) (Worcester)
...
Ebdomada prima post Natale domini

℃ In primis for expensis on howsolde xxxij s. j d. vnde seyny Money iiij s.   20
Item rewarded to iiij pleyeres of glowceter A pon sonday
when þe balyffes & þe xxiiij^ti dyned with ⌊me in þe
grete hall   iij s. iiij d.⌋ |
Item rewardes for presantes & oþer ij d. xx d. iiij d. to William lewter
for pleyng & syngyng in the halydays be fore me iij s. iiij d./ viij d....   25
...
Item to syngares of carolles iiij d. ij d. ij d. iiij d. iiij d./ rewardes to
Richard tovye of london xx d.
...

    30

(13–19 January) (Worcester)
Ebdomada iij.ᵃ

℃ In primis for expensis on howsolde xvj s. x d. ob. vnde seyny money
iiij s./ half A byff ix s. ij d.
Item rewardes iiij d. ij d. iiij d. xij d. to pleyeres of seynt kenelmes   35
[vi] xij d./ ij d.
...

9/ þe balyffes: *Humphry Debitote and John Coleman, high and low bailiffs for 1520–1*

f 48   *(10–16 February) (Worcester)*
...

Ebdomada vij^a quyttyde sonday

℃ Item for expens*is* on howsolde xx s. vij d. vnde ij pleyer*es* xij d.

Item reward*es* to Mynstrell*es* & oth*er*   viij d. iiij d. iiij d. ij d./   5
v d. iiij d. vj d. viij d.

Item payd to Mawte catur for wasshyng of Roger Knytt*es*
geere   iiij d.
...
                                                                                                          10

(17–23 February) (Worcester)
Ebdomada octaua

℃ In *p*rimis for expens*is* on howsolde x s. viij d. ⌈ob.⌉ vnde ⌈of⌉ ij pleyer*es*
xij d.
...
                                                                                                          15

f 48v   *(24 February–2 March) (Worcester)*
...

Ebdomada ix.^a

℃ In *p*rimis for expens*is* on howsolde xv s. v d. ob. vnde ij pleyer*es* xij d.   20
...

(3–9 March) (Worcester)
Ebdomada x^a

℃ In *p*rimis for expens*is* on howsolde xiij s. iij d. ob. vnde ij pleyer*es* xij d.   25
...

f 49   *(10–16 March) (Worcester)*

Ebdomada xj^a   30

℃ In *p*rimis for expens*is* on howsolde xv s. iij d. ob. vnde ij pleyer*es* xij d.
...

(17–23 March) (Worcester)
Ebdomada xij^a [palme sonday]   35

In *p*rimis for expens*is* on howsolde xxix s. xj d. ob. palme sonday &
o*ur* lady day in þe same/ ⌈ij⌉ pleyer*es* xij d. ...
...

(Quarterly summary)   40
S*um*ma toci*us* q*u*arterij in exp*e*ns*is* hospicij d*omi*ni
prioris   xiij li. ij s. x d. ob

vnde Seyny Money & pleyer*es*   xxxij s. iiij d.

...

f 49v   *(7–13 April) (Worcester)*

...   5

Ebdomada iij^a

C In p*rim*is for expens*is* on howsold þ*is* Wycke xiiij s. vj d. vnde seyny
Money iiij s.
Item reward*es* to wyett þe mynstrell xij d. reward*es* at Ou*er*bury &
cropthorn iiij s. ⌐to boxes &c⌐   10

...

(14–20 April) (Worcester)

Ebdomada iiij^{ta}

C In p*rim*is for expens*is* on howsolde þ*is* Wycke xiij s. j d. vnde seyny   15
Money iiij s. viij d.
...to c*er*ten p*er*sons & boxes at hervynton iiij s. iiij d.
It*em* to mawte cat*ur* for wasshing of Rog*er* Kny3thes
geere   iiij d./ iiij d. ij d.
Item payd to Iohn Taylo*ur* for cloth. lynyng & makyng   20
of Rog*er* Kny3thes coote   [viij d.] ⌐iiij s. viij d.⌐

...

C þe kyng*es*   Item to þe kyng*es* mynstrell*es*   x s.
Mynstrell*es*
...
                                                                                 25

f 50   *(5–11 May) (Worcester)*

...

Ebdomada vij^a in Rogacione

C In p*rim*is for expens*is* on howsold þ*is* Wycke [xvj s. v d.] xx s. vj d.
vnde [seyny Money] ⌐pleyer*es*⌐ [iiij s.] xij d.   30

...

It*em* for A pey*er* of showes to roger kny3th vj d....

...

(19–25 May) (Worcester)   35
Ebdomada ix. In [die] pentecosten
In p*rim*is for expens*is* on howsolde þ*is* wycke xix s. vij d. ob. vnde
ij pleyer*es* xij d./ vltra A calf// ⌊price iij s.⌋

...

1521–2
Account Book of Prior William More   WCL: A11
f 53v*   *(10–16 November) (Worcester)*
...

Ebdomada vij^a

℃ In *primis* for expens*is* on howsolde þ*is* wycke xviij s. iiij d. vnde seyny
Money iiij s.
...

Item rewardes to the kynges joguler ⌈Thomas brandon⌉ iij s. iiij d.
...

(1–7 December) (Worcester)
Ebdomada x^a Aduent sonday

℃ In *primis* for expens*is* on howsolde þ*is* wycke xx s. ix d. vnde ij pleyer*es*
xij d.
...

f 54   *(8–14 December) (Worcester)*

Ebdomada xj^a

℃ In *primis* for expens*is* on howsolde þ*is* wycke xix s. ix d. vnde ij
pleyer*es* xij d.
...

(15–21 December) (Worcester)
Ebdomada xij^a

℃ In *primis* for expens*is* on howsolde þ*is* wycke xiiij s. xj d. vnde ij
pleyer*es* xij d.
...

Item to Mawte catur for wesshing & mendyng of Roger
Kny3thes geere   vij d.
...

f 54v   *(22–8 December) (Worcester)*

Ebdomada prima in Natale d*omi*ni   °1521°

℃ In *primis* for expens*is* on howsold þ*is* wycke xxiiij s. ij d./ ⌈vnde ij
pleyer*es* xij d.⌉ vltra A byff *price* xvj s. v d.
...

Item to syngeres of carralles xiiij d./ viiij d./ vijj d./
...

40/ vijj d. *for* vij d. *or* viij d.

(29 December–4 January) (Worcester)
Ebdomada ij.^{da}

ℂ In primis for expensis on howsolde þis wycke xxxj s. ix d. ob. vnde
seyny Money iiij s. ⌈& balys dynyd with me in þe grete hall with þe
xxiiij⌉   5
Item rewardes to ij childurn þat [tumbed] tumbled before
me & þe balyffes & oþers   xij d.

...

wyne   ℂ Item for x galandes & half of wyne red & claret spended &
fat in þe town when þe balyffes & xxiiij^{ti} dyned with me A   10
pon seynt thomas day   viij s. ix d.
Item a pottel & A quarte of Mawmesey to þe brawne at
Dynar   xij d.

...
                                                                          15

(5–11 January) (Worcester)
Ebdomada iij^a

ℂ In primis for expensis on howsolde þis wycke xxij s. vnde seyny
Money iiij s.
Item rewardes x d. to pleyeres A pon twelpff day with   20
mynstrelles   iij s. iiij d. viij d.
Item rewardes   iiij d. iiij d. iiij d. xx d.
Item for Mawmesey A quarte to brawne a pon
twelffday   iiij d. / iiij d.
...
                                                                          25

f 55v   *(2–8 March) (Worcester)*
...
Ebdomada xj.^a quyttyde sonday
ℂ In primis for expensis on howsolde þis wycke xxv s. ix d. vnde ij   30
pleyeres xij d.
Item rewardes to Iohn Harper A pon quyttyde sonday viij d. / iiij d. /
viij d.
...
                                                                          35

(9–15 March) (Worcester)
Ebdomada xij^a
ℂ In primis for expensis on howsolde þis wycke xj s. xj d. ˏ⌈ob.⌉ vnde
ij pleyeres xij d.
...
                                                                          40

4/ balys: *John Hall and Hugh Dee, high and low bailiffs for 1521-2*

(16–22 March) (Worcester)
Ebdomada xiij^a

℃ In *pri*mis for expens*is* on howsolde þ*is* wycke xij s. iiij d. ob. vnde
ij pleyer*es* xij d.

…   5

f 56v   *(23–9 March) (Worcester)*

°1522° Ebdomada *pri*ma in Annu*n*ciacione beate marie

℃ In *pri*mis for expens*is* on howsolde þ*is* wycke xviij s. ix d. ob. vnde   10
ij pleyer*es* ⌐xij d.⌐

…

(30 March–5 April) (Worcester)
Ebdomada ij^{da}   15

℃ In *pri*mis for expens*is* on howsolde þ*is* wycke xv s. iiij d./ vnde ij
pleyer*es* xij d.

…

(6–12 April) (Worcester)   20
Ebdomada iij^a

℃ In *pri*mis for expens*is* on howsolde þ*is* wycke xv s. j d. vnde [sey] ij
pleyer*es* xij d.

…

25

f 57   *(13–19 April) (Worcester)*

Ebdomada iiij^{ta} þe palmeson wycke

℃ In *pri*mis for expens*is* on howsold þ*is* wycke xxiiij s. iiij d./ ⌐þe abbot
of hales⌐ vnde ij pleyer*es* xij d.   30

…

(20–6 April) (Worcester)
Ebdomada.v.^{ta} þe Ester wycke

℃ In *pri*mis for expens*is* on howsolde þ*is* Wycke xxxj s. j d. ob. ij pleyer*es* 35
xij d.

…

29–30/ þe abbot of hales: *Edmund Greyne, abbot of Halesowen, elected 1505*

f 57v   *(25–31 May) (Worcester)*
...

Ebdomada xᵃ þe Rogacion wyck

C In primis for expensis on howsolde þis Wycke xxv s./ vnde ij pleyeres
xij d.   5
...

f 58   *(8–14 June) (Worcester)*
...

Ebdomada xijᵃ whitsonday   10

C In primis for expensis on howsolde þis wycke xxix s. iiij d./ vnde ij
pleyeres xij d.
...

(Quarterly summary)   15
Seyny Money þis quarter ⌈with pleyeres⌉   xxxj s.

f 58v   *(6–12 July) (Worcester)*
...

Ebdomada iijᵃ   20

C In primis for expensis on howsolde þis Wycke xviij s. viij d. ob. vnde
seyny Money iiij s.
...

þe kynges   Item to þe kynges Mynstrelles   x s.
mynstrelles
...   25

f 59   *(27 July–2 August) (Worcester)*

Ebdomada vjᵗᵃ

C In primis for expensis on howsolde þis wycke xj s. xj d. ob. vnde   30
seyny money iiij s. the sessheons
Item rewardes iiij d./ ...
to þe chaplen for certen causes of Roger kny3th xx d.
Item rewardes   viij d./ ij s./ viij d.
...   35

1522–3
Account Book of Prior William More   WCL: A11
f 3v*   *(Autumn) (Worcester)*
...   40

In expensis of doctor Neckham master foxforde comissary &c

Iorneyng In visitacion to pershorre lyuyng in ye townne at my cost.

...

f 4

...   5

Item At bristowe to supper bred & Ale ij s./ kychyn iiij s.
Item for wynne xj d./ to ye waytes viij d.
Item for Almes viij d./ for expensis at tauerne vj d.
Item for wynne to dyner & Supper xvj d./ for horssemete xv s. vj d.
Item for fyer & candills & drynckyng at our ynne   v s.   10
Item spended for our meles dyner & supper at
Robert pepes   x s.
Item to ye seruauntes ⌊there⌋ vj d./ for Almes ij d.
Item to ye Sadler x d./ to ye Smyth xv d.
Item to ye Sextens expensis at tauerne viij d./ to ye Sumner of bristo   15
xvj d.

...

f 61   (16–22 November) (Worcester)
...   20
                        Ebdomada octaua
℃ In primis for expensis on howsolde þis wycke xvj s. x d. vnde seyny
money iiij s.

...

Item to Iohn taylor for ij peticootes for Roger   25
kny3th with þe makyng   iiij s. ij d.

(23–9 November) (Worcester)
                        Ebdomada ix^a
℃ In primis for expensis on howsolde þis wycke xviij s. ij d. vnde seyny   30
money iiij s.
...
Item for clolthe & mendyng of Roger Kny3ths Coote   xiiij d.
...

8/ expensis: *mark of abbreviation missing over second* e
10/ drynckyng: *mark of abbreviation missing*
11/ spended: *mark of abbreviation missing*
30/ expensis: *mark of abbreviation missing over* e
33/ clolthe *for* clothe

f 61v   *(30 November–6 December) (Worcester)*

Ebdomada xᵃ aduent sonday
℃ In primis for expensis on howsold þis Wycke xxiiij s. vnde ij pleyeres
xij d.   5
...

(7–13 December) (Worcester)
Ebdomada xjᵃ
℃ In primis for expensis on howsold þis wycke xviij s. j d. vnde ij pleyeres 10
xij d.
...

f 62*   *(14–20 December) (Worcester)*
                                                                                               15
Ebdomada xijᵃ
℃ In primis for expensis on howsold þis wycke xiiij s. iij d. vnde ij
pleyeres xij d.
...
Item for A peyer of shoes to Roger Kny3th vij d. Item A fustian coote   20
to thomas herforde viij s. j d.
...

(Quarterly summary)
Summa in Expensis hospicij hoc quaterno   x li. iiij s. v d. ob.   25
vnde Seyny Money & pleyeres   xxxix s.
...

f 62v   *(21–7 December) (Worcester)*
                                                                                               30
Ebdomada prima in Natale domini °1522°
In primis for expensis on howsolde þis wycke xxvij s. vnde ij pleyeres
xij d. ⌜vltra A byff price xv s. viij d.⌝
Item rewardes to syngeres of carralles on cristmas day   iij s. iiij d.
...   35
℃ Item for swete wyne on cristmas day & at ny3th ij s.
...

(28 December–3 January) (Worcester)
Ebdomada ij^{da}

❡ In primis for expensis on howsolde þis wycke xxiij s. viij d. ob. vnde
seyny Money iiij s.

Item rewardes to William synger xx d./ iiij d./ to syngeres of carawles   5
xvj d./

...

(4–10 January) (Worcester)
Ebdomada iij^a   10

❡ In primis for expensis on howsold þis Wycke xxx s. v d. ob. vnde
seyny Money iiij s. ⌈þe balyffes & citesens dyned with me in þe grete
hall⌉

Item rewardes for caralles &c xij d. xij d. viij d./ to a seruantes of mr
wye xij d.   15

Item rewardes iij s. iiij d. to mr leylande

wynne   Item for wyne when þe balys & xxiiij^{ti} dyned with me. viz. A pottel
iij s. x d.   & A quarter of Mawmesey xij d./ A galand of Osey xvj d./ A galand
of redwyne x d.

Item A pottell of Secke at þe sesshions viij d. *Summa*   iij s. x d.   20
Summa   vij s.

...

f 63   *(1–7 February) (Worcester)*

...   25

Ebdomada vij^a

❡ In primis for expensis on howsold þis Wycke xix s. vnde seyny Money
iiij s./

...

þe kynges   Item rewarded to Thomas brandon þe kynges Iugeler   iij s. iiij d.   30
Iogolar
...

(15–21 February) (Worcester)
Ebdomada ix^a quyttyde sonday

❡ In primis for expensis on howsolde þis wycke xxiij s. vij d. ob. vnde   35
ij pleyeres xij d.

12/ þe balyffes: Richard Carn and William Serjant, high and low bailiffs for 1522–3
14/ seruantes for seruant

wyne   Item for Swete wyne A pon quyttyde sonday   ij s. viij d.
dowbelet   Item rewardes to dyuers Mynstrelles þat day iij s. viij d./ to Iohn
taylour for my dowblet xvij d.
...

    5

(22–8 February) (Worcester)
Ebdomada x^a

℃ In primis for expensis on howsolde þis wycke x s. viij d. ob. vnde ij
pleyeres xij d.
...   10

f 63v *(1–7 March) (Worcester)*

Ebdomada xj^a

℃ In primis for expensis on howsolde þis wycke xxv s. ix d. vnde ij   15
pleyeres xij d. ⌈this wyke þe vice collector was with me⌉
...

(8–14 March) (Worcester)
Ebdomada xij^a   20

℃ In primis for expensis on howsolde xvj s. x d. vnde ij pleyeres [ij s.]
xij d.
...

(15–21 March) (Worcester)   25
Ebdomada xiij^a

℃ In primis for expensis on howsolde þis Wycke xviij s. ij d. vnde ij
pleyeres [ij s.] xij d.
...

   30

(Quarterly summary)
Seyny Money & pleyeres þis quarter   xxxv s.
...

f 64 *(22–8 March) (Worcester)*   35

°1523°Ebdomada prima in Annunciacione beate marie

℃ In primis for expensis on howsolde þis Wycke xxiij s. viij d. vnde ij
pleyeres [ij s.] ⌈xij d.⌉
...   40

(29 March–4 April) (Worcester)
                    Ebdomada ijᵃ. in Ramis palmar*um*
ℂ In *primis* for expen*sis* on howsolde þ*is* Wycke xxv s. ij d. ob./ vnde
ij pleyer*es* xij d.
…   5

f 64v   *(5–11 April) (Worcester)*

                    Ebdomada iijᵃ Est*er* Day
ℂ In *primis* for expen*sis* on howsolde þ*is* wycke xxx s. viij d. vnde ij   10
pleyer*es* xij d.
…

f 65*   *(10–16 May) (Worcester)*
                                                                            15
                    Ebdomada octaua þe rogacion wycke
ℂ In *primis* for expen*sis* on howsolde þ*is* wycke xxvij s. xj d. ob. vnde
ij pleyer*es* xij d.
It*em* reward*es* to þe showe of seynt pet*ures* xij d./ iiij d. iiij d. xx d.
iiij d.   20
…

(24–30 May) (Worcester)
                    Ebdomada xᵃ. dies pentecostes
ℂ In *primis* for expen*sis* on howsold þ*is* wycke xxiiij s. iiij d. vnde ij   25
pleyer*es* xij d.
…

f 67v   *(30 August–5 September) (Worcester)*
…   30
                    Ebdomada xjᵃ
ℂ In *primis* for expen*sis* on howsold þ*is* Wycke xiij s. v d. vnde seyny
Money iiij s.
…

the kyng*es*   Item to the kyng*es* Mynstrell*es*   x s.   35
Mynstrell*es*   Item reward*es* to Iohn þe clerke of seynt Elyns viij d./ to Ric*hard*
parker at seynt ⌊gylles xx d.⌋

1523-4
Account Book of Prior William More WCL: A11
f 70 *(29 November-5 December) (Worcester)*
...

                   Ebdomada xᵃ [aduent*us* domini] Aduent*us* domini 5
C In *primis* for expens*is* on howsold þ*is* wycke xxiij s. ij d. ⌐ob.¬ vnde
[seyny money] ⌐ij pleyer*es* xij d.¬
...

(6-12 December) (Worcester) 10
               Ebdomada xj[j]ᵃ
C In *primis* for expens*is* on howsolde þ*is* wycke xvij s. ix d. vnde ij
pleyer*es* xij d.
...
15

(13-19 December) (Worcester)
              Ebdomada xij[j]ᵃ
C In *primis* for expens*is* on howsold þ*is* Wycke xiiij s. iij d. ob. vnde
ij pleyer*es* xij d.
...
20

f 70v
...
Item for carralls on cristmas day fryday & seynt sthevens
day.   xij d. 25
Item A pottel of rumney on cristmas day at ny3th þe balys
& ⌐þe¬ xxiiijᵗⁱ· in þe grete hall   vj d.
Item for wafur*es* at þat tyme   ij d.

(20-6 December) (Worcester) 30
              Ebdomada xiijᵃ in þe cristmas wocke
C Item for expens*is* on howsolde in þe Cristmas wycke ⌐þe day A pon
fryday¬ xx s. xj d. ob. vnde ij pleyer*es* ⌊xij d.⌋

(Quarterly summary) 35
S*umm*a toci*us* q*u*arterij in Expens*is* hospicij   x li. xvj s. viij d.
vnde seyny Money & pleyer*es* þ*is* q*u*arter   x li. j s. viij d.
...

26/ þe balys: *Hugh Dee and Richard Billford, high and low bailiffs for 1523-4* f 70v   *(27 December–2 January) (Worcester)*

°1523° Ebdomada jᵃ post Natale*m* Do*m*i*ni*.
seynt Ioh*anne*s day sonday

ℭ In p*r*imis for expen*sis* on howsolde þis Wycke xxv s. viij d. vnde seyny   5
Money iiij s. ⌜//Item An Ox p*r*ice xx s.⌝
Item rewarde*s* for caralle*s*   x. d. xij d. vj d.
                                                                     viij d. viij d.

...
                                                                                          10

f 71   *(10–16 January) (Worcester)*

Ebdomada iij.ᶜⁱᵃ
ℭ In p*r*imis for expen*sis* on howsolde þis wycke xij s. ix d. vnde seyny
Money/ iiij s.   15

...

Item rewarde*s* vj d. ⌜to broke þe mynstrell⌝/
to þe ij scholar*es*   iij s. iiij d./ viij d./ vj d.
                                                       iiij d. vj d. vj d.

...   20
Item to Mawte cat*ur* for wasshyng of Roge*r* knyghte*s*
geere   iiij d.

...

f 71v*   *(7–13 February) (Worcester)*   25

Ebdomada vijᵃ   [qy] quyttyde sonday
ℭ In p*r*imis for expen*sis* on howsold þis wycke xxj s. v d./ vnde ij pleyer*es*
xij d.
Item in rewarde*s* to Mynstrelle*s* on quyttyde sonday   xx d./ xij d./   30
                                                                     iiij d. xij d.

...

(14–20 February) (Worcester)
Ebdomada octaua   35
ℭ In p*r*imis for expen*sis* on howsold þis wycke xj s. vnde [ij] ij pleyer*es*
xij d.

...

(21–7 February) (Worcester)
Ebdomada ix^a

℃ In primis for expensis on howsold þis wycke xiij s. xj d. ob. vnde ij
pleyeres xij d.

...   5

(28 February–5 March) (Worcester)
Ebdomada x^a

℃ In primis for expensis on howsold þis wycke xxj s. ob. vnde ij pleyeres
xij d.   10

...

⟨......⟩ a New sewte to Roger Kn⟨y3th.....⟩

f 72   *(6–12 March) (Worcester)*

15

Ebdomada xj^a

℃ In primis for expensis on howsold þis wycke xij s. xj d. ob. vnde ij
pleyeres xij d.

...   20

(13–19 March) (Worcester)
Ebdomada xij^a [pal]

℃ In primis for expensis on howsold þis wycke xiij s. ix d. vnde ij pleyeres
xij d.

...   25

(20–6 March) (Worcester)
Ebdomada xiij^a in ramis palmarum

℃ In primis for expensis on howsold ˌ⌐þis¬ wycke xxiiij s. iij d. vnde ij
pleyeres xij d.   30

...

f 72v*   *(Quarterly summary)*

...

Summa tocius quarterij in Expensis hospicij   xij ˌ⌐li.¬ v s. vij d.   35
vnde seyny Money & pleyeres   xxxj s.

...

(3–9 April) (Courting)
Ebdomada ij^{da} beyng at courtyng

℃ In primis for expensis on howsold þis wycke xj s. ix d. vnde seyny
Money iij s. iiij d.
Item to tumbleres   viij d. iiij d. xij d.   5
…

f 73   *(17–23 April) (Courting)*
…
Ebdomada iiij.ª beyng at courtyng   10

℃ Item for expensis þis wycke on howsolde vj s. x d. ob. vnde seyny
Money iiij s.
In rewardes to Thomas þe kynges Ioguler   iij s. iiij d. / xij d. xij d.
…

                                                                  15

(1–7 May) (Worcester)
Ebdomada vj^{ta} the rogacion wycke

℃ In primis for expensis on howsold þis wycke xxiij s. x d. vnde ij
pleyeres xij d.
…   20

f 73v   *(15–21 May) (Worcester)*

Ebdomada octaua dies pentecoste

℃ In primis for expensis on howsolde þis wycke xxvij s. vij d. vnde ij 25
pleyeres xij d.
…

ff 74v–5*   *(17–23 July) (Crowle)*
…   30
Ebdomada iiij.^{ta} at crowle

℃ In primis for expensis on howsolde þis wycke xviij s. ob. vnde seyny
Money ⌊iiij s.⌋//
…
Item to wyett þe Mynstrell viij d./ …   35
…

(24–30 July) (Crowle)

Ebdomada v.^{ta} at crowle

℃ In *pr*imis for expen*sis* on howsolde þ*is* wyff xix s. ix d. ob. vnde seyny
money ⌐iiij s.⌐//

...   5

þe kyng*es*   Item to þe kyng*es* Mynstrell*es*   x s.
Mynstrell*es*
...

1524–5
Account Book of Prior William More   WCL: A11   10
f 76v*   *(2–8 October) (Grimley)*

...

Ebdomada .ij.^{da} at grymley

℃ In *pr*imis for expen*sis* on howsold þis wycke xiiij s. iiij d./ vnde seyny
Money .iiij s.   15

...

þe kyng*es*   Item to Iohn Englisshe & othe*r* þe kyng*es* pleyer*es*   x s.
pleyer*es*
...

f 77v   *(27 November–3 December) (Worcester)*   20

...

Ebdomada x.^a aduen*tus* do*m*ini at w*ur*ceter

℃ In *pr*imis for expen*sis* on howsold þis wycke xxv s. x d. vnde ij pleyer*es*
xij d.
...   25

(4–10 December) (Worcester)

Ebdomada xj.^a at W*ur*ceter

℃ In *pr*imis for expen*sis* on howsold þis wycke xix s. viij d./ vnde ij
pleyer*es* xij d.   30
...

(11–17 December) (Worcester)

Ebdomada xij^a at W*ur*ceter

℃ In *pr*imis for expen*sis* on howsold þis wycke xiiij s. ix d. vnde ij   35
pleyer*es* xij d.
...

3/ wyff *for* wycke

(18–24 December) (Worcester)
Ebdomada xiij.ª at Wurceter

℃ In primis for expensis on howsold þis wycke xv s. x d. vnde ij pleyeres
xij d.

...   5

f 78   *(Quarterly summary)*

...

Summa tocius quarterij in Expensis Hospicij xj li. iiij s. xj d. vnde
seyny money ⌐&⌐ pleyeres þis quarter xxxix s. iiij d.   10

...

(25–31 December) (Worcester)
°1524° Ebdomada prima in Natale Domini

℃ In primis for expensis on howsolde þis wycke xxxv s. j d. ⌐þe balys   15
dyned with me seynt Iohn day⌐
Item An Ox. price xvj d./ ij pleyeres ⌐xij d.⌐

...

Item to syngeres of caralles   ij d. iiij d. xij d.
                                                vij d. vj d. iiij d.   20
wyne   Item for wyne for þe baylis & citezens on cristmas Day after
        Euensong/ a pottel of Mawmesey. viij d./ A pottell of Rumney vj
        d./ A pottell off Rynneshewyne viij d.

...

wyne   Item for wy[s]yne when þe baylys & dyuers of þe worshipfulles xj   25
        dyned with me on seynt ⌊Iohns day iiij s. viij d.⌋

...

f 80v   *(16–22 April) (Worcester)*
...   30
Ebdomada iiij^{ta} in pascha at Wurceter

℃ In primis for expensis on howsold þis wycke   xxxv s.
Item rewardes ij s./ iiij d. iiij d. to þe kynges berewarde xx d./ iiij
d./ iiij d./ iiij d.

...   35

<hr>

15/ þe balys: *John Coleman and Walter Stone, high and low bailiffs for 1524–5*

f 81   *(7–13 May) (Crowle)*

...

Ebdomada vijᵃ at crowle

℃ In *primis* for expen*sis* on howsold þ*is* wycke xx s. ij d. vnde seyny
money iiij s.   5

...

þe kyng*es*
Mynstrell*es*

Item to þe kyng*es* mynstrell*es* x s.

...

f 81v   *(21–7 May) (Worcester)*   10

...

Ebdomada ixᵃ Rogacion wycke at w*u*rceter

℃ In *primis* for expen*sis* on howsold þ*is* wycke xxiiij s. iij d. vnde ij
pleyer*es* xij d.

...   15

(4–10 June) (Worcester)

Ebdomada xjᵃ at w*u*rceter d⟨ie⟩ pentecosten

℃ In *primis* for expen*sis* on howsolde þ*is* wycke xxix s. ij d. vnde ij
pleyer*es* xij d.   20

...

Item to thomas brandon þe kyng*es* Ioogler & *ser*uant   iij s. viij d.

...

f 82*   *(11–17 June) (Worcester)*   25

Ebdomada xijᵃ at w*u*rceter trinite sonday

℃ In *primis* for expen*sis* on howsolde þ*is* wycke xxxj s. x d. ob. vnde
seyny money iiij s.
Item reward*es* to vij dawncer*es* of claynes on trinite sonday xx d.   30

...

f 84*   *(17–23 September) (Battenhall)*

Ebdomada xiijᵃ at batnall   35

℃ In *primis* for expen*sis* on howsold þ*is* wycke xvij s. ij d. vnde seyny
Money iiij s.
Item to the pryncesse Mynstrell*es*   iiij s./

...

18/ pentecosten *for* pentecostes

1525-6
Account Book of Prior William More   WCL: A11
f 86   *(3-9 December) (Battenhall, Worcester)*

Ebdomada x^a advent sonday at batnall & wurceter

5

℃ In *pri*mis for expens*is* on howsolde þ*is* wycke [xv s. xij d. ob.] ⌐xxix
s. xj d.⌐. vnde ij pleyer*es* xij d.
Ite*m* to Mynstrell*es* viij d./ xx d./...

...

10

(10-16 December) (Battenhall)
Ebdomada xj.^a at batnall

℃ In *pri*mis for expens*is* on howsolde þ*is* wycke xv s. iiij d. ob. vnde
ij pleyer*es* xij d.

...

15

f 86v   *(Quarterly summary)*

...

S*um*ma toci*us* quart*er*ij in expens*is* hospicij xj li. viij d./ vnde seyny
money & pleyer*es*. xxxvij s. iiij d.

20

...

(24-30 December) (Worcester)
°1525°   Ebdomada *pri*ma in Natale d*omi*ni at w*ur*ceter

℃ In *pri*mis for expens*is* on howsold þ*is* wycke xxxiiij s. viij d. ob. vnde   25
ij pleyer*es* ⌐xij d.⌐
...to synger*es* of carrall*es* on cristmas day xvj d.
Item to synger*es* of carrall*es* on seynt sthevens day   viij d./ viij d.

wyne   Item for wyne owt of þe towne for þe balys
& oth*er*s   iij s. vj d./ ⌐viij d.⌐   30
                                                     viij d. viij d.

f 87*   *(31 December-6 January) (Worcester)*

Ebdomada ij^{da} newer*es* yeven   35
at W*ur*ceter þe balis & ⌐all⌐ skarlett gownes dyned w*ith* me
℃ Item for expens*is* on howsolde þ*is* wycke xxvj s. ix d. ob. [ij pleyer*es*]
seyny Money iiij s.

29/ þe balys: *Philip Haverd and William Harden, high and low bailiffs for 1525-6*

Item to iiij pleyeres iij s. iiij d./ ...

...

f 87v*   (11–17 February) (Worcester)

...   5

Ebdomada octaua at wurceter þe princes
beyng here quyttyde sonday

℃ In primis for expensis on howsolde xxij s. iij d. [vnde ij]

Item rewardes to Mynstrelles xx d./ rewardes to certen of

þe princes seruantes   vj s. viij d.   10

Item rewardes   viij d./ xx d. viij d. xij d.

...

f 88   (18–24 February) (Worcester)

...   15

Ebdomada ix^a at Wurceter þe princes beyng here

℃ In primis for expensis on howsolde þis wycke xiij s. vij d./ vnde ij

pleyeres xij d.

...

                                                                                20

(25 February–3 March) (Worcester)

Ebdomada [i]x.^{a} at Wurceter the princes beyng at batnall

℃ In primis for expensis on howsolde þis wycke xj s. x d. xix d./ vnde

ij pleyeres xij d.   25

...

(4–10 March) (Worcester)

Ebdomada xj^a at wurceter the prynces beyng at batnall   30

℃ In primis for expensis on howsold xj s. x d./ vnde ij pleyeres

xij d.

...

f 88v   (11–17 March) (Worcester)   35

Ebdomada xjj^a at wurceter. the princes beyng at batnall

℃ In primis for expensis on howsold þis wycke xiij s. ob. vnde ij pleyeres

xij d.

...   40

(18–24 March) (Worcester)

   Ebdomada xiij at w*ur*ceter. the princes beyng at batnall
⟪ In p*ri*mis for expens*is* on howsolde þ*is* wycke xvij s. [v] x d. ob. vnde
ij pleyer*es* xij d.   5
…

(Quarterly summary)

Seyny money ₍ᴧ₎ ⌜& pleyer*es*⌝ this quarter   xxix s. iiij d. 10
…

f 89 *(1–7 April) (Worcester)*
…
    Ebdomada ij.ᵈᵃ at w*ur*ceter. þe prynces   15
      beyng at w*ur*ceter Ester day
⟪ In p*ri*mis for expens*is* on howsold þ*is* wycke xxx s. ob. vnde ij pleyer*es*
xij d.
…
                           20

f 89v *(22–8 April) (Grimley)*
…
    Ebdomada v.ᵗᵃ at grymley
⟪ In p*ri*mis for expens*is* on howsold þ*is* wycke xviij s. x d. vnde seyny
money iiij s.   25
…

the kynges Item reward*es* to þe kyng*es* Mynstrell*es* x s. to A noþ*er* Minstrel viij d.
Mynstrel*es*
…

(6–12 May) (Worcester)   30

    Ebdomada vijᵃ at w*ur*ceter þe rogacion wycke
⟪ In p*ri*mis for expens*is* on howsold þ*is* wycke xxv s. viij d. / ij pleyer*es*
xij d.
In reward*es* to þe princes s*er*uant*es* to þe wyne xij d. /
Item ⌜daunc*e*r*es*⌝   xij d. / viij d. 35
Item to bery by A byll   iij s. iiij d. ij d.
the prynces Item to the prynces pleyer*es* vj s. / reward*es* viij d.
pleyer*es*
…

f 90   *(20–6 May) (Worcester, Battenhall)*
...

Ebdomada Nona at Wurceter & parte at batnall/
ebdomada pentecosten

℃ In primis for expensis on howsold þis wycke xxvij s. j d. vnde ij   5
pleyeres xij d.
...

f 92   *(19–25 August) (Worcester)*
...   10

   Ebdomada ixᵃ at wurceter þe princes beyng here til wennesday.
℃ In primis for expensis on howsolde þis wycke xxxj s. iij d. ob. vnde
seyny mo⌊ney⌋ ⌐iiij s.⌐
Item to thomas brandon the kynges Ioguler   iij s. iiij d.
...   15

1526–7
Account Book of Prior William More   WCL: A11
f 93v*   *(7–13 October) (Worcester)*
...   20

Ebdomada ij.ᵈᵃ at wurceter

℃ In primis for expensis on howsold xxiij s. vj d. ob./ seyny Money iiij s.
...

Mynstrelles   Item to þe princesse Mynstrelles   iij s. iiij d.
...   25

f 95   *(27 January–2 February) (Worcester)*

Ebdomada vjᵗᵃ at wurceter

℃ In primis for expensis on howsolde þis wycke xxiiij s. viij d./ vnde   30
seyny money iiij s.
...

Item to my lady princes mynstrell   xx d.
...
                                                                                 35

f 95v   *(3–9 March) (Worcester, Grimley)*
...

Ebdomada xj.ᵃ quyttyde sonday/ parte at grymley

℃ In primis for expensis on howsolde þis wycke xxvj s. iij d. ob./ vnde
[seyny] Money ⌐ij pleyeres⌐ xij d.   40

4/ pentecosten *for* pentecostes

In rewardes on Mynstrelles   xx d./ viij d.// viij d.
...

f 96   *(10–16 March) (Grimley)*

                           Ebdomada xij^a quadragesima at grymley

℃ In primis for expensis on howsold þis wycke xxj s. viij d. ij pleyeres
xij d.
...

(17–23 March) (Grimley)
                      Ebdomada xiij.^{a} at grymley

℃ In primis for expensis on howsolde þis wycke xxiiij s. viij d./ vnde
ij pleyeres ⌐xij d.⌐
...

f 96v   *(24–30 March) (Grimley)*

            °1527° Ebdomada prima in Annunciacione beate marie
                              at grymley

℃ In primis for expensis on howsold þis wycke xxiij s. vij d./ vnde ij
pleyeres ⌐xij d.⌐
...

(31 March–6 April) (Grimley)
                      Ebdomada ij.^{da} at grymley

℃ In primis for expensis on howsold xxij s. ij d./ vnde ij pleyeres xij d.
...

(7–13 April) (Grimley)
                 Ebdomada iij.^{a} at grymley. in passione domini

℃ In primis for expensis þis wycke xxx s. xj d./ vnde ij pleyeres xij d.
...

f 97   *(14–20 April) (Worcester)*

                 Ebdomada iiij^{ta} in ramis palmarum at wurceter

℃ In primis for expensis on howsold þis wycke xxxiiij s. j d. vnde ij
pleyeres xij d.
...

(21–7 April) (Worcester, Battenhall)
         Ebdomada v.ᵗᵃ pascha. at wᵣceter & batnall
Item for expensᵢₛ on howsolde þᵢₛ wycke xxxiij s. ix d./ ij pleyerₑₛ xij d.
…

                                                              5

f 97v   *(28 April–4 May) (Grimley)*

             Ebdomada vj.ᵗᵃ low sonday at grymley
℃ In primis for expensᵢₛ on howsold þᵢₛ wycke xxij s. iij d. ob. vnde
seyny money ⌈iiij s. viij d.⌉   10
…
Item to þe may[⟨.⟩]dens at grymley for syngyng on
maye day   xvj d./ xij d.
…

                                                              15

(19–25 May) (Grimley)
             Ebdomada ix.ᵃ at grymley
℃ In primis for expensᵢₛ on howsold þᵢₛ wycke xxix s. iij d. ob./ vnde
seyny money ⌈iiij s. viij d.⌉
…   20

f 98
…
        ⟨þe kyn⟩gₑₛ   Item to the kyngₑₛ mynstrellₑₛ   x. s.
        mynstrellₑₛ   …   25

(26 May–1 June) (Worcester)
         Ebdomada x.ᵃ at wᵣceter þe rogacion wycke
℃ In primis for expensᵢₛ on howsold þᵢₛ wycke xxiij s. ix d. ob./ vnde
ij pleyerₑₛ xij d.   30
…

(9–15 June) (Worcester)
         Ebdomada xijᵃ at Wᵣceter in pentecosten
℃ In primis for expensᵢₛ on howsolde þᵢₛ wycke xxx s. viij d. ob./ ij 35
pleyerₑₛ xij d.
…

f 99v*   *(18–24 August) (Crowle)*

...

Ebdomada ix.ª at crowle

ℭ In primis for expensis on howsolde þis wycke xxiij s. ij d. ob./ vnde
seyny money ⌐iiij s. viij d.⌐   5

the kynges   Item to the kynges pleyeres. Iohn slye & his company   vj s. viij d.
pleyeres
...

1527–8
Account Book of Prior William More   WCL: A11   10
f 101   *(6–12 October) (Grimley)*

Ebdomada ij.ᵈᵃ at grymley

ℭ In primis for expensis on howsold þis wycke xxv s. v d. ob./ vnde
seyny Money ⌐iiij s. viij d.⌐   15
...

branden   Item to thomas brandan þe kynges Iogeller at grymley   iij s. iiij d.
þe Iogyller   Item to his chylde for tumblyng   viij d.
...

                                                                              20

f 102v   *(1–7 December) (Battenhall)*

Ebdomada x.ª advent sonday/ At batnall

ℭ In primis for expensis on howsolde þis wycke xxxij s. x d.// ⌐ij pleyeres
xij d.⌐   25
...

(8–14 December) (Battenhall)
Ebdomada xjª at batnall die concepcionis beate marie

ℭ In primis for expensis on howsolde þis wycke xxiiij s. v d. ij pleyeres   30
xij d.
...

(15–21 December) (Battenhall)
Ebdomada xij.ª at batnall   35

ℭ In primis for expensis on howsolde þis wycke xvj s. xj d./ vnde ij
pleyeres xij d.
...

f 103v   *(22–8 December) (Worcester)*

°1527° Ebdomada prima in Natale Domini. hoc Anno
exstat ⟨die⟩ mercurij

℃ In primis for expensis on howsold þis cristmas wycke iij li. vij d. ob./   5
ij pleyeres ⌐xij d.⌐
Item rewardes to William poole   xx d. xij d.
Item for syngyng of carrolles on cristmas day & to
Mynstrelles   ij s. vj d. xvj d.
...   10

Item for wyne for þe baylys x d. for wafferres ⌐iij dosen⌐ & cakes vj d.
wyne   Item for swete wyne at dyner & supper [& oþer]
cristmas wycke   iij s. iij d.
...
                                                                            15

f 103v   *(29 December–4 January) (Battenhall)*
...
Ebdomada ij.ᵈᵃ seynt thomas day at batnall
℃ In primis for expensis on howsold þis wycke xxxj s. iiij d./ vnde seyny
Money ⌐iiij s.⌐//.   20
...

Item to [re] Mynstrelles & syngeres of carralles   xij d./ iiij d.
...

(5–11 January) (Battenhall)   25
Ebdomada iij.ᵃ xijᵗʰ yeven/ at batnall
℃ In primis for expensis on howsolde xxix s. vj d. vnde seyny Money
iiij s. viij d.
Item rewardes for carralles xij d./ to mynstrelles ij s./
...   30
wyne   Item Swete wyne & other wyne on twelfday   ij s. viij d. ij.d. ij d.
...

f 104v   *(2–8 February) (Battenhall)*
...   35
Ebdomada vijᵃ candilmas day at batnall
℃ In primis for expensis on howsold þis wycke xxviij s. xj d. vnde seyny
money iiij s.
...

11/ þe baylys: *Richard Billford and Thomas Bullingham, high and low bailiffs for 1527–8*

Item to A Iogeller   xij d.

...

f 105   *(23–9 February) (Grimley)*

...   5

              Ebdomada x.ᵃ quyttydes sonday. at grymley

C In primis for expensis on howsolde xxviij s. xj d. ob. vnde ij pleyeres
xij d.

...

mynstrelles   Item to Mynstrelles on quyttyde sonday   ij s.   10

wyne   Item for ij galandes of wyne on quyttyde sonday to dyner ij s./ a
quarte of mawme⌊sey iiij d.⌋

...

(1–7 March) (Grimley)   15

              Ebdomada xj.ᵃ at grymley

C In primis for expensis on howsold xxiiij s. viij d. ob. vnde ij pleyeres
xij d.

...

                                                                         20

f 105v   *(8–14 March) (Grimley)*

...

              Ebdomada xij.ᵃ at grymley

C In primis for expensis on howsolde þis wycke xix s. x d. vnde ij pleyeres
xij d.   25

...

(15–21 March) (Grimley)

              Ebdomada xiij.ᵃ at grymley seynt benettes day.

C In primis for expensis on howsold xxj s. xj d./ vnde [seyny] ⌜pleyeres⌝   30
Money xij d.

...

(Quarterly summary)

Summa tocius quarterij in Expensis hospicij xviij li. ⟨iij s. xj d.⟩ vnde   35
seyny money & pleyeres xlj s.

...

f 106   *(22–8 March) (Grimley)*

°1528° Ebdomada prima in Annunciacione Anno [domini]
henrici octaui xix° at grymley
C In primis for expensis on howsolde xxviij s. x d. ob./ vnde ij pleyeres   5
xij d.
…

(29 March–4 April) (Grimley)
Ebdomada ijᵈᵃ at grymley paussheon sonday   10
C In primis for expensis on howsolde xxiiij s. ix d./ vnde ij pleyeres xij d.
…

(5–11 April) (Worcester)
Ebdomada iij.ᵃ palme sonday/ at wurceter   15
C In primis for expensis on howsolde þis wycke xxiij s. x d. ob./ vnde
ij pleyeres. xij d.
…

f 106v   *(12–18 April) (Worcester, Grimley)*   20
…
Ebdomada iiij.ᵗᵃ Ester day at wurceter & grymley
C In primis for expensis on howsold þis wycke xxxvij s. v d. vnde ij
pleyeres xij d.
…   25

f 107   *(26 April–2 May) (Grimley)*
…
Ebdomada vj.ᵗᵃ at grymley
C In primis for expensis on howsolde þis wycke xxxv s./ vnde seyny   30
money .iiij s. viij d.
Item to a mynstrell of sir george throckmorton   xij d./
Item rewardes viij d. viij d./ on may day to maydens at grymley
xvj d./ xij d.
…   35

(3–9 May) (Crowle)
Ebdomada vij.ᵃ at crowle
C In primis for expensis on howsold þis wycke xxxvij s. j d. ob. vnde
seyny Money iiij s.   40

Item rewardes iiij s./ to þe box at bredicote viij d./ to harry dewrant
xx d./ xij d.

Item to syngeres on may day at wurceter   xij d./ iiij d.

...

Item to þe Mayndens ⌈box⌉ at crowle   viij d./   5

...

the kynges   Item to kynges Mynstrelles   x s.
Mynstrelles
...

f 107v   *(17–23 May)* *(Worcester, Battenhall)*   10

...

       Ebdomada ixª Rogacion wycke at wurceter and batnall
℃ In primis for expensis on howsolde þis wycke xxxij s. j d. vnde ij
pleyeres xij d.

...   15

(31 May–6 June) *(Worcester, Crowle)*
       Ebdomada xjª [at] Pentecostes at wurceter & crowle.
℃ In primis for expensis on howsolde þis wycke xliij s. iiij d. ob. vnde
ij pleyeres xij d.   20

...

f 108

...

Item to iiij syngeres on our dedicacion day in   25
þe morenyng   viij d.

...

(Quarterly summary)
Summa tocius quarterij in Expensis Hospicij xxj li. xvj s. vj d. ob.   30
vnde Seyney money & pleyeres this quarter xxxvj s. viij d.

...

f 108v   *(5–11 July)* *(Crowle)*
...   35
       Ebdomada iijª at crowle
In primis in expensis on howsolde þis wycke xxv s. vij d. vnde seyny
Money iiij s.
Item rewardes iiij s./ xx d. iiij d. iij s.

5/ Mayndens *for* Maydens

Wyne iij s.   Item wyne xij d./ ij s. vj d. to the bonfyer at crowle on seynt thomas
nyht vj d.

Summa   xvj s.

(12–18 July) (Crowle)   5
...

Ebdomada iiij^{ta} at crowle. þis wycke þe sessheons
℃ In primis for expensis on howsold þis wycke xvj s. ix d. ob. vnde
seyny Money iiij s. viij d.
...   10
Item to Wyet þe mynstrell[es]   xij d./
...

f 110*   *(13–19 September) (Grimley)*
...   15
Ebdomada xiiij.ª at Grymley.
℃ In primis for expensis on howsold xxj s. xj d./ vnde seyny money iiij
s. viij d.
...
the kynges Item to Iohn sly & his felowes the kynges pleyeres [x]   vj s. viij d.   20
pleyeres   ...

1528–9
Account Book of Prior William More   WCL: A11
f 111*   *(4–10 October) (Grimley)*   25
...
[Ebdo] Ebdomada ij.^{da} at grymley
℃ In primis for expensis on howsold þis wycke xxx s. ix d./ vnde seyny
Money iiij s. viij d.
thomas brandon Item to thomas brandon the kynges Iogeller At Wurceter   30
the kynges   seynt oswaldes day   /iij s. iiij d.
Iogeller
wyne   Item for wyne seynt Oswaldes day   xviij d. xij d. iij d.
...

(11–17 October) (Grimley)   35
Ebdomada iij^a at grymley
℃ In primis for expensis on howsold þis wycke xxvij s. iiij d./ vnde
seyny money iiij s. viij d.
þe kynges   Item rewardes to the kynges Mynstrelles   iij s. iiij d./
mynstrelles ...   40

f 112   *(29 November–5 December) (Battenhall)*

...

Ebdomada x.ª Aduent sonday/ at batnall

℃ In primis for expensis on howsold this wycke xxxiiij s. xj d./ vnde ij
pleyeres xij d.   5
In rewardes to Mynstrelles on Advent sonday   xij d./ xij d. xx d./
                                                             [to] xvj d.

wyne.   Item for wyne on advent sonday   iiij s. x d./ iij d.

...

                                                                        10

f 112v   *(6–12 December) (Battenhall)*

Ebdomada xj.ª at Batnall

℃ In primis for expensis on howsolde þis wycke xxiiij s. iij d. ob./ vnde
ij pleyeres xij d.   15

...

(13–19 December) (Battenhall)
Ebdomada xij.ª at batnall

℃ In primis for expensis on howsolde þis wycke xvij s. x d./ vnde ij   20
pleyeres xij d.

...

(20–6 December) (Worcester, Battenhall)
Ebdomada xiij.ª parte of þe wycke at batnall/   25
& cristmas day. fryday

℃ In primis for expensis on howsolde þis wycke xxxij s. iiij d./ vnde ij
pleyeres xij d.

...

                                                                        30

(Quarterly summary)
Summa tocius quarterij in Expensis hospicij xvj li. iiij s. viij d.
Vnde seyny Money þis quarter with pleyeres xlij s.

...

                                                                        35

f 113   *(27 December–2 January) (Battenhall)*

°1528° Ebdomada prima in Natale Domini parte at batnall.
dies natalis domini extat die veneris hoc Anno

A byff   ℃ In primis for expensis on howsolde þis wycke [att] cristmas wycke 40
xlvj s. viij d. ob./ unde seyny money. ⌐iiij s.⌐

...

Item rewardes to Mynstrelles & syngeres of caralles
on cristmas day ·   xx d.

wyne for
þe bayliffes
on cristmas
day

Item for wyne for þe baylifes & other on cristmas day after [euesh]
evensong viz A quarte of mawmesey iiij d./ A pottell of secke vj d./
A galand of claret xij d./ for wafures iiij d. for kakes ij d.   5

...

(3–9 January) (Battenhall)

Ebdomada ij.^{da} parte at batnall/
þe bayles dyned *with* me *with* oþer of them   10
℃ In *pri*mis for expen*sis* on howsold þ*is* wycke xlvj s. iij d./ vnde seyny
Money iiij s. viij d.
In rewardes to iiij pleyeres of coventrie. on sonday when
þe bayliffes dyned *with* me   iij s. iiij d.

...   15

wyne   Item for mawemesey red & claret when þe baylys dyned
with me   vij s. x d.

...

f 113v   *(7–13 February) (Battenhall)*   20
...

Ebdomada vij.^a at batnall/ quyttyde sonday
℃ In *pri*mis for expen*sis* on howsolde xxxiiij s. ix d. ob./ ij pleyeres xij d.
It*em* to mynstrelles on quyttyde sonday   ij s. viij d.
wyne   Item for wyne all man*er* on þat day   vj s. viij d.   25

...

Item to the kynges berewarde at batnall/ havy*ng* ⌈ij⌉
beres there   xx d.

...

      30

f 114   *(14–20 February) (Grimley)*

Ebdomada octaua at grymley/ D*omi*nica prima .xl.^e
℃ In *pri*mis for expen*sis* on howsolde þ*is* wycke xxiiij s. vj d./ vnde ij
pleyeres xij d./   35

...

3/ þe baylifes: *William Stone and John Fathers, high and low bailiffs for 1528–9*

(21–7 February) (Worcester, Grimley)
        Ebdomada Nona/ at wurceter & grymley/ the sessheons/
❡ In primis for expensis on howsold þis wycke xviij s. j d./ ij pleyeres
xij d.
...   5

(28 February–6 March) (Grimley)
        Ebdomada x.ᵃ seynt oswaldes day at grymley
❡ In primis for expensis on howsolde xxx s./ vnde ij pleyeres xij d./
...   10

(7–13 March) (Battenhall)
            Ebdomada xj.ᵃ at batnall
❡ In primis for expensis on howsolde þis wycke xxij s. ij d./ vnde ij
pleyeres xij d.   15
...

f 114v   *(14–20 March) (Battenhall)*

            Ebdomada xij.ᵃ passion sonday/ at Batnall   20
❡ In primis for expensis on howsold this wycke xviij s. j d. ob./ vnde
ij pleyeres xij d.
...

(21–7 March) (Worcester, Battenhall)   25
        Ebdomada xiij.ᵃ palme sonday/ at wurceter & batnall
❡ In primis for expensis on howsold þis wycke xxxiiij s. viij d./ ij pleyeres
xij d.
...

                                                                                      30

(Quarterly summary)
Seyny Money & pleyeres þis quarter   xxxj s. viij d.
...

f 115   *(28 March–3 April) (Worcester)*   35

            °1529° Ebdomada prima in festo Pasche
❡ In primis for expensis on howsolde þis wycke iij li. iiij s. ij d./ vnde
ij pleyeres xij d.
...   40

f 115v*   *(18–24 April) (Battenhall)*

Ebdomada iiij.ta at batnall

C In primis for expensis on howsolde þis wycke xxxij s. x d. Vnde seyny
Money iiij s.   5

þe kynges   Item rewardes to the kynges Mynstrelles   x s.
Mynstrelles
...

(2–8 May) (Battenhall, Worcester)

Ebdomada vj.ta at batnall & wurceter/ the rogacion Wycke.   10

C In primis for expensis on howsolde þis wycke xxxvj s. v d./ Vnde ij
pleyeres xij d.
...

(16–22 May) (Worcester, Battenhall)   15

Ebdomada Octaua. Whitsonwycke/ parte at wurceter/
& parte at batnall

C In primis for expensis on howsold þis wycke [⟨.....⟩] lj s. v d. . Vnde
ij pleyeres xij d.
Item rewardes to certen yong men ‸⌜of seynt Elyns⌝   20
þat pleyd Robyn Whod   xij d.
...

f 116   *(30 May–5 June) (Crowle)*

25

Ebdomada decima at Crowle

C In primis for expensis on howsold þis Wycke xxvj s. xj d. vnde seyny
money iiij s.
...

In rewardes xij d./ to Wyet þe mynstrell xij d./ ⌜grymhull⌝ xx d. iiij d.   30
...

(6–12 June) (Crowle)

Ebdomada xj.a at crowle. þe dedicacion wycke

C In primis for expensis on howsolde þis wycke xxxix s. x d./ vnde   35
seyny money iiij s.
...

Item to mynstrelles on our dedicacion day   xxij d.
...

f 117   *(11–17 July) (Grimley)*

Ebdomada iij.ª at Grymley
℃ In *pri*mis for expens*is* on howsolde þ*is* wycke xxvj s. x d. vnde seyny
Money iiij s.   5

...

thomas brandon Item to thomas brandon the Kyng*es* Iogeller   iij s. iiij d.
          Item to A mynstrell of þe Dowke of Suffock*es*   ij s.

...
                                                                                    10

(18–24 July) (Worcester, Grimley)
Ebdomada iiij.ᵗᵃ at w*ur*cet*er* & grymley. the Sessheons
℃ In *pri*mis for expens*is* on howsolde þ*is* wycke xviij s. iij d. .Vnde
seyny Money iiij s.

...   15

my lord   Item to my lord cardinall*es* Mynstrell*es*   iiij s.
cardinall*es*
mynstrell*es*   ...

f 117v   *(29 August–4 September) (Grimley)*
...   20

Ebdomada x.ª at grymley
℃ In *pri*mis for expens*is* on howsold þ*is* wycke xxviij s. ix d./ vnde seyny
Money iiij s.

...

the kyng*es*   Item to Iohn englisshe & his iiij felowes þe kyng*es* pleyer*es* vj s. viij d. 25
pleyer*es*   ...

1529–30
Account Book of Prior William More   WCL: A11
f 119*   *(19–25 December) (Battenhall)*   30

Ebdomada xij.ª at batnall
℃ In *pri*mis for expens*is* on howsolde xx s. v d./ ij pleyer*es* xij d.
...
                                                                                    35

(26 December–1 January) (Worcester)
Ebdomada prima in Natale d*omi*ni at W*ur*cet*er* °1529°
℃ In *pri*mis for expens*is* on howsolde þ*is* wycke xlvj s. ij d. ob./ vnde
seyny money iiij s.
⟨℃ A⟩ byff   Item payd for A byff ⌐for cristmas⌐   xix s. ix d.   40

16/ my lord cardinall*es*: *Thomas, Cardinal Wolsey*

Item rewardes on cristmas day for carralles xiiij d./ on monday xv d.

…

f 119v   *(16–22 January) (Battenhall)*

…   5

Ebdomada iiij.^{ta} at Batnall

℃ In primis for expensis on howsolde þis wycke xxvij s. xj d./ vnde
seyny money iiij s.

…

Item to iiij pleyeres of wurceter on seynt Wlstans day   ij s. viij d.   10

…

wyne   Item spendid on seynt Wlstans day   ij s. iiij d.

…

f 120   *(20–6 February) (Grimley)*   15

…

Ebdomada nona. At Grymley. þe Sessheons þis wycke

℃ In primis for expensis on howsolde þis wycke xviij s. iiij d. ob. Vnde
seyny Money iiij s.

…   20

In rewardes iiij d./ to Mynstrelles xij d./ viij d. xij d.
Item to my lord of feryes pleyeres ij s. viij d.

…

f 120v   *(27 February–5 March) (Grimley)*   25

Dominica decima at Grymley. quyttyde sonday

℃ In primis for expensis on howsold þis wycke xl s. x d. Vnde ij pleyeres
xij d.
Item gyff to mynstrelles on quyttyde sonday   iiij s. iiij d.   30

…

(6–12 March) (Grimley)
Ebdomada xj^a at grymley

In primis for expensis on howsolde þis wycke xxiiij s. viij d. vnde ij   35
pleyeres xij d.

…

(13–19 March) (Grimley)
Ebdomada xij.ª at [gy] grymley
℃ In primis for expensis on howsold þis wycke xxj s. iiij d./ vnde ij
pleyeres xij d.
...   5

(20–6 March) (Grimley)
Ebdomada xiij.ª at grymley
℃ In primis for expensis on howsolde þis wycke xxviij s. ix d. ob./ Vnde
ij pleyeres xij d.   10
...

f 121a*   *(17–23 April) (Worcester, Battenhall)*

Ebdomada iiij.ᵗᵃ Ester day/ at Worceter & batnall   15
°in anno 1530°
℃ In primis for expensis on howsolde xxxvij s. x d. ob./ vnde ij pleyeres
xij d.
...
                                                                                       20

(15–21 May) (The More)
Ebdomada octaua at the more
℃ In primis for expensis on howsolde þis wycke xxj s. vij d. vnde seyny
Money iiij s.
...   25
Item for costes & expensis at pensax churche Ale   iiij s. vj d.
...

f 121av*   *(22–8 May) (The More)*
                                                                                       30
Ebdomada Nona. at þe more the Rogacion wycke
℃ In primis for expensis on howsolde þis wycke   xxiij s. xj d.
...
Item to pleyeres at þe more on þe Assencion day to þe vce
of A churche   ij s. iiij d.   35
...

(29 May–4 June) (The More)
Ebdomada xª. at þe more
℃ In primis for expensis on howsolde þis wycke xxxiiij s. iiij d./ vnde 40
seyny money iiij s.
...

þe churche Ale | Item to þe churche Ale at grymley   vij s. vj d.
at grymley &
a pley.   ...

(5–11 June) (Worcester)
               Ebdomada xj.ª Whitsonday. at Worceter   5
℃ In primis for expensis on howsolde þis wycke lij s. iiij d./ ij pleyeres
xij d.
...

Item to the syngers on our dedicacion day in þe morenyng   xvj d.
...   10

(12–18 June) (Worcester, Battenhall)
           Ebdomada xij.ª trinite sonday. at Wurceter & batnall
℃ In primis for expensis on howsold þis wycke xxxvij s. x d. vnde seyny
money iiij s.   15
...

Item gyff to þe dawnceres of claynes xx d./ to þe box of Robyn hood
&c xij d.
...
                                                                                     20

f 121b   (26 June–2 July) (Battenhall)
...
       °1530° Ebdomada prima post festum Natiuitatis Sancti
             Iohannis Baptiste. at Batnall
℃ In primis for expensis on howsolde þis [q] wycke xxiiij s. ij d. ob.   25
vnde seyny money iiij s.
...
the kynges   Item to the kynges mynstrelles   x s.
mynstrelles   ...
                                                                                     30

(3–9 July) (Crowle)
           Ebdomada ij^da at Crowle
In primis for expensis on howsolde þis wycke xxxiij s. xj d. Vnde
seyny money iiij s.
Item rewardes xij d. ij s. xij d.   35
the bonfyur   Item spende at þe boonfyur at þe crosse in crowle on seynt thomas
at crowle   nyght Amonges the hole neypurs of þe seid towne iij d pens in kakes
A pottell & A quarte of red wyne. A pottell of secke vj d.
                    Summa   iiij s. ix d.

...   40

f 121bv   *(24–30 July) (Crowle)*

...

Ebdomada v.^{ta} at Crowle. seynt Iames day.

℃ In primis for expensis on howsolde þis wycke xvij s. ij d./ vnde seyny
money iiij s.   5

...

Item rewardes to mynstrelles & oþer at master wynteres
at seynt Iames day   ij s. iiij d.

...

                                                                                                      10

f 122   *(14–20 August) (Worcester, Crowle)*

...

Ebdomada Octaua at wurceter & crowle. monday
the Assumpcion of our lady/ the Abbottes of Glowceter
& Euesham beyng here with oþer   15

℃ In primis for expensis on howsold þis wycke xlvij s. ix d. vnde seyny
Money iiij s.
In rewardes to Mynstrelles our lady day   iiij s.

...

                                                                                                      20

1530–1
Account Book of Prior William More   WCL: A11
f 124   *(6–12 November) (Grimley)*

...

Ebdomada vj.^{ta} at grymley   25

℃ In primis for expensis on howsold þis wycke xxviij s. ob./ vnde seyny
Money iiij s.

...

thomas brandon   Item to thomas brandan the kynges Ioguller   iij s. iiij d.

...   30

f 124v   *(27 November–3 December) (Battenhall)*

...

Ebdomada Nona Advent sonday/ At Batnall

℃ In primis for expensis on howsolde þis wycke xxix s. vij d. [v] vnde   35
ij playeres xij d.

14/ the Abbottes: *William Parker or Malvern, abbot of Gloucester, elected 1514, and Clement
Litchfield, abbot of Evesham, 1514–39*

In rewardes to mynstrelles   iij s. iiij d./ viij d.
                                                    viij d. viij d.

...

(4–10 December) (Battenhall)   5
     Ebdomada x.ª at batnall
ℭ In primis for expensis on howsolde þis wycke xxiij s. vij d. ob./ vnde
ij pleyeres xij d.

...
                                                                       10

f 125   *(11–17 December) (Battenhall)*

     Ebdomada xj.ª at batnall
ℭ In primis for expensis on howsold þis wycke xv s. xj d. ob./ vnde ij
pleyeres xij d.   15

...

(18–24 December) (Battenhall)
     Ebdomada xij.ª at batnall
ℭ In primis for expensis on howsold þis wycke xiiij s. xj d./ vnde ij   20
pleyeres xij d.

...

(Quarterly summary)
Summa tocius quarterij in Expensis hospicij xv li. iij s.   25
vnde Seyny Money & pleyeres xxxvj s.

...

f 125v   *(25–31 December) (Worcester)*
                                                                       30
Ebdoma prima in Natale Domini. extat hoc Anno in dominica die
ℭ In primis for expensis on howsolde þis wycke iij li. vij d. ob. vnde
seyny [Mone] ij pleyeres xij d.
byff   Item for A byff At cristmas wycke price   xviij s. iiij d.
Item rewardes to singeres of carralles cristmas   35
day ⌈&c⌉   viij d. vj d. x d.

...

wyne   Item for wyne ⌈& wafferes⌉ for master baliffes & þe oþer of þe Citie

31/ Ebdoma *for* Ebdomada
38/ master baliffes: *William Porter and Thomas Browne, high and low bailiffs for 1530–1*

on cristmas day at nyght videli*cet* waff*eres* iiij dosen ⌐iiij d.¬ iij d.
[dosen] ⌐in¬ kak*es* A pottell of secke vj d./ clarett

wyne   Item for ⌐swete¬ wyne as mawmesey & Secke ˄⌐& red
wyne¬ *þis* wycke   v s. vj d.

...   5

Item gyff to philip *þe* harper for his beyng ⌐wi*th* me¬ til
after Neweyer*es* day   iij s. iiij d.

...

f 126   *(15–21 January) (Battenhall)*   10

Ebdomada iiij.ᵗᵃ at batnall/. thursday seynt Wlstans day
C In *pri*mis for expens*is* on howsold *þis* wycke xxviij s. vij d. ob./ vnde
seyny Money iiij s.
In reward*es* to Roger bury to his wedyng on seynt maures   15
day in Ianuar*y*   xxx s./

...

Item reward*es* to Mynstrell*es* at *þe* weddyng   xviij d./ xij d.

...
                                                                          20

(19–25 February) (Worcester)
        Ebdomada Nona at W*u*rceter/ quyttyde sonday
C In *pri*mis for expens*is* on howsold *þis* wycke xxx s. iij d. ob./ ij pleyer*es*
xij d.

...   25

f 126v

...

Item to Mynstrell*es* on quyttyde sonday   xviij d./

...   30

(26 February–4 March) (Worcester)
        Ebdomada decima at w*u*rceter j.ᵐᵃ ebd*omada* quadragesime/
                this wyck *þe* sessheons fryday. setterday
C In *pri*mis for expens*is* on howsold *þis* wycke xxvij s. viij d. vnde ij   35
pleyer*es* xij d.

...

(5–11 March) (Battenhall, Worcester)
        Ebdomada undecima at batnall & w*u*rceter   40
C In *pri*mis for expens*is* on howsold *þis* wycke xviij s. vj d./ vnde ij
pleyer*es* xij d.

...

(12–18 March) *(Grimley)*
                    Ebdomada xij.ᵃ at Grymley
℃ In *pr*imis for expens*is* on howsolde þis wycke xxv s. viij d. ob./ Vnde
ij pleyer*es* [x d.] xij d.
…   5

f 127   *(19–25 March)* *(Grimley, Worcester)*

                    Ebdomada xiij.ᵃ At grymley & w*ur*ceter
℃ In *pr*imis for expens*is* on howsolde þis wycke xxxj s. ix d./ vnde ij   10
pleyer*es* xij d./
…

(Quarterly summary)
S*umm*a toci*us* quarterij in Expens*is* hospicij   xvij li. iij s. j d.   15
Vnde seyny Money & pleyer*es* þis qu*a*rter   xxij s.
…

f 127v   *(26 March–1 April)* *(Grimley)*
                                                                             20
   °1531° Ebdomada *pr*ima post Annu*n*ciacione*m* beate marie
        passion sonday At grymley/ beyng disyeasid þis wycke
℃ In *pr*imis for expens*is* on howsolde þis wycke xxx s. vj d. vnde ij
pleyer*es* xij d.
…   25

(9–15 April) *(Grimley)*

   Ebdomada iijᵃ· Ester day at grymley. beyng disyeased ⌊þis wycke⌋
℃ In *pr*imis for expens*is* on howsold þis wycke   xxxij s. xj d.   30
Item spend at the churche Ale at grymley on
blake monday   iij s. viij d.
…

f 128*   *(30 April–6 May)* *(Grimley)*   35

                    Ebdomada vjᵗᵃ· at grymley
℃ In *pr*imis for expens*is* on howsold þis wycke xxvij s. xj d. vnde seyny
money iiij s.
…   40

Item rewarde*s* to [that] them þ*at* singeth on Maye
Mornyng Men & Women at grymley   iij s.
…

(7–13 May) (Grimley)
　　　　　　Ebdomada vij^{a.} at grymley
℃ In primis for expens*is* on howsold þ*is* wycke xxvj s. ij d. ob. vnde seyny
Money iiij s.
In reward*es* to þe boxe at þe showe of seynt pet*ures* xij d./ to other   5
boxes xvj d. xij d. xij d. iij s. iiij d.
…

(14–20 May) (Worcester, Battenhall)
　　　　　　　　　　　　　　　　　　　　　　　　　　　10
　　　　Ebdomada octaua. Rogacion Wycke at w*ur*ceter & batnall
℃ In primis for expens*is* on howsold þ*is* wycke xxxvj s. x d./ vnde ij
pleyer*es* xij d.
…
Item to þe daunc*eres* of seynt sewthans   xij d.   15
…

f 128v*   *(28 May–3 June) (Worcester, Battenhall)*

　　　　Ebdomada x.^a Whitsonday at W*ur*ceter & batnall   20
℃ In primis for expens*is* on howsold þ*is* Wycke. xlix s. x d./ vnde ij
pleyer*es* xij d.
…
Item for ij shurt*es* for leonard stanley ij s. ij d./ & A peyer of showe*s*
vij d.   25
…
singer*es* Item to þe singer*es* of þe towne on o*ur* dedicacion day in
þe morenyng   xvj d.
Item to mynstrell*es* on o*ur* dedicacion day xij d./ to dawnc*eres* of þe
p*ar*asshe xx d.   30
…

(11–17 June) (Crowle)
　　　　Ebdomada xij^a at crowle/ seynt Wlstans day
℃ In primis for expens*is* on howsold þ*is* Wycke xxviij s. xj d./ vnde   35
seyny Money iiij s.
…
Item to Wyet þe Mynstrell   xij d.
…

f 129*   *(9–15 July) (Crowle)*

...

Ebdomada iij.ª at crowle

℃ In primis for expensis on howsolde þis wycke xxiiij s. v d. Vnde seyny
Money iiij s.   5

...

⟨þe princes⟩   Item ⌈to⌉ William slye & iij other þe princes pleyeres   v s.
pleyeres
...

(16–22 July) (Crowle)   10
Ebdomada iiij.ᵗᵃ at Crowell/ tewesday sessheons

℃ In primis for expensis on howsolde þis wycke xiiij s. ix d./ vnde seyny
Money iiij s.

...

⟨the kynges   Item to the kynges Mynstrelles. his shambulles   x s.   15
mynstrelles⟩

f 129v*   *(23–9 July) (Crowle)*

Ebdomada v.ᵗᵃ at Crowle. seynt Iames & [seynt] Anne day

℃ In primis for expensis on howsolde þis wycke xvij s. vj d. Vnde seyny   20
money. iiij s.
In rewardes to the tenantes of clyve. pleying with Robyn
Whot Mayde Marion & other   vj s. viij d.
Item Rewardes   xvj d. xvj d. xx d.
                                                                  xij d. xvj d.   25

...

(30 July–5 August) (Battenhall)
Ebdomada vj.ᵗᵃ at batnall

℃ In primis for expensis on howsolde þis wycke xvij s. xj d. vnde seyny   30
money iiij s.

...

Item to A Mynstrell of my lord of Arunedell   xvj d.

...

                                                                                35

(13–19 August) (Worcester)
Ebdomada octaua at ⌈wurceter⌉ [batnall] þe Assumpcion of our lady

℃ In primis for expensis on howsolde þis wycke xxviij s. vj d. ob./ vnde
seyny money iiij s.

...   40

In rewardes iiij d. viij d./ vj s. viij d./ to A Mynstrell xij d./ xij d.
viij d./ xxij d.

Item for A peyer of hoses for leonard stanley   ij s. iiij d./ xij d.
...

f 130   *(27 August–2 September) (Worcester)*
...   5
                    Ebdomada xª at Wurcester
In primis for expensis on howsolde þis wycke xxvij s. ix d/ vnde seyny
Money iiij s.
...
Item spend at seynt gyles at þe parkeres Ale   10
& offryng   ij s.
...

(10–16 September) (Grimley)
...   15
                Ebdomada xij.ª at Grymley beyng disyeased
℃ In primis for expensis on howsolde þis wycke xxj s. vj d. ob./ vnde
seyny money iiij s.
...
thomas brandon Item to thomas brandon the kynges Ioguler   iij s. iiij d.   20
...

1531–2
Account Book of Prior William More   WCL: A11
f 132   *(3–9 December) (Battenhall)*   25

                Ebdomada x.ª aduent sonday/ At batnall
℃ In primis for expensis on howsold þis wycke   xxxj s. j d. ij d.
Item to Mynstrelles on aduent sonday   ij s./ xx d.
...   30

(17–23 December) (Battenhall)
                Ebdomada xijª at batnall
In primis for expensis on howsold this wycke xix s.
...   35
Item for certen geere to leonarde stanley & þe page of
þe kychion   ij s.
...

f 132v   *(24–30 December) (Worcester)*

°1531° Ebdomada prima in Natale domini
⌐at Wurceter⌐./ monday/

℃ In primis for expensis on howsolde þis wycke   iij li. iij s. iiij d.   5
In rewardes to syngeres of caralles   viij d. xij d.
                                                                    viij d. viij d.

Item for wyne on crist[a]mas day for master baylys & other after
Even song vidz A quarte of mawmesey ⌐iiij d.⌐ ⌊& A pottell of secke
vj d.⌋   10
Item for [i]ij dosen of wafures ⌐ij d.⌐ [iij dosen/] for cakes   ij d.

...

Item to Mynstrelles   xij d.

...
                                                                                   15

(31 December–6 January) (Worcester, Battenhall)

Ebdomada ij.^da at Wurceter & batnall/ Newyeres day þe
baylyffes &c. dyned with me
℃ In primis for expensis on howsold this wycke. monday Newyeresday   20
the bayles & other dyned with me/ xxxij s. ob.

...

Item rewardes for carralles   xij d. xij d.

...

Item to iiij pleyeres Apon Neweyeres day. the baylyffes   25
dynyng with me with others   v.s

...

f 133   *(4–10 February) (Battenhall)*

...   30
Ebdomada vij^a at batnall
In primis for expensis on howsold þis wycke   xviiij s. viij d.

...

Item to Iohn taylour for geere for leonard stanley & for
Richard of þe kycheon   ij s. j d.   35

...

8/ master baylys: *Richard Cooper and John Brangham, high and low bailiffs for 1531–2*

(11–17 February) (Battenhall)

...

           Ebdomada Octaua. quyttite sonday. at batnall

℃ In *primis* for expen*sis* on howsolde þ*is* wycke   xxvj s. viij d. ob.

...

Item to Mynstrell*es* on quyttite sonday   xviij d.

...

f 133v *(10–16 March) (Battenhall)*

...

       Ebdomada xij.ª at batnall/ seynt gregory day tewesday

℃ In *primis* for expen*sis* on howsold þ*is* wycke   xvij s. v d.

Item to the prynces bereward*es* xvj d. viij d./...

...

f 134v *(7–13 April) (Battenhall)*

...

          Ebdomada iij.ª at batnall/ lowe sonday

℃ In *primis* for expen*sis* on howsold þ*is* wycke   xxvij s. xj s.

...

Item reward*es* xvj d. ij s./ to mynstrell*es* xij d.

...

f 135* *(14–20 April) (Battenhall)*

             Ebdomada iiij.ᵗᵃ at batnall

℃ In *primis* for expen*sis* on howsold þ*is* wycke   xxviij s. x d. iiij d.

It*em* reward*es* xxij d./ xij d./ to A mynstrell [v]viij d./ viij d. xvj d./
iij s. iiij d./ v s.

...

(28 April–4 May) (Crowle)

           Ebdomada vj.ᵗᵃ at crowle

℃ In *primis* for expen*sis* on howsold þ*is* wycke   xxviij s. vj d.

...

Item to the yong Men of crowle for singyng on Maij day
in þe Morenyng   xvj d.
Item to Mr talbott*es* Mynstrell   xij d.
Item to the Maydens of crowle for syngyng on holyrowde day in the
Morenyng. toward [t] o*ur* lady lyght xx d./ & to oþ*er* syng*eres* xij d.

...

(5–11 May) (Worcester)

      Ebdomada vij.ª at [cro] Wurceter. the rogacion wycke.
℃ In primis for expensis on howsold þis wycke   xxxiiij s. ij d. ob.
...
Item to Mynstrelles & Iogulares on sonday   iij s. iiij d.
...

f 135v   *(12–18 May) (Crowle)*

      Ebdomada octaua at crowle
℃ In primis for expensis on howsold þis wycke   xxx s. ix d.
...
Item for A shurt to Leonar stanley   xvj d.
...
Item at Hymulton to ther churche Ale   ij s. vj d.
...

f 136   *(2–8 June) (Crowle)*

      Ebdomada xj.ª At Crowle. þis wycke our dedicacion day
℃ In primis for expensis on howsold þis wycke   xxx s. ix d. ob.
In rewardes   xij d. vj d.
Item to Wyet the Mynstrell at crowle   xij d.
...
Item rewarded to Anne parsons for kepyng of
leonard stanley beyng syke.   ij s.
the kynges Item rewardes to the kynges Mynstrelles   x s.
Mynstrelles Item to the syngeres in þe dedicacion day in
þe Morenyng   xij d.
...

(9–15 June) (Crowle)
      Ebdomada xij.ª at crowle
℃ In primis for expensis on howsold þis wycke   xxx s. vij d. ob.
...
Item for rayment for leonard stanley   xiij s. iiij d.
Item to Mynstrelles   viij d. / iiij d. xij d.
...

16/ Hymulton: *Himbleton, Worcestershire*

f 137   *(25–31 August) (Crowle)*

...

Ebdomada.x.ª at crowle

℃ In primis for expensis on howsold this wycke   xxvij s. iij d. ob.

...

a bagge   Item for A bagge pype   ij s viij d.
pype

...

f 137v   *(8–14 September) (Crowle)*

...

Ebdomada xij.ª þe Natiuite of our lady. At crowle

℃ In primis for expensis on howsolde this wycke   xxviij s. x d. ob.
In rewardes to Mynstrelles on our lady day   xij d. viij d. xij d.
                                                       iiij d./ xij d.

...

Item for expensis at Iohn Walcroft þe keper of hallowe
parke at his Ale   ij s. iiij d.

...

(15–21 September) (Crowle)

Ebdomada xiij.ª at Crowle

℃ In primis for expensis on howsold this wycke   xxvij s. vj d.

...

⟨Thomas   Item to thomas brandon the kynges Ioguler. at crowle   iij s. iiij d.
Bran⟩den

...

(22–8 September) (Crowle)

Ebdomada xiiijª· at Crowle

⟨℃ In primis⟩ for expensis on howsold þis wycke   xxvij s. vj d.

...

⟨........⟩es at þe churche Ale at hymulton   x s./ iiij s.

...

1532–3
Account Book of Prior William More   WCL: A11
f 138v   *(13–19 October) (Grimley)*

...

Ebdomada iij.ª At grymley

℃ In primis for expensis on howsold this wycke   xxvj s.

...

29,31/ ⟨℃ In primis⟩, ⟨........⟩es: *part of folio missing*   31/ hymulton: *Himbleton, Worcestershire*

Item to A Mynstrell   xij d.

...

f 139v   *(1–7 December)* *(Grimley)*

Ebdomada Decima. aduent sonday. At grymley
℃ In *primis* for expens*is* on howsold this wycke   xxix s. iiij d.
Item to Mynstrell*es* on advent sonday at grymley   xviij d.

...

f 140   *(22–8 December)* *(Worcester)*

°1532° Ebdomada prima ˌ⌐at W*ur*ceter⌐ Ante festu*m* Natiuitat*is*
domini q*uod* extat die mercur[yy]⌐ij⌐
℃ In *primis* for expens*is* on howsolde this wycke þe cristmas wycke   15
xliiij s./ ix d. Vl*tra* in byff xij s.
In reward*es* to synger*es* of caroll*es* þe xij days   ij s. viij d.

...

...to Mynstrell*es* & synger*es* of [cal] carall*es* on cristmas day xvj d./
...   20
Item for Swete ˌ⌐wyne⌐ at cristmas wycke   iij s. iiij d.
Item for wafur*es* ˌ⌐ij d.⌐ & cak*es* ˌ⌐ij d.⌐ on cristmas nyght when master
baylys & other wer w*ith* me after euensong It*em* for wyne A pottell
of Secke vj d. & red & clarett
...   25

(29 December–4 January) *(Worcester)*
Ebdomada ij.^da At w*ur*ceter/ sonday seynt thomas day.
þe baylys ˌdyned w*ith* meˌ
℃ In *primis* for expens*is* on howsold this wycke/   lj s. xj d. ob.   30
...
Item to iij Mynstrell*es* beyng w*ith* me all the xij days   vij s.

f 140v   *(26 January–1 February)* *(Battenhall)*
...   35
Ebdomada vj.^ta At Batnall
℃ In *primis* for expens*is* on howsolde this wycke   xxviij s. x d.
...
Item to Iohn Slye & his compani beyng the kyng*es* pleyers   v s.
...   40

wyne

Mynstrell*es*

the kyng*es*
pleyer*es*

22–3/ master baylys: *Thomas Browne and Robert Luddington, high and low bailiffs for 1532–3* f 141   *(23 February–1 March) (Battenhall, Worcester)*

…

Ebdomada x.ᵃ [Advent] ⌐quyttid⌐ sonday. *parte* at batnall þ*is*
wycke þe sessheons ⌊was fryday & setterday⌋

℃ In *pri*mis for expensis on howsold this wycke   xxvij s. vj d.   5

…

Item rewarde*s* to Mynstrelle*s* A pon quyttyde sonday   iiij s.

Item for wyne bowght on quyttyte sonday   v s.

…

10

f 142   *(13–19 April) (Worcester)*

…

Ebdomada iij.ᵃ Est*er* yeven at w*ur*ceter

℃ In *pri*mis for expens*is* on howsold this wycke lix s./ vl*tr*a xxj d.

In rewarde*s* to dy*uer*s s*er*uantes ⌐& frynde*s*⌐ A yenst Est*er*   15

viz stanley Ric*hard* of þe kychion &c   xx s.

…

Item to on pye A Mynstrell   xx d.

…

Item to the churche Ale at grymley in þe Est*er* wycke   20

thursday   iij s. iiij d.

…

(27 April–3 May) (Battenhall)

Ebdomada vᵗᵃ At batnall   25

℃ In *pri*mis for expens*is* on howsold this wycke   xxxv s.

…

Item to Iohn Acton Will*i*am Parker & Iohn tylar for syng

at batnall on Maij Morenyng   xij d.

Item to iiij of w*ur*ceter singyng men for þe same syngyng   xvj d.   30

…

f 142v*   *(4–10 May) (Crowle)*

Ebdomada Sexta At Crowle   35

℃ In *pri*mis for expens*is* on howsold this wycke   xxxiij s. v d.

…

Item to the mayde*s* of Crowle for syngyng in

þe Morenyng   xij d.

…   40

28/ syng *for* synging

(11–17 May) (Crowle)
                    Ebdomada vij.ᵃ at Crowle
℃ In primis for expensis on howsold this Wycke   xxvij d. ix d.
Item to the Ale at crowle churche hows   xvj d.
...   5

(25–31 May) (Crowle)
                    Ebdomada ix.ᵃ at Crowle
℃ In primis for expensis on howsold this Wycke   xxvij s. xj d.
...   10
Item to my lord markas berewarde   xvj d.
...

f 143 *(1–7 June) (Worcester)*
                                                                              15
         Ebdomada .x.ᵃ at Wurceter. the Whitsonday wycke.
℃ In primis for expensis on howsold this wycke   xlj s. xj d.
In rewardes to Mynstrelles on Whitsonday   xij d. vj d.
...
Item rewardes to the churche Ales of seynt Elens &   20
seynt mihelles   ij s. iiij d.
...

(8–14 June) (Worcester)
         Ebdomada xj.ᵃ at wurceter/ trinite wycke.   25
                    & þe sessheons of peasse.
℃ In primis for expensis on howsolde þis wycke   xlvj s. xj d.
...to wyett þe Mynstrell xij d.
...
                                                                              30

(15–21 June) (Crowle)
                    Ebdomada xij.ᵃ At Crowle
℃ In primis for expensis on howsold þis wycke   xxviij s. x d.
...
wyne   Item for v galandes of wyne of red & clarett for þe   35
       v pageontes and oþer tymes   v s. vj d.
...

f 143v* *(6–12 July) (Battenhall)*
...   40
                    Ebdomada iij.ᵃ at Batnall
℃ In primis for expensis on howsold þis wycke   xxvij s. x d.

the pley at
hynwyckes hull

In rewardes [⟨at⟩] to alhaland churche at the pley holden at
hynwyckes hull seynt thomas yeven beyng sonday. & on
seynt thomas day beyng monday. Whiche pley was kept
to the profett of alhaland churche   vj s. viij d.
...   5

(20–6 July) (Worcester)
                Ebdomada quinta. at Worceter./ the sessheons
℃ In primis for expensis on howsold this Wycke   xix s. x d.
...   10

f 144

the kynges mynstrelles†
Item to iij of the kynges Mynstrelles with þe schombulles vij s. vj d.   15

wyne
Item for wyne this wycke   iij s. j d.
...

(3–9 August) (Grimley)
                Ebdomada vij.ᵃ at grymley   20
℃ In primis for expensis on howsold this wycke   xxij s. x d.
...

norton ale
Item to the churche Ale at kynges Norton   vij s. vj d.
Item to Iohn taylour as by A byll concernyng
leonard stanley   vij s. j d.   25
...

f 144v   (7–13 September) (Crowle)

                Ebdomada xij.ᵃ at Crowle/ þe Natiuite   30
                of our lady þis wycke.
℃ In primis for expensis on howsold this wycke   xliij s.
...
Item to Mynstrelles Apon our lady day   ij s. iiij d.
...   35

(21–7 September) (Crowle)
                Ebdomada xiiij.ᵃ At Crowle
℃ In primis for expensis on howsold this wycke xxxix s. viij d./ xij
warkemen at crowle Mott   40

In rewardes to te dewke of suffolke trumpeteres   ij s.

...

1533–4
Account Book of Prior William More   WCL: A11   5
f 145v*   *(5–11 October)* *(Worcester)*

...

Ebdomada ijᵃ. At Wurceter
℃ In primis for expensis on howsold this wycke xlij s. iiij d./ the
sessheons   10

...

Item rewarded to Auncelme of crowle to his Ale   xx d.

...

(12–18 October)   15
Ebdomada iijᵃ. At Crowle
℃ In primis for expensis on howsold þis wycke   xxxiiij s. vj d.
the quenes   In rewardes to thomas Evance & his ij felowes the kynges
mynstrelles   mynstrelles   v s.

...   20

f 146v   *(30 November–6 December)* *(Worcester, Battenhall)*

...

Ebdomada x.ᵃ Aduent sonday/
At wurceter & batnall   25
℃ In primis for expensis on howsold this wycke   xxxv s. iij d.

...

wyne   Item for swete wyne on aduent sonday   xij d.
              Item to mynstrelles on aduent sonday   vj d.

...   30

ij balys   Item for ij litle balys of yerne to blow with   xx d.
of yern
              ...

f 147   *(7–13 December)* *(Battenhall)*

                                                                   35

Ebdomada xj.ᵃ At batnall. our lady day monday
℃ In primis for expensis on howsold this wycke   xxv s. xj d.

...

1/ te *for* the

Item to ij mynstrelles of master talbottes & master
throckmortons   ij s.
...

(21–7 December)   5

<blockquote>
Ebdomada xiij.ᵃ at batnall/ þe thursday
after ˏʳisˋ cristmas day
</blockquote>

℃ In primis for expensis on howsold þis wycke   xlviij s. ix d. ob./
...   10
Item on cristomas day to mynstrelles & singyng of
carralles   xij d.
Item for ij pens in cakes & ij d. in waffures for þe baylys & oþer/
for muscadell vj d. Secke iij d.
...   15

f 147v   *(28 December–3 January) (Worcester)*

<blockquote>
∘1533∘ Ebdomada prima post Natalem domini/ At wurceter
</blockquote>

℃ In primis for expensis on howsold þis wycke. this   20
sonday Innocence day. the baylyffes dyned with me
with other states of the citie   lvj s. x d.
In rewardes for carolles   xij d. vj d. [xij d.]
...
                                                                                                25

(4–10 January) (Worcester, Battenhall)

<blockquote>
Ebdomada ij.ᵈᵃ at wurceter & batnall/ tewesday xijᵗʰ day
</blockquote>

℃ In primis for expensis on howsold þis wycke   xlij s. j d.
Item to iiij pleyeres at dyner on þe Epiphanie day   iij s. iiij d.   30
...

f 148   *(1–7 February) (Battenhall)*
...

<blockquote>
Ebdomada Sexta At Batnall   35
</blockquote>

℃ In primis for expensis on howsold this wycke   xxxv s. x d.
...
Item to A mynstrell   viij d.
...

13/ þe baylys: *John Brangham and Humphry Bartford, high and low bailiffs for 1533–4*

(15–21 February) (Worcester)
  Ebdomada octaua. quyttite sonday./ on monday I rod to London
℃ In primis for expens*is* on howsold   xxj s. ij d.
  Item rewardes to mynstrell*es*   xx d. xij d.
  …   5

f 150* *(19–25 April) (Crowle)*
  …
                          Ebdomada v.^ta at Crowle.
℃ In primis for expens*is* on howsold this Wycke   xxxiij s. vij d.   10
  Item to iiij syngyng men craftesmen of W*ur*ceter vpon
  seynt georg*es* day in the morenyng at crowle   xvj d.
  …

(26 April–2 May) (Crowle)   15
                          Ebdomada vj.^ta at Crowle
℃ Expens*is* on howsold this wycke   xxxiij s. iij d.
  …
  Item to vj mayd*es* at crowle þat did syng in the morenyng
  on seynt philip & Iacob day   xvj d.   20
  …

(3–9 May) (Crowle)
                          Ebdomada vij.^a At crowle
℃ Item for expens*is* on howsold this wycke   xxxj s. x d.   25
the kynges   Item to ⌈iiij⌉ the kyng*es* mynstrell*es*   vij s. vj d.
mynstrelles Item rewardes xiiij d. to pleyer*es* xvj d./ v s. iiij d./ xvj d. ij s./ to þe
             sheowe of seynt Elynes xij d./
  …
                                                                                   30
f 150v* *(17–23 May) (Crowle)*

                          Ebdomada ix.^a at Crowle
℃ In primis for expens*is* on howsold this wycke   xxxiij s. v d.
  Item rewardes to sheowe of seynt Sewthans   xx d.   35
  …

(24–30 May) (Worcester, Crowle)
              Ebdomada x^a at wurceter ⌈& crowle⌉. Whitsonday
℃ In primis for expens*is* on howsold this wycke   ⌐   xlix s.   40
  …

Item to the box of seynt Andros sheowe on þer
dedic*acion* day   xij d. [&]

…

Item to seynt Elyns churche Ale   xij d.

…   5

f 151   *(31 May–6 June) (Worcester)*

Ebdomada xj.ª trinite sonday. At wurceter
þe sessheons tewesday   10
ℂ In p*ri*mis for expens*is* on howsold this wycke xlj s. viij d. vlt*ra* þe
sessheons vj s. viij d.
In reward*es* to the dawncer*es* of claynes   xx d.

…

the quenes   Item reward*es* to þe quenes pleyer*es*. Iohn slye &   15
pleyer*es*   iij other   vij s. vj d.
Thomas brandon Item to thomas brandon the kyng*es* Iogular   iij s. iiij d.

…

(7–13 June) (Grimley)   20
Ebdomada xij.ª ower dedicacion day sonday/ At grymley.
ℂ In p*ri*mis for expens*is* on howsold this wycke   xxxj s. x d.
In reward*es* to þe synger*es* in þe morenyng on þe
Dedicacion day   xx d.

…   25

f 151v*   *(12–18 July) (Grimley)*

…

Ebdomada iiij.ᵗᵃ at Grymley
ℂ In p*ri*mis for expens*is* on howsold this wycke   xxxvj s. x d.   30
the berewarde   In reward*es* to my lord markas bereward   xx d.
In reward*es*   xij d. viij d. xij d. xvj d.

…

Item to philipp by a byll for the bonfyer at grymley xj d.

…   35

f 152v*   *(23–9 August) (Grimley)*

…

Ebdomada x.ª at grymley
ℂ In p*ri*mis for expens*is* on howsold this wycke   xxx s. ij d.   40

…

Wyet
þe mynstrell   Item to Wyett þe mynstrell at grymley   xx d.

...

(30 August–5 September) *(Grimley, Worcester)*

                                                                                    5

                Ebdomada xjᵃ at grymley *parte*/ master bonar beyng here
C In *primis* for expens*is* on howsold þ*is* wycke xxxj s. v d. vltra x s. ij d.
        In rewardes   ij s. iiij d./ xij d./ ij s./
                                                             xx d. xij d. xij d.

        Item to William Colburne for seynt gyles Ale   ij s.   10

...

(6–12 September) *(Worcester, Grimley)*

                Ebdomada xij.ᵃ At wurce*ter* & grymley. the Natiuite of *our* lady 15
C In *primis* for expens*is* on howsold this wycke   xxxvj s. vj d.

        ...

        Item to mynstrell*es* on *our* lady day Natiuite   xx d. xvj d. xvj d.

        ...

the kynges   Item to vj of the kyng*es* mynstrell*es*. beyng haggebusshes   x s.   20
mynstrell*es*
        ...

f 153   *(20–6 September)*

                    Ebdomada xiiij.ᵃ At Crowle   25
C In *primis* for expens*is* on howsold this wycke   xxviij s. viij d.

        ...

the quenes   Item to thomas Evance & his felowes þe quenes
mynstrell*es*   mynstrell*es* on Myhelmas yeven   vj s. viij d.

        ...   30

1534–5
Account Book of Prior William More   WCL: A11
f 153v   *(18–24 October)* *(Crowle)*

        ...   35

                    Ebdomada iiij.ᵗᵃ at Crowle
C In *primis* for expens*is* on howsold this wycke   xxviij s. x d.

        ...

A bereward   Item to A bereward of my lord of derbie at Crowle w*ith*
              his ber*es*   xx d.   40

        ...

f 154   *(25–31 October) (Crowle)*
                    Ebdomada v.^{ta} At Crowle
℃ In primis for expensis on howsold this wycke   xxvij s. viij d.
…

A Ioguller   Item to William *(blank)* A Ioguller at crowle   xij d. …   5

f 154v   *(29 November–5 December) (Grimley)*
…
                    Ebdomada x^a at grymley/ Aduent sonday
℃ In primis for expensis on howsold this wycke   xl s v d.   10
In rewardes to mynstrelles on aduent sonday   ij s. iiij d.
…

wyne   Item for claret & secke wynes on advent sonday   vj s. j d.
…
                                                                                  15

f 155   *(20–6 December) (Grimley)*
…
                    Ebdomada xiij.^a at grymley. fryday cristmas day
℃ In primis for expensis on howsold this wycke   xl s. v d.
Item vpon cristmas day to mynstrelles   xij d.   20
…
Item for master baylys & other on cristmas day at nyght

wyne for   A galand of claret ⌐viij d.⌐/ A pottell of Secke ⌐vj d.⌐/ A
þe balys   pottell of muscadell ⌐vj d.⌐   xvj d. iiij d.
Item cakes ij d./ & waferes ij d.   25

f 155v   *(27 December–2 January) (Worcester)*

          °1534° Ebdomada prima in Natale domini at wurceter
℃ In primis for expensis on howsold this wycke/ the bayliffes & ther   30
wyffes & other of þe citie with ther wyffes xviij. dyned with me sonday
seynt Iohns day iij li. iij s. xj d. ⌐vltra byff xij s.⌐
…

✓   Item to mynstrelles Innocentes day & A popet pleyer   ij s.
Item to singeres of carrowles   viij d.   35
pleyeres   Item to iiij pleyeres on Innocenses day   ij s. viij d.
Item rewardes   xvj d. ij s. ij s.
…

22/ master baylys: *Robert Luddington and Roger Ward, high and low bailiffs for 1534-5*

f 156   *(7–13 February) (Grimley)*

...

Ebdomada vij.ª at grymley/
this is quyttyde sonday

℃ In primis for expensis on howsold this wycke   xxxvij s. ij d.   5

...

Item to mynstrelles on quyttyde sonday   iij s. iiij d.

...

f 157*   *(25 April–1 May) (Battenhall)*   10

°1535° Ebdomada v.ᵗᵃ At batn⟨all⟩

℃ In primis for expensis on howsold þis wycke   ⟨...⟩

...

⟨t⟩he kynges   Item to iij of the kynges mynstrelles ˏ⸢at   15
mynstrelles   batna⟨ll⟩⸣   ⟨.....⟩

the kynges   Item to iiij of the kynges pleyeres at Wurceter   ⟨...⟩
pleyeres

(2–8 May) (Worcester)

Ebdomada vj.ᵗᵃ At Wurcet⟨er⟩   20

℃ In primis for expensis on howsold this wycke   ⟨...⟩

...

In rewardes xij d. iij s./ x d./ to A berewarde xij d./ xij d.
xij ⟨d....⟩

...   25

(9–15 May) (Battenhall)

Ebdomada vij.ª at batnall

℃ In primis for expensis on howsold this wycke   xxviij s. x d.
In rewardes to Edward porter iij s. iiij d./ to þe pleyeres of seynt   30
petures xij d.

...

f 157v   *(30 May–5 June) (Battenhall)*

...   35

⟨Ebdo⟩mada Decima At batnall

⟨**℃** In primis for expensis⟩ on howsold this wycke   xxix s. viij d.

...

⟨R⟩obyn Whod & litle Iohn of Ombursley   xij d.

...   40

(6–12 June) (Battenhall)
         Ebdomada xj.ᵃ at batnall þe dedicacion day

⟨**℄**⟩ In primis for expensis on howsold þis wycke   xxxv s. v d.

…

Item rewardes to certen singeres on þe dedicacion day in   5
þe morenyng   ij s. iiij d.

⟨the⟩ quenes   Item to William slye & his compeny beyng the quenes
pleyeres   pleyeres   vij s. vj d.

Item to the dewke of suffolke mynstrell   ⌜x⌝ xij d.

…   10

PAKINGTON OF WESTWOOD PARK

1584
Account Book of Sir John Pakington   SHRO: BA 3835/16(ii)3   15
f [10v]

…

Item to A northern bagpiper   xij d.

…

APPENDIX 1
Post-1642 Pageant House Leases

12 feet wide

The pageant houses near St Martin's Gate in Worcester's Cornmarket first appear in a lease of 1492/3, where their location is used to clarify the position of the leased land. References to the pageant houses continue through the sixteenth century; there were apparently two such buildings (see Worcester Rent Roll, 1605–6) and by 1583–4 they were no longer used to house 'pageants,' though their traditional name persisted through the seventeenth century. Their exact location in the Cornmarket is uncertain enough that I include these two leases of the property from the later seventeenth century. Three leases were drawn up, in 1659, 1680/1, and 1682. The texts of all three are identical except for the names of the principals and the later leases have therefore not been transcribed. The 1680/1 lease includes an assignment on the dorse, however, and this has been transcribed.

Worcester, St Helen's Record Office, BA 5955/7/iv; 16 September 1659; English; parchment; single sheet; 460mm x 644mm, bottom 34mm folded over; decorated initial at beginning.

Worcester, St Helen's Record Office, BA 5955/7/iia; 5 January 1680/1; English; parchment; single sheet; 460mm x 644mm, bottom 34mm folded over; a copy of above with assignment on dorse.

1659
Pageant House Lease   SHRO: BA 5955/7/iv
single sheet   *(16 September)*

This Indenture made the sixteenth day of September in the yeare of   5
our Lord God (according to the account now vsed in England) one
thousand six hundred ffiftie and Nine, Betweene the Master wardens
and Comonalty of Weavers Walkers and Clothiers within the Citty
and County of the Citty of Worcester on the one parte And Thomas
Not the Elder of the sayd Citty of Worcester and County of the same   10
Citty Walker and Clothier on the other parte Witnesseth That the
sayd Master Wardens and Comonalty of Weavers, Walkers and

Clothiers aswell for and in Consideracion of the yearely Rents
hereafter in and by these presents mencioned expressed and reserved,
to bee payd in Maner as is hereafter sett downe, And for and in hope
of performance, of all and every the Covenants promises and grants,
in these presents mencioned and Conteyned, as alsoe for diverse other   5
goods causes and valuable consideracions them herevnto moveing,
Have demised, granted, leased, sett, and to farme letten, And by these
presents doe demise, grant, lease, sett and to farme lett vnto the sayd
Thomas Nott his Executours Administratours & Assignes and every
of them, all that theyr Messuage or Tenement withall and singular   10
the appertenaunces to the sayd Messuage or Tenement belonging or
apperteyning lying and being in the parrish of St Martin in the sayd
City of Worcester, neere vnto the Corne markett of the sayd Citty,
And is adioyning on the South side to a house or Tenement now in
the possession or occupacion of Thomas Hill Blacksmith, And on   15
the East side to the Towne wall, And on the North side to a house
or Tenement now in the possession of Iohn Oliver And on the West
side to a way that leadeth from the foregate to the sayd Cornemarkett
And Alsoe all and singular, buildings Chambers, Shopps, lights,
wayes, entryes, easements, profitts, Comodyties, and advantages   20
whatsoever, to the sayd Messuage or Tenement belonging or in any
wise apperteyning, To have and to hould all and singular the sayd
Messuage or Tenement, and all other the premisses with theyr and
every of theyr appertenances and every parte and parcell thereof vnto
the sayd Thomas Nott his Executours Administratours and Assignes   25
from the Nine and twentieth day of this instant September, vnto the
end and tearme, and for and dureing the full tearme of Thirty and
Seaven yeares from thence next ensueing and fully to bee compleate
& ended, yeelding and paying therefore yearely and every yeare
dureing the sayd Tearme vnto the sayd Master wardens and   30
Comonalty of Weavers, Walker & Clothiers within the sayd Citty
of Worcester and to their Successours, or vnto their Sufficient Deputie,
or Attorney in that behalfe appoynted the yearely Rent or Summe
of Tirty three shillings and foure pence of Lawfull english money at
foure vsuall dayes or tymes in the yeare that is to say the ffive and   35
twentieth day of December, the ffive and twentieth day of March,
the ffoure and twentieth day of Iune and the Nine and twentieth day
of September, by even and equall porcions, the first payment thereof
to begin vpon the ffive and twentieth day of December next after the
date of these presents, And if it shall hapen the sayd yearely rent of   40

31/ Walker for Walkers   34/ Tirty for Thirty

Thirtie three shillings and ffoure pence to bee behinde and vnpayd in
parte or in all, by the space of Twentie dayes next after any of the sayd
dayes of payment on which the same ought to bee payd as aforesayd,
the same being lawfully demanded, that then and from thencefourth
it shall and may bee lawfull to and for the sayd Master wardens and   5
Comonalty of Weaver Walkers & Clothiers and theyr Successors and
theyr Assignes into all the sayd demised premises with the
appertenaunces and every parte and parcell thereof to reenter and the
same to repossesse, and have againe as in theyr former Estate or Estates
these presents or any herein Conteyned to the Contrary thereof in   10
any wise notwithstanding And the sayd Thomas Nott for himselfe
his Executours Administratours and Assignes and for Every of them
doth hereby Covenant promise and grant to and with the sayd Master
wardens and Comonalty of Weavers, Walkers, and Clothiers their
Successours & Assigns and every of them That hee the sayd Thomas   15
Nott his Executours Administratours or Assignes or some of them
at his and theyr owne proper Costes and Charges shall and will from
tyme to tyme and at all tymes hereafter when and as often as neede
shall require well and sufficiently repayr vphold susteyne, maynteyne
amend and keepe, all and singular the sayd demised premisses and   20
every parte and parcell thereof together with the pavements of the
soyle thereto belonging as alsoe soe much of the Towne Wall as is
adioyning to the sayd Messuage or Tenement in by and with all
needefull and necessary repayracions dureing the sayd tearme, And
the sayd premisses and every parte and parcell thereof, being so   25
sufficiently, repayred, vpholden, susteyned maynteyned amended
paved and kept, in the end of the sayd Tearme shall leave and yeeld
vp vnto the sayd Master wardens and Comonalty of Weavers Walkers
and Clothiers theyr successours or Assignes, And the sayd Thomas
Nott for himselfe his Executours Administratours and Assignes and   30
for every of them doth Covenant, promise and agree to and with the
sayd Master wardens and Comonalty of Weavers Walkers and
Clothiers theyr Successours and Assignes and to and with every of
them by these presents that they the sayd Master wardens and
Comonalty of Weavers Walkers and Clothiers theyr Successours and   35
Assignes shall and may twice in every yeare (at theyr Convenient
leasure) dureing the aforesayd tearme into the sayd Messuage or
Tenement and every parte and parcell thereof to enter and veiwe and
see whether the sayd House or Tenement and every parte thereof bee
well and sufficiently repayred and amended according to the true   40

6/ Weaver *for* Weavers   36/ may *for* may have leave (?)

intent and meaning of these presents And the sayd Thomas Nott for
himselfe his Executours Administratours and Assignes and for every
of them doth Covenant promise and grant to and with the sayd Master
wardens and Comonalty of Weavers Walkers and Clothiers their
Sucessors and Assignes and to and with every of them by these presents   5
That hee the sayd Thomas Nott his Executours Administratours and
Assignes shall not, nor will not, dureing the aforesayd tearme of Thirty
and Seaven yeares grant Assigne or sett over the sayd Messuage or
Tenement or any parte thereof to any person or persons whatsoever
(except to his wife Child or Children) for any tyme or terme in this   10
Indenture mencioned without the speciall lycense and Consent of the
sayd Master wardens and Comonalty of Weavers Walkers & Clothiers
aforesayd therevnto first had and obteyned in writeing vnder the Seale
of the Corporacion, And the sayd Master Wardens and Comonalty
of Weavers Walkers & Clothiers for themselves theyr Successours   15
and Assignes and for every of them doe Covenant promise and grant
to and with the sayd Thomas Nott his Executours Administratours
and Assignes, and to and with every of them by these presents, That
hee the sayd Thomas Not his Executours Administratours & Assignes
and every of them for the yearely Rent herein before reserved and   20
by and vnder the Covenants herein Conteyned shall and may
peaceably and quietly have, hold, vse, occupie possesse and enioy all
and singular the sayd demised premisses and every parte and parcell
thereof dureing the aforesayd tearme without any lett, trouble,
eviccion, eieccion expulcion disturbance, clayme, denyall or demands   25
of them the sayd Master wardens and Comonalty of Weavers, Walkers
& Clothiers theyr Successours or Assignes or of any other person or
persons whatsoever lawfully clayming or to Clayme from by or vnder
them or any of them In witness whereof the sayd Thomas Nott hath
herevnto put his hand and seale the day and yeare aboue written/   30

single sheet verso

Sealed and Delivered in the presence of   35
        Kenelm Wilkes
        Raphe Billingsley
        William Cole
        William Baker
Counterparte of Thomas Nott Esquire   40

5/ Sucessors for Successors

°Writings belonging to the Pagen house
Lease for 37 years Date 1659°

1680/1
Pageant House Lease   SHRO: BA 5955/7/iia   5
single sheet verso   *(5 January)*

Memor*andum* That Henry Evans of the City of Wor*cester* Clothier
and Elizabeth his wife Daughter and Adm*inistrat*rix of the goods and
Cha*ttelles* of the *wi*thin named Thomas Nott ffor and in consideracion 10
of the ffull som*me* of five pounds of lawfull money of England to
them in hand paid by Richard Evans of the same City Clothier Doe
hereby graunt Assigne and Sett over vnto the Said Richard Evans his
Ex*ecutou*rs Adm*ini*stratou*r*s & Assignes All and Singuler the *wi*thin
Demised Mesuage or tenem*ent* and *p*remisses *wi*th the appertena*u*nces 15
And all their and eyther of their right title estate intrest terme of yeares
claime & Demand therein or thereto together *wi*th this Indenture of
lease To haue and to hold the said graunted and assigned *p*remisses
*wi*th the appertena*u*nces and the said Indent⟨ure⟩ of lease to him the
said Richard Evans his Ex*ecutou*rs & Assignes from the Date hereof   20
for and Dureing all the rest and residue of the *wi*thin menc*i*oned terme
of yeares yett to come & vnexpired in as large and ample manner as
they the said Henry Evans and Elizabeth his wife or eyther of them
might or ought to have hold or enioyed the same In Wittnes whereof
they the said Henry Evans and Elizabeth his wife have hereunto putt   25
their hands and seales this ffifth Day of Ianuary 1681
Sealed and Deliuered by Eliz*abeth*   ye Marke of
Evans in *p*resence of *(signed)* Iohn ffry/.   Elizabeth E Evans
Sealed and Deliuered by Henry Evans   *(signed)* Henry Evans
in *p*resence of *(signed)* Iohn ffry.   30
            (signed) Will*i*am Holkman

2/ 37 *corrected in pencil from* 39
28/ *Elizabeth Evans signed with her personal mark*

APPENDIX 2
Documents Preserved in Worcester Repositories

The documents in this appendix, though now in Worcester archives, are relevant to an area wider than the county itself. Their application is in both cases to the whole country and they have been included here since they cannot be conveniently localized and will therefore not fit precisely within the scope of any of the volumes in this series.

The first document is a manuscript copy of Henry VIII's proclamation of 22 July 1541 (*STC*: 7795) prohibiting the observance of a variety of saints' days and feasts, including several whose traditional celebration involved disguisings, song, and dance. The text was copied into a miscellaneous volume at Worcester Cathedral containing, in addition to a register of letters and proclamations, a variety of inventories and accounts for receipts and expenditures.

The proclamation is clearly intended to abolish the boy bishop's mass and sermon, along with the traditional money-gathering in which he and his fellow choristers went from house to house. It is therefore interesting to note that the canons' bakehouse rolls of Hereford Cathedral still record a payment '*paruo Episcopo pro vino existenti ad missam*' in 1543–4 (p 119 above). The most natural interpretation of this is that the chapter had chosen to disregard the proclamation; evasion of uncongenial royal edicts about religious practice was by no means uncommon in Tudor England, particularly in places relatively remote from the seat of government where the infraction was less likely to be found out. On the other hand, it is not impossible that, while discontinuing the traditional observances as the royal proclamation required, the chapter at Hereford continued to recognize a boy whom the choristers elected as their bishop and to give him his accustomed perquisite on Holy Innocents' Day, even though he no longer had any special duties to perform then.

Worcester, Cathedral Library, A12; early 16th c.; Latin and English; paper; i + 175 + i; 320mm x 220mm; foliated 1–23, 23, 24–144, 144, 145–173; 19th c. suede binding (spine much damaged). Includes inventories, accounts, and register.

The second document is a performing licence from the master of the revels, Sir Henry Herbert, whose principal residence was at Ribbesford, Worcestershire. Herbert's period of tenure in the office is a matter of considerable complexity; although he styled himself 'master of the Revels' from about 1623 on, he formally received a grant in 1629 of the reversion of the office on the death of both Ben Jonson (d. 1635) and Sir John Ashley (d. 1641). Herbert may very well have bought out Jonson's and Ashley's interest. Despite these complications, he was undisputedly in charge of the office in 1631 for all practical purposes (see DNB).

Thomas and Cicely Peadle (p 539, l. 42–p 540, l. 1) were very likely members of the well-known performing family whose name is also spelled 'Pedel.' Although their relationships are not clearly known, three other members of the family, Abraham, William, and Jacob, performed in Germany as part of the company of English actors in the service of John Sigismund, elector of Brandenburg, during the years 1614–15. By 1623 Abraham was playing at the Fortune, probably as a member of the palsgrave's men. William appears in a variety of provincial records as a pantomimist and acrobat from 1616–39, though the later records may refer to his son of the same name, first mentioned as a performer in 1620. Jacob, who seems to have been the eldest of the Peadles, also performed in Germany in 1597 in Thomas Sackville's company. (See Murray, *English Dramatic Companies*, vol 2, pp 248, 253, 342, 346; Chambers, *The Elizabethan Stage*, vol 2, p 332; and Nungezer, *A Dictionary of Actors*, pp 270–1.)

The presence of this document in the Worcester Record Office is not easy to explain, but the possibility should not be ignored that it may have been forfeit within the county for some infraction of its terms.

Worcester, St Helen's Record Office, BA 4935/xxxiv; 1631; English; paper; single sheet; 265mm x 210mm; decorated initial at beginning, some words in display head.

1541
Royal Proclamation   WCL: A12
ff 149–50   (22 July)

> A proclamacion deuised by the kynges maiestie. by the advice   5
> of hys hyghnes councell the xxij day of Iuly: in the xxxiij yere
> of hys maiesties reygne.
>
> ffor as moche as the feastes of sayncte luke and Seyncte Marke
> Euangelistes: Occurrynge with thyn the termes holden at   10
> Westminster/ And also the feaste of Sayncte Mary magdalen fallynge
> within the tyme of harueste were Amongest other abrogated and
> comaunded. to be obserued as holy dayes:/ the kynges hyghnes
> considerynge that the same saynctes ben often and many tymes
> mentioned in playne and manyffeste scripture. wylleth and   15
> comaundeth. that the said iij feastes from hensforthe shalbe celebrated

13/ not *omitted after* comaunded

and kepte holy dayes: As in tymes past they haue ben vsed And
further. more where as in dyuers parties of thys realme Sayncte Markes
day hath ben vsed as A fastynge day. And in Some other places of thys
hys realme: the people haue vsed customably to eate flesshe: The
kynges most gracious maiestie wyllynge an vniforme maner and   5
fasshion ther in to be obserued throughoute this hys realme and
Dominions of the same/ And for that the day of no Sayncte hath ben
vsed to be fasted: but only the said day of Saynt Marke. Wylleth and
comaundeth that from hensforth through. oute all thys hys realme
the sayd. of sayncte Marke shall no⟨t⟩ be taken ne kept [and ta] as   10
fastynge day. but yt shalbe laufull to All and euery hys gracis
subiecte⟨s⟩ to eate flesshe or suche other meat as to them shalbe thought
expedient without gru‸ᵣd¹ge or scruple of conscience And where also
as by the variable and vncertayne fallynge of the feaste of Easter The
feast of the Inuencion of the Crosse comonlye called saynct Elyns   15
day for the moost parte | chaunceth within Easter terme holden at
Westminster. and yet some yere out of the sayd terme ambiguitie and
dout hath reson Amonges subiettes whether the sayd feast shulde be
celebrate and kept holy day or no. The kynges moost benigne grace
of hys Infynite goodnes willyng one vniforme order herein to be   20
obserued Amonge all hys faythfull subiettes/ Ordenyth And
comaundeth. that as the sayd feast fallynge within the terme ys not
kept holyday. So lykewyse at Altymes from hensforth yt shal not be
obserued accepted ne taken as holyday/ Though yt fall out of the
terme/ but that yt shalbe laufull vn to all the kynges subiectes. to vse   25
and excersise all Maner of labures and occupacions as of Any other
workynday/ And lykewyse the exaltacion of the Crosse fallynge in
harueste or out of harueste shalnot be kept as holy day/ but that all
the kynges subiettes to vse all maner labures as of Any other Workyng
day/ Also where as the day of saynt larance fallyng within the tyme   30
of haruest was abrogated and comaunded not to be obserued as holy
day. And yet that not withstandyng many of the kynges subiettes
doth obserue and kepe the feast vpon the yeven. thynckyng them self
to be bound in consciens so to do in as moche as ‸ᵣin¹ the abrogacion
of the holy day. ther was no expresse Mencion made of the takyng   35
Away of the faste vpon the yeven. som other lyke as in deed yt was
ment at the makynge of the sayd ordynance. doth omyt as we the
fastyng of the sayd yeven. as the haloweng of the day/ The kynge
oure souerayn lord wyllynge to remoue and put Away from Amonges
hys lege people all occasion of variance dyuersite discord. discencion   40

10/ sayd *for* sayd day   37/ we *for* well (?)

or debate/ And to stablesshe them all in on conformable and vniforme
ordre in all suche publyque obseruaunce declareth and comaundeth
that from hensforth. the sayd yeven of saynct larance shal not be taken
ne kept as A fastynge day/ but that yt may be laufull to all and euery
his gracys louyng subiettes to eate flesshe and all other kyndes of   5
meates without Any gruge or scruple of consciens/ And where as
heretofore dyuerse and many supersticious and chyldesshe
obseruacions hath be vsed and yet to thys day ar obserued and kept
in many and sondry parties of thys Realme: As vpon saynct Nicholas.
Saynct kateryn. Saynt Clement. the holy Innocentes And suche lyke   10
chyldern be strangely dect and appareled to counturfett prystes/
bisshops/ And women/ And so be [with] led with songes and Daunces
from howse to howse blessyng the people and getheryng of money.
And boys do synge Masse and preche in the pulpytt with suche other
vnfyttyng and inconuenient vsages/ rather to the derysyon then to   15
Any trewe glorye of god or honoure of hys saynctes/ The kynges
maiestie therfor Myndynge nothyng so Moche as to Auaunce the
trew glory of god without vayne | supersticion willeth and comaundeth
that from hensforth all suche supersticious obseruacions be left and
clerely extinguesshed throughout all thys hys realme and Domynyons   20
for as Moche as the same do resemble rather the vnlaufull supersticion
of gentilite then the pure and syncere Religion of Criste/   God
saue the kynge/
        Thomas Berthelet regius Impressor excudebat
        Cum priuilegio ad Imprimendum solum Anno domini   25
        millesimo d. [xxxiij]. xlj.

1631

Licence from the Master of the Revels   SHRO: BA 4935/xxxiv
single sheet   *(29 August)*   30

To all Maiors, Sheriffes, Iustices of the Peace, Bayliffes, Constables,
Headborroughes and all other his Maiesties Officers, true Leigemen
and Subiectes and to euery of them Greeting Knowe yee that whereas
the Kings most Excellent Maiestie hath graunted vnto the Master of   35
the Revells a Comission vnder the great Seale of England, Giveing
thereby charge with full power and authoritie to the said Master of
the Revells and his deputie for the ordering Reformeing authorizing
and putting downe of all and euery playes, Players and Playmakers
as of all other Shewes whatsoeuer in all places within his Maiesties   40
Realme of England as well within ffranchises and Liberties as without
I haue by these presentes Licensed and authorized Sisley Peadle;

Thomas Peadle her sonne Elias Grundling and three more in theire
Company to vse and exercise daunceing on the Roapes, Tumbling,
Maulling and other such like ffeates which they or any of them are
practized in or can performe Requireing you and euery of you in his
Maiestes name to suffer and permitt them the said Sisley Peadle,   5
Thomas Peadle, Elias Grundling and theire said assotiates quietly to
passe and to sett forth and shewe those thinges before mencioned
with such musiccke drumme or Trumpettes as they shall thinke fitting
for the same ffrom time to time and att all time and times without
any of your Lettes or molestacion within any of your Liberties and   10
places of Iurisdiccion Townes Corporate Citties or Borroughes
wheresoeuer within the Realme of England, and alsoe to be aydeing
and assisting vnto them if any wrong or Iniury shall be offered vnto
them or any of them They behaueing themselues honestly and
according to the Lawes of this Realme and forbearing to make shewe   15
on the Saboth day &c in the time of devine service you affording
them your Townehalls, Mootehalls, Guildhalls or some convenient
place to shewe in And what Company soeuer eyther Stage Players
or such as make shewe of mocions and strange Sightes shall repaire
vnto any of your Townes Corporate, Citties Boroughes or Villages   20
not haueing theire authoritie ymediatlie from me or confirmed by me
and Sealed with the Seale of the Office of the Revells That forthwith
you seize and take from them any Graunt or Comission whatsoeuer
they beare and send yt to me According to those Warrantes directed
to you the Mayors, Sheriffes, Iustices of the Peace, Bayliffes   25
Constables of all Townes Corporate, Citties Boroughes or Villages
heretofore by the right honorable the Lord Chamberlaine of the Kings
Maiesties most Honorable household And if you finde any traveyling
without License That forthwith you apprehend and imprison them
or give them such condigne punishment as in your discretions they   30
shall deserue Prouided that this License continue in force but for and
dureing the terme and space of one whole yeare and noe Longer next
ensueing the date hereof Giuen att his Maiesties Office of the Revells
vnder my hand and the Seale of the said Office the nyne and twentieth
daie of August In the Seaventh yeare of the Raigne of our most gracious   35
Soueraigne Lord Charles by the grace of God King of England
Scotland ffraunce and Ireland defender of the faith &c Annoque
domini One thousand sixe hundred

26/ One thousand sixe hundred: *remainder of year date missing where bottom of page cut off*

Prior More's Household Players

The accounting procedures and contents of Prior More's Account Book have been discussed in the Introduction (pp 304–5 and 307–8). This appendix provides a clarification of the weekly payments among More's household expenses which alternate between payments to two players and payments to the fund of 'seyny' money, that is, money given in support of the kitchen for monks who had been routinely bled (see p 291, endnote to HRO f 28). The relationship between these payments, other than the fact of their alternation, is obscure.

Prior More specified no 'seyny'/players' payments in the first year of his priorate, 1518–19, nor any after his thirteenth year, 1530–1. The normal pattern was: payments for 'seyny' money for the first nine weeks of Michaelmas term, payments to players during Advent and the week of Christmas (normally four weeks, but possibly five), payments for 'seyny' money until Quinquagesima week, then payments to players during Lent and Easter week, and finally payments for 'seyny' money for the remainder of the year, with the exception of Rogation week and Whitsun week when payments are again made to players. Thus players' payments may be made for thirteen or fourteen weeks out of fifty-two.

The whole of this pattern is not followed every year. In 1519–20, there is no payment of either kind listed for most of the weeks in which players' payments are usually found in later years. The next year, 1520–1, also contains some gaps: there are no payments of either kind listed for the first week of Advent, Holy Week, or Easter week. In 1523–4 no payment of either kind was made in Easter week and in 1525–6 the third week of Advent, Quinquagesima week, and Holy Week are similarly without payments.

In other years, the omission of the players' payments is connected with the prior's absences in London or with his illness. In 1524–5, the prior was in London from the eighth week of Christmas term until Lady Day. No payments for the two players were made while he was away, although Quinquagesima week, when such payments usually started again, was the third week of his stay. In fact, no payments were made of either kind during Lent or at Easter in 1524–5, even after the prior's return. Curiously, 'seyny' payments were made for his household the first two weeks of his stay in London: only the players' payment was suspended during and immediately after the trip. In 1526–7, the prior spent thirteen weeks during the Michaelmas and Christmas terms in London, including the weeks of Advent when players' payments were usually made. Once again, the 'seyny' payments continued in his absence, but the players' payments are not recorded. In 1529–30, a six-week absence in London during Michaelmas term caused both the players' payments and the 'seyny' payments to be suspended. The next year an illness during Holy Week, Easter week, and the following week caused two players' payments not to be made, although the expected 'seyny' payment the week of Low Sunday was made.

Is it possible that the players' payments were considered by the prior as primarily personal, rather than as a household expense? His absences from Worcester and his illness consistently caused a suspension in these payments, while 'seyny' money payments more frequently continued during an absence. This is shown in the years cited above, as well as by a seven-week absence in London in 1522–3, during which 'seyny' payments continued. Unfortunately there is simply too little evidence, and all of it indirect, to allow any conclusions to be drawn.

The following table summarizes Prior More's weekly payments for 'seyny' money or to two players. The weeks are listed according to the ecclesiastical terms which form the basis for the prior's bookkeeping, beginning on 29 September with Michaelmas term (12–13 weeks), Christmas term (12–13 weeks), Annunciation term (12–13 weeks), and St John Baptist term (13–14 weeks).

Abbreviations

P	payments to two players
S	payments for 'seyny' money
N	no payment
(L)	Prior More in London

1519–20	Payment	Number of Weeks
Michaelmas 1–8	S	8
Michaelmas 9 (Advent)	N	1
Michaelmas 10–12	P	3
Christmas 1	N	1
Christmas 2–8	S	7
Christmas 9–12	N (L)	4
Christmas 13–		
Annunciation 3 (Easter)	N	4
Annunciation 4–7	S	4
Annunciation 8 (Rogation)	N	1
Annunciation 9	S	1
Annunciation 10 (Whitsun)	N	1
Annunciation 11–		
St John Baptist 14	S	17

1520–1	Payment	Number of Weeks
Michaelmas 1–9	S	9
Michaelmas 10 (Advent)	N	1
Michaelmas 11–13	P	3
Christmas 1–6	S	6
Christmas 7–12	P	6
Annunciation 1–2 (Easter)	N	2
Annunciation 3–6	S	4
Annunciation 7 (Rogation)	P	1
Annunciation 8	S	1
Annunciation 9 (Whitsun)	P	1
Annunciation 10– St John Baptist 14	S	18

1521–2		
Michaelmas 1–9	S	9
Michaelmas 10 (Advent)– Christmas 1	P	4
Christmas 2–10	S	9
Christmas 11 (Quinquagesima)– Annunciation 5 (Easter)	P	8
Annunciation 6	S	1
Annunciation 7–8	S (L)	2
Annunciation 9	S	1
Annunciation 10 (Rogation)	P	1
Annunciation 11	S	1
Annunciation 12 (Whitsun)	P	1
Annunciation 13	S	1
St John Baptist 1	N	1
St John Baptist 2–14	S	13

1522–3		
Michaelmas 1–9	S	9
Michaelmas 10 (Advent)– Christmas 1	P	4
Christmas 2–8	S	7
Christmas 9 (Quinquagesima)– Annunciation 3 (Easter)	P	8
Annunciation 4–7	S	4
Annunciation 8 (Rogation)	P	1
Annunciation 9	S	1
Annunciation 10 (Whitsun)	P	1

1522–3 *(cont)*	Payment	Number of Weeks
Annunciation 11–		
St John Baptist 4	S (L)	7
St John Baptist 5–14	S	10
1523–4		
Michaelmas 1–9	S	9
Michaelmas 10 (Advent)–13	P	4
Christmas 1–6	S	6
Christmas 7 (Quinquagesima)–13	P	7
Annunciation 1 (Easter)	N	1
Annunciation 2–5	S	4
Annunciation 6 (Rogation)	P	1
Annunciation 7	S	1
Annunciation 8 (Whitsun)	P	1
Annunciation 9–		
St John Baptist 13	S	18
1524–5		
Michaelmas 1–9	S	9
Michaelmas 10 (Advent)–13	P	4
Christmas 1	N	1
Christmas 2–7	S	6
Christmas 8–9	S (L)	2
Christmas 10–13	N (L)	4
Annunciation 1–4 (Easter)	N	4
Annunciation 5–8	S	4
Annunciation 9 (Rogation)	P	1
Annunciation 10	S	1
Annunciation 11 (Whitsun)	P	1
Annunciation 12–		
St John Baptist 1	S	3
St John Baptist 2	N	1
St John Baptist 3–14	S	12
1525–6		
Michaelmas 1–9	S	9
Michaelmas 10 (Advent)–11	P	2
Michaelmas 12	N	1
Christmas 1	P	1
Christmas 2–7	S	6
Christmas 8 (Quinquagesima)	N	1

1525–6 *(cont)*	Payment	Number of Weeks
Christmas 9–13	P	5
Annunciation 1	N	1
Annunciation 2 (Easter)	P	1
Annunciation 3–6	S	4
Annunciation 7 (Rogation)	P	1
Annunciation 8	S	1
Annunciation 9 (Whitsun)	P	1
Annunciation 10–		
St John Baptist 14	S	18

1526–7		
Michaelmas 1–3	S	3
Michaelmas 4–9	S (L)	6
Michaelmas 10 (Advent)–		
Christmas 1	N (L)	4
Christmas 2–4	S (L)	3
Christmas 5	S (L, Worcester)	1
Christmas 6–10	S	5
Christmas 11 (Quinquagesima)–		
Annunciation 5 (Easter)	P	8
Annunciation 6–9	S	4
Annunciation 10 (Rogation)	P	1
Annunciation 11	S	1
Annunciation 12 (Whitsun)	P	1
Annunciation 13–		
St John Baptist 14	S	15

1527–8		
Michaelmas 1–9	S	9
Michaelmas 10 (Advent)–		
Christmas 1	P	4
Christmas 2–9	S	8
Christmas 10 (Quinquagesima)–		
Annunciation 4 (Easter)	P	8
Annunciation 5–8	S	4
Annunciation 9 (Rogation)	P	1
Annunciation 10	S	1
Annunciation 11 (Whitsun)	P	1
Annunciation 12–		
St John Baptist 14	S	16

1528–9	**Payment**	**Number of Weeks**
Michaelmas 1–9	S	9
Michaelmas 10 (Advent)–13	P	4
Christmas 1–6	S	6
Christmas 7 (Quinquagesima)–		
Annunciation 1 (Easter)	P	8
Annunciation 2–5	S	4
Annunciation 6 (Rogation)	P	1
Annunciation 7	S	1
Annunciation 8 (Whitsun)	P	1
Annunciation 9–		
St John Baptist 11	S	16
(rest missing)		

1529–30		
Michaelmas 1–4	S	4
Michaelmas 5–10	N (L)	6
Michaelmas 11	N	1
Michaelmas 12	P	1
Christmas 1–9	S	9
Christmas 10 (Quinquagesima)–13	P	4
Annunciation 1–3 (missing)	—	3
Annunciation 4 (Easter)	P	1
Annunciation 5–8	S	4
Annunciation 9 (Rogation)	N	1
Annunciation 10	S	1
Annunciation 11 (Whitsun)	P	1
Annunciation 12–		
St John Baptist 14	S	16

1530–1		
Michaelmas 1–8	S	8
Michaelmas 9 (Advent)–		
Christmas 1	P	5
Christmas 2–5	S	4
Christmas 6–8	N (L)	3
Christmas 9 (Quinquagesima)–		
Annunciation 1	P	6
Annunciation 2 (ill)–3 (Easter) (ill)	N	2
Annunciation 4 (ill)–7	S	4
Annunciation 8 (Rogation)	P	1
Annunciation 9	S	1

1530–1	Payment	Number of Weeks
Annunciation 10 (Whitsun)	P	1
Annunciation 11–St John Baptist 14		
(St John Baptist 12 ill)	S	17

APPENDIX 4
Saints' Days and Festivals

The following table contains the dates for all the feast days to which reference is made in the documents. The exact dates of moveable feasts are given in textual footnotes. See also the tables in C.R. Cheney, *Handbook of Dates for Students of English History*, pp 84–161.

Advent Sunday	nearest Sunday to feast of St Andrew (30 November)
St Anne	26 July
Ascension Day	Thursday after Rogation Sunday, ie, 40 days after Easter
St Benedict (Benet)	21 March
Black Monday	Easter Monday, the Monday after Easter
Candlemas	2 February
St Catherine	25 November
Christmas	25 December
Circumcision	1 January
St Clement	23 November
Corpus Christi Day	Thursday after Trinity Sunday, the eighth Sunday after Easter
Dedication Day, Worcester Priory	6 June
Easter	Sunday after the first full moon on or following 21 March
Epiphany	6 January
St George	23 April
St Gregory	12 March
St Helen	see Holy Cross, invention of
Hock Days	second Monday and Tuesday after Easter
Holy Cross	
exaltation of	14 September
invention of	3 May

Holy Innocents' Day	28 December
Holy Rood Day	*see* Holy Cross, invention of
St James	25 July
St John the Baptist, nativity of	24 June
St John the Evangelist	27 December
Lady Day	25 March
St Lawrence	10 August
Low Sunday	Sunday after Easter
St Luke	18 October
St Mark	25 April
St Mary the Virgin	
annunciation to	25 March
assumption of	15 August
conception of	8 December
nativity of	8 September
purification of	2 February
St Mary Magdalene	22 July
St Maurus	15 January
May Day	1 May
St Michael (Michaelmas)	29 September
Midsummer	24 June
New Year's Day	1 January
St Nicholas	6 December
St Oswald, bishop of Worcester	28 February
St Oswald, king and martyr	
feast of	5 August
translation of	8 October
Palm Sunday	sixth Sunday in Lent
Passion Sunday	fifth Sunday in Lent
Pentecost	seventh Sunday after Easter
Sts Philip and Jacob	1 May
Quadragesima Sunday	first Sunday in Lent
Quinquagesima (Quittide)	Sunday before Ash Wednesday
Rogation Sunday	fifth Sunday after Easter
St Stephen	26 December
St Thomas, archbishop and martyr	
feast of	29 December
translation of	7 July
Trinity Sunday	Sunday after Pentecost, ie, eighth Sunday after Easter
Twelfth Day	6 January
Whitsunday	*see* Pentecost
St Wulfstan	19 January

Translations

ABIGAIL ANN YOUNG

DIOCESE OF WORCESTER

1240
Constitutions of Bishop Walter Cantilupe   LPL: MS 171
f 41v*   *(26 July) (Part 1, On the state of the church: chapter 4,
Concerning churchyards)*

...

We believe that churchyards also, which contain the bodies of those
who are to be saved, many of whom now cleansed await the (white)
robe of their glorification, are dishonourably disfigured by the filth
of dumb animals. Therefore we also order that they should be properly
fenced in by a hedge or wall, canonically compelling to do this those
to whom (responsibility for) their enclosure is known to belong.

(We forbid) the rectors and priests of churches also to pasture their
animals in the churchyards or even to allow (them) to enter. But if they
presume (to do so) they should be aware that they will be seriously
punished.

Also, to preserve reverence for the churchyard as well as the church
we forbid markets to be held in churchyards or other consecrated
places – or indeed anywhere else on Sundays – or legal cases involving
bloodshed to be tried. Neither shall there be unsuitable plays/
pastimes, especially on the eves of the saints and (on) the (patronal?)
feasts of the church, because we know that such things bring shame
to the saints rather than honour to those presuming (to take part in
them) and also to the priests who support the doing of these things
when they have been canonically restrained (from doing so). Neither
shall there be any buildings in churchyards, except perhaps if a period
of war makes it necessary and if (any buildings) were erected, they
should be torn down....

f 45v* *(Chapter 29, Concerning wanton behaviour)*

...It ought also to be asked whether the canon of the mass be properly
restored in all churches. We also forbid clerics from being present at
ᵛ unsuitable plays/pastimes or dances or from playing at gambling or
dice. And they shall not undertake for games/pastimes of the king and
queen to take place, nor for quintains to be set up, nor for public
wrestling rings to be put up, nor (shall they tolerate) unsuitable guild
ales (?), especially (those involving) traders and outsiders which we
completely forbid to take place (and) through which we know that
many dangers arise....

...

f 47v   *(Part 2, On the correction of priests: chapter 33)*

Moreover we order that there be no carriage (of goods) on feast- days
and holy days, nor any markets, and if any should be found to have
been at fault in this (respect) and do not cease after being warned, they
would be called before the chapter and there seriously punished. We
order that the same (restrictions) as there are about markets be
observed concerning games/pastimes on consecrated ground so that
they will not take place....

1391
Register of Bishop Henry Wakefield   SHRO: BA 2648/4/iv
ff 86–6v*   *(20–1 November)* *(Orders for the appointment and
conduct of stipendiary chaplains)*
...
...Nor shall they (the chaplains) then be allowed to wander about in
the nave of the church to which they have been admitted | as is
described above, either in the churchyard or elsewhere in the field.
And if they receive a reminder and reproof about these (matters) from
those who are then in charge of the churches, they should not behave
stubbornly towards them on account of that nor show themselves to
be puffed up and they will not by the occasion of such a reproof stir
up others who help them in their insolent behaviour or succour them
(to do) anything against the rectors, vicars, or their deputies. Instead
they will show themselves to be humble in all these abovesaid matters
and offer deserved respect. But those said priests are to begin their own
masses on the said Sundays and holy days or when the body of some
dead person is present right after the gospel reading of the principal
mass and not before unless the permission of the rector, vicar, or other

spiritual deputy has been obtained beforehand. In fact the aforesaid priests are not to detract from rectors or vicars of churches or chapels when they celebrate, but are to learn with the psalmist to keep watch over their tongues. Likewise (we order) that they not frequent taverns, shows, or other disreputable places, nor harmful and illicit plays/ pastimes, but that they behave in a priestly fashion in their appearance and their manners lest their ministry – God forbid! – fall into blame, scandal, or neglect....

...

1450

Notebook of John Lawern   Bodl.: MS Bodley 692
f 163v*   *(6 April) (Letter from John Carpenter, bishop of Worcester, to John Lawern)*

⟨John⟩ by divine permission bishop of Worcester to his beloved sons in Christ Master John Lawern, STD, almoner of our cathedral church of Worcester, and each and every rector, vicar, or chaplain whomsoever having a cure (of souls and) established in our diocese. Greetings, ⟨grace, and blessing *(?)*⟩. An unmistakable rumour of grief has filled the inner reaches of our spirit with bitterness about a noxious corruption tending to reduce persons of either sex to a state of (spiritual) illness which, we are sorry to say, we should think has escaped the notice of none of you. (For you must have known) how on one set day usually, alas, when the solemn feast of Easter has ended (*ie,* at the conclusion of the quindene of Easter) women feign to bind men, and on another (*or* the next) day men feign to bind women, and to do other things – would that they were not dishonourable or worse! – in full view of passers-by, even pretending to increase church profit but earning a loss (*literally,* damnation) for the soul under false pretences. Many scandals arise from the occasion of these activities, and adulteries and other outrageous crimes are committed as a clear offence to God, a very serious danger to the souls of those committing them, and a pernicious example to others. Therefore we, wishing to provide an opportune remedy for this malignant disease and this false perfection insofar as the Almighty has granted us, lest hereafter more serious wrongs be committed under the guise (and) appearance of devotion, entrust (this task) to you jointly and severally and strictly order (you) under pain of disobedience and contempt, enjoining that you warn peremptorily (and) generally each and every one of our subjects of either sex, whom we ourselves thus also warn by the tenor of this present (letter) to cease and desist from these bindings and unsuitable pastimes on the hitherto usual days, commonly called 'hock days,' as is described above, on pain of greater excommunication to be fulminated bitterly against those contravening or not obeying these our orders without any special treatment but also with the full force of the law. In addition we order you under penalty of law that at once after the receipt of the present (letter) you will make the aforementioned (facts) known publicly in sermons and in your aforesaid churches in time of divine service when the greater part of the people will be there. And you will clearly inform us or the officer presiding over our consistory court of Worcester on any day when the consistory court meets before the feast of Pentecost next to come of the names and surnames of those who are delinquent after your – nay rather our – order has been lawfully posted for them about the aforementioned matters, (either) by your letters patent authentically sealed or else in person verbally. Given under our seal 'ad causas' in our castle of Hartlebury on 6 April AD 1450 and in the seventh year of our consecration.

...

ALDERMINSTER

1612
Visitation Act Book   SHRO: BA 2884
f 26v*   *(23 October)*
...

Let the churchwarden call (him) for presentment.†
'Ex officio' proceedings of the lord (judge) against Christopher Hawten.

Detected for being at a bear-baiting on the sabbath day. °On 23 October he appeared and confessed. Therefore the lord (judge) enjoined on him a canonical penance, (to be performed) once in linen clothing and once in the usual garb, and to certify (his compliance) on the next (court day). On 13 November (he was) excommunicated.°

An excommunication was promulgated.

...

f 27*   *(4 November)*
...

'Ex officio' proceedings of the lord (judge) against Thomas Greene. For being at the bear-baiting °at Laughton. He did not appear. (He was) excommunicated.°

Excommunication

'Ex officio' proceedings of the lord against Richard Bowlton.

In the
same place
(Detected) in like manner. (Cited?) in like manner. °(He was)
excommunicated.°

ALVECHURCH

1611
Visitation Act Book   SHRO: BA 2884
f 161*   *(July)*
...
An excommunication was promulgated.   °(He was) absolved.°†
'Ex officio' proceedings of the lord (judge) against Edward
Bartlemewe, alias Heath.
For playing an interlude with various others at the time of divine
service. (He was) cited (to appear) by Coombie (but) did not appear.
(He was) excommunicated.

...

f 161v   *(31 July)*
...
'Ex officio' proceedings of the lord (judge) against Ralph Lyddiat.
Detected for playing in a stage play upon the sabbath days and upon
St Peter's Day in time of divine service. On the last day of July 1611

Dismissal
the said Ralph Lyddiat appeared and because he confessed his fault the
lord (judge) dismissed him with a warning.

An excommunication was promulgated.†
Certificate†

In the
same place
'Ex officio' proceedings of the lord (judge) against John Lyddiat.
(Detected) in like manner. (He was) excommunicated.

In the
same place
'Ex officio' proceedings of the lord (judge) against John Lilley.
(Detected) in like manner. (He was) dismissed with a warning.

Dismissal
In the
same place
'Ex officio' proceedings of the lord (judge) against Richard Davis.
(Detected) in like manner. (He was) dismissed with a warning.

Dismissal

In the same place†
'Ex officio' proceedings of the lord (judge) against William More.
(Detected) in like manner. On that day (he was) cited by Coombie.

Excommu-
nication
Afterwards he appeared (but) the penalty was held over until the next
(court day). °On 22 November (he was) excommunicated.°

BAYTON

1611/12
Archdeaconry of Ludlow Acts of Office   HRO: box 35, vol 131
p 88   *(26 February)*

*Proceedings of the court held in the parish church of Ludlow before
Master Silas Griffithes, STD, deputy of James Bailie, LLD, official
principal.*

Dismissal | William Phillipes
Was present at a bull-baiting at Bayton on a Sunday. He was warned
to be present today to reply, etc.
On that day the said William Phillipes appeared and upon an
examination of the case the lord (deputy) dismissed him with a
warning.
...

BEOLEY

1611
Visitation Act Book   SHRO: BA 2884
f 160   *(5 July)*

'Ex officio' proceedings of the lord (judge) against John Butcher.
For proclaiming a play in the church on the sabbath day. °He appeared
and confessed. Therefore the lord (judge) enjoined him to
acknowledge (his) fault according to the form of the schedule and to
certify (his compliance) on the next (court day).° °On 27 September
Excommu- | (he was) summoned. Since he did not certify, (he was)
nication | excommunicated.°
...

BEWDLEY

1615–16
Diocese of Hereford Acts of Office   HRO: box 24a (formerly 18), vol 70
f [136v]*   *(5 September)*
...
Dismissal | John Brigges for dancing on Sunday. On 5 September aforesaid he

Bewdley

appeared and upon an examination of the article he was dismissed with a warning, etc.

BRADLEY

1617/18
Visitation Act Book   SHRO: BA 2760
ff 321v–2*   *(27 February)*
…
Against Thomas Paddye
Detected for dancing upon Whitson Tuesday in time of divine service. °Although cited by Wall, he did not appear, etc. On 13 March (he was)

Dismissal

dismissed with a warning.°

(13 March)
Against John Sale (Detected) in like manner. °Although (he was) cited by Wall on 13 March, he did not appear, etc.° On 15 March 1617 (he was) dismissed with a warning.

Against William Sale (Detected) in like manner. °Although he was) cited, he did not certify. (Penalty) was reserved until the next (court day).°

Against Humphrey Faukes (Detected) in like manner. °(His case was dealt with) in like manner.°

Against William Lewe (Detected) in like manner. °(He was) cited and dismissed.°

…

They appeared and submitted themselves and the lord (judge) enjoined (on them) to acknowledge (their) fault before the minister, church-wardens, and four parishioners and to certify (their compliance) on the next (court day).

CROWLE

1611
Visitation Act Book   SHRO: BA 2884
f 251   *(10 May)*

...

Dismissal

Excommu-
nication
Absolution
Dismissal

'Ex officio' proceedings of the lord (judge) against Richard Chaundler.
For playing on his fiddle on Low Sunday last in time of divine service.
(He was) enjoined to perform penance according to the form of the
schedule. °(He was) excommunicated.°

...

f 252v*

[(They were) excommunicated for not certifying payment (of court fees)
⟨........⟩.] Dismissal†
'Ex officio' proceedings of the lord (judge) against Richard Auster,
John Horniblow, (and) John Davies.
For dancing at time of divine service. °(Having been cited) by ways
and means, etc, they appeared and confessed. Therefore the lord
(judge) enjoined on them a canonical penance in the usual garb
according to the form and to certify (their compliance) on the next
(court day).° °They certified on 18 July 1611 and were dismissed.°

...

EVESHAM

1300–1
Royal Wardrobe Accounts of Edward I   BL: Add. 7966A
f 66*   *(20 November–19 November)*

...

Fiddlers

To Gilbert of York and William Hathewy, fiddlers,
making their minstrelsy before the king, by the gift of the
same king, that is, 13s 4d for the aforesaid Gilbert and
6s 8d for the aforesaid William by his (the king's) own
hands in the same place on 2 April.   Total: 20s.

...

GRAFTON FLYFORD

1615/16
Visitation Act Book of William Swaddon, Archdeacon of Worcester
SHRO: BA 2512
pp 195–6*   *(24 February)*
...
George Heming
Then the lord decreed a penance should be performed before the
minister and churchwardens.†

Dismissal

He (was) detected for setting and suffering dancing in his new barn
floor the 18th of June 1615 at time of divine service. °On 24 February
1615 he appeared before the lord archdeacon and when the article had
been charged against him, he confessed the article and submitted
himself, etc. Therefore the lord (archdeacon) ordered him to
acknowledge (his) fault before the minister and the entire congregation
at the time of divine service next Sunday immediately before the
reading of the second lesson and to certify (his compliance) on the next
(court day). °°At that time he certified the completion of penance and
(was) dismissed. °

Against Robert Heming

Dismissal

For dancing there at that time. On 24 February 1615 he appeared and
confessed that he was present with the dancers but not at time of divine
service. Therefore the lord (archdeacon) dismissed the same (Robert)
with a warning because he took an oath to the truth of the foregoing./

Against Ralph Kinges
°On the like (charge). Although (he was) cited in church by Master

Cited at
North Piddle.

Stonehall just as he himself (Stonehall) affirmed in court earlier, (and)
therefore publicly summoned, he did not appear on 24 February 1615,
and because (he was) a poor man, (he was) dismissed on the
information of Master Stonehall from any penalty if he be guilty, etc. °

Against William Elletes

Dismissal

°On the like (charge). Although (he was) cited in church by Master
Stonehall, just as he himself (Stonehall) affirmed earlier, (and) publicly
summoned, he did not appear on 24 February 1615, (but) the penalty
is reserved until the next (court day). Later he was dismissed using the
form for a poor man. °

Lawford.
(He was) cited
on the next
(court day).

Against Thomas Haye
On the like (charge). °According to the account of Smith, the apparitor, Haye has gone away.°

Dismissal

Against Thomas Woolner
On the like (charge). °On 24 February 1615 he appeared and confessed the article. Therefore the lord dismissed him with a warning.°

[(She was) cited
on the next
(court day).]

Against Alice Heming (his) wife
On the like (charge). °On 18 January 1616 (she was cited ?).° °According to the account of ⟨...⟩ the apparitor, (she has) died.°

Dismissal

Against Thomas Dugard, musician
For playing to the dancers at that time. °On 24 February 1615 according, etc, he appeared and when the article had been charged against him, he confessed that he was absent from evening prayers and, as for the other part of this article, he denied the same upon his oath. Therefore the lord (archdeacon) ordered him to acknowledge (his) fault before the minister and churchwardens according to the form given to him, etc.° °Then he certified the completion of penance and (was) dismissed.°

Dismissal

Against Walter Arnoll
On the like (charge). On 24 February 1615 (he was dealt with) in like manner.
°Ask for the names of the others who were dancing at that time.°

GREAT MALVERN

1613
Visitation Act Book   SHRO: BA 2760
f 330*   *(7 October)*

'Ex officio' proceedings of the lord (judge) against George Farse, alias Barber.
For playing on his drum in service time to draw the youth from church to the offence of (the) minister and the better disposed of the parish.

An excommu-
nication
was promul-
gated.

°(Having been cited) by ways and means (to appear) on 7 October, he did not appear (and was) excommunicated.°

...

KEMPSEY

1300–1
Royal Wardrobe Accounts of Edward I   BL: Add. 7966A
f 66v*   *(20 November–19 November)*

...

The king's
fiddlers

To Henry and Gerard, German fiddlers, the king's
minstrels, of the king's gift (and) by his own hands at
Kempsey on 29 April, to each of them 13s 4d   26s 8d

...

LINDRIDGE

1572/3
Diocese of Hereford Acts of Office   HRO: box 19, vol 72
f [24v]*   *(30 January)*

*Proceedings of the court held in the parish church of Whitbourne before
John Scory, bishop of Hereford, and in the presence of Edward
Langford, notary public and principal registrar.*

...

Thomas Parker, alias Tynckar, of the parish of Stockton, (having
been) cited, etc, did not appear in person (and) therefore (he was)
excommunicated. Afterwards on 2 March he appeared and confesses
that he did play upon the tabor. Therefore the lord (bishop) imposed
penances on him, (to be performed) on the next Sunday in the church
of Eastham and on the following Sunday in the church of Lindridge.
On 27 March he did not appear although (he was) publicly summoned.
Therefore (he was) suspended. Afterwards he appeared, etc, and so
(was) dismissed.

f [25]*   *(2 March)*

...

'Ex officio' proceedings of the lord (bishop) against William Morton
of the same (parish of Lindridge).
He appeared on 2 March and confesses that he was one of them that
carried the cowlstaff. Therefore the lord (bishop) warned (him) and
imposed penances, that is, (to be performed) on the next Sunday in
the church of Lindridge and on the following Sunday in the church
of Eastham, and to certify (his compliance) on 27 March. On that
day and in that place he did not appear, although (he was) summoned.
Therefore (he was) suspended.

MARTIN HUSSINGTREE

1617
Visitation Act Book   SHRO: BA 2760
f 113   *(17 December)*

…

Against Master Griffin Glinn
Detected for causing a puppet play to be in the chancel. °On 17
December he did not appear, although (he had been) cited by
Coombie. Therefore the lord decreed that he should be suspended
from his office and benefice.° °On 20 December 1617 upon the
submission of the said Glinn in the lord bishop's palace, the same lord
bishop revoked the suspension imposed on him elsewhere, etc, and
warned him to appear on the next court day, that is, on 16 January
next, in the consistory.°°He appeared and confessed, whereupon the
lord (judge) enjoined (on him) to appear before the lord bishop in the
afternoon. (Although he was) cited by Coombie, he did not appear
(and) having been excommunicated, he was referred to the lord bishop
(later ?) in the afternoon.° °Then the lord (bishop) absolved him and
ordered (him) to appear on the next (court day).°

°[Excommu-
nication]°

°Suspension°

°It is
revoked.°

PERSHORE

1495–6
Account Roll of Abbot John Pypulton   PRO: SC6/Henry VII/1704
mb 7   *(External expenses)*

…And in gifts and rewards given to minstrels of the lord king and of
other lords, £6.…

1612/13
Visitation Act Book   SHRO: BA 2884
f 279   *(12 February)*

…

Pershore
Holy Cross

He is ill.

'Ex officio' proceedings of the lord
(judge) against
John George.
John Cosnet.
Thomas Morris (who was dealt
with) like Cosnet.
Roger Edge (who was dealt with)
like Cosnet.

For playing of a stage play on
the sabbath day at time of
divine service. On 12 February
1612 Cosnet appeared and the
lord enjoined him to
acknowledge (his) fault before
the minister, churchwardens,
and ten parishioners according,

Richard Nashe (who was dealt
with) like Cosnet.

etc, after morning prayer and
to certify (his compliance) on
the next (court day).

Richard Bell
On 12 February 1612, (he was) cited in church as appears in the
certificate (and) summoned; when he did not appear the penalty (was)
reserved until the next (court day).

Matthew Davies (who was dealt with) like Cosnet.

John Greneway (who was dealt with) like Cosnet entirely.

He is ill.   Samuel Costell
He (was) cited in church and the penalty (was) reserved until the next
(court day).

f 280

...

'Ex officio' proceedings of the lord (judge) against William Phelps.
Detected for being a minstrel; (he) did play at the said stage play. The
Dismissal   said Phelps appeared in person and on his previous oath he denies
that he played at time of divine service and was at part of evening
prayers. Thereupon the lord (judge) dismissed him graciously with a
warning, etc.

'Ex officio' proceedings of the lord (judge) against Thomas Sharman.
(Detected) in like manner. On 12 February 1612 he appeared and the
lord (judge) ordered him to acknowledge (his) fault before the minister
(and) churchwardens according to form and to certify (his compliance)
on the next (court day). °The penalty (was) reserved until the next
(court day) on 12 March 1612 next.°

...

REDDITCH

1628
Recognizance of John Woodyne
HWRO: Quarter Sessions Records 110:54/45
single sheet *(20 October)*

Worcester   Be it known that on 20 October in the fourth year of our lord Charles,
sessions   by the grace of God king of England, Scotland, France, and Ireland,

defender of the faith, etc, John Woodyne of Redditch in the aforesaid county, victualler, came in his own person before us, John Culpeper and Edward Cookes, esquires, two justices of the said lord king assigned to keep the peace in the said county, and acknowledged that he was bound to the said lord king for £10. And Thomas Sore, husbandman, and Edward Vaughan, yeoman, both of Redditch aforesaid, came then and there in their own persons in like manner as guarantors for the aforesaid John Woodyne and acknowledged that each individually was in like manner under pain of £5. These (sums) they agreed would be levied from their goods, chattels, lands, and holdings to the use of the now lord king himself, (and to the use of) his heirs and successors, if the same John Woodyne should fail in the following condition:
(English follows).

RIBBESFORD

1616
Archdeaconry of Ludlow Acts of Office   HRO: box 36, vol 134
f [35]*   *(30 July)*

Proceedings of the court held in the parish church of Ludlow before Master Silas Griffithes, STD, vicar general of Robert Bennett, bishop of Hereford.

Dismissal | Thomas Weaver detected for dancing the morris on the Lord's Day and providing himself for it at the time of divine service and sermon and for many misdemeanours then committed.
°The said Thomas Weaver appeared in person before the lord vicar general, etc, on 30 July 1616 in the church of Ludlow and when the article had been charged against him he confessed that it was true and submitted himself, etc. Therefore the lord warned him that henceforth, etc. And so (he was) dismissed.°

Dismissal | John Budd on the like (charge).
On that day (his case was dealt with) in like manner.

Dismissal | William Lake, alias Lloid, on the like (charge).
On that day (his case was dealt with) in like manner.

Dismissal | William Sparrie on the like (charge).
On that day (his case was dealt with) in like manner.

Dismissal   Thomas Nashe on the like (charge).
               On that day (his case was dealt with) in like manner.

Dismissal   Edward Parker on the like (charge).
               On that day (his case was dealt with) in like manner.

               (23 September)
Dismissal   Thomas Lucas the younger on the like (charge). Although (he was)
               cited, etc, (and) summoned (to appear) on 23 September 1616
               aforesaid, etc, he did not appear, etc. Then upon an examination of
               the case, the lord (judge) dismissed him.

               Thomas Hayward the younger on the like (charge). Although (he was)
               cited, etc, and summoned (to appear) in person on 23 September
               aforesaid, etc, he did not appear, etc. (He was) excommunicated.

               (5 September)
Dismissal   °John Brigges on the like (charge). On 5 September aforesaid he
               appeared and cleared himself upon his oath, etc. Therefore he was
               dismissed for cause.°
               ...

               1616
               Diocese of Hereford Acts of Office   HRO: box 24a (formerly 18), vol 70
               f [129v]*   *(5 September)*
               ...
               Thomas Aston the elder
               Affirmed that stage plays were made by the Holy Ghost and the word
               of God was but man's invention.
               Cited on the next (court day). °See below.°†
               °On 5 September aforesaid in the parish church of Ludlow before the
               lord vicar general, etc, the said Thomas Aston appeared in person and
               when the article had been charged against him, etc, he denied that it
               was true. Therefore he has to clear himself on the next (court day),
23 September   etc, with six compurgators, etc, after making a proclamation, etc, in
               this place, that is, on 23 September instant, under penalty of law. And
               the lord (vicar general) decreed that John Hailes should be cited in
               particular in court. On 23 September 1616 in the church of Ludlow
               before the lord vicar general, etc, the said Aston appeared. The lord
               graciously assigned him (a new date) as above on the next (court day),

that is, 15 October aforesaid, in this place after the aforesaid John
Hailes had been warned, etc.°

...

f [138]*   *(15 October)*

Thomas Aston the elder has to clear himself with six compurgators,
etc, upon the article that he affirmed not that stage plays were made
by the Holy Ghost and that the word of God was but man's invention.

Dismissal On 15 October 1616 in the church of Ludlow before the reverend
Master Silas Griffithes, STD, vicar general, etc, the said Aston appeared
in person and produced these men as his compurgators, John Gillam
and John Stephens, after he had given notice and no opposition had
occurred, etc. (So) the said Aston swore to his innocence and the said
compurgators to their respective belief. Therefore the lord (vicar
general) pronounced, etc (*ie*, that he had failed in his compurgation
because he had not produced the required number of compurgators),
and dismissed him from his office.

1618
Archdeaconry of Hereford Acts of Office   HRO: box 24, vol 90
f [279v]*   *(11 November)*

*Proceedings of the court held in the parish church of Ludlow before
Master Gabriel Wallwin, MA, deputy of Master Oliver Lloid, LLD, vicar
general of Francis Godwin, bishop of Hereford.*

...

Thomas Gunghe for being disguised contrary to the 30th article.
°Having been cited, etc, by public decree (to appear) on 11 November
aforesaid (and) summoned, etc, he did not appear, etc. (He was)
excommunicated.°

ROCK

1613–14
Archdeaconry of Ludlow Acts of Office   HRO: box 35, vol 132
ff [73v–4]*   *(14 December)*

...

Cleobury
Mortimer William Mundaie of the same parish (was) detected by the
churchwardens of Rock for acting a stage play upon a Sunday after
evening prayer. Having been sought (to appear) on 14 December
aforesaid, etc, (and then) by ways and means (to appear) on the next

(court day), etc, (and) cited (to appear) on 8 February aforesaid, etc,
according to the apparitor's certificate, etc, (and) summoned, etc, (he
did not appear and was) excommunicated. |

(18 January)
John Bathe of the same (parish) on the like (charge). On 18 January
1613 in the church of Ludlow before Dr Griffithes, deputy, etc, he
appeared and when the article had been charged against him, he
confessed that it was true.

...

f [105v]   *(8 February)*

...

Dismissal	Thomas Watmor			Against Walter Pother for
Neen Savage	William Norden			profaning the sabbath, that
	Thomas Turnor			is, for acting upon a stage at
	John Turnor	They were present.		the Rock. On 8 February
	Richard Piper			1613 he appeared before Dr
	Richard Piper			Griffithes, surrogate, etc,
	Thomas Warrold			and confessed that the article,

Dismissal
Neen Savage

Thomas Watmor
William Norden
Thomas Turnor
John Turnor   They were present.
Richard Piper
Richard Piper
Thomas Warrold

Against Walter Pother for
profaning the sabbath, that
is, for acting upon a stage at
the Rock. On 8 February
1613 he appeared before Dr
Griffithes, surrogate, etc,
and confessed that the article,
etc, (*ie*, that it was true).
Therefore the lord
(surrogate) imposed penance
on him (of) one day of
penance according to the
form of the schedule, etc, in
the parish of Rock and
(ordered him) to certify (his
compliance) on the next
(court day). °Then the lord
(judge) dismissed him with a
warning.°

UPTON ON SEVERN

1629
Indictment of John Jones   HWRO: Quarter Sessions Records 110:55/31
single sheet*   *(24 June)*

Worcester   The jurors for the lord king upon their oath present that John Jones
late of the parish of St Michael in Bedwardine in the county of
Worcester, labourer, devised a scheme whereby the people of the now

lord king could very subtly subvert and annul the law of this realm
of England on 24 June in the fifth year of the reign of lord Charles,
now king of England, etc, at Upton upon Severn in the county of
Worcester by means of a deceitfully and falsely counterfeited letter
under the name of Henry Herbert, knight, master of the revels, in
English 'master of the Revells,' containing this gist, that is: *(English)*.
And since the same John Jones thus ⟨...⟩ the said forgery, how he could
have sealed the said forgery ⟨...⟩ he placed and attached and since the
forgery thus as is said above ⟨...⟩ upon Severn aforesaid in the aforesaid
county and in various other places of the same ⟨...⟩ the king's lieges
and subjects, he received in the said now lord king's ⟨...⟩ against the
form of the statute decreed and provided in this circumstance.
...

WORCESTER

1186–90
Gerald of Wales' Gemma Ecclesiastica   LPL: MS 236
f 51v*   *(Distinction 1, chapter 43)*
...
That people ought not to occupy their time in dances and songs in
churches and churchyards.
We have it on the authority of the council of Toledo – in 'De
Consecratione', distinction 3 – that in fact people ought not to occupy
their time on saints' festivals in dances and songs about the churches
and churchyards, but only in the divine offices:

> There is an irreverent custom which the common people
> usually follow during saints' festivals. People who ought to
> attend to the divine offices stay up late over vile dances, not
> only singing wicked songs but also disturbing the offices of
> the devout. And indeed the holy council entrusts the rooting
> out of this practice from every province to the care of priests
> and judges.

On this point, Augustine (writes): 'Let no one do anything in a place
of prayer except what is appropriate to the purpose for which it was
made and whence it takes its name.'
(We also have) the example of a priest in the district of Worcester

who one morning when he was dressed for mass in his priestly
vestments and standing set apart at the altar for the greeting to the
people, that is, 'The Lord be with you,' spoke (instead) before
everyone, chanting in a loud voice in the English language, in this way,
'Swete lamman dhin are.' The gist of this phrase might be 'sweet
mistress, your lover begs your aid.' (He put in) that part of the song –
which they call a refreit or refrain – because he had heard it all night
long as the dances went around the church, (the part) to which they
kept on returning. (It came to him) out of (all) the rest of (his) thoughts
for the mouth customarily speaks out of the fullness of the heart.

However, acting on the occurrence of this event, the bishop of that
place, William, that is, (William) de Northall, issued a public
prohibition through the synods and chapters under threat of anathema
that that song should not be sung henceforth throughout his diocese
(or during his episcopate) on account of the painful recollection which
could recall the crime to mind.

...

1337–8
Cellarer's Account Roll   WCL: C606
mb 1*   *(Gifts and grants)*

...

...Likewise in gifts given to three minstrels of the earl of Lancaster,
18d.... In gifts given to the earl of Warwick's minstrel/s, 3s 4d.... In
gifts to the earl of Warwick's harper, ⟨....⟩....In gifts to the lord prior's
minstrel/s at the More, 4d....

...

1344–5
Cellarer's Account Roll   WCL: C59
mb 2*   *(Gifts and grants)*

...

...Likewise to minstrel/s of the same, 4s. Likewise to the queen's
harper, 2s.... (Spent) on the lord prior's gifts to four minstrels of the
earl of Warwick in Easter week, 6s 8d. Likewise to three other
minstrels on the feast of Cor⟨pus Christi⟩, 5s.... Likewise to John atte
Lee's minstrel/s, 6d.... Likewise 3s 6d (were) gi⟨ven⟩ to minstrel/s
during the lord prior's tourn.... Likewise to minstrel/s on Palm
Sunday, 6s.

...

1345-6
Cellarer's Account Roll WCL: C60
mb 2*   *(Gifts and grants)*
...
...Likewise (spent on gifts given) to Sir Hugh Despenser's minstrel/s, 4s.... Likewise to Sir Edmund de Hereford's minstrels, 2s.... Likewise to minstrels at Easter, 12d. Likewise to minstrels on the feast of Corpus Christi, 2s.... Likewise 18d on gifts given to John Talbot's minstrel/s on occasion.... Likewise 4s for the abbot of Gloucester's harper on two occasions ... (and) 6s 6d on gifts for minstrels at Cleeve and Blackwell during the prior's tourn....
...

1347-8
Cellarer's Account Roll St George's Chapel, Windsor: xi E 37
mb 1d   *(Expenses)*
...
Likewise (spent on) the abbot of Gloucester's minstrel/s, 2s. Likewise for John Talbot's minstrel, 2s. Likewise for minstrel/s on various other festivals, 2s.... Likewise for Earl Arundel's minstrel/s, 2s.... Likewise for minstrel/s during the lord prior's tourn, 2s....
...

1351-2
Cellarer's Account Roll WCL: C53a
mb 1d   *(30 September–7 September) (Expenses)*
...
...(Spent) on gifts given the earl of Warwick's minstrel/s, 12d. Likewise (spent) on the abbot of Evesham's servant/s, 2s....
...

1391-2
Cellarer's Account Roll WCL: C74
mb 2   *(29 September–26 March) (Gifts and grants)*
...
...Likewise (spent) on a gift to minstrel/s, 2s in addition to (*or* in accordance with) the lord prior's commons (*ie,* the amount of commons available to the lord prior for guests.)
...

1445–6
Prior's Account Roll   WCL: C396
mb 3*   *(Gifts and grants)*
...

...Likewise 13s 4d (were spent) for the lord king's minstrel/s at Bevere.
Likewise 10s (for those) of the lord duke of Gloucester. Likewise 6s
8d (for those) of the lord duke of Warwick. Likewise 20d for one
minstrel of the lord duke of Buckingham. Likewise 20d for the lord
bishop of Durham's minstrel/s. Likewise 3s 4d for the lord of
Worcester's minstrel/s (?). Likewise 20d for various others at various
times. Likewise 6s 8d for the lord duke of Exeter's minstrel/s. Likewise
6s 8d for the lord of Salisbury's minstrel/s. Likewise 10s for the lord
of Suffolk's minstrel/s.... Likewise 6s 8d for various players of the
town on Epiphany night....
...

1446–7
Prior's Account Roll   WCL: C397
mb 1   *(Gifts and grants)*
...

...Likewise 20d (were spent) for the lord duke of York's minstrel/s.
Likewise 2⟨.⟩ for John Lynley, a minstrel.... Likewise 6s 8d for the
lord duke of York's minstrel/s. Likewise 6s 8d for the lord duke of
Buckingham's minstrel/s. Likewise 10s for the lord of Suffolk's
minstrel/s. Likewise 20d for one harper of Sir Roland Leynthale....
Likewise 8d for one harper. Likewise 12d for one other harper....
Likewise 13s 4d for the lord king's minstrel/s....

mb 2

Likewise 13s 4d for player/s on the feast of Corpus Christi....
...

1447–8
Prior's Account Roll   WCL: C398
mb 2*   *(Gifts and grants)*
...

...Likewise 12d (were spent) for the minstrel/s of the town of
Worcester on the first Sunday of the Lord's Advent.... Likewise 3s
4d for the lord earl of Arundel's minstrel/s. Likewise 3s 4d for Sir

Edmund Hungerford's minstrel/s. Likewise 20d for one minstrel of Sir Walter Devereux. Likewise 20d for one minstrel of the lady duchess (of) Warwick.... Likewise 20d for Sir Walter Devereux's minstrel/s....

...

1451–2
Prior's Account Roll   WCL: C399
mb 1*   *(30 September–30 September) (Gifts and grants)*
...
...Likewise for minstrel/s of William Lucy, knight, 2s. Likewise for minstrel/s, 2s. Likewise for the duke of Buckingham's minstrel/s, 6s 8d. Likewise for the lord earl of Warwick's minstrel/s, 6s 8d....

mb 3
...
Likewise for the lord duke of Exeter's minstrel/s, 6s ⟨....⟩...

...

1463–4
Prior's Account Roll   WCL: C401
mb 1   *(Gifts and grants)*
...
£7 19s 2d (were spent) on gifts given to various household servants of the lord king and to the minstrels of the same on various occasions this year together with gifts given to various household servants of the dukes, earls, and other magistrates this year....

...

1464–5
Prior's Account Roll   WCL: C402
mb 1   *(Gifts and grants)*
...
£6 19s 2d (were spent) on gifts given to various household servants of the lord king and queen and to the minstrels of the same together with gifts given to various household servants of the dukes and earls, barons, and other magnates....

...

1466–7
Cellarer's Account Roll WCL: C97
mb 3* (Gifts and grants)

…

…Likewise 2s this year for various players in the town of Worcester.
Likewise 3s this year for various players at Claines Aston and
Powick.…

…

1469–70
Prior's Account Roll WCL: C403
mb 2 (Gifts and rewards)

…

And he accounts for £25 3s 11 ½d (spent) on gifts given to household
servants of the lord king and to the servants and minstrels of various
gentlemen (and) lords for the period of this account as appears in the
small book of the same lord prior.…

…

c 1470–80
Cellarer's Account Roll HCL: R707
mb 5* (Gifts from the king)

…

…And 6s given to players of the churches of All Saints, St Helen, St
Swithin, St Alban, St Peter, and St Michael in Worcester, that is, 12d
to each church.… And *(blank)* given to [the players of] John Yonge,
sheriff, for his work on the inquest made about waste.… And 12d
given at Hocktide to the house/s of mendicants (*ie*, mendicant friars)
for torches to be made in various churches.…

…

1470–1
Prior's Account Roll WCL: C404
mb 2 (Gifts and rewards)

…

…And in rewards to minstrels of the lord king and other lords during
the time of this account, £21 ⌜£10 13s 4d⌝.…

…

1471–2
Prior's Account Roll   HCL: R708
mb 2   *(Gifts and rewards)*

...

...And in rewards given to minstrel/s of the said lord king, the duke
of Clarence, and other lords for the time of this account, £12 19s 9d....

1472–3
Prior's Account Roll   WCL: C405
mb 2   *(Gifts and rewards)*

...

...And (he accounts for) £11 8s 6d (spent) on gifts given to various
minstrels of the lord king, the queen, the prince, the dukes of Clarence
(and) Gloucester, and of other lords and magnates....

...

1478–9
Prior's Account Roll   WCL: C406
mb 1d   *(Gifts and rewards)*

...

And he accounts for £24 18s 8d as a payment (spent) on gifts given
to the servants of the lord king, the queen, the prince, (and) the duke
of Gloucester, to various household servants of various lords, and
various performers of the aforesaid together with gifts given to various
persons bringing presents and other payments as appears in the small
book of the lord prior and (of) John Brooke this year....

...

1481–2
Prior's Account Roll   WCL: C407
mb 2   *(Gifts and rewards)*

...

...And (he accounts for) £29 7s (as a payment spent) on gifts or rewards
given to the household servants of the lord king, the queen, the lord
prince, the duke of Gloucester, the duke of York, the earl of
Northumberland, (and) the earl of Arundel, to various lawyers, and
to minstrels of the aforesaid lords together with gifts given to various
persons bringing rents and other payments with gifts and grants as in
the small book of the aforesaid prior....

1486–7
Prior's Account Roll WCL: C409
mb 3 *(Gifts and rewards)*

...

And he accounts for £50 10s 4d in rewards given to servants of the lord
king and to servants of other lords visiting this year on many
(occasions), that is, within the time of this account, together with
rewards given to various persons bringing presents and to minstrels
as appears more fully in detail in the small book of the said lord (prior)
now rendering account for this year.

...

1490–1
Prior's Account Roll WCL: C411
mb 2 *(Gifts, rewards, and alms)*

...

And (he accounts for) £37 5s in rewards given to servants of the lord
king (and) the duke of Bedford, to minstrels and players of various
lords (and) gentlemen at the session of the justices of the lord king,
also to well-wishers and benefactors and many other persons bringing
presents, with alms given to scholars and the more needy as appears
in the small book of the said lord prior.

...

1492/3
Lease of Property Adjacent to the Pageant House
SHRO: BA 5234/23(ii)
single sheet* *(20 February) (Lease)*

To all the faithful in Christ to whom this present indenture shall come,
William Lane and Thomas Cirkeyn, the lord king's bailiffs for the city
of Worcester; John Frethorn and John Jones, aldermen of the same
city; Richard Cetull and Thomas Wighan, treasurers of the same;
William Joly, John Mores, John Payne, Richard Mors, John Malpas,
and Thomas Swynerten, citizens of the same city, (send) greeting in
the Lord. Know ye that we, by the assent and consent of the entire
community of the aforesaid city, have given over, granted, and leased
to Richard Griffith, carpenter, one vacant piece of land situate in the
Cornmarket of the aforesaid city, near the St Martin's gate there,
containing in length, (beginning) from the wall of the aforesaid city

(and measuring) from east to west, twenty-eight royal feet and in width, (beginning) from the wall of the aforesaid gate (and measuring) from north to south, fifteen royal feet. We have also given over and granted to the aforesaid Richard Griffith another vacant piece of land situate in the southern section of the aforesaid market, containing in length, (beginning) from the wall of the aforesaid city (and measuring) from east to west, thirty-eight royal feet and in width, (beginning) from the houses called the pageant houses (and measuring) from south to north, twelve royal feet. We have also given over and granted to the said Richard Griffith another vacant piece of land situate in length between the aforesaid vacant pieces of land and in width between the aforesaid wall and the market house there. The aforesaid vacant pieces of land (are to be) had and held by the aforesaid Richard Griffith and his assigns from the feast of the Annunciation of St Mary the Virgin next after the date of the present (indenture) until the conclusion of a term of eighty-one years next following thereafter and to be fully completed. They will pay for them annually to the treasurers of Worcester for the time being two shillings sterling at two times a year, that is, at the feasts of St Michael the Archangel and the Annunciation of St Mary the Virgin, in equal parts. And the aforesaid Richard Griffith and his assigns will make anew and construct within seven years next following the date of the present (indenture) upon the aforesaid two pieces of land two buildings, one of which will contain two bays (?), at their own costs and expenses, and they will repair, keep up, and maintain at their own costs and expenses well and sufficiently the same buildings thus built and until the end of their aforesaid term they will let the well and sufficiently repaired (buildings). They will not bear or pay any other charges whatever pertaining to the aforesaid pieces of land or which ought to be paid for the entire term aforesaid. And the aforesaid Richard Griffith and his assigns shall not grant or demise their rights or term-interest in the aforesaid pieces of land nor any section of them except only to citizens or a citizen of the aforesaid city and to one or ones remaining within the said city and to one or ones to whom our treasurers for the time being give their consent. And if it happens that the aforesaid rent is partly or wholly in arrears or unpaid for the space of one month after any aforenamed feast on which it should be paid, our treasurers for the time being will then be fully empowered to enter the aforesaid pieces of land and to distrain and take away, drive off, and keep by them the distraints, if any are lawfully seized, until the aforesaid rent together with arrears of the same, if any, is fully satisfied and paid.

And if the aforesaid rent is partly or wholly in arrears or unpaid for the space of a quarter-year after any aforementioned feast, or if the aforesaid two buildings are not newly built before the end of the term set out above, or if the same buildings are not well and sufficiently repaired, kept up, and maintained, or if the same Richard Griffith or his assigns grant or lease their rights or term-interest in the aforesaid pieces of land or any section thereof contrary to the aforesaid form, then our treasurers of the aforesaid city for the time being will be fully empowered on our own behalf and that of the community of the aforesaid city to re-enter the aforesaid pieces of land and any part thereof and to expell and remove the said Richard Griffith and his assigns totally from them and resume our present rights (therein), this indenture not withstanding in any particular. And we, the said bailiffs, aldermen, treasurers, citizens, and the whole community of the aforesaid city warrant the aforesaid pieces of land to the aforesaid Richard Griffith and his assigns according to the aforementioned manner and form against all persons and defend (their rights in the land) during the aforesaid term by the present (indenture). In testimony of which fact, we the aforesaid bailiffs, aldermen, treasurers, and citizens by the assent of the community of the aforesaid city have affixed our common seal to one part of this indenture remaining in the keeping of the aforesaid Richard Griffith, (and) the aforesaid Richard Griffith affixed his seal to the other part of the same indenture remaining in the keeping of us, the aforesaid bailiffs, aldermen, treasurers, citizens, and community of the aforesaid city. Witnesses: John Porter, John Croke, Thomas Grene, Thomas Radnor, William Codon, and others. Given at Worcester on the 20th of February in the eighth year of the reign of King Henry the seventh after the conquest of England.

I, Codon, have subscribed.

1607
Indictment of John Hart   HWRO: Quarter Sessions Records 110:42/53
single sheet*

Worcester

The jurors for the lord king present upon their oath that one John Hart, labourer, of Anserwick in the aforesaid county did on 5 June in the fifth year of the reign of our lord James by the grace of God king of England, Scotland, France, and Ireland (and) defender of the faith, etc, that is, the fifth year in England, France, and Ireland and the fortieth year in Scotland, within his own messuage situate in the aforesaid Anserwick in the aforesaid county and on various other times and occasions both before and afterwards, keep and have as a host in his said messuage various unlawful entertainments, that is, dancing at the time of the celebration of divine service, held both on the said day in the said year and on various other times and occasions in the said messuage among various persons of bad reputation and dishonest conversation to the great injury of all the people of the now lord king and contrary to the peace of the said now lord king, his crown and dignity, etc.

William Payton, proc'

ENDNOTES

347 LPL: MS 171 f 41v
Walter Cantilupe, the uncle of St Thomas Cantilupe, bishop of Hereford (1275–82), became bishop of Worcester in 1237, serving until his death in 1266. His constitutions reflect a considerable amount of administrative originality, with such matters as proper clerical conduct dealt with in detail. They are in two parts, the first more general than the second. The chapters are consecutively numbered throughout the two parts, however. All the chapters in the first section have topical headings but there are no such headings for the chapters in the second part. No register survives from his episcopate. The entry is not dated in the Lambeth Palace copy, but in the copy in BL: Cotton Claudius A viii, f 212v, it is dated 'in crastino Sancti Iacobi apostoli.'

348 LPL: MS 171 f 45v
Although the phrase 'in omnibus ecclesijs' (l.3) is not repeated, some of the subsequent prohibitions make better sense if the bishop was concerned to keep churches and churchyards free from secular activities. One characteristic of the reform movement in the medieval church from the late eleventh century onward was an ever-increasing desire to separate the sacred from the profane. This concern explains what connection exists in the bishop's mind between correct behaviour in clerics and correct performance of the liturgy (see l.3–4): only a pure priest can say a proper mass. Such a desire for separation also underlies the order that sacred persons, priests, may not take part in popular lay pastimes (ll.4–5). Since the bishop cannot have intended by the further prohibitions (ll.5–8) to order his clergy to stop all wrestling, for instance, in the diocese, it seems safe to assume that the clergy are also being ordered not to allow other such pastimes to take place on sacred ground. This makes better sense too of the extension of the final prohibition by 'omnino' (l.7): if 'gilde' are entirely banned only if made up of 'mercatores' and 'peregrini,' then the original order must be restrictive rather than prohibitive.

It is not possible to be precise about the meaning of most of the terms used to describe these forbidden activities. If the phrase 'ludis inhonestis' (l.4) was followed at once by 'aleas' and 'taxillos,' (l.5) then we might safely deduce that we have here a precursor of the later usage in which the phrase usually refers to gambling. But associated as it is immediately with dances ('correis,' l.5), its meaning cannot be so restricted. 'Aleas' and 'taxillos' refer to two popular forms of gaming. 'Alea,' according to Isidore, was a game played with a board, dice, counters or men, and a dice-box (Isidore of Seville, *Etymologiae*, W. M. Lindsay (ed), vol 2 (Oxford, 1911), book 18, chapter 60). 'Taxilli' were (originally bone) dice. So in one blow, the bishop forbids his priests to engage in games of chance, whether straight dice games or board games in which dice were used to determine the moves of pieces. Of the remaining four activities, which priests were forbidden to allow, two are apparently sports (l.6). Priests were not to allow wrestling or the military exercises of the knightly classes to occur. Without more precise information as to the time of year, it is hard to know what the 'ludos ... de rege & regina' (ll.5–6) might be. Perhaps some sort of May or summer games with lords and ladies had been brought to Cantilupe's attention. The 'gildas inhonestas' are a bit difficult to understand. The reading of C, 'gildales' (l.39) seems helpful: it is likely an English word provided by the scribe as a clarification of an obscure sense of 'gilda' used by the bishop: 'guild ales' instead of 'guilds.' The *Dictionary of Medieval Latin* cites several examples of 'gilda' in contexts which involve drinking. Presumably then the 'gilde inhoneste' were gatherings of a guild held not directly for a pious purpose, such as maintaining a light or a chapel, for which the guild was founded, but for ale-drinking or even ale-selling. The probable gloss 'gildales' and the mention of 'mercatores' and 'peregrini' provide a clue to what the bishop is really trying to stop, ie, guild ales, ales held by guilds, doubtless in churchyards, to raise money. The bishop wished to restrict guild ales as a money-making enterprise, but when professional buyers and sellers and outsiders were involved, he wanted to put an end to them altogether.

348–9   SHRO: BA 2648/4/iv   ff 86–6v
Henry Wakefield was elected in 1375 and served until 1395. This letter covering the activities of stipendiary priests was sent by William Courtenay, archbishop of Canterbury, on 28 April 1391 and forwarded to Worcester by Robert Braybrooke, bishop of London, on 26 October. The second part of the text is concerned with the publication and observation of the mandate. Most of the Latin text is printed in D. Wilkins, *Concilia Magnae Britanniae et Hiberniae ab anno MCCCL ad annum MDXLV*, vol 3 (London, 1737), 213–14 and a summary is given in *A Calendar of the Register of Henry Wakefield*, W.P. Marett (ed), nos 633–4, pp 100–1.

349–50   Bodl.: MS Bodley 692   f 163v
Bishop John Carpenter presumably addressed this letter dealing with clerical conduct to his clergy generally. John Lawern, then almoner of Worcester Priory, copied it on a blank folio at the end of the notebook of lectures and sermons which he had kept earlier as a student at Gloucester College, Oxford. Lawern entered the priory by 1433 and was ordained on 18 September 1434. He was at Oxford from c 1442–9, taking his STB by 1445 and his STD on 9 April 1448. Returning to Worcester Priory, he served as almoner in 1448–9, sacrist from 1458 until at least 1460, and became subprior in 1474 (see A.B. Emden, *A Biographical Register of the University of Oxford to A.D. 1500*, vol 2 (Oxford, 1958), 1112).

350   Dr Williams's Library: Roger Morrice MSS L(3)   p 12
Except for the few weeks during which the proclamation of 6 August 1549 placed a general ban on plays until All Saints' Day (1 November), control of dramatic performances (particularly within the church) was left to the individual diocese, at least until 1553. Hooper's visitation articles and interrogatories were first composed for the diocese of Gloucester in 1551 during the last year of his episcopate there; it is likely that the same articles were administered in Worcester diocese the following year after Hooper's translation. Hooper's interrogatory

is based on the seventeenth article of Bishop Bonner's 1542 injunctions to the clergy, which prohibits 'any manner of common plays, games, or interludes, to be played, set forth, or declared, within their churches...' (Frere and Kennedy, *Visitation Articles and Injunctions*, vol 2, pp 88, 267, 291; *Later Writings of Bishop Hooper*, Charles Nevinson (ed), Parker Society (Cambridge, 1852), xix). The immediate cause of the 1549 proclamation was the performance of plays which contained 'matter tending to sedition, and contemning of sundry good orders and laws: whereby were grown, and daily did grow and ensue much disquiet, division, tumults and uproars within the realm', (quoted in R.W. Dixon, *History of the Church of England*, vol 3 (London, 1885), 123n–4n).

350   WCL: A14   f 47
The articles are not in fact dated, but the 1577 date (the first year of Whitgift's episcopate) is clear from the surrounding documents. Whitgift's Article 29 is based on Article 61 of Archbishop Edmund Grindal's 1571 Articles for the Province of York (see Frere and Kennedy, *Visitation Articles and Injunctions*, vol 3, p 271).

351   STC: 10367   p 11
The eighty-eighth Canon, promulgated in 1604, forbade the profanation of church, chapel, or churchyard by 'plays, feasts, banquets, suppers, church ales, drinkings, temporal courts, or leets, lay-juries, musters, or any other profane usage' (Edward Cardwell, *Synodalia*, vol 1 (Oxford, 1842), 296).

355   SHRO: BA 2884   ff 26v, 27
The parish of Alderminster (situated about five miles south of Stratford on Avon) together with the parishes of Tredington, Shipston on Stour, and Tidmington to the south formed an island of Worcestershire within Warwickshire's borders.
    The 'acta' paragraph on the previous page (f 26) describes a court session held on 11 September. It is clear from internal evidence, however, that Hawten's case was not heard before the session of 23 October, at which he appeared. The entry for the session of 13 November, at which he was to certify his penance, is highly abridged, but it is most likely that the excommunication resulted from a failure to appear and certify.
    The entry on f 27 has been assigned to the parish in which the case was heard rather than the parish of the event, since it is not possible to identify Laughton specifically among the many possible candidates (none of them in either Worcestershire or Warwickshire).

355–6   SHRO: BA 2884   f 161
This entry falls between sessions dated 5 July (f 160) and 30 July (at the bottom of f 161). However, the two previous cases on f 161 are dated 20 and 19 July respectively, so it is likely that this case was heard at a session on or after 19 July and before 30 July.

356   HRO: box 35, vol 132   f [41]
'eundem ffranciscum' (l. 35) refers to Francis Rogers, curate of Dowles, subject of the previous prosecution for improper solemnization of a marriage. Both prosecutions were heard in Ribbesford cum Bewdley.

357   SHRO: BA 5013/2   f [31]
Payments for the purchase of barley are included even when there is no explicit receipt for
a church ale, on the grounds that such a purchase is itself evidence that an ale may have occurred.

357–8   SHRO: BA 5013/2   f [31v]
The list of churchwardens at the head of the account gives the names Thomas Placum and
John Smith, but the account rendering gives Thomas Placum and Robert Smith. Both John
and Robert Smith appear as churchwardens in other years and I have assumed that because
of either an error or a change of churchwardens during the year, the names of those rendering
the accounts are accurate.

359   SHRO: BA 5013/2   f [34v]
There appears to be a year missing here; the previous rendering is clearly dated the second
Friday after Easter 1539 (for 1538–9) and the following rendering is dated on the same day
1542 (for 1541–2). The intervening rendering has no date, although a later antiquarian hand
has added 'in the year of our lorde M.cccccxl.' It is not possible to be certain whether this
entry refers to 1539–40 or to 1540–1.

360   SHRO: BA 5013/2   f [4v]
The whole entry has been cancelled administratively with two diagonal lines and one vertical
line.

360   PRO: PROB 10 Box 70 1571–Feb. A–W   f 53
William Sheldon, a dyer by trade, became well known as a tapestry weaver. He retired from
the family home at Beoley in 1534 to Skilts, just over the Warwickshire border, where he
died on 23 December 1570. He was buried at the family estate at Beoley. The will is very
long, with elaborate provisions for his tapestry-weaving business and its weavers. The material
possessions in the will show his considerable wealth (see E.A.B. Barnard, *The Sheldons* (Cambridge, 1936), 11–27).

362   HWRO: BA 8681/236(i)   p 238
'my Lord President' (l.22) is Henry Herbert, earl of Pembroke, who served as lord president
of the Council in the Marches of Wales from 1586 until his death in 1600/1.

362–3   SHRO: BA 8681/236(i)   pp 312, 331
Edward, Lord Zouche (p 362, l.40), served as lord president of the Council in the Marches
of Wales from 1602–7 and was succeeded by Ralph, Lord Eure. 'my lordes' (p 363, l.9) probably refers to one of these men.
   Part of the account heading which applies to the entry on p 331 is missing; the date 1607
is visible, as is a reference to wardens chosen on 10 December 1606. The date 1607 appears
in various places in the account and a new heading on p 333 notes that the accounts were
passed to new wardens in April of 1608. Thus it seems likely that this account covers the
period 10 December 1606–April 1608.

363   HWRO: BA 8681/236(i)   p 399
No end date is given for this account, which is described simply as beginning at Michaelmas 1615. It may end at Michaelmas 1616, but since the 1616–17 accounts begin on St Andrew's Day (30 November) 1616, the previous day (29 November) seems a more likely closing date.

'mie lordes' (l. 18) is probably a reference to the lord president of the Council in the Marches. Lord Eure (1558–1617) served as lord president of the Council in the Marches of Wales from 1607–17.

363   HRO: box 24a (formerly 18), vol 70   f [136v]
The preceding 'acta' paragraph (f 128) describes a court session of 30 July. There is no evidence here however that Brigges' case was heard before 5 September when he appeared.

364–7   Wing: C6272   pp 97–102
John Hammond (p 364, l.6) paid first fruits in the parish of Ribbesford cum Bewdley on 2 March 1614. His name appears several times in the register and he held the living until some time before 1630, when it went to John Boraston. A John Hammond from Shropshire matriculated from Corpus Christi College, Oxford in 1597 and took his BA from Christ Church on 15 February 1600/1, so it is possible, as J.A.W. Bennett and H.R. Trevor-Roper suggest (*The Poems of Richard Corbett* (Oxford, 1955), 131), that Hammond and Corbett may have known each other as undergraduates. The poem cannot be dated more precisely than Hammond's tenure at Bewdley, although it may very well have been prompted in part by the publication of James I's *Book of Sports* (London, 1618; STC: 9238.9).

The Blackfriars Church (p 364, l.10) was the centre of some of the most extreme puritan preaching. John Hopkins and Thomas Sternhold (p 364, l.17) were principal versifiers of *The Whole Book of Psalms*, which had been appended to the Book of Common Prayer in 1562 (Bennett and Trevor-Roper, *Poems of Richard Corbett*, p 131). The small pleated ruff and the goggle eye (p 365, l.18) were alleged puritan attributes which inspired a considerable amount of satire, such as the 'small printed ruffs' of *Bartholomew Fair*, III, ii; see also the references cited under Goggle *sb* 2 in the OED.

367–8   SHRO: BA 2760   ff 321v–2
John Sale (p 368, l.2) was apparently not cited to appear on 27 February but only on 13 March. It is impossible, given the text of the entries and the hand of the registrar, to decide whether the last three accused named (p 368, ll.6–15) were considered first on 27 February or 13 March.

368–9   SHRO: BA 2302/2 (345)   single sheet
'Doctor Helmes' (p 368, l.24) is Christopher Helme, LLD, chancellor of the diocese of Worcester from 1618 to 1628 (Anthony Wood, *Athenae Oxonienses*, Philip Bliss (ed) (London, 1815), vol 2, col 267).

369   SHRO: BA 2884   f 252v
Three different hands appear in this entry. 'Officium ... Horniblow' (l.23) and 'ffor ... divinorum' (l.25) are written in the first hand; the other names (ll.23–4), 'vijs et modis ... in

proximo' (ll.25–7), and the first four lines of marginalia are written in the second. The last line of marginalia and 'cert*ificaverunt* ... dimiss*i*' (l.28) are in a third hand.

371   HWRO: BA 1006/33/596   mb 1d
The intriguing mention of 'Midso*m*mer' (l.6), especially in conjunction with the word 'Company' (l.5), has led to the inclusion of such an unusual and large payment in this collection. However, it is difficult to explain what Francis Alexanders and his company are being paid for or who they were. The context of this payment is a series of legal charges, paid out by the bailiff 'in the busines betweene Salwarp and o*ur* Towne concerninge Leiwnes.' (Salwarpe, an adjacent parish, takes its name from the river upon which both it and Droitwich stand. A 'leiwne' (*OED* Lewn) is a church rate.) Whatever Alexanders did clearly involved him in a personal legal action, for in the same set of payments, the bailiff paid 6s 2d 'for Charges of a Lattitat ag*ainst* ffr*ancis* Allexanders in the same busines.' (A writ of 'latitat' was issued by the court if a sheriff reported that a person whom he was sent to arrest could not be found. Presumably the town was assisting Alexanders with court charges incurred on its behalf.)

   The phrase 'Castinge open the Com*m*ons (l.6) is unclear in such a context. Perhaps the dispute over church rates involved a question of the exact status of land held by the town to be common or to involve a public right of way, which Droitwich attempted to solve by having it cast open, that is, by unilaterally opening it up to public access, possibly by the removal of fences or some other obstacles. There was apparently a custom of lighting Midsummer bonfires in the fields, described thus by Aubrey: 'In Herefordshire, and also in Somersetshire, on Midsommer-eve, they make fires in the Fields in the waies: *sc.* to Blesse, the Apples. I have seen the same custome in Somersetshire, 1685; but there they doe it only for the custome-sake' (*Remaines of Gentilisme and Judaisme* in *John Aubrey: Three Prose Works*, J. Buchanan-Brown (ed) (Carbondale, Illinois, 1972), 143). We may therefore speculate whether such a custom influenced the timing of an effort to secure the status of certain common land or rights of way.

371   SHRO: BA 2302/2/(374)   single sheet
The document is undated; the previous document is dated July 1624, the following document October 1624, but since they are loose papers this may be irrelevant. The puritanical Gerard Prior (ll.15m, 17), vicar of Eldersfield, had a long-standing quarrel with his parishioners over the subject of Sunday sports. On the basis of this letter Prior was bound over to appear at the sessions, where he was charged by his parishioners with irreverence and immorality. The diocesan clergy petitioned for his restoration and Archdeacon Swaddon supported him as did the archbishop. The case was eventually decided in Prior's favour (*Calendar of State Papers, Domestic Series, of the Reign of James* I, vol 9, 1611–1618, Mary Anne Everett Green (ed) (London, 1858; rpt 1967), 164; vol 10, 1619–1623, pp 72–3, 78). A section of the first paragraph, from 'the Kinges' (l.19) to the end ('vse it,' l.26) is written at the foot of the sheet; the two parts of this paragraph are marked off by two horizontal lines.

   'St Peeters tide' (l.28) probably refers to the season following the feast of Sts Peter and Paul (29 June).

372   BL: Add. 7966A   f 66
Another copy of the payment to Gilbert of York and William Hathewy (l.7) is in

PRO: E101/359/5, f 1v (a fragment of a Wardrobe Account Journal); the entry notes that 2 April is Easter Sunday (see Bullock-Davies, *Register of Royal and Baronial Domestic Minstrels*, p 226).

376–7 STC: 772.3 sigs B–C

Robert Armin was the son of a tailor in King's Lynn, Norfolk, though the date of his birth is not known. From 1581–92 he was apprenticed to a goldsmith in London; sometime after 1594 he joined the company of William Brydges, Lord Chandos, which toured the West Midlands during the period 1595–7. Further information on the company's touring during this period may be found in Audrey Douglas and Peter Greenfield (eds), *Cumberland/Westmorland/Gloucestershire*, Records of Early English Drama (Toronto, 1986) and in the forthcoming REED volume for Shropshire/Staffordshire. Many of the anecdotes in *Foole vpon Foole* derive from these travels. By the time of the publication of *Foole vpon Foole*, Armin was back in London and by August of 1600 he was playing at the Globe Theatre, probably as a member of the chamberlain's men. *Foole vpon Foole* elaborates on the distinction between natural and artificial fools and Armin takes some care to leave open the question of the nature of his own fooling. He remained a member of the chamberlain's/king's company from 1600 to 1610, acting the fool roles in many of Shakespeare's plays (Touchstone, Feste, Thersites, and the fool in *King Lear* among others). He died in 1616. See Nungezer, *A Dictionary of Actors*, pp 15–20 and David Wiles, *Shakespeare's Clown: Actor and Text in the Elizabethan Playhouse* (Cambridge, 1987), 136–58, especially 139–43.

377–9 SHRO: BA 2512 pp 195–6

We are fortunate to have the actual date of the offence, 18 June 1615. The Worcester court did not proceed as quickly in this case as the Hereford court did in the case printed under Ashperton (p 62). The date assigned to this entry is that of the court session to which most of the accused were cited, 24 February 1615/16, held before the archdeacon. However, Alice Heming (p 378, l.32) was apparently not cited before the session of 18 January 1616/17. Possibly this delay was the result of an illness which also caused her death.

379 SHRO: BA 2760 f 330

The preceding 'acta' paragraph (f 328v) describes a court session of 9 September. There is no mention made of any consideration of Farse's case before 7 October when he failed to appear. But the fact that the citation for 7 October was by ways and means ('vijs et modis,' l.17) implies a previous citation which either could not be served or was not effective. There is no way to tell whether that citation was for 9 September or for another intervening session.

379 BL: Add. 7966A f 66v

The name 'Girardo' (l.26) may be an error for 'Cunrad' or 'Conrad'; the evidence available from other royal household accounts of the period suggests that the king's three German fiddlers were named Henry, Conrad, and Conrad (see Constance Bullock-Davies, *Menestrellorum Multitudo*, pp 106–8). There are two payments to Henry and one of the Conrads on f 67 of this MS, as well as in BL: Add. 35292, f 29v, where they are paid a mark's wages at Dunfermline, and in PRO: E101/369/11, f 102v (see Constance Bullock-Davies, *Register of Royal and Baronial Minstrels*, pp 37–8, 68–9).

A rough version of this account survives as PRO: E101/359/5. This payment was entered on f 3v: '…Duob*us* Gigatorib*us* Alemann*is* de dono R*egis* ij marce….' In her *Register*, p 58, Bullock-Davies mistakenly dates this payment in the draft account to the following day, Sunday, 30 April 1301.

379–80   BL: Egerton 2570   ff 3v–4
The details of circumstances under which the puritan divine Richard Baxter was invited to Kidderminster are given in the Introduction, p 300. A firm parliamentarian in a county well-known as a royalist stronghold, Baxter was forced to withdraw to Gloucester in 1642 (*DNB*).

381   HRO: box 19, vol 72   ff [24v, 25]
Although only one of these accused, Morton, (l.32) was from the parish of Lindridge, both Parkar (l.22) and Morton are ordered to do penance in Lindridge and in Eastham. It therefore seems likely that the offence took place in both parishes (they are contiguous) and that Parkar's taboring accompanied the cowlstaff riding in which Morton was involved. Carrying someone on a cowlstaff, or 'riding,' was one of the traditional elements of a charivari. See Herefordshire Introduction, pp 15 and 47, n 53 and p 275, endnote to HRO: box 17, vol 66, ff [228v, 229].

382–3   HWRO: Quarter Sessions Records   110:29/67   single sheet
'ffortingtons' (p 382, l.17) refers to the parish of Forthampton, Gloucestershire, about three miles southeast of Longdon. The statute for the control of rogues, vagabonds, and sturdy beggars (p 383, ll.3–4) was revised extensively by Elizabeth on 9 February 1597/8 and was confirmed in 1601. James confirmed the statute in 1603/4 and amended it somewhat in 1609/10. The rogues at whom the statute was directed are defined in Elizabeth's 1597/8 version: 'All p*er*sons calling themselves Schollers going about begging, all Seafaring-men p*re*tending losses of their Shipp*es* or Good*es* on the Sea going about the Country begging, all idle p*er*sons going about in any Cuntry eyther begging or using any subtile Crafte or unlawfull Games and Play*es*, or fayning themselves to have knowledge in Phisiognomye Palmestry or other like crafty Scyence, or p*re*tending that they can tell Destenyes Fortunes or such other like fantasticall Ymagynac*i*ons; all p*er*sons that be or utter themselves to be Proctors P*ro*curors Patent Gatherers or Collectors for Gaols Prisons or Hospitall*es*; all Fencers Bearewardes common Players of Enterlud*es* and Minstrell*es* wandring abroade, (other then Players of Enterlud*es* belonging to any Baron of this Realme, or any other honorable P*er*sonage of greater Degree, to be auctoryzed to play, under the Hand and Seale of Armes of such Baron or P*er*sonage); all Juglers Tynkers Pedlers and Petty Chapmen wandring abroade; all wandering p*er*sons and comm*on* Labourers being p*er*sons able in bodye using loytering and refusing to worcke for such reasonable Wag*es* as is taxed or comm*only* gyven in such Part*es* where such p*er*sons do or shall happen to dwell or abide, not having lyving otherwyse to maynteyne themselves; all p*er*sons delivered out of Gaol*es* that begg for their Fees, or otherwise do travayle begging; all such p*er*sons as shall wander abroade begging p*re*tending loss*es* by Fyre or otherwise; and all such p*er*sons not being Fellons wandering and p*re*tending themselves to be Egipcyans, or wandering in the Habite Forme or Attyre of counterfayte Egipcians; shalbe taken adjudged and deemed Rogues Vagabond*es* and Sturdy Begg*er*s, and shall susteyne such Payne and Punyshment as by this Acte is in that behalfe appointed' (*The Statutes of the Realm*, A. Luders et al (eds), vol 4, pt 2 (London, 1819), 899. The edition was set with

special diplomatic type repesenting common abbreviation symbols; I have expanded them with italics.)

384–5 SHRO: BA 2302/2(414) single sheet
William Warmestrey (p 384, l.31) was the diocesan registrar; the office of registrar had been in his family since 1544.

387–8 HRO: box 36, vol 134 f [35–5v]
Despite the date provided by the preceding 'acta' paragraph (f [20]), 23 May 1615, these cases were apparently first heard at a session of 30 July 1616 before the vicar general, who can be identified from elsewhere as Silas Griffithes. The final three accused were only cited for appearances in September, however – Lucas and Hayward on the twenty-third and Brigges on the fifth. From entries in Acts of Office vol 70 also describing cases heard on those dates, we may infer that Dr Griffithes also presided over the court on those days.

388–9 HRO: box 24a (formerly 18), vol 70 ff [129v, 138]
The preceding 'acta' paragraph (f [128]) describes a court session of 30 July (probably the same session reported in part of Acts of Office vol 134, printed on pp 387–8 above). This case, however, was clearly first heard at the session of 5 September. It is not clear who Hailes (p 389, l.6) was, nor what connection he had with Aston or this case. The account of Aston's reappearance to certify on 15 October (p 389, ll.17–25) suggests he may have held office in the church, but efforts to discover more about him, like those to identify Hailes, have been unsuccessful.

389 HRO: box 24, vol 90 f [279v]
Only the date of the session at which Gunghe was excommunicated for non-appearance is mentioned in the entry, 11 November. The fact that he was cited by public decree ('per publicum edictum,' l.36), however, implies that this is the final citation in a series. So although there is no explicit mention of it, we may infer at least an attempted citation for 20 October, the session described in the 'acta' paragraph on f [277], and probably also a citation by ways and means for an intervening session.

This charge clearly does not refer to the Articles of Religion of 1562 (and subsequent reprints), in which Article 30 refers to the denial of communion. Rather it derives from the Royal Injunctions first promulgated by Elizabeth in 1559 and regularly confirmed, in which Article 30 discusses the apparel of ministers, enjoining them to wear 'seemly habits, garments, and such square caps, as were most commonly and orderly received in the latter year of the reign of King Edward VI' (Frere and Kennedy, *Visitation Articles and Injunctions*, vol 3, p 20). The 1559 injunction is an expansion of Bishop Hooper's thirtieth interrogatory for the diocese of Gloucester and Worcester in 1551–2: 'Item, whether they go in sober, modest, and comely apparel, without any cuts, jaggs, or such like external and undecentness not to be used in our ministers of the church' (*Later Writings of Bishop Hooper*, Charles Nevinson (ed), Parker Society (Cambridge, 1852), 147.)

390 HRO: box 35, vol 132 ff [73v–4]
It is difficult to assign a date to the first case on f [73v]. These cases follow an 'acta' paragraph

on f [66] which describes a session on 23 November, but it seems that Mundaie was first cited to appear on 14 December. In fact, he never did appear and was excommunicated at a session held on 8 February 1613/14. In the prosecution of both Mundaie and Bathe, 'eadem' (ll. 7 and 14) refers to their home parish, the Shropshire parish of Cleobury Mortimer, as indicated by the marginal heading.

392   HWRO: Quarter Sessions Records 110:21/68   single sheet
Carrying upon a cowlstaff was one of the traditional elements of a charivari, often, as here, accompanied by 'rough music,' the banging of metal objects and other sounds of improvised percussion. The curate's position is no insurance against a charivari; in *Arden of Feversham* the constable is 'carried ... about the fields on a coltstaffe.' See Herefordshire Introduction, pp 15 and 47, n 53, and p 275, endnote to HRO: box 17, vol 66 ff [228v, 229].

392–3   STC: 772.3   sigs C–Cv
See p 585, endnote to STC: 772.3 sigs B–C above.

394–5   HWRO: Quarter Sessions Records 110:55/31   single sheet
The document is very badly damaged. A triangular section covering about a third of the total area from the right-hand side has disintegrated. The size of the gaps in the text is indicated in the textual notes.

395–6   LPL: MS 236   f 51v
Gerald of Wales (Giraldus Cambrensis, c 1146–c 1223) probably wrote his *Gemma Ecclesiastica* around 1197, during his stay at Lincoln and prior to his abortive election as bishop of St David's on 29 June 1198. During Gerald's lengthy suit to the Vatican to have his election approved, the pope expressed his particular interest in the *Gemma Ecclesiastica*, recommending it to the cardinals, although Gerald's suit was denied. The *Gemma* is a series of exemplary tales laid out in two 'distinctiones,' dealing respectively with the sacraments and with the clerical life. The tale printed here is from the first distinction; the date given for the story is that of the episcopate of William of Northall (see p 396, ll. 12–13), who held the see of Worcester from 1186 until his death in 1190. The *Gemma Ecclesiastica* was edited by J.S. Brewer, *Giraldi Cambrensis Opera*, Rolls Series, 21 (London, 1862).
    The corrections to the quotation from Gratian are taken from the *Decretum*; the presence of these errors would suggest that Brewer's theory that Gerald (a strict canonist) oversaw the production of the unique manuscript is highly unlikely. Bartlett discusses the possibility that the manuscript might be a later recension (Robert Bartlett, *Gerald of Wales 1146–1223* (Oxford, 1982), 218).

396   WCL: C51a   mb 1   col 2
The roll covers the usual Michaelmas – Michaelmas period, but this section of the prior's expenses is dated separately, from the Sunday in the octave of Sts Peter and Paul to the Annunciation.

396   WCL: C482   mb 1   col 2
Although this entry cannot be fixed in any chronological order, it does follow a series of payments relating to a visit by Queen Isabella.

396–7   WCL: C606   mb 1
The hamlet of 'the More' (p 397, l.3), situated in the parish of Lindridge, appears in documents
of the twelfth century as 'la Mora' and retains the definite article into the sixteenth century.
It was the birthplace of Prior William More, extracts from whose Account Book appear in
the Households section for the years 1518–35.

397   WCL: C58   mb 2
The new prior was Simon de Botiler, who assumed the office on the elevation of Wulstan
de Bransford to the bishopric.

397   WCL: C59   mb 2
A piece is torn from the right-hand margin and the name at the end of the previous line is
missing. Therefore, the person referred to by 'eiusdem' (l.18) cannot be identified. 'Iohannis
atte Lee' (l.21) may be one of several persons of this name (or its variants John de Lee, John
de la Lee, John du Lee) who appear in the patent rolls of the 1340s. Although it is not possible
to separate these persons entirely, one man stands out with strong Worcestershire connections:
he is appointed collector for the ninth of lambs, fleeces, and sheaves for Worcester in 1341,
as commissioner of oyer and terminer in 1340 and 1341, and as justice of the peace in 1341
(*Calendar of Patent Rolls Edward III*, vol 5 (London, 1900), 112, 153, 217; *Calendar of Close
Rolls Edward III*, vol 6 (London, 1902), 20). A variety of further West Midlands appointments
in Staffordshire, Warwickshire, Herefordshire, and Gloucestershire may appertain to the
same person, but it is not possible to be sure. The prior's tourn or visitation ('in torno,' l.22)
occurred annually, though it does not appear to have been on a set date.

397–8   WCL: C60   mb 2
'domini Edmundi de Hereforde' (p 397, l.31) cannot be identified. Contemporary records
reveal no persons who might reasonably be referred to as 'Edmund de Hereford.' There was
no Edmund among the members of the de Bohun family (the earls of Hereford), nor was
the bishop or the county sheriff named Edmund. John Talbot (p 397, l.33) would presumably
be of the great border Talbot family who later became the earls of Shrewsbury, though his
name does not appear in Talbot documents of the mid-fourteenth century. The manors of
Cleeve Prior and Blackwell (p 398, l.1) belonged to the priory, under the control, respectively,
of the prior and the cellarer.

399   WCL: C396   mb 3
'Beuerey' (l.20) presumably refers to the tiny hamlet of Bevere, 4 km north-north-west of
Worcester, or perhaps to a nearby manor or other house. From the sums involved in these
payments it would seem likely that the word 'Mynstrell'' is generally plural here unless otherwise indicated.

400   WCL: C398   mb 2
The Devereux family ('domini Walteri Deverose,' l.17) had estates in Herefordshire from
the time of William I and Walter was a traditional family name with a representative in almost
every generation. A Sir Walter Devereux married the heiress of Lord Ferrers, of Chartley,
Staffordshire, and was summoned to parliament by that title in 1461. He was very likely the
patron of these minstrels (Walter Bourchier Devereux, *Lives and Letters of the Devereux*,

Earls of Essex, vol 1 (London, 1853), 3). His relationship to the Walter Devereux who became in 1550–1 the first Viscount Hereford is uncertain. See p 279, endnote to HRO, f 39.

400   WCL: C399   mb 1
William Lucy (l.33) (1398–1466) served as sheriff of Warwickshire and Leicestershire in 1435 (*List of Sheriffs for England and Wales, from the Earliest Times to 1831*, Lists and Indexes, 9, PRO (London, 1898, rpt 1963), 145).

401   SHRO: BA 9360/C–2   f [1]
In an earlier ordinance of 1392 for the better regulation of the bailiffs and the rendering of their accounts (HWRO: BA 9360/A23 box 4) two aldermen were appointed as well as two bailiffs. It contains no reference to the administration of the pageants (see Dyer, *City of Worcester*, p 190).

403–4   WCL: C97   mb 3
'Claynes Aston' (p 404, l.1) must refer to the Cistercian convent of St Mary Magdalene, known as Whistones, in the parish of Claines just outside the Foregate of the city. The convent has often been confused with White Ladies' Aston (as in VCH: *Worcestershire*, vol 2, p 90), a parish lying southeast of the city where the convent owned lands (Knowles and Hadcock, *Medieval Religious Houses*, p 276).

404   HCL: R707   mb 5
The roll may be dated approximately by the name of the cellarer, Nicholas Hanbury, who appears frequently in other rolls through the 1470s.

406–11   BL: Cotton Julius B xii   ff 13v–17
This passage follows on directly from the account of the First Provincial Progress of Henry VII to York (see Alexandra F. Johnston and Margaret Rogerson (eds), *York*, vol 1, Records of Early English Drama (Toronto, 1979), 146–52) and is immediately followed by the accounts for Hereford (see above, pp 113–15) and Gloucester (see Douglas and Greenfield (eds), *Cumberland/Westmorland/Gloucestershire*, REED, pp 291–2). For the itinerary of the progress, see p 279, endnote to BL: Cotton Julius B xii, ff 17–18. The herald's account of the stay in Worcester gives no indication of why the king did not hear the pageant which had been prepared. The verses transcribed in fact comprise three speeches by reciters representing King Henry VI, the Virgin Mary, and a gatekeeper ('Ianitor,' p 409, l.12); but since the herald has not supplied either a marginal note or a heading for the Virgin's speech, it is not perfectly clear where it begins. The most likely starting point, however, would seem to be 'O Eternal god' (p 408, l.31). John Meagher has suggested that the speeches are given in the wrong order and that the seven-stanza speech of the gatekeeper should in fact begin the pageant (John C. Meagher, 'The First Progress of Henry VII,' *Renaissance Drama*, ns, 1 (1968), 61). The Latin lines beginning this speech (p 409, ll.13–15) are a pastiche of reminiscences of various passages in the Vulgate Bible.
    The stanza of King Henry VI's speech beginning 'And Here thou may dere Cousyn un⌜dre⌝stande' (p 407, ll.1–7) is obscure even by the standard of the rest of the text, largely because the scribe used so little punctuation, but also because of its complex syntax and lexical

peculiarities. Hence readers may find a paraphrase helpful: 'And here you may, dear kinsman, understand (that) this poor city, with humble reverence, has put into my hand a poor petition, beseeching me, (out) of my benevolence, to recite it at length to your magnificence; to which (task) I must apply my pitiful heart, and thus proceed, whoever cares to hear, forthwith...'
For the sense assumed for 'in place' (l.7) see OED Place *sb* 19a; this idiom, however, is not impressively well attested, and it is possible that both here and in the most closely parallel passage that the OED cites for this sense the phrase is a nearly meaningless tag put in to make up metre and rhyme. The forms 'this' and 'Whos' (l.7) are probably not scribal errors for 'thus' and 'whoso' but rather legitimate variants; see OED This *adv*; Whoso. For other individual words, see the English Glossary. On the elaborate diplomacy involved in the pageant, see Meagher, pp 60–7 and Introduction, p 309.

412–13   SHRO: BA 5234/23(ii)   single sheet
This is the earliest surviving document to mention the Worcester pageant houses in the
Cornmarket. The pageant houses are peripheral to the main purpose of this document, which uses their location to define one boundary of another plot of land: 'continent*em* ... in latitud*ine* a domib*us* vocat*is* le pageantehous*es* ... duodecem pedes regal*es*/' (p 412, ll.21–4). This suggests that they may have been adjacent, but provides little more information. Subsequent leases, however, mention only one pageant house in the Cornmarket. A second pageant house appears in a rent roll of 1605–6 (p 451), but is not localized. How many pageant houses there were remains an open question, as does their precise location. The Codon who witnessed the document (p 413, l.42) was William Codon, the town clerk.

416   SHRO: BA 9360/C–2   f [37v]
The ordinance concerning church ales suggests that such occasions provided a common mode of parochial fund raising among the Worcester city parishes, though there is little evidence of this in the Records. Prior More's household accounts include payments to church ales at St Helen's in 1533 (p 521, l.20) and 1534 (p 526, l.4), and at St Michael's in 1533 (p 521, l.21). The only church ale payment to survive from the meagre churchwardens' accounts of the city parishes is the following entry for the year 1543 in the accounts of St Michael's in Bedwardine (SHRO: BA 2335/16b (iii) f 5):

...
Item rec*eived* at Whitson[day] tyde for the churche ale   viij s.
...

   This entry gives little hint of the festivities that may have taken place on such an occasion (unlike the fuller accounts from Badsey, pp 357–60, and South Littleton, p 391). However it does indicate the date on which the churchwardens received the proceeds and thus the time of year at which the ale took place.

417–22   BL: Harley 425 ff 69–70
This narrative of a twelve-year-old child's imprisonment for reading the Bible in English and composing an anti-catholic ballad was condensed by Foxe, who assumed it to have been written by Davis himself. Although the story is presented as a third-person narrative, this should not preclude the possibility that Davis is in fact the author. Foxe adds that in 1596 Davis was still alive and serving as a minister in the Church of England. (See *Actes and*

monuments of these latter and perillous dayes, touching matters of the church. Now againe, recognised, perused, the fift time imprinted, 2 vols (London, 1596; STC: 11226), 1879–80.) The story was published by John Gough Nichols in *Narratives of the Days of the Reformation, Chiefly from the Manuscripts of John Foxe the Martyrologist*, Camden Society, 77 (London, 1859), 60–8.

The Act of the Six Articles (1539) (see p 417, l.38) was intended to prevent the spread in England of certain reformed doctrines by maintaining more traditional catholic teaching on such subjects as transubstantiation and clerical celibacy. Some at least of those called papist in this text are probably so characterized because of support for these articles rather than any loyalty to the pope or to the Roman Catholic church.

Nichols has identified most of the people referred to in this passage. He also points out that Parton's popish book 'named The hunting of the hare with curres and bandoges,' (p 418, l.14) is not known, but appears to be a reply to *The huntyng & fyndyng out of the romishe fox* (STC: 24353), published in 1543 by William Turner under the pseudonym of William Wraughton. Nichols identifies William Dodding and Richard Dabitote (p 420, l.18) as the bailiffs in 1545–6. Nash's list for this year gives the former's name as Dodington, but the correct name is given in 1543, when he served as low bailiff (see Nash, *Collections for the History of Worcestershire*, vol 2, Appendix, p cxii). Nichols also points out that Richard Bullingham (p 420, ll.20–1) served as low bailiff in 1561 and high bailiff in 1563. His brother, Nicholas Bullingham (p 420, ll.21–2), educated at Oxford and Cambridge, served as bishop of Lincoln from 1560 until his translation to Worcester in 1571, where he died in 1576 (see A.B. Emden, *A Biographical Register of the University of Oxford A.D. 1501 to 1540* (Oxford, 1974), 83; John Venn and J.A. Venn, *Alumni Cantabrigienses*, Pt 1 (Cambridge, 1922), 252). The following have also been identified: Robert Youle (p 420, l.38) served as low bailiff in 1545–6 and later on three occasions as high bailiff; Henry Jolliffe and Richard Eure (p 421, ll.21–2) were appointed prebendaries by the dean and chapter's foundation charter of 24 January 1541/2; Sir William Portman (p 421, l.39) was judge of the King's Bench from 1547 and later chief justice; Sir Edward Mervyn (p 421, l.40) was judge of King's Bench from 1541. (See Nichols, *Narratives of the Reformation*, pp 61n, 65n–68n.) Sir John Bourn (p 421, ll.41–2), a resident of Battenhall, Worcestershire, served as privy councillor and secretary under Mary (1553–8), holding a variety of offices in Worcestershire (S.T. Bindoff, *The House of Commons 1509–1558*, vol 1 (London, 1982), 466–8).

422   HWRO: BA 3585 1556:152A   mb 1
It is likely that Specheley was storing the players' costumes, rather than that he owned costumes of such great value.

424   SHRO: BA 9360/A–14   f 104v
According to John Noake, the liveries (l.35) were blue with cocked hats, though such a description would suggest that he is referring to a later period (*Notes and Queries for Worcestershire*, p 214).

425–8   SHRO: BA 9360/A–14   ff 122–3
Queen Elizabeth arrived in Worcester on Saturday, 13 August, having spent the previous two nights at Hartlebury with Dr Nicholas Bullingham, the bishop of Worcester. Since

9 July, her progress had included stops at Kenilworth, Lichfield, Stafford, and Chillington Hall. Following her visit to Worcester, the queen went on to Gloucester, returning to Woodstock at the beginning of September. (See Nichols, *The Progresses and Public Processions of Queen Elizabeth*, vol 1, pp 426–600.)

Christopher Dighton (p 426, l.17) served as governor of the Worcester Free School from 1561 to 1581. He was twice bailiff, in 1559–60 and 1574–5 (hence his prominence during the royal visit), and served as member of parliament for the city in 1572. (Nash, *Collections for the History of Worcestershire*, vol 2, p cxii; W.R. Buchanan-Dunlop, 'Old Worcestershire Families III: Dighton,' *TRWAS*, ns, 22 (1946), 84–7; P.H. Hasler, *The House of Commons 1558–1603*, vol 2 (London, 1981), 39.)

428–39   SHRO: BA 9360/A–14   ff 123–8
For the orator's speech, described on p 429, ll.21–5, see pp 439–42. The orator, as is clear from the description of the ceremony and the payments to him, was a Mr Bell, or, as it is sometimes written, Bellue. The boys' speeches (p 430, ll.19–21 and 29–31) do not in fact appear in the Chamber Order Book, perhaps because of the lack of room which the writer complains of earlier.

William Wyatt (p 430, l.31m) served as Worcester's town clerk from 1599 to 1631. Much of the second Chamber Order Book is in his hand (Bond (ed), *The Chamber Order Book of Worcester, 1602–1650*, p 31). Mr Stayner (p 432, l.23) is John Rowland, who is generally referred to in documents as John Rowland alias Steyner. Rowland, perhaps a member of the guild of the Holy Trinity, was one of the six Worcester citizens who acquired ownership of the Trinity Hall at the dissolution of the guild. He was one of the six 'descretiste cittizens' appointed as governors of the Free School in 1561 (*VCH: Worcestershire*, vol 2, p 293; vol 4, p 479). John Habington (1515–81) of Hindlip, Worcestershire (see p 432, l.35), was cofferer to Queen Elizabeth. His son Thomas, implicated in the Babington plot, was pardoned on the condition that he remain within the county. He retired to Hindlip, where he compiled an extraordinary collection of material towards a history of Worcestershire, *A Survey of Worcestershire by Thomas Habington*, 2 vols, John Amphlett (ed), WHS (Oxford, 1894–9). For his pedigree, see Nash, *Collections for the History of Worcestershire*, vol 1, page facing p 588.

439–42   SHRO: BA 9360/A–14   ff 9–10
'Worfarius,' king of Mercia (p 439, l.23), is almost certainly Wulfhere, who was placed on the throne in 659, three years after the death of his father, Penda, and ruled until 674 (Bede, *Historia Ecclesiastica*, Bertram Colgrave and R.A.B. Mynors (eds) (Oxford, 1969), book 3, chapters 24, 30). He is commonly styled the first Christian king of Mercia by chroniclers such as Florence of Worcester, who notes that 'regum Merciorum primus fidem et lavacrum sanctæ regenerationis accepit' (*Florentii Wigorniensis Monachi Chronicon ex Chronicis*, Benjamin Thorpe (ed), vol 1 (London, 1848), 32). The town clerk's spelling of his name is a bit odd and must derive from a Latinization like 'Wulferius.' Matthew Paris latinized the name to 'Wlferius' (*Chronica Majora*, Henry Richards Luard (ed), Rolls Series, 57, vol 1 (London, 1866), 291), though many of the other chroniclers retain the form 'Wulfere' or 'Wulfhere.' We must of course remember that the copy of the oration may have been taken down by dictation.

The school to which the orator refers (p 440, ll.15–20) was the Free School, the predecessor of the Royal Grammar School. A school had existed in Worcester from the late thirteenth century; in the early sixteenth century it was endowed by the Trinity guild, though in the early 1540s the guild had stopped supporting the schoolmaster. In 1547, John Oliver, BA, was appointed to the post and the school was revived. He abandoned his position in 1553 after a dispute over wages. The school was refounded by letters patent on 28 February 1560/1 as the Free School, to provide preparatory work for the King's School, the former cathedral school (see Nicholas Orme, 'The Medieval Schools of Worcestershire,' pp 43–51; *VCH: Worcestershire*, vol 4, pp 478–9, 491).

The 'fewe word*es*' of the orator (p 442, l.24) and Queen Elizabeth's reply do not appear in the Chamber Order Book. Edward Danniell (p 442, l.27) was the town clerk and the scribe who wrote the document.

445   HWRO: BA 3585 1575:97   mb 2, single sheet
His possession of 'players geare' (p 444, l.38) in addition to viols and recorders (p 444, l.39; p 445, l.1) suggests that Harry Smythe was one of the Worcester waits. The term is most commonly used to indicate actors' costumes and properties, but in the household of a musician the possibility should not be discounted that the 'geare' might be waits' liveries or paraphernalia. The 'boys' (p 445, l.10) to whom Smythe leaves his instruments and books are likely apprentices. That Smythe was also a maker of musical instruments is suggested by the references, in the bequest to his wife, to 'tymber,' 'wares ... readie made,' (p 445, ll.8–9) and 'tolles' (tools) (p 445, l.9).

445   SHRO: BA 9360/A–14   f 133v
Richard Durant, or Dyrham, (ll.25–6) appears regularly in the two Chamber Order Books. He may very well have already been one of the Forty-eight by this date, for leases of civic property frequently were granted to members of the chambers. He was certainly a member of the lower chamber in 1588 when his name appears in the list of members; he afterwards became a member of the Twenty-four, serving as auditor for the upper chamber in 1602–3. In 1583–4 he leased 'the vacant place where the pagant*es* do stand' for the term of sixty-one years and the lease appears to have been renewed by his son Robert on 20 February 1617–18 (Bond (ed), *The Chamber Order Book of Worcester, 1602–1650*, pp 63, 150).

445–7   WCL: B1872   f 1v
Although the document is clearly dated 3 December 1576, the 1578 dates at p 446, l.21 and p 447, l.6 would suggest that it may be a later copy of an inventory made in 1576. There is no evidence of a second or later hand.

448   SHRO: BA 9360/A–10   f [173v]
A total sum for all the allowances is given at the end of the paragraph: 'Cviij li. ij s. xj d.' It is of some interest that the corporation hired players in this year and several other times before the end of the century. From 1582–3 until 1600, with the exception of 1597–8, the city was consistently operating at a deficit. The players were important enough for their appearances to have continued (see Dyer, *City of Worcester*, p 221).

448   SHRO: BA 9360/A–10   f [182v]
A total sum is given for the paragraph: 'Clxxv li. xv. s v d.'

449   SHRO: BA 9360/A–10   f [186]
A total sum is given for the paragraph: 'lxviij li. viij s. viij d.'

449   HWRO: BA 3585 1594:28m   single mb dorse
The mere existence of a play-text such as 'the comedie of midas' (l.21) in a library does not, of course, constitute evidence for performance and in many cases I have disregarded such records, especially when the library was relatively large and the play-text just as likely to have been used for teaching or scholastic purposes (for example, the copy of Terence which may have belonged to the Worcester Priory library discussed by H.M. Bannister, 'Bishop Roger of Worcester and the Church of Keynsham, with a List of Vestments and Books Possibly Belonging to Worcester,' *English Historical Review*, 32 (1917), 388–91). On the other hand, a single play-text, especially in private hands, may be quite important. The existence of a play-book in Hereford in 1439–40 (see above, p 112) is, of course, quite useless as evidence that the city had a play cycle, but it may nonetheless indicate performance of some kind in a way that a copy of Terence likely does not. Worcester tradesmen may have had some involvement in the production of plays, however (see above, p 422, William Specheley's probate inventory, and endnote). I have therefore included documents recording play-texts (especially contemporary texts) in private hands, omitting those cases where the owner is clearly a book-collector. John Lyly's *Midas* was first performed in 1589 and was printed in 1592 (STC: 17083).
  This entry in Evans' probate inventory is a later addition. The initial inventory of 23 March was witnessed by Christopher Elgar and Geoffrey Humffreys; the additions (unwitnessed) were made on 18 May 1594.

449   SHRO: BA 9360/A–10   f [209v]
A total sum is given for the paragraph: 'xliiij li. ij d. ob.'

449   SHRO: BA 9360/A–10   f [215]
A total sum is given for the paragraph: 'xliiij li. iiij s. j d.'

450   SHRO: BA 9360/A–10   f [221]
A total sum is given for the paragraph: 'lvij li. j s. v d.'

450   SHRO: BA 9360/A–14   f 203v
Early references to this document, such as Noake's (*Worcestershire in Olden Times*, p 138), have referred to it as pertaining to the 'corvisors.' The order clearly involves payment by the city to a group of musicians to act as the city's waits and has nothing to do with the corvisors or shoemakers. Noake saw the problem and questioned if 'corvisors' might mean 'choristers,' a meaning for which there is no evidence. That these musicians are being hired at the bishop's request may suggest, as Dyer says, that 'a group of church musicians was made into the city waits' (Dyer, *The City of Worcester*, p 251).
  I have transcribed this word as 'Cornitors' (l.12), a form of OED Corneter, which at this date must have meant a player of the cornetto (see EG cornett). It is clear from the cathedral accounts of 1619 that cornetto players were hired to play with the choir; the cornetto was a normal waits' instrument.

450   SHRO: BA 9360/A–10   f [228]
The guests entertained this year include William Stanley, 15th earl of Derby; Gervase
Babington, bishop of Worcester (1597–1610); Sir John Pakington (see Introduction p 305);
and Sir Henry Bromley of Holt Castle, Worcestershire and Shrawardine Castle, Shropshire.
Bromley served as MP for Worcestershire in 1593 and 1604 and as JP from c 1591–1601. He
was sheriff of the county in 1591–2 (*Complete Peerage*, vol 4, pp 213–14; Hasler, *The House
of Commons, 1558–1603*, vol 1, p 491).

450   SHRO: BA 9360/A–10   f [234]
A total sum is given for the paragraph: 'lxj li. xiiij s. j d.'

451   SHRO: BA 9360/A–17   p 6
✓The final payment (ll. 14–15) is the only indication that Worcester had two pageant houses.
The pageant house referred to earlier (ll. 6–7) appears frequently in the Chamber Order Book
and was leased for many years to Richard Durant.

451   HWRO: Quarter Sessions Records   110:42/53   single sheet
The place of Hart's residence, Anserwick (ll. 23 and 27), cannot be precisely located; it is
not the name of a borough or parish in the county. I have therefore put this document under
Worcester, where the court met. It is difficult to expand 'proc' (l. 35) any further. The obvious
candidates, 'proctor' or 'procurator' are ruled out by context. They refer to attorneys in
ecclesiastical or equity courts, but this document comes from a common law court, of which
Payton was likely an officer or clerk.

451–2   BL: Royal 18 B vii   f 1v
The case is cited by T.W. Hancock, *Collections Historical and Archaeological Relating to
Montgomeryshire and its Borders*, vol 19 (London, 1886), 252. Hancock notes that the court
was sitting at Ludlow, though this information is not given in the manuscript.

452   SHRO: BA 3585 1618:154   single sheet
The will was probated before Dr Christopher Helme, chancellor of the diocese from 1618
to 1628, acting for Bishop John Thornborough.

453   WCL: A26   f 77
Although this payment is not strictly within the usual guidelines for REED documents, it is
of some importance for it provides likely evidence for the hiring of one of the city waits to
play with the cathedral choir, a practice for which the documentation is not extensive. That
the player is not in the regular employ of the cathedral (as the musicians in the civic order
concerning the waits in 1598–9 (see p 450, ll. 12–18) may have been) is implied by the fact
that it is an isolated payment. The Norwich waits played frequently in the cathedral (many
of them were singingmen as well); see David Galloway (ed), *Norwich*, Records of Early
English Drama (Toronto, 1984), xl–xli.

456–7   PRO: SP 16/298   p 84
The author of this report is the notorious Dean Roger Mainwaring, who had got himself

into serious trouble in 1627 by preaching two highly absolutist sermons before the king. He was appointed dean of Worcester in 1633. In 1640, as bishop of St David's, Mainwaring was accused of 'popish innovations' and this report to Laud was cited as evidence, especially item 14, that 'the Kings Schollers being 40, vsually comeing Tumultuouselye into ye Chore, I ordered to come in binatim; and to doe reuerence Toward ye Altar.' Some of Mainwaring's reforms were clearly for the best: 'Thousands of Rolls lyeing in ye Tower saued from vtter perisheing: by remoueinge them from a dampe Stone wall; and from vnder a wyndow, where ye rayne beate in vppon Them.'

Dr Nathaniel Tomkins (p 457, l.5), prebendary of Worcester, was the son of the composer, Thomas Tomkins, who spent much of his life as organist at Worcester Cathedral. (See *DNB*, 'Manwaring,' 'Tomkins'; *The New Grove Dictionary of Music and Musicians*, Stanley Sadie (ed) (London, 1980), 'Thomas Tomkins.')

The first six items of the report are preceded by an 'x,' and three items (6, 11, 17) are marked by a slash ('/'). Both these markings appear to be in a later hand.

458   WRO: BA 9360/A–6   p [71]
The Liber Legum (Civic Miscellany 2) contains several entries at this time in which the words 'the king's majesty's' have been replaced by 'his' and 'the king's subjects' by 'the people.' It seems likely that a parliamentarian was at work in the town clerk's office.

459–60   WCL: A11   f 30v
The year (l.23) has been added at a later time; the hand is very similar to the main hand of the accounts and may well be the same. Apart from Prior More's regular payments to carollers (p 459, ll.28–9; p 460, ll. 5–8) at the Christmas season, there is further evidence for the importance of this tradition in Worcester. The Selden manuscript (Bodl.: MS Arch. Selden B. 26), one of the principal sources for fifteenth-century carols, was compiled in Worcester and was the property of Bishop John Alcock, who was at Worcester from 1476 to 1486, though the collection of carols antedates his episcopate. Richard Leighton Green (*The Early English Carols*, 2nd ed (Oxford, 1977), 314–15) suggests that the origin of such a collection may be suggested by the payments in the week of Nativity 1 to carollers and to Richard Skryvener, the prior's scribe. The sizeable payment of 5s 8d to Skryvener between the payments for carols may indicate that he was collecting the singers' repertoire. As Green notes, 'This is a large payment, possibly at overtime rates, to a scribe, who would not usually be working on Christmas Day' (p 315). Skryvener was certainly capable of writing music; on f 30 (Advent Sunday 1518) he is paid 4s for writing 'ij quer*es* of A New masbocke.' Green's argument is not very strong, however; other payments to Skryvener are equally large (he was paid a total of 6s 8d for copying during the first week of Advent 1518) and there is no clear indication in the account entry that the payment is made for services on Christmas Day. Furthermore, the payment to Skryvener is not the only one to intervene between the payments to the carollers. Green's theory does, however, remain an interesting possibility.

Roger Knight (p 460, ll. 28–9), who was likely the prior's fool, figures prominently in the Account Book, with regular payments for his clothing, shoes, and laundry. Later in the year's accounts (see below, p 461, ll. 7–8) and again in Advent 1520 (see below, p 468, ll. 23–4), the prior paid for motley for Knight. No payments are made to him in wages, which must have been paid from another source. Payments for Knight's clothes and laundry cease abruptly in 1523, when he must have died or been dismissed. Further payments over the next few years in clothing and laundry to Leonard Stanley suggest that Knight's position may have been filled. Though occasional payments for shoes or clothing are made to other persons, Knight and Stanley are the only servants of the prior whose laundry bills are regularly paid. Although Stanley is never identified as the prior's fool, it must be remembered that apart from the two payments for motley, no such identification is given for Knight either.

Bailiff's names are given in the footnotes according to the list in Nash, *Collections for the History of Worcestershire*, vol 2, Appendix, pp cxi–cxiii.

460   WCL: A11   f 31v
The prior's scribe regularly refers to Quinquagesima as 'quyttide' (see l.35).

461   WCL: A11   f 33
This is the first of two payments for motley for Knight, suggesting that he was the prior's fool. The second is on f 46v (see below, p 468, ll.23–4). John Taylour (l.6) was the prior's tailor; Maude Catur (l.9) the washerwoman. Payments to both of them are frequent in the Account Book. I have included these payments only when they appear to refer to Roger Knight's 'geere.'

461   WCL: A11   f 33v
'Stoke' (l.26) is probably Stoke Prior; the manor belonged to the priory.

461–2   WCL: A11   f 34
Daniel of Pershore (p 461, ll.34–5) is likely one of the monks of the priory. On entering the order the monks generally took the name of their native town. The church of St Michael's in Bedwardine (p 462, l.1) physically adjoined the cathedral at the north-west corner until its demolition in 1840 and the parish included the cathedral precincts. The early accounts of the parish contain no references to players. They were edited by John Amphlett, *The Churchwardens' Accounts of St Michael's in Bedwardine, Worcester, from 1539 to 1603*, WHS (Oxford, 1896).

462–3   WCL: A11   ff 35, 35v, 36
I have given no dates for most of the weeks in this term, since the scribe has added an extra week between the first week of John the Baptist and what is given as the twelfth week, containing the feast of the Nativity of the Virgin. This feast should in fact come in the eleventh week. Unfortunately it is not possible to tell from the information in the entries where in this period the extra week has been added.

Two payments are made for the Parker's ale (p 463, l.27) at St Giles, the second occurring at the beginning of September 1531 (f 130, p 514, ll.10–11), that is, within a week of the time of year of this entry. A further payment, also probably for the ale, is made at the same time of year in 1523 and the recipient is identified as Richard Parker at St Giles (f 67v, p 480, ll.36–7). The first part of this entry is a payment to 'Iohn þe clerke of seynt Elyns' and it may well be that Richard Parker is the clerk of St Giles. The chapel of St Giles was connected with the prior in two ways. First, it was located on the prior's estate at Peachley, about three miles west of Worcester. Second, it was tied indirectly with the parish of Grimley, site of one of the prior's favourite manors: St Giles' chapel was subordinate to the chapel at Hallow, the manor of which Peachley estate was part, and that chapelry was annexed to the church of the neighbouring parish, Grimley (*vch*: *Worcestershire*, vol 3, pp 370–1).

The players (p 463, l.37) are from the parish of Martley, Worcestershire.

464   wcl: A11   f 38
Similar payments to 'ij pleyers' (l.12) are made on a regular basis, generally during the seasons of Lent and Advent, over the next twelve years. On the significance of these payments, see Introduction, pp 307–8, and Appendix 3.

465   wcl: A11   f 39
A rip in the bottom right corner of the folio has caused the loss of some of the text of week three (ll.17–18).

465–6   wcl: A11   f 40
During week nine, 19–25 February, the prior was in London for the first part of the week, but the payment to the minstrel John Harper (p 466, ll.5–6) was made in Worcester.

466   wcl: A11   f 40v
The extraordinary payment to the king's juggler and his harper (ll.13–14) may very well be due to the fact that the blind harper has the same name as the prior. Glimpses of such sentiment are not infrequent in the accounts.

466   wcl: A11   f 41v
'þe kynge*s* Mynstrelle*s*' (l.23) appear regularly in the prior's accounts. The patent of 24 April 1469 licensing the king's minstrels was reviewed and continued by an inspeximus dated 23 January 1519/20. At that time the members were John Gilmyn, Thomas Grenyng, Thomas Spence, Thomas Mayowe, John Abes, Thomas Pygyn, William Kirkeby, and John Rippys (?) (*Letters and Papers, Foreign and Domestic, of the Reign of Henry viii*, J.S. Brewer (arr and cat), vol 3, pt 1 (London, 1867), 204).

466–7   wcl: A11   ff 42, 42v
The scribe has made a dating error here in 'Ebdomada x^a' (p 466, l.28) and the previous two weeks are both numbered 'ix.' This week should therefore be numbered 'xj,' though the designation as Trinity Sunday is correct. Similarly, the week designated 'xij^a' on f 42v (p 467, l.2) should be numbered 'xiij.'

St Peter's (p 467, l.6) parish lay along the London road, on the route to the prior's manor at Battenhall. A further payment to the parish's players is made in May 1535 (f 157, p 529, ll.30–1).

468   wcl: A11   f 46v
The payments in week ten include a variety of other purchases of cloth which were not specifically related to Roger Knight's clothing (ll.23–4). This is the second mention of motley made up specifically for Knight, suggesting he was the prior's fool. The first is on f 33 (see above, p 461, ll.7–8).

468–9 WCL: A11 ff 47–7v

The chapel of St Kenelm (p 469, l.35) was located in the Clent Hills in the parish of Romsley in the northern part of the county, a few miles south of Halesowen. However, it was attached to the parish of Clent. It was an important pilgrimage site through the Middle Ages (*VCH: Worcestershire* vol 2, p 163; vol 3, p 150; Nash, *Collections for the History of Worcestershire*, vol 1, p 519).

472 WCL: A11 f 53v

Payments to Thomas Brandon (l.9), the king's juggler, continue from 1521 to 1533; once his son appears with him as a tumbler. Brandon is well-known from other sources; payments to him are found in Cambridge in 1532–3 (Alan H. Nelson (ed), *Cambridge*, Records of Early English Drama, vol 1 (Toronto, 1989), 106), Devon in 1533–4 (John M. Wasson (ed), *Devon*, Records of Early English Drama, (Toronto, 1986), 133), and in Shrewsbury on five occasions from 1522–3 to 1537–8 (J.A.B. Somerset (ed), Shropshire/Staffordshire, Records of Early English Drama, forthcoming). Subsequent REED volumes are likely to provide further information on his career.

475–6 WCL: A11 f 3v

The visitation mentioned in p 476, l.1 was part of a set of visitations undertaken during the vacancy of the see of Worcester in the autumn of 1522 and the winter of 1522/3. The prior appointed a member of his priory, Roger Neckham, as diocesan visitor during the vacancy. Neckham, who was to be deeply involved in the disputes leading to More's eventual removal from the priorate in the mid-1530s (*VCH: Worcestershire*, vol 2, pp 109–10), is usually identified as subprior but in this appointment he is called, perhaps erroneously, sacrist (f 2). Little is known of Foxforde except what can be garnered from this account book. He appears to have accompanied Neckham on the visitation in his capacity as commissary during vacancy (p 475, l.41) and may have been vicar general or guardian of spiritualities during that period. We know from a later payment (f 83v) that he became a doctor (in laws?) in 1525. Unlike Neckham he is never called 'dan' and so was probably not a monk of the priory.

477 WCL: A11 f 62

A tear in the folio does not affect the text.

480 WCL: A11 f 65

The precise meaning of 'showe' (l.19) in this context is not clear, but it would seem to be *OED* 13, an extraordinary pageant, procession, or spectacle. The prior makes payments to several other Worcester parishes for their 'shows,' all in May 1534 (St Helen's, St Swithin's, St Andrew's) (p 525, ll.28, 35; p 526, l.1). The St Peter's payment would confirm that the 'show' generally took place in May. On St Peter's, Worcestershire see above, p 599, endnote to WCL: A11 ff 42, 42v.

482–3 WCL: A11 f 71v

The final entry in week ten (p 483, l.12) has been damaged by a tear through the foot of f 71v.

483–4 WCL: A11 f 72v

The place where the prior spent weeks two and three (p 484, ll.2–14) has not been positively identified; it could perhaps be Cortington, Wiltshire (also known as Corton).

484–5 WCL: A11   ff 74v–5
The parish of Crowle was the site of one of the prior's manors where, as the Account Book indicates, he spent a good deal of time.

485 WCL: A11   f 76v
John English (l.17) first appears in the Exchequer accounts as court interluder to Henry VII in 1494, a post he continued to hold under Henry VIII. He appears to have been the leader of the players and his name is found frequently in royal accounts until 1531. He played for Prior More again at the end of August 1529 (p 504, l.25). (See Chambers, *The Mediaeval Stage*, vol 2, p 187; *The Elizabethan Stage*, vol 2, p 78; Edwin Nungezer, *A Dictionary of Actors* (New Haven, 1929), 130.)

487 WCL: A11   f 82
The suburb of Claines (l.30) lay immediately outside the Foregate of the city to the north, along the road to Droitwich and Kidderminster. Dancers from the parish entertained the prior regularly at this time of year.

487 WCL: A11   f 84
The princess (l.38) was Princess Mary, daughter of Henry VIII, later Queen Mary.

488–9 WCL: A11   f 87
At the time of Elizabeth I's visit of 1575, and presumably earlier as well, the bailiffs, aldermen, and high chamberlain wore scarlet gowns (p 488, l.36). Members of the upper chamber of Worcester's civic government, the Twenty-four, who had previously served as bailiffs (a large proportion of the group), wore scarlet trimmed with black. The rest of the Twenty-four wore gowns of murrey (mulberry purple) and the Forty-eight (the lower house of civic administration) wore violet. Thus by entertaining the scarlet gowns, the prior was entertaining the most powerful members of the civic oligarchy.

489 WCL: A11   f 87v
Princess Mary (see l.6) remained the prior's guest from the beginning of January through mid-April, returning for a further two weeks in August.

491 WCL: A11   f 93v
The usual Advent payments to two players and other entertainers do not appear this year, since the prior was in London from the week of 21 October until 24 January.

494 WCL: A11   f 99v
John Slye (l.6), or Slee, was a member of Queen Jane Seymour's players for an uncertain period before her death in 1537. Sometime in 1538 he was named in a Chancery suit concerning the hire of a horse used to carry the players' costumes (PRO: Chancery Proceedings, Bundle 931/11/Y cited and printed in C.C. Stopes, *Shakespeare's Environment* (London, 1914), 236). Chamber accounts show that he was one of the court interluders in the service of Henry VIII in 1539–40 and probably was earlier as well, as this payment would suggest. (Chambers,

The Elizabethan Stage, vol 2, p 79 n 3, 80 n 5; Edwin Nungezer, *A Dictionary of Actors*, p 331.) Slye played twice more before Prior More, in September 1528 (p 499, l.20) and at the end of January 1532/3 (p 519, l.39). In all these payments the ensemble is called 'the king*es* players.' However, the last time he is paid, in the spring of 1534 (p 526, ll.15–16), the ensemble is called the 'quenes pleyer*es*.'

499   WCL: A11   f 110
There are no explicit accounts for the following week, 20–6 September. The present week is given as the last week of the accounting year and the next accounts given are for 27 September–3 October, the first week of the following year. This accounting for week fourteen may possibly cover two weeks.

499   WCL: A11   f 111
'seynt Oswald*es* day' (l.32) must be the feast of the translation of St Oswald, the king and martyr, 8 October, rather than his better-known feast on 5 August.

503   WCL: A11   f 115v
The city parish of St Helen's (l.20) lies to the north of the cathedral; churchwardens' accounts survive for the years 1519–20, but contain no references to players. The St Helen's accounts were included in John Amphlett (ed), *The Churchwardens' Accounts of St Michael's in Bedwardine*, pp 1–8.

504–5   WCL: A11   f 119
The usual payments to two players in the two weeks previous to week twelve are missing this year because the prior was in London.

506–7   WCL: A11   ff 121a, 121av
The More is the village of the prior's birth; born William Peres, in traditional monastic fashion he took the name of his village upon entering the monastery. See above, pp 396, l.31–397, l.3 and endnote.

511–12   WCL: A11   f 128
On St Peter's parish (p 512, l.5), see above, p 599, endnote to WCL: A11 ff 42, 42v. St Swithin's (p 512, l.15) is a central city parish, situated between the High Street and the city walls to the east.

512   WCL: A11   f 128v
Since 'þe p*a*rasshe' (ll.29–30) could not refer to Worcester, it is probable that the reference is to Battenhall, where (as the heading indicates) the prior spent part of the week.

513   WCL: A11   f 129
'Will*i*am slye' (l.7) is clearly not the William Sly who was a member of the chamberlain's men in 1598 and died in 1608. No records have been published concerning Princess Mary's players, but the grouping (Sly as leader and three others) would show them to be an ensemble similar to the king's players. William may well be related to John Slye, who is paid as leader of the king's players in 1527, 1528, and 1532/3, and of the queen's players in 1534.

513–14 WCL: A11 f 129v
The manor of Cleeve Prior ('clyve,' p 513, l.22), north-east of Evesham, belonged to the priory.

516–17 WCL: A11 f 135
Although Cheney (*Handbook of Dates for Students of English History*, p 53) identifies Holy Rood Day (p 516, l.39) as the feast of the Exaltation of the Cross on 14 September, the term was in fact used indifferently in the Middle Ages, and down at least into the seventeenth century, for both the Exaltation and the Invention of the Cross on 3 May; see OED Rood Day and MED holi rode. Since Prior More uses the term in a set of accounts for the week of 28 April–4 May, he clearly intends the Invention.

520–1 WCL: A11 f 142v
The patron of 'my lord markas berewarde' (p 521, l.11) cannot be identified with certainty. There were two marquesses in the English peerage at the time: Henry Courtenay, marquess of Exeter, and Henry Grey, marquess of Dorset. For particulars of both, see below, Patrons and Travelling Companies, under Lord Marquess.

521–2 WCL: A11 f 143v
All Hallows' (p 522, l.1), or All Saints', is a central city parish. Henwick Hall ('hynwyck*es* hull,' p 522, l. 2) lay to the west of the city, along the west bank of the Severn in the parish of Hallow. The manor belonged to the prior; in 1533 he rented Henwick farm to a Mr Hall whose family held the lease until 1665 (*VCH: Worcestershire*, vol 3, p 368).

523 WCL: A11 f 145v
Prior More made two payments to Thomas Evance (l. 18), the second in September 1534 (p 527, ll.28–9). Although the text of this first payment names the king as Evance's patron, both the marginal note (ll.18–19m) and the second payment agree in calling him and his two companions the queen's minstrels. That suggests that 'kyng*es*' (l.18) in this case is an error.

525–6 WCL: A11 ff 150, 150v
On the parishes of St Helen's (p 525, l.28) and St Swithin's (p 525, l.35), see above, p 602 (endnotes to WCL: A11 ff 115v and 128). St Andrew's (p 526, l.1), a central city parish, lies along the river to the west of St Helen's.

526 WCL: A11 f 151v
For 'my lord markas' (l.31) see above, p 603; endnote to WCL: A11 f 142v.

526–7 WCL: A11 f 152v
The six sackbut-playing minstrels of the king (p 527, l.20) are very likely to have included the Bassano brothers, Anthony, Alvise, Jasper, and John, who came to the court from Venice in 1531 to serve in Henry VIII's shawm and sackbut ensemble, only to return to Venice after a few years. Anthony returned to England in 1538, followed shortly by his brothers Alvise, Jacopo, Jasper, John, and Baptista. The Bassano family formed the nucleus of the royal wind band until the middle of the seventeenth century (see David Lasocki, 'The Bassanos: Anglo-Venetian and Venetian,' *Early Music*, 14, pt 4 (1986), 558–60).

529   WCL: A11   f 157

A leaf has been torn out and there is a break from mid-March until 25 April. On St Peter's parish (ll.30–1), see above, p 599, endnote to WCL: A11 f 42v.

PATRONS AND TRAVELLING COMPANIES, GLOSSARIES, AND INDEX

Patrons and
Travelling Companies

The following list has two sections. The first lists companies alphabetically by patron, according to the principal title under which the playing companies and entertainers appear. Cross-references to the principal title are given from other titles named in the Records. The second section lists companies which are identified by place of origin.

The biographical information supplied here has come entirely from printed sources, the chief of which are the following: S.T Bindoff (ed), *The History of Parliament: The House of Commons 1509–1558*, 3 vols (London, 1982); *Calendar of Patent Rolls* (edited through 1576); *Calendar of State Papers*; G[eorge] E[dward] C[okayne], *The Complete Peerage…*; *The Dictionary of National Biography*; James E. Doyle, *The Official Baronage of England Showing the Succession, Dignities, and Offices of Every Peer from 1066 to 1885*, 3 vols (London, 1886); P.W. Hasler (ed), *The History of Parliament: The House of Commons 1558–1603*, 3 vols (London, 1981); *Letters and Papers, Foreign and Domestic, Henry VIII*, 21 vols and Addenda (London, 1864–1932); F. Maurice Powicke and E.B. Fryde (eds), *Handbook of British Chronology*; and Josiah C. Wedgwood and Anne D. Holt, *History of Parliament: Biographies of the Members of the Commons House 1439–1509* (London, 1936).

All dates are given in accordance with the style in the sources used. The authorities sometimes disagree over the dates of birth, death, creation, succession, and office tenure. Where this evidence conflicts, dates given in the *Calendar of State Papers*, *Calendar of Patent Rolls*, and lists based on primary sources such as the following are preferred: *List of Sheriffs for England and Wales from the Earliest Times to A.D. 1831*, Public Record Office, Lists and Indexes, no 9 (London, 1898); J.H. Gleason, *The Justices of the Peace in England: 1558 to 1640* (Oxford, 1969); and J.C. Sainty, 'Lieutenants of Counties, 1585–1642,' *Bulletin of the Institute of Historical Research*, Special Supplement, no 8 (May, 1970).

Normally, each patron entry is divided into four sections. The first lists relevant personal data and titles of nobility with dates. Succession numbers are given only for the most important titles and for titles given in the Records. These numbers follow the absolute sequence given in *The Complete Peerage* rather than the relative ones which begin afresh with each new creation. Knighthood dates are included only for minor gentry not possessing higher titles. The second section lists appointments showing connections local to Herefordshire/Worcestershire and surrounding counties and includes those known to have been used in titles of playing companies. Purely expeditionary military titles have been largely omitted, along with most minor Scottish and Irish landed titles. For patrons holding peerage titles, minor civil commissions not given in *The Complete Peerage* and *The Dictionary of National Biography* have been omitted. Readers desiring further information on these patrons are advised to consult the *Calendar of Patent Rolls* and *Letters and Papers of Henry VIII*.

Where possible, the date of an appointment is taken from the date of a document assigning that position. If the appointment is stated in the document to be 'for life,' then these words follow the title of that post. If the original document has not been edited and a secondary source is used which states 'until death,' then this form appears. Otherwise dates of appointment and termination are given, if available. If the length of time an office is held is not known, then only the date of appointment is given. Alternatively, if the only evidence comes from a source dated some time during the period of tenure, then the word 'by' and a date appears. If only the date of termination is known, 'until' is used. Finally, if no dates at all are available, 'nd' follows the title of the appointment. A '?' following a date indicates uncertainty regarding the dating of a document in the sources or differentiation in the case of several patrons by the same name who might have held the post. For all minor commissions such as commissions of the peace (JP), years only are given. If the dates of these commissions cover several years in sequence, then the earliest and latest years of the sequence are separated by a dash.

The third section, for which information is often incomplete or unavailable, contains the names and locations of the patron's principal seats and locations of other properties he or she is known to have held. Extensive property lists have been condensed. Place names for which no standard modern spelling is available are enclosed in single quotes to indicate spelling from the original source.

The fourth section is an annotated index by date of the appearances of each patron's company or companies in the Records. Following the date are the page numbers in parentheses where the citations occur. If a patron's company appears under a title other than the usual or principal one, this other title is in parentheses next to the designation of the company. Companies named according to a patron's civil appointment are indexed under the name of that post as it appears in the Records: for example, 'Lord President of the Council in the Marches.' All other companies appear under their patron's principal landed title. If a patron has more than one type of company, all entries for a given type are grouped together in chronological order. Each group of entries is then listed according to the earliest year that company appears in the Records. If two or more companies first appear in the same year, alphabetical order is followed.

The reader may also wish to refer to the Index for additional references to some of the patrons and to various unnamed companies and their players. Where it has been possible to identify a patron of an unnamed company, the reference has been included here; otherwise such references are only in the Index. Persons referred to as 'seruientes' are included among the listed companies as 'servants' although those referred to as 'famuli' are not. It seems probable that 'seruientes' might be 'men' in the sense of 'performers' or 'players.' 'Famuli' seems more likely to refer to such persons as household servants, that is, those working in the household or with its head, petty serjeants of the Crown, or even labourers. Noble patrons are listed in the Index under their family names or, in the case of women, under their maiden names.

Abbreviations

acc	acceded	JP	Justice of the Peace
adm	admiral	jt	joint
bapt	baptized	kt	knight
capt	captain	lieut	lieutenant
comm	commissioner	MP	Member of Parliament
cr	created	nd	no date
custos rot	custos rotulorum	PC	Privy Councillor
d.	died	pres	president
gov	governor	succ	succeeded

Companies Named by Patron

Abbot (Evesham)
William de Boys (?–6 Jun 1367), elected 1 Jan 1344/5, confirmed 20 Mar 1344/5, installed 16 May 1345.

minstrel/s	Worc	Worcester	1351–2 (398)

Abbot (Gloucester)
Adam of Staunton (?–1351), abbot of Gloucester after 28 Feb 1336/7.

harper	Worc	Worcester	1345–6 (397)
minstrel/s	Worc	Worcester	1347–8 (398)

Abbot (Reading)
Robert de Burghate (?–after 1290), abbot of Reading, royal assent given 15 Jul 1269, resigned 26 October 1290.

harper	1289–90 (189)

Arundel
Richard FitzAlan (c 1313–24 Jan 1375/6), probably restored as 14th earl of Arundel and Baron Kedy, Kedewy, Clun, Oswestry Dec 1331; cr Baron Bromfield and Yale 18 Jan 1354; succ as 10th earl of Surrey and Warenne 31 Aug 1361. Keeper for life Castle Chirk, Denbighshire, Wales, 13 Sept 1333; justice of North Wales during pleasure 8 Nov 1334, for life 10 Mar 1337; gov Caernarvon Castle, Caernarvonshire, Wales, 12 Jul 1339; JP Shrops 1344–5, 1351–3, 1356; sheriff Shrops 10 Mar 1345; jt guardian of England 1 Jul 1355. Lands in Wales and various counties including Shrops and Staff.

minstrel/s	Worc	Worcester	1347–8 (398)

William FitzAlan (or Mautravers) (23 Nov 1417–87), succ as 21st earl of Arundel 24 Apr 1438. JP Shrops 1440–1, 1443–5, 1448–9, 1453–4, 1457–8, 1460–2, 1466, 1468–9, 1471, 1473–5, 1477–8, 1480, 1483, 1485–6, Glouc 1441, 1444–6, 1448–9, 1451–2, 1454–8, 1460, 1462, 1464, 1468–71, 1473–5, 1477, 1479, 1481, 1483–5; justice in eyre south of Trent 19 Dec 1459–61 and 1 Jul 1483–5. Seat at Arundel Castle, Suss.

minstrel/s	Worc	Worcester	1447–8 (400)
			1481–2 (405)

William FitzAlan (c 1476–23 Jan 1543/4), styled Lord Mautravers 1487–1524, succ as 23rd earl of Arundel 25 Oct 1524. JP Shrops 1526, 1529, 1531, 1536, 1538–9, Worc 1531–2, 1537–40, 1542. Lands in Wales and various counties.

minstrel	Worc	Battenhall	1530–1 (513)

Beauchamp

William Beauchamp (?–8 May 1411), kt by 1375, Lord Bergavenny 1392. Keeper of Feckenham Forest, Worc, for life 1377; keeper of castle and county of Pembroke, castle and lordship of Cilgerran, Pembrokeshire, Wales, during minority of John Hastings, earl of Pembroke, 9 Mar 1378–4 Feb 1389/90 (revoked); lord chamberlain 1380; capt of Calais 1383–90 (dismissed); justice of South Wales for life 30 Oct 1399–27 Aug 1401 (removed from office); governor of castle and county of Pembroke and lord of Tenby and Cilgerran, Pembrokeshire, Wales, 29 Nov 1399–1403; JP Heref 1404–8, Warw 1401, 1404–7, Worc 1405–7, 1410; king's lieut in South Wales and the Marches during pleasure 23 May 1405. Lands in Wales and various counties including Glouc, Heref, London, Shrops, Staff, Warw, Worc.

minstrels	Worc	Worcester	1395–6 (399)

Bedford

Jasper Tudor (c 1430–21 Dec 1495), cr 16th earl of Pembroke by 20 Jan 1452/3 and 3rd duke of Bedford 27 Oct 1485; attainted 4 Nov 1461; restored 1470–1; attainted 1471; fled England after 4 May 1471; restored to earldom 12 Dec 1485. JP Heref 1456–60, 1470, 1486–7, 1492–5, Glouc 1470, 1485–90, 1493–4, Worc 1485–9, 1493–4, Shrops 1490, 1493, Warw 1490–1, 1493–4, Staff 1493; constable castles of Aberystwyth, Cardiganshire, Carmarthen, Carmarthenshire, and Denbigh, Denbighshire, Wales, 1457; comm of array South Wales and the Marches 1470/1; constable Gloucester Castle, Glouc, 14 Feb 1470/1; PC 27 Oct 1485; chief justice South Wales for life 13 Dec 1485; lord deputy of Ireland 11 Mar 1486–94; lieut of Ireland 1 Oct 1488; earl marshal of England 1492. Seat at Pembroke Castle, Pembrokeshire, Wales; lands in Wales and various counties including Glouc, Shrops, Warw, and Worc.

servant/s	Worc	Worcester	1490–1 (411)

Belknap

Edward Belknap (c 1465–before 26 Mar 1520/1), kt by 20 Feb 1512/13. JP Warw 1491, 1493–4, 1496–7, 1499, 1503, 1506–7, 1509–12, 1514; keeper Wedgnock Park, Warw, for life, sole 24 Apr 1492 and jt 15 Feb 1511; sheriff Warw 5 Nov 1501; constable Warwick Castle, Warw, during pleasure, sole 11 Feb 1502 and jt 15 Feb 1511; steward of various manors in Warw, sole 11 Feb 1502 and jt 15 Feb 1511. Seat at Weston, Warw; lands in various counties including Staff, Warw, and Worc.

players	Worc	Worcester	1518–19 (460)
			1519–20 (465)

Berkeley

Henry Berkeley (26 Nov 1534–26 Nov 1613), succ as 7th Lord Berkeley at birth. Keeper of Kingswood Forest, Glouc, for life 26 Jun 1559; JP Glouc 1562, 1564; lord lieut 13 Aug 1603 and vice-adm Glouc 14 Nov 1603 until death. Principal residences at Yate Court and Berkeley Castle, Glouc, and Caludon Castle near Coventry,

Warw; lands in various counties including Glouc and Warw.

players	Heref	Leominster	1600–1 (147)

Bishop (of Durham)

Robert Neville (1404–9 Jan 1457). Bishop of Salisbury by provision 9 Jul 1427, temporalities restored 10 Oct 1427, consecrated 26 Oct 1427; bishop of Durham, elected and translated 27 Jan 1438, temporalities restored 8 Apr 1438, installed 11 Apr 1441.

minstrel/s	Worc	Worcester	1445–6 (399)

Buckingham

Humphrey Stafford (15 Aug 1402–10 Jul 1460), succ as 6th earl of Stafford and 7th Baron Stafford 21 Jul 1403, 5th earl of Buckingham 16 Oct 1438, and cr 1st duke of Buckingham 14 Sept 1444. JP Heref 1423–4, 1427–8, 1431–3, 1435, 1437, 1441, 1443, 1451, 1453, 1455–60, Shrops 1423–4, 1426, 1430–2, 1439–41, 1443–5, 1448–9, 1453–4, 1457–8, Warw 1424, 1433–4, 1439–45, 1449, 1452–5, 1457–9, Staff 1430, 1432, 1439, 1441–2, 1446, 1449, 1453–4, 1456, 1459–60; PC 15 Feb 1424; sheriff Hereford 4 Nov 1446. Seats at Stafford Castle, Staff, and Writtle, Essex, from 1421 and Maxstoke Castle, Warw, from 1438; lands in Wales and various counties including Brecon Castle, Brecknockshire.

minstrel	Worc	Worcester	1445–6 (399)
minstrel/s	Worc	Worcester	1446–7 (399)
			1451–2 (400)

Edward Stafford (3 Feb 1477/8–17 May 1521), restored as 3rd duke of Buckingham, 8th earl of Stafford, 7th earl of Buckingham, and 9th Baron Stafford Nov 1485. JP Glouc 1500–6, 1508, 1510–11, 1513–15, 1520, Heref 1503, 1505, 1507, 1509–10, 1513–15, 1521, Warw 1503, 1506–7, 1509–11, 1514–15, Shrops 1503–4, 1510–11, 1513–14, Staff 1503–4, 1508, 1509–11, 1514, 1520; PC 1509; imprisoned in Tower 16 Apr 1521; beheaded 17 May 1521. Seats at Thornbury, Glouc, and Brecon Castle, Brecknockshire, Wales; lands in many counties including Glouc, Warw, and Worc.

harper	Worc	Worcester	1518–19 (459)

Cardinal

Thomas Wolsey (c 1475–29 Nov 1530). Dean of Hereford by 4 Jun 1509–3 Dec 1512; PC by 1511; bishop of Lincoln, temporalities restored 4 Mar 1514 and consecrated 26 Mar 1514; archbishop of York, temporalities restored 5 Aug 1514 and translated 15 Sept 1514; cardinal after 10 Sept 1515; lord chancellor 24 Dec 1515; bishop of Bath and Wells 'in commendam' 27 Jul 1518 and temporalities granted 26 Aug 1518; JP Glouc 1520, 1522, 1524–25, 1528, Staff 1520, 1522–3, 1526, Heref 1521–2, 1525, 1528, Shrops 1521–3, 1526, 1529, Warw 1522, 1524, 1529, Worc 1522, 1524, 1526; bishop of Durham 'in commendam' 21 Mar 1523 and temporalities restored 30 Apr 1523; bishop of Winchester 'in commendam' 8 Feb 1529 and temporalities restored 6 Apr 1529.

| singer | Worc | Worcester | 1518–19 (463) |
| minstrels | Worc | Worcester/Grimley | 1528–9 (504) |

Chandos
William Brydges (after 1548–18 Nov 1602), succ as 4th Baron Chandos 21 Feb 1593/4. MP Glouc 1584–7; member, Council in the Marches of Wales, May 1594; lord lieut Glouc 9 Sept 1595 until death. Seat at Sudeley Castle, Glouc.

| players | Heref | Leominster | 1597–8 (146) |
| | Worc | Evesham | c 1600 (376–7) |

Clarence
George Plantagenet (21 Oct 1449–18 Feb 1477/8), son of Richard, 3rd duke of York, qv, cr 3rd duke of Clarence 28 Jun 1461 and 17th earl of Warwick and 12th earl of Salisbury 25 Mar 1471/2. Chief gov of Ireland Feb 1461/2–Mar 1469/70 and 1472; JP Shrops 1466, 1468–71, 1473–5, 1477, Warw 1466, 1468–75, Staff 1468–75, Worc 1469, 1471, 1473–5, 1477, Glouc 1470–1, 1473–5, 1477, Heref 1470, 1473–6; chief justice in eyre south of Trent for life 3 Sept 1468; lord chamberlain 20 May 1471/2; attainted 8 Feb 1477/8 and executed 18 Feb 1477/8. Seat at Warwick Castle, Warw; lands in many counties including Warw.

| minstrel/s | Worc | Worcester | 1471–2 (405) |
| | | | 1472–3 (405) |

Derby
Edward Stanley (10 May 1509–24 Oct 1572), probably styled Lord Strange until he succ as 12th earl of Derby, 11th Lord Strange, 4th Lord Stanley, and lord of the Isle of Man 23 May 1521. PC 9 Aug 1551, 17 Aug 1553, and 24 Nov 1558. Seats at Lathom and Knowsley, Lanc and Knockin, Shrops; lands in various counties.

| bearward | Worc | Crowle | 1534–5 (527) |

William Stanley (c 1561–29 Sept 1642), succ as 15th earl of Derby 16 Apr 1594; confirmed in the lordship of the Isle of Man 7 Jul 1609. PC Mar–May 1603; member, Council in the Marches of Wales, by 1617. Seats at Lathom and Knowsley, Lanc.

players	Heref	Leominster	1597–8 (146)
			1616–17 (148)
			1619–20 (149)

Despenser
Hugh Despenser (c 1308–8 Feb 1348/9), Lord le Despenser by writ 15 Nov 1338. Imprisoned in Bristol Castle, Glouc, 15 Dec 1328–5 Jul 1331; imprisoned in the Tower before 20 Dec 1344. Lands in Wales and various counties including Glouc, Warw, and Worc.

| minstrel/s | Worc | Worcester | 1345–6 (397) |

Devereux

Walter Devereux (c 1432–22 Aug 1485), cr 2nd Lord Ferrers 1461. MP Heref 1460;
JP Heref 1461–3, 1473–6, 1481, 1483–4, Glouc 1462, 1464, 1468–9, 1471, 1473–5,
1477, 1479, 1481, 1483–5, Shrops 1471, 1474–5, 1477–8, 1480, 1483, Worc 1474;
constable Aberystwyth Castle, Cardiganshire, Wales, for life 18 Jun 1463; jt keeper
Haye Park, Heref, for life 10 Aug 1464; constable and steward, castles and lordships
of Brecon, Brecknockshire, Wales, and Hay, Heref, 16 Nov 1469; sheriff
Caernarvonshire and master forester Snowdon, Caernarvonshire, Wales, for life
28 Jul 1470; attainted 7 Nov 1485 as of from 21 Aug 1485. Seat at Weobley,
Heref; lands in various counties including Glouc, Heref, Shrops, Staff, and
Warw.

minstrel/s	Worc	Worcester	1447–8 (400)

Dudley

Edward Sutton or Dudley (bapt 17 Sept 1567–23 Jun 1643), succ as 5th Lord Dudley
by 12 Aug 1586. MP Staff 1584; JP Staff by 1585 and Worc 1608, 1626, 1636. Seat at
Dudley Castle, Staff.

players	Heref	Leominster	1600–1 (147)
	Worc	Worcester	1625–6 (455)

Exeter (duke)

John Holand (29 Mar 1395 or 1396–5 Aug 1447), restored in blood and succ as 14th
earl of Huntingdon 1417; cr 3rd duke of Exeter 6 Jan 1443/4. Constable of the
Tower, sole 20 Aug 1420 and jt 28 Feb 1446/7; PC 24 Nov 1426; JP Heref 1427–8,
1431–3, 1435, 1437, 1441, 1443; deputy marshal of England 15 Nov 1432–12
Sept 1436; lord high adm during pleasure, sole 2 Oct 1435 and jt 14 Feb 1445/6. Seat at
Barnstaple, Devon, London residence at Coldharbour; lands in Wales and various
counties including Wilts.

minstrel/s	Worc	Worcester	1445–6 (399)

Henry Holand (27 Jun 1430–Sept 1475), son of John, 3rd duke of Exeter, qv, succ
as 4th duke of Exeter and 15th earl of Huntingdon 5 Aug 1447. Lord high adm, jt
14 Feb 1445/6 and sole 5 Aug 1447–60; constable of the Tower, jt 28 Feb 1447 and
sole 6 Aug 1447–60; attainted 4 Nov 1461; fled to Flanders 1463–Feb 1470/1; held
in custody 26 May 1471–20 May 1475. Seat at Barnstaple, Devon, London residence
at Coldharbour; lands in Wales and many counties.

minstrel/s	Worc	Worcester	1451–2 (401)

Ferrers

Walter Devereux (c 1488–17 Sept 1558), succ as 4th Baron Ferrers 1501; cr 1st
Viscount Hereford 2 Feb 1549/50. Jt constable Warwick Castle, Warw, jt steward
various manors in Warw for life 15 Feb 1510/11; member, Council in the Marches
of Wales, 10 Aug 1513; JP Heref 1513–15, 1521–2, 1525, 1528, 1531–2, 1538, 1540–1,

1543–4, 1547, 1554, Flintshire, Wales, 1515, Glouc 1515, 1522, 1524–5, 1528, 1531–2, 1537, 1539–40, 1542–5, 1547, 1554, Shrops 1515, 1522–3, 1526, 1531–2, 1536, 1538–9, 1543, 1547, 1554, South Wales and Marches 1515, Worc 1515, 1522, 1524, 1526, 1531–2, 1537–40, 1542–5, 1547, 1554, Staff 1522–3, 1526, 1531–2, 1536, 1538, 1540, 1543–5, 1547, 1554, Warw 1539, 1542–5, 1547, Monmouthshire, Wales 1543–4; steward of lands in Warw and steward of crown lands in Wales, Staff, Shrops 29 Mar 1522; chief justice for life South Wales 22 Aug 1525; steward of South Wales 1526; constable Llanddewibrefi Castle, Cardiganshire, Wales by 1536. Principal seat Chartley, Staff; lands in Wales and various counties including Glouc, Heref, Staff, and Warw.

players	Worc	Grimley	1529–30 (505)

Gardin
Arnold de Gardin (before 1280–after 1305), knight of Flanders, in service of Arnold Guillelmi, Count Daudoyns (1299); envoy of John, count of Namur 1303.

minstrel	Heref	Abbey Dore	1303 (187)

Gloucester (abbot) *see under* Abbot

Gloucester (duke)
Humphrey of Lancaster (3 Oct 1390–23 Feb 1446/7), 4th son of Henry IV, *qv*, cr 2nd duke of Gloucester and 14th earl of Pembroke 16 May 1414. Lord chamberlain during pleasure 7 May 1413 and 30 Nov 1422; PC by 10 Apr 1415; chief justice and warden of forests south of Trent for life 27 Jan 1415/16; JP Glouc 1416, Heref 1437, 1441, 1443; keeper of the realm and deputy of the king 30 Dec 1419 and 23 Apr 1430; regent May 1422; protector 5 Dec 1422; constable Gloucester Castle, Glouc, during pleasure 10 Dec 1422; justice Chester, Ches, and North Wales, 10 May 1427–19 Feb 1440 and Anglesey and Flintshire, Wales, during pleasure 16 Mar 1437; lieut Marches of Wales 1 Nov 1435. Principal seat at Greenwich, Kent; London residence at Baynard's Castle; lands in Wales and many counties, including Glouc.

minstrel	Worc	Worcester	1445–6 (399)

Richard Plantagenet (2 Oct 1452–22 Aug 1485), son of Richard Plantagenet, 3rd duke of York, *qv*, and Cecily Neville; cr 3rd duke of Gloucester 1 Nov 1461; protector of the realm 9 Apr 1483; acc as Richard III 26 Jun 1483; crowned 6 Jul 1483.

minstrel/s	Worc	Worcester	1472–3 (405)
			1481–2 (405)
servant/s	Worc	Worcester	1478–9 (405)

Hereford
Edmund de Hereford. Not identified.

minstrels	Worc	Worcester	1345–6 (397).

Hungerford
Edmund Hungerford (d. by 1470). Sheriff Glouc 7 Nov 1436 and 5 Nov 1464; JP Glouc 1448–9, 1451–2, 1454–8; jt constable Cardiff Castle, Glamorgan, and master forester Glamorgan, both in Wales, 2 Aug 1448. Residence at Suckley, Worc; lands in various counties including Worc.

minstrel/s	Worc	Worcester	1447–8 (400)

Huntingdon
George Hastings (c 1540–30 Dec 1604), succ as 21st earl of Huntingdon and Baron Hastings, Hungerford, Botreaux, Moleyns, Moels 14 Dec 1595. Seat at Loughborough, Leic.

players	Heref	Leominster	1602–3 (147)

King
Edward Plantagenet (17 or 18 Jun 1239–7 Jul 1307), son of Henry III and Eleanor of Provence; acc as Edward I 16 Nov 1272; crowned 19 Aug 1274.

minstrels	Worc	Kempsey	1300–1 (379)

Henry of Windsor (6 Dec 1421–21 May 1471), son of Henry V and Catherine of Valois; acc as Henry VI 1 Sept 1422; proclaimed king of France 21 Oct 1422 (John, 1st duke of Bedford, appointed protector 5 Dec 1422); crowned king of England 6 Nov 1429 and of France 16 Dec 1431; deposed 4 Mar 1461; restored 3 Oct 1470; crowned 13 Oct 1470; deposed finally 11 Apr 1471.

minstrel/s	Worc	Bevere	1445–6 (399)
	Worc	Worcester	1446–7 (400)

Edward of York (28 Apr 1442–9 Apr 1483), son of Richard Plantagenet, 3rd duke of York, qv, and Cecily Neville; acc as Edward IV 4 Mar 1461; crowned 28 Jun 1461; fled England 3 Oct 1470–14 Mar 1471; restored 11 Apr 1471.

minstrel/s	Worc	Worcester	1463–4 (401)
			1464–5 (401)
			1470–1 (404)
			1471–2 (405)
			1472–3 (405)
			1481–2 (405)
servant/s	Worc	Worcester	1478–9 (405)

Henry Tudor 'of Richmond' (28 Jan 1457–21 Apr 1509), son of Edmund Tudor, earl of Richmond, and Margaret Beaufort; acc as Henry VII 22 Aug 1485; crowned 30 Oct 1485.

servants	Worc	Worcester	1486–7 (411)
servant/s	Worc	Worcester	1490–1 (411)

minstrel/s	Worc	Pershore	1495–6 (385)

Henry Tudor (28 Jun 1491–28 Jan 1547), son of Henry VII, *qv*, and Elizabeth of York; cr prince of Wales 18 Feb 1503; acc as Henry VIII 22 Apr 1509; crowned 24 Jun 1509.

minstrel/s	Worc	Worcester	1517–18 (417)
minstrels	Worc	Worcester	1518–19 (461)
			1519–20 (466)
			1520–1 (471)
			1521–2 (475)
			1522–3 (480)
	Worc	Crowle	1523–4 (485)
			1524–5 (487)
	Worc	Grimley	1525–6 (490)
			1526–7 (493)
	Worc	Crowle	1527–8 (498)
	Worc	Grimley	1528–9 (499)
	Worc	Battenhall	1528–9 (503)
			1529–30 (507)
	Worc	Crowle	1530–1 (513)
			1531–2 (517)
	Worc	Worcester	1532–3 (522)
	Worc	Crowle	1533–4 (525)
minstrel/s	Heref	Hereford	1533–4 (119)
minstrels	Worc	Worcester/Grimley	1533–4 (527)
	Worc	Battenhall	1534–5 (529)
harper	Worc	Worcester	1518–19 (459)
			1519–20 (466)
juggler	Worc	Worcester	1518–19 (462)
			1519–20 (466)
			1520–1 (468)
			1521–2 (472)
			1522–3 (478)
		'Courting'	1523–4 (484)
	Worc	Worcester	1524–5 (487)
			1525–6 (491)
	Worc	Grimley	1527–8 (494)
	Worc	Worcester	1528–9 (499)
	Worc	Grimley	1528–9 (504)
			1530–1 (508, 514)
	Worc	Crowle	1531–2 (518)
	Worc	Worcester	1533–4 (526)
bearward	Worc	Worcester	1524–5 (486)
	Worc	Battenhall	1528–9 (501)

players	Worc	Grimley	1524–5 (485)
	Worc	Crowle	1526–7 (494)
	Worc	Grimley	1527–8 (499)
			1528–9 (504)
	Worc	Battenhall	1532–3 (519)
	Worc	Worcester	1534–5 (529)

Edward Tudor (12 Oct 1537–6 Jul 1553), son of Henry VIII, *qv*, and Jane Seymour; acc as Edward VI 21 Jan 1547; crowned 20 Feb 1547. Edward Seymour, 5th duke of Somerset, appointed protector.

minstrel/s	Heref	Hereford	1553–4 (121)

James Stuart (19 Jun 1566–27 Mar 1625), son of Henry, Lord Darnley, and Mary Stuart, queen of Scots; acc as James VI of Scotland 24 Jul 1567 and as James I of England 24 Mar 1603; crowned 25 Jul 1603.

trumpeters	Worc	Bewdley	1616–17 (363)
players	Worc	Worcester	1623–4 (454)

Charles Stuart (19 Nov 1600–30 Jan 1649), son of James VI (of Scotland) and I (of England), *qv*, and Anne of Denmark, *qv*; cr prince of Wales 4 Nov 1616; acc as Charles I 27 Mar 1625; crowned 2 Feb 1625; beheaded 30 Jan 1649.

players (as prince)	Heref	Leominster	1616–17 (149)
	Worc	Worcester	1624–5 (454)
players	Worc	Worcester	1630–1 (455)
			1631–2 (456)
revellers	Worc	Worcester	1624–5 (454)

See also Richard Plantagenet *under* **Gloucester** (duke)

King of Bohemia
Frederick Wittelsbach (26 Aug 1596–29 Nov 1632), son of Palsgrave Frederick IV and Louisa Juliana of Orange–Nassau; succ as palsgrave of the Rhine 19 Sept 1610; married Elizabeth Stuart, *qv* (*under* **Princess**) 14 Feb 1613; crowned king of Bohemia 4 Nov 1619; deposed 8 Nov 1619.

players	Heref	Leominster	1619–20 (149)

Lady Elizabeth *see* Elizabeth Stuart *under* **Princess**

Lancaster
Henry of Lancaster (*c* 1281–22 Sept 1345), cr Lord Lancaster 6 Feb 1298/9; cr 9th earl of Leicester 29 Mar 1324; cr 3rd earl of Lancaster by 26 Oct 1326. Possibly cr steward of England 29 Mar 1324; constable Abergavenny Castle, Monmouthshire,

Wales, 25 Oct 1326, Kenilworth Castle, Warw, 27 Nov 1326; chief guardian of king Jan 1327; JP Warw and Worc 1338. Lands in Wales and various counties including Glouc and Staff.

minstrels	Worc	Worcester	1337–8 (396)

Lee

John atte Lee. Not identified (see p 589, endnote to WCL: C59 mb 2).

minstrel/s	Worc	Worcester	1344–5 (397)

Leicester

Robert Dudley (24 Jun 1532 or 1533–4 Sept 1588), cr baron of Denbigh, Denbighshire, Wales, 28 Sept, and 14th earl of Leicester 29 Sept 1564; imprisoned Jul 1553; attainted 22 Jan 1553/4; pardoned 18 Oct 1554; restored in blood 7 Mar 1557/8. PC 23 Apr 1559; lord lieut Warw 10 May 1559, Worc 20 Nov 1569–15 Nov 1570; JP Heref, Warw, and Worc 1562, 1564, 1584; custos rot Warw 1568; high steward Glouc 1570 until death; chancellor and chamberlain, Anglesey, Caernarvonshire, and Merioneth, all in Wales, 26 Sept 1578; lord steward of the household 1 Nov 1584–8; warden and chief justice in eyre south of Trent 25 Nov 1585 until death. Seat at Kenilworth, Warw, estate at Drayton Basset, Staff; lands in Wales and many counties including Shrops, Staff, Warw, and Worc; granted lordship of Denbighshire, Wales, including Denbigh Castle and borough of Chirk, 1563, and lands in various parts of England and Wales from 1563.

players	Worc	Bewdley	1573–4 (361)
musicians	Worc	Worcester	1575 (437)

Leynthale

Roland Leynthale (c 1390–before 19 Dec 1450), kt by 20 Mar 1415. JP Shrops 1413, Heref 1422–3; sheriff Hereford 13 Nov 1423; constable and steward, castle and town of Haverfordwest, Wales, by 28 Jan 1442. Residence in city of Hereford; lands in Wales and various counties including Heref and Warw.

harper	Worc	Worcester	1446–7 (400)

Lord Marquess

Henry Courtenay (c 1498–9 Dec 1538), succ as 19th earl of Devon Dec 1512; cr 1st marquess of Exeter 18 Jun 1525. PC 1520; attainted and beheaded 9 Jan 1538/9. Seat at Tiverton Castle, Devon; lands in various counties.

or

Henry Grey (17 Jan 1517–23 Feb 1554), styled Lord Grey until he succ as 6th marquess of Dorset, 9th Lord Ferrers, 9th Lord Harington, 4th Lord Bonville, and possibly Lord Astley 10 Oct 1530; cr 7th duke of Suffolk 11 Oct 1551. JP Warw

1539, 1542, 1545, 1547; chief justice in eyre south of Trent 2 Feb 1549/50–3; PC 11 Dec 1549–53; steward, royal honours and lordships in Warw; attainted and beheaded 23 Feb 1554. Seats at Chewton, Somers, and Bradgate and Groby, Leic; lands in various counties including Warw, property in London.

| bearward | Worc | Crowle | 1532–3 (521) |
| | Worc | Grimley | 1533–4 (526) |

Lord President of the Council in the Marches of Wales

Henry Herbert (after 1538–19 Jan 1601), styled Lord Herbert 1551 until he succ as 21st earl of Pembroke and Baron Herbert of Cardiff, Glamorgan, Wales 17 Mar 1569/70. Constable and keeper of Bristol Castle, Glouc, steward and keeper of lordship of Dinas and steward of manor of Brecon and constable and porter of Brecon Castle, all in Brecknockshire, Wales, all for life 15 May 1570; constable of St Briavel's Castle, keeper of the forest of Dean, and bailiff of the manor of Lydney, all in Glouc, for life by 18 Nov 1577; comm for piracy, Pembrokeshire, Wales, by 7 Jan 1579; JP Worc 1584; lord pres of the Council in the Marches of Wales Mar 1586 until death; vice-adm of South Wales c 1586; lord lieut Heref, Shrops, Worc, and Wales 24 Feb 1587; custos rot for Glamorgan, nd, and Monmouthshire, both in Wales, 18 Feb 1594. Seat at Cardiff Castle, Glamorgan, Wales, residence at Ludlow Castle, Shrops.

| players | Worc | Bewdley | 1593–4 (362) |
| players (as earl) | Worc | Bewdley | 1598–9 (362) |

Ralph Eure (24 Sept 1558–1 Apr 1617), succ as 3rd Lord Eure 12 Feb 1593/4. Lord pres, Council in the Marches of Wales, and lord lieut Heref, Shrops, Worc, and Wales 12 Sept 1607–17. Seats at Ingleby, Greenhow, Malton, and Stokesley, all in Yorks, NR.

| players | Worc | Bewdley | 1615–16 (363) |

Lucy

William Lucy (c 1404–10 Jul 1460), kt before 9 Jul 1432. Sheriff Warw 1435, 1449, Heref 1440, 1459. Seat at Wicken, Northants; lands in Wales and various counties including Glouc, Heref, Shrops, and Worc.

| minstrel/s | Worc | Worcester | 1451–2 (400) |

Master of the King's Horse

Henry Guildford (1489–before 22 May 1532). Master of the king's horse 6 Nov 1515–18 Jul 1522; comptroller of the household by 1 Sept 1522. Residence in London; lands in Warw.

| minstrel | Worc | Worcester | 1518–19 (463) |

Mortimer

Edmund de Mortimer (*c* 1251–17 Jul 1304), Lord Mortimer by writ 24 Jun 1295. Keeper of Oswestry Castle and hundred, Shrops, 8 Aug 1282; jt keeper Ystrad Tywi, Carmarthenshire, and Cardigan, Cardiganshire, both in Wales, during pleasure, 5 Dec 1287. Seat at Wigmore, Heref; lands in Wales and various counties including Glouc, Heref, Shrops, and Worc.

harper			1289–90 (189)

Northumberland

Henry Percy (*c* 1449–28 Apr 1489), restored as 8th earl of Northumberland 25 Mar 1470; succ as Lord Poynings Feb 1483/4. Imprisoned *c* 1464; removed to the Tower after Sept 1465–27 Oct 1469; lord chamberlain 30 Nov 1483–22 Aug 1485. Lands in various counties.

minstrel/s	Worc	Worcester	1481–2 (405)

Pembroke *see* Henry Herbert *under* **Lord President of the Council in the Marches of Wales**

Pippard

Ralph Pippard (d. before 10 Jul 1303). Lands in various counties.

harper			1289–90 (189)

Prince

Edward Plantagenet (2 or 3 Nov 1470–*c* Aug 1483), son of Edward IV, *qv (under* **King**), and Elizabeth Wydevill, *qv (under* **Queen**); cr prince of Wales 26 Jun 1471; acc as Edward V 9 Apr 1483; deposed 25 Jun 1483.

minstrel/s	Worc	Worcester	1472–3 (405)
			1481–2 (405)
servant/s	Worc	Worcester	1478–9 (405)

See also Charles Stuart *under* **King**

Princess

Elizabeth Stuart (mid-Aug 1596–13 Feb 1662), daughter of James VI (of Scotland) and I (of England), *qv (under* **King**), and Anne of Denmark, *qv (under* **Queen**); married Frederick V, elector palatine, *qv (under* **King of Bohemia**) 14 Feb 1613; crowned queen of Bohemia 7 Nov 1619.

players (as Lady Elizabeth)	Heref	Leominster	1613–14 (148)
			1616–17 (148)
			1619–20 (149)
servants (as Lady Elizabeth)	Worc	Worcester	1624–5 (454)

See also Mary Tudor *under* **Queen**

Prior (Worcester)
Wulstan de Bransford (*c* 1284–6 August 1349). Elected 23 Nov 1317 and installed 30 Nov 1317; elected bishop of Worcester 4 Jan 1338/9, consecrated 21 Mar 1338/9, enthroned 28 Mar 1338/9.

minstrel/s	Worc	Worcester	1337–9 (397)

Queen
Philippa of Hainault (*c* 1314–69), married Edward III 30 Jan 1327/8; crowned 4 Mar 1330.

harper	Worc	Worcester	1344–5 (397)

Elizabeth Wydevill (*c* 1437–8 Jun 1492), daughter of Richard Wydevill, 1st Earl Rivers, and Jaquetta de Luxembourg; married Sir John Grey (d 1461), nd, and Edward IV, *qv* (*under* **King**), 1 May 1464; crowned 26 May 1465.

minstrel/s	Worc	Worcester	1464–5 (401)
			1472–3 (405)
			1481–2? (405)
servant/s	Worc	Worcester	1478–9 (405)

Katherine of Arragon (16 Dec 1485–7 Jan 1536), daughter of Fernando v of Castile and Arragon and Isabel of Castile and Leon, Spain; married Arthur, prince of Wales (d. 2 Apr 1502), 14 Nov 1501, and Henry VIII, *qv* (*under* **King**), 11 Jun 1509; crowned 24 Jun 1509; marriage declared null and void 23 May 1533.

minstrel/s	Worc	Worcester	1517–18 (417)

Anne Boleyn (1507–19 May 1536), daughter of Thomas Boleyn, 12th earl of Wiltshire, and Elizabeth Howard; married Henry VIII, *qv* (*under* **King**), 25 Jan 1533; crowned 1 Jun 1533; beheaded 19 May 1536.

minstrels	Worc	Crowle	1533–4 (523)
	Worc	Worcester/Grimley	1533–4 (527)
players	Worc	Worcester	1533–4 (526)
	Worc	Battenhall	1534–5 (530)

Mary Tudor (18 Feb 1515/16–17 Nov 1558), daughter of Henry VIII, *qv* (*under* **King**), and Katherine of Arragon, *qv*; acc as Mary I of England 19 Jul 1553; crowned 1 Oct 1553; married 25 Jul 1554, Philip, king of Naples and Jerusalem, and king of Spain from 16 Jan 1556.

minstrels (as princess)	Worc	Battenhall	1524–5 (487)
minstrel (as princess)	Worc	Worcester	1526–7 (491)
minstrel/s	Heref	Hereford	1553–4 (121)

players (as princess)	Worc	Worcester	1525–6 (490)
	Worc	Crowle	1530–1 (513)
servants (as princess)	Worc	Worcester	1525–6 (489, 490)
bearwards (as princess)	Worc	Battenhall	1531–2 (516)

Elizabeth Tudor (7 Sept 1533–24 Mar 1603), daughter of Henry VIII, *qv* (*under* **King**), and Anne Boleyn, *qv*; acc as Elizabeth I 17 Nov 1558; crowned 15 Jan 1559.

players	Worc	Bewdley	1571–2 (361)
	Worc	Worcester	1586–7 (448)
			1587–8 (448)
			1591–2 (449)
			1595–6 (449)
	Heref	Leominster	1596–7 (146)
	Worc	Worcester	1596–7 (449)
			1597–8 (450)
	Heref	Leominster	1600–1 (147)
musicians	Worc	Worcester	1575 (438)
trumpeters	Worc	Worcester	1575 (437)
			1591–2 (449)

Anne of Denmark (12 Dec 1574–2 Mar 1619), daughter of Frederick II of Denmark and Norway and Sophia of Mecklenburg; married James VI of Scotland (later James I of England), *qv* (*under* **King**), 20 Aug 1589; crowned queen of England 25 Jul 1603.

players	Heref	Leominster	1616–17 (149)
			1618–19 (149)

Reading *see under* **Abbot** (Reading)

Salisbury
Richard Neville (*c* 1400–30 or 31 Dec 1460), 10th earl of Salisbury by right of marriage, approved 3 May 1429 and confirmed 4 May 1442. PC 12 Nov 1437; lord chancellor 2 Apr 1454–7 Mar 1455; JP Glouc 1460; lord chamberlain 29 Oct 1460 until death. Seat at Middleham Castle, Yorks, NR.

minstrel/s	Worc	Worcester	1445–6 (399)

Shrewsbury
George Talbot (1468–26 Jul 1538), succ as 7th earl of Shrewsbury, 9th Lord Furnivalle, Lord Talbot, Lord Strange, and earl of Waterford, Ireland, 28 Jun 1473. JP Heref 1486, 1492–6, Shrops 1486–7, 1490, 1493, 1496–7, 1502–4, 1510–14, 1521–3, 1526, 1529, 1531, 1536, 1538, Staff 1486–7, 1493, 1496, 1499, 1501–4, 1508–11, 1514, 1520, 1522–3, 1526, 1531–2, 1536, 1538, Worc 1486–9, 1493–4, 1497, 1500–2, 1504–7, 1510–15, 1522, 1526, 1531–2, 1537–8; comm of musters Shrops and Staff

23 Dec 1488; steward manor of Morfe, Staff, 22 Aug 1493, and honour of Tutbury, Derb and Staff, 18 Nov 1529; comm of array Derb and Staff 1496, 1513, Worc 1496, Shrops 1513; lord steward of the household by 20 Jul 1506 until death; chamberlain of the exchequer, sole 14 May 1509 and jt 17 Jul 1527; PC by Jul 1512. Seat at Sheffield Castle, Yorks, WR, London residence at Coldharbour; lands in various counties including Shrops.

| minstrels | Worc | Worcester | 1518–19 (463) |

Stafford

Edward Stafford (17 Jan 1535/6–18 Oct 1603), succ as 12th Baron Stafford 1 Jan 1565/6. MP Staff 1558 and 1559; lord lieut Staff 1559?; justice in eyre and lieut, Needwood Forest, Staff, 13 May 1559; justice and ranger, forest of Cannock, Staff, 24 Sept 1560; jt comm of musters Staff by 8 Aug 1569; JP Glouc, Shrops, and Staff by 1573/4, Montgomeryshire, Wales, by 1591; vice-adm Glouc 1587; member, Council in the Marches of Wales, Aug 1601. Seat at Stafford Castle, Staff.

| players | Heref | Leominster | 1599–1600 (147) |

Suffolk

William de la Pole (16 Oct 1396–2 May 1450), succ as 8th earl of Suffolk 25 Oct 1415; cr 1st marquess of Suffolk 14 Sept 1444, 15th earl of Pembroke 23 Feb 1446/7, and 1st duke of Suffolk 2 Jun 1448. PC 30 Nov 1431; lord steward of the household between 26 Oct 1432 and 14 Aug 1433–50; chief justice South Wales by 28 Jul 1438–Feb 1439/40 and Chester, Ches, and North Wales, sole 19 Feb 1439/40 and jt 1 Dec 1443; JP Staff 1439, Warw 1439–46, 1449; lord chamberlain for life 24 Feb 1446/7; lord high adm 9 Aug 1447; imprisoned in the Tower 28 Jan 1449/50; released 19 Mar 1449/50; banished as of 1 May 1450; beheaded 2 May 1450. Seat at Wingfield, Suff.

| minstrel/s | Worc | Worcester | 1445–6 (399) |
| | | | 1446–7 (400) |

Charles Brandon (c 1484–22 Aug 1545), cr 5th Viscount Lisle 15 May 1513 and 4th duke of Suffolk 1 Feb 1513/14; surrendered viscountcy 20 Apr 1523. Chamberlain North Wales during pleasure 22 Nov 1509; PC before 15 May 1513 until death; steward various manors in Glouc, Warw, and Worc 6 Jun 1513; earl marshal 21 May 1524–20 May 1533; pres, privy council, Feb 1529/30 until death; JP Glouc 1531, 1537, 1539–40, 1542, 1544, Heref 1531, 1538, 1540–1, 1543, Shrops 1531, 1536, 1538–9, 1543, Staff 1531–2, 1536, 1538, 1540, 1543–4, Warw 1531–2, 1537–9, 1542, 1544–5, Worc 1531–2, 1537–40, 1542, 1544, Monmouthshire, Wales, 1543–4; chief justice in eyre south of Trent 27 Nov 1534 until death; lord steward of the household before 13 Apr 1540 until death. Seat at Tattershall Castle, Linc; lands in various counties.

| minstrel | Worc | Grimley | 1528–9 (504) |

	Worc	Battenhall	1534–5 (530)
trumpeters	Worc	Crowle	1532–3 (523)

Sussex

Robert Radcliffe (12 Jun 1573–22 Sept 1629), son of Henry, 9th earl of Sussex, styled Lord FitzWalter until he succ as 10th earl of Sussex, 5th Viscount and 11th Lord FitzWalter 14 Dec 1593. Sold ancestral estate of New Hall, Boreham, Essex, Jul 1622; family estate at Attleborough, Norf.

players	Heref	Leominster	1616–17 (148)

Sutton

Probably
Sir William de Sutton (before 1270–after 1324). Chief justice North Wales 1303, 1325; keeper of Warwick Castle, Warw, 1321. Lands in various counties including Warw.

minstrel	Heref	Abbey Dore	1303 (187)

Talbot

John Talbot (d. before 23 Nov 1355). Residence at Richard's Castle, Heref; lands in various counties including Heref, Shrops, and Worc.

minstrel/s	Worc	Worcester	1345–6 (397)
	Worc	Worcester	1347–8 (398)

Gilbert Talbot (by 1479–22 Oct 1542), kt 14 Oct 1513. JP Worc 1506–7, 1510–15, 1524, 1526, 1531–2, 1537–8, 1542; comm subsidy Worc 1 Aug 1524; MP Worc 1529, 1536, 1542; comm of gaol delivery Worcester Castle, Worc, 20 Jun 1530; comm of oyer and terminer Glouc, Heref, and Worc 4 July 1538–9; comm musters Worc 1539; sheriff Worc 17 Nov 1539. Seat at Grafton Manor, Worc; lands in various counties, including Shrops and Worc.

minstrel	Worc	Crowle	1531–2 (516)
	Worc	Battenhall	1533–4 (524)

Throckmorton

George Throckmorton (c 1489–6 Aug 1552), kt before 1516. Steward of the lordship of Yardeley, Worc, during pleasure 4 Feb 1512; sheriff Warw Nov 1525–7, 1533–4, Worc 1528, 1539–44; high steward Evesham Abbey, Worc, 1527–38; steward of the bishop of Worcester's land in Warw and Worc 1528–40; MP Warw 1529; JP Warw 1531–2, 1537, 1542, Worc 1531–2, 1537, 1542, Glouc 1547; steward of various
manors, Warw, 4 Jul 1431; imprisoned in the Tower by Jan 1536; released by 25 Jan 1537; imprisoned again by 16 Oct 1537; released by Nov 1539. Residence at Coughton, Warw; lands in various counties including Heref, Warw, and Worc.

minstrel	Worc	Grimley	1527–8 (497)

	Worc	Battenhall	1533–4 (524)

Tregoz
John de Tregoz (d before 6 Sept 1300), summoned to parliament as Lord Tregoz 26 Jan 1296/7; kt of the shire, Heref, 1297 until death. Lands in various counties including Heref.

harper	Heref	Sugwas	1289–90 (189)

Warnecombe
James Warnecombe (c 1522–21 Feb 1580/1). Escheator Heref and the Marches of Wales 1548–9; recorder Ludlow, Shrops, 1551–63; standing council of Leominster, Heref, by 1552; MP Ludlow, Shrops, 1554, Leominster 1555, Heref 1563, city of Hereford 1571–2; JP Heref 1554, 1569, 1570–1; mayor of Hereford 1571–2, 1578–9; sheriff Heref 1576–7.

minstrels	Heref	Leominster	1571–2 (145)

Warwick (duke)
Henry de Beauchamp (22 Mar 1424/5–11 Jun 1446), styled Lord Despenser until 1439; succ as 14th earl of Warwick 30 Apr 1439 and Lord Burghersh 27 Dec 1439; cr 1st duke of Warwick 5 Apr 1445. Hereditary chamberlain of the exchequer; hereditary constable of Worcester Castle, Worc, and St Briavel's Castle, Glouc; hereditary sheriff of Worc; JP Glouc, Warw, and Worc 1446. Seat at Elmley Castle, Worc; lands in Wales and various counties including Glouc, Heref, Staff, Warw, and Worc.

minstrel/s	Worc	Worcester	1445–6 (399)

Warwick (duchess)
Cecily Neville (c 1425–28 Jul 1450), 2nd daughter of Richard Neville, 10th earl of Salisbury qv; married Henry de Beauchamp, 1st duke of Warwick qv, 1434; married John Tiptoft, 4th earl of Worcester, 1449. Sheriff Worc 5 June 1449 until death. Lands in Wales and various counties including Glouc and Worc. Seat at Hanley Castle, Worc.

minstrel/s	Worc	Worcester	1447–8 (400)

Warwick (earl)
Thomas de Beauchamp (prob 14 Feb 1313/14–13 Nov 1369), succ as 11th earl of Warwick 12 Aug 1315. Hereditary chamberlain of the exchequer; hereditary constable of Worcester Castle, Worc; sheriff Worc 10 Dec 1330, and Warw for life 26 Jun 1344; JP Warw 1332, 1338, 1345, 1351–3, 1367–8, Worc 1332, 1338, 1351–4, 1367–9; marshal of England, 10 Feb 1343/4. Seat at Elmley Castle, Worc; lands in Wales and various counties including Glouc, Heref, Staff, Warw, and Worc.

harper	Worc	Worcester	1337–8 (397)
minstrel/s	Worc	Worcester	1337–8 (397)

minstrels	Worc	Worcester	1338–9 (397)
			1344–5 (397)
			1346–7? (398)
			1351–2 (398)

Richard Neville (22 Nov 1428–14 Apr 1471), son of Richard, 10th earl of Salisbury, *qv*, in right of marriage styled Lord Bergavenny; confirmed in the earldom of Warwick 23 Jul 1449 and cr 16th earl of Warwick 2 Mar 1449/50; succ as 11th earl of Salisbury 30 or 31 Dec 1460. Hereditary sheriff Worc 28 Jul 1450–70; chamberlain of the exchequer 6 Dec 1450; JP Warw 1452–5, 1457–61, 1464–6, 1468–70, Staff 1454, 1456, 1459, 1461, 1463–5, 1467–70, Worc 1454, 1458–9, 1461, 1464, 1469, 1471, Glouc 1454–8, 1460, 1462, 1464, 1468–70, Heref 1455–9, 1461–3, 1470, Shrops 1460–2, 1466, 1468–70; PC by 6 Dec 1453; steward, Monmouth and castles of Grosmont, Skenfrith, and Whitecastle, all in Monmouthshire, Wales, 31 May 1455, manor of Feckenham, Worc, 7 May 1461; attainted 20 Nov 1459; attainder reversed Oct 1460; keeper Newport Castle, Monmouthshire, Wales, 4 Nov 1460 and 21 Feb 1470/1, Brecon Castle, Brecknockshire, Wales, sole 4 Nov 1460 and jt 14 Feb 1470/1, and Goodrich Castle, Monmouthshire, Wales, 4 Nov 1460 and 7 May 1461; lord chamberlain 22 Jan 1460/1 and 7 May 1461; master forester forest of Needwood, Staff, 4 Nov 1461; constable and steward Tutbury, Staff, 4 Nov 1461 and Kenilworth Castle, Warw, 14 Feb 1467/8; lord high adm 13 Feb–Jul 1462 and 2 Jan 1470/1. Seats at Middleham and Sheriff Hutton, Yorks, NR; held castle and honour of Abergavenny, Monmouthshire, Wales; lands in Wales and various counties.

| minstrel/s | Worc | Worcester | 1451–2 (401) |

Worcester
Edward Somerset (*c* 1550–3 Mar 1627/8), styled Lord Herbert until he succ as 9th earl of Worcester and Baron Herbert 21 Feb 1588/9. Member, Council in the Marches of Wales, 16 Dec 1590; PC 29 Jun 1601; lord lieut Glamorgan and Monmouthshire, both in Wales, sole 17 Jul 1602 and jt 3 Dec 1626 until death; custos rot Monmouthshire, Wales, Jun 1603; JP Worc 1608, 1626; lord keeper of the privy seal 2 Jan 1615/16 until death. Seat at Raglan, Monmouthshire, Wales, residence at Hackney, Midd.

| players | Heref | Leominster | 1600–1 (147) |

York
Richard of York or Plantagenet (21 Sept 1411–30 Dec 1460), succ as 3rd duke of York 25 Oct 1415 and 6th earl of March, Lord Mortimer of Wigmore, Heref, and 9th earl of Ulster 18 Jan 1425; restored as 5th earl of Cambridge by 19 May 1426; probably resigned earldom of March between Sept and Dec 1445. JP Shrops 1432, 1439–41, 1443–5, 1448–9, 1453–4, 1457–8, 1460, Glouc 1433, 1435, 1437–41, 1444–6, 1448–9, 1451–2, 1454–8, 1460, Worc 1433, 1435, 1437, 1440, 1443, 1451, 1454, 1458–9, Heref 1437, 1441, 1443, 1451, 1453, 1455–9, Staff 1454, 1456, 1459; PC

24 Feb 1439; justice in eyre south of Trent 14 Jul 1447–Jul 1453; lieut Ireland 29 Sept 1447–Mar 1452/3 and 1 Dec 1454–9; protector of the realm 3 Apr 1454–Feb 1454/5 and 19 Nov 1455–25 Feb 1455/6; constable, castles of Aberystwyth, Cardiganshire, and Carmarthen and Carreg Cennen, Carmarthenshire, all in Wales, 2 Jun 1455–Apr 1457; attainted 20 Nov 1459; declared heir to the throne 25 Oct 1460. Seat at Fotheringay, Northants; lands in various counties including Heref.

minstrel/s	Worc	Worcester	1446–7 (399)

Richard of Shrewsbury or Plantagenet (17 August 1473–after 16 Jun 1483), 2nd son of Edward IV, *qv* (*under* **King**), cr 5th duke of York 28 May 1474, 7th earl of Nottingham 12 Jun 1476, and 5th duke of Norfolk and earl of Warenne 7 Feb 1476/7. Lord lieut Ireland 5 May 1479; imprisoned in the Tower 16 Jun 1483; probably murdered a few months later. Lands in many counties.

minstrel/s	Worc	Worcester	1481–2 (405)

Companies Named by Location

Claines, Worc

dancers	Worc	Worcester	1524–5 (487)
		Worcester/Battenhall	1529–30 (507)
		Worcester	1533–4 (526)

Cleeve Prior, Worc

players	Worc	Crowle	1530–1 (513)

Coventry, Warw

players	Worc	Battenhall	1528–9 (501)

Evesham, Worc

players	Worc	Worcester	1519–20 (465)

Gloucester, Glouc

players	Worc	Worcester	1520–1 (469)

Hereford, Heref

waits	Heref	Leominster	1572–3 (145)
	Heref	Holme Lacy	1640–1 (196)

Martley, Worc

players	Worc	Worcester	1518–19 (463)

Ombersley, Worc

players	Worc	Battenhall	1534–5 (529)

St Kenelm's Chapel, Worc

players	Worc	Worcester	1520–1 (469)

Warwick, Warw

waits	Worc	Droitwich	1522–3 (370)

Worcester, Worc

players	Worc	Battenhall	1529–30 (505)
players (St Peter's)	Worc	Battenhall	1534–5 (529)
singing men	Worc	Battenhall	1532–3 (520)
	Worc	Crowle	1533–4 (525)
waits	Heref	Hereford	1641–2 (193)

Glossaries: Introduction

The purpose of the glossaries is to assist the reader in working through the text. The criteria for the selection of glossary entries are discussed below, under the headings Latin Glossary and English Glossary. The glossaries include words found in records printed or quoted in the Introduction, Records, Appendixes, and Endnotes. Definitions are given only for those senses of a particular word which are used in the records printed in these two collections. Within references, page and line numbers are separated by an oblique stroke. Words occurring within marginalia are indicated by a lower-case 'm' following the page and line reference. Manuscript capitalization has not been preserved; however, if proper names are glossed, they are capitalized in accordance with modern usage.

Latin Glossary

Words are included in the Latin Glossary if they are not to be found in the *Oxford Latin Dictionary* (OLD), now the standard reference work for classical Latin. Words listed in the OLD whose meaning has changed or become restricted in medieval or Renaissance usage are also glossed. If a word is found in the OLD, but appears in the text in an obscure spelling or anomalous inflectional form for which the OLD provides no cross-reference, that word has been included and its standard lexical entry form indicated, without giving a definition. If the spelling variants or anomalous inflectional forms have been treated as scribal errors and more correct forms given in textual notes, the forms thus noted are not repeated in the glossary.

Most of the Latin words used in the records are common classical words whose spelling has changed, if at all, according to common medieval variations. The results of these common variations are not treated here as new words, nor are forms of glossed words resulting from such variations cross-referenced. These variations are:

ML *c* for CL *t* before *i*
ML *cc* for CL *ct* before *i*
ML *d* for CL *t* in a final position
ML *e* for CL *ae* or *oe*
ML *ff* for CL *f*, common in an initial position
ML addition of *h*
ML omission of CL *h*
ML variation between *i* and *e* before another vowel

ML *n* for CL *m* before another nasal
Intrusion of ML *p* in CL consonant cluster *mm* or *ms*
ML doubling of CL single consonants
ML singling of CL double consonants

No attempt has been made to correct these spellings to classical norms: rather, scribal practice has been followed in such cases. Where the same word occurs in spellings which differ according to the list above, the most common spelling (or the earliest, when numbers of occurrences are roughly equal) is treated as standard and used for the headword. However, we have conformed to the practice of the *OLD* as regards 'i/j' and 'u/v' variation: in this glossary only the letter forms 'i' and 'u' are used. If a noun of the first declension appears only in documents whose scribes consistently used classical orthography, its genitive singular is listed as '-ae'; otherwise the ML '-e' is used.

All listed variant spellings will be found under the headword, at the end of the definition, set apart in boldface type. Where the variant spelling would not closely follow the headword alphabetically, it is also listed separately and cross-referenced to the main entry.

It is difficult to know in some cases whether certain words are being used in a CL sense or in one of the modified senses acquired in Anglo-Latin usage during the Middle Ages. In these circumstances, the range of possibilities has been fully indicated under the appropriate lexical entry. (When it seems useful to indicate the possibility that a given sense was intended in a given passage, even if no certainty exists, a '?' is added after the appropriate page and line reference under that sense.) Unclear, technical, or archaic terms, especially those pertaining to canon or common law, performance, and music, are usually given a stock translation equivalent, but receive a fuller treatment in the glossary.

As a rule, only one occurrence of each word, or each form of each word, will be listed for each collection; 'etc' or 'et al' following a reference means that there are more occurrences of that word or form in that collection. The one occurrence listed is either the sole occurrence or the first chronologically. Since this volume covers two counties and is arranged by locality, the examples cited are not necessarily the first to occur in the page order of the Records; the other occurrence(s) indicated by 'etc' may in fact precede the first occurrence in page order. Page order has only been used if there are two earliest occurrences in different documents assigned to the same year. In such cases, the chronologically first occurrence which also appears earliest in page order is given. Multiple occurrences of each sense may be listed for words defined in more than one sense; in fact all possible occurrences of a given sense may be listed if it is difficult to distinguish the senses in context. Page and line references to different collections are separated by a semicolon.

All headwords are given in a standard dictionary form: nouns are listed by nominative, genitive, and gender; adjectives by the terminations of the nominative singular or, in the case of adjectives of one termination, by the nominative and genitive; verbs by their principal parts. The abbreviation *qv* is used to refer the reader to the definition of the word in the *Oxford Latin Dictionary*; for internal cross-references or references to works other than the *OLD*, the expression *see* has been used. Cross-references to other words in the glossary with related meanings are introduced by *see also*. The expression 'etc' used after an occurrence indicates the existence of further occurrences of that word or sense in other documents. A single occurrence followed by 'et al' indicates that, although there are other occurrences of that word or sense, its use is restricted to a single document; for purposes of this glossary, the eight Star Chamber documents printed under Goodrich in Herefordshire and the run of entries from Prior More's account book printed under Households in Worcestershire have each been treated as a single document.

English Glossary

The English glossary is not meant to be exhaustive, but only 1/ to define words or record senses that are genuinely obsolete or likely to be mistaken by a modern reader and 2/ to give the modern equivalents of spellings that would puzzle a beginner. Accordingly words and senses given in *The Concise Oxford Dictionary* have usually been passed over, and these include archaic words and phrases still familiar to most educated readers, such as 'doth,' 'herein,' 'spake,' 'hight,' and 'vpon paine of.' The reader is also assumed to be familiar with such common spelling alternations as au/a, c/s, ea/e, i/e, i/j, i/y, oo/ou, s/z, and u/v, and accordingly forms offering no other difficulty have usually been passed over. So have forms produced by a scribe's failure to mark a common abbreviation, when these are reasonably transparent (eg, 'preservacon'), and such easily recognized combinations of the definite article with a following noun as 'thoccupacion' and 'thaudyte.' Abbreviations are also mostly omitted. Forms such as 'yem' for 'them,' in which a 'þ' identical in shape with 'y' has been transcribed as 'y,' are, however, glossed for the benefit of readers unfamiliar with that convention.

To these general rules there are two exceptions. First, fuller treatment has been given to words and phrases likely to be of special interest to users of a REED volume; these include terms for articles of dress (eg, 'dowblet,' 'ierkyn') and for textiles and other materials used in performance (eg, 'buffin') and the specialized vocabulary of pastimes and the performing arts (eg, 'feates of activety,' 'virginalls'). Second, encyclopedic information on political or social history has been provided where it seemed necessary to an understanding of the text.

The glossary follows normal alphabetical order; 'ȝ' follows 'y' and 'þ' follows 't.' Normal headword forms are the uninflected singular for nouns and the infinitive for verbs, but nouns occurring only in the plural or possessive and verbs occurring only in one participial or finite form are entered under the form that actually occurs. Similarly, verbal nouns are subsumed under the infinitive when other parts of the same verb also occur in the text, and adverbs are entered under the related adjective when that also occurs.

Fully glossed words appearing in a variety of spellings are entered under the one most often found in the text. When two spellings are equally or nearly equally common, the one nearer modern usage is used as headword. Other spellings of these words are cross-referenced to the main entry from their alphabetical places, except where the cross-reference would come within two entries of the main entry. All noted variants are listed within the main entry, in alphabetical order under each grammatical form.

Unfamiliar spellings of words not fully glossed appear in their alphabetical places, but several may be grouped into a single entry where that can cause the reader no confusion. Forms corrected in the footnotes or cancelled and replaced by the original scribe are not normally entered.

For every word, sense, and variant recorded, the glossary cites the earliest example occurring in the Records as a whole. In some entries the earliest example from each county is cited. Since this volume covers two counties and is arranged by locality, the examples cited are not necessarily the first to occur in the page order of the Records. When two citations are given without 'etc,' that means that the form or sense in question occurs only twice. Otherwise further occurrences are represented by 'etc,' except when it is deemed advisable to alert the reader that the sense in question applies in particular later passages.

Where the definition begins by repeating the headword in a different spelling, the latter is normally the headword in the *Oxford English Dictionary* and further information can be found there. Occasionally it has been thought advisable to cite the authority followed or succinctly indicate the glossarians' reasoning process and this information is then given within square brackets at the end of the entry. When a dictionary entry is cited there, the headword is given exactly as it appears in the source. For the authorities used, see 'Works Consulted' below.

Anglo-Norman Texts

There is no glossary for the Anglo-Norman document in the Herefordshire Households section. Although sufficiently involved to qualify for translation by REED guidelines, it contains little vocabulary not found in standard reference works for French. That vocabulary is treated in textual notes to the Records.

Works Consulted

Black's Law Dictionary. Henry Campbell Black (ed). 5th ed (St Paul, 1979). [*Black's*]

Cheney, C.R. *Handbook of Dates for Students of English History.* Corrected ed (London, 1978).

The Concise Oxford Dictionary of Current English. 7th ed (Oxford, 1982).

Cunnington, C. Willett and Phillis Cunnington. *Handbook of English Costume in the Sixteenth Century.* Rev ed (London, 1970).

– *Handbook of English Costume in the Seventeenth Century.* 3rd ed (London, 1972).

Dearmer, Percy. *The Ornaments of the Ministers.* 2nd ed (London, 1920).

Dictionary of Medieval Latin from British Sources. R.E. Latham and D.R. Howlett (eds). Fascicules 1–4: A–H (London, 1975–1989). [*DML*]

Dyer, Alan D. *The City of Worcester in the Sixteenth Century* (Leicester, 1973).

Encyclopædia Britannica. 11th ed (Cambridge, 1910).

The English Dialect Dictionary. Joseph Wright (ed). 6 vols (London, 1898–1905). [*EDD*]

Latham, R.E. *Revised Medieval Latin Word-List from British and Irish Sources* (London, 1965).

Micklethwaite, J.T. *The Ornaments of the Rubric.* Alcuin Club Tracts 1 (London, 1897).

Middle English Dictionary. Hans Kurath and Sherman M. Kuhn, et al (eds). Fascicules A.1– S.12 (Ann Arbor, 1956–89). [*MED*]

Munrow, David. *Instruments of the Middle Ages and Renaissance* (London, 1976).

The Oxford Dictionary of the Christian Church. F.L. Cross and E.A. Livingstone (eds). 2nd ed with corrections (Oxford, 1978).

The Oxford English Dictionary. Compact ed. 2 vols (Oxford, 1971). [*OED*]

Oxford Latin Dictionary. P.G.W. Glare (ed) (Oxford, 1982). [*OLD*]

Page, Christopher. *Voices and Instruments of the Middle Ages.* Appendix 1 (London, 1987).

Robbins, Rossell Hope (ed). *Early English Christmas Carols* (New York and London, 1961).

Rodes, Robert E. Jr. *Lay Authority and Reformation in the English Church: Edward I to the Civil War* (Notre Dame and London, 1982).

Strutt, Joseph. *The Sports and Pastimes of the People of England.* Rev ed. J. Charles Cox (ed) (London, 1903; rpt Detroit, 1968).

Young, Abigail Ann. 'Plays and Players: the Latin Terms for Performance.' *REEDN* 9, no 2 (1984), 56–62 and 10, no 1 (1985), 9–16.

Abbreviations

abbrev	abbreviation	Lk	Luke
abl	ablative	m	masculine
acc	accusative	ME	Middle English
adj	adjective	Mk	Mark
adv	adverb	ML	Medieval Latin
AL	Anglo-Latin	Mt	Matthew
art	article	n	noun
attr	attributive	nt	neuter
CL	Classical Latin	NT	New Testament
coll	collective	OT	Old Testament
comm	common gender	p	participle
comp	compound	pa	past tense
conj	conjunction	pass	passive voice
cp	compare	per	person
dat	dative	phr	phrase
E	English	pl	plural
EG	English Glossary	poss	possessive
ext	extension	pp	past participle
F	French	ppl	participial
f	feminine	pr	present tense
fig	figuratively	prep	preposition
gen	genitive	pron	pronoun
Gk	Greek	prp	present participle
imper	imperative	refl	reflexive
indecl	indeclinable	sbst	substantive
inf	infinitive	sg	singular
interj	interjection	subj	subjunctive
intr	intransitive	superl	superlative
L	Latin	tr	transitive
LG	Latin Glossary	v	verb
lit	literally	vb	verbal

Latin Glossary

ABIGAIL ANN YOUNG

abbas, -atis *n m* abbot, head of a monastery 189/9, etc; 397/34, etc

absolucio, -onis *n f* absolution, the formal assurance of forgiveness from sin or remission of the penalty incurred for committing a sin in ecclesiastical law 99/35, etc; 369/17m

absoluo, -ere, -ui, -utum *v tr* to absolve from sin or from penalty for a sin, bestow forgiveness 171/20, etc; 356/3m, etc

abusus, -us *n m* misuse, abuse, used of a custom or practice 57/15

accedo, -dere, -ssi, -ssum *v intr with* 'ad' *and acc* to come to, attend, *here found only as prp* 99/9m

accepto, -are, -aui, -atum *v tr* to receive or accept (something) as true or sufficient 150/18, etc

accido, -ere, -i *v intr* to fall within a certain period of time (*defined by abl phr or* 'infra' *with acc*) 111/2, etc

actus, -us *n m* legal proceedings, action, here used of ecclesiastical courts 183/40, etc

adinuicem *prep phr* ad inuicem *written as one word and used for adv* inuicem *qv*

adiungo, -gere, -xi, -ctum *v tr* to join to, add to, assign to, *here used in error for* **iniungo** *qv* 154/24

admitto, -ittere, -isi, -issum, *v tr* to admit (a cleric) to a cure of souls in a given church, here as an assistant 348/23

admoneo, -ere, -ui, -itum *v tr* to warn, used of a judge in a church court 146/7, etc; 388/4

admonicio, -onis *n f* formal warning given by a judge to a defendant at dismissal enjoining better behaviour in future 154/40, etc; 392/3

adnullo, -are, -aui, -atum *v tr* to bring to no effect, annul (eg, a law or rule) 394/9

adpresens *adv* at the present time, now 99/9; **ad presens** 98/11

adtunc *adv* at that time, then 70/30, etc

aduentus, -us *n m lit* coming, arrival, *here in idiom* aduentus domini *lit* the Lord's coming, *hence* Advent, the liturgical season serving as a preparation for the celebration of the Incarnation at Christmas 400/14 or the first Sunday in Advent 468/19, et al

aedituus, -i *n m* in CL one who has charge of a temple, in AL a churchwarden 180/11, et al

aldermannus, -i *n m* alderman, a civic officer, here found only in Worcester 412/8, et al; *see* EG **alderman**

alea, -e *n f* a game of chance played with dice on a board, *here in idiom* ludere ad aleas to play at 'alea,' *hence* to gamble 348/5

alias *adv* 1. elsewhere 99/10, etc; 348/24, etc; 2. else 350/10; 3. with alternate names, alias 146/1, etc; 381/22, etc

allego, -are, -aui, -atum *v tr* to allege, to state or claim (something) formally in court as true or sufficient 140/38, etc

Allemannus, -a, -um *adj* German 379/26

Altissimus, -i *sbst m* the most high, used as a divine title 349/27

altram, altri, altrum *for* **alteram, alteri, alterum** *syncopated forms of* **alter, altera, alterum** *qv*

amendacio, -onis *n f* amendment of life, improvement in conduct 172/10

amoueo, -ouere, -oui, -otum *v tr* to cause (someone) to be legally removed from possession of a landholding 413/25

anathema, -atis *n nt lit* something accursed, *by ext* formal declaration of excommunication or other canonical censure 57/21/; 396/13

Anglia, -e *n f* England 94/6; 396/3, etc

Anglicanus, -a, -um *adj* of or pertaining to England, English 445/16

Anglice *adv* in the English language 97/28, etc; 394/12

Anglicus, -a, -um *adj* of or pertaining to England, English 396/9

animal, -alis *n nt* wild animal, beast 347/8; also referring to domesticated animals put to graze or kept in a pasture 347/12

annexit *for* **adnexuit** *3rd per pa of* **adnecto** *qv*

annunciacio, -onis *n f* announcement, here always the announcement by an angel to the Virgin Mary of the impending birth of Christ (Lk 1.26–38), *hence* the feast of the Annunciation commemorating this event 474/9, et al; *see also* **festum** *sense 2*

apediamentum, -i *n nt* hindrance, impediment 200/26; **apodiamentum** 200/30 (*possibly a variant of* **impedimentum** *qv but more probably an independent formation on the same root*)

apostolus, -i *n m* apostle, one of the first followers of Jesus 57/8 (in reference to St Paul); *see also* **festum** *sense 2*

apparitor, -oris *n m* apparitor, officer of the ecclesiastical courts with special responsibility for delivering citations to appear in court to accused persons 167/32, etc; 390/11, etc

archangelus, -i *n m* archangel, one of the highest order of angels; *see* **festum** *sense 2*

archidiaconus, -i *n m* archdeacon, cleric

appointed by a bishop to assist him principally in administering justice and in supervising parochial clergy 377/39

aretro *adv* in arrears, used of payments of money 413/8, et al

aries, -etis *n m lit* a ram, *by ext* a sort of post, or quintain, used as a jousting target for military exercises and competitions (so-called because of its shape or appearance?) *here in idiom* **arietes leuare** to put up such quintains, *hence* to hold such exercises or contest? 348/6

armiger, -eri *n m lit* one who bears arms, in AL used as a title, esquire 387/3

arreagia, -e *nf* arrears, used of payments of money 413/13

ars, -tis *n f see* **magister** *sense 2*

articulo, -are, -aui, -atum *v tr* to set out charges in the form of an article 70/21, et al

articulum, -i *n nt* article, a charge or list of charges laid against a person in court 97/15, etc; 392/2, etc

assensus, -us *n m* agreement, assent, here formal consent of a governing body, eg, a town council or group of officials 412/12, et al

assignatus, -i *sbst m* assign, a person to whom another has assigned, or made over, rights in property or in receivable sums of money 412/29, et al

atrium, -ii *n nt* in a Roman house the first main room or entrance hall, traditionally open to the sky, *here by ext* **ecclesie atrium** the court or yard of a church, churchyard 347/12

attachio, -are, -aui, -atum *v tr* to attach, to subject (someone) to attachment, or seizure, of their person or goods; here used of arrest in the event of failure to return a wrongfully detained book or its value 112/25

attempto, -are, -aui, -atum *v tr* try, attempt 99/37

auctenticus, -a, -um *adj* having authority, authentic, real, here used of a seal 58/2

bacchalaureus, -i *n m* bachelor, one holding the lowest academic degree in a given faculty, *here in idiom* **in legibus bacchalaureus** bachelor of laws, LLB; the pl 'legibus' formerly indicated a degree in both laws, that is, canon and civil, but after the teaching of canon law was forbidden at the universities by Henry VIII, the degree was presumably in civil law only and retained the pl by custom 151/15–16, etc

balliuus, -i *n m* bailiff, a civic officer, here found only in Worcester 412/7, et al; *see* EG **baylyff**

baptista, -e *n m* baptist, one who baptizes; *see* **festum** *sense 2 and* **natiuitas**

baro, -onis *n m* baron, lowest rank in the hereditary peerage 401/26

beatus, -a, -um *adj* blessed, used as the title for a saint, especially the Virgin Mary; *see* **dies** *sense 5,* **festum** *sense 2*

Bedefordia, -e *n f* Bedford, name of a duchy 411/31

benediccio, -onis *n f* blessing 98/11, et al

benefactor, -oris *n m* benefactor, here a patron of a religious house 411/34

beneficium, -ii *n nt* 1. benefit, freely-bestowed gift, *here in idioms with attr gen* **absolucionis beneficium** 99/35, etc; **beneficium sanitatis** 200/24; 2. benefice, an ecclesiastical appointment, often one to a parish and involving a cure of souls 383/35

billa, -e *n f* indictment, *here in idiom* **billa uera** true bill, the decision of a grand jury that sufficient evidence exists for a valid indictment 370/6

binatim *adv* two by two, in pairs 597/5

camera, -e *n f* room, chamber, *here in idiom* **camera stellata** Star Chamber, the king's council sitting as a court 96/15; *see* p 21

camerarius, -ii *n m* chamberlain, a civic officer, here found only in Worcester 412/9, et al; *see* EG **chamberlayne**

campana, -e *n f* bell, here one of a set of bells rung as part of the formal declaration of excommunication 99/32

campus, -i *n m lit* a field, here referring to land pertaining to a church building but apparently in some way distinct from the churchyard, possibly land extending beyond or around the churchyard 348/24; *cp* DML fasc 2:C **campus** 2b

cancelarius, -ii *n m* chancellor, deputy of a bishop with primarily administrative and judicial responsibility, here the chancellor of Hereford Cathedral 98/10

cancerosus, -a, -um *adj* cankerous, malignant 349/27

canon, -onis *n m lit* a model or standard, hence 1. **canon misse** the canon of the mass, the invariable central portion of the service comprising the eucharistic prayer 348/3; 2. **sacri canones** sacred canons, the authoritative precepts of ecclesiastical law, *hence used collectively,* canon law 57/15–16

canonice *adv* canonically, in accordance with a specific canon or with canon law in general 347/9, et al

canonicus, -a, -um *adj* canonical, pertaining or appropriate to a specific canon or to canon law in general 98/31, et al; 369/26, etc

canonicus, -i *sbst m* canon, an ordained member of a secular cathedral chapter, here used of canons of Hereford Cathedral 201/1, etc

canticum, -i *n nt* secular song; although the original CL sense of a sung passage in comedy is probably no longer meant, the negative connotations attached to comedy in the patristic period probably influenced the use of the word in the canons of the third council of Toledo (589) quoted here by Gerald of Wales 395/27

cantilena, -e *n f* secular song, ballad, often with negative associations or connotations. Gerald of Wales' use of the word implies certain characteristics of a 'cantilena': a) that it was a popular or folk song; b) that it was closely associated with, and sung while, dancing; and c) that it normally had a refrain. Although the small number of occurrences in this or previous collections makes it difficult to determine if this usage is idiosyncratic, the word is elsewhere associated with the E 'carol' and 'balet,' and the CL meaning is 'refrain' 188/38; 395/20, et al; *see* EG **carrall**, REED *Cambridge* LG **cantilena** and EG **balet, carol,** and OLD **cantilena**

capella, -e *n f* chapel 348/36

capellanus, -i *n m* chaplain, a priest having charge of a chapel 349/14

capitulum, -i *n nt* chapter 1. an organized and partially self-governing body of secular clerics serving a cathedral or collegiate church, here used of a chapter meeting called for disciplinary purposes 348/14, 396/14?; 2. one of the subdivisions making up a collection of canons or statutes, hence a regulation 396/14?; 3. any subdivision of a longer work 442/9m

caput, -itis *n nt lit in* CL head, *hence by ext* a beginning, *and further by ext* beginning of a text, hence a section or passage of a text, *here in idiom* **secundum caput** the second lesson or passage appointed to be read at morning or evening prayer 378/3–4

carragium, -ii *n nt* act of carrying or carting, carriage of goods 348/12 (*pl used as coll*)

castrum, -i *n nt* castle 350/12

catallum, -i *n nt* chattel, moveable property 387/10

cathedralis, -e *adj* of or pertaining to the see of a bishop or his church, *here in idiom* **ecclesia cathedralis** cathedral church 57/27, etc; 349/13

causa, -e *n f* 1. cause, reason 140/29, etc; 2. law case, the proceedings arising from it, or the matter thereof 171/29, etc; 360/23, etc; **sanguinis causa** a case involving bloodshed 347/16; 3. *by ext of sense 2 in*

idiom **sigillum nostrum ad causas** apparently the name of a seal used by the bishop of Worcester chiefly for judicial business 350/11–12

cedula, -e *n f see* **schedula** *sense 2*

celebro, -are, -aui, -atum *v tr* 1. *absolutely*, to celebrate mass 348/36; 2. to celebrate other divine services 451/30

censura, -e *n f* censure, rebuke, punishment 99/2, et al

cereus, -i *n m* processional candle 98/1, et al

certificarium, -ii *n nt* certificate, a document introduced in court to verify a statement or compliance with an order, or the act of producing such a document; certificates often were not separate pieces of parchment or paper but rather were written on the backs of citations of schedules of penance 171/11, etc; 356/14m, etc; *see also* **forma** *sense 1,* **schedula**

certifico, -are, -aui, -atum *v tr* 1. to inform 57/31; 350/11; 2. to certify formally (one's compliance with a court order, here with an order to perform public penance) 97/17, etc; 381/28, etc

ceruix, -icis *n f* neck, *here in idiom* **ceruicem erigere** to be stiff-necked, *hence* stubborn in resistance or proud 348/26

chorea, -e *n f* dance, originally a round dance; it was sometimes used in AL for a folk or country dance; in 396/7 it describes a dance which took place around a church and was accompanied by singing; **correa** 348/5

Christianus, -a, -um *adj* Christian 98/15; *m pl as sbst* Christian people, Christians 98/13, etc

cimiterium, -ii *n nt* churchyard 97/28; 395/20, etc; **cymiterium** 347/20

circiter *adv for* **circa** *prep qv*

circumcisio, -onis *n f* circumcision, *here in idiom* **in circumcisione domini** on the feast of the Circumcision, 1 January 465/3

citacio, -onis *n f* citation, a document summoning an accused person to appear before an ecclesiastical court 57/28, etc

citharedes, -i *n m* in CL one who plays the lyre; in medieval English usage one who plays the harp; possibly a generic term applied to players of plucked-string instruments, both with and without fingerboards 397/18, etc; *second declension forms* **citharedus** 397/2; **citheredus** 106/40

citharista, -e *n m* harper, player on a stringed instrument 200/21, etc; *see also* **citharedes** *which is derived from the same root*

citherazator, -oris *n m* harper, player on a stringed instrument 400/3, et al; *see also* **citharedes** *which is derived from the same root*

cito, -are, -aui, -atum *v tr* cite, issue a citation (to appear before an ecclesiastical court) 57/26, etc; 381/22, etc

Clarencia, -e *n f* Clarence, name of a duchy 405/5, etc

claua, -e *n f see* **seruiens** *sense 2*

clausio, -onis *n f* an enclosed area, enclosure 347/10

clericalis, -e *adj* of or pertaining to a cleric, clerical 356/37

clericus, -i *n m* clerk, cleric, one in holy orders 72/25, etc; 348/4

cohercio, -onis *n f for* **coercitio** *qv*

comes, -itis *n m* earl, a peer ranking above a viscount but below a marquess 396/35, etc

comitatus, -us *n m* county 451/23, etc

commissarius, -ii *n m* commissary, judge presiding over a bishop's or archdeacon's court on his behalf, the chief judicial officer of a diocese 57/27; 445/15

communa, -e *n f* commons, the standard daily provision of supplies, usually foodstuffs, made for each member of a community, or the monetary value thereof 113/2, etc; 398/34

communis, -e *adj* common, communal, of or pertaining to a community, in this case a city 413/34

communitas, -atis *n f* community,

commonalty, commons (of a city or town) 412/13, et al

communiter *adv* in ordinary language, in English (as opposed to Latin) 349/35

compareo, -ere, -ui *v intr* to appear before a judge to answer charges, here used of appearances before a bishop or one of his officers in an ecclesiastical court 57/26, etc; 381/23, etc

comparitio, -onis *n f* appearance before a judge, here in an ecclesiastical court 71/30

compotus, -i *n m* account, formal accounting made of the receipts and disbursements of a corporate body, *here in idiom* **tempus (huius) compoti** (this) accounting period, the period of time covered in a given account 111/20, etc; 404/9–10, etc

compurgator, -oris *n m* compurgator, one who supports the oath of an accused party by his own oath; in ecclesiastical courts this process, called compurgation, was a means by which the accused could be cleared of a charge 389/21, et al

computacio, -onis *n f* calculation, reckoning, *here in idiom* **secundum computacionem ecclesie Anglicane** according to the reckoning of the English church, used of dates to describe the English custom, retained formally until 1752, of treating Lady Day, 25 March, as the start of a new calendar year (*see* Cheney, pp 4–5) 445/16; although the phr 'iuxta computacionem ecclesie Anglicane' does not occur in full, the abbreviated expression **iuxta &c** after dates presumably stands for it 64/32, etc; 378/36–7

computo, -are, -aui, -atum *v tr* 1. calculate the cost of, account for spending on 106/33, etc; 404/8, etc; 2. render an account 411/17

concensus, -us *n m for* **consensus** *qv*

concilium, -ii *n nt* church council, an assembly of bishops and other clerics for the purpose of deciding theological and doctrinal issues 395/24, et al

condicio, -onis *n f* 1. condition, stipulation (of a bond) 387/12; 2. station of life, *in idiom* **libere condicionis** of a free status, ie, not a villein, a status which persisted in law until the early 17th c. 112/22

confessio, -onis *n f* statement, acknowledgment (in response to a charge) 150/17, etc

confiteor, -fiteri, -fessus sum *v intr* to make a statement, claim, acknowledge 62/31, etc; 390/29

congregacio, -onis *n f* gathering together, meeting, here a gathering of people in church for a service, congregation 73/28; 378/2

conquestus, -us *n m* Norman conquest 413/40

consecracio, -onis *n f* consecration; *lit* the act of making holy, here the act of ordaining a bishop 350/14; also as a title **de consecratione**, part three of Gratian's *Decretum* 395/24

consistorialis, -e *adj* of or pertaining to a consistory court, *in idiom* **locus consistorialis** the site of such a court, consistory 66/5, etc; *see also* **dies** *sense 7*

consistorium, -ii *n nt* consistory, originally a council-chamber in a bishop's residence which became the site of a court meeting under the bishop or his deputy, later such a court 350/8 or any chamber in which it met 383/39; in Hereford there was a dean's consistory as well as a bishop's consistory

consocius, -ii *n m* accomplice, fellow, partner 62/29m

continuo, -are, -aui, -atum *v tr* to adjourn or postpone legal proceedings to another day or time, *used absolutely* 184/25 *or with* **causam** 181/29; 2. to extend the deadline for the fulfilment of a condition of dismissal from a church court, here always the deadline for producing a certificate 171/16, 64/16

contradictio, -onis *n f* opposition, gainsaying, here specifically a challenge to the validity of a compurgation 389/22

contradictor, -oris *n m* one who is disobedient 57/22

contrado, -dere, -didi, -ditum *v tr* hand over, deliver 169/36

contrafactus, -a, -um *pp* having been counterfeited or forged 394/11

contrauenio, -ire, -i, -tum *v tr* to violate or contravene (eg, an order or decree) 99/1, et al; 350/1

contumax, -acis *adj* contumacious, guilty of the offence, punishable by excommunication, of contumacy, a refusal to comply with a citation, sentence, or other order of an ecclesiastical court or its officers 64/6, etc

conuentus, -us *n m* convent, religious house, used for houses of friars as well as of monks and nuns 404/22 (*in form* **couet'**), etc

corona, -e *n f* crown, here standing symbolically for royal authority, the Crown 451/34

corpus, -oris *n nt* 1. body, one's person 112/25; 2. a dead body, corpse 347/6, etc; 3. *in idiom* **corpus Christi** the eucharistic body of Christ; *see* **dies** *sense 6*, **festum** *sense 2*

correa, -e *n f see* **chorea**

creator, -oris *n m* creator, used as a divine title 98/18, et al

credulitas, -atis *n f* act of trusting or believing, belief 389/24

crux, -cis *n f* cross, here always used of the cross of Christ 1. *fig* for Christ's saving work 99/21; 2. in the name of a festival; *see* **festum** *sense 2*; 3. in the name of a parish **Parshore St Crucis** Pershore Holy Cross 385/42–3m

cultus, -us *n m* religious practice, observance 57/6

curatus, -i *n m* curate, any priest having the cure of souls 72/25; 349/14

curia, -e *n f* law court 159/16, etc

custos, -odis *n m* guardian, keeper, here used

of a cleric appointed to watch over the tomb of a locally venerated bishop 200/13, et al

cymiterium, -ii *n nt see* **cimiterium**

dampnabiliter *adv* in a manner worthy of condemnation 57/24

dampnum, -i *n nt* 1. financial loss; 2. condemnation, damnation; the occurrence on 349/22 is a play on the two senses

deauratus, -a, -um *adj* gilt, covered or ornamented with gold paint or leaf, here referring to clothing, *hence possibly used idiomatically* **pannus deauratus** cloth of gold 99/39

decanatus, -us *n m* deanery, an administrative division of a diocese, more properly called a rural deanery, under the supervision of a priest known as the rural dean; in some dioceses, such as Hereford, the deaneries were used as court divisions for the ecclesiastical courts 182/29m

decanus, -i *n m* dean, administrative head of a cathedral chapter, who also sat as judge of his consistory court in Hereford 98/10, etc

dedimus potestatem *vb phr* name of a writ issued to empower commissioners to take statements on oath from persons involved in a suit before Star Chamber; apparently the name of this writ and a style of cause were normally written on the dorse of interrogatories used, or answers taken, by commissioners in a given suit 88/41, et al

denarius, -ii *n m* a penny 200/32; 397/1, et al; *also in idiom* **denarii missales** masspence, money given as an offering at mass, here apparently money given the boy bishop by the chapter for his offering 100/38-9

denouo *adv* anew, afresh 412/36; **de nouo** 413/17

denunciacio, -onis *n f* denunciation, a public proclamation of guilt or excommunication made against a person charged in an ecclesiastical court 153/19

denuncio, -are, -aui, -atum *v tr* to denounce (someone), proclaim (someone) as guilty of an offence, or as having been excommunicated for an offence, against canon law 99/33, etc

deputatus, -i *n m* deputy, a judge delegated by a superior to hear cases on his behalf 171/14, etc; 390/16

detego, -gere, -xi, -ctum *v tr lit* to uncover, expose, *here as legal term* to detect, to allege formally before church authorities that a given person has committed a canonical offence 97/14, etc; 356/8, etc

detencio, -onis *n f* detention, the act of wrongfully withholding goods lawfully acquired from their owner, eg, refusing to return goods left in one's possession by the owner for a term at the end of that term; also the name of an action at law for the recovery of goods wrongfully detained 112/23; *see Black's* **Detinue**

diaconus, -i *n m* deacon, a member of the lowest of the three major orders of clergy, the other two being bishop, 'episcopus,' and priest, 'presbyter' or 'sacerdos' 98/1

dies, diei *n m or f* 1. day 187/7, etc; 372/11, etc; 2. day of the week: **dies dominicus** 99/31-2, etc; 347/15-16, etc *or* **dominicus dies solis** 174/10 Sunday; **dies Iouis** Thursday 160/41; **dies lune** Monday 64/3 (also found with 'dies' understood 79/24); **dies Martis** Tuesday 98/32; **dies Mercurij** Wednesday 98/20, et al; 519/14; **dies Veneris** Friday 500/39; 3. day as a measurement of time 100/3, etc; 4. day set aside for a special purpose: referring to one or both of the hock days 349/19, 349/20, 349/34; **dies installacionis domini prioris** the lord prior's installation day 397/15-16; **dies paraseue** *lit* day of preparation, Good Friday, Friday before Easter 200/14-15; 5. a saint's day: **dies concepcionis beate Marie** the Conception of St Mary,

8 December 494/29; **dies Innocencium** 100/17, etc *or* **dies sanctorum Innocencium** 102/18, etc *or* **dies festi sanctorum Innocencium** 100/31 (Holy) Innocents' Day, 28 December; **dies sancti Michaelis** St Michael's Day, Michaelmas, 29 September 100/6; **dies natiuitatis beate Marie** the Nativity of St Mary, 8 September 396/23; 6. a feast day: **dies festiuus** 73/28; 348/12, etc; **dies corporis Christi** Corpus Christi Day, Thursday after Trinity Sunday 399/13; **dies palmarum** *lit* day of palms, Palm Sunday 397/22–3; **dies Pentecostes** Pentecost, Whitsunday, Sunday fifty days after Easter 480/24, et al; **dies rogacionum** Rogation Days, the Monday, Tuesday, and Wednesday before Ascension Day 340/n 97; **dies sancte Trinitatis** Trinity Sunday, the Sunday after Pentecost 466/28; 7. *in various idioms*: **dies consistorialis** day upon which a consistory court could meet 350/9; **dies iuridicus** court day, day upon which legal business could be conducted 57/28; 383/38; **dies penitencialis** day of penance, a day, usually a Sunday, assigned by a church court for a penance, such as public confession, to be performed 97/16, etc; 390/32–3 (*see also* **penitencia**); **his nostris diebus** in our own time 396/3

dimissio, -onis *n f* dismissal of defendant from further proceedings, usually upon payment of court expenses and/or a fine 97/31m, etc; 391/42m, etc

dimitto, -ittere, -isi, -issum *v tr* 1. to demise, to convey or grant title or possession of property by will or lease 413/3, 413/20; 2. to lease, let *absolutely* 412/42; *in idiom with* **ad firmam** 412/13–14; 3. to release, set free 200/28; 4. to dismiss or release (an accused person) from court without further charges, punishments, or citations pending, usually upon payment of court

expenses and/or a fine 63/15, etc; 381/28, etc

diocesis, -is *n f* diocese, administrative district under the authority of a bishop 57/20, etc; 349/15

dismissus *for* **dimissus** *pp of* **dimitto**

dissolucio, -onis *n f* 1. easing, slackening (eg, of a rule or order); *or* 2. dissolute behaviour, immorality; the occurrence on 188/38 may represent a play on both senses; it is hard to decide which is primary

distinctio, -onis *n f lit* the act of separating into sections or a section so created, *hence* distinction, a subdivision of a longer work, here one of the subdivisions into which the parts of Gratian's *Decretum* are divided 395/25

districcio, -onis *n f* 1. stricture, punishment 98/31, et al; 2. distraint, the act of seizing goods, etc, for non-payment of rent or other obligation, or the goods so seized 413/11

distringo, -ngere, -nxi, -ctum *v tr* to distrain, to seize goods, etc, as distraints 413/11

diuinus, -a, -um *adj* 1. divine, pertaining to or suitable for God 98/9, etc; 349/11; 2. *with* **officium** divine office, the set of daily prayers and scriptural readings to be said by religious at the canonical hours 57/23; 395/26, et al; 3. *as nt pl sbst by ext of sense 2* **diuina** 167/31, etc; 350/5, etc *or in sg idiom* **diuina seruitia** 451/30 divine service, an unspecified liturgical service, often used to refer to the main worship service at a parish church on any Sunday

doctor, -oris *n m* doctor, one holding the highest academic degree in a given faculty; used as a title with names 70/34, et al; 390/16 (*in form* **docorem**), etc; *in idiom* **legum doctor**, doctor of laws, LLD; the pl 'legum' formerly indicated a degree in both laws, that is, canon and civil, but after the teaching of canon law was forbidden at the universities by Henry VIII, the degree was presumably in civil law only and

retained the pl by custom 143/1, etc;
445/14, etc

domina, -e *n f* lady, title of royalty, peeress,
or peer's wife 107/1; 400/17

dominicus, -a, -um *adj* of or pertaining to
the Lord: *f sg as sbst* Lord's Day, Sunday
400/14; *see also* **dies** *sense 2*

dominus, -i *n m* 1. the Lord, title of God or
Christ 100/10, etc; 396/9, etc; 2. lord: title
of bishop 200/9, et al; 399/23, etc; abbot
189/9; prior 397/2, etc; royalty 187/14,
etc; 399/20, etc; peer 399/20, etc; various
ecclesiastical officials and judges 98/10,
etc; 381/25, etc; 3. Sir: title of priest 200/6,
et al or knight 189/13, etc; 400/2, etc; *see
also* **officium** *sense 2*

domus, -us *n f* 1. house, home 69/32, et al;
in various idioms: **domus domini** the
Lord's house, a church 57/5; **domus
mercati** market house, building in a
market area for the use of buyers and sellers
412/27; 2. pageant house 412/23

dorsum, -i *n nt* dorse, the back of a sheet of
paper or parchment 171/17, etc

draco, -onis *n m lit* dragon, *here by ext* the
name of a banner or streamer, perhaps in
the shape of a dragon, traditionally carried
in liturgical Rogation processions 340/n 97

ducissa, -e *n f* duchess, whether a peeress in
her own right or the wife of a duke 400/17

duplex, -icis *sbst nt* a double portion, here
probably a double portion of daily
provisions or commons 339/n 82; *see also*
communa

dux, -cis *n m* duke, highest rank of the
hereditary peerage 399/21, etc

ebdomada, -e *n f* week 397/19, etc

Eboracum, -i *n nt* York, name of a town and
royal duchy 372/7, etc

ecclesia, -e *n f* 1. specific church or church
building 98/11, etc; 347/11, etc; 2. the
church as a corporate or spiritual body
99/34, etc; 445/16; *see also* **cathedralis,
computacio, parochialis**

ecclesiasticus, -a, -um *adj* ecclesiastical, of
or pertaining to the church 99/2, et al

edictum, -i *n nt* order, decree, edict, here
used to refer to a form of citation ('per
publicum edictum') used as a final resort
by ecclesiastical authorities when previous
attempts to serve a citation personally
and/or by ways and means had been
unsuccessful or at least had failed to compel
an appearance by the accused person; such
a citation appears to have taken the form
of an order, the 'edictum,' posted or
proclaimed at the parish church of the
accused 146/2–3, etc; 389/36

elemosinarius, -ii *n m* almoner, officer
charged with dispensing alms 349/13

elimozina, -e *n f* alms, charitable gift 411/34

emano, -are, -aui, -atum *v intr* to come
forward, be promulgated, used of a legal
order or decision, especially from a bishop
or his court 68/21m, etc; 356/2m, etc

enormis, -e *adj lit* exceeding the standard,
excessive, *hence* outrageous, awful 349/24

enterludium, -ii *n nt see* **interludium**

epiphania, -e *n f* epiphany, revelation, here
used of the revealing of Christ to the
gentiles (Mt 2.1–12) or the liturgical
festival commemorating it; *see* **nox** *sense 2*

episcopatus, -us *n m lit* the office or function
of a bishop, *here by ext* the area under a
bishop's authority, diocese, or the period
of time during which a given person holds
a see, episcopate; the former seems more
likely in context on 396/16

episcopus, -i *n m* 1. bishop, member of the
highest of the major orders of clergy, the
other two being deacon, 'diaconus,' and
priest, 'presbyter' or 'sacerdos' 98/9, etc;
396/12, etc; 2. *in idiom* **episcopus** 100/24
or **episcopus paruorum** 100/17 *or* **paruus
episcopus** 100/31, etc, little bishop, a name
for the boy bishop, a boy, usually a
choirboy, chosen to act as a mock bishop
in liturgical and other observances on the
feast of the Holy Innocents

equitatura, -e *n f* act of riding 99/39

euangelium, -ii *n nt* gospel, here referring to the gospel reading in a mass or other liturgical service 65/10, etc; 348/33

examinacio, -onis *n f* judicial examination of a case or charge 167/33, etc; 392/2, etc

examino, -are, -aui, -atum *v tr* to examine (a person or a case) judicially, used of a judge 167/33, etc; 388/23

Excetria, -e *n f* Exeter, the name of a duchy 401/3

excommunicacio, -onis *n f* excommunication, ecclesiastical penalty under which the guilty party was punished by exclusion from the sacraments and especially the reception of communion; at various times, further disabilities were imposed as well, such as exclusion from all social intercourse with other church members 100/2, etc; 356/1, etc; the latter, more severe, form is also called **excommunicacio maior** greater excommunication 350/1

excommunico, -are, -aui, -atum *v tr* to excommunicate, impose the penalty of excommunication on someone 99/25, etc; 381/23, etc

excreto, -ere, -i, -tum *v tr* to cause to grow, increase 349/22

excudo, -dere, -ssi, -ssum *v tr lit* to strike or hammer, *hence* to print 539/24

execucio, -onis *n f* execution, carrying out (eg, of a sentence) 100/8, etc

executor, -oris, *n m* executor, a man who oversees the due execution of the various clauses and bequests in a will and is accountable to the ecclesiastical authorities for so doing 452/37

executrix, -icis *n f* executrix, a woman, often the widow of the testator, who oversees the due execution of the various clauses and bequests in a will and is accountable to the ecclesiastical authorities for so doing 445/15

exhennia, -e *n f* gift, present 411/16; **exemia** 405/37; *neuter forms* **exennium** 405/25; **exhennium** 411/34

explanendum *gerund for* **explanandum** *from* **explano** *qv*

exto, -are, -aui, -atum *v intr for* **exsto** *qv*

extraho, -here, -xi, -ctum *v tr* to copy out, make a copy of 65/10, etc

extunc *adv* from then on, thenceforward 412/31, et al

familia, -e *n f* household, an extended family group which includes everyone living under the authority of the head of the household 200/8; *cp* **parentela**

famulus, -i *n m* servant, especially one who is a member of the 'familia,' household servant 401/10, etc

feodum, -i *n nt* fee, here a court fee assessed on accused persons for court appearances, citations, and other acts of church courts and their officers 97/25m, etc

feretrum, -i *n nt* portable shrine, eg, for relics, here probably a monstrance for bearing and displaying consecrated eucharistic bread in a Corpus Christi procession 340/n 97

festiuus, -a, -um *adj* of or pertaining to a festival or feast, festive; *see* **dies** *sense* 6

festum, -i *n nt* 1. festival, feast 347/17, etc; 2. a specific festival: **festum annunciacionis beate Marie uirginis** feast of the Annunciation of St Mary the Virgin, 25 March 412/29–30, et al; **festum beati Bartolomei apostoli** feast of St Bartholomew the Apostle, 24 August 98/21; **festum corporis Christi** feast of Corpus Christi, Thursday after Trinity Sunday 397/20, etc; **festum Innocencium** 98/2–3 *or* **festum omnium sanctorum Innocencium** 111/18–19 *or* **festum sanctorum Innocencium** 100/31, etc, feast of (all) the (Holy) Innocents, 28 December; **festum inuencionis sancte crucis** feast of the Invention (or Finding)

of the Holy Cross, 3 May 113/33–4;
festum natale domini 400/25–6 *or* **festum
natiuitatis domini** 519/13–14 Christmas,
25 December; **festum natiuitatis sancti
Iohannis Baptiste** feast of the Nativity of
St John the Baptist, 24 June 507/23–4;
festum Paschatis 349/19–20 *or* **festum
Pasche** 502/37 Easter, Sunday after the full
moon on or following 21 March; **festum
Pentecostes** Pentecost, Whitsunday,
Sunday fifty days following Easter 350/9;
festum sancti Iohannis feast of St John,
27 December 98/1; **festum sancti
Michaelis archangeli** feast of St Michael
the Archangel, Michaelmas, 29 September
412/34; **festum sancti Stephani** feast of
St Stephen, 26 December 97/41–98/1
fidedignus, -i *n m* trustworthy person
99/19
fidelis, -is *sbst comm* faithful believer, *here in
pl* the faithful 57/11; 412/6
fides, -ei *n f* 1. (religious) faith 98/24, etc;
451/25, etc; 2. oath, *here in idiom* **facere
fidem** to swear an oath 142/12, etc;
378/10–11
filius, -ii *n m* son 62/15; *used in various idioms*
1. of a symbolic or spiritual relationship
between a bishop and the clergy of his
diocese, especially his administrative
subordinates 98/10, et al; 349/12; 2. to
describe one embodying a quality or
activity of which he is said to be the son,
here **iniquitatis seu rebellionis filii** sons of
iniquity or rebellion, that is, evil or
rebellious men 99/20
firma, -e *n f* rental, leasing 412/13
Flandria, -e *n f* Flanders, a district of the
Low Countries 187/12m
forma, -e *n f* 1. a form of words, formula,
here often the form of words used in the
public confession imposed as penance by
church courts or a written copy thereof
169/24, etc; 361/3, etc or the form of words
used to dismiss a person excused by
poverty from any court fees 378/22 or

possibly the form of words used to certify
the carrying out of an order 184/3;
2. tenor, purport, terms (eg, of a statute
or agreement) 99/19; 413/21, et al; *see also*
certificarium, schedula
Francia, -e *n f* France 94/6; 451/25, et al;
Frauncia 386/43
Froma Episcopi *n phr* Bishops Frome, name
of a parish 65/22m

gardianus, -i *n m* churchwarden 167/35, etc;
355/11m, etc
generalis, -e *adj see* **uicarius** *sense 3*
generosus, -i *n m* gentleman 119/2, etc;
404/9, etc
gero, -rere, -ssi, -stum *v tr* to bear or carry;
here in various idioms 1. **bene gerendo**
acting well, behaving properly, a condition
of a bond to keep the peace 383/20;
2. **uices gerens** *see* **uicis** *sense 2*
gestus, -us *n m* behaviour, manner 349/2
gigator, -oris *n m* one who plays a 'giga,'
probably a rebec or pear-shaped bowed
stringed instrument; *hence* possibly used
as a generic term for a player of bowed,
as opposed to plucked-string, instruments,
fiddler 379/26m, et al
gilda, -e *n f lit* guild, an association or
confraternity of people having some
common purpose and brought together
for mutual benefit and the pursuit of that
purpose, eg, a religious guild dedicated to
honouring a saint by maintaining a light
or chapel in his or her honour; *here by ext*
a meeting of such a body 348/6; *see* DML
fasc 4: F–H **gilda** 2a,b *and* pp 579–80,
(endnote to LPL: MS 171 f 45v)
gildales *n pl probably an English gloss*; *see* EG
gildales 348/39
glorificacio, -onis *n f* glorification, act of
making glorious or bright 347/7
Gloucestria, -e *n f* Gloucester, name of a
town and of a royal duchy 397/34, etc;
Gloucestra 398/17; **Glowcestria** 405/14,
etc

gracia, -e *n f* 1. mercy, forgiveness, favour 98/16, 185/15, *hence in idioms* **cum gracia** with remission (a form of 'dimissus' should probably be understood), apparently a kind of dismissal from an ecclesiastical court which also implies the forgiveness of a previous excommunication or of a required court fee 171/28m, etc *and* **ex gracia** graciously, mercifully, used of the actions of a judge 175/19, etc; 386/26, etc; 2. grace, a divine gift operating in human beings to sanctify, regenerate, and strengthen 98/11, et al; 3. grace, divine favour 451/24, etc

granum, -i *n nt* grain of corn, *here in idiom* **mercatum granorum** Cornmarket 412/15

harparator, -oris *n m* harper, one who plays upon a harp, possibly a generic term for players upon plucked-string, as opposed to bowed, instruments 189/16, et al

Herefordensis, -is *n m* Hereford, name of a town and of a diocese 98/9, et al

Herefordia, -e *n f* Hereford, name of a town and of a diocese 200/13, etc

Hibernia, -e *n f* Ireland 94/6; 451/25, etc

historia, -e *n f lit* story, account, *often by ext* the visual representation of a story, picture; here the exact sense cannot be determined 118/36

histrio, -onis *n m* entertainer; in CL actor of the better sort; in later, eg, patristic, Latin, performer in the often obscene farces or ritual drama of the later Empire; in AL usage, usually a generic term, synonymous with 'menestrallus' and 'mimus,' which frequently refers to a musician; often the exact sense cannot be determined; here in the employ of a town 400/25

hospicium, -ii *n nt* household 464/22, et al

hostilitas, -atis *n f* war, hostilities 347/21

immediate *adv* immediately, at once 64/38, etc; 378/3

impressor, -oris *n m* printer 539/24

imprimo, -mere, -ssi, -ssum *v tr* to print; *see* **priuilegium**

incurro, -rere, -ri, -sum *v tr* incur, bring (a penalty) upon oneself 57/24

indentatus, -a, -um *adj* indented, that is, having the top or bottom edge cut on a zigzag, used of either half of a legal document drawn up in duplicate on a single sheet and then separated by cutting along a zigzag line; one half was given to each party affected by the document, and the matching indentations authenticate the halves 412/6

indentura, -e *n f* indenture, an indented legal document, often a deed of conveyance 413/31, et al

informacio, -onis *n f* information, specifically that laid before a court in the course of proceedings 171/30; 378/17

infra *prep* within 1. used of extent of space 97/28, etc; 413/5, etc; 2. used of a period of time 100/2–3, etc; 411/15, etc

inhibicio, -onis *n f* prohibition, order forbidding some activity 99/16

iniquitas, -atis *n f* evil, wrong-doing, iniquity 99/20

Innocentes, -cium *sbst m* the (Holy) Innocents, the children of Bethlehem killed by Herod in an attempt to kill the infant Jesus (Mt 2.16–18); *see* **dies** *sense 5,* **festum** *sense 2*

innodo, -are, -aui, -atum *v tr* involve with 100/2

inobediencia, -e *n f* disobedience 349/31

inquisitio, -onis *n f* inquest, a judicial inquiry made on behalf of the Crown under the direction of a royal officer, here **inquisitio de uasto** an inquest concerning possible waste committed by tenants of the Crown 404/21–2; *see also* **uastum**

insolutus, -a, -um *adj* unpaid, here used of rent 413/8, et al

installacio, -onis *n f* installation, ceremony in which an abbot or prior formally assumed his office; *see* **dies** *sense 4*

instans, -ntis *adj* present, instant, used of dates 98/20, etc; 389/5

interludium, -ii *n nt* interlude 57/19, etc; **enterludium** 121/35

interminacio, -onis *n f* threat, danger 57/21; 396/13

intimacio, -onis *n f* announcement, here specifically the public prior announcement of one's intention to seek to clear oneself by compurgation; such an announcement was required to allow challenges to be made at the time of compurgation 389/22

inuencio, -onis *n f* act of discovering or finding something; *see* **festum** *sense 2*

inuentarium, -ii *n nt* inventory, a legally certified list and valuation of all possessions, receivables, and debts of a person at the time of his or her death made for probate purposes under the direction of a court 445/17, et al

ioculo, -are, -aui, -atum *v tr* to jest, to provide amusement or entertainment 99/28

iocus, -i *n m, nt in pl* in CL jest, joke, usually verbal; in AL amusement, entertainment, recreation, or trick (eg, of a performing animal) 451/29

iudicialiter *adv* in a manner suitable to a court, judicially 71/31

iuridicus, -a, -um *adj see* **dies** *sense 7*

iusticiarius, -ii *n m* judge, justice (eg, of the peace or of assizes) 411/33, etc

iuxta *prep* according to 97/31, etc; 361/3, etc; *see also* **computacio**

Lancastria, -e *n f* Lancaster, name of an earldom 396/35

le, la forms of the Romance definite article used to signal the beginning of an English word or phr in an otherwise Latin passage 397/3, 412/23

lectio, -onis *n f* (public) reading, act of reading aloud 65/9, etc; 378/3

lectus, -us *n m* (public) reading, act of reading aloud 348/32

leuo, -are, -aui, -atum *v tr lit* to lift up, raise, erect, *in legal idiom* to raise or levy money posted as a bond in the event that specified conditions are not met 387/11; *see also* **aries**

lex, legis *n f* law 394/8; *see also* **bacchalaureus, doctor, peritus**

liber, -era, -erum *adj* free; *see* **condicio** *sense 2*

liberacio, -onis *n f* delivery (of money or goods) 108/19

libero, -are, -aui, -atum *v tr* to deliver, to hand over (eg, a payment) 101/12, etc

libra, -e *n f* pound (currency denomination) 387/5, et al

licencia, -e *n f* permission 348/33

ligacio, -onis *n f* act of fastening or binding 349/34

ligeus, -i *n m* liege, liege subject 395/10

linteum, -i *n nt* piece of linen clothing 355/10

littera, -e *n f lit* a letter of the alphabet, *in pl* letter, epistle 394/11, *also in idiom* **littere patentes** letters patent, a type of formal communication sent in the form of a letter not closed by a seal 58/1; 350/10

Londonium, -ii *n nt* London, name of a city 189/13, et al

ludo, -dere, -si, -sum *v tr* to play, with various significances 1. to play a sport or game 348/5; 2. used without specification, to play, to play music (?) 99/28; 3. *prp as sbst* player, participant in an unspecified sport, pastime, or play 399/13, etc

ludus, -i *n m* game, game of chance, sport, play, pastime; it is not always easy to determine which sense is meant in a given context, but the following senses may be distinguished 1. game of chance **ludi inhonesti** 348/4?, **ludi noxii & illiciti** 349/1; 2. folk game, popular pastime **ludi inhonesti** 348/4?, 349/34 (referring to hock day activities), **ludi de rege & regina** (probably a summer game with a summer king and queen) 348/5; 3. play of an unspecified kind **ludi siue interludia**

57/19; 4. stage play **ludi theatrales** 57/7, 57/7m; sense unclear 348/15

lusio, -onis *n f* play of an unspecified kind but clearly in a written form, play-text 112/23

lusor, -oris *n m* player 1. participant in an interlude 121/35, 122/8, 122/19; 2. participant in an unspecified play or pastime 123/40, 138/18, 138/33; 404/18, 411/24

luminare, -is *n nt* light, a processional torch or candle 340/n 97

magister, -tri *n m* 1. one who has authority or rank, master, used as a title with names 200/34, etc; 349/12, etc; 2. *with* **artium** 167/12–13, etc, *or* **in artibus** 161/18, et al, master of arts, MA, one holding the highest degree obtainable in the arts faculty of a university, and the prerequisite for entering one of the other faculties; 3. as a title of office; **magister reuellorum** master of the revels, an officer of the royal household in charge of entertainment for the court 394/12

magnas, -atis *n m* magnate, member of the gentry, peer, or other person of importance 398/8, etc

maintentus, -a, -um *pp see* **manuteneo**

manucaptor, -oris *n m* one who acts as a pledge for another's performance of a task or obligation, guarantor 387/8

manus, -us *n f* hand 1. *lit* expressing direct agency 372/10, 379/27; 2. *fig* expressing authority 409/14; 3. *by synecdoche* a person, especially in idiom after **purgare se** to express the number of compurgators required by a church court for a given party to be cleared from a charge (*using abl sg plus an ordinal or distributive number*), eg, 'ad purgandum se (cum) quarta manu' to clear oneself with four compurgators; *see* **purgo**

manuteneo, -ere, -ui, -tum *v tr* to maintain,

keep up 412/40; *pp in form* **maintentus** 413/19

marchio, -onis *n m* marquess, a peer ranking next below a duke 400/1

matutinus, -a, -um *adj* of or pertaining to morning; *nt sg used as sbst* matins, one of the canonical hours making up the divine office of clerics; despite its name, matins is the night office, being said at midnight or 2 AM under strict Benedictine observance 98/2, etc; *see also* **prex**

medietas, -atis *n f* half 113/26, etc

mendicans, -ntis *sbst m lit* one who begs, *by ext* a member of one of the mendicant orders, a friar 404/22

menestralcia, -e *n f* service due from a 'menestrallus,' usually referring to musical performance; *here in idiom* **faciens menestralciam** doing or carrying out such service 187/9, etc; 372/8

menestrallus, -i *n m lit* a servant (*from* CL 'minister' *plus diminutive suffix*) 1. minstrel; usually 'menestrallus' appears to refer to a performer, probably a musician and often a member of the household of a royal, ecclesiastical, noble, or other important person; a synonym of 'mimus' and 'histrio,' it is the most commonly used term of the three in this collection 189/12, etc; 396/23, etc; 2. in conjunction with a specific appositive, a particular kind of musician: **gigatores ... menestralli** 379/26, **uidilator menestrallus** 187/7; **ministrallus** 119/1, etc (*third declension forms* 121/21, 121/24); 399/5, etc, **ministrellus** 398/27, etc, **minstrallus** 398/34, etc, **mynstrellus** 399/20, etc

mercatum, -i *n nt* 1. market, a place set aside for the buying and selling of goods 412/15, et al; *see also* **domus** *sense 1*, **granum**; 2. fair, market 347/16, et al

meritum, -i *n nt* merit, deserts; the usage here reflects the view of late medieval piety that it was possible for the devout to appropriate merit from the good deeds of saints so as to effect cures and other benefits 200/19, et al

messuagium, -ii *n nt* one's principal dwelling together with the outbuildings and land appertaining to it 451/26, et al

miles, -itis *n m* knight 394/12

mimus, -i *n m* in CL an actor of the less savoury sort, and often in late Latin a synonym for 'pantomimus,' a performer in pantomime; in AL usually a generic term for an entertainer, probably a musician of some kind: 1. performer in the employ of a town 400/25; 2. performer in the employ of a royal, noble, or other important person 405/24

minister, -tri *n m* 1. *lit* servant; *by ext* with reference to Mk 10.43–5, clergyman, minister, specifically the incumbent of a parish 142/33, etc; 361/3, etc; 2. possibly used for its diminutive 'ministrallus' (*see* **menestrallus**) 398/27

ministrallus, ministrellus, minstrallus *see* **menestrallus**

minucio, -onis *n f* loss, lessening, *here in idiom with* 'sanguinis' (188/36) *or without* 'sanguinis' (339/n 82) blood-letting

minuo, -uere, -ui, -utum *v tr* to bleed (a person) for medicinal purposes 188/37, et al

miraculose *adv* miraculously, in the manner of a miracle 200/18

miraculum, -i *n nt* miracle, wondrous act or sign 200/11, et al

miseracio, -onis *n f* mercy 98/9

missa, -e *n f* mass, liturgical celebration of the eucharist 99/32, etc; 396/7, etc

missalis, -e *adj* of or pertaining to a mass; *see* **denarius**

modus, -i *n m* way, means 98/35, etc; 396/10, etc; *see also* **uia**

Mortuummare, Mortuimaris *n nt* Latinization of Mortimer; this L form of the E surname is based on a false etymology of the name 'de Mortimer' from F 'de Morte Mer,' ie, from the Dead Sea 189/16

mynstrellus, -i *n m see* **menestrallus**

natalis, -e *adj* of or relating to birth; *nt sg as sbst plus* **domini** Christmas 459/23, et al; *see also* **festum** *sense 2*

natiuitas, -atis *n f* birth, *in idiom* **post natiuitatem sancti Iohannis Baptiste** after the feast of the Nativity of St John Baptist, 24 June 462/15; *see also* **dies** *sense 5,* **festum** *sense 2*

nauis, -is *n f lit* ship, *here in idiom* **nauis ecclesie** nave of a church, main central body of a church building between the chancel and the west doors 348/23

nocturnus, -a, -um *adj* of or pertaining to night; *nt sg used as sbst* nocturns, the night office; it may refer to part of matins which, despite its name, was said at night, or collectively to matins and lauds, which were said consecutively at night or early in the morning; the occurrence on 113/32–3 clearly represents the former usage, those on 112/38 and 113/17 are ambiguous

nocumentum, -i *n nt* injury, hurt, harm 451/32

Northhumbria, -e *n f* Northumberland, the name of an earldom 405/34

notarius, -ii *n m* notary, person authorized to draw up and attest to various public and legal documents, thus giving such documents an authoritative status at law; often, as here, notaries served as registrars of ecclesiastical courts 71/21, etc

noto, -are, -aui, -atum *v tr* to note, to bring (someone) to the attention of a church for a canonical offence 167/30, etc

nox, -ctis *n f* 1. *lit* night, night-time 396/6; 2. the eve of a feast day, so called from the liturgical convention of beginning the observance of a holy day at sunset on the previous day; **nox Epiphanie** Epiphany Eve, that is, Twelfth Night 399/27

nullatinus *adv for* **nullatenus**; *see* OLD **nullus, -a, -um** *and* **tenus**²

nuncius, -ii *n m in* CL a messenger, but here probably groom 189/12; 417/26

obediencia, -e *n f* obedience, here used with special reference to the obedience owed by a cleric to the bishop of the diocese in which he has a benefice 98/30, etc

oblacio, -onis *n f* alms, offerings, gift 102/18, etc

oblator, -oris *n m lit* one who offers, *hence either* 1. one who gives alms, especially on behalf of another, an almoner *or* 2. (*by ext from the use of the root verb 'offero' to describe the offering of the eucharist*) one who makes eucharistic wafers; the former seems more likely than the latter 189/14

officium, -ii *n nt* 1. office, position, duty, task 99/29; 389/24, etc; 2. *by ext* **officium** 165/19 *or* **officium domini** 381/32, etc office, a church court acting 'ex officio' on information received and not as the result of promotion; what criminal proceedings are to the common law courts, office proceedings are to the church courts; 3. divine office 395/28; *see* **diuinus** *sense 2*

onero, -are, -aui, -atum *v tr* to bind someone by an oath, swear someone to an oath (*used with acc of the person and simple abl of the oath*) 185/38–186/1

oracio, -onis *n f* prayer 57/9, *et al; in idiom* **uespertine oraciones** evening prayer, the post-Reformation evening office of the Church of England, a conflation of the pre-Reformation offices of vespers and compline 63/13

oratorium, -ii *n nt lit* a place of prayer; *hence* oratory, church, chapel 396/1

ordinacio, -onis *n f* 1. ordinance, regulation, order 188/39; 2. ordination, sacramental rite conferring holy orders, usually used of ordination to priesthood, but here of the consecration of a priest to the episcopal order 99/3

Oxonia, -e *n f* Oxford 189/14

paena, -e *n f over-corrected form of* **poena** *qv*

pallatium, -ii *n nt* palace, *here in idiom* **pallatium domini episcopi** the lord bishop's palace, that is, the official residence of the diocesan bishop, which in Worcester diocese apparently contained a court 383/36

palma, -e *n f* palm tree; *see* **dies** *sense 6*, **ramus**

pannus, -i *n m* cloth, a piece of cloth, *hence in pl* clothing, *here in phr* **panni serici** silk clothing 99/39; *see also* **deauratus**

papirus, -i *n m* paper 111/11; **paupirus** 111/2

paraseues, -e *n f* preparation (from Gk παρασκευή); *see* **dies** *sense 4*

parcella, -e *n f* parcel, small plot of land, apparently a section of a 'placea' 413/4, *et al*

parentela, -e *n f* kindred, kinship group, a group of people connected by ties of blood (as opposed to 'familia,' a group of people connected by living under a common authority and often in a common residence) 200/8

parochia, -e *n f* parish, the smallest distinct unit of ecclesiastical jurisdiction and Christian ministry, each parish having its own church, priest, wardens, and tithes 63/12, etc; 381/22, etc

parochialis, -e *adj* of or pertaining to a parish, *here in idiom* **ecclesia parochialis** parish church 97/17, etc; 389/1

parochianus, -i *n m* parishioner, member of a parish 175/4; 386/5, etc

particulariter *adv* in detail, item by item 411/16

Pascha, -e *n f* Easter, festival celebrating the resurrection of Christ 96/14; 397/32, etc; *also in form* **Pascha, -atis** *n nt* 349/20, etc; *see also* **festum** *sense 2*

paschalis, -e *adj* of or pertaining to Easter, *hence* **ebdomada paschalis** Easter week, probably the octave of Easter 397/19–20

passio, -onis *n f* 1. suffering, *here in idiom* **in passione domini** on Passion Sunday, the fifth Sunday of Lent, the Sunday before

Palm Sunday 492/31; 2. *lit* that which occurs to or befalls one, *here in idiom* **passiones planetarum**; in the technical terminology of pre-Copernican astronomy, the 'passiones,' also known as 'accidentes' or 'phainomena,' are the apparent discrepancies or alterations which can be observed in the planets, such as changing of orbital speed or direction; the occurrence on 449/20 is probably the title of a treatise dealing with the resolution of the apparent contradictions between the observed 'passiones' and the theoretical assumptions according to the developed Ptolemaic system, a process often known as saving the 'phainomena'

pauperinus, -a, -um *adj* poor 378/16

paupirus, -i *n m see* **papirus**

peculiaris, -e *adj* belonging to a particular person, peculiar, *here in idiom* **peculiaris iurisdiccio** peculiar jurisdiction, a jurisdiction acquired by an ecclesiastic over a district which would otherwise be within the jurisdictional area of another 70/20, et al

penitencia, -e *n f* penance, act of contrition or restitution imposed by ecclesiastical authorities upon persons guilty of canonical offences; in case of moral offences such as sabbath breaking, penance often took the form of public confession on a set day or series of days 97/32, etc; 381/25, etc

penitencialis, -e *adj* pertaining or appropriate to a penitent, suitable for penance 97/16, etc; 390/33

Pentecostes, -es *n f* Pentecost, Whitsunday, Sunday fifty days following Easter 471/36, et al; *see also* **dies** *sense 6,* **festum** *sense 2;* **Pentecosta** 484/24

peregrinus, -i *sbst comm* foreigner, alien, *hence* stranger, outsider 348/7

peremptorie *adv* in a peremptory manner 349/32

peritus, -i *sbst m* person skilled or knowledgeable in a certain field, *here in idiom* **legis periti** persons knowledgeable in the law, legists, lawyers 405/35

persona, -e *n f* person 451/31; *in various idioms:* **in persona sua** in one's own person, personally 387/2, et al; **in persona** *plus gen* indicates the individual through whom one acts or receives by proxy 171/28–9, 159/30

personaliter *adv* in person, personally 67/21, etc; 350/11, etc

perturbator, -oris *n m* one who disrupts or disorganizes, a disturber of order 57/23

pes, pedis *n m* foot; 1. *lit* of the foot and ankle 200/21, et al; 2. *in idiom* **pes regalis** royal foot, probably the standard or assize foot, a legally established standard measure enforced by royal officers 412/17–18, et al

placea, -e *n f* a piece or plot (of land), a lot 412/14, et al

placitum, -i *n nt* judicial plea 112/23, *hence* a court 348/15

planeta, -e *n f* planet; *see* **passio** *sense 2*

plegius, -ii *n m* 1. guarantor, one who acts as a pledge for another's performance of a task or obligation 112/24; 2. *by ext* the pledge or bond given by a guarantor 112/24m

portatilis, -e *adj* portable 98/2

prebenda, -e *n f* prebend, *lit* an endowment established to support a member of a cathedral or other collegiate chapter, a cathedral benefice, *by ext* the district of a cathedral's holdings whose revenues supported a member of the chapter and over which he might acquire a peculiar jurisdiction 71/27, etc

prebendarius, -ii *n m* prebendary, member of a cathedral chapter supported by a prebend 70/20, etc

preconizacio, -onis *n f* summoning, a formal call made in a church court summoning a cited party three times by name in an audible voice to appear before the court 181/16

preconizo, -are, -aui, -atum *v tr* to summon (someone) formally (eg, to appear in an ecclesiastical court) 97/30, etc; 381/27, etc

predico, -are, -aui, -atum *v tr* 1. to say before or above 349/35, *hence pp as adj* aforesaid 99/27, etc; 350/5, etc; 2. to say in the presence of, proclaim, *hence* preach 98/25

prefigo, -gere, -xi, -xum *v tr* to fix or determine (eg, date) 58/1

prenominatus, -a, -um *pp* having been named or specified earlier 413/9, et al

preobtentus, -a, -um *pp* having been obtained or gotten earlier 348/34

presbyter, -eri *n m* priest, member of the second of the three major orders of clergy, also referred to as 'sacerdos,' the other two being bishop, 'episcopus,' and deacon, 'diaconus' 200/6; 348/31, et al

presentacio, -onis *n f* presentment, the act of presenting a person or persons as guilty of canonical offences or a written copy of the name(s) and charge(s) reported at a presentment; presentments were originally made by churchwardens but later by parish clergy as well 175/4

presentamentum, -i *n nt* presentment, the act of presenting a person or persons as guilty of canonical offences or a written copy of the name(s) and charge(s) reported at a presentment; presentments were originally made by churchwardens but later by parish clergy as well 151/1, etc

presento, -are, -aui, -atum *v tr* 1. to present (someone) as guilty of a canonical offence, used of churchwardens and/or parish clergy 175/30, etc; 2. *in an absolute sense* to make presentment, present a list of persons guilty of canonical offences, used of churchwardens and/or parish clergy 69/19; 355/12m; 3. to present a decision that someone is guilty of an indictable offence, used of a grand jury 451/22, etc

presidens, -ntis *sbst m* one who presides, presiding officer, president 350/8

presto, -are, -iti, -atum *v tr* to furnish, provide, *here in idiom* **iuramentum prestare** to swear or take an oath 143/7–8, etc; 389/23

presumo, -ere, -psi, -ptum *v tr* to take upon oneself (to do something), used of violators of rules or orders 98/19, et al; 347/13

presumptor, -oris *n m* one who presumes (to do something), used of a violator of rules or orders 347/19

preuius, -a, -um *adj* previous, prior 386/21, etc

prex, -ecis *n f* (*here only found in pl* **preces, -cum**) prayers, here always referring to one of the two post-Reformation offices of the Church of England: **preces matutine** morning prayer, matins, the morning office based upon the pre-Reformation offices of matins and prime 386/5–6; **uespertine preces** or **preces uespertine** evening prayer, evensong, the evening office based upon the pre-Reformation offices of vespers and compline 66/38, etc; 378/38; where **preces** occurs unmodified (142/34, etc) it is impossible to be sure which is meant although context suggests that the principal Sunday service is being referred to

prima, -e *sbst f* prime, one of the canonical hours making up the divine office of clerics; prime was said at the first hour of the day, conventionally 6 AM, whence the name is derived 200/15, et al

princeps, -ipis *n m* prince, son of the king 187/8, et al; 405/13, etc

prior, -oris *n m* prior, head of a priory, here used of the head of the Benedictine cathedral priory at Worcester 397/2, etc

priuilegium, -ii *n nt* privilege, a special right or exemption, *here in idiom* **cum privilegio ad imprimendum solum** using the privilege of acting as sole printer 539/25

probo, -are, -aui, -atum *v tr* to prove or obtain probate of, used of a will 445/14, etc

processio, -onis *n f* 1. liturgical procession

98/2; 2. civic procession in honour of a religious festival, here the feast of Corpus Christi 118/35

proclamacio, -onis *n f* announcement, here the public prior announcement of one's intention to seek to clear oneself of a charge by compurgation; such an announcement was required to allow challenges to be made at the time of compurgation 66/18, etc; 389/4

professor, -oris *n m here in idiom* **sacre theologie professor** one holding the highest degree obtainable in the divinity faculty, doctor of sacred theology, STD 67/20, etc; 349/12, etc

prophanacio, -onis *n f* act of profaning or desecrating, profanation 169/5

propheta, -e *n m* a prophet, here one of the authors of the prophetic books of the Old Testament 57/5

prouideor, -deri, -isus sum *v tr deponent form of* **prouideo** *qv*

prouincia, -e *n f* province, district of ecclesiastical administration; since the text quoted by Gerald of Wales on 395/29 was originally promulgated by the third council of Toledo, the original reference is to the districts of ecclesiastical administration in sixth-century Spain

psalmista, -e *n f* psalmist, here used of King David, believed to have been the author of the book of Psalms 348/36

psaltator, -oris *n m* a dancer; the spelling with initial 'p' is based on a confusion with or a false etymology from 'psallere,' to play a plucked-string instrument (the root from which 'psalterium' and 'psaltery' derive); the actual root is that of 'saltare,' to dance; there is insufficient context to determine the type of dance 180/32, et al

puer, -eri *n m* boy, here a choirboy 98/3

purgacio, -onis *n f* compurgation, a form of proof used in church courts whereby the accused demonstrated innocence by an oath supported by the oaths of others of

the same sex and status called compurgators; the number of supporters required was set by the court on a case by case basis 164/29, et al

purgo, -are, -aui, -atum *v tr* cleanse, clear 140/30; *also in refl sense* to clear oneself from an accusation by means of an oath or with compurgators 150/23, etc; 388/32, et al; *see* **manus** *sense 3*

Quadragesima *n indecl lit* forty, *here used idiomatically as n f* Lent, the forty days preceding Easter 501/33 (*in form* **xl.ᵉ.**), et al; *hence by ext* the first Sunday in Lent 492/6

quarterium, -ii *n nt* 1. quarter, one of the four terms into which a year is divided 110/5; 413/16, etc; 2. farthing, the fourth part of a penny 111/28, etc

quaternum, -i *n nt (from* CL 'quaterni' four each, four apiece) 1. *lit* quire, strictly a gathering of four sheets folded to produce eight leaves or sixteen pages, *hence possibly* any gathering of sheets, here a booklet formed from a single quire and used for financial records, specifically one which contains the detailed accounting on which finished accounts are based 404/10, etc; 2. quarter, one of the four terms into which a year is divided 464/22, et al

quindena, -e *n f* quindene, the fifteenth day after a holy day, here **xvⁿᵃ Pasche** the quindene of Easter, the usual day on which the Easter law term began 96/14; *see* Cheney pp 65–9, 70

Quinquagesima *n indecl lit* fifty, here the Sunday before Ash Wednesday, so-called because it is fifty days before Easter 460/33

Radingum, -i *n nt* Reading, name of a town and its abbey 189/9

ramus, -i *n m* branch, *here in idiom* **in ramis palmarum** on Palm Sunday, the Sunday before Easter 480/2, et al recessus, -us *n m lit* the act of going away, *hence* leaving, departure 187/10

recognosco, -oscere, -oui, -otum *v tr* to acknowledge, used especially in bonds to acknowledge that a given amount of money has been posted 387/8, *hence in idiom* recognoscere se debere *plus* (a sum of money) to acknowledge that one is bound (for a given amount) 387/5

rector, -oris *n m* rector, priest having responsibility for and authority over a parish and entitled to enjoy its tithes 174/40, etc; 347/11, etc

redditum, -i *n nt* act of returning or restoring 112/25

refectoria, -e *n f* refrain (of a song) 396/5

refractoria, -e *n f* refrain, 'refreit' (of a song) 396/5

refricatio, -onis *n f* reawakening of painful feelings, *here in idiom* memorie refricatio painful recollection 396/15

regalis, -e *adj see* pes *sense 2*

regardum, -i *n nt* reward, gratuity, customary payment 411/13, etc; rewardum 404/30, etc

regina, -e *n f* queen, here used of reigning monarch 121/21 and of the wife of the king 107/1; 397/18, etc; *see also* ludus *sense 2*

registrarius, -ii *n m* registrar, court official, usually a notary, who recorded proceedings before church courts and kept the various court records 161/2

regius, -a, -um *adj* of or pertaining to a king, royal 539/24

regnum, -i *n nt* 1. reign 92/17, et al; 413/39, etc; 2. kingdom, realm 409/14

reintro, -are, -aui, -atum *v tr* to reenter, to take possession again of land from a defaulting lessee 413/24

religio, -onis *n f* religious practice, devotion, Christian devotion 57/6

religiosus, -i *sbst m* member of a religious community, eg, a monk or canon regular, a religious 395/28 (*the apparent occurrence of the adj on 395/26 is a scribal error for*

a form of irreligiosus, -a, -um *qv*)

renouo, -are, -aui, -atum *v tr* to renew, resume, repeat, *hence as a legal idiom* to carry or hold over (eg, court proceedings), used of a judge 183/32, etc

reparo, -are, -aui, -atum *v tr* to mend, repair, fix 412/40, et al

requisicio, -onis *n f* request 171/20

residuacio, -onis *n f* a recurrent illness or fever, *here used fig* 349/17

respectiue *adv* respectively 389/24

reuellum, -i *n nt see* magister *sense 3*

rewardum, -i *n nt see* regardum

rex, regis *n m* 1. king, reigning monarch 189/12, etc; 372/9, etc; 2. title of an OT book Regum Liber one of the four Vulgate books of Kings; these are usually divided in English Bibles into two books of Samuel and two books of Kings; the specific reference here is to 2 Samuel 442/8m; *see also* ludus *sense 2*

rogacio, -onis *n f lit* the act of asking, here Rogation Sunday, the Sunday before Pentecost 471/28; *see also* dies *sense 6*

sabbatum, -i *n nt* sabbath, here Sunday, conceived of as a Christian sabbath to which all OT sabbatarian regulations apply 390/23

Sabrina, -e *n f* Severn, name of a river 394/10, et al

sacerdos, -otis *n m* priest, a member of the second of the three major orders of clergy, also referred to as 'presbyter,' the other two being deacon, 'diaconus,' and bishop, 'episcopus' 98/1; 395/29, etc

sacerdotalis, -e *adj* of or pertaining to a priest, priestly 349/2; *nt pl as sbst* priestly vestments 396/8

salio, -ire, -ii, -tum *v intr lit* to leap, *here by ext* (*and possibly influenced by its compound* salto *qv*) to dance 379/6

saltor, -oris *n m lit* one who leaps, *here by attraction to the sense of* saltator *qv*, dancer 378/9

saluator, -oris, *n m* saviour, one who saves, here always used in reference to Jesus 98/12, etc

salus, -utis *n f in* CL, health, often used in conventional good wishes in epistolary salutations; in Christian usage, salvation; here used in salutations in a play upon both senses 98/11, et al; 349/15, etc

sanctus, -a, -um *adj* holy or blessed, used of qualities 57/18, institutions 99/34; 396/1, or persons 200/19, et al; 404/18, etc; *m pl as sbst* holy ones, saints 395/22, etc; *see also* **dies** *senses 5, 6,* **festum** *sense 2*

sanguis, -inis *n m* blood; *see* **causa** *sense 2,* **minucio**

scandalum, -i *n nt* scandal, discredit 98/27, et al; 349/3, etc

schedula, -e *n f* 1. *lit* schedule, especially a schedule of penitential forms to be imposed on those guilty of canonical offences 71/35?, 184/36, 185/23, 186/7[1], 186/26; 369/17; 2. *by ext of sense 1* the form, formula, or form of words, contained therein or a copy thereof 71/35?, 71/36, 185/24, 186/7[2], 186/27; *see also* **certificarium, forma; cedula** 167/34; **scedula** 361/3, 390/32 (*both in sense 2*)

scituatus, -a, -um *adj see* **situatus, -a, -um**

scolaris, -e *sbst m* scholar, student 411/35

Scotia, -e *n f* Scotland 94/7; 451/25, etc

septimana, -e *n f* week, *here in idiom* **dies solis ultimus ad septimanam** *lit,* Sunday last by a week, *hence* Sunday a week ago, Sunday of last week 174/10

sericus, -a, -um *adj* silken; *see* **pannus**

sermo, -onis *n m* sermon 350/4

serua, -e *n f* (female) servant, maid servant 170/33, etc

seruiens, -ntis *sbst m* 1. servant 404/8, etc; 2. *in idiom* **seruiens ad clauam** serjeant-at-mace, a royal officer 118/34

seruitia, -e *n f* service; *see* **diuinus** *sense 3*

seruus, -i *n m* (male) servant 72/30; **seruius** 150/18m; **seruuus** 174/30

sessio, -onis *n f* session, sitting (of a court),

here in pl idiom sessions, ie, sittings of the court of quarter sessions 386/42m

set *conj for* **sed** *qv*

sigillo, -are, -aui, -atum *v tr* to seal, affix a seal to 350/11, etc

sigillum, -i *n nt* seal; *see* **causa** *sense 3*

signum, -i *n nt* sign, here the personal sign used by an illiterate person instead of a signature 371/36

sinodus, -i *n m* synod, a local council, here specifically a diocesan council made up of the bishop and other clergy, meeting to discuss and decide issues of doctrine and conduct 396/14

situatus, -a, -um *adj* located, situated 412/15, et al; **scituatus** 451/27

solem(p)nis, -e *adj* 1. solemn, ceremonious, partaking of religious rites: **dies solempnes** holy days 348/12; **solempne festum** holy festival 349/19; *hence n pl as sbst* solemn religious service, often specifically a high mass 99/32; **diuinorum solemnia** 71/24 probably refers to the two main Sunday services of morning and evening prayer; 2. formal 98/26?; 3. customary, traditional 98/26? (*for senses 2 and 3 cp the quotation from Martial under* OLD **sollennis** 2)

solempnitas, -atis *n f* solemn, celebration, religious festival 395/22, et al

solidus, -i *n m* shilling, one-twentieth of a pound 412/33

solomodo *adv for* **solummodo** *qv*

specifico, -are, -aui, -atum *v tr* to specify, to make a detailed list of 152/18, et al

spiritualis, -e *adj* spiritual; *nt pl as sbst* **spiritualia** spiritualities, the rights, revenues, and powers of a bishop which were considered to belong exclusively to his spiritual authority and position; where necessary a bishop might delegate part of the responsibility for his spiritualities to a vicar general 71/21; *see also* **uicarius** *sense 3*

sporta, -e *n f lit* basket, hamper, but here clearly something much larger, apparently a pallet or litter made of basketwork in or on which a crippled person could be carried about 200/16, et al

sterlingi, -orum *n m (found in coll pl)* sterling, used of currency 412/33

subditus, -a, -um *adj* under the authority of, subject to (some person or authority) 70/19, 71/26; *m as sbst* a subject (eg, of a king or bishop) 349/32, etc

submissio, -onis *n f* submission, part of the process whereby an accused person in a church court first confesses to, and then submits to the sentence of, a judge; here the part apparently stands for the whole process 383/35

submitto, -ittere, -isi, -issum *v tr here in refl sense* to submit oneself (to the judgment or sentence of a court), used of defendants pleading guilty in a church court 68/26, etc; 378/1, etc

superuenio, -enire, -eni, -entum *v tr* to come in from outside, visit 411/14

supraiuratus, -a, -um *pp* having been sworn before 200/7, et al

surrogatus, -i *n m* surrogate, a judge in the church courts who acts as a deputy to a bishop, archdeacon, or other ecclesiastic; it was customary in many dioceses to appoint permanent surrogates who were legally trained to preside over the bishop's or archdeacon's court 167/13, etc; 390/28

suspendo, -dere, -di -sum *v tr* 1. to suspend a cleric from his office or revenues for a limited time 383/34; 2. to suspend a lay person from reception of the sacraments for a limited time 381/27, et al

suspensio, -onis *n f* 1. suspension of a cleric from his office and revenues for a limited time 383/36m, et al *(in form* **suspencio**); 2. suspension of a lay person from reception of the sacraments for a limited time 68/22m, etc

taberna, -e *n f lit* a shop, but usually in AL a tavern, alehouse, inn 348/37

taxillus, -i *n m (from* CL 'talus,' *knucklebone,*

plus diminutive suffix) a small die or playing piece in the shape of a die, *here in idiom* **ludere ad taxillos**, to play at 'taxilli,' hence to game or gamble with dice or similar objects 348/5

templum, -i *n nt* temple, here a Christian church, with reference to the NT episode of the cleansing of the Temple in Jerusalem (Mt 21.12–16 and parallels) 57/8

tempus, -oris *n nt* 1. time, occasion 100/3, etc; 347/20, etc: *in this sense often found with gen of specification defining the nature of the occasion*; 2. period of time 200/20: *here often in idiom* **tempus (huius) compoti**, *see* **compotus**; 3. *in various idioms: in attr phr* **qui pro tempore fuerint** for the time being 412/32–3, et al; **tunc temporis** then, at that time 379/6

tenementum, -i *n nt* 1. building 412/38, et al; 2. tenement, freehold interest other than in land 387/10

teneo, -ere, -ui, -tum *v tr* to hold 1. to hold one's body or limbs in a certain way *(with predicative modifiers)* 200/28; 2. to hold a meeting or event 347/16; 3. to hold property 412/28; 4. to have an obligation (to do something), have (to do something) 57/15, etc; 5. *in pass plus* 'pro' to be held or regarded as (something) 181/17

terminus, -i *n m* 1. a set date fixed for some purpose 57/31; 412/33; 2. term, a set period of time, eg, that for which a lease runs 412/30, 412/41, 413/1, 413/17, 413/30; 3. term, an interest acquired in land by virtue, and for the set time period, of a lease 413/3, 413/20

testifico, -are, -aui, -atum *v tr active form of deponent* **testificor** *qv*

theatralis, -e *adj see* **ludus** *sense 4*

theologia, -e *n f* theology, theological study, divinity; *see* **professor**

thesaurarius, -ii *n m* treasurer, here the financial officer of a cathedral chapter 97/41

Toletanus, -a, -um *adj* of or pertaining to Toledo, a city in Spain 395/24

tornus, -i *n m* tourn, here a regular series of visits made by a prior of the manors and dependent houses of the priory 397/22, etc

torticium, -ii *n nt* torch or possibly processional candle 404/22

Trinitas, -atis *n f* Trinity; *see* **dies** *sense 6*

tumulus, -i *n m* in CL a burial mound, here a tomb or tomb-shrine within a church building 200/13, etc

turpiloquium, -ii *n nt* rude, shameful, or crude speech, bad language 57/8

uaco, -are, -aui, -atum *v intr* 1. to give one's time to, devote oneself to (*with dat*) 395/23; 2. (of statutes, etc) to be void 424/12m

uastum, -i *n nt* waste, any action taken by a tenant of freehold property which tends to reduce its value for the owner or the owner's heirs 404/22

uespera, -e *n f* vespers, one of the canonical hours making up the divine office of clerics; despite its name, also the L word for evening, vespers was usually said before dark, in the late afternoon or early evening 98/2

uespertinus, -a, -um *adj* of or pertaining to evening; *see* **oracio, prex**

uestis, -is *n f* clothing, *here in idiom* **consuete uestes** customary clothing, that is, the clothing usually required of penitents, a white linen robe 369/27, etc

uestitus, -us *n m* clothing, *here in idiom* **usualis uestitus (suus)** (their) usual clothing, that is, the clothing usually required of penitents, a white linen robe 140/34, etc

uexilla, -e *n f* banner carried in liturgical processions 340/n 97

uia, -e *n f* way, *here in idiom* **uijs et modis** by ways and means, the name of a form of citation which seems to have been issued when an apparitor was unable to serve the original citation personally; the citation by ways and means apparently authorized an apparitor to deliver the citation by whatever way seemed appropriate 69/2, etc; 369/25, etc

uicarius, -ii *n m* vicar 1. one who acts as a deputy for a rector who cannot discharge his duties in a parish 167/34, etc; 348/28, etc; *also in idiom* **perpetuus uicarius** perpetual vicar, ie, one appointed as a vicar for life 200/6; 2. assistant or deputy for a member of a cathedral chapter, often in carrying out choir duties 200/13; 3. *in idiom* **uicarius generalis (in spiritualibus)** vicar general (for spiritualities), an official appointed by a bishop to act as his deputy in all matters pertaining to the spiritualities of the diocese 66/22, etc; 388/1–2, et al; *in form* **uicario &c** 452/40; *see also* **spiritualis**

uicecomes, -itis *n m* sheriff, an officer of the Crown with various responsibilities within a given county 404/21

uicis (*gen*) *n f* (*nom sg is lacking*) 1. occasion, time 451/28; *in various idioms*: **ad diuersas uices** on various occasions 399/24, etc; **per uices** on occasion 397/33, et al; **trina uice** three times 64/5, etc; 2. part or function filled by a person (in rotation is implied), *hence in idiom* **uices gerens** one filling another's role, a deputy 98/10–11, et al; 348/28; **uices gerens spiritualiter** one filling another's role in a spiritual way or a way pertaining to spiritual duties, spiritual deputy, here referring to one acting for a priest 348/34

uictualia, -ium *sbst nt* victuals, necessary supplies, especially foodstuffs 188/39

uicus, -i *n m* street 98/35, et al

uidillator, -oris *n m lit* one who plays upon a fiddle; *by ext* possibly a general term for one who plays upon a bowed, as opposed to a plucked-string, instrument 187/7; **uidulator** 372/8, et al

uielator, -oris *n m* one who plays upon a fiddle, fiddler 189/13; *see also* **uidillator**

uigil, -ilis *n m* watchman or wait; here there is insufficient context to determine which sense is primary, and in fact one need not preclude the other 189/8

uigilia, -e *n f* eve of a festival or saint's day 347/17

uilipensus, -a, -um *adj* worthless, of no value 99/24

uilla, -e *n f* town 399/27, etc

uirgo, -inis *n f* virgin; *see* **festum** *sense 2*

uis, uis *n f* power, strength, ability, *here in idiom* **in uim iuramenti** (**sui**) by virtue of (his or her) oath 169/14–15, etc; 378/39, etc

uituperium, -ii *n nt* censure, scorn, vituperation 99/23; 349/3

wafferarius, -ii *n m* waferer, *lit* one who makes wafers. Waferers and 'menestralli' are sometimes mentioned in close association, as here. It is not clear whether they ought to be classified with minstrels, either in that word's general sense of 'servant' or more specifically as a kind of entertainer; *see* pp 291–2 (endnote to Bodl.: MS Lat. hist. d. 1(R) mb 3d) 189/15

warantizo, -are, -aui, -atum *v tr* to warrant or guarantee something to someone (ie, their possession of it) 413/30

Waruicum, -i *n nt* Warwick, name of an earldom and duchy 397/1, etc

Wia, -e *n f* Wye, name of a river 184/33m

Wigornia, -e *n f* Worcester, name of a town, county, and diocese 396/3, etc; **Wygornia** 349/11, etc

ymmo *particle for* **immo** *qv*

ymus, -a, -um *adj for* **imus** *qv*

ystrio, -onis *n m see* **histrio**

ystrionatus, -us *n m* the state of being an entertainer 99/29; *see also* **histrio**

English Glossary

WILLIAM COOKE / ANNE QUICK

abbetment *n* abetting, encouragement; **abbetments** *pl* 90/17; **abbetements** 92/1

abilitie *n* 1. wealth, means 440/34; **habilitie** 441/12, 442/15; in some of these occurrences the meaning may shade into 2. capacity, faculty; **abilitie** 435/18

aboutes *prep* about 75/25

abrogatt *pp* abrogated, cancelled 118/1

accomplites *n pl* accomplices 82/20, etc

accompt *n* account 120/30, 120/33; **accompte** 402/10, etc; **accoumpte** 437/17; **accomptes** *pl* 403/25

accoumpted *pp* taken into account, bothered about 441/20

acknowledinge *prp error for* acknowledging 83/29

a cownt *n* account 444/1, etc

activety *see* **feates of activety**

adiugged *pp* adjudged 121/8

admitted *see* **admyt**

admyracion *n* wonder 420/29

admyt *v* 1. accept, receive (into a certain body, as of a certain rank) 123/25; **admytted** *pp* 415/9, etc; 2. permit; **admitted** *pp* 387/15

advantage of excepcion *legal phr* the right to take exception; the respondent to a bill of complaint uses the phrase to mean that he reserves the right to challenge statements and allegations made in the bill 79/36; **advantages of exception** *pl* 86/15, 90/7; **advauntages of exception** 89/18

aell *see* **ale**

afore *adv* before 402/31, 415/22; **afor** 115/14

against *prep* in preparation for 421/33; **agenst** 439/1; **a yenst** 520/15

agon *adv* ago 131/3

agood *art and adj* a good 138/2

agre *v* agree 123/32, 123/33; **agred** *pp* 119/28, 120/11; **agreid** 385/25, 385/29

aill *see* **ale**

alderman *n* in most English cities and boroughs, a member of the governing corporation; in Worcester the word refers to one of two civic officials concerned chiefly with economic regulation; **aldermans** *poss* 191/4, etc; **aldermen** *pl* 117/10, etc; **aldremen** 118/12, 415/33

ale *n* a festival or gathering at which ale was drunk 463/27, etc; **ales** *pl* 417/18; **alys** 416/21m; **church ale** *n comp* ale held at or under the auspices of a church 358/24, etc; **church aell** 360/6; **churche ale** 462/38, etc; **chwrche ale** 391/8, etc; **churchales** *pl* 351/23; **church-ales** 351/7, 581/19; **church alis** 416/23; **churche ales** 521/20; **geve aill** *n phr* give-ale: a public ale and/or amusement put on to raise funds 118/15, 118/21; **Whittson-ale** Whitsun ale, ale held at Whitsuntide 367/7

ale taster *n comp* ale-conner, an officer appointed to examine or try the ale sold in his district; **ale tasters** *pl* 417/13

alhaland *n comp poss* All Hallows', All Saints' 522/4

allewey *see* **alwey**

alsaulte *v* assault 95/24

alwey *adv* always 402/29; **allewey** 415/17

alys *see* **ale**

ambiguitie *n* uncertainty 538/17

amend *v* repair 533/20; **amended** *pp* 533/26, 533/40

amner *n* almoner, an official distributor of the alms of another (a functionary in a religious institution or in the household of a person of rank) 437/3

amonges *prep* amongst 507/37, etc; **amongest** 537/12

ane *art* an 81/27, 81/34

angell *n* angel, an English gold coin, valued by 1575 at 10s; **angells** *pl* 426/24

annexted *pp* annexed, appended 117/21; **anyxste** 444/19

annoied *pp* affected in a way which interferes with its proper action 60/17

answered *pp* answered for, accounted for 446/13

anuyte *n* annuity, yearly grant, allowance 120/6; **anuytes** *pl* 120/16, etc

anyxste *see* **annexted**

apertenaunce *see* **appertenaunce**

a perythe *v pr 3 sg* appeareth, appears 444/18

apon *prep* upon 460/35, etc; **a pon** 460/8, etc

apottell *see* **pottell**

apoynt *v* appoint, decide; **apoynting** *vb n* 448/1; **a poyntid** *pp* 423/7

apparaunt *adj* apparent 375/40, 436/37, etc

apparitor *n* officer of the ecclesiastical courts with special responsibility for delivering to accused persons citations to appear in court 384/28

appertenaunce *n* appurtenance, thing belonging (to something); **apertenaunce** 406/15; **appertenaunces** *pl* 532/11, etc; **thappertenaunces** *art and n pl* 410/17

apperteygnyth *v pr 3 sg* is proper, is suitable 441/13 [*OED* Appertain *v* 3, 4]

appeyred *pp* damaged, deteriorated 121/5

appointement *n* order, direction 148/9, etc; **appointment** 148/5, etc; **appoynement** 149/21; **appoyntmentt** 120/26

apprentiswod *n* apprenticehood, apprenticeship 415/19

are *n* grace, favour 396/11 [*OED* Ore¹, *MED* or(e *n* (2)]

aright *art and adj* a right, ie, a true 376/38

armes *n pl* 1. heraldic insignia; *in phr* **her maiesties armes** the queen's coat of arms 425/19; **the queenes armes** 425/31; **officers of armes** *pl* heralds and their assistants, who regulated the use of coats of arms 411/6; 2. *in phr* **seriauntes at(t) armes** *see* **seriant**

armiger *n* one entitled to bear heraldic arms 452/11

a rowe *adv* a-row, in a row 435/7

arst *see* **earste**

article *n* 1. a distinct charge or count in an accusation or indictment; **articles** *pl* 144/10; 2. a separate clause or provision of a statute, enactment, or agreement 88/24; **articles** *pl* 401/33, etc; *in phr* **the vi. articles** 417/38, 419/4; *see* pp 591–2 (endnote to BL: Harley 425 ff 69–70); **the six articles** 421/22; **the sixe articles** 419/12–13

asseses *n pl* assessments 427/7 [*OED* Assess(e, *sb*]

assistance *n coll* a body of helpers 394/24; **assistances** *pl* 394/28 [*OED* Assistance 4]

assuer *v* assure 433/25, 435/26

attempt *n* warlike enterprise; attack, assault; **attemptes** *pl* 439/19

atturned *pp in phr* **atturned tenant** agreed formally to be the tenant of (someone into whose possession an estate has passed) 80/5 [*OED* Attorn *v*]

auaunce *v* advance 539/17

auctoryte *n* authority 119/31

auctoryzed *pp* authorized 586/34

auez *see* **vous auez**

aunsweare *v* answer 77/1; **aunswered** *pa 3 sg* 375/17

aunswere *n* answer, response 79/33, 375/14, etc; **aunswer** 79/38

avauntage *n* advantage 416/26
avoyded *pp* invalidated, quashed 88/27, 92/9
awne *adj* own 188/20
awnswer *n* answer 84/22
a yenst *see* **against**

bagge *see* **clerke**
bailieffes, bailiff(es) *see* **baylyff**
bailly *n* bailiff (*see* **baylyff** 1.) 402/8, etc;
　baillie 416/25, etc; **bayly** 145/23; **baillies**
　pl 416/8, etc; **balies** 465/6; **balis** 488/36;
　ballies 415/33, 416/4; **balyes** 464/34,
　465/11; **balys** 460/17, etc; **bayles** 460/13,
　etc; **baylis** 486/21; **baylys** 486/25, etc; **hie**
　baylie *n phr* the senior of the two
　Worcester city bailiffs 443/3; **low baylie** *n*
　phr the junior of the two Worcester city
　bailiffs 425/5; **lowe bailie** 443/3–4
baiting *see* **bull baiting**
balde *adj* bold 439/17
baliffes *see* **baylyff**
ballet *n* ballad, a popular song, especially one
　celebrating or scurrilously attacking
　persons or institutions 419/13, 421/23;
　ballettes *pl* 453/28m, 453/30; **balletts**
　458/10
ballies *see* **bailly**
balliffes, balyffes *see* **baylyff**
balyes, balys *see* **bailly**
balys *n pl in phr* **balys of yerne to blow with**
　balls(?) of iron (or yarn?) to blow with: *of*
　uncertain meaning, possibly some kind of
　musical instrument 523/31; **balys of yern**
　523/31–32m
band *see* **ruffe band**
bandog *n* a dog kept tied or chained up, either
　to guard a house or on account of its
　ferocity; generally, a mastiff or blood-
　hound; **bandoges** *pl* 418/14
barbour *n* barber or barber-surgeon
　(someone who combines barbering with
　blood-letting, tooth extraction, and minor
　surgery); **barbours** *pl* 116/15
batries *n pl* batteries 89/29
battails *n pl* battles 126/29

bayles, baylie, baylis, bayly(s) *see* **bailly**
baylyff *n* 1. bailiff, generally a municipal
　officer; in Bewdley, the bailiff was one of
　the two governing officers of the city; in
　Worcester, the two bailiffs were the chief
　executive officers of the city; in Hereford,
　they were subordinate to the mayor;
　baylief 149/20, 149/30; **bayliffe** 299/9,
　299/10; **bailieffes** *poss* 148/15, etc; **baylifes**
　363/35; **bayliffes** 367/26; **bailiffes** *pl*
　447/18; **baliffes** 509/38; **ballifes** 423/8;
　balyffes 469/9, etc; **bayliefes** 450/15;
　baylifes 501/3; **bayliffes** 420/18, 501/4m,
　etc; **baylifs** 375/36; **baylyffes** 426/4m,
　515/19, etc; **baylyffs** 447/38, 448/9; **high**
　baylyff *n phr* the senior of the two
　Worcester bailiffs 426/18m, 437/17; **highe**
　baylyff 426/17, 426/26; **lowebaylef** *n phr*
　the junior of the two Worcester bailiffs
　420/38; **lowe baylyff** 429/17; 2. steward;
　bailiff 189/29; *see also* **bailly**
beare *see* **bere**
bearebaytinge *n* form of entertainment in
　which dogs were set on a bear chained to
　a stake 355/8, 355/17
bearward *see* **berewarde**
becheching *prp error for* beseeching (?) 407/4
beedle *n* beadle, minor town official; **beedles**
　pl 190/12, etc
behoffe *n* behoof, benefit 120/7; **behove** 121/11
beholding *pp* beholden 125/19
bellman *n* someone paid to go round the
　streets of a town and make public
　announcements, to which he attracts
　attention by ringing a bell 438/17; **belman**
　116/21
ben *v pr 3 pl* are 402/9, etc
benesoun *n* benison 409/33
benevolence *n* gift or grant of money 124/33,
　450/14, 450/17
benne *pp* been 121/13
bere *n* bear, ie, performing bear; **beare** 363/9;
　beres *pl* 501/28, 527/40
bere *v in phr* **as myghty lyon bere the even**
　bear thyself even as a mighty lion 408/3

berewarde *n* bearward, keeper of a bear, who leads it about 486/33, etc; **bearward** 370/14m; **bereward** 526/31, etc; **berward** 370/14; **bearewardes** *pl* 586/31; **berewardes** 516/13

besene *pp* beseen, apparelled 115/2

beside *adv* besides, also 186/4

beynde *prep* behind 435/6

bicawes *conj* because 418/30, etc

biforn *prep* before 403/8

bine *pp* been 423/12

birdinge peece *n comp* birding piece, a gun for shooting birds 78/22

Black-fryers *n phr pl* Black Friars, the Friars Preachers or Dominicans, a mendicant order, or the church named for them 364/10; *see* p 583 (endnote to Wing: C6272 pp 97–102)

black garde *n phr* the lowest menials in the royal household, who had charge of kitchen utensils 438/9

Blake Monday *n phr* Black Monday, Easter Monday 511/32

bochours *n pl* butchers 115/33

boke *n* book 423/39; **bokes** *pl* 191/14

bold *adj in v phr* **shalbe bold with hym** shall venture (to request) of him 432/33

bollrynge *n comp* bullring, the place where bulls were baited (*see* **bull baiting**) 362/13; **bolrynge** 362/7

boltes *n pl* bolts, fetters 421/4; **bolts** 420/40

bone-setter *n comp* one who sets dislocated or broken bones 130/27

bonfyer *n* bonfire 499/1, 526/34; **bonfyur** 507/36m; **boonfyur** 507/36

boody *n* body 414/36

boordes *see* **table boordes**

boords *see* **shoppe-boords**

boote *n* avail, use 393/37; the phrase **there was no little boote to bid runne** is puzzling; had 'no' been cancelled, it might be paraphrased 'there was little use in bidding (someone) run (for help)'

boren *pp* borne, carried 431/15

bottels *n pl in phr* **gentlemen of the bottels**

gentlemen in charge of the royal wine cellar 438/8 [*MED* botel *n* (1)]

bottome *n* core around which thread, etc, is wound 135/16

bouldenethe *v pr 3 sg* emboldens 124/12

box *n* money-box; *here often* a collecting-box for a particular parish or group 498/1, etc; **boxe** 512/5; **boxes** *pl* 471/10, etc

boye *n* boy, young man; *here often with sense* servant, apprentice 373/29, etc; **boyes** *pl* 445/10

boylyng howse *n comp in phr* **officers of the boylyng howse** boilers of food (as opposed to, eg, bakers), part of the kitchen staff of the royal household 438/11

brauies *n pl* error (*anticipating* **brauely** *in the same line*) for armies, *or syncopated form of* braveries, ie, things to be exhibited *or* (band of) gallants, *or nonce-form combining* brave *and* armies 127/3 [*OED* Brave *a sb int* B 1; Bravery 3d, 5]

breache *n* failure to fulfil agreements 441/15

bredyth *n* breadth 445/29, 445/30; **bredeth** 445/28

breeches *n pl* short trousers which varied in shape and length in the 16th and 17th centuries, but were nearly always worn over stockings and never came much below the knee 131/21(2); **breches** 447/10

breecht *v pa 3 pl* whipped 377/21

brennyng *prp* burning 416/4; **brennynge** 403/8

bretherne *n pl* brethren 1. fellow members of the governing corporation of the town 117/16, etc; **breethern** 424/33, etc; **brethen** (*error for* brethren?) 448/15; **brethern** 118/12, etc; **brethren** 123/15, etc; **brethrene** 465/6; 2. fellow members of a guild; **bretherne** 117/16, 117/18

bridgwardens *n comp pl* keepers of a bridge; until 1605, the Bewdley bridgewardens also accounted for civic receipts and expenditures; they also acted as church-wardens for the bridge chapel 299/11

brigge *n* bridge 114/1

brome *n* broom 420/6

browed *see* **on browed**

browtht *pp* brought 421/22

bruers *n pl* brewers 417/12, etc

bruge *n* bridge 462/10

buffin *n* a kind of grogram, a coarse fabric of silk, mohair, and wool, or of these mixed (often stiffened) with gum 132/30

bull baiting *n comp* the setting of dogs on a chained or tied bull; in the 16th century, bulls to be slaughtered were always baited first, in the belief that this would render the meat more wholesome; but later, and especially under the Puritans, the belief lapsed and bull-baiting was seen (and condemned) as primarily an entertainment 360/20

butt shoote *n phr* butt's length, the distance between two archery butts, ie, the length of a shooting-range, as a measure of distance 370/25

buxome *adj* indulgent, favourable 275/15

buysshopp *n* bishop 431/5, etc; **busshop** 450/25; **buishops** *poss* 450/13; **bushops** 189/29; **buysshops** 431/19, 436/5m; **buysshopps** *pl* 436/39m

bycawes *conj* because 418/24

byff *n* beef 469/4, etc

by for *prep* before 414/19, etc; **by fore** 415/17, 415/20

byne *pp* been 423/4

byng *prp* being 443/20

caled *pp* called, named 417/35, etc; **calle** *error for* called(?) 421/21

can cup *n comp* a cup made of metal 437/24

canne *v pr 3 sg* knows, has practical knowledge of 403/2

cantting *vb n* canting, speaking the special jargon of some group (eg, thieves, vagabonds) (?) 191/10

canuazed *pp* canvassed: scrutinized, investigated 373/2

capp *n* cap, a kind of headgear generally distinguished from a hat by being made of

soft material and, in this period, by having a very short brim or no brim; **cappes** *pl* 134/30, 447/12; **capps** 457/4; **square caps** *n phr pl* perhaps the soft brimless bonnets with square crowns and side-flaps (which could be turned down over the ears, or buttoned at the top) often worn by men in the early 16th century 587/36; **Iewes cap** *n phr* cap characteristically worn by Jews (perhaps like those seen in play-text illustrations of Jews, hats with high conical crowns and narrow brims) 132/32, 132/33

cappers *n pl* makers of caps 116/7, 116/31

caps *n* copse, underbrush, underwood 81/29

caralles, carawles *see* **carrall**

caranto *n* coranto, a kind of dance 133/39

cardeners *n pl* cordwainers, shoemakers, organized as a craft guild 116/30

carpettes *n pl* pieces of thick woven fabric, commonly used in the 16th and 17th centuries to cover benches and tables, including church altars 447/1, **carpetts** 457/4

carrall *n* carol, a song of a particular kind, originating in England and having set stanzas which alternate with a burden; the earliest carols, which commemorate Christmas and the lesser feasts of the Christmas season, were probably used as extra-liturgical Christmas processional hymns; later, carols were sung at other semi-religious public ceremonies; **caralles** *pl* 464/31, etc; **carawles** 478/5; **carolles** 469/27, etc; **carralles** 460/5, etc; **carralls** 481/24; **carroldes** 469/11; **carrolles** 495/8; **carrowles** 528/35 [Robbins]

carriages *n pl* acts of conveyance, carryings 286/40

carringe *vb n* carrying 454/33

castinge *vb n* 1. opening suddenly, throwing open 371/6; 2. digging out, clearing out; **castyng** 120/25

catholik *n* an adherent of the doctrines and practices of the unreformed church 420/39;

cp **papist** *and see* pp 591–2 (endnote to BL: Harley 425 ff 69–70)

cattell *n coll* 1. livestock 59/39, etc; **cattle** 352/8; 2. personal property; **cattell** 423/31

causes *n pl* cases 188/5

cawsey *n* causey, causeway; **cawseyes** *pl* 120/24, 121/5

ceacesed *pl* ceased 368/27

cedule *n* a paper appended to a document and containing explanatory or supplementary matter 117/21

celebrate *adj* celebrated, observed 538/19

cemytory *n* cemetery, burying-ground 415/43

cercuets *n pl* judicial circuits 31/21

cessith *v pr 3 sg* ceaseth, puts a stop to (something) 114/34

cesterne *n* cistern, a pond or natural depression containing water 409/38

cettie *n* city 422/26

chaf *n* rage, passion 421/24 [*OED* Chafe *sb*]

chains *see* **hanged in chains**

challenge *v* lay claim to, claim as one's due 365/38

chamber *n* 1. in Hereford, the governing body of the city; **chambour** 121/12; 2. in Worcester, applied to the two bodies (the Twenty-Four and the Forty-Eight) who made up the town council, and also to the council as a whole; **chamber** 426/15, 447/35; **chamberes** *pl* 426/34; 3. a particular session of the town council 426/17, 458/27

chamberlayne *n* 1. in Hereford, civic officials who accounted for civic receipts and expenditures; **chamberleyns** *pl* 121/9, 121/11; **chamborleyns** 121/12; 2. in Worcester, civic officers responsible for collecting the city's regular revenues and spending them on public business, a job which included supervising public works and maintaining the city's stock of house property; **chamberlayne** 426/4, etc; **chamberlaines** *pl* 447/19, 457/21; **chamberlaynes** 425/30, etc; **chamberlens**

443/23, etc; **chamburleyns** 415/33; 3. *in phr* **lord chamberlaine** lord chamberlain of the household, one of the chief officers of the royal household 540/27; **lord chamberlayne** 433/36, etc; **lorde chaumberlayn** 411/1–2

chapelens *n pl* chaplains 115/6

chapiter *n* chapter; governing body of a cathedral church or monastery 446/2; *in comp* **chapitr howse** chapter house, the room or building where the chapter met 188/23

chardeginge *prp* charging 384/29

chargeable *adj* expensive 80/3

chargies *n pl* charges, costs 438/24

chattell *n* cattle, livestock 60/18

chaumberlayn *see* **chamberlayne**

chaundler *n* chandler, maker or seller of candles; sometimes, a dealer in provisions in general; **chaundelers** *pl* 116/6; **chawnlers** 443/16

childern *n pl* children 460/17, etc; **childurn** 473/6; **chyldern** 539/11

chore *n* choir 597/4

christen *adj* Christian 439/23

church aell, church ale, church alis *see* **ale**

churchard *n comp* churchyard 81/21, etc

churche ale, chwrche ale *see* **ale**

churche hows *n comp* a building belonging to, and usually adjoining, a church, and commonly used for church ales or other parish feasts 521/4

chylders *n pl* children 124/22

cite *n* city 118/12, etc; **citte** 423/21, 423/22

citesyn *n* citizen, ie, an inhabitant of a city or town, especially one possessing civic rights or privileges; **citezen** 417/6; **citticen** 450/17; **citesens** *pl* 401/34, etc; **citesyns** 430/16, etc; **citeyzens** 465/12; **citezens** 118/18, 486/21; **cytesyns** 426/38, etc; **cytysyns** 434/12

cleane *adj of uncertain meaning; perhaps* 'innocent,' 'simple,' as those words are applied to persons deficient in sense or intelligence *or perhaps* 'utter,' 'complete' 376/26, etc

clearke *n* 1. cleric 90/37, etc; **clarke** 80/15, 89/14; **clerke** 75/10, 78/42, 480/36; **clearks** *pl* 135/26; 2. *probably* the senior clerk of a court, possibly of chancery; **clarke** 94/12; 3. *in phr* **clerk of the markett** royal officer who attends fairs and markets to keep the standard of weights and measures 438/6; **clerke of the pettie bagge** *n phr* a minor officer of the court of chancery 75/15

cloath *n attr* cloth 131/21

cloke *n* cloak; an overgarment of varying style and length, hooded or hoodless, sometimes having sleeves 124/31, 431/1, etc; **cloake** 134/15

closer *n* close, cloister 187/28

coates *see* **coote**

cockes of the game *n phr pl* fighting cocks 126/29

cockny-endes of the worlde *n phr* used in punning reference to the supposed weakness and effeminacy of Londoners/ townsmen ('cockney' bears both these meanings and can also mean a coddled, 'soft,' effeminate person); there is a further pun on 'end' ('boundary' and 'remnant,' 'fragment'), and perhaps, with humorous inversion of the claim that London is the centre of the kingdom and the provinces remote and unimportant, a pun on 'end of the world'/'ends of the earth' 134/14

cognizances *n pl* marks, emblems 275/16

colectures *n pl* collectors 120/37; **collectures** 121/7

colen *proper n* Cologne 116/20

colestaffe *see* **cowlestaffe**

colour *n* pretext, pretence 88/14; **collor** 85/6; **color** 81/36; **coulor** 419/21; **cullor** 420/10

coltstaffe *see* **cowlestaffe**

comen *adj* common 414/25, etc; **commen** 415/38; **comyn** 402/8, etc; *pl used as n* the common people; **comens** 416/25, 416/31; **comyns** 403/20

comissary *n* bishop's judicial deputy 475/41; *see* p 600 (endnote to WCL: A11 f 3v)

commons *n pl in phr* **castinge open the commons** *of uncertain meaning; perhaps refers to* breaking down fences or gates as a way of securing the status of common land or a right of way 371/6; *see* p 584 (endnote to HWRO: BA 1006/33/596 mb 1d)

common weale *n comp* commonweal, community 439/32

commorant *adj* dwelling, resident 369/3

comonalty *n* commonalty, common people (of a town) or members (of a guild) 531/8, etc; **commonalte** 118/13

company *n* a body of persons combined or incorporated for some common object, *here especially*: 1. a group of musicians, actors, or other entertainers 122/36, etc; **compani** 519/39; **companie** 129/14, etc; **compeny** 530/8; **companies** *pl* 197/7, 456/6; 2. a trade guild; **companie** 129/14, etc; **companye** 423/10; **companeis** *pl* 423/11; **companeys** 423/5; **companies** 129/13; **companis** 422/40; 3. the governing body of a town; **company** 148/6, 148/98, 148/15 (these occurrences may belong to sense 1)

complainant *n* plaintiff 79/34, etc; **complaynant** 84/18, etc

composicion *n* written agreement 117/28, 117/35; **composysyon** 117/10; **composycions** *pl* 119/38; **composycyons** 119/39

comyn *v* talk, converse 402/34 [*OED* Common *v* 6]

comyn *see* **comen**

concealement *n* in legal language, intentional suppression (of some fact) 63/28

conceite *n* conception, notion 371/21, 373/9

condescended *pp* agreed, conceded 119/28; **condescendyd** 120/11

confederacie *n* league for an unlawful or evil purpose; conspiracy 75/18; **confederaces** *pl* 85/35; **confederacies** 78/28, etc

conforme *adj* conformable 384/22

consoulting *prp* consulting 418/4

constable *n* officer of a parish or township appointed to act as keeper of the peace 74/18, etc; **cunstable** 92/36; **constabelles** *pl* 443/35, etc; **constables** 427/12, etc

constableshipp *n* the office of constable 85/7

consyons *n* conscience 117/31

contentacion *n* contentment, satisfaction 123/28

contentt *v* satisfy by making full payment 120/5

contre *n* country, region 118/15

contributory *n* person or group of persons who contribute (eg, to a common fund); **contributories** *pl* 403/25, 403/31

contributory *adj* contributing, obliged to contribute (eg, to a common fund) 402/9, etc; **contributorye** 403/2

coole staffe *see* cowlestaffe

cooper *n* maker of casks and similar vessels 368/37

coote *n* 1. coat, sometimes a sleeveless close-fitting garment coming no lower than the waist, sometimes a loose-fitting one with skirts and sleeves 462/23, etc; **coates** *pl* 132/29, 457/4; 2. *attr in comp* cote cloth a piece of cloth intended to be made into a coat; **cote clothes** *pl* 438/16

cope *n* a cape-like church vestment, open in front, reaching to the ankles, fitted with a real or vestigial hood, and often richly embroidered or otherwise ornamented; retained in cathedrals in the reformed English church to be worn by the chief ministers at the communion 447/2; **copes** *pl* 457/3

cornett *n* cornetto, a wind instrument (not to be confused with the modern cornet); **cornettes** *pl* 431/14, 432/12; **cornetts** 453/21

cornitors *n pl* players of the cornetto 450/12; *see* p 595 (endnote to SHRO: BA 9360/A–14 f 203v)

coroune *n* crown 410/19

corporall *adj in phr* corporall othes oaths ratified by touching a physical object (after the Reformation, the Bible or New Testament) 94/11

correcion *n error (?) for* correccion, ie, correction 78/36

corviser *n* shoemaker 136/23; 136/25; **corvicer** 142/37; **corvesers** *pl* 117/8

cosed *pp of uncertain meaning, perhaps* exercised by running 380/37 [*OED* Course *v* 9]

cosyn *n* cousin, kinsman 406/30

cotche *n* coach 432/1, 433/6

cotchemen *n comp pl* coachmen 437/33

cotcher *n error for* cotche, ie, coach (?) *or form of* coachee, ie, coach (?) 431/25

cote *see* coote

cotes *see* sault cotes

coulor *see* colour

countenance *n* comportment, bearing 429/34

counterfayte *adj* counterfeit, fake, pretended 586/42

cowle *n* 1. a tub or large vessel for water, etc, especially applied to one with two handles which could be borne by two men on cowlstaff; 2. such a vessel of a particular size, used to measure ale 417/12

cowlestaffe *n* 1. cowlstaff, a stout pole or staff used to carry cowls (*see* cowle) and other burdens; 2. *in phr* cary ... vpon a colestaffe to set astride a pole and carry in derision around the streets 72/19; **carried ... on a coltstaffe** 588/11; **caryed the coole staffe** 381/33–4; **putt ... vpon a cowlestaffe** 392/19; **carried vpon a cowlstaffe** 275/17

Cowleyan *adj of uncertain meaning*; perhaps in reference to Cowley, near Oxford, an area with strong morris dance associations 125/13

cownt *see* a cownt

crafte *n* fraud, trickery 586/27

crafty *adj* deceitful, fraudulent 586/29

cresset *n* an iron vessel, hung from a pole or building, containing coal, wood, etc, to be burnt for light 403/8, 416/3

Cristen *adj* Christian 114/11

cullor *see* **colour**

cunstable *see* **constable**

cuntriman *n* fellow countryman, person from the same region 370/32

cuntry *n* country, region, district 586/27

cupbord *n* cupboard, *here probably* a court cupboard or sideboard; **cupbord clothes** *n comp pl* cloths for the top of a sideboard 447/5

curate *n* incumbent, minister in charge of a parish 369/5; **curat** 392/19

cure *n* care 143/27, 406/32

cussyon *n* cushion 446/31; **cussyons** *pl* 446/29, etc; **cuyssons** 446/28

customably *adv* according to custom 538/4

customed *pp* well supplied with customers, doing a good business 372/30

cutts *n pl* ornamental slashes or indentations in the fabric of a garment, sometimes revealing fabric of another colour underneath 587/40

cytay *n* city 117/5; **cyte** 401/35, 423/20

cytesyns, cytysyns *see* **citesyn**

damaske *n* a rich silk fabric with an elaborate design woven into the texture; any fabric of wool, linen, or cotton woven in the same way was also called damask 446/36

dame *n* mistress 445/12

dar *v pr 1 sg* dare 114/19

dayle *adv* daily 118/2

decessed *pp* deceased 436/36, 437/15

deckydd *pp* decked, adorned 430/18; **deckyd** 430/26; **dect** 539/11

dedicacion *n in comp* **dedicacion day** the anniversary of the dedication of a church, observed as a festival 461/35, etc; **dedicacion wycke** the octave of such a festival 503/34

default *n* fault 59/29, etc

defaute *n* default 402/7, etc; **defaut** 403/14; **defawte** 414/24; **defautes** *pl* 417/14

defeature *n* defeat (as a candidate) 124/17

defy'd *pp* renounced, rejected 364/16

delyured *pp* delivered, handed over 443/21

demene *v* 1. manage, govern; 417/8; **demeaned** *pp* 403/32; 2. charge, assess; **demened** 402/36; **demeanid** 417/4 [OED Demean *v*¹ 3, 4, 5; MED demeinen *v* 1, 3, 4]

demised *pp* transferred, conveyed (of real property) 532/7, etc

demurer *n* demurrer 83/26, 83/36

depravinge *vb n* vilifying, defaming 79/42

depute *n* deputy 403/13, etc

deserte *n* good deed, benefit 439/33; **desertes** *pl* 432/22

desessed *pp* deceased 444/31

despite *n in phr* **in despite of** in spite of 175/2

devoure *n in v phr* **put theym silf in devoure** make an attempt, do what they can 407/34

dewke *n* duke 523/1, 530/9; **dewkes** *poss* 459/18

dhin *pron poss* thine 396/11

di *abbrev for* L dimidium, *used with the meaning of* E a half 445/29

diet *n and adj* daily provsion of food; board 454/31; **diett** 438/35

dilectable *adj* delectable, delightful 430/20

diligence *n in v phr* **done their diligence** exerted themselves, done their utmost 353/19, 353/40

dinner *see* **dyner**

disfraunchesing *vb n* being disfranchised, being deprived of citizenship (here, in a town) and its privileges 416/2

disgysse *v* masquerade 416/26; **disgised** *pp* disguised: *here probably* dressed in clothing inappropriate to one's station and calling 389/35; *see* p 587 (endnote to HRO: box 24, vol 90 f [279v])

dishabiting *vb n* being deprived of its inhabitants 6/32

disyeased *ppl adj* diseased, sick 511/29, 514/16; **disyeasid** 511/22

doctours *n pl* learned men 116/25

doen *see* **doone**

dole *n* grief, lamentation 132/9

dooble *adv in phr* **double gylte** twice-gilt 429/34

doone *pp* done 374/22, 429/20, etc; **doon** 369/2, 432/40; **doen** 76/29, 77/41

dooth *v pr 3 sg* doth, does 115/13; **doothe** 441/27; **dotth** 123/33

doozen *n* dozen 134/22

dowblet *n* doublet, in the 16th century, generally a man's garment for the upper body, always close-fitting but varying in cut, sometimes having skirts, always having sleeves (though these were sometimes detachable), worn over the shirt (or waistcoat if present) 479/3; **dowbelet** 479/2m; **doublettes** *pl* 426/9

dowke *n* duke 504/8

dowre *n* dower, dowry 408/36

drad *adj* dread 414/10

draper *n* maker of or dealer in cloth 422/26, 423/32; **drapers** *pl* 116/24

drapinge *vb n* weaving or making into cloth 144/37; **draping** 303/8

dressed *pp* made ready 425/35m

drifat *n* dry vat, a cask or barrel to contain dry things; **drifats** *pl* 374/27; **dryfats** 375/31 [*OED* Fat *sb*¹ 3]

drum-minor *n phr* second drummer 128/33–4

dryve *v* draw, propel; **dryven** 423/18; **dryvyng** *vb n* 423/18m

duc *n* duke 410/38

duety *n* duty 143/26; *in pl in v phr* **doon their duties** expressed deference or respect 432/40

dyner *n* the main meal of the day, eaten, in the 16th and 17th centuries, in the middle of the day 466/34, etc; **dinner** 139/15, 392/35; **dynar** 473/13; **dynner** 74/25, etc

dyspence *n* expenditure 120/31 [*OED* Dispense *sb*¹ 1]

dyspend *v* spend 120/23; **dyspended** *pp* 121/4 [*OED* Dispend *v*]

dysport *n* recreation 188/12

dyvert *v* turn aside out of one's course, digress 439/13

earste *adv* formerly, before 441/22; **arst** 406/25

ech 1. *pron* each 373/36; 2. *adj* every 372/36; **eche** 373/17

effecte *n* purport, tenor 430/21, etc

effectuall *adj* (of a complaint) one which is strictly valid in law 88/25, 92/8

egally *adv* equally 415/29, etc; **egallye** 414/26

egging *vb n* incitement, urging on 365/4

Egipcians *n pl* gypsies 586/42; **Egipcyans** 586/42

eieccion *n* ejection 534/25

enbrace *v* incline (?) 407/6

enchaced *pp in phr* **gilte enchaced plate** silver plate, gilded and engraved, or silver plate, engraved, with the engraved designs gilded 432/26

encreaced *pp* increased 123/4

encrese *n* increase, profit 402/22; **encresse** 415/1

endauour *n* endeavour 385/2

endewed *v pa 3 pl* endowed 439/30

enformant *n* an officer of the court making a formal accusation 452/11

enquest(es) *see* **inqueste**

ensuen *v* ensue, follow 406/8

entayle *n* secured inheritance 367/6

entended *pp* proposed, planned out 440/22

entent *n* intention 74/30, 114/29, etc; **thentent** *art and n* 95/5; **to thentent** *prep phr* with the intention 77/41, 95/39; **to thentente** 118/16–17

enterlude *n* light or humorous play; **enterludes** *pl* 188/11, 351/17, etc; **interludes** 581/2; **enterlude players** *n phr pl* 452/2

enterteyne *v* make hospitable provision for (the wants of a guest) 75/2; **enterteyned** *pa 3 sg* 432/25

entre *n* 1. entrance into a place; doorway 115/1, 115/17; **entryes** *pl* 532/20; 2. entrance, admission into a group 402/36, 417/5; **entree** 402/33

enyoie *v* enjoy 402/24; **enyoye** 415/3; **enyoyed** *pa 3 pl* 120/1

equitie *n* justice administered according to fairness as contrasted with the strictly formulated rules of common law; certain courts, such as the court of Star Chamber, were established with the intention of administering equity rather than common law 80/12

er *v pr 3 pl* are 188/21

es *v pr 3 sg* is 187/25, etc

esquyer *n* esquire, a title of rank, usually appended to a man's name, originally given to those who were gentry but not knights 119/18, etc; **esquier** 137/40; **esquire** 421/42, 534/40; **esquyre** 124/5; **esquiers** *pl* 126/15

estatte *n* estate, ie, state, condition 118/3

Ester *n and adj* Easter 191/26, 474/34, etc

euery *adj* each (of) 539/34, etc; **everie** 137/26; **every** 120/2, etc

even *see* **bere** *v*

evening prayer *n phr* the afternoon or evening service of public worship of the Church of England 172/24–5, etc; **euening prayer** 180/23, etc; **eueninge praier** 165/21, etc; **evening praier** 65/4, etc; **eveninge praier** 67/15, etc; **eveninge prayer** 142/1, etc; **evenyng prayer** 63/12; **evening prayers** *pl with same sense as sg* 386/25; **eveninge prayers** 382/28; *cp* LG oracio

examynat *n* examinate, a person under examination, either as witness or as accused person 95/20, etc; **examinat** 95/13, 95/15, **examynatt** 95/15

excepcion *see* **advantage of excepcion**

expence *n* expending, outpouring (of resources, etc) 442/13

exsekutrix *n* executrix 445/7

faced *pp* (of a garment) trimmed, having certain portions covered with another material 426/8, 429/2

fachion *see* **fauchion**

factor *n* agent 175/3

fader *n* father 188/5, etc; **ffader** 408/32

faier *n* fair 191/31, 191/31m

faier *adj* fair 426/11, etc

falchion *see* **fauchion**

falne *pp* fallen 136/8

farme *n in v phr* **to farme lett** to let at a fixed rent 532/8; **to farme letten** *pp phr* 532/7

fat *pp* obtained (?) 473/10 [*OED* Fet *v* 3, Fetch *v* 5]

fauchion *n* falchion, broad, curved sword 81/17, etc; **fachion** 95/16; **falchion** 95/14, 95/16; **ffauchion** 91/5, etc; **ffawchin** 77/40; **ffawchyn** 78/23; **fouchion** 84/37

fayning *prp* feigning 586/28

fealte *pp* felt 440/3

feates of activety *n phr pl* shows of athletic ability 394/26

fencers *n pl* professional swordsmen, fencers who fence in public shows 586/31

fer *adv* for 406/13

feste *n* 1. feast (as religious anniversary) 401/36; **ffest** 414/9; 2. public entertainment of some kind; **festes** *pl* 188/3

fested *pp* feasted 435/25m

fetching *vb n* performing 130/36

ffacte *n* deed 419/34; **ffactes** 120/32

ffader *see* **fader**

ffauchion, ffawchin, ffawchyn *see* **fauchion**

ffawne *v in phr* **ffawne ffreendshipp** make an ingratiating pretence of friendship 418/36 [*OED* Fawn *v*[1] 3, Fain *v* 1 b, Feign *v* 8; there appears to be some blending of these meanings]

ffayne *adj* obliged by circumstances 421/3

ffeared *pp* frightened, scared 421/10

ffest *see* **feste**

ffieft *adj* fifth 92/31

fflacchers *n pl* fletchers, makers or sellers of arrows 116/14

ffleme *n* stream, river 116/29 [*OED* Fleam *sb*[2] 1]

ffootemen *see* **footemen**

fforrest bill *see* **forrest bill**

ffraunchis *n* franchise, the district over which the privilege of a corporation extends 414/7

ffree *adj* admitted to the privileges of a guild or city 415/23

ffrontique *adj* frantic, ragingly or violently mad 421/18

ffynd *see* **fynde**

fifte *adj* fifth 74/17, 74/22

flawne *n* some kind of sweet cake or tart, usually flat; sometimes mentioned together with custards and cheesecakes 393/8, 393/10 [*OED* Flawn; *OED Supplement* Flan]

flea *v* flay 125/26

focalia *L sbst pl used here as E n pl; lit* things of the hearth; *here* opposed to **sacra**, sacred things; *hence*, domestic utensils as opposed to objects used in religious observance 457/2

foole *n* 1. one born or become deficient in reason or intellect; a simpleton; 2. one who professionally conterfeits folly for the entertainment of others; a jester, clown; since 'natural' or born fools were often employed as fools of the second kind in great households, it is often difficult (as it is here) to distinguish between the two meanings 376/26, etc

foormes *n pl* forms, benches 454/33

foorth *adv* forward (ie, into the street) 448/1

footemen *n pl* servants on foot attending a rider 434/12; **ffootemen** 437/30

forbede *v pr 1 pl* forbid 188/11; **forbedyng** *prp* 188/1

foreplotted *pp* contrived beforehand 89/34

foreyn *n* stranger, outsider; someone not a resident 417/15 [*OED* Foreign B 1 b]

forfaycture *n* forfeiture 423/9

forfett *v* forfeit 414/36; **forfettin** *vb n* 423/23

formal *adj* valid in form only 82/40

forrest bill *n comp* a tool made up of a curved blade mounted on a long straight handle, used for lopping undergrowth and overgrowth in forests 76/32; **fforrest bill** 76/21–2; **fforrest bylles** *pl* 136/35; *cp* **hedge-bill**

forseyn *pp* foreseen, provided for beforehand 402/29

forte *prep comp* for to, ie, to 408/36

fouchion *see* **fauchion**

fourme *n* form, ie, guise, outward appearance 422/9

foyle *n* fencer's foil, a kind of light sword, with a blunt edge and a button on the point 134/19

foynd *see* **fynde**

foyson *n* foison, abundance 408/21

frended *pp* joined in friendship 440/37

freres *n attr perhaps* frieze, a woollen cloth with a heavy nap on one side 446/30, 447/9

frerez *n pl* friars 114/3

fronts *n pl* frontals, pieces of fabric, often richly embroidered or otherwise decorated, and used to cover the front of an altar, being either stretched on a frame or hung with rings from a rod and weighted 457/4

fructifull *adj* fruitful, beneficial 410/35

fryndes *n pl* friends 520/15

furnace *n* boiler, cauldron 370/35

furnishe keeper *n comp of uncertain meaning, perhaps* keeper of a furnace (ie, a smelting furnace, kiln, the fireplace of a forge, etc) 160/39 [*OED* Furnace *sb*, MED furnaise]

furnyture *n* furnishing, equipping 442/2

furthewith *adv* forthwith, immediately 425/29

fustian *n attr* a fabric of cotton and flax, or flax mixed with wool, and having a silky finish; used as a substitute for velvet, and very popular 477/20

fylde *n* field 432/38; **fyldes** *pl* 434/8

fynde *v* provide, supply 403/8; **ffynd** 416/3; **foynd ... in** *v phr* supply with 432/31–2

Fyve Portes *n phr pl* the Cinque Ports, a group of ports, originally numbering five, on the south-east coast of England, with peculiar responsibilities and privileges; *in phr* **warden of the Fyve Portes** a royal officer overseeing the Ports and with maritime jurisdiction over adjacent waters 437/14

galand *n* gallon 478/18(2), etc; **galandes** *pl* 473/9, etc; **gallandes** 454/29, 454/30

galliard *n* quick and lively dance in triple time for two persons 133/38

gambouls *n pl* gambols, capers, leaps, friskings 125/36

game *n* amusement, sport, pastime 118/15, etc; **games** *pl* 58/35, 350/24, etc; *see also* **cockes of the game**

garboyle *n* garboil, brawl, hurly-burly 82/8

garde *see* **black garde**

gardians *n pl* churchwardens 68/20 [Latham, warda]

garnysshe *n* garnish, a set of vessels for table use 446/17

gatt *v pa 3 sg* got 95/16

geate *v* get 122/41

geave *v* give 122/38, 123/1

geder *v* gather 416/23, 417/17; **gederyng** *vb n* 357/8, 416/20, etc; **gedering** 416/21m; *in comp* **gederyng money** 358/32

geere *n* gear; *in most of these occurrences* apparel 460/28, etc; **geare** 444/38; **gere** 447/18

Gentiles *n pl* gentlefolk, persons of gentle birth 393/16 [*OED* Gentle *a* and *sb* B 1]

gentilite *n* the state of being a gentile or non-Christian 539/22 [*OED* Gentility]

gentle *adj* generous, noble, courteous 434/5; **gentil** 406/30

gentleman vssher *n* man of birth, who, as officer of the royal household, escorted persons of high rank; **gentlemen vsshers** *pl* 430/10

gethur *v* gather 391/16, 391/26; **getheryng** 462/10, 539/13

geve *v* give 117/22, etc; **geven** *pp* 431/12, etc; **gevyng** *vb n* 118/21; *in comp* **thankes gevyng** thanksgiving 435/4–5

geve aill *see* **ale**

gildales *n pl probably* guild-ales, festive gatherings, sponsored by guilds, at which ale was drunk 348/39; *see pp* 579–80 (endnote to LPL: MS 171 f 45v)

gleeke *n* a card game played by three people, using forty-four cards 133/10

glouers *n pl* makers or sellers of gloves 115/30

goggle eye *n comp* protuberant, prominent eye(s) 365/18; see p 583 (endnote to Wing: C6272 pp 97–102)

goly *proper name* Goliath 410/1

gonnys *n pl* guns 416/28

goo *v* go 115/15, etc

goodman *n* title used before the name of a man under the rank of gentleman 453/20

gowne *n* 1. a garment worn by both sexes, hanging from the shoulders but before 1600 often girt at the waist, and usually reaching well below the knee 447/9, etc; **gownd** 147/13; 2. a gown of a particular colour or mix of colours, worn by town officials as a badge of office; **gownes** *pl* 426/8, etc; 3. *by metonymy*, officials of a particular rank; **skarlett gownes** *n phr pl* those entitled to wear scarlet gowns 488/36; *see p* 601 (endnote to WCL: A11 f 87)

gowte *n* gout 135/21; *in phr* **running gowte** some disease characterized by a running issue or by rapid movement from one part of the body to another; *possibly* gonorrhea 135/23 [*OED* Gout *sb*¹ 1 a and d and Running *ppl a* 6 b]

gowtie *adj* gouty, afflicted with gout 135/13

grasse crosse *n comp* the cross situated near the junction of the High Street and Broad Street in Worcester; the name used for the junction itself 425/35, etc

grauntfather *n* grandfather 439/35, 440/4

grayne *n in phr* **in grayne** (dyed) in grain, dyed in a fast colour or thoroughly 426/11, etc

grest *n* footboard; *here probably* step; **grestes** *pl* 432/6 [*OED* Grece, Grest]

greven *v pr 3 pl refl in phr* **greven theym** (they) grieve themselves 407/25 [*MED* greven 3d (b)]

groomes *n pl* serving-men 133/25

grudge *n* doubt, misgiving 538/13; **gruge** 539/6

guift *n* gift 450/14

gultie *adj* guilty 83/13

gunnys *n pl* guns 417/18

gyder *see* to gyder

gyff *pp* given 505/30, etc

gyldmarchaunttes *n pl* members of the
merchants' guild or guild merchant (*see*
yeld marchaunt) 120/15

habilitie *see* abilitie

hakebuttes *n pl* 1. sackbuts 431/15, 432/13;
2. players of sackbuts; haggebusshes
527/20

hall dayes *n phr pl* the days when a court sat
117/14 [*OED* Hall *sb* 13]

hallinge *prp* hauling, dragging 85/16

haloweng *vb n* hallowing, keeping holy
538/38

halydays *see* holiday

hande maide *n comp* handmaid, female
servant (with reference to Lk 1.38) 408/33

hanged in chains *ppl phr* (of a corpse)
executed by hanging and left chained to
the gallows to rot and be picked clean by
birds and wild beasts, a form of execution
reserved for especially odious crimes 376/5

happelie *adv* happily, fortunately 440/3

harbengers *n pl* harbingers, officers in the
royal household who went before the
retinue as it travelled to secure lodgings
437/28

harde *v pa 3 sg* heard 406/9, etc; hard 410/30

harnes *n* harness, defensive armour 116/29

harnesid *pp* harnessed, wearing defensive
armour 403/12; herneysid 416/9

hartyst *adj superl* heartiest 118/11

hast *n* haste 75/40, 76/5

hazard *n* a game of chance played with dice
133/10

head *n* skin or membrane of a drum; heades
pl 125/11

headborroughes *n pl* headboroughs, petty
constables 539/33

healthfull *adj* healthy 134/25

heap *n* a great company, multitude 127/30;
vpon heapes in crowds, in great numbers
423/8

heder *adv* hither, to here 407/19

hedge-bill *n comp* a tool made up of a curved
blade mounted on a long straight handle,
used for lopping and pruning hedges
81/27–8; *cp* forrest bill

henne feast *n comp* 145/24, 145/26; *see* p 284
(endnote to HRO f [3v])

hensfurth *adv in phr* from hensfurth from
henceforth, from now on 415/7;
ffromhensfurth 415/42; fromhensfurth
415/28

herneysid *see* harnesid

hertely *adv* heartily 409/17, 409/27

herytique *n* heretic 420/13, etc; heretique
421/13; heritique 420/36, 421/25

hether *adv* hither, to here 419/6

hetherunto *adv* hitherto, until now 117/24

hevyn *n* heaven 115/13

hey *n* hay, a country dance like a reel, with
a winding movement 125/37

heyer *n* heir 436/37

highe *adj* 1. of persons, denoting seniority
of rank or appointment; *in phr* highe
baylyff senior bailiff 426/17, 426/26; high
baylyff 426/18m, 437/17; hie baylie 443/3;
highe chamberlayne senior chamberlain
428/35, etc; high chamberlayne 426/4,
426/5–6m; highe constable chief
constable 383/17; highe shrifes *poss* high
sheriff's 430/28–9m; 2. of things, denoting
prime importance; *in phr* highe streete the
main street, High Street 425/24; highe
warde probably the ward of the main
business district, containing the high street
427/11–12, 428/6; hye warde 444/10

hignes *n error for* highnes, ie, highness
435/17

his *pron poss* its 414/31, etc

his *the poss suffix* often written and construed
in the 15th–17th centuries as a separate
word 362/22, etc

hit *pron* it 414/16, etc

hobby-horse *n comp* in the morris dance, a
figure of a horse, made of wicker or other
light material and worn by one of the
performers 133/33, etc; hobbie-horse

126/34, etc; **hobbi-horse** 127/36, 132/34; **hobbie-horses** *poss* 131/3

hodiwinking *vb n comp in phr* **a hodiwinking** a-hoodwinking, taking part in the game of blindman's buff 66/37

hokday *n comp* Hockday, the second Tuesday after Easter, widely kept as a popular festival 402/13, 404/22; **hok dayes** *pl* the second Monday and Tuesday after Easter 349/35

hold *n* a particularly secure cell within a prison 421/7 [*OED* Hold *sb*[1] 13 and Hole *sb* 2 b]

hold *v in phr* **hold crafte** ply a craft or trade 402/32

holden *pp* held 401/35, etc; **holdyn** 402/13

hole *adj* whole 401/34, etc

holiday *n comp* a day of special religious observance, often accompanied by public rejoicing 353/25, etc; **holi-day** 134/7; **holieday** 158/11; **holyday** 538/23, 538/24; **holy day** 538/19, etc; **halydays** *pl* 469/25; **holidaies** 351/9, etc; **holidayes** 353/32; **holiedayes** 84/3, 370/4; **hollidaies** 163/20, etc; **holydaies** 188/4, 352/15; **holy daies** 74/29; **holy-dayes** 59/6, etc; **holye dayes** 143/32–3

Holyrowde Day *n phr* Holy Rood Day or Holy Cross Day, the feast of the Invention of the Cross, 3 May 516/39; *see* p 603 (endnote to WCL: A11 f 135)

honourable *adj used as n pl* honourable persons 430/27

hoole *adj* whole 414/6

hoorson *n comp* whoreson, ie, whore's son; but here, as commonly, merely a term of abuse 420/24

horne-pypes *n pl* hornpipes, wind instruments, either the three-holed pipes usually played with tabors, or pipes partly or wholly made out of horn; 2. lively and vigorous dances done to these (context suggests the writer had both senses in mind) 125/37

horsemeate *n comp* horse-fodder 438/36; **horssemete** 476/9

hoses *n pl in phr* **a peyer of hoses** men's nether garment consisting of breeches and stockings sewn together 514/1

hosier *n* one who makes and deals in hose and underwear 131/20

houre *n* time; *here*, the appointed time for outside brewers to buy barley and malt in Worcester market, after townsfolk had had first choice 417/15

housband *n* husband 418/26, etc

howgh hoo *interj* ho-ho, expressing derision 421/12

howsis *n pl* houses 385/32, 385/34

howsold *n* household 462/8, etc; **howshold** 436/29, etc; **howsolde** 459/16, etc; **howswold** 465/5

hull *n* hall 522/2, 522/2m

humble *adv* humbly 138/11

hye *see* **highe**

iavellinges *n pl* javelins 136/35

idle *adj* groundless 83/40

ierkyn *n* jerkin, a close-fitting man's jacket, sometimes sleeveless, having skirts of varying length and fullness 447/10, 447/12

Iewes cap *see* **capp**

impannell *v* empanel, enrol 128/22

impotent *adj* decrepit 86/28

incontinent *adv* straightway, without delay 419/15

inconuenient *adj* unsuitable 539/15

incorporat *adj* incorporated 120/21

indevor *v* endeavour 82/25

indewed *pp* endued, furnished 418/3

indifferent *adj* moderate, fairly great 372/32

infanterie *n* infantry (*used fig and with an ironic pun on the nonce-sense* troop of infants) 128/31

inforced *pp* enforced, ie, obliged 78/24

inforth *see* **with inforth**

iniust *adj* unjust 89/20 [*OED* Injust]

inne *n error for* end (?) 454/3m

Innocentes Day *n phr* the feast of the Holy

Innocents, commemorating the children massacred by Herod, 28 December 528/34; **Innocence Day** 524/21; **Innocenses Day** 528/36; **the Holy Innocentes** 539/10

inobedience *n* disobedience 188/18

inowghe *adj* enough 419/32; *adv* 422/1

in pontificalibus *L phr* in episcopal vestments and insignia 410/33

inqueste *n* 1. *generally*, a body of men appointed to hold a legal inquiry; in Hereford, three inquests were sworn in annually at the Law Day before Michaelmas 123/32, etc; **enquest** 138/7; **inquest** 120/17, 120/18; **in qwest** 138/8; **enquest** *pl* 123/16; **enquestes** 119/29, etc; **in quest** 138/4; **inquestes** 120/35, etc; 2. the Great Inquest: in Hereford, an important administrative body which also functioned as a judicial body at the two annual Law Days; **Great Inquest** *n phr* 138/9; **Grete Inquest** 124/31; in Worcester, presiding at a thrice-annual Law Day, the Great Inquest (a jury made up of prominent citizens) dealt with breaches of the law and made and amended by-laws; **Grete Enquest** 402/13, 417/13

interludes *see* **enterlude**

interteynement *n* entertainment 435/38, 436/8

intreat *v in phr* **evill intreat** ill-treat 88/15; **evill intreate** 77/27

Inuencion of the Crosse *n phr* the finding of Christ's cross by St Helen, commemorated on 3 May 538/15

inuetorye *n* inventory 444/30 [*OED* Invitory]

invented *v pa 3 pl* planned, plotted 418/5, 418/23

invexions *n pl* invections, ie, invectives 80/12

iogeller *n* juggler, professional buffoon or merry-maker 494/17, etc; **iogellar** 462/31; **iogolar** 478/31m; **iogular** 526/17; **ioguler** 468/15, etc; **ioguller** 508/29, etc; **iogyller**

462/18, 494/18m; **ioogler** 487/22; **iugeler** 466/13, 478/30; **joguler** 472/9; **iogulares** *pl* 517/6

iolly *adj* 1. high-hearted, cheerful 392/40; 2. fresh and lively (with overtone of sense amorous or lustful) 365/15; 3. fine, excellent (here used ironically, perhaps with reference to the pride of those who really have nothing to be proud of); **ioly** 420/39; **ʒolye** 418/3 [*OED* Jolly *a* and *adv* 3, 5, 6, 7, 12 and 12 b]

iorneymen *n comp pl* journeymen, qualified craftsmen working for master 402/37, etc; **iornemen** 117/8, 403/3

iorneyng *prp* journeying 476/1

ioule *n* jowl 129/6

ipocras *n* hippocras, wine flavoured with herbs and spices 433/22, 438/37

Iudasly *adv* traitorously, like Judas Iscariot 420/4

iuell *see* **mathematicall iuell**

iugeler *see* **iogeller**

iugge *n* judge 411/2

iuggement *n* judgment 114/27

Iulij *n* July 425/13

iuuentus *L n* youth 134/38

ize *n* ice 377/12, etc

jaggs *n pl* jags, ornamental indentations or slashes in the fabric of a garment, sometimes revealing fabric of another colour underneath 587/40

joguler *see* **iogeller**

Kings bookes *n phr pl in phr* **in the Kings bookes** on the taxation lists 129/37

knottes *n pl* knobs, ornaments carved in relief 425/33

knuppes *n pl* knops, small rounded knobs or lumps at the end of an object or on its stem 446/12

knyght marshall *n phr* an officer of the royal household, with jurisdiction over offences committed within its bounds and verges 438/4

kychion *n* kitchen 514/37; **kycheon** 515/35; **kychyn** 476/6, etc

kynnerede *n* kindred 409/29

lady of misrule *n phr* a woman chosen to preside over Christmas revels, which commonly involved practical jokes and inversion of the usual social hierarchy 174/9; *cp* **lord of misrule**

ladyes of honour *n phr pl* gentlewomen attending a queen or other lady of rank, ladies-in-waiting 437/6–7m; *cp* **maydens of honour**

laid *pp* alleged 83/1

lamman *n* leman, ie, sweetheart, beloved 396/11

largez *n* largess, money or gifts freely bestowed 411/5

larums *n pl* alarms 135/36

lasse *adj* less 407/25

lasse *see* **vn lasse**

latte *adjectival n in phr* **of latte** of late 117/20

laundar *see* **lawnder**

Lawday *n comp* Law Day, day when inquests were sworn (*see* **inqueste**) 402/13, etc; **Law Day** 417/10, etc; **Lawe Day** 119/30, 123/16; **Lawe Daye** 122/30, etc

lawgh *v pa 3 sg* laughed 421/12

lawnder *n* laundry, washing 462/40, 467/17; **laundar** 462/23 [MED lavendrie *n*]

lay-iuries *n phr* juries for secular courts 60/15; **laye iuries** 351/23–4; **lay-juries** 59/36, etc

least *conj* lest 419/5, 422/12; **leaste** 373/29

leefe *n* leave, ie, permission 187/29

leere *adj* riderless 431/32 [OED Leer *a*[1] 2]

leet *n* 1. a local court of record, held once a year in a hundred, lordship, or manor before the lord or his steward to view frankpledges, to present by jury crimes perpetrated within its jurisdiction, and to punish trivial misdemeanours; **leets** *pl* 59/36, etc; 2. the area of jurisdiction of such a court; **lete** 385/30

lefull *adj* lawful 415/11 [OED Leeful]

lege *adj* liege, bound by a tie of allegiance 453/32, 538/40

leighmen *n pl* liegemen 394/15

lementacion *n* lamentation 116/5

lenuoy *n* conclusion, parting words 133/22, 133/24 [OED L'envoy, lenvoy *sb*]

lete *see* **leet**

lett *n* hindrance, obstruction 534/24; **lettes** *pl* 540/10

lett, letten *see* **farme**

letters missiue *n phr pl* a letter or letters from the sovereign or other high authority to some person or body, giving an order, recommendation, or permission 144/9, 144/23

levey *n* levy 402/11

lewter *n* luter, lute player 469/12, 469/24

leyff *n* leave, permission 118/21

leyved *pp* levied 121/2; **leyveydid** *error for* leyveyid (?) 414/32

liberte *n* 1. liberty, a district exempt from the usual authority, particularly, the territory of a borough, as exempt from the jurisdiction of the sheriff of the surrounding county 414/7, etc; **liberties** *pl coll* 425/26, etc; 2. **libertes** *pl* liberties, freedoms 117/35

licke *adj* like, similar 119/39

lickwyse *adv* likewise 128/33

lie *v* spend the night, stay over (on a visit); **lay** *pa 3 sg* 435/32; **lieng** *prp* 432/23, etc

lif *n* life 81/20, 407/18; **lief** 79/42; **liff** 114/31, 408/28

lifeting *vb n* lifting 133/36

light *n* 1. a lighted lamp, torch, or candle, particularly one kept burning before a religious image as a mark of honour or carried in a religious procession; **lyght** 516/40; **lightes** *pl* 402/26, etc; **lightz** 402/23, 402/37; 2. an opening admitting light, such as a window or a glazed door; **lights** *pl* 532/19; 3. lungs; **lights** *pl* 131/33

limit *n* an administrative subdivision; *here* of a country 383/17

linnen-armourers *n comp pl* makers and

sellers of quilted linen adjuncts to armour 134/10

litter men *n comp pl* litter-bearers, bearers of curtained couches for transporting people 437/33

lock *n* tuft 421/4

loffe *n* loaf 339/n 83; *possibly pl*; it is not clear either whether **past loffe** is to be taken as a compound, meaning a loaf or loaves made with larded dough (?), or the words are to construed separately; *see also* **past**

loftie trickes *n phr* acrobatic feats, tumbling 130/36 [*OED* Lofty *a*]

logge *v pr 1 sg* lodge 406/25

loke *v* look; **loke** *imper* 419/27; **loked** *pa 1 sg* 420/13; **lokid** *pp* 420/31; *in comp* **longe-loked** long sought, long looked for 418/34

loost *v pa 1 sg* lost 114/31

loouing *prp* loving 374/20

lord of misrule *n phr* man chosen to preside over Christmas revels, which commonly involved practical jokes and inversion of the usual social hierarchy 174/1; **lordes of misrule** *pl* 58/21–2, 58/24–5; **lords of misrule** 58/10, etc; *cp* **lady of misrule**

lowe baylyff *n phr* low bailiff, junior bailiff (*see* **baylyff**) 429/17; **lowe bailie** 443/3–4; **lowebaylef** 420/38; *cp* **highe**

luste *v pr subj 3 sg* list, may be pleased 407/7; *see* pp 590–1 (endnote to BL: Cotton Julius B xii ff 13v–17)

lyff *n* life 436/14; **lyffe** 442/23

lyggyng *vb n* lying 188/4

lyght *see* **light**

lyghtyng *prp* alighting, dismounting 432/40

lyon *see* **bere**

lyuerey *n* livery; 1. distinctive clothing given by a magnate or corporate body to a retainer (such as a town wait) as a mark of office and part payment for his services 426/10, etc; **lyueres** *pl* 423/21; **lyuereys** 424/35, etc; 2. a similar allowance of food; **lyvereys** *pl* 339/n 83

made way *n phr* a road or passage specially constructed 432/39; **made wayes** *pl* 435/31

magames *see* **maygames**

mahumed *pp* maimed 76/28

Maide-Marrian *n phr* Maid Marian, the legendary sweetheart of Robin Hood, a traditional personage in the morris dance 132/1, etc; **Maide-Marrion** 132/34; **Mayd-Marian** 125/32; **Mayd-Marion** 135/34–5; **Mayde Marion** 513/23

Maij *n* May 516/36, 520/29

maister *n* master 118/11, etc

makers of wayes *n phr pl probably* the staff of the surveyor of the ways, a royal official who went ahead of the retinue to ensure that the proposed route was passable 437/34; **way men** *with same sense* 437/34

male *see* **yoman**

man *n* workman or serving-man 438/13, etc; **men** 438/7, etc

mannerly *adv* suitably, properly 409/25

marchandise *n* merchandise 351/19

marchaunt *see* **yeld marchaunt**

mare *v* mar 422/12

markes *n pl* monetary units, each equal to two thirds of a pound or 13s 4d 137/6

marques *n* marquess 437/7; **markas** *poss* marquess' 521/11, 526/31; **marques** *poss in phr* **the lady marques of Northampton widowe** the lady the marquess of Northampton's widow 437/6

marshales of the field *n phr* officers charged with the arrangement of ceremonies, here especially with keeping a place clear for the morris dancers 129/28

marshall *see* **knyght marshall**

masbocke *n comp* mass-book, missal 597/35

master *n* 1. a craftsman or tradesman carrying on his own business and having full membership in his guild 415/8; **maister** 402/32, 403/19; **maisters** *pl* 403/17; **masters** 414/25, etc; 2. *in phr* (of various royal officials) **master of the queenes maiesties horses** the master of the horse, officer managing the royal stables

433/16–17; **masters of the courte of requestes** *pl* chief officials of a court for the relief of persons petitioning the sovereign 437/5; *see also* **revells**

mastershyppes *n pl* title of address given to persons commonly styled master, such as civic dignitaries 117/7, etc

match *n* compact, agreement 76/11

materiall *adj* (of a complaint) essential, that which is a necessary part 88/25, 92/8 [*Black's* Material allegation]

mathematicall iuell *n phr* a mathematical or astronomical instrument (?); *or*, the title of an unidentified book (?) 449/20

matier *n* matter 403/6

maulling *vb n* engaging in mutual combat with mauls or hammers (?) 540/3

mawmesey *n* malmsey, a strong sweet wine first made in Greece but later imitated in the Iberian countries 459/26, etc; **mawemesey** 501/16

Mayde Marion *see* **Maide-Marrian**

maydens of honour *n phr pl* unmarried ladies, usually of noble birth, attending on a queen or princess 431/33; *cp* **ladyes of honour**

Mayd-Marian, Mayd-Marion *see* **Maide-Marrian**

maydons *n pl* maidens 391/16

maygames *n comp pl* may games, traditional games played or rites observed at the beginning of May 382/13; **magames** (*for* maygames?) 80/21

may gaminge *vb n comp in phr* **a may gaminge** taking part in the traditional games or rites of May 66/1

mayhemed *pp* maimed 78/27

meary *adj* merry 80/26

meat *n* food (not necessarily flesh) 538/12; **meate** 75/1, 421/20; **meates** *pl* kinds of food 539/6

medle *adj* middle 439/23

meery *adj* merry 430/28

meire *n* mayor 114/1

meke *adj* gentle, not wrathful or exacting

409/25; **mek** 406/27; **mekely** *adv* humbly 407/22

mekellmass *see* **Mighelmas**

meknesse *n* gentleness, absence of rigour 406/33

mensinger *n* messenger 462/20

mercer *n* 1. a dealer in textiles; **mercers** *pl* 116/25; **mersers** 443/12; 2. a seller of sundry small items; **merces** *pl* 372/25

merchant *see* **yeld marchaunt**

merveile *n* marvel 441/33

merveled *v pa 3 sg* marvelled 434/11

mervelous *adj* marvellous 433/13

Mighelmas *n comp* Michaelmas, the feast of St Michael and all angels, 29 September 420/38; **Mekellmass** 443/24; **Mighellmas** 420/19; **Myhelmas** 527/29

minister *n* minister 368/38

minstrel(l) *see* **mynstrell**

missiue *see* **letters missiue**

moche *adj and adv* much 408/39, etc

mocions *see* **motion**

mode *n* mood, ie, disposition, temperament 409/25

moder *n* mother 188/5, 408/9

Moneday *n* Monday 432/19, etc

moneth *n* month 188/22, etc

monstruous *adj* monstrous 373/8

mony *adj* 415/39

moore *adj* 114/1

moorning verses *n comp* mourning verses, elegies 191/9

moost *adj* most, greatest 114/11, etc; **mooste** 118/11, 168/27

mootehalls *n comp pl* town halls 540/17

morenyng *n* morning 498/26, etc

morris *n* a kind of traditional dance, usually performed in costume 128/27, etc; **morish** 280/28; **morrice** 169/31, etc; **morrices** *pl* 382/13, 382/27; *in comp* **morrice dance** 172/4; **morrice daunce** 170/33–4; **morris dance** 133/12; **morris daunce** 125/33, etc; **morrice daunces** *pl* 169/12

morris dancer *n comp* one who dances a morris; **morrice dauncer** 142/28;

moris-dauncers *pl* 125/16; **morrice
dauncers** 172/22, 383/21; **morris-dancers**
130/14, 136/6–7; **morris-dauncers** 133/31

motion *n* 1. a proposal 126/31; 2. a puppet
play or other public show 394/24; **mocions**
pl 395/1, 540/19

motley *n* a worsted of mixed colours giving
a mottled effect 468/23; **moteley** 461/7

mought *v pa 2 sg* might 429/35

mountebanke *n* an entertainer who performs
tricks; a clown or juggler 455/25

mucisians *see* **musitian**

mumchance *n comp* a game of chance played
with dice 133/10

murrey *n* mulberry colour, purplish red, but
having a considerable variation in hue
426/10, etc

murther *v* murder 382/16; **murthered**
pp 91/13, 91/34

murtherers *n pl* murderers 421/36

muscadell *n* muscatel, a strong sweet wine
made from the muscat or similar grape
524/14, 528/24

musick *n coll* a band of musicians 191/3,
195/15, etc; **musicke** 194/32, etc

musitian *n* musician 448/10m, 453/20;
musition 128/34m; **musycion** 123/19;
musysian 448/11; **mucisians** *pl* 437/37;
musisians 191/34; **musitians** 132/27,
132/28; **musitions** 128/33, etc; **musycians**
360/32

mutton *n coll* loose women, prostitutes
(slang) 134/6

Myhelmas *see* **Mighelmas**

mynstrell *n* a professional entertainer using
music, singing, storytelling, juggling, etc
461/34, etc; **minstrel** 490/27; **minstrell**
73/31, etc; **minstrelles** *pl* 63/41, 64/17;
minstrells 182/11; **mynstreles** 490/28m;
mynstrelles 460/35, etc; **mynstrells**
385/32

mynstrelseys *n pl* minstrelsies, minstrels'
performances 188/11

myrthe *n* diversion, pleasurable entertainment 431/23

myskyns *n pl* mixens, laystalls, places where
dung and refuse were laid 425/20

ne *adv* nor 415/7, etc

neb *n* nib 126/9

neight *n* night 139/24

ner *adv* near 406/13

nether *conj* neither, nor 441/13

nevew *n* nephew, ie, male kinsman 406/11

neweres *n phr poss* New Year's 488/35;
Neweyeres 465/5, etc

neypurs *n pl* neighbours 507/37

Nisi Prius court *L and E n phr* the room in
the Worcester Guildhall where judges of
assize tried civil causes 311/10, 311/15

nixt *adj* next 431/29

nokwise *adv* wedgewise, like a slice of a
pie (?) 445/29 [*OED* Nock *sb*¹ 1 c?]

nomeber *n* number 426/7, etc

noon *pron and adj* none, no 188/1, 188/2

note *n* 1. sign, indication 418/33; 2. song
432/12

nother *quasi-pron in phr* **a nother** another
114/22, etc; **a noþer** 490/27

nowne *quasi-pron in phr* **my nowne** mine
own, ie, my own 420/14

noyse *n* music 432/11; *in phr* **lowde noyce**
loud music, especially that of shawms
123/27

ny3th *n* night 459/27, etc; **nyht** 499/2

ob *abbrev for* L obolus, *frequently used in* E
context for halfpenny 459/8, etc

occasion *n in phr* **vppon no occasion** without
any (good) reason 124/15–16

occupacion *n* a trade or other calling
organized into a guild 415/7, etc;
occupazione 443/13; **occupacions** *pl*
119/23, etc

occupie *v* to ply (a trade or other calling)
402/35, etc; **occupy** 415/7

occupier *n* craftsman or tradesman 372/31

odde *adj* unspecified or unmatched additional
(used of amounts of money, years, etc)
446/21; **ode** 124/10

oes *n pl* pains that make one cry out 135/24

on *adj and pron* one 187/30, etc

on browed *pp* unbrewed 391/17–18

one *prep* on 169/32, etc

ons *adv* once 145/4

oon *adj and pron* one 402/7, etc

oon *prep* on 416/8

op *prep* up 127/1

opteynyng *prp* obtaining 409/33

or *conj* ere, before 407/22, 421/10

orator *n* 1. petitioner 122/33, etc; **orators** *poss* 123/3; **orators** *pl* 117/7, etc; **oratours** 407/10, 407/37; 2. official speaking for civic corporation on ceremonial occasions; **oratour** 429/11, etc

ordene *v* ordain, ie, decree or enact; **ordenyth** *pr 3 sg* 538/21; **ordenid** *pp* 415/41, etc

ornaments *n pl* accessories or furnishings belonging to a church and used for its worship, including the vestments of its ministers and such fixtures as bells and organs 457/1, 457/3

osey *n* sweet wine of Alsace 469/10, 478/18

oste *n* oast, ie, kiln for drying malt or hops 417/16

oþer *pron pl* others 508/7, etc

ouer *prep in phr* **ouer that** besides that 416/2

oune *adj* own 115/5, 115/6; **ovne** 410/28

ownckle *n* uncle 417/37, etc; **ownkle** 419/30

oxe-leach *n comp* ox leech, ie, cattle doctor 125/17; **oxleach** 125/5

pageant *n* 1. a public spectacle, sometimes genuinely dramatic but often a tableau, either stationary or mounted and taken through the streets 402/14, etc; **pageaunt** 114/9, 114/23; **paiaunt** 115/1; **pageantes** *pl* 402/21, etc; **pageauntes** 403/24; **pageaunttes** 119/26, 120/4; **pagentes** 402/3, 403/32; **pageontes** 521/36; **paiantes** 115/27; 2. a platform or stage for a pageant;

pageaunt 430/18, 430/26; **pageauntes** *pl* 425/34, 425/34m; 3. a wagon or other mount for a paraded pageant; **pagantes** *pl* 447/35, 447/37m; **pageants** 447/28; *in comp* **pageant howse** a building where these were kept 447/20; **pagent howse** 451/7, 451/15; **pagen house** 535/1; **pageon howse** 445/28, etc; **pageantehouses** *pl* 412/23; 4. *metaphorically*, a drama; **pageant** 374/33

palaice *n* palace 431/19; **pallaice** 431/18m

Palmeson wycke *quasi-n phr* Palmsun week, the week beginning with Palm Sunday 474/28 [*OED* Palm Sunday]

pamenttes *n pl* pavements 120/25

pamphilletts *n pl* pamphlets 191/9; **pamflets** 191/9m

papist *n properly*, a supporter of the papal claims and the doctrines and religious practices commended by the pope; *but here, used loosely for* a supporter of the conservative customs and teachings retained by the Church of England down to the death of Henry VIII 418/2; **papest** 421/8; **papestes** *pl* 418/34; **papists** 419/29; *see* pp 591–2 (endnote to BL: Harley 425 ff 69–70)

parasshe *n* parish 512/30; **pariche** 82/38

parcell gylte *adj phr* parcel gilt, partly gilt, used especially of silver ware having the inner surface gilt 446/10

part *n* a role in a dance, pageant, or dramatic piece 136/13; **partes** *pl* 58/23, 350/33; **parts** 58/11, 351/18

parties *n pl* parts 538/2, 539/9

past *n* paste, ie, larded dough (?) 339/n 83; *see also* **loffe**

paste *adj* past 122/35

patent gatherers *n phr pl* persons possessing letters patent authorizing them to collect alms for distressed persons or charitable institutions 586/31

paule *n* pall, coffin cover 446/37

Paussheon Sonday *n phr* Passion Sunday, the fifth Sunday in Lent 497/10

payer *n* pair 420/40, 447/10

payyd *pp* paid 357/30, etc

peasse *n* peace 521/26

pee *n* the letter P; **pees** *pl* 393/22

peece *n* 1. a piece of plate; *here* a silver cup 442/17; 2. a firearm 82/16, etc; *see also* **birdinge peece**

pens *n pl* pence 507/37, 524/13

perfytt *adj* perfect 442/3

perythe *see* **a perythe**

pescods *n pl* pea-pods, peas in the pod 393/8 [*OED* Peasecod]

pese *n in phr* **the pese** the piece, ie, per head, each 443/1, 443/6

pestel *n* pestle 373/40, 374/5; **pestell** 373/38

pettie *see* **clearke**

pety coote *n* a kind of waistcoat; in the period of these occurrences, it was a waist-length underdoublet, usually quilted, sleeveless or having sleeves (which might be detachable) 467/38; **peticootes** *pl* 476/25

peyer *n* pair 462/40, etc

pilde *pp* pilled, ie, tonsured 418/39

pistles *see* **pystle**

pitefull *adj* pitiful 407/6

place *n in phr* **in place** immediately, forthwith (?) 407/7; *see* pp 590–1 (endnote to BL: Cotton Julius B xii ff 13v–17)

plaide, plaie, plaies *see* **play** *n and v*

plaiers, plairs *see* **players**

plaintief *n* plaintiff 85/23

plaisters *n pl* plasters 129/15

platformes *n pl* plans, schemes 373/1

play *n* a dramatic piece or other public spectacle 373/27, etc; **plaie** 424/6, etc; **playe** 375/3, etc; **pley** 507/3m, etc; **plaies** *pl* 58/25, etc; **playes** 416/23, etc; **plays** 350/34; **pleyes** 416/19; **pleys** 417/16; *see also* **puppett playe**

play *v* 1. perform a dramatic piece or other public spectacle 416/26, etc; **pleyd** *pa 3 pl* 503/21; **played** *pp* 423/18, etc; **pleying** *prp* 513/22; **playeinge** *vb n* 356/8; **playenge** 455/33; **playing** 356/1, etc; *fig* **plaide** *pp* 374/33; 2. *intr* (of a play or spectacle)

be performed; **pley** *pr subj 3 pl* 414/30; **pleye** 414/29; **pleyng** *vb n* 414/28; 3. perform on a musical instrument or instruments; **play** 123/23; **playe** 392/21; **played** *pa 3 sg* 128/36; 386/25; **played** *pa 3 pl* 174/19; **plaieinge** *vb n* 151/14, 163/1; **plaieng** 167/30, etc; **plaienge** 161/12; **plaing** 182/11, 145/37; **playeing** 168/12; **playeinge** 66/14, etc; **playeng** 145/25; **playenge** 379/15; **playing** 378/36, etc; **playinge** 448/11m, etc; **pleyng** 469/12, 469/25; 4. disport or divert oneself; **play** 145/5; 5. accomplish, execute (tricks); **playing** *vb n* 134/16

players *n pl* performers, usually actors of dramatic pieces but sometimes used of other entertainers 362/22, 425/5, etc; **plaiers** 361/16m, etc; **plairs** 147/18; **playeres** 508/36; **pleyars** 361/35; **pleyeres** 460/19, etc; **pleyers** 464/12, 519/39; **players** *pl poss* 444/38, etc; **pleyars** 422/31, 422/31m; *in phr* **players of enterludes** 351/17, etc; *see* **enterlude, popet pleyer, stage players,** *and* **waite plaiers**

playmakers *n comp pl* producers of plays or other public spectacles 394/20, 539/39

playsterers *n pl* plasterers 374/23

pleasaunce *n* pleasure 114/28

ples *v* please 117/32

pley(e), pleyd, pleying, pleyng *see* **play** *n and v*

pleyars, pleyer(e)s *see* **players**

pleyer *see* **popet pleyer**

plumbe pottage *n comp* plum pottage or plum porridge, a boiled dish containing dried plums or other fruit and cereal, the precursor of modern plum pudding 393/8

pollytike *adj* politic, sagacious 439/35

pon *see* **apon**

pontificalibus *see* **in pontificalibus**

poorpos *n* purpose 421/35

popet pleyer *n comp* puppet player, puppeteer 528/34

popez *n poss* pope's 410/36

porpotte *n* purport 118/1

port townes *n phr pl* market towns (not necessarily on the coast or a navigable river) 188/2

poste master *n comp* the master of the posts, the officer in charge of the royal post-messengers 438/3; **post maisters** *poss* 438/13

poticary *n* apothecary, one who stored, compounded, and sold medicaments of all kinds 417/37

pottage *see* **plumbe pottage**

pottell *n* pottle, a half a gallon, or a vessel of that size 469/10, etc; **potell** 469/10; **pottel** 473/12, etc; **apottell** *art and n* 145/22(2)

pourpose *n* purpose 419/19

poyntid *see* **apoynt**

praier *n in phr* **divyne praier** public worship 72/22; *cp* **evening prayer**

praysed *pp* appraised 422/27, 423/40; **preysed** 422/32, 423/33; **prysed** 453/7

preachers *n pl* clergy of the Church of England licensed to preach 376/10

preachinge minister *n phr* a clergyman of the Church of England licensed to preach 89/21

prenounce *v* pronounce 392/38

prescripcion *n* right established by long usage 83/40

present *v* bring (a fact, complaint, or accused person) before a court or other authority 417/14, etc

present potte *n phr* a votive flagon (?) 446/15; **present pottes** *pl* 446/18

preste *adj* ready and willing 408/32 [*OED* Prest *a and adv*]

pretenced *pp* pretended 77/17

prevent *v* anticipate, forestall 456/6, etc; **prevente** 455/33; **preuented** *pa 3 sg* 374/31; **prevented** 421/37; **prevented** *pp* 364/14

prevocacion *n* provocation 81/15

preysed *see* **praysed**

price *n* worth, estimation 409/21

primero *n* a card game similar to ombre but played with six cards per hand instead of nine, usually for stakes 133/10 [*OED* Primero; Strutt]

princes *n* 1. princess, sovereign's daughter 489/16, etc; **prynces** 489/30; **princes** *poss* princess' 490/35, etc; **princesse** 491/24; **prynces** 490/38, etc; **pryncesse** 487/38; 2. *poss* prince's, of the king's son and heir; **princes** 149/3

priste *n* priest 422/3; **pristes** *pl* 418/39, etc; **prystes** 539/11

prive *n* privy, ie, lavatory 421/7

prive *adv* privy, secret 75/22

privelagid *pp* privileged 415/36

privitie *n* secret counsel (implying consent) 78/1

probacion *n* proof 115/9

proctors *n pl* persons authorized to collect alms for lepers or others not allowed to do so for themselves, or for charitable institutions 586/30

procurement *n* prompting, contriving 78/2

procurors *n pl* persons authorized to collect alms for lepers or others not allowed to do so for themselves, or for charitable institutions 586/30

profanes *n* profaneness 371/30

proffe *n* proof 441/35, etc

pronosticate *v* prognosticate, foretell 441/27

prosession tyme *n phr* procession time, Rogationtide 466/33

prosterne *v* lay low 410/1

providinge *vb n* preparing 387/39

provytt *n* profit 118/22

prynces(se) *see* **princes**

prysed *see* **praysed**

prystes *see* **priste**

pudding pyes *n comp pl* baked dough puddings containing meat, not unlike modern toad-in-the-hole 393/8

puppett playe *n comp* puppet play, drama acted by puppets 383/32

putt *v in phr* **putt in colors** paint, decorate with colours 426/1

pystle *n* epistle, the first lesson at the communion, usually taken from the New Testament epistles 432/14; **pistles** *pl* 423/40

qu *abbrev for* L quarterium, *meaning* a fourth part, *frequently used in* E *context for* farthing 359/24

quack-salver *n comp* a medical charlatan, a pedlar of sham remedies and treatments 129/12

quere *see* **quyer**

quest *n* inquest, judicial inquiry 421/32; *in apparent pl (by false word division)* **in quest** *see* **inqueste**

quest-men *n pl* sidesmen, churchwardens' assistants charged with investigating the moral and religious conduct of parishioners 353/18, 353/39

quoyne *n* coin 430/2

quyer *n* 1. choir, a band of trained singers in a church 431/6; **quere** 115/18; 2. choir or quire, the part of a church where singers and other musicians normally perform 432/8m, 446/27; **quyre** 432/12, 453/21

Quyttyde Sonday *n phr* Shrove Sunday, ie, the Sunday before Shrove Tuesday, 470/3, etc; **Quyttid Sonday** 466/5–6, 520/3; **Quyttides Sonday** 461/1; **Quyttite Sonday** 516/6, etc; **Quyttydes Sonday** 496/6; **Quyttyte Sonday** 520/8

qwest *see* **inqueste**

radde *pp* read 120/34

raged *pp* enraged 421/11

range *v pa 3 sg* rang 392/21

recorde *n in phr* **God to recorde** as God is our witness 410/23

recorder *n* a borough magistrate, usually presiding over the local court 425/38, etc

redwyne *n phr* red wine 478/19

refusse *v* refuse 117/24

register *n* registrar 419/17

rehersid *pp* rehearsed, ie, enumerated 415/17, etc; **rehersed** 120/33

relyeffe *n* relief 117/16

remevede *v pa 3 sg* removed, changed abode 113/41; **remeuid** *pp* 144/37

reparacions *n pl* repairs 120/26; **repayracions** 533/24

replenyshed *pp* filled 435/3

requestes *see* **master**

rescous *n* rescue 77/35

resetteth *v pr 3 sg* harbours 370/1

reseuyd *pp* received 357/8, etc

reson *pp* risen, arisen 538/18

resonablelie *adv* reasonably 85/22

retynewe *n* retinue 434/14

revelers *n pl in phr* **the kinges revelers** the king's players 454/22

revell *v* hold a festivity with entertainment 416/26

revells *n coll* an office of the royal household responsible for festivities and for regulating public performances 540/22, 540/33; *in phr* **master of the revells** the head of that office 394/12, etc

revels *n pl* festivities with entertainment 370/34; **revelles** 416/19, 416/19m

reuelyng *vb n* revelling, festivity (not necessarily riotous) 188/12

ring *n* a set of church bells 126/3

ripe *n* bank, shore 370/26

rithmes *n* rhymes 364/16 [OED Rhythm *sb 1*]

robing *vb n in phr* **robing the devill**, robbing the devil, cheating the devil (the sense seems to be that, by making his rounds, a night watchman prevents evil deeds to which the devil would otherwise incite people) 421/10

Robyn Whod *proper n phr* Robin Hood, the legendary outlaw chief, a frequent personage in folk plays 462/9, etc; **Robyn Whot** 513/22–3

rochett *n* rochet, an ample ankle-length garment of white linen, with full sleeves gathered at the wrist, the usual dress of a bishop of the Church of England 431/6

rod *v pa 1 sg* rode 356/36, 525/2

Rogacion wycke *n phr* Rogation week, the fifth week after Easter, containing the

Rogation days 480/16, etc; **Rogacion wyck** 475/3

rome *n* 1. room, ie, place, post 123/20; **roome** 428/37; 2. room, ie, chamber 81/3

roobez *n pl* robes 410/31

roode *v pa 3 sg* rode 113/41

routously *adj* with unlawful purpose 77/10, 77/15

rowt *n* 1. an unruly mob or troupe 380/4, 380/27; **routes** *pl* 365/30; 2. a gathering for unlawful purposes; **routes** *pl* 83/9, etc; **routs** 85/38, etc

ruffe band *n comp possibly* a falling band, the loose flat collar worn underneath, or instead of, a ruff; *possibly* one of the wrist bands or flat cuffs worn under hand ruffs 449/19

rumney *n* a sweet wine of Greek origin 459/26, etc

ruynowes *adj* ruinous, decrepit 120/24, 121/5

Rynneshewyne *n phr* Rhenish wine 486/23

ryotours *n pl* rioters 137/2, 137/16; **ryottors,** 137/9; **ryottours** 137/18, 137/19

ryson *pp* risen 442/1

saboath *n, usually attr* sabbath, applied to Sunday, the Christian day of rest, as it is understood to correspond with Saturday, the Jewish sabbath 150/13, etc; **sabaoth** 356/18, etc; **sabbaoth** 286/39; **sabboth** 370/4, etc; **saboathe** 169/11, etc; **saboth** 67/3, etc; *in comp* **saboathday** 184/34

sacke *see* **secke**

sacra L *sbst pl used here as* E *n pl* sacred things 457/2

sad *adj* grave 406/19, 419/28

sadler *n* saddler, maker and seller of saddles and of leather goods in general 476/14; **sadlers** *pl* saddlers as an organized guild 116/28

saffe *adj* safe, secure 420/23

saltes *n pl* salt-cellars 446/8

salues *n* salves, healing ointments 129/15

sanguinitie *n* consanguinity, kinship 409/4

saples *adj* sapless, ie, lacking vitality 128/6

sariant *see* **seriant**

sartayne *adj* certain 385/25

satten *n* satin 426/9, etc; **satene** 410/33

sault cotes *n comp pl* salt-houses, buildings in which salt is made 370/35

saulters *n pl* salters, makers and sellers of salt 370/31

saveguarde *n* safeguard 78/25; **savegardge** 95/16

scarlett *n* fine woollen cloth often but not always of a bright red colour approaching orange, commonly used for the robes of civic and other dignitaries 426/5, etc; **scarlet** 132/33; **skarlett** 429/2; *in phr* **skarlett gownes** men who, as current or former office-holders, were entitled to wear scarlet robes 488/36

sceane *n* scene, ie, spectacle or tableau 128/15, 128/19

scholares *n pl* scholars, ie, monks attached to a religious house but supported while studying at a university (?) 482/18

schombulles *see* **shambulles**

scituacion *n* situation, location 439/17

seche *v* seek 402/4, 414/17

secke *n* sack, sweet white wine from Spain or the Canary Islands 478/20, etc; **sacke** 454/29; **seck** 145/22

secte *n* religious party 418/3

seelie *adj* helpless and deserving pity 80/23 [*OED* Seely *a* 6]

seller *n* cellar 373/24, etc

sensede *v pa 3 pl* censed, presented with wafts of burning incense by way of honour 114/23

seny money *see* **seyny money**

seravantes *n pl error for* servantes, ie, servants 80/22

seriant *n* 1. serjeant, a minor municipal officer; **seriauntes** *pl* 430/8, etc; *in phr* **seriauntes at armes** municipal officers charged with enforcing the judicial and administrative decrees of the corporation 437/29; **seriauntes att armes** 431/29;

2. an officer of a guild 115/35m, 116/2;
sariant 116/13

sermonde *n* sermon 115/20, 410/35

seruiceable *adj* ready and willing to do service
439/18

sessheons *n pl* sessions, periodic sittings of
county or borough magistrates to try cases
and issue orders 475/31, etc; sesshions
478/20; sessions 392/12

sett *v* conclude (a lease) 532/8; sett *pp* 532/7;
in phr sett forth *pa 1 sg* publish (a book)
364/20; sett forth *pp* 143/34; sett forth
present (a play or other show) 540/7;
settyng ffurthe *vb n* 120/3; settyng
furthe 424/6; sett foreward produce (a
play or pageant) 119/25; sett in colors *pp*
painted, decorated with colour 462/2; sett
in ... colour 425/18; sett out ... with
colours 425/30; sett over convey
(property) 534/8, 535/13; set vppe crafte
start up trade or business 403/16; set vp
... crafte 415/7–8, 415/11–12

Saturday *n* Saturday 428/19, etc; Setterday
510/34, 520/4

sewte *n* suit 483/12

sextend *adj* sixteenth 188/27; sextene 188/25

seyny money *n comp* 464/23, etc; seny
money 339/n 82, 468/40–1; seyney
money 498/31; *see* Worcestershire
Introduction, pp 307–8 *and* Worcestershire Appendix 3

shale *v pr* shall 422/42, etc

shalmes *n pl* shawms 123/27

shambulles *n pl* shawm players 513/15;
schombulles 522/15

shellinges *n pl* the branches and other outer
parts of flax plants, stripped from the bolls
or useful inner stalks by the process called
rippling 374/25

shent *pp* scolded 419/5

sheowe *see* showe

sheowes *see* showes

shere *n* shire, county 436/1

sheth *n* sheath 93/14

shew *n see* showe

shewe *v* show 428/28, etc; shew 126/38;
sheweth *pr 3 sg* 74/13, 143/26; shewethe
122/31; shewythe 117/7; sheweth *pr 3 pl*
115/9; shewed *pa 3 sg* 431/36; shewyng
prp 432/7; shewed *pp* 426/30, etc; shewyd
415/20

shewers *n pl* showers 135/2

shippeskins *n pl* sheepskins, fleeces 421/5

shoppe-boords *n comp pl* the counters (in old
times usually giving directly on to the
street) on which tradesmen displayed their
goods and did their business; tailors
commonly sat right on theirs, crosslegged,
to work 134/4

Shore Thursday *n phr* Sheer Thursday, ie,
Maundy Thursday, the Thursday before
Easter 115/29

shos *see* showes

shote *v pr subj 3 sg* shoot 416/28, 417/18

showe *n* 1. public spectacle or display 480/19,
512/5; sheowe 525/28, etc; shew 379/40,
etc; shewes *pl* 423/11, etc; shews 380/34;
2. outward appearance, pretence; show
373/20

showes *n pl* shoes 467/16, etc; sheowes
462/40; shos 468/6

showmakers *n pl* shoemakers, organized as
a trade guild 443/17

shreeve *n* sheriff 435/40; shrifes *poss* 430/29m

shull *v pr 3 pl* shall 402/9, etc

sid *n* side 82/5

side-men *n pl* sidesmen, churchwardens'
assistants charged, among other things,
with investigating the moral and religious
conduct of parishioners 365/25, etc

signior *n* gentleman, man of rank (*but here
used ironically with pun on* senior, 'elder')
134/34

sill *v* sell 415/42, 417/19; sill *pr subj 3 sg* 417/6

simnells *n pl* simnels, bread or buns made of
fine flour 454/31

singleman *n comp* unmarried man, bachelor
368/37

sircomspecte *adj* circumspect 418/21

sirplices *see* surpleses

sith *conj* since 406/30; **syth** 442/15

sithence *conj* since 124/15; **sithence** *prep* 124/17; **sithens** 68/21; **sythence** *adv* 382/25, 453/6

sixte *adj* sixth 440/1; **syxt** 119/20; **sixts** *poss* 129/19

skarlett *see* scarlett

skarse *adv* scarce, ie, scarcely 420/30

sklender *adj* slender, ie, slight 432/28

skynners *n* preparers and purveyors of animal skins, organized as a guild 116/11

sleeues *n pl* sleeves; *in phr* **hanging sleeues** decorative sleeves which might be attached to the arm at various points; those actually worn were most commonly attached at the shoulder, with the arms emerging from slits above or at the elbow, leaving the rest of the sleeve to dangle decoratively 132/30; **hie sleeues** *of uncertain meaning, perhaps* sleeves full to the elbow and then close fitting to the wrist, in the fashion of some men's garments of the early 16th century (these are, according to the text, 'gathered at the elbowes,' which fits the definition) 132/29; **a peyer of sleves** detachable sleeves, fastened at the armhole by points or buttons 467/26–7

sling *n* a long, narrow field or other strip of land 452/18 [*EDD* Sling *sb²*]

small leg *n phr* the calf, the part of the leg that extends from knee to ankle; **small legs** *pl* 420/40 [*OED* Small *a and sb²* B 6]

sockes *n pl* socks, usually worn with boots or buskins, sometimes to protect fine understockings from contact with the boot 467/38

sodainly *adv* suddenly 376/36

soiles *see* soyle

soke *v pa 3 sg* sucked 408/34

solempne *adj* solemn 431/14

some *n* sum, total, amount 443/26, etc; **somme** 120/6, etc; **sommes** *pl* 120/20, etc

somer poole *n comp* summer pole, maypole 62/29

Soneday *n* Sunday 431/24, 431/24m

soo *adv* so 420/27

sot *n* 1. habitual drunkard 380/32; 2. fool; **sotte** 442/20

soueryan *adj error for* souerayn, ie, sovereign 414/10

southren *adj* southern 125/12

sowdiers *n poss* soldier's 442/19

soyle *n* 1. soil, ie, ground 533/23; 2. muddy or filthy places; **soiles** *pl* 425/23m; **soyles** 425/22, 425/27 [*EDD* Soil *sb²* 1]

spawles *v pr 3 sg* spawls, spits coarsely and copiously 135/24

spectacles *n pl* public shows for entertainment ✓ 188/3

spended *pp* (of food or drink) spent, ie, consumed 473/9

spones *n pl* spoons 446/12, 446/14

stablesshe *v* establish 539/1

staff torches *n phr pl* torches carried on staffs 430/17, 433/12

stage *n* a platform for a play or other public ✓ spectacle 430/20m, etc; **stages** *pl* 425/34, etc

stage play *n comp* a play performed on a stage ✓ 385/42, 386/23; **stage plaie** 390/8; **stagge playe** 356/8; **stage plaies** *pl* 388/39, 389/16; **stageplayes** 380/34

stage players *n comp* actors 540/18

stambring *prp* stammering 376/37

states *n pl* dignitaries 524/22

stede *n* stead 120/3

steward *n* a guild officer, usually ranking next after the aldermen 403/17; **stuard** 403/19; **stewardes** *pl* 402/9, etc; **stewards** 423/5; **stewyerdes** 444/17; **stuardes** 402/10

stewardship *n* the office of a steward, *here,* of a borough official 195/27

stile *n* style, full title 115/21

still *v* distil 419/9, 419/32

stockings *n pl here probably* breeches and long tailored stockings sewn together to produce a single garment 132/31

stonding *prp* standing 420/2

stoole-ball *n comp* a game like cricket but

simpler, in that there were no fielders, a common stool took the place of the wicket, and its keeper had no bat; traditionally played between men and women as an Easter game 60/15 [*OED* Stool-ball; Strutt]

stoup *v* stoop; **stouped** *pa 3 sg* 373/41; **stouping** *prp* 373/37

strak *v pa 3 sg* struck 434/24; **strake** 95/13, 383/4; **strake** *pa 3 pl* 91/12

strangers *n pl* outsiders, persons not belonging to a given community 402/38, 417/17

strayt *adj* strait, ie, restricted, confined 435/14

stricke *v* strike 95/24; **strickinge** *prp* 87/39

striff *n* strife 114/34

stript *pp* striped 132/30

strooke *v pa 3 sg* struck 82/17, 374/17

strucken *pp in phr* **strucken in yeares** stricken in years, advanced in age 129/21

stryke *n pl* strike, a measure of grain, usually the same as a bushel 357/30, etc; **strycke** 391/17

stuard *see* **steward**

stublefylde *n comp* stubble field 435/5

sturdy beggers *n phr pl* beggars who were able-bodied and apt to be violent 586/43

stutted *v pa 3 sg* stuttered 392/37 [*OED* Stut *v*[1]]

stycke *n* the customary length (varying according to the material) of a piece or roll of certain textile fabrics 468/23; **styckes** *pl* 468/23

stypell *n* steeple 362/8

subarbez *n pl* suburbs 402/33

subiettes *n pl* subjects 538/29, etc

subsidie man *n phr* a man wealthy enough to be liable to the kind of tax called a subsidy, a man of considerable means 129/33–4, etc

substanciall *adj* 1. effectual, in force 402/3, 414/16; 2. essential, fundamental; **substancyalle** 187/24

subtile *adj* subtle, ie, devious 586/27

suerly *adv* surely 408/18

suggestyon *n* false representation 407/13

suger *n* sugar 450/24; **sugger** 147/15

suict *n* suit 89/25

sumes *n pl* sums 439/4

sumner *n* summoner, an officer of a court (usually a church court) who delivered citations and warnings to accused persons to appear there 476/15

sumtyme *adv phr* at one time, formerly 406/20, etc

supplyance *n* supply 138/2

supportacion *n* support 115/11

suppryoresse *n* subprioress, prioress' deputy 188/16

surete *n* surety, certainty 402/15

surpleses *n pl* surplices, ample, ankle-length garments of white linen, with bell-shaped hanging sleeves, the characteristic dress of Anglican clergy and their assistants when officiating 431/7; **sirplices** 370/2

surseassed *pp* surceased, ie, stopped, discontinued 119/28

surveigh *n* survey, surveying 449/21

sustre *n* sister 187/27; **sustres** *pl* 188/21, 188/24

suytt *n* suit 188/19

swoord *n* sword 84/38

sworne man *n phr* sidesman, churchwarden's assistant 174/18

swound *n* swoon 393/35

syd *n* side 95/14

syke *adj* sick 414/36, 517/27

syns *adv* since, afterwards 144/34

syth *see* **sith**

sythence *see* **sithence**

syxt *see* **sixte**

table boordes *n comp pl* boards forming the top of a table 454/33

tabor *n* a small drum, especially one used as an accompaniment to a pipe 129/10, etc; **taber** 381/24, etc; **tabour** 365/27; **tabors** *pl* 125/30; *in comp* **taber-man** 125/17, 125/21; **taber playing** 179/38

taborer *n* tabor player 169/1, etc; **taberer** 125/13; **taberor** 63/14

tabring work *n comp* work of playing the tabor 134/42

tanners *n pl* those who turned raw hides into leather by tanning, organized as a craft guild 115/28

tapur *n* taper, ie, a wax candle not necessarily slender 358/17; **tapers** *pl* 402/24; **tapurs** 414/40

tary *v* 1. tarry, ie, delay 114/36, 115/15; 2. await; **tarried** *pa 3 sg* 431/2

taxed *pp* fixed by lawful authority 586/37

tearme *n* term, period 532/27, etc

tenderyng *prp* caring about, being concerned for 440/16

testament *n* New Testament 417/39, etc

thandes *n phr pl* the hands 432/25

thankfull *adj* thankworthy, deserving thanks 439/33

thend *art and n in adv phr* **to thend** to the end, so as 76/35, 93/9; **to thende** 76/41, 92/35

thentent(e) *see* **entent**

ther *pron poss* their 407/36, etc

thereffore *adv* therefor, for that reason, on that account 117/26, 117/27

thes *pron* this 120/12

thew *v error for* shew, ie, show 134/37

theym *pron* them 403/18, etc

theymsilf *pron 3 pl* themselves 407/30

thir *pron* these 187/24

this *adv* thus 407/7; *see* pp 590–1 (endnote to BL: Cotton Julius B xii ff 13v–17)

this *pron pl* these 418/39, 419/32

tho *adv* then 430/23

thoos *pron pl* those 408/1; **thoose** 95/5; **thos** 441/24; **thowes** 444/17

thorowe *prep* through 375/2; **thorowgh** 421/6

threasurer *n* treasurer 434/3; **thresarour** 434/3m; **thresorer** 446/1, 447/5; **thresurer** 436/28; **thresurour** 436/21

threasury *n* treasury 426/33

threed *n* thread 134/11

thretin *v* threaten 418/18

thrid *adj* third 138/7

througe *prep error for* throughe, ie, through 81/29

throwly *adv* thoroughly 122/37

thyn *see* **with thyn**

times *n pl in phr* **at times** *error for* at all times 84/25–6

tipling *prp* 1. retailing strong drink; *or, less probably,* 2. drinking intoxicating liquor (perhaps to excess) 353/30, 354/19; **tipling** *vb n* 172/37; **tiplinge** 457/19

tissue *see* **tysshew**

titill *n* title 410/19

to *adv* too 383/9

to *adj* two 421/20

to gyder *adv* together 188/16

toke *v pa 3 sg* took 419/29, etc

toked *v pa 3 sg* punished, chastised 410/5 [*OED* Tuck *v*¹ 1]

tolles *n pl* tools 445/9

tollshopp *n comp* guild-hall, city hall 435/34, 438/30; **towleshopp** 420/17

too *adj* two 424/23, etc

toyes *n pl* frivolous antics 72/21

trainsents *n pl* train-scents, dead animals or other objects trained (ie, dragged) along the ground to make a scent for hounds to follow; *hence*, the sport of exercising horses and hounds by that means 133/9

translate *adj* translated, transported 406/24

travayle *n* travel 89/22

travayle *v* travel 586/40

traves *n* a small compartment shut off with a curtain or screen in a hall, a church, or the like 432/9 [*OED* Traverse *sb* 14]

tresorie *n* treasury 443/8, 443/10

tresour *n* treasury 402/12, etc; **tresur** 414/21, etc; **tresure** 416/22

trouth *n* troth, fidelity 403/26

trumpetor *n* trumpet player 454/32; **trompeters** *pl* 437/32, 449/12; **trumpeteres** 523/1; **trumpeters** 363/36

trym *adj* good, well made (a vague term of approval) 418/15

trymmyng *vb n* dressing up and otherwise arraying, making neat or smart 438/26 tumbled *v pa 3 pl* tumbled, did acrobatics 473/6

tumbleres *n pl* tumblers, acrobats 484/5

tumbling *vb n* tumbling, acrobatics 540/2; tumbleing 394/25; tumblying 494/18

tumultuating *prp* apt to make tumults or disturbances 380/28

tuneable *adj* melodious, harmonious 129/4

turkeye colour *n phr* a bright blue, obtained from a dye thought to come from the Ottoman Empire 430/9

turne-ups *n pl* turnips 136/4

Tweire-pipe *n comp* Twire-pipe, apparently the name of a proverbial or mythical taborer 125/12 [*cp OED* Twire-pipe]

Twelf Day *n phr* Twelfth Day or Epiphany, the twelfth day after Christmas (6 January) 190/26; Twelfday 495/31; Twelffday 473/24; Twelpff Day 473/20

twenteth *adj* twentieth 74/22, 75/26; twentith 84/7, 434/36

twine *v in phr* twine or untwine squirm (?) 418/20 [*OED* Twine *v*¹ 8]

two hand-sword man *n comp* a man able to wield a two-handed sword 132/13–14

twooe *adv* too 122/35

Twysday *n* Tuesday 432/34

tymber *n coll* wood available for building or other working (not necessarily already felled) 445/8

tynkers *n pl* a class of vagabonds, some of whom ostensibly earned their living as menders of kitchen utensils, but who were generally reputed thieves and tricksters 586/35

tyrement *n* articles of dress collectively 422/31

tysshew *n* tissue, a variety of cloth of gold, made of precious metals and silk in twisted threads 446/32, 447/11; tissue 410/32; tyshew 447/10; tyssew 446/34; tyssue 446/29

þat *pron* that 416/28, etc

þe *art* the 415/40, etc

þer *pron poss* their 415/5, etc

þis *pron* this 459/16, etc

unquiete *v pr 3 pl* disturb 350/22

untwine *see* twine

unwildy *adv* unwieldly, ungainly 365/5

utter *v refl* pass (oneself) off 586/30

vaulting-schoole *n comp* brothel 135/10–11

vce *n* use 506/34

velom-spotted *pp comp* vellum-spotted, ie, spotted like old vellum (?) *or error for* venom-spotted, ie, stained with venom (?) 125/29

ventred *v pa 3 sg* ventured 376/27

veraly *adv* verily, truly 115/14; verely 114/15

vicar *n* a salaried clergyman in actual charge of a parish church where the nominal rector, who received the tithes, was a layman, corporation, or disabled cleric 75/10, etc

vice collector *n comp* deputy collector 479/16

vidz *abbrev for L* videlicet *used with the meaning of E* to wit *or* namely 515/9; vz 425/18

vintner *n* wine-merchant 134/21; vynteners *pl* vintners organized as a trade guild 116/17

virginalls *n pl* a keyboard musical instrument, usually having the strings laid parallel to the keyboard 452/31, 453/13

vmble *adj* humble 117/7

vnce *n* ounce 437/22, 437/26; vnces *pl* 437/21, 437/25

vndeseuerable *adj* undisseverable, inseparable 408/25

vndue *adj* unjust 439/18

vngle *n* uncle 409/34

vn lasse *conj* unless 403/13

vn to *prep* unto 415/20–1, etc

vous auez *F vb phr* you have, ie, you have a complete jury (a traditional law-French phrase) 128/24

vpholden *pp* upheld 533/26; **vp houlden** 175/3

vse *v* 1. employ 374/23, etc; **vsyng** *prp* 430/4; **vsed** *pp* 453/38, 143/28; **vsid** 416/36; **vsyd** 402/24; 2. be accustomed 351/20; **vsed** *pp* accustomed 414/27, etc; **vsid** 415/3, 415/31; 3. ply, practise (a trade or pastime); **vse** *v inf* 538/25, etc; **vsed** *pp* 539/8, etc; 4. keep, observe (a holy day or custom); **vsed** *pp* 117/27, 538/1, 538/3; 5. treat; **vsed** *pp* 60/21

vsshers *see* **gentleman vssher**

vssue *v* issue 82/13

vsyng *prp* using 430/4

vtteraunce *n* utterance, ie, disposal of goods by trade 372/35

vyalls *n pl* viols, bowed instruments with six strings 444/39, 445/10

vynteners *see* **vintner**

vytteling howse *n comp* victualling-house 385/29–30

vz *see* **vidz**

wacche *n* watch, ie, a revel held on the eve of a festival 403/10, 403/12; **wach** 416/2m; **wache** 416/9, 417/8; **wathe** *error for* watche 416/5

waffures *n pl* wafers, thin, crisp cakes, often eaten with wine, 464/36, etc; **wafferes** 509/38, etc; **wafferres** 495/11; **wafures** 481/28, etc; **wafurnes** 469/10

wagen *n* wagon, ie, carriage 431/26

waieng *prp* weighing 437/25

waightes *see* **wayte**

waite plaiers *n comp pl* players on waits' instruments, waits 450/35

waites *see* **wayte**

waitshippe *n* office of a wait 124/13

waker *n* watchman 421/6

walker *n* fuller, one who whitens and thickens cloth 392/14, etc; **walkers** *pl* fullers

organized as a craft guild 115/30, etc; **walkeres** 444/17, 444/18

ward *n* an administrative division of a borough 444/1, 444/7; **warde** 443/37, 444/10

warden *n* 1. a member of the governing body of a guild 403/19; **wardens** *pl* 403/1, etc; **wardeyns** 403/10, 403/17; **wordeyns** 402/34; 2. *in phr* **warden of the Fyve Portes** *see* **Fyve Portes**

ware *adj* aware 392/40

ware *v pa 3 pl* were 421/28

warke *n* work 461/6

warkemen *n comp pl* workmen 522/40

wast *v* waste 130/2

watche & ward *n phr* guard by night 374/38

wathe *see* **wacche**

wayeng *prp* weighing 437/21

way men *n comp see* **makers of wayes**

wayte *n* 1. a musician retained by a town or other corporation 123/25; *in phr* **head wayte** chief wait 123/19; *in pl* a band of such musicians; **waightes** 450/12m, 450/13; **waites** 124/32, etc; **waits** 190/2; **waytes** 476/7, etc; **wayts** 129/9; **waytyes** 370/17; 2. waits' instruments, shawms; **waytes** 362/39, 448/12, 448/12m; *see also* **waite plaiers**

waytyng maydens *n phr pl* waiting maids, superior female servants attending a lady 431/33–4

weare *v pa 3 pl* were 419/3, etc; **weare** *subj pa 3 sg* 418/37

weaver *n* one who gains a living by weaving fabric 392/15; *in pl* weavers organized as a trade guild; **weavers** 451/14, etc; **wevers** 447/27; *in comp* **silke-weauer** 126/3

wedyng *n* wedding 510/15

weele *n* weal, prosperity 402/28

wele *adv* well 114/19

wesshing *vb n* washing 472/30

westerne-men *n phr* men of the south-western counties 125/35

wevers *see* **weaver**

wex *n* wax 415/15, 415/22

wezand *n* weasand, ie, windpipe, gullet 374/14

wherefore *adv* wherefor, for which 83/2

wheþer *conj* whether 402/14

whiflers *n pl* attendants who kept the way or space clear for a public spectacle, particularly for a morris dance 129/29, etc; **wiflers** 132/35

whiles *conj* whilst 128/12, 350/23

whitlyme *v* white-lime, distemper with white-wash 425/29

Whitson *quasi-proper adj* of Whitsunday or Pentecost, the church festival seven weeks after Easter; *in phr or comp* **Whitson holiedaies** *pl* the holy days of Whit-tide, Whitsunday and the two days following 84/3; **Whitson Munday** the Monday after Whitsunday 384/19–20; **Whitson-Tewesdaye** the Tuesday after Whitsunday 367/36; **Whitsontyd** Whit-tide, Whitsunday and the days after 360/6; **Whitson weeke** the week beginning with Whitsunday 74/21–2, etc; **Whitsonwycke** 503/16; **Whittson-Ale** a parish festival at Whit-tide 367/7; **Wytsone even** the eve of Whitsunday 406/6

whome *n* home 422/4

whos *pron* whoso, whoever 407/7; *see* pp 590–1 (endnote to BL: Cotton Julius B xii ff 13v–17)

whuling *vb n* howling, moaning 125/13 [*OED* Whewl *v*]

Wichemen *n comp pl* men of a salt-works, salt-makers; *here specifically*, the men of Droitwich 370/31 [*OED* Wich]

wicke *n* week 465/34; **wike** 460/26

wief *n* wife 136/34, etc; **wif** 418/35; **wiff** 114/33

wiflers *see* **whiflers**

withall *prep phr* with all 532/10

with inforth *adv comp* within, inside 188/14

without that *conj phr* (the above) notwithstanding 88/23, 92/6

withseyng *vb n* withsaying, ie, contradiction or denial 415/12

with thyn *prep* within 537/10

wocke *n* week 481/31

woes *v pr 3 sg* woos 366/4

wordeyns *see* **warden**

workynday *n comp* working day 538/27

worshipfulles *n pl* persons entitled to be called worshipful 486/25

wostid *n* worsted 191/39

wrastling *prp* wrestling 135/8

wretyn *pp* written 118/26

wright *v* write 419/9, etc; **wright** *imper sg* 419/6; **wrighting** *vb n* 419/29, etc; **wrightinge** 419/16

wrought *pp* worked, ie, put to work, employed 441/5

wull *v pr 3 sg* will 415/23

wycke *n* week 459/16, etc; **wyck** 465/5, etc; **wyke** 479/16

wyff *n* wife 437/15, etc; **wyf** 418/27; **wyffes** *pl* 528/31(2)

wylfulle *adj* wilfull, ie, voluntary 187/25

wynne *n* wine 476/9, 478/17m

Wystone *see* **Whitson**

yat *pron and conj* that 372/26, etc

yave *v pa 3 sg* gave 410/3

yche *adj* each 188/22

ye *art* the 374/25, etc

ye *interj* yea, yes 93/1, 433/8, etc

yeald *see* **yeld**

yee *pron* you 133/8, etc

yeld *n* 1. guild, ie, guild merchant 402/20, etc; **yelde** 424/26; 2. guild-hall; **yeald** 453/39; *see also* **yeld hall** *and* **yeld marchaunt**

yelde *v* yield 410/27, etc; **yeald** 455/24; **yelde** *pr 3 sg error for* yeldes 442/2; **yeldyng** *prp* 429/18

yeld hall *n comp* guild-hall, city hall 414/8, etc; **yeald hall** 454/1–2; **yelde hall** 425/11–12

yeld marchaunt *n phr* guild merchant, an association of merchants and tradesmen, originally to promote and regulate trade, but which in Worcester as elsewhere became in time largely identical with the civic government 401/35; **yelde merchaunt** 414/7–8

yem *pron* them 380/1, etc

yenst *see* **against**

yere *n pl* years 538/17

yerle *n* earl 431/31, etc

yerly *adv* yearly 402/4, etc; **yerelye** 117/12; 117/14; **yerlye** 119/25

yern *n* iron; or yarn (?) 523/32m; **yerne** 523/31

yerre *adv* ere, ie, sooner 360/33

yes *n pl* eyes 435/29, 441/36

yeven *n* even, ie, eve of a church feast or other festival 488/35, etc

yevenyng *art and n* th'evening, ie, the evening 433/4

yife *v pr 3 sg subj* give 188/1

yoman *n* a petty officer in a great household *attr* 339/n 83; *pl in phr* **yomen of the male** officers of the royal household in charge of baggage 438/1 [*OED* Mail *sb*³ 1]

youngman *n phr* 1. young man 376/12; *pl* **youngmen** 372/25; 2. *more particularly*, the young men of a particular place, organized as a charitable guild; **youmen** 391/26; **yongemenys** *pl poss* 357/38

ȝolye *see* **iolly**

Index

The index combines subjects with names, book or play titles, and places in a single listing. When identical headwords occur in more than one category, the order is names of persons, titles of nobility, names of places, subjects, and titles of books or plays; thus 'Worcester, earl of' precedes 'Worcester, Worc.'

Place-names and given names appear in the modern form where that can be ascertained and titles and family names of nobility and other public figures in forms commonly used by modern historians. Other surnames are usually cited in the most common form occurring in the text, except that capitalization and the use of i/j and u/v have here been assimilated to modern usage. Surnames and place-names are regularly followed by any variant spellings (in parentheses), but these are given for titles only where clarity requires them. Nobles are entered under their family names with cross-references from any titles which occur in the text or apparatus and royalty under their regnal or given names. Saints' names are indexed under 'St,' alphabetized as if spelt out. The chief sources used for identifying persons were *The Dictionary of National Biography*, F. Maurice Powicke and E.B. Fryde (eds), *Handbook of British Chronology*, 2nd ed (London, 1961), and Treadway R. Nash, *Collections for the History of Worcestershire*. Sources for the identification of royalty and nobility are specified in the headnote to 'Patrons and Travelling Companies,' to which the index refers throughout.

The format for names and titles has largely been taken from R.F. Hunnisett, *Indexing for Editors* (Leicester, 1972). Hence members of noble families have usually been distinguished by their family relationships when those are known rather than by succession numbers, but when required for clarity, succession numbers have been used following *The Complete Peerage*. Occupations are specified only when considered relevant (eg, 'Peadle, Abraham, player').

Certain broad topics such as 'costume, articles of' and 'musical instruments' are given to aid research. The pertinent members of these classes are then mostly either listed as subentries or referred to by cross-references.

RECORDS OF EARLY ENGLISH DRAMA

Suggested in 407.

Terence-copy n on p. 595

Thomas Tonlin's son
involved in donation.
p. 457.

[devil grimace at Worcester Cath!
p. 447.

— which chs 14.

See: (ed.) Leonard Cantor,
The English Med. Landscape
(1982)
(cit p. 334)

? a writs
will pp 444-5

prohibitions
347 + frons 551-2

Baxter 379-80

Royal injunctions against vagabonds — p. 586

King's jingle 600

Bibles.
✓
585